Lecture Notes in Computer Science

Lecture Notes in Artificial Intelligence 16013
Founding Editor

Jörg Siekmann

Series Editors

Randy Goebel, *University of Alberta, Edmonton, Canada*
Wolfgang Wahlster, *DFKI, Berlin, Germany*
Zhi-Hua Zhou, *Nanjing University, Nanjing, China*

The series Lecture Notes in Artificial Intelligence (LNAI) was established in 1988 as a topical subseries of LNCS devoted to artificial intelligence.

The series publishes state-of-the-art research results at a high level. As with the LNCS mother series, the mission of the series is to serve the international R & D community by providing an invaluable service, mainly focused on the publication of conference and workshop proceedings and postproceedings.

Rita P. Ribeiro · Bernhard Pfahringer ·
Nathalie Japkowicz · Pedro Larrañaga ·
Alípio M. Jorge · Carlos Soares ·
Pedro H. Abreu · João Gama
Editors

Machine Learning and Knowledge Discovery in Databases

Research Track

European Conference, ECML PKDD 2025
Porto, Portugal, September 15–19, 2025
Proceedings, Part I

Editors
Rita P. Ribeiro ⓘ
University of Porto
Porto, Portugal

Bernhard Pfahringer ⓘ
University of Waikato
Hamilton, Waikato, New Zealand

Nathalie Japkowicz ⓘ
American University
Washington, D.C., WA, USA

Pedro Larrañaga ⓘ
Technical University of Madrid
Boadilla del Monte, Madrid, Spain

Alípio M. Jorge ⓘ
University of Porto
Porto, Portugal

Carlos Soares ⓘ
University of Porto
Porto, Portugal

Pedro H. Abreu ⓘ
University of Coimbra
Coimbra, Portugal

João Gama ⓘ
University of Porto
Porto, Portugal

ISSN 0302-9743   ISSN 1611-3349 (electronic)
Lecture Notes in Artificial Intelligence
ISBN 978-3-032-05961-1   ISBN 978-3-032-05962-8 (eBook)
https://doi.org/10.1007/978-3-032-05962-8

LNCS Sublibrary: SL7 – Artificial Intelligence

© The Editor(s) (if applicable) and The Author(s), under exclusive license
to Springer Nature Switzerland AG 2026
Chapters "Optimizing and Tuning Fairness in Machine Learning: An Augmented Lagrangian Method with a Performance Budget" and "InfoClus: Informative Clustering of High-Dimensional Data Embeddings" are licensed under the terms of the Creative Commons Attribution 4.0 International License (http://creativecommons.org/licenses/by/4.0/). For further details see license information in the chapters.

This work is subject to copyright. All rights are solely and exclusively licensed by the Publisher, whether the whole or part of the material is concerned, specifically the rights of translation, reprinting, reuse of illustrations, recitation, broadcasting, reproduction on microfilms or in any other physical way, and transmission or information storage and retrieval, electronic adaptation, computer software, or by similar or dissimilar methodology now known or hereafter developed.
The use of general descriptive names, registered names, trademarks, service marks, etc. in this publication does not imply, even in the absence of a specific statement, that such names are exempt from the relevant protective laws and regulations and therefore free for general use.
The publisher, the authors and the editors are safe to assume that the advice and information in this book are believed to be true and accurate at the date of publication. Neither the publisher nor the authors or the editors give a warranty, expressed or implied, with respect to the material contained herein or for any errors or omissions that may have been made. The publisher remains neutral with regard to jurisdictional claims in published maps and institutional affiliations.

This Springer imprint is published by the registered company Springer Nature Switzerland AG
The registered company address is: Gewerbestrasse 11, 6330 Cham, Switzerland

If disposing of this product, please recycle the paper.

Preface

The 2025 edition of the European Conference on Machine Learning and Principles and Practice of Knowledge Discovery in Databases (ECML PKDD 2025) was held in the vibrant city of Porto, Portugal on September 15–19, 2025. This marks a significant return of the conference to Porto, following successful editions in 2005 and 2015, underscoring the city's enduring appeal as a hub for scientific exchange.

The annual ECML PKDD conference stands as a premier worldwide platform dedicated to showcasing the latest advancements and fostering insightful discussions in the fields of machine learning and knowledge discovery in databases. Held jointly since 2001, ECML PKDD has firmly established its reputation as the leading European conference in these disciplines. It provides researchers and practitioners with an unparalleled opportunity to exchange knowledge, share innovative ideas, and explore the latest technical advancements. Furthermore, the conference deeply values the synergy between foundational theoretical advances and groundbreaking practical data science applications, actively encouraging contributions that demonstrate how Machine Learning and Data Mining are being effectively employed to address complex real-world challenges.

A Hub for Responsible AI and Cutting-Edge Research

As the technological landscape continues to evolve and societal needs shift, the conference remains committed to adapting to and reflecting these dynamic changes. This year's event saw a robust engagement from the global research community with a substantial increase in the number of submissions.

The three main conference days were organised into five distinct tracks:

- The Research Track received an impressive number of 924 submissions, with 226 papers ultimately accepted, reflecting a highly competitive acceptance rate of 24.5%.
- The Applied Data Science Track received a total of 299 submissions, accepting 74 papers, resulting in an acceptance rate of 24.7%.
- The Journal Track continued to bridge the gap between conference and journal publications, accepting 43 papers (27 for the Machine Learning journal and 16 for the Data Mining and Knowledge Discovery journal) out of 297 submissions.
- The Nectar Track, focusing on recent scientific advances at the frontier of machine learning and data mining, received 30 submissions.
- The Demo Track showcased practical applications and prototypes, accepting 15 papers from a total of 30 submissions.

These proceedings cover the papers accepted in the Research and Applied Data Science tracks.

The high quality and diversity of the accepted papers across all tracks underscore the continued vitality and intellectual breadth of the machine learning and data mining communities. We extend our sincere gratitude to all authors for their valuable contributions, to the program committee members and reviewers for their diligent efforts in ensuring the rigorous double-blind review process, and to the organising committee for their tireless work in making ECML PKDD 2025 a resounding success. We believe these proceedings will serve as a valuable resource, inspiring future research and innovation in these rapidly advancing fields.

This year's conference featured seven insightful keynote talks that focused on crucial and emerging areas within Responsible AI, including trustworthy AI, interpretability, and explainability. The keynotes also explored fundamental theoretical issues, covering causality, neural-symbolic systems, large language models (LLMs), and AI for science. We were honoured to host leading experts who shared their valuable perspectives:

- Cynthia Rudin (Duke University) presented on "Many Good Models Lead to …";
- Elias Bareinboim (Columbia University) discussed "Towards Causal Artificial Intelligence";
- Francisco Herrera (University of Granada) addressed "Not Just a Trend: Institutionalizing XAI for Responsible and Compliant AI Systems";
- Mirella Lapata (University of Edinburgh) explored "Compositional Intelligence: Coordinating Multiple LLMs for Complex Tasks";
- Nuria Oliver (ELLIS Alicante Foundation, Spain) spoke on "Towards a Fairer World: Uncovering and Addressing Human and Algorithmic Biases";
- Pedro Domingos (University of Washington) shared insights on "A Simple Unification of Neural and Symbolic AI"; and
- Sašo Džeroski (Jožef Stefan Institute, Slovenia) presented on "Artificial Intelligence for Science".

Fostering Diversity and Inclusion

Our Diversity and Inclusion initiative proudly awarded 10 scholarship grants of €500 to early-career researchers. These grants enabled individuals from developing countries and communities underrepresented in science and technology to attend the conference, present their work, and become integral members of the ECML PKDD community.

Acknowledging Our Contributors and Supporters

We extend our sincere gratitude to everyone who contributed to making ECML PKDD 2025 such a success. Our heartfelt thanks go to the authors, workshop and tutorial organisers, and all participants for their valuable scientific contributions.

An outstanding conference program would not be possible without the immense dedication and substantial time investment from our area chairs, program committee, and organising committee. The smooth execution of the event was also largely due to the hard work of our many volunteers and session chairs. A special acknowledgement goes to the local organisers for meticulously handling every detail, making the conference a truly memorable experience.

Finally, we are incredibly grateful for the generous financial support from our wonderful sponsors. We also appreciate Springer's ongoing support and Microsoft's provision of their CMT software for conference management, as well as their continued assistance. Our sincere thanks also go to the ECML PKDD Steering Committee for their invaluable advice and guidance over the past two years.

September 2025

João Gama
Pedro H. Abreu
Alípio M. Jorge
Carlos Soares
Rita P. Ribeiro
Pedro Larrañaga
Nathalie Japkowicz
Bernhard Pfahringer
Inês Dutra
Mykola Pechenizkiy
Sepideh Pashami
Paulo Cortez

Organization

Honorary Chair

Pavel Brazdil — University of Porto, Portugal

General Chairs

João Gama — University of Porto, Portugal
Pedro H. Abreu — University of Coimbra, Portugal
Alípio M. Jorge — University of Porto, Portugal
Carlos Soares — University of Porto, Portugal

Research Track Program Chairs

Bernhard Pfahringer — University of Waikato, New Zealand
Nathalie Japkowicz — American University, USA
Pedro Larrañaga — Technical University of Madrid, Spain
Rita P. Ribeiro — University of Porto, Portugal

Applied Data Science Track Program Chairs

Inês Dutra — University of Porto, Portugal
Mykola Pechenisky — TU Eindhoven, The Netherlands
Paulo Cortez — University of Minho, Portugal
Sepideh Pashami — Halmstad University, Sweden

Journal Track Chairs

Ana Carolina Lorena — Instituto Tecnológico de Aeronáutica, Brazil
Arlindo Oliveira — Instituto Superior Técnico, Portugal
Concha Bielza — Technical University of Madrid, Spain
Longbing Cao — Macquarie University, Australia
Tiago Almeida — Federal University of São Carlos, Brazil

Nectar Track Chairs

Ricard Gavaldà
Riccardo Guidotti
Amalfi Analytics, Spain
University of Pisa, Italy

Demo Track Chairs

Arian Pasquali
Nuno Moniz
Faktion, Belgium
University of Notre Dame, USA

Local Chairs

Bruno Veloso
Rita Nogueira
Shazia Tabassum
University of Porto, Portugal
INESC TEC, Portugal
INESC TEC, Portugal

Workshop Chairs

Irena Koprinska
João Mendes Moreira
Paula Branco
University of Sydney, Australia
University of Porto, Portugal
University of Ottawa, Canada

Tutorial Chairs

Alicia Troncoso
Nikolaj Tatti
Universidad Pablo de Olavide, Spain
University of Helsinki, Finland

PhD Forum Chairs

Raquel Sebastião
Yun Sing Koh
Polytechnic Institute of Viseu, Portugal
University of Auckland, New Zealand

Awards Committee Chairs

André Carvalho   University of São Paulo, Brazil
Amparo Alonso-Betanzos   University of A Coruña, Spain
Katharina Morik   TU Dortmund, Germany
Vítor Santos Costa   University of Porto, Portugal

Proceedings Chairs

João Vinagre   European Commission (JRC), Spain
Miriam Santos   University of Porto, Portugal
Shazia Tabassum   INESC TEC, Portugal

Diversity and Inclusion Chairs

Inês Sousa   Fraunhofer, Portugal
Zahraa Abdallah   University of Bristol, UK

Discovery Challenge Chairs

Carlos Ferreira   Polytechnic Institute of Porto, Portugal
Peter van der Putten   Leiden University, The Netherlands
Rui Camacho   University of Porto, Portugal

Panel Chairs

Pedro H. Abreu   University of Coimbra, Portugal
Paula Brito   University of Porto, Portugal

Publicity Chair

Carlos Ferreira   Polytechnic Institute of Porto, Portugal

Sponsorship Chairs

Mariam Berry	BNP Paribas, France
Nuno Moutinho	University of Porto, Portugal
Rui Teles	Accenture, Portugal

Social Media Chairs

Luis Roque	ZAAI.ai, Portugal
Ricardo Pereira	University of Coimbra, Portugal
Dalila Teixeira	Creative Matter, USA

Web Chair

Thiago Andrade	University of Porto, Portugal

Senior Program Committee – Research Track

Adam Jatowt	University of Innsbruck, Austria
Andrea Passerini	University of Trento, Italy
Anthony Bagnall	University of Southampton, UK
Arno Knobbe	Leiden University, Netherlands
Arno Siebes	Universiteit Utrecht, Netherlands
Arto Klami	University of Helsinki, Finland
Bernhard Pfahringer	University of Waikato, New Zealand
Bettina Berendt	TU Berlin, Germany
Celine Robardet	INSA Lyon, France
Celine Vens	KU Leuven, Belgium
Cesar Ferri	Universitat Politècnica Valencia, Spain
Charalampos Tsourakakis	Boston University, USA
Chedy Raissi	Inria, France
Chen Gong	Nanjing University of Science and Technology, China
Danai Koutra	University of Michigan, USA
Dimitrios Gunopulos	University of Athens, Greece
Donato Malerba	Università degli Studi di Bari Aldo Moro, Italy
Dragi Kocev	Jožef Stefan Institute, Slovenia
Dunja Mladenic	Jožef Stefan Institute, Slovenia
Eirini Ntoutsi	Universität der Bundeswehr München, Germany

Emmanuel Müller	TU Dortmund, Germany
Ernestina Menasalvas	Universidad Politécnica de Madrid, Spain
Esther Galbrun	University of Eastern Finland, Finland
Evaggelia Pitoura	University of Ioannina, Greece
Evangelos Papalexakis	University of California, Riverside, USA
Fabio A. Stella	University of Milano-Bicocca, Italy
Fabrizio Costa	Exeter University, UK
Fragkiskos Malliaros	CentraleSupélec, France
Georg Krempl	Utrecht University, Netherlands
Georgiana Ifrim	University College Dublin, Ireland
Gustavo Batista	University of New South Wales, Australia
Heikki Mannila	Aalto University, Finland
Hendrik Blockeel	KU Leuven, Belgium
Henrik Bostrom	KTH Royal Institute of Technology, Sweden
Henry Gouk	University of Edinburgh, UK
Ioannis Katakis	University of Nicosia, Cyprus
Jan N. Van Rijn	LIACS, Leiden University, Netherlands
Jefrey Lijffijt	Ghent University, Belgium
Jerzy Stefanowski	Poznań University of Technology, Poland
Jesse Davis	KU Leuven, Belgium
Jesse Read	Ecole Polytechnique, France
Jessica Lin	George Mason University, USA
Jesus Cerquides	IIIA-CSIC, Spain
Jilles Vreeken	CISPA Helmholtz Center for Information Security, Germany
João Gama	INESC TEC - LIAAD, Portugal
Jörg Wicker	University of Auckland, New Zealand
José Hernández-Orallo	Universitat Politècnica de Valencia, Spain
Junming Shao	University of Electronic Science and Technology of China, China
Kai Puolamaki	University of Helsinki, Finland
Manfred Jaeger	Aalborg University, Denmark
Marius Kloft	TU Kaiserslautern, Germany
Marius Lindauer	Leibniz University Hannover, Germany
Mark Last	Ben-Gurion University of the Negev, Israel
Matthias Renz	University of Kiel, Germany
Matthias Schubert	Ludwig-Maximilians-Universität München, Germany
Michele Lombardi	University of Bologna, Italy
Michèle Sebag	LISN CNRS, France
Nathalie Japkowicz	American University, USA
Paolo Frasconi	Università degli Studi di Firenze, Italy

Parisa Kordjamshidi	Michigan State University, USA
Pasquale Minervini	University of Edinburgh, UK
Pauli Miettinen	University of Eastern Finland, Finland
Pedro Larrañaga	Technical University of Madrid, Spain
Peer Kroger	Christian-Albrechts-Universität Kiel, Germany
Peter Flach	University of Bristol, UK
Ricardo B. Prudencio	Universidade Federal de Pernambuco, Brazil
Rita P. Ribeiro	University of Porto and INESC TEC, Portugal
Salvatore Ruggieri	University of Pisa, Italy
Sebastijan Dumancic	TU Delft, Netherlands
Sibylle Hess	TU Eindhoven, Netherlands
Sicco Verwer	Delft University of Technology, Netherlands
Siegfried Nijssen	Université catholique de Louvain, Belgium
Sophie Fellenz	RPTU Kaiserslautern-Landau, Germany
Stefano Ferilli	University of Bari, Italy
Stratis Ioannidis	Northeastern University, USA
Szymon Jaroszewicz	Polish Academy of Sciences, Poland
Tijl De Bie	Ghent University, Belgium
Ulf Brefeld	Leuphana University of Lüneburg, Germany
Varvara Vetrova	University of Canterbury, New Zealand
Wannes Meert	KU Leuven, Belgium
Wei Ye	Tongji University, China
Wenbin Zhang	Florida International University, USA
Willem Waegeman	Universiteit Gent, Belgium
Wouter Duivesteijn	Technische Universiteit Eindhoven, Netherlands
Xiao Luo	University of California, Los Angeles, USA
Yun Sing Koh	University of Auckland, New Zealand
Zied Bouraoui	CRIL CNRS and Université d'Artois, France

Senior Program Committee – Applied Data Science Track

Albrecht Zimmermann	Université de Caen Normandie, France
Andreas Hotho	University of Würzburg, Germany
Anirban Dasgupta	IIT Gandhinagar, India
Anna Monreale	University of Pisa, Italy
Annalisa Appice	University of Bari Aldo Moro, Italy
Bruno Cremilleux	Université de Caen Normandie, France
Carlotta Domeniconi	George Mason University, USA
Dejing Dou	BCG, USA
Fabio Pinelli	IMT Lucca, Italy
Fuzhen Zhuang	Beihang University, China

Gabor Melli	PredictionWorks, USA
Giuseppe Manco	ICAR-CNR, Italy
Glenn Fung	Independent Researcher, USA
Grzegorz Nalepa	Jagiellonian University, Poland
Hui Xiong	Hong Kong University of Science and Technology (Guangzhou), China
Inês Dutra	University of Porto, Portugal
Ioanna Miliou	Stockholm University, Sweden
Ira Assent	Aarhus University, Denmark
Jiayu Zhou	Michigan State University, USA
Jiliang Tang	Michigan State University, USA
Jingrui He	University of Illinois at Urbana-Champaign, USA
João Gama	INESC TEC - LIAAD, Portugal
Jose A. Gamez	Universidad de Castilla-La Mancha, Spain
Ke Liang	National University of Defense Technology, China
Kurt Driessens	Maastricht University, Netherlands
Lars Kotthoff	University of Wyoming, USA
Liang Sun	Alibaba Group, China
Martin Atzmueller	Osnabrück University and DFKI, Germany
Michael R. Berthold	KNIME, Germany
Michelangelo Ceci	University of Bari, Italy
Min-Ling Zhang	Southeast University, China
Mykola Pechenizkiy	TU Eindhoven, Netherlands
Myra Spiliopoulou	Otto-von-Guericke-Universität Magdeburg, Germany
Niklas Lavesson	Blekinge Institute of Technology, Sweden
Nikolaj Tatti	Helsinki University, Finland
Panagiotis Papapetrou	Stockholm University, Sweden
Paolo Frasconi	Università degli Studi di Firenze, Italy
Paulo Cortez	University of Minho, Portugal
Peggy Cellier	INSA Rennes, IRISA, France
Rayid Ghani	Carnegie Mellon University, USA
Sahar Asadi	King (Microsoft), UK
Sandeep Tata	Google, USA
Sepideh Pashami	Halmstad University, Sweden
Slawomir Nowaczyk	Halmstad University, Sweden
Sriparna Saha	IIT Patna, India
Thomas Liebig	TU Dortmund, Germany
Thomas Seidl	LMU Munich, Germany
Tom Diethe	AstraZeneca, UK
Tony Lindgren	Stockholm University, Sweden

Vincent S. Tseng National Yang Ming Chiao Tung University, Taiwan
Vítor Santos Costa Universidade do Porto, Portugal
Xingquan Zhu Florida Atlantic University, USA
Yi Chang Jilin University, China
Yinglong Xia Meta, USA
Yongxin Tong Beihang University, China
Yun Sing Koh University of Auckland, New Zealand
Zhaochun Ren Shandong University, China
Zheng Wang Alibaba DAMO Academy, China
Zhiwei (Tony) Qin Lyft, USA

Program Committee – Research Track

Christoph Bergmeir Monash University, Australia
A. K. M. Mahbubur Rahman Independent University, Bangladesh
Abdulhakim Qahtan Utrecht University, Netherlands
Abhishek A. Fujitsu Research, India
Acar Tamersoy Microsoft, USA
Ad Feelders Universiteit Utrecht, Netherlands
Adam Goodge I2R, A*STAR, Singapore
Adele Jia China Agricultural University, China
Adem Kikaj KU Leuven, Belgium
Aditya Mohan Leibniz Universität Hannover, Germany
Ajay A. Mahimkar AT&T, USA
Akka Zemmari Université de Bordeaux, France
Akshay Sethi MasterCard, USA
Alborz Geramifard Meta, USA
Alessandro Antonucci IDSIA, Switzerland
Alessandro Melchiorre Johannes Kepler University Linz, Austria
Alexander Dockhorn Leibniz University Hannover, Germany
Alexander Schiendorfer Technische Hochschule Ingolstadt, Germany
Alexander Schulz CITEC, Bielefeld University, Germany
Alexandre Termier Université de Rennes 1, France
Alexandre Verine Ecole Normale Supérieure - PSL, France
Alexandru C. Mara Ghent University, Belgium
Ali Ayadi University of Strasbourg, France
Ali Ismail-Fawaz IRIMAS, Université de Haute-Alsace, France
Alicja Wieczorkowska Polish-Japanese Academy of Information Technology, Poland
Alipio M. G. Jorge INESC TEC/University of Porto, Portugal

Alireza Gharahighehi	KU Leuven, Belgium
Alistair Shilton	Deakin University, Australia
Alneu A. Lopes	University of São Paulo, Brazil
Alper Demir	Izmir University of Economics, Turkey
Alvaro Figueira	CRACS and Universidade do Porto, Portugal
Amal Saadallah	TU Dortmund, Germany
Aman Chadha	Stanford University and Amazon, USA
Amer Krivosija	TU Dortmund, Germany
Amir H. Payberah	KTH Royal Institute of Technology, Sweden
Ammar Shaker	NEC Laboratories Europe, Europe
Ana Rita Nogueira	INESC TEC, Portugal
Anand Paul	Louisiana State University HSC, USA
Anastasios Gounaris	Aristotle University of Thessaloniki, Greece
Andre V. Carreiro	Fraunhofer Portugal AICOS, Portugal
André C. P. L. F. de Carvalho	University of São Paulo, Brazil
Andrea Cossu	University of Pisa, Italy
Andrea Mastropietro	University of Bonn, Germany
Andrea Pugnana	University of Trento, Italy
Andrea Tagarelli	DIMES - UNICAL, Italy
Andreas Bender	LMU Munich, Germany
Andreas Nürnberger	Otto-von-Guericke-Universität Magdeburg, Germany
Andreas Schwung	Fachhochschule Südwestfalen, Germany
Andrei Paleyes	University of Cambridge, UK
Andrzej Skowron	University of Warsaw, Poland
Andy Song	RMIT University, Australia
Angelica Liguori	ICAR-CNR, Italy
Anirban Dasgupta	IIT Gandhinagar, India
Anke Meyer-Baese	Florida State University, USA
Anna Beer	University of Vienna, Austria
Anna Krause	Universität Wurzburg and Chair X Data Science, Germany
Anna Monreale	University of Pisa, Italy
Annelot W. Bosman	Universiteit Leiden, Netherlands
Antoine Caradot	Hubert Curien Laboratory, France
Antonio Bahamonde	University of Oviedo, Spain
Antonio Mastropietro	Università di Pisa, Italy
Antonio Pellicani	Università degli Studi di Bari, Aldo Moro, Italy
Antonis Matakos	Aalto University, Finland
Antti Laaksonen	University of Helsinki, Finland
Aomar Osmani	LIPN-UMR CNRS, France
Aonghus Lawlor	University College Dublin, Ireland

Aparna S. Varde	Montclair State University, USA
Apostolos N. Papadopoulos	Aristotle University of Thessaloniki, Greece
Aritra Konar	KU Leuven, Belgium
Arjun Roy	Freie Universität Berlin, Germany
Arthur Charpentier	UQAM, Canada
Arunas Lipnickas	Kaunas University of Technology, Lithuania
Atsuhiro Takasu	National Institute of Informatics, Japan
Aurora Esteban	University of Cordoba, Spain
Baosheng Zhang	Tsinghua University, China
Barbara Toniella Corradini	University of Florence and University of Siena, Italy
Bardh Prenkaj	Technical University of Munich, Germany
Barry O'Sullivan	University College Cork, Ireland
Beilun Wang	Southeast University, China
Benjamin Halstead	University of Auckland, New Zealand
Benjamin Paassen	Bielefeld University, Germany
Benjamin Quost	Université de Technologie de Compiègne, France
Benoit Frenay	University of Namur, Belgium
Bernardo Moreno Sanchez	University of Helsinki, Finland
Bernhard Pfahringer	University of Waikato, New Zealand
Bertrand Cuissart	University of Caen, France
Bin Liu	Chongqing University of Posts and Telecommunications, China
Bin Shi	Xi'an Jiaotong University, China
Bin Wu	Zhengzhou University, China
Bin Zhou	National University of Defense Technology, China
Bitao Peng	Guangdong University of Foreign Studies, China
Bo Kang	Ghent University, Belgium
Bogdan Cautis	Université Paris-Saclay, France
Bojan Evkoski	Central European University, Hungary
Boshen Shi	Institute of Computing Technology, Chinese Academy of Sciences, China
Boualem Benatallah	Dublin City University, Ireland
Brandon Gower-Winter	Utrecht University, Netherlands
Bunil K. Balabantaray	NIT Meghalaya, India
Carlos Ferreira	INESC TEC, Portugal
Carlos Monserrat-Aranda	Universitat Politècnica de Valencia, Spain
Carson K. Leung	University of Manitoba, Canada
Catarina Silva	University of Coimbra, Portugal
Cecile Capponi	Aix-Marseille University, France
Celine Rouveirol	LIPN Université de Sorbonne Paris Nord, France

Cesar H. G. Andrade	Porto University, Portugal
Chandrajit Bajaj	University of Texas, Austin, USA
Chang Rajani	University of Helsinki, Finland
Charlotte Laclau	Polytechnique Institute, Télécom Paris, France
Charlotte Pelletier	Université de Bretagne du Sud, France
Chen Wang	DATA61, CSIRO, Australia
Cheng Cheng	Carnegie Mellon University, USA
Cheng Xie	Yunnan University, China
Chenglin Wang	East China Normal University, China
Chenwang Wu	University of Science and Technology of China, China
Chiara Pugliese	IIT Institute of National Research Council, Italy
Chien-Liang Liu	National Chiao Tung University, Taiwan
Chihiro Maru	Chuo University, Japan
Chongsheng Zhang	Henan University, China
Christian Beecks	FernUniversität in Hagen, Germany
Christian M. M. Frey	University of Technology Nuremberg, Germany
Christian Hakert	TU Dortmund, Germany
Christine Largeron	LabHC Lyon University, France
Christophe Rigotti	INSA Lyon, France
Christophe Rodrigues	DVRC Pôle universitaire Léonard de Vinci, France
Christos Anagnostopoulos	University of Glasgow, UK
Christos Diou Harokopio	University of Athens, Greece
Chuan Qin	Chinese Academy of Sciences, China
Chunchun Chen	Tongji University, China
Chunyao Song	Nankai University, China
Claire Nedellec	INRAE, MaIAGE, France
Claudio Borile	CENTAI Institute, Italy
Claudio Gallicchio	University of Pisa, Italy
Claudius Zelenka	Kiel University, Germany
Colin Bellinger	NRC and Dalhousie University, Canada
Collin Leiber	Aalto University, Finland
Cong Qi	New Jersey Institute of Technology, USA
Congfeng Cao	University of Amsterdam, Netherlands
Corrado Loglisci	Università degli Studi di Bari, Aldo Moro, Italy
Cuicui Luo	University of Chinese Academy of Sciences, China
Cuneyt G. Akcora	University of Central Florida, USA
Cynthia C. S. Liem	Delft University of Technology, Netherlands
Dalius Matuzevicius	Vilnius Gediminas Technical University, Lithuania

Dan Li	Sun Yat-sen University, China
Danai Koutra	University of Michigan, USA
Dang Nguyen	Deakin University, Australia
Daniel Neider	TU Dortmund, Germany
Daniel Schlor	Universität Würzburg, Germany
Danil Provodin	TU Eindhoven, Netherlands
Danyang Xiao	Sun Yat-sen University, China
Dario Garcia-Gasulla	Barcelona Supercomputing Center (BSC), Spain
Dario Garigliotti	University of Bergen, Norway
Darius Plonis	Vilnius Gediminas Technical University, Lithuania
Dariusz Brzezinski	Poznań University of Technology, Poland
David Gomez	Universidad Politecnica de Madrid, Spain
David Holzmüller	University of Stuttgart, Germany
David Q. Sun	Apple, USA
Davide Evangelista	University of Bologna, Italy
Debo Cheng	University of South Australia, Australia
Deepayan Chakrabarti	University of Texas at Austin, USA
Deng-Bao Wang	Southeast University, China
Denilson Barbosa	University of Alberta, Canada
Denis Huseljic	University of Kassel, Germany
Denis Lukovnikov	Ruhr-Universität Bochum, Germany
Destercke Sebastien	UTC, France
Di Jin	TikTok, USA
Di Wu	Chongqing Institute of Green and Intelligent Technology, Chinese Academy of Sciences, China
Diana Benavides Prado	University of Auckland, New Zealand
Dianhui Wang	Independent Researcher, Australia
Diego Carrera	STMicroelectronics, Switzerland
Diletta Chiaro	Università degli Studi di Napoli Federico II, Italy
Dimitri Staufer	TU Berlin, Germany
Dimitrios Katsaros	University of Thessaly, Greece
Dimitrios Rafailidis	University of Thessaly, France
Dino Ienco	INRAE, France
Dmitry Kobak	University of Tübingen, Germany
Domenico Redavid	University of Bari, Italy
Dominik M. Endres	Philipps-Universität Marburg, Germany
Dominique Gay	Université de La Réunion, France
Dong Li	Baylor University, USA
Duarte Folgado	Fraunhofer Portugal AICOS, Portugal
Duo Xu	Georgia Institute of Technology, USA

Edoardo Serra	Boise State University, USA
Edouard Fouche	Karlsruhe Institute of Technology (KIT), Germany
Eduardo F. Montesuma	Université Paris-Saclay, France
Edward Apeh	Bournemouth University, UK
Edwin Simpson	University of Bristol, UK
Ehsan Aminian	INESC TEC, Portugal
Ekaterina Antonenko	Mines Paris - PSL, France
Eliana Pastor	Politecnico di Torino, Italy
Emanuela Marasco	George Mason University, USA
Emilio Dorigatti	LMU Munich, Germany
Emilio Parrado-Hernandez	Universidad Carlos III de Madrid, Spain
Emmanouil Krasanakis	CERTH, Greece
Emmanouil Panagiotou	Freie Universität Berlin, Germany
Emre Gursoy	Koc University, Turkey
Engelbert Mephu Nguifo	Université Clermont Auvergne, CNRS, LIMOS, France
Eran Treister	Ben-Gurion University of the Negev, Israel
Erasmo Purificato	Otto-von-Guericke Universität Magdeburg, Germany
Erik Novak	Jožef Stefan Institute, Slovenia
Erwan Le Merrer	Inria, France
Esra Akbas	Georgia State University, USA
Esther-Lydia Silva-Ramirez	Universidad de Cadiz, Spain
Evaldas Vaičiukynas	Kaunas University of Technology, Lithuania
Evangelos Kanoulas	University of Amsterdam, Netherlands
Evelin Amorim	INESC TEC, Portugal
Fabian C. Spaeh	Boston University, USA
Fabio Fassetti	Università della Calabria, Italy
Fabio Fumarola	Prometeia, Italy
Fabio Mercorio	University of Milan-Bicocca, Italy
Fabio Vandin	University of Padova, Italy
Fandel Lin	University of Southern California, USA
Federica Granese	Inria, Université Côte d'Azur, France
Federico Baldo	University of Bologna, Italy
Federico Sabbatini	National Institute for Nuclear Physics (INFN), Italy
Feifan Zhang	China Agricultural University, China
Felipe Kenji Nakano	KU Leuven, Belgium
Fernando Martinez-Plumed	Universitat Politècnica de Valencia, Spain
Filipe Rodrigues	Technical University of Denmark (DTU), Denmark

Flavio Giobergia	Politecnico di Torino, Italy
Florent Masseglia	Inria, France
Florian Beck	JKU Linz, Austria
Florian Lemmerich	University of Passau, Germany
Francesca Naretto	University of Pisa, Italy
Francesco Piccialli	University of Naples Federico II, Italy
Francesco Renna	Universidade do Porto, Portugal
Francisco Pereira	DTU, Denmark
Franco Raimondi	Gran Sasso Science Institute, Italy
Frederic Koriche	Université d'Artois, CRIL CNRS, France
Frederic Pennerath	CentraleSupélec - LORIA, France
Furong Peng	Shanxi University, China
Gabriel Marques Tavares	LMU Munich, Germany
Gabriele Sartor	University of Turin, Italy
Gabriele Venturato	KU Leuven, Belgium
Gaetan De Waele	Ghent University, Belgium
Gaia Saveri	University of Trieste, Italy
Gang Li	Deakin University, Australia
Gaoyuan Du	Amazon, USA
Gavin Smith	University of Nottingham, UK
Geming Xia	National University of Defense Technology, China
Geng Zhao	Heidelberg University, Germany
Gennaro Vessio	University of Bari Aldo Moro, Italy
Geoffrey I. Webb	Monash, Australia
Georgia Baltsou	Centre for Research & Technology, Greece
Geraldin Nanfack	Concordia University, Canada
Germain Forestier	University of Haute Alsace, France
Gerrit Grossmann	DFKI, Germany
Gerrit J. J. van den Burg	Alan Turing Institute, UK
Gherardo Varando	Universitat de Valencia, Spain
Giacomo Medda	University of Cagliari, Italy
Gilberto Bernardes	INESC TEC and University of Porto, Portugal
Giorgio Venturin	University of Padova, Italy
Giovanna Castellano	University of Bari Aldo Moro, Italy
Giovanni Ponti	ENEA, Italy
Giovanni Stilo	Università degli Studi dell'Aquila, Italy
Gisele Pappa	UFMG, Brazil
Giuseppe Manco	ICAR-CNR, IT, Italy
Gizem Gezici	Scuola Normale Superiore, Italy
Gjergji Kasneci	TU Munich, Germany
Goreti Marreiros	ISEP/GECAD, Portugal

Graziella De Martino	University of Bari, Aldo Moro, Italy
Grazina Korvel	Vilnius University, Lithuania
Grigorios Tsoumakas	Aristotle University of Thessaloniki, Greece
Guangyin Jin	National University of Defense Technology, China
Guangzhong Sun	University of Science and Technology of China, China
Guanjin Wang	Murdoch University, Australia
Guilherme Weigert	Cassales University of Waikato, New Zealand
Guillaume Derval	UC Louvain - ICTEAM, Belgium
Guorui Quan	University of Manchester, UK
Guoxi Zhang	Beijing Institute of General Artificial Intelligence, China
Gustau Camps-Valls	Universitat de Valencia, Spain
Gustav Sir	Czech Technical University, Czech Republic
Gustavo Batista	University of New South Wales, Australia
Hachem Kadri	Aix-Marseille University, France
Hadi Asghari	Humboldt Institute for Internet and Society, Germany
Haifeng Sun	University of Science and Technology of China, China
Haihui Fan	Institute of Information Engineering, Chinese Academy of Sciences, China
Haizhou Du	Shanghai University of Electric Power, China
Hajer Salem	AUDENSIEL, France
Hakim Hacid	TII, United Arab Emirates
Hamid Bouchachia	Bournemouth University, UK
Han Wang	Xidian University, China
Hang Yu	Shanghai University, China
Hanna Sumita	Institute of Science Tokyo, Japan
Hao Niu	KDDI Research, Japan
Hao Xue	University of New South Wales, Australia
Hao Yan	Carleton University, Canada
Haowen Zhang	Zhejiang Sci-Tech University, China
Harsh Borse	IIT Kharagpur, India
Heitor M. Gomes	Victoria University of Wellington, New Zealand
Helder Oliveira	FCUP and INESC TEC, Portugal
Helge Langseth	Norwegian University of Science and Technology, Norway
Hendrik Blockeel	KU Leuven, Belgium
Henrique O. Marques	University of Southern Denmark, Denmark
Henryk Maciejewski	Wroclaw University of Science and Technology, Poland

Hideaki Ishibashi	Kyushu Institute of Technology, Japan
Hilde J. P. Weerts	Eindhoven University of Technology, Netherlands
Holger Froening	University of Heidelberg, Germany
Holger Karl	HPI, Germany
Hongbo Bo	University of Bristol, UK
Hongyang Chen	Zhejiang Lab, China
Hua Chu	Xidian University, China
Huaiyu Wan	Beijing Jiaotong University, China
Huaming Chen	University of Sydney, Australia
Huandong Wang	Tsinghua University, China
Huanlai Xing	Southwest Jiaotong University, China
Hui Ji	University of Pittsburgh, USA
Hui (Wendy) Wang	Stevens Institute of Technology, USA
Huiping Chen	University of Birmingham, UK
Humberto Bustince	Universidad Publica de Navarra, Spain
Huong Ha	RMIT University, Australia
Idir Benouaret	Epita Research Laboratory, France
Ines Sousa	Fraunhofer AICOS, Portugal
Ingo Thon	Siemens AG, Germany
Inigo Jauregi Unanue	University of Technology Sydney, Australia
Ioannis Sarridis	Centre for Research & Technology, Greece
Issam Falih	Université Clermont Auvergne, CNRS, LIMOS, France
Ivan Vankov	iris.ai, Norway
Ivor Cribben	University of Alberta, Canada
Jaemin Yoo	KAIST, South Korea
Jakir Hossain	University at Buffalo, USA
Jakub Klikowski	Wroclaw University of Science and Technology, Poland
Jalaj Bhandari	Columbia University, USA
Jaleed Khan	University of Oxford, UK
James Goulding	University of Nottingham, UK
Jan Kalina	Czech Academy of Sciences, Czech Republic
Jan P. Mielniczuk	Polish Academy of Sciences, Poland
Jan Ramon	Inria, France
Jan Verwaeren	Ghent University, Belgium
Jannis Brugger	TU Darmstadt, Germany
Jean-Marc Andreoli	Naverlabs Europe, Netherlands
Jedrzej Potoniec	Poznań University of Technology, Poland
Jeronimo Arenas-Garcia	Universidad Carlos III de Madrid, Spain
Jhony H. Giraldo	Télécom Paris, Institut Polytechnique de Paris, France

Jia Cai	Guangdong University of Finance and Economics, China
Jiahui Jin	Southeast University, China
Jiang Zhong	Independent Researcher, China
Jianwu Wang	University of Maryland, Baltimore County, USA
Jiawei Chen	Tianjin University, China
Jiaxin Ding	Shanghai Jiao Tong University, China
Jidong Yuan	Beijing Jiaotong University, China
Jie Song	Zhejiang University, China
Jie Wu	Fudan University, China
Jie Yang	University of Wollongong, China
Jimeng Shi	Florida International University, USA
Jin Chen	Hong Kong University of Science and Technology, China
Jin Liang	South China Normal University, China
Jing Ren	NUDT, China
Jing Wang	Amazon, USA
Jinghui Zhong	South China University of Technology, China
Jingtao Ding	Tsinghua University, China
Jinli Zhang	Beijing University of Technology, China
Jiri Sima	Czech Academy of Sciences, Czech Republic
João Gama	University of Porto, Portugal
Joao Mendes-Moreira	University of Porto, Portugal
Joao Vinagre	European Commission (JRC), Spain
Joaquim Silva	NOVA LINCS, Universidade Nova de Lisboa, Portugal
Jochen De Weerdt	KU Leuven, Belgium
Joe Mellor	University of Edinburgh, UK
Johanne Cohen	LISN-CNRS, France
Johannes Jakubik	IBM Research, USA
John W. Sheppard	Montana State University, USA
Jonata Tyska Carvalho	Federal University of Santa Catarina, Brazil
Jordi Guitart	Barcelona Supercomputing Center (BSC), Spain
Joris Mattheijssens	Ghent University, Belgium
Jose M. Costa Pereira	University of Porto, Portugal
Jose Oramas	University of Antwerp, sqIRL/IDLab, imec, Belgium
Jose Tomas Palma	University of Murcia, Spain
Joydeep Chandra	Indian Institute of Technology, Patna, India
Juan A. Botia	University of Murcia, Spain
Juan Rodriguez	Universidad de Burgos, Spain
Jukka Heikkonen	University of Turku, Finland

Julien Delaunay	Inria, France
Julien Ferry	Polytechnique Montreal, Canada
Julien Perez	EPITA, France
Jun Zhuang	Boise State University, USA
Jun Yu Hou	Nanjing University, China
Junbo Zhang	JD Intelligent Cities Research, USA
Junze Liu	University of California, Irvine, USA
Jurgita Kapočiūtė-Dzikienė	Tilde SIA, University of Latvia and Tilde IT, Vytautas Magnus University, Lithuania
Justina Mandravickaitė	Vytautas Magnus University, Lithuania
Kamil Adamczewski	Max Planck Institute for Intelligent Systems, Germany
Kamil Michal Ksiazek	Jagiellonian University, Poland
Karim Radouane	Université Sorbonne Paris Nord, France
Kary Framing	Umeå University, Sweden
Katerina Taskova	University of Auckland, New Zealand
Katharina Dost	Jožef Stefan Institute, Slovenia
Kaushik Roy	University of South Carolina, USA
Kejia Chen	Nanjing University of Posts and Telecommunications, China
Ken Kobayashi	Tokyo Institute of Technology, Japan
Khaled Mohammed Saifuddin	Northeastern University, USA
Khalid Benabdeslem	Université de Lyon 1, France
Kim Thang Nguyen	LIG, University Grenoble-Alpes, France
Kira Maag	Heinrich-Heine-Universität Düsseldorf, Germany
Koji Maruhashi	Fujitsu Research, Japan
Koyel Mukherjee	Adobe Research, USA
Kristen M. Scott	KU Leuven, Belgium
Krzysztof Ruda	Polish Academy of Sciences, Poland
Krzysztof Slot	Lodz University of Technology, Poland
Kuldeep Singh	Cerence, Germany
Kushankur Ghosh	University of Alberta, Canada
Lamine Diop	EPITA, France
Latifa Oukhellou	IFSTTAR, France
Laurence Park	Western Sydney University, Australia
Laurens Devos	KU Leuven, Belgium
Len Feremans	Universiteit Antwerpen, Belgium
Lena Wiese	Goethe University Frankfurt, Germany
Lenaig Cornanguer	CISPA Helmholtz Center for Information Security, Germany
Lennert De Smet	KU Leuven, Belgium
Lev Reyzin	University of Illinois at Chicago, USA

Li Wang	National University of Defense Technology, China
Liang Du	Shanxi University, China
Lianyong Qi	China University of Petroleum (East China), China
Lijie Hu	King Abdullah University of Science and Technology, Saudi Arabia
Lijing Zhu	Bowling Green State University, USA
Lingling Zhang	Capital Normal University, China
Lingyue Fu	Shanghai Jiao Tong University, China
Linh Le Pham Van	Deakin University, Australia
Livio Bioglio	University of Turin, Italy
Lixing Yu	Yunnan University, China
Liyan Song	Harbin Institute of Technology, China
Longlong Sun	Chang'an University, China
Luca Corbucci	University of Pisa, Italy
Luca Ferragina	University of Calabria, Italy
Luca Romeo	University of Macerata, Italy
Lucas Pereira	LARSyS, Tecnico Lisboa, Portugal
Luciano Caroprese	ICAR-CNR, Italy
Ludovico Boratto	University of Cagliari, Italy
Luis Rei	Jožef Stefan Institute, Slovenia
Mahardhika Pratama	University of South Australia, Australia
Maiju Karjalainen	University of Eastern Finland, Finland
Makoto Onizuka	Osaka University, Japan
Manali Sharma	Samsung, South Korea
Maneet Singh	MasterCard, India
Manuel M. Garcia-Piqueras	Universidad de Castilla La Mancha, Spain
Manuele Bicego	University of Verona, Italy
Mao A. Cheng	University of California, Berkeley, USA
Marc Plantevit	EPITA, France
Marc Tommasi	Lille University, France
Marcel Wever	Leibniz University Hannover, Germany
Marcilio de Souto	LIFO/Université d'Orleans, France
Marco Lippi	University of Florence, Italy
Marco Loog	Radboud University, Netherlands
Marco Mellia	Politecnico di Torino, Italy
Marco Podda	University of Pisa, Italy
Marco Polignano	Università di Bari, Italy
Marco Viviani	Università degli Studi di Milano Bicocca, Italy
Maria Vasconcelos	Fraunhofer Portugal AICOS, Portugal
Maria Sofia Bucarelli	Sapienza University of Rome, Italy

Mariana Oliveira	Universidade do Porto, Portugal
Mariana Vargas Vieyra	MostlyAI, Austria
Marielle Malfante	CEA, France
Marina Litvak	Shamoon College of Engineering, Israel
Mario Antunes	Universidade de Aveiro, Portugal
Mario Andres Munoz	University of Melbourne, Australia
Marius Koppel	Johannes Gutenberg University Mainz, Germany
Mark Junjie Li	Shenzhen University, China
Marko Robnik-Sikonja	University of Ljubljana, Slovenia
Marta Soare	Université d'Orleans, France
Martin Holena	Czech Academy of Sciences, Czech Republic
Martin Pilat	Charles University, Czech Republic
Martino Ciaperoni	Aalto University, Finland
Marwan Hassani	TU Eindhoven, Netherlands
Masahiro Suzuki	University of Tokyo, Japan
Massimo Guarascio	ICAR-CNR, Italy
Matej Mihelcic	University of Zagreb, Croatia
Mathias Verbeke	KU Leuven, Belgium
Mathieu Lefort	Université de Lyon, France
Matteo Francobaldi	University of Bologna, Italy
Matteo Riondato	Amherst College, USA
Matteo Salis	University of Turin, Italy
Matthew B. Middlehurst	University of Southampton, UK
Matthia Sabatelli	University of Groningen, Netherlands
Mattia Cerrato	JGU Mainz, Germany
Mattia Setzu	University of Pisa, Italy
Mattis Hartwig	German Research Center for Artificial Intelligence, Germany
Matyas Bohacek	Stanford University, USA
Maximilian T. Fischer	University of Konstanz, Germany
Maximilian Münch	University of Applied Sciences, Würzburg-Schweinfurt, Germany
Maximilian Stubbemann	University of Hildesheim, Germany
Maximilian Thiessen	TU Wien, Austria
Maximilian von Zastrow	Southern Denmark University, Denmark
Megha Khosla	TU Delft, Netherlands
Meiyun Zuo	Renmin University of China, China
Meng Liu	National University of Defense Technology, China
Mengying Zhu	Zhejiang University, China
Michael Granitzer	University of Passau, Germany
Michael B. Ito	University of Michigan, USA

Michael G. Madden	National University of Ireland, Galway, Ireland
Michal Wozniak	Wroclaw University of Science and Technology, Poland
Michele Fontana	Università di Pisa, Italy
Michiel Stock	Ghent University, Belgium
Miguel Rocha	University of Minho, Portugal
Miguel Silva	INESC TEC, Portugal
Mike Holenderski	Eindhoven University of Technology, Netherlands
Milos Savic	University of Novi Sad, Serbia
Mina Rezaei	LMU Munich, Germany
Minh P. Nguyen	University of Texas, Austin, USA
Minyoung Choe	Korea Advanced Institute of Science and Technology, South Korea
Minyu Chen	Shanghai Jiaotong University, China
Miquel Perello-Nieto	University of Bristol, UK
Mira Kristin Jurgens	Ghent University, Belgium
Miriam Santos	University of Porto, Portugal
Mirko Bunse	TU Dortmund, Germany
Mirko Polato	University of Turin, Italy
Mitra Baratchi	LIACS, University of Leiden, Netherlands
Mohammed Elbamby	Telefonica Scientific Research, Spain
Moises Rocha dos Santos	University of Porto, Portugal
Monowar Bhuyan	Umeå University, Sweden
Morteza Rakhshaninejad	Ghent University, Belgium
Mounim A. El Yacoubi	Télécom SudParis, France
Muhammad Rajabinasab	University of Southern Denmark, Denmark
Muhao Guo	Arizona State University, USA
Mustapha Lebbah	Paris Saclay University-Versailles, France
Nabeel Hussain Syed	Rheinland-Pfälzische Technische Universität, Kaiserslautern-Landau, Germany
Nandyala Hemachandra	Indian Institute of Technology Bombay, India
Nannan Wu	Tianjin University, China
Nanqing Dong	Shanghai Artificial Intelligence Laboratory, China
Naresh Manwani	International Institute of Information Technology, Hyderabad, India
Natan Tourne	Ghent University, Belgium
Nate Veldt	Texas A&M, USA
Nathalie Japkowicz	American University, USA
Natthawut Kertkeidkachorn	Japan Advanced Institute of Science and Technology (JAIST), Japan
Ngoc-Son Vu	ENSEA, France
Nhat-Tan Bui	University of Arkansas, USA

Nian Li	Tsinghua University, China
Nick Lim	University of Waikato, New Zealand
Nico Piatkowski	Fraunhofer IAIS, Germany
Nicolas Roque dos Santos	University of São Paulo, Brazil
Niklas A. Strauss	LMU Munich, Germany
Nikolaj Tatti	Helsinki University, Finland
Nikolaos Nikolaou	University College London, UK
Nikolaos Stylianou	Information Technologies Institute, Greece
Nikos Kanakaris	University of Southern California, USA
Ning Xu	Southeast University, China
Nripsuta Saxena	University of Southern California, USA
Nuwan Gunasekara	Halmstad University, Sweden
Olga Kurasova	Vilnius University, Lithuania
Olga Slizovskaia	AstraZeneca, UK
Olivier Teste	IRIT, University of Toulouse, France
Oswald C.	NIT Trichy, India
Oswaldo Solarte-Pabon	Universidad del Valle, Colombia
Ozge Alacam	University of Bielefeld, Germany
P. S. Sastry	Indian Institute of Science, India
Pablo Olmos	Universidad Carlos III de Madrid, Spain
Panagiotis Karras	University of Copenhagen, Denmark
Panagiotis Symeonidis	University of the Aegean, Greece
Pance Panov	Jožef Stefan Institute, Slovenia
Paolo Bonetti	Politecnico di Milano, Italy
Paolo Merialdo	Università degli Studi Roma Tre, Italy
Paolo Mignone	University of Bari Aldo Moro, Italy
Pascal Welke	TU Wien, Austria
Patrick Y. Wu	American University, USA
Paul Caillon	LAMSADE Université Paris Dauphine - PSL, France
Paul Davidsson	Malmo University, Sweden
Paul Prasse	University of Potsdam, Germany
Paulo J. Azevedo	Universidade do Minho, Portugal
Pawel Teisseyre	Warsaw University of Technology, Poland
Pawel Zyblewski	Wroclaw University of Science and Technology, Poland
Pedro G. Ferreira	University of Porto, Portugal
Pedro Larrañaga	Technical University of Madrid, Spain
Pedro Ribeiro	University of Porto, Portugal
Pedro H. Abreu	CISUC, Portugal
Peijie Sun	Tsinghua University, China
Peng Wu	Shanghai Jiao Tong University, China

Pengpeng Qiao	Institute of Science Tokyo, Japan
Peter Karsmakers	KU Leuven, Belgium
Peter Schneider-Kamp	SDU, Denmark
Peter van der Putten	Leiden University, Netherlands
Petia Georgieva	University of Aveiro, Portugal
Philipp Vaeth	Technical University of Applied Sciences Würzburg-Schweinfurt and Universität Bielefeld, Germany
Philippe Preux	Inria, France
Phung Lai	SUNY-Albany, USA
Pierre Geurts	Montefiore Institute, University of Liège, Belgium
Pierre Monnin	Université Côte d'Azur, Inria, CNRS, I3S, France
Pierre Schaus	UC Louvain, Belgium
Pierre Wolinski	Paris Dauphine University - PSL, France
Pieter Robberechts	KU Leuven, Belgium
Pietro Sabatino	ICAR-CNR, Italy
Pingchuan Ma	HKUST, China
Piotr Habas	Amazon, USA
Piotr Lipinski	University of Wroclaw, Poland
Piotr Porwik	University of Silesia, Katowice, Poland
Prithwish Chakraborty	IBM Corporation, USA
Lucie Flek	Marburg University, Germany
Przemyslaw Biecek	Warsaw University of Technology, Poland
Qiang Sheng	Institute of Computing Technology, Chinese Academy of Sciences, China
Qiang Zhou	Nanjing University of Aeronautics and Astronautics, China
Rafet Sifa	Fraunhofer IAIS, Germany
Raha Moraffah	Arizona State University, USA
Raivydas Simanas	Vilnius University, Lithuania
Rajeev Rastogi	Amazon, USA
Ranya Almohsen	Baylor College of Medicine, USA
Raphael Romero	Ghent University, Belgium
Raquel Sebastiao	ESTGV-IPV & IEETA-UA, Portugal
Ravi Kolla	Sony Research India, India
Raza Ul Mustafa	Loyola University, USA
Remy Cazabet	Université de Lyon 1, France
Renhe Jiang	University of Tokyo, Japan
Reza Akbarinia	Inria, France
Ricardo P. M. Cruz	University of Porto (FEUP), Portugal
Ricardo B. Prudencio	Universidade Federal de Pernambuco, Brazil
Ricardo Rios	Federal University of Bahia, Brazil

Ricardo Santos	Fraunhofer Portugal AICOS, Portugal
Riccardo Guidotti	University of Pisa, Italy
Robertas Damasevicius	Vytautas Magnus University, Lithuania
Roberto Corizzo	American University, USA
Roberto Interdonato	CIRAD, France
Rocio Chongtay	University of Southern Denmark, Denmark
Rohit Babbar	University of Bath, UK and Aalto University, Finland
Romain Tavenard	Université de Rennes, LETG/IRISA, France
Rosana Veroneze	LBiC, Italy
Ruggero G. Pensa	University of Turin, Italy
Rui Meng	BNU-HKBU United International College, USA
Rui Yu	University of Louisville, USA
Ruixuan Liu	Emory University, USA
Runqun Xiong	Southeast University, China
Runxue Bao	University of Pittsburgh, USA
Ruochun Jin	National University of Defense Technology, China
Ruta Juozaitiene	Vytautas Magnus University, Lithuania
Rytis Maskeliunas	Polsl, Poland
Salvatore Ruggieri	University of Pisa, Italy
Sam Verboven	Vrije Universiteit Brussel, Belgium
Sangkyun Lee	Korea University, South Korea
Sara Abdali	University of California, Riverside, USA
Sarah Masud	LCS2, IIIT-D, India
Sarwan Ali	Georgia State University, USA
Satoru Koda	Fujitsu Limited, Japan
Sebastian Buschjager	Lamarr Institute for ML and AI, Germany
Sebastian Jimenez	Ghent University, Belgium
Sebastian Meznar	Jožef Stefan Institute, Ljubljana, Slovenia
Sebastian Ventura Soto	University of Cordoba, Spain
Sebastien Razakarivony	Safran, France
Selpi Selpi	Chalmers University of Technology, Sweden
Sergio Greco	University of Calabria, Italy
Sergio Jesus	Feedzai, Portugal
Sha Lu	University of South Australia, Australia
Shalini Priya	Indian Institute of Technology Patna, India
Shanqing Guo	Shandong University, China
Shaofu Yang	Southeast University, China
Shazia Tabassum	INESCTEC, Portugal
Shengxiang Gao	Kunming University of Science and Technology, China

Shichao Pei	University of Massachusetts, Boston, USA
Shin Matsushima	University of Tokyo, Japan
Shin-ichi Maeda	Preferred Networks, Japan
Shiwen Ni	Chinese Academy of Sciences, China
Shiyou Qian	Shanghai Jiao Tong University, China
Shu Zhao	Anhui University, China
Shuai Li	University of Cambridge, UK and University of Tokyo, Japan, Tsinghua University, China
Shuang Cheng	Institute of Computing Technology, Chinese Academy of Sciences, China
Shubhranshu Shekhar	Brandeis University, USA
Shurui Cao	Carnegie Mellon University, USA
Shuteng Niu	Mayo Clinic, USA
Siamak Ghodsi	Leibniz University of Hannover, Germany
Sihai Zhang	University of Science and Technology of China, China
Silvia Chiusano	Politecnico di Torino, Italy
Silviu Maniu	Université de Grenoble Alpes, France
Simon Gottschalk	L3S Research Center, Leibniz Universität Hannover, Germany
Simona Nistico	University of Calabria, Italy
Simone Angarano	Politecnico di Torino, Italy
Sinong Zhao	Nankai University, China
Siwei Wang	Intelligent Game and Decision Lab, China
Sofoklis Kitharidis	LIACS, Netherlands
Songlin Du	University of Melbourne, Australia
Songlin Du	Southeast University, China
Soumyajit Chatterjee	Nokia Bell Labs, USA
Sourav Dutta	Huawei Research Centre, China
Stefan Duffner	University of Lyon, France
Stefan Heindorf	Paderborn University, Germany
Stefan Kesselheim	Forschungszentrum Jülich, Germany
Stefano Bortoli	Huawei Research Center, China
Stefanos Vrochidis	Information Technologies Institute, CERTH, Greece
Steffen Thoma	FZI Research Center for Information Technology, Germany
Stephan Doerfel	Kiel University of Applied Sciences, Germany
Steven D. Prestwich	University College Cork, Ireland
Suman Banerjee	IIT Jammu, India
Sunil Aryal	Deakin University, Australia
Surabhi Adhikari	Columbia University, USA

Susan McKeever	TU Dublin, Ireland
Swati Swati	Universität der Bundeswehr München, Germany
Szymon Wojciechowski	Wroclaw University of Science and Technology, Poland
Talip Ucar	AstraZeneca, UK
Taro Tezuka	University of Tsukuba, Japan
Tatiana Passali	Aristotle University of Thessaloniki, Greece
Tatiane Nogueira Rios	UFBA, Brazil
Telmo M. Silva Filho	University of Bristol, UK
Teng Lin	Hong Kong University of Technology (Guangzhou), China
Teng Zhang	Huazhong University of Science and Technology, China
Thach Le Nguyen	Insight Centre, Ireland
Thang Duy Dang	Fujitsu Limited, Japan
Thanh-Son Nguyen	A*STAR, Singapore
Theresa Eimer	Leibniz University Hannover, Germany
Thiago Andrade	INESC TEC & University of Porto, Portugal
Thomas Bonald	Telecom Paris, France
Thomas Guyet	Inria, Centre de Lyon, France
Thomas Lampert	University of Strasbourg, France
Thomas L. Lee	University of Edinburgh, UK
Thomas Mortier	Ghent University, Belgium
Tianyi Chen	Boston University, USA
Tie Luo	University of Kentucky, USA
Tiehang Duan	Mayo Clinic, USA
Tijl De Bie	Ghent University, Belgium
Timilehin B. Aderinola	University College Dublin, Ireland
Timo Bertram	Johannes-Kepler Universität, Germany
Timo Ropinski	Ulm University, Germany
Tobias A. Hille	University of Kassel, Germany
Tom Hanika	University of Hildesheim, Germany
Tomas Kliegr	University of Economics, Prague, Czech Republic
Tomasz Michalak	University of Warsaw and Ideas NCBiR, Poland
Tomasz Walkowiak	Wroclaw University of Science and Technology, Poland
Tommaso Zoppi	University of Florence, Italy
Tong Li	Hong Kong University of Technology, China
Tong Mo	Peking University, China
Tongya Zheng	Hangzhou City University, China
Tonio Weidler	Maastricht University, Netherlands
Tony Lindgren	Stockholm University, Sweden

Tsunenori Mine	Kyushu University, Japan
Tuan Le	New Mexico State University, USA
Tuwe Lofstrom	Jönköping University, Sweden
Ulf Johansson	Jönköping University, Sweden
Vadim Ermolayev	Ukrainian Catholic University, Ukraine
Vahan Martirosyan	CentraleSupélec, Belgium
Vana Kalogeraki	Athens University of Economics and Business, Greece
Vanessa Gomez-Verdejo	Universidad Carlos III de Madrid, Spain
Vasileios Iosifidis	SCHUFA Holding, Germany
Vasilis Gkolemis	ATHENA RC, Greece
Victor Charpenay	Mines Saint-Etienne, France
Vincent Derkinderen	KU Leuven, Belgium
Vincent Lemaire	Orange Research, France
Vincenzo Pasquadibisceglie	University of Bari, Aldo Moro, Italy
Virginijus Marcinkevicius	Vilnius University, Lithuania
Vitor Cerqueira	University of Porto, Portugal
Vivek Kumar	Universität der Bundeswehr München, Germany
Vivek Srikumar	University of Utah, USA
Wagner Meira Jr.	UFMG, Brazil
Wei Wu	Ben Gurion University of the Negev, Israel
Weichen Li	RPTU Kaiserslautern-Landau, Germany
Weifeng Xu	Independent Researcher, China
Weike Pan	Shenzhen University, China
Weiwei Jiang	Beijing University of Posts and Telecommunications, China
Weiwei Sun	Carnegie Mellon University, USA
Weiwei Yuan	Nanjing University of Aeronautics and Astronautics, China
Weixiong Rao	Tongji University, China
Wen-Bo Xie	Southwest Petroleum University, China
Wenhao Li	Tongji University, China
Wenhao Zheng	Shopee, Singapore
Wenjie Feng	National University of Singapore, Singapore
Wenjie Xi	George Mason University, USA
Wenshui Luo	Nanjing University of Science and Technology, China
Wentao Yu	Nanjing University of Science and Technology, China
Wenzhe Yi	Wuhan University, China
Wenzhong Li	Nanjing University, China
Wojciech Rejchel	Nicolaus Copernicus University, Torun, Poland

Xi Jiang	Southern University of Science and Technology, China
Xiang Li	East China Normal University, China
Xiang Lian	Kent State University, USA
Xiao Ma	Beijing University of Posts and Telecommunications, China
Xiao Zhang	Shandong University, China
Xiaobing Zhou	Yunnan University, China
Xiaofeng Cao	University of Technology Sydney, Australia
Xiaofeng Gao	Shanghai Jiaotong University, China
Xiaojun Chen	Institute of Information Engineering, Chinese Academy of Sciences, China
Xiao-Jun Zeng	University of Manchester, UK
Xiaoming Zhang	Beihang University, China
Xiaoting Zhao	Etsy, USA
Xiaowei Mao	Beijing Jiaotong University, China
Xiaoyu Shi	Chinese Academy of Sciences, China
Xin Du	University of Edinburgh, UK
Xin Qin	California State University, Long Beach, USA
Xing Tang	Tencent, China
Xing Xing	Tongji University, China
Xinning Zhu	Beijing University of Posts and Telecommunications, China
Xinpeng Lv	National University of Defense Technology, China
Xintao Wu	University of Arkansas, USA
Xinyang Zhang	University of Illinois at Urbana-Champaign, USA
Xinyu Guan	Xi'an Jiaotong University, China
Xixun Lin	Chinese Academy of Sciences, China
Xiyue Zhang	University of Bristol, UK
Xuan-Hong Dang	IBM T.J. Watson Research Center, USA
Xue Li	University of Queensland, Australia
Xue Yan	Institute of Automation, Chinese Academy of Sciences, China
Xuefeng Chen	Chongqing University, China
Xuemin Wang	Guilin University of Electronic Technology, China
Yachuan Zhang	East China University of Science and Technology, China
Yan Zhang	Peking University, China
Yang Li	University of North Carolina at Chapel Hill, USA
Yang Shu	East China Normal University, China
Yang Wei	Nanjing University of Science and Technology, China

Yanhao Wang	East China Normal University, China
Yanmin Zhu	Shanghai Jiao Tong University, China
Yansong Y. L. Li	University of Ottawa, Canada
Yao-Xiang Ding	Nanjing University, China
Yaqi Xie	Carnegie Mellon University, USA
Yasutoshi Ida	NTT, Japan
Yaying Zhang	Tongji University, China
Ye Zhu	Deakin University, Australia
Yeon-Chang Lee	Ulsan National Institute of Science and Technology, South Korea
Yexiang Xue	Purdue University, USA
Yi Wang	Xinjiang Technical Institute of Physics and Chemistry, Chinese Academy of Sciences, China
Yifeng Gao	University of Texas, Rio Grande Valley, USA
Yilun Jin	Hong Kong University of Science and Technology, China
Yin Zhang	University of Electronic Science and Technology of China, China
Ying Chen	RMIT University, Australia
Yinsheng Li	Fudan University, China
Yong Li	Huawei European Research Center, China
Yongyu Wang	JD Logistics, China
Youhei Akimoto	University of Tsukuba/RIKEN AIP, Japan
You-Wei Luo	Sun Yat-sen University and Jiaying University, China
Yuchen Li	Baidu, China
Yuchen Yang	Harbin Institute of Technology, China
Yudi Zhang	Eindhoven University of Technology, Netherlands
Yuhao Li	University of Melbourne, Australia
Yuheng Jia	Southeast University, China
Yujia Zheng	CMU, USA
Yulong Pei	TU Eindhoven, Netherlands
Yuncheng Jiang	South China Normal University, China
Yuntao Shou	Xi'an Jiaotong University, China
Yunyun Wang	Nanjing University of Posts and Telecommunications, China
Yutong Ye	East China Normal University, China
Yuzhou Chen	University of California, Riverside, USA
Zahraa Abdallah	University of Bristol, UK
Zaineb Chelly Dagdia	UVSQ, Paris-Saclay, France
Zehua Cheng	University of Oxford, UK
Zeyu Chen	University of Auckland, New Zealand

Zhaocheng Ge	Huazhong University of Science and Technology, China
Zhe Yang	Soochow University, China
Zhen Liu	Guangdong University of Foreign Studies, China
Zheng Chen	Osaka University, Japan
Zhenghao Liu	Northeastern University, China
Zhenyu Yang	Macquarie University, Australia
Zhi Li	Tsinghua University, China
Zhichao Han	ETHZ, Switzerland
Zhihui Wang	Fudan University, China
Zhilong Shan	South China Normal University, China
Zhipeng Yin	Florida International University, USA
Zhipeng Zou	Nanjing University of Science and Technology, China
Zhiwen Xiao	Southwest Jiaotong University, China
Zhiwen Zhang	LocationMind, Japan
Zhixin Li	Guangxi Normal University, China
Zhiyong Cheng	Shandong Academy of Sciences, China
Zhong Chen	Southern Illinois University, USA
Zhong Li	Leiden University, Netherlands
Zhong Zhang	Tsinghua University, China
Zhongjing Yu	Peking University, China
Zhuang Liu	Dongbei University of Finance and Economics, China
Zhuo Cao	Forschungszentrum Jülich, Germany
Zhuoming Xie	Guangdong University of Technology, China
Zhuoqun Li	Louisiana State University, USA
Zicheng Zhao	Nanjing University of Science and Technology, China
Zichong Wang	Florida International University, USA
Zifeng Ding	University of Cambridge, UK
Ziheng Chen	Walmart, USA
Zijie J. Wang	Georgia Tech, USA
Zirui Zhuang	Beijing University of Posts and Telecommunications, China
Zixing Song	Chinese University of Hong Kong, China
Ziyu Wang	University of Tokyo, Japan
Ziyue Li	University of Cologne, Germany
Zongxia Xie	Tianjin University, China
Zongyue Li	LMU Munich, Germany
Zuojin Tang	Zhejiang University, China

List of Editors

Bernhard Pfahringer	University of Waikato, New Zealand
Nathalie Japkowicz	American University, USA
Pedro Larrañaga	Technical University of Madrid, Spain
Rita P. Ribeiro	University of Porto, Portugal
Alípio M. Jorge	University of Porto, Portugal
Carlos Soares	University of Porto, Portugal
João Gama	University of Porto, Portugal
Pedro H. Abreu	University of Coimbra, Portugal

Program Committee – Applied Data Science Track

Nasrullah Sheikh	IBM Research, USA
Aakarsh Malhotra	MasterCard, USA
Aakash Goel	Amazon, USA
Abdoulaye Sakho	Artefact, France
Abhijeet Pendyala	Ruhr-Universität Bochum, Germany
Abu Shad Ahammed	University of Siegen, Germany
Adi Lin	Didi, China
Aditya Gautam	Meta, USA
Ahmed K. Mohamed	Meta, USA
Akihiro Yoshida	Kyushu University, Japan
Akshay Sethi	MasterCard, USA
Alejandro Kuratomi	Stockholm University, Sweden
Alessandro Gambetti	Nova School of Business and Economics, Portugal
Alessandro Leite	INSA Rouen, Inria, France
Alessio Russo	Politecnico di Milano, Italy
Alex Beeson	University of Warwick, UK
Alexander Galozy	Halmstad University, Sweden
Alexander Karlsson	University of Skovde, Sweden
Alexander Kovalenko	Czech Technical University in Prague, Czech Republic
Alexey Zaytsev	Skoltech, Russia
Alina Bazarova	Forschungszentrum Jülich, Germany
Alix Lheritier	Amadeus SAS, France
Allan Tucker	Brunel University London, UK
Alvaro Figueira	CRACS and Universidade do Porto, Portugal
Aman Gulati	Amazon, USA
Amira Soliman	Halmstad University, Sweden

Organization

Ana Gjorgjevikj	Jožef Stefan Institute, Slovenia
Anders Holst	RISE SICS, Sweden
André C. P. L. F. de Carvalho	University of São Paulo, Brazil
Andrea Seveso	University of Milan-Bicocca, Italy
Andreas Bender	LMU Munich, Germany
Andreas Henelius	Independent Researcher, Finland
Andreas Holzinger	University of Natural Resources and Life Sciences, Vienna, Austria
Andrei Shelopugin	Independent Researcher, Brazil
Angelo Impedovo	Niuma, Italy
Aniket Chakrabarti	Amazon, USA
Animesh Prasad	Roku, USA
Anisio Lacerda	UFMG, Brazil
Anli Ji	Georgia State University, USA
Antoine Doucet	La Rochelle Université, France
Anton Borg	Blekinge Institute of Technology, Sweden
Antonio Bevilacqua	Meetecho, Italy
Antonis Klironomos	University of Mannheim, Germany
Aron Henriksson	Stockholm University, Sweden
Artur Chudzik	Polish-Japanese Academy of Information Technology, Poland
Arun Venkitaraman	EPFL, Switzerland
Arunabha Choudhury	ASML, Netherlands
Asem Omari	Higher Colleges of Technology, UAE
Ashman Mehra	Birla Institute of Technology and Science, India
Ashwani Rao	Amazon, USA
Asier Rodriguez	BBVA, Spain
Asma Atamna	Ruhr-Universität Bochum, Germany
Atiye Sadat Hashemi	Halmstad University, Sweden
Atul Anand Gopalakrishnan	SUNY Buffalo, USA
Avani Wildani	Emory University, USA
Aviv Rovshitz	Ben-Gurion University of the Negev, Israel
Axel Brando	Barcelona Supercomputing Center (BSC) and Universitat de Barcelona (UB), Spain
Azadeh Alavi	RMIT University, Australia
Beihong Jin	Institute of Software, China
Benoit Frenay	University of Namur, Belgium
Berkay Aydin	Georgia State University, USA
Bijaya Adhikari	University of Iowa, USA
Bin Li	Alibaba Group, China
Bo Pang	University of Auckland, New Zealand
Bogdan Ruszczak	Opole University of Technology, Poland

Bohao Qu	Agency for Science, China
Bruno Veloso	INESC TEC, FEP-UP, Portugal
Buyue Qian	Xi'an Jiaotong University, China
Camille Kurtz	Université Paris Cité, France
Cangbai Li	Guangdong University of Technology, China
Carlo Metta	ISTI CNR, Italy
Carlos N. Silla	Pontifical Catholic University of Paraná (PUCPR), Brazil
Cecile Bothorel	IMT Atlantique, France
Cesar Ferri	Universitat Politècnica Valencia, Spain
Chang Li	Apple, USA
Chang-Dong Wang	Sun Yat-sen University, China
Chaofan Li	Karlsruhe Institute of Technology, Germany
Chaoyuan Zuo	Nankai University, China
Chen Gao	Tsinghua University, China
Chen Li	Computer Network Information Center, China
Chen Zhao	Baylor University, USA
Chen-Wei Chang	Virginia Tech, USA
Chenxi Xue	Nanjing Normal University, China
Chongke Bi	Tianjin University, China
Christian M. Adriano	Hasso-Plattner Institute, Germany
Christophe Rodrigues	DVRC Pôle universitaire Léonard de Vinci, France
Chuan Li	Sorbonne University, LIPADE, France
Chunhui Zhang	Dartmouth College, USA
Cristina Soguero Ruiz	Rey Juan Carlos University, Spain
Daheng Wang	Amazon, USA
Daifeng Li	Sun Yat-sen University, China
Damien Fay	HPE Labs, Ireland
Dania Herzalla	Technology Innovation Institute, UAE
Daniel Lemire	University of Quebec (TELUQ), Canada
Daniel Trejo Banos	SDSC, USA
Daochen Zha	Rice University, USA
Dawei Cheng	Tongji University, China
Dayne Freitag	SRI International, USA
Di Yao	Institute of Computing Technology, China
Dimitris Nick Dimitriadis	Aristotle University of Thessaloniki, Greece
Diogo F. Soares	Universidade de Lisboa, Portugal
Dirk Pflueger	University of Stuttgart, Germany
Doheon Han	University of Notre Dame, USA
Dongxiang Zhang	Zhejiang University, China
Dongxiao Yu	Shandong University, China

Dugang Liu	Guangdong Laboratory of Artificial Intelligence and Digital Economy (Shenzen), China
Ece Calikus	Uppsala University, Sweden
Edwyn Brient	Thales LAS/Mines Paris PSL, France
Efstathios Stamatatos	University of the Aegean, Greece
Elaine Faria	UFU, Brazil
Elio Masciari	University of Naples, Italy
Emilie Devijver	Université Grenoble Alpes, Inria, CNRS, Grenoble INP, LIG, France
Emmanuelle Claeys	IRIT, France
Enayat Rajabi	Halmstad University, Sweden
Enda Barrett	University of Galway, Ireland
Enyan Dai	Hong Kong University of Science and Technology (Guangzhou), China
Eric Peukert	ScaDS.AI, Germany
Eric Sanjuan	Avignon University, France
Erik Frisk	Linköping University, Sweden
Eui-Hong (Sam) Han	The Washington Post, USA
Eunil Park	Sungkyunkwan University, South Korea
Fabio Carrara	CNR-ISTI, Italy
Fabiola Pereira	Federal University of Uberlandia, Brazil
Fan Yang	Rice University, USA
Fangzhao Wu	MSRA, China
Fangzhou Shi	Didi Chuxing, China
Fathima Nuzla Ismail	State University of New York, USA
Flavio Bertini	University of Parma, Italy
Francesco Dente	EURECOM, France
Francesco Guerra	University of Modena e Reggio Emilia, Italy
Francesco Scala	CNR-ICAR, Italy
Francesco Spinnato	University of Pisa, Italy
Francesco Paolo Nerini	Sapienza University of Rome, Italy
Francisco P. Romero	UCLM, Spain
Franco Maria Nardini	ISTI-CNR, Italy
Francois Schwarzentruber	ENS Lyon, France
Fudong Lin	University of Delaware, USA
Gabriel Augusto Pinheiro	UNIFESP, Brazil
Gan Sun	South China University of Technology, China
Gargi Srivastava	Rajiv Gandhi Institute of Petroleum Technology Jais, India
Giacomo Boracchi	Politecnico di Milano, Italy
Giuseppe Garofalo	DistriNet, KU Leuven, Belgium
Giuseppina Andresini	University of Bari Aldo Moro, Italy

Goran Falkman	University of Skovde, Sweden
Grzegorz Nalepa	Jagiellonian University, Poland
Guanggang Geng	Jinan University, China
Guojun Liang	Halmstad University, Sweden
Haifang Li	Baidu, China
Haina Tang	University of Chinese Academy of Sciences, China
Hancheng Ge	Amazon, USA
Hao Li	National University of Defense Technology, China
Haohui Chen	CSIRO, Australia
Haomin Yu	Aalborg University, Denmark
Haoyi Xiong	Baidu, China
Hiba Najjar	DFKI, Germany
Hillol Kargupta	Agnik, USA
Hong Zhou	Meta, USA
Hongbin Pei	Xi'an Jiao Tong University, China
Hou-Wan Long	Chinese University of Hong Kong, China
Hua Wei	Arizona State University, USA
Huaiyuan Yao	Xi'an Jiaotong University, China
Huan Song	Amazon, USA
Hubert Baniecki	University of Warsaw, Poland
Hyunsung Kim	KAIST, Fitogether, South Korea
Ibtihal El Mimouni	Inria, France
Ildar Baimuratov	L3S Research Center, Germany
Ilir Jusufi	Blekinge Institute of Technology, Sweden
Inaam Ashraf	Bielefeld University, Germany
Ines Sousa	Fraunhofer AICOS, Portugal
Iris Heerlien	Saxion, Netherlands
Isak Samsten	Stockholm University, Sweden
Ishan Verma	TCS Research, India
Ismail Hakki Toroslu	METU, Turkey
Ivan Carrera	EPN, Ecuador
Jaakko Hollmen	Stockholm University, Sweden
Jairo Cugliari	Laboratoire ERIC, France
Jakub Nalepa	Silesian University of Technology, Poland
Jelica Vasiljević	Hoffmann-La Roche, Switzerland
Jens Lundstrom	Halmstad University, Sweden
Jesse Davis	KU Leuven, Belgium
Jiahui Bai	Meta, USA
Jiajun Gu	Carnegie Mellon University, USA
Jiali Pan	Department of Information Management, USA

Jian Yu	Auckland University of Technology, New Zealand
Jiangbin Zheng	Westlake University, China
Jianhua Yin	Shandong University, China
Jingbo Zhou	Baidu, China
Jingjing Liu	MD Anderson Cancer Center, USA
Jingwen Shi	Michigan State University, USA
Jingxuan Wei	University of Chinese Academy of Sciences, China
Jinyoung Han	Sungkyunkwan University, South Korea
Jiue-An Yang	City of Hope Beckman Research Institute, USA
Joao R. Campos	University of Coimbra, Portugal
Jochen De Weerdt	KU Leuven, Belgium
Joe Tekli	Lebanese American University, Lebanon
Joel Ky	University of Lorraine, CNRS, Inria, France
John McCall	Robert Gordon University, UK
John Mitros	University College Dublin, Ireland
Jonas Fischer	Ruhr-Universität Bochum, Germany
Jonas Nordqvist	Linnaeus University, Sweden
Joydeep Chandra	Indian Institute of Technology Patna, India
Julian Martin Rodemann	LMU Munich, Germany
Jun Shen	University of Wollongong, Australia
Junichi Tatemura	Google, USA
Junxuan Li	Microsoft, USA
Jyun-Yu Jiang	Amazon Science, USA
Kai Wang	Shanghai Jiao Tong University, China
Kaiping Zheng	National University of Singapore, Singapore
Kaiwen Dong	University of Notre Dame, USA
Katarzyna Bozek	University of Cologne, Germany
Katerina Schindlerova	UniVie, Austria
Katharina Dost	Jožef Stefan Institute, Slovenia
Katsiaryna Mirylenka	Zalando SE, Germany
Keith Burghardt	ISI, Germany
Klaus Brinker	Hamm-Lippstadt University of Applied Sciences, Germany
Koki Kawabata	Osaka University, Japan
Korbinian Randl	Stockholm University, Sweden
Krzysztof Krawiec	Poznań University of Technology, Poland
Krzysztof Kutt	Jagiellonian University, Poland
Kwan Hui Lim	Singapore University of Technology and Design, Singapore
Lamija Lemes	University of Zenica, Bosnia & Herzegovina
Le Nguyen	University of Oulu, Finland

Lei Li	Hong Kong University of Science and Technology (Guangzhou), China
Lei Liu	York University, Canada
Li Liu	Chongqing University, China
Li Zhang	University College London, UK
Liang Tang	Google, USA
Liang Tong	NEC Labs America, USA
Liang Wang	Alibaba Group, China
Lina Yao	University of New South Wales, Australia
Lingxiao Li	Michigan State University, USA
Lingyang Chu	McMaster University, Canada
Lixin Zou	Wuhan University, China
Lluis Garcia-Pueyo	Meta, USA
Lou Salaun	Nokia Bell Labs, USA
Luca Corbucci	University of Pisa, Italy
Luca Pappalardo	ISTI, Italy
Luca Romeo	University of Macerata, Italy
Luis Ferreira	Olympus Medical Products Portugal, Portugal
Luis Miguel Matos	ALGORITMI Centre, Portugal
Lukas Grasmann	TU Wien, Austria
Lukas Pensel	Johannes Gutenberg University Mainz, Germany
Maciej Grzenda	Warsaw University of Technology, Poland
Maciej Piernik	Poznań University of Technology, Poland
Madiraju Srilakshmi	Dream Sports, India
Mads C. Hansen	A.P. Moller-Maersk, Denmark
Mahardhika Pratama	University of South Australia, Australia
Mahmoud Rahat	Halmstad University, Sweden
Man Tianxing	Jilin University, China
Manish Gupta	Microsoft, USA
Manos Papagelis	York University, Canada
Manuel Lopes	Instituto Tecnico Superior, Portugal
Manuel Portela	Universitat Pompeu Fabra, Spain
Marc Tommasi	Lille University, France
Marco Fisichella	Leibniz Universität, Hannover, Germany
Maria Riveiro	Jonkoping University, Sweden
Maria Ulan	RISE Research Institutes of Sweden, Sweden
Marian Scuturici	LIRIS, France
Marianne Clausel	IECL, France
Mario Doller	University of Applied Sciences, Kufstein, Austria
Marius Schwammle	DLR/BT, Germany
Markus Gotz	Karlsruhe Institute of Technology (KIT), Germany

Markus Leyser	Technische Universität Dresden, Germany
Martin Boldt	Blekinge Institute of Technology, Sweden
Martin Mladenov	Google, USA
Martin Vita	Institute of Physics, Czech Academy of Sciences, Czech Republic
Matthias Demant	Fraunhofer ISE, Germany
Matthias Galipaud	SDSC, Switzerland
Matthias Petri	Amazon, USA
Matthieu Latapy	CNRS, France
Maurice Van Keulen	University of Twente, Netherlands
Maxime Cordy	University of Luxembourg, Luxembourg
Maxwell J. Jacobson	Purdue University, USA
Md Nahid Hasan	Miami University, USA
Md Zia Ullah	Edinburgh Napier University, UK
Mehtab Alam Syed	CIRAD, France
Melanie Neubauer	University of Leoben, Austria
Meng Chen	Shandong University, China
Mengxuan Zhang	Australian National University, Australia
Miao Fan	NavInfo, China
Michael Bain	University of New South Wales, Australia
Michele Bernardini	Uni eCampus.It, Italy
Michiel Dhont	EluciDATA Lab of Sirris, Belgium
Mickael Coustaty	L3i Laboratory, France
Miguel Couceiro	LORIA, France
Mihaela Mitici	Utrecht University, Netherlands
Min Lee	Singapore Management University, Singapore
Min Hun Lee	Singapore Management University, Singapore
Mina Rezaei	LMU Munich, Germany
Ming Ma	Inner Mongolia University, China
Minghao Chen	Tencent, China
Mirco Nanni	CNR-ISTI Pisa, Italy
Mirjam Wattenhofer	Google, USA
Mirko Marras	University of Cagliari, Italy
Mitra Heidari	University of Melbourne, Australia
Modesto Castrillon-Santana	Universidad de Las Palmas de Gran Canaria, Spain
Mohammadmehdi Saberioon	German Research Centre for Geosciences, Germany
Mohammed Amer	Fujitsu Research of Europe, Germany
Mohammed Ghaith Altarabichi	Halmstad University, Sweden
Mojgan Kouhounestani	University of Melbourne, Australia
Moonki Hong	Sogang University, South Korea

Munira Syed	Procter & Gamble, USA
Nan Li	Microsoft, USA
Narendhar Gugulothu	TCS Research, India
Nedra Mellouli	LIASD, Portugal
Ngoc Son Le	University of Hildesheim, Germany
Niklas Lavesson	Blekinge Institute of Technology, Sweden
Niraj Kumar	Fujitsu, Japan
Nitish Kumar	MasterCard, USA
Nuno Cruz Garcia	FCUL, Portugal
Nuno R. P. S. Guimaraes	INESC TEC, University of Porto, Portugal
Nuwan Gunasekara	Halmstad University, Sweden
Pablo Picazo-Sanchez	Halmstad University, Sweden
Pablo Torrijos Arenas	Universidad de Castilla-La Mancha, Spain
Pablo Jose Del Moral Pastor	Ekkono.ai, Finland
Pan He	Auburn University, USA
Panagiotis Kanellopoulos	University of Essex, UK
Panagiotis Papadakos	FORTH-ICS, Greece
Pandey Shourya Prasad	International Institute of Information Technology, Bangalore, India
Panpan Xu	Amazon AWS, USA
Paola Velardi	Sapienza University of Rome, Italy
Paolo Cintia	Kode, Italy
Pascal Plettenberg	Intelligent Embedded Systems, Italy
Paul Boniol	Inria, France
Pavel Blinov	Sber AI Lab, Russia
Pawel Parczyk	Wroclaw University of Science and Technology, Poland
Pedro M. Ferreira	University of Lisbon, Portugal
Pedro Seber	MIT, USA
Peng Qiao	NUDT, China
Pengyuan Wang	University of Georgia, USA
Petr Olegovich Sokerin	Skoltech, Russia
Philipp Bach	University of Hamburg, Germany
Philipp Froehlich	TU Darmstadt, Germany
Philipp Schmidt	Amazon Research, USA
Philipp Zech	University of Innsbruck, Austria
Pinar Karagoz	Middle East Technical University (METU), Turkey
Ping Luo	Chinese Academy of Sciences, China
Po Yang	University of Sheffield, UK
Pop Petrica	Technical University of Cluj-Napoca, Romania
Prathap Manohar Joshi R	Zoho Corporation, India

Praveen Borra	Florida Atlantic University, USA
Praveen Paruchuri	IIIT Hyderabad, India
Qian Li	Curtin University, Australia
Qihang Yao	Georgia Institute of Technology, USA
Qiwei Han	Nova School of Business and Economics, Portugal
Quentin Duchemin	Université Gustave Eiffel, France
Radu Tudor Ionescu	University of Bucharest, Romania
Rafal Kucharski	Jagiellonian University, Poland
Rafet Sifa	Fraunhofer IAIS & University of Bonn, Germany
Ramasamy Savitha	I2R A*STAR, Singapore
Ran Yu	DSIS Research Group, Singapore
Ranga Raju Vatsavai	North Carolina State University, USA
Raphael Couturier	University of Bourgogne Franche-Comte (UBFC), France
Renato M. Assuncao	ESRI, USA
Renaud Lambiotte	University of Oxford, UK
Reuben Kshitiz Borrison	ABB, Switzerland
Reza Shirvany	Zalando SE, Germany
Ricardo R. Pereira	Feedzai, Portugal
Riccardo Rosati	Università Politecnica delle Marche, Ancona, Italy
Richard Allmendinger	University of Manchester, UK
Richard Nordsieck	XITASO GmbH IT and Software Solutions, Germany
Richi Nayak	Queensland University of Technology, Australia
Roberto Trasarti	CNR, Italy
Rogerio Luis de C. Costa	Polytechnic of Leiria, Portugal
Romain Ilbert	Huawei Paris Research Center, France
Roy Ka-Wei Lee	Singapore University of Technology and Design, Singapore
Ruilin Wang	University of Aberdeen, UK
Sabrina Gaito	Università degli Studi di Milano, Italy
Sai Karthikeya Vemuri	Computer Vision Group Jena, Italy
Saisubramaniam Gopalakrishnan	Quantiphi, USA
Sajjad Shumaly	Max-Planck-Institut for Polymer Research, Germany
Salvatore Rinzivillo	KDD Lab, ISTI, CNR, Italy
Samaneh Shafee	LASIGE, Portugal
Sandra Wissing	Fachhochschule Münster, Germany
Sarwan Ali	Georgia State University, USA
Sebastian Becker	Fraunhofer ISST, Germany

Sebastian Honel	Linnaeus University, Sweden
Selin Colakhasanoglu	Saxion University of Applied Sciences, Netherlands
Senzhang Wang	Central South University, China
Sepideh Nahali	York University, Canada
Shahrooz Abghari	Blekinge Institute of Technology, Sweden
Shahroz Tariq	CSIRO, Australia
Shang Yanlei	BUPT, China
Shen Liang	Paris Cité University, France
Shengheng Liu	Southeast University, China
Shereen Elsayed	University of Hildesheim, Germany
Shi-ting Wen	NingboTech University, China
Shiv Krishna Jaiswal	Walmart Global Tech, USA
Shoujin Wang	Macquarie University, Australia
Shuai Li	University of Cambridge, UK and University of Tokyo, UK
Shuchu Han	Capital One Financial Group, Japan
Simon F. Weinberger	EssilorLuxottica, France
Siyuan Chen	Guangzhou University, China
Snehanshu Saha	BITS Pilani Goa Campus, India
Souhaib Ben Taieb	University of Mons, Abu Dhabi
Sriparna Saha	IIT Patna, India
Stefan Rueping	Fraunhofer IAIS, Germany
Stephane Chretien	Université Lyon 2, France
Sunil Aryal	Deakin University, Australia
Susana Ladra	University of A Coruña, Spain
Szymon Bobek	Jagiellonian University, Poland
Szymon Jaroszewicz	Institute of Computer Science, Poland
Szymon Wilk	Poznań University of Technology, Poland
Tanel Tammet	Tallinn University of Technology, Estonia
Thanh Thi Nguyen	Monash University, Australia
Thiago Zangato	Université Sorbonne Paris Nord, France
Theodora Tsikrika	Information Technologies Institute, Greece
Thibault Girardin	Université Jean Monnet, France
Thomas Czernichow	Darwinlabs, Portugal
Thorsteinn Rognvaldsson	Halmstad University, Sweden
Tiago Mendes-Neves	FEUP/INESC TEC, Portugal
Tianshu Yu	Chinese University of Hong Kong (Shenzhen), China
Ting Su	Imperial College London, UK
Tingrui Qiao	University of Auckland, New Zealand
Tobias Glasmachers	Ruhr-Universität Bochum, Germany

Tomas Olsson	RISE SICS, Sweden
Tome Eftimov	Jožef Stefan Institute, Slovenia
Topon Paul	Toshiba Corporation, Japan
Tsuyoshi Okita	Kyushu Institute of Technology, Japan
Unmesh Padalkar	Dream Sports, India
Vahid Shahrivari Joghan	Utrecht University, Netherlands
Valerio Bonsignori	Unipisa, Italy
Vanessa Borst	University of Würzburg, Germany
Venkata Sai Prakash Mukkamala	Quantiphi Analytics, USA
Veselka Boeva	Blekinge Institute of Technology, Sweden
Viacheslav Komisarenko	University of Tartu, Estonia
Vikas Gupta	HPCL, India
Vinayak Gupta	University of Washington, Seattle, USA
Vincent Auriau	Artefact Research Center, France
Vincenzo Pasquadibisceglie	University of Bari, Aldo Moro, Italy
Vincenzo Scotti	KASTEL, Germany
Vinothkumar Kolluru	Stevens Institute of Technology, USA
Vladimir Mic	Aarhus University, Denmark
Wang-Zhou Dai	Nanjing University, China
Wee Siong Ng	Institute for Infocomm Research, Singapore
Wei Cheng	NEC Laboratories America, USA
Wei Li	Harbin Engineering University, China
Wei Wang	Tsinghua University, China
Wei-Peng Chen	Fujitsu Research of America, USA
Wentao Wang	Michigan State University, USA
Wentao Wu	Microsoft Research, USA
Wray Buntine	VinUniversity, Vietnam
Xianchao Wu	Nvidia, USA
Xiang Lian	Kent State University, USA
Xianli Zhang	Xi'an Jiaotong University, China
Xiaobo Jin	Xi'an Jiaotong-Liverpool University, China
Xiaofei Zhou	University of Chinese Academy of Sciences, China
Xiaofeng Gao	Shanghai Jiaotong University, China
Xiaolin Han	Northwestern Polytechnical University, China
Xin Huang	Hong Kong Baptist University, China
Xin Liu	East China Normal University, China
Xing Tang	Tencent, China
Xiuqiang He	Tencent, China
Xiuyuan Hu	Tsinghua University, China
Xueping Peng	University of Technology Sydney, Australia
Yanchang Zhao	CSIRO, Australia

Yang Guo	Xidian University Hangzhou Institute of Technology, China
Yang Song	Apple, USA
Yijun Zhao	Fordham University, USA
Yinghui Wu	Case Western Reserve University, USA
Yingzhen Lin	Harbin Institute of Technology (Shenzhen), China
Yintao Yu	University of Illinois at Urbana-Champaign, USA
Yixiang Fang	Chinese University of Hong Kong, China
Yixuan Cao	Institute of Computing Technology, China
Yizheng Huang	York University, Canada
Yongchao Liu	Ant Group, China
Yu Huang	Indiana University, USA
Yu Wang	University of Oregon, USA
Yuantao Fan	Halmstad University, Sweden
Yucheng Zhou	University of Macau, China
Yue Shi	Meta, USA
Yueyuan Zheng	Beihang University, China
Yunchuan Shi	University of Sydney, Australia
Yunjun Gao	Zhejiang University, China
Yuting Ding	Southeast University, China
Yuzhuo Li	University of Auckland, New Zealand
Zahra Kharazian	Stockholm University, Sweden
Zahra Taghiyarrenani	Halmstad University, Sweden
Zahraa Abdallah	University of Bristol, UK
Zeyi Wen	Hong Kong University of Science and Technology (Guangzhou), China
Zeyu Zhu	National University of Defense Technology, China
Zhanyu Liu	Shanghai Jiao Tong University, China
Zhaogeng Liu	Jilin University, China
Zhaohui Liang	National Library of Medicine, USA
Zhen Zhang	Shandong University, China
Zhendong Chu	Squirrel Ai Learning, China
Zheng Zhang	University of California, USA
Zhengze Li	University of Göttingen, Germany
Zhibin Gu	Hebei Normal University, China
Zhuang Liu	Dongbei University of Finance and Economics, China
Ziyu Guan	Xidian University, China
Zoltan Miklos	Université de Rennes, France
Zunlei Feng	Zhejiang University, China

Program Committee – Demo Track

Andrzej Wójtowicz	Adam Mickiewicz University, Poznań, Poland
Anna Sokol	University of Notre Dame, USA
Arian Pasquali	Faktion AI, Belgium
Bruno Veloso	INESC TEC - FEP-UP, Portugal
Chongsheng Zhang	Henan University, China
Christos Doulkeridis	University of Piraeus, Greece
Danqing Zhang	PathOnAI.org, USA
Fátima Rodrigues	INESC TEC, Portugal
Grigorii Khvatskii	University of Notre Dame, USA
Joe Germino	University of Notre Dame, USA
Jungwon Seo	University of Stavanger, Norway
Ke Li	University of Exeter, England
Manfred Jaeger	Aalborg University, Denmark
Marcin Luckner	Warsaw University of Technology, Poland
Mehwish Alam	Institut Polytechnique de Paris, France
Nuno Moniz	University of Notre Dame, USA
Tânia Carvalho	FCUP, Portugal
Vitor Cerqueira	FEUP, Portugal
Wei-Wei Du	National Yang Ming Chiao Tung University, Taiwan

Additional Reviewers

Andrea D'Angelo
Patrick Altmeyer
Guiseppina Adresini
Vedangi Bengali
Michele Bernardini
Zhi Cao
Louis Carpentier
Alessio Cascione
Lilia Chebbah
Meng Ding
Roberto Esposito
Alina Fastowski
Roger Ferrod
Michele Fontana
Chang Gong
Michal Grzejdziak-Zdziarski
Paul Hahn

Antonia Hain
Md Athikul Islam
Michael Ito
Philipp Jahn
Rahul Kumar
Bishal Lakha
Yuwen Liu
Jerry Lonlac
Shijie Luo
Francesca Naretto
Navid Nobani
Diego Coello de Portugal
Joana Santos
Francesco Scala
Richard Serrano
Nuno Silva
Francesco Spinnato

Pedro C. Vieira
Xiao Wang
Yunyun Wang
Qi Wen
Jianye Xie

Huaiyuan Yao
Yutong Ye
Obaidullah Zaland
Efstratios Zaradoukas
Nan Zhang

Sponsors

Diamond

Platinum

liv   Organization

Gold

Silver

Bronze

Other Sponsors

Partners

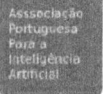

Keynotes

Many Good Models Leads to ...

Cynthia Rudin

Duke University, USA

Abstract. As it turns out, many good models leads to amazing things! The Rashomon Effect, coined by Leo Breiman, describes the phenomenon that there exist many equally good predictive models for the same dataset.

This phenomenon happens for many real datasets, and when it does it sparks both magic and consternation, but mostly magic. In light of the Rashomon Effect, my collaborators and I propose to reshape the way we think about machine learning, particularly for tabular data problems in the nondeterministic (noisy) setting. I'll address how the Rashomon Effect impacts (1) the existence of simple-yet-accurate models, (2) flexibility to address user preferences, such as fairness and monotonicity, without losing performance, (3) uncertainty in predictions, fairness, and explanations, (4) reliable variable importance, (5) algorithm choice, specifically, providing advanced knowledge of which algorithms might be suitable for a given problem, and (6) public policy. I'll also discuss a theory of when the Rashomon Effect occurs and why: interestingly, noise in data leads to a large Rashomon Effect. My goal is to illustrate how the Rashomon Effect can have a massive impact on the use of machine learning for complex problems in society.

Towards Causal Artificial Intelligence

Elias Bareinboim

Columbia University, USA

Abstract. While a significant portion of AI scientists and engineers believe we are on the verge of achieving highly general forms of AI, I offer a critical appraisal of this view through a causal lens. In particular, building on foundational developments in the field, I will present my perspective on the relationship between intelligence and causality – and the central role of the latter in building intelligent systems and advancing credible data science.

I frame this discussion in terms of five core capabilities that we should expect from an intelligent AI system: performing causal reasoning and articulating explanations; making precise, surgical, and sample-efficient decisions; generalizing across changing conditions and environments; generating and simulating in a causally consistent manner; and learning causal structures and variables.

In this talk, I will elaborate on this perspective and share current progress toward building causally intelligent AI systems. A more detailed discussion of this thesis is provided in my forthcoming textbook, a draft of which is available here: https://causalai-book.net/.

Not Just a Trend: Institutionalizing XAI for Responsible and Compliant AI Systems

Francisco Herrera

Granada University, Spain

Abstract. As artificial intelligence (AI) systems increasingly mediate decisions in high-stakes domains – from healthcare and finance to public policy – the demand for explainable AI (XAI) has grown rapidly. Yet many current XAI approaches remain disconnected from the practical needs of stakeholders and the requirements of emerging regulatory frameworks. This talk argues that XAI must not be treated as a passing trend or optional technical add-on, but as a foundational principle in the design and deployment of AI systems. We critically examine the state of the field, exposing the gap between model-centric explainability and stakeholder-centric accountability. In response, we propose a framework that aligns explainability with legal, ethical, and social responsibilities, emphasizing co-design with affected users, sensitivity to institutional contexts, and governance over opacity. Our goal is to advance XAI from superficial compliance toward deeply integrated transparency that fosters trust, accountability, and responsible innovation.

Compositional Intelligence: Coordinating Multiple LLMs for Complex Tasks

Mirella Lapata

University of Edinburgh, UK

Abstract. Recent years have witnessed the rise of increasingly larger and more sophisticated language models (LMs) capable of performing every task imaginable, sometimes at (super)human level. In this talk, I will argue that in many realistic scenarios, solely relying on a single general-purpose LLM is suboptimal. A single LLM is likely to underrepresent real-world data distributions, heterogeneous skills, and task-specific requirements. Instead, I will discuss multi-LLM collaboration as an alternative to monolithic generative modeling. By orchestrating multiple LLMs, each with distinct roles, perspectives, or competencies, we can achieve more effective problem-solving while being more inclusive and explainable. I will illustrate this approach through two case studies: narrative story generation and visual question answering, showing how a society of agents can collectively tackle complex tasks while pursuing complementary subgoals. Additionally, I will explore how these agent societies leverage reasoning to improve performance.

Towards a Fairer World: Uncovering and Addressing Human and Algorithmic Biases

Nuria Oliver

ELLIS Alicante Foundation, Spain

Abstract. In my talk, I will first briefly present ELLIS Alicante1, the only ELLIS unit that has been created from scratch as a non-profit research foundation devoted to responsible AI for Social Good. Next, I will provide an overview of AI with a focus on the ethical implications and limitations of today's AI systems, including algorithmic discrimination and bias. On this topic, I will present a few examples of our work on uncovering and mitigating both human and algorithmic biases with AI.

On the human front, I will present the body of work that we have carried out in the context of AI-based beauty filters that are so popular on social media. On the algorithmic front, I will explain the main approaches to address algorithmic discrimination and I will present three novel methods to achieve fairer decisions.

Tensor Logic: A Simple Unification of Neural and Symbolic AI

Pedro Domingos

University of Washington, USA

Abstract. Deep learning has achieved remarkable successes in language generation and other tasks, but is extremely opaque and notoriously unreliable. Both of these problems can be overcome by combining it with the sound reasoning and transparent knowledge representation capabilities of symbolic AI. Tensor logic accomplishes this by unifying tensor algebra and logic programming, the formal languages underlying respectively deep learning and symbolic AI. Tensor logic is based on the observation that predicates are compactly represented Boolean tensors, and can be straightforwardly extended to compactly represent numeric ones. The two key constructs in tensor logic are tensor join and project, numeric operations that generalize database join and project. A tensor logic program is a set of tensor equations, each expressing a tensor as a series of tensor joins, a tensor project, and a univariate nonlinearity applied elementwise. Tensor logic programs can succinctly encode most deep architectures and symbolic AI systems, and many new combinations.

In this talk I will describe the foundations and main features of tensor logic, and present efficient inference and learning algorithms for it. A system based on tensor logic achieves state-of-the-art results on a suite of language and reasoning tasks. How tensor logic will fare on trillion-token corpora and associated tasks remains an open question.

Artificial Intelligence for Science

Sašo Džeroski

Jožef Stefan Institute, Slovenia

Abstract. Artificial intelligence is already transforming science, with its future impact expected to be even greater. Realizing this potential requires addressing key scientific challenges, such as ensuring explainability (of models and their predictions), learning effectively from limited data, and integrating data with prior domain knowledge. It also requires the provision of support for open and reproducible science through formalizing and sharing scientific knowledge.

I will present an overview of my research on the development of AI methods suitable for use in science. These include methods for explainable machine learning – including multi-target prediction and relational learning – that deliver accurate yet interpretable models suitable for complex scientific domains. These methods have been applied in environmental science, life science and materials science. Learning from limited data is critical in science. I will discuss two complementary approaches: semi-supervised learning, which leverages unlabeled data directly, together with labeled data, and foundation models, which use representations learned from vast unlabeled data to support downstream tasks with minimal supervision, i.e., limited amounts of labeled data. Both paradigms expand AI's reach into data-scarce scientific problems.

I will then present our work on automated scientific modeling, where we learn interpretable models of dynamical systems – such as process-based models and differential equations – from time series data and domain knowledge. Finally, I will highlight the role of ontologies and semantic technologies in experimental computer science, including machine learning and optimization. In these areas, we have developed ontologies for the representation and annotation of both data and other artefacts produced by science, such as algorithms, models, and results of experiments.

Contents – Part I

Anomaly and Outlier Detection

Robust Gaussian Process Regression with Huber Likelihood and Projection Pursuit 3
   Pooja Algikar and Lamine Mili

Enriching Category Representations with LLMs Towards Robust Zero-Shot OOD Detection 20
   Dian Chao, Yuxuan Zhang, Luping Zhou, and Yang Yang

GLADMamba: Unsupervised Graph-Level Anomaly Detection Powered by Selective State Space Model 37
   Yali Fu, Jindong Li, Qi Wang, and Qianli Xing

SODA: Out-of-Distribution Detection in Domain-Shifted Point Clouds via Neighborhood Propagation 55
   Adam Goodge, Bryan Hooi, Jingyi Liao, Yongyi Su, Wee Siong Ng, Xun Xu, and Xulei Yang

Unsupervised Surrogate Anomaly Detection 71
   Simon Klüttermann, Tim Katzke, and Emmanuel Müller

Multivariate Time Series Anomaly Prediction Based on Forecasting and Reconstruction Using Transformer with Temporal and Feature-Wise Attention 89
   Chihiro Maru, Masato Oguchi, and Ichiro Kobayashi

Improving Novel Anomaly Detection with Domain-Invariant Latent Representations 106
   Padmaksha Roy, Ming Jin, Himanshu Singhal, Tyler Cody, and Kevin Choi

Evidential Spectrum-Aware Contrastive Learning for OOD Detection in Dynamic Graphs 124
   Nan Sun, Xixun Lin, Zhiheng Zhou, Yanmin Shang, Zhenlin Cheng, and Yanan Cao

HAGAN: Homophily-Aware Generative Adversarial Network for Graph Anomaly Detection 141
   Wenkai Wang, Fan Gao, and Meihong Wang

RandomAD: A Random Kernel-Based Anomaly Detector for Time Series 159
Wenjie Xi and Jessica Lin

HCT: A Hierarchical Contrastive Learning Framework for Transferable
Graph Anomaly Detection 176
Jiawei Ye, Hongyi Li, Qinlin Xie, Sicheng Liang, Yu Liu, and Jie Wu

Bias and Fairness

Fair and Privacy-Preserving Synthetic Data Generation
via Clustering-Based Variational Autoencoder and Adversarially
Debiased Wasserstein Generative Adversarial Networks with Gradient
Penalty 195
Malek Adouani and Zaineb Chelly Dagdia

Optimizing and Tuning Fairness in Machine Learning: An Augmented
Lagrangian Method with a Performance Budget 213
Michele Fontana, Francesca Naretto, and Anna Monreale

Better Features, Better Calibration: A Simple Fix for Overconfident
Networks 231
Soumya Suvra Ghosal, Ramya Hebbalaguppe, and Dinesh Manocha

Bias vs Bias Dawn of Justice: A Fair Fight in Recommendation Systems 248
Tahsin Alamgir Kheya, Mohamed Reda Bouadjenek, and Sunil Aryal

What Large Language Models Do Not Talk About: An Empirical Study
of Moderation and Censorship Practices 265
*Sander Noels, Guillaume Bied, Maarten Buyl, Alexander Rogiers,
Yousra Fettach, Jefrey Lijffijt, and Tijl De Bie*

Fair Associative Co-clustering 282
Federico Peiretti and Ruggero G. Pensa

DispaRisk: Assessing Fairness Through Usable Information 301
Jonathan Vasquez, Carlotta Domeniconi, and Huzefa Rangwala

Analyzing and Correcting Biased Machine Learning-Based Tuning
of Weight Shrinkage in Forecast Combination 319
Veronika Wachslander

Redefining Fairness: A Multi-dimensional Perspective and Integrated
Evaluation Framework 336
*Zichong Wang, Zhipeng Yin, Zhen Liu, Roland H. C. Yap,
Xiaocai Zhang, Shu Hu, and Wenbin Zhang*

Fairness-Aware Graph Representation Learning with Limited
Demographic Information 354
   Zichong Wang, Zhipeng Yin, Liping Yang, Jun Zhuang, Rui Yu,
   Qingzhao Kong, and Wenbin Zhang

Constrained Optimization to Improve Critical Rare Classes Performance
Within the Top-Ranking Part 372
   Yuxin Ying, Fuzhen Zhuang, Ziyi Liu, Dingyuan Zhu, Daixin Wang,
   and Xiaobo Qin

Causality

Counterfactual Robustness: A Framework to Analyze the Robustness
of Causal Generative Models Across Interventions 391
   Manal Benhamza, Marianne Clausel, and Myriam Tami

KANITE: Kolmogorov–Arnold Networks for ITE Estimation 409
   Eshan Mehendale, Abhinav Thorat, Ravi Kolla, and Niranjan Pedanekar

Advanced Strategic Improvement with Decision Interactions 426
   Wenjing Yang, Xinpeng Lv, Yunxin Mao, Liyang Xu, Ruochun Jin,
   Huan Chen, Jing Ren, Jinxuan Yang, Yuanlong Chen, and Haotian Wang

Clustering

TreeDiffusion: Hierarchical Generative Clustering for Conditional
Diffusion 447
   Jorge da Silva Gonçalves, Laura Manduchi, Moritz Vandenhirtz,
   and Julia E. Vogt

Late Fusion Multiple Kernel Clustering Refined via Optimal Linear Graph
Filtering 463
   Henghui Jiang, Yiqing Guo, Yan Chen, and Liang Du

InfoClus: Informative Clustering of High-Dimensional Data Embeddings .. 480
   Fuyin Lai, Edith Heiter, Guillaume Bied, and Jefrey Lijffijt

Unimodal Strategies in Density-Based Clustering 498
   Oron Nir, Jay Tenenbaum, and Ariel Shamir

Author Index 515

Anomaly and Outlier Detection

Robust Gaussian Process Regression with Huber Likelihood and Projection Pursuit

Pooja Algikar[✉] and Lamine Mili

Virginia Tech, Falls Church, VA 22043, USA
{apooja19,lmili}@vt.edu

Abstract. Outliers in both covariates and output responses pose significant challenges for Gaussian Process (GP) regression models. We present a novel GP regression approach that effectively integrates the Huber likelihood into the GP framework—with additional parameters that can be set before inference. Specifically, we model the likelihood of observed outputs using the Huber probability distribution: this reduces deviations caused by output outliers. For covariate outliers, we introduce projection pursuit weights—attenuating their influence on the model. To address the analytically intractable, yet unimodal, posterior distribution, We employ Laplace approximation and, separately, Gibbs sampling within a Markov Chain Monte Carlo (MCMC) framework. We simplify Gibbs sampling by expressing the likelihood associated with outlying points as normally distributed through the scale mixture representation of the Laplace distribution. This work is particularly important in the field of transmission spectroscopy—where noisy measurements are often neglected in the estimation of planet-to-star radius ratios. We demonstrate the robustness and effectiveness of our method through extensive experiments on synthetic and real-world datasets.

Keywords: Covariate and Response Outliers · Transmission Spectroscopy

1 Introduction

Bayesian inference which is based on Gaussian likelihood is known to be sensitive to extreme observations and gross errors, called outliers. The estimation of parameters in Gaussian processes (GPs) is affected in non-Gaussian error settings as the predictive uncertainty assigns equal confidence to the measurements, regardless of whether they are outliers or not. We illustrate this problem in a numerical example. Let us consider a 2-d sinc function $y(x) = \text{sinc}(x) + e$, where $x = \sqrt{(x_1^2 + x_2^2)}$ with an additive error that follows the Student's t-distribution

---

Supplementary Information The online version contains supplementary material available at https://doi.org/10.1007/978-3-032-05962-8_1.

© The Author(s), under exclusive license to Springer Nature Switzerland AG 2026
R. P. Ribeiro et al. (Eds.): ECML PKDD 2025, LNAI 16013, pp. 3–19, 2026.
https://doi.org/10.1007/978-3-032-05962-8_1

with 10 degrees of freedom $e \sim$ Student's-t(2). We add additional large outliers $y^{(l)}$ with magnitude close to 0.8 and $x_1^{(l)}$. Figure 1(a) shows the predicted values at test points $x = [-10, 10]$, obtained from standard.

Existing studies addressing the outlier problem in GP regression use various approaches to define the likelihood. Two common strategies are: (1) using a mixture of two normal distributions or (2) employing heavy-tailed distributions. Most of these methods assume the error distribution is known a priori—a condition that is often unrealistic in practical applications. Moreover, their robustness is questionable when faced with extreme observations that do not correspond to the non-normal distribution their heavy tailed likelihood is specified to capture. These models typically struggle to handle both general noise patterns and large errors in covariate and response dimensions, often attempting to fit extreme values. We show this shortcoming in Fig. 1(b) with the sinc function data for the GP with the Student's t-likelihood and employing the MCMC integration approximation method. We notice that the model overfits when large outliers $x_1^{(l)}$ and $y^{(l)}$ occur simultaneously, as the Student's-t likelihood can effectively compensates only for errors in $y^{(l)}$.

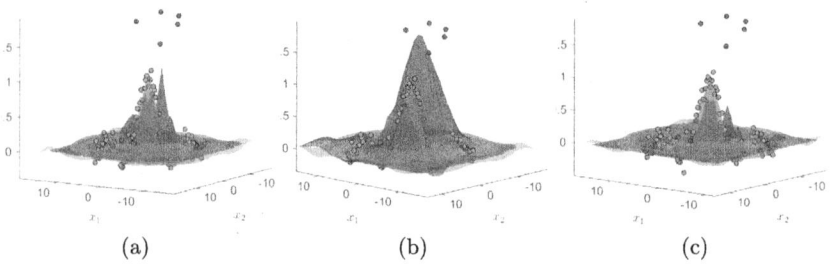

Fig. 1. Predictions for sinc2d(x): (a) standard GP, (b) Student's t-likelihood via MCMC, (c) GP with Huber likelihood. The red surface shows the mean of the model predictions, the grey surface represents the true sinc2d function, red dots are outliers, and green dots are training points fitting sinc2d. The proposed GP with Huber likelihood and projection pursuit weights demonstrates robustness to the outliers $\{y^{(l)}, x^{(l)}\}$.

In this paper, we propose a new way of handling extreme outliers in covariate space and output responses that models the likelihood of the observed data using Huber density function. We significantly enhance downweighting of the outliers compared to the earlier work by [1], which was limited to handling outliers only in the output responses with added hyperparameters (β, c).

2 Related Work

Goldberg et al. [11] introduced a dual-model Gaussian process framework to account for covariate-dependent noise. The first Gaussian process model governs the output process y, while the second Gaussian process governs the noise process. [31] investigated heavy-tailed error distributions that are constructed as scale mixtures of normal distributions, which are also used for specifying a priori distribution based on the earlier ideas suggested by [6,24]. By doing so, the prior distribution discounts any observations highlighting inconsistency between likelihood and prior. Along the same line, [7] assumed a super heavy-tailed error distribution dependent on an explanatory variable to make the estimation of the population mean and ratios robust to outliers. [16] extended a mixture of two normal distributions, one to model small errors in regular observations and a second one to model large errors in outlying observations. However, [22] questioned the adequacy of the two-model approach. They proposed instead twin GP that allow us to choose between the distribution of the regular observations and that of the outliers. [16] suggested a GP with a Laplace likelihood model that utilizes a scale mixture representation of Laplace noise distribution where the variance follows an exponential distribution. [30] proposed a GP model based on the Student's t-likelihood function, where the noise is modeled as a scale mixture of Gaussian distributions. Unfortunately with the non-Gaussian likelihood, the Bayesian inference becomes analytically intractable. Consequently, various advanced approximation methods were proposed [5,14,16,25,30] to overcome the convergence failure of the classical approximation methods such as expectation propagation [21], Markov Chain Monte Carlo [23], variational Bayes [9], and Laplace approximation [32]. More recently, [2,17] presented a robust variants of GPs for datasets with substantial contamination removing the outlier data based on trimming parameters in iterative manner.

In GP regression models with Student's t-likelihoods [16], a scale-mixture representation of the Student's t-distribution is utilized. A variational approximation is devised presuming the Gaussian likelihood whose individual variances are Gamma distributed. Combined with the Kullback-Leibler divergence, $\mathrm{KL}(q||p)$, between the true posterior, p, and the approximation, q, an expectation maximization (EM)-type algorithm is implemented. As for the models with Laplace likelihoods, the scale mixture model yields a unimodal posterior enabling the implementation of the EP approximation and the MCMC sampling. Here, a Laplace approximation is inappropriate because the discontinuous derivatives of the Laplace likelihood at zero may cause the Hessian matrix to be undefined.

3 Contributions

[1] proposed a robust Gaussian Process (GP) regression method that leverages generalized Bayesian inference to preserve computational conjugacy. Their method handles outliers in the output responses through weighting mechanism J in the noise term: $\sigma^2 J_{ii} = \sigma^2 \left(1 + r_i^2/c^2\right)$, where r_i is the residual associated with i^{th} data point $r_i = y_i - m(\boldsymbol{x}_i)$ and c is the threshold parameter. However, a potential limitation of this approach is that it may not adequately account for outliers in the output response, $y_i^{(l)}, y_j^{(c)}$, when they occur alongside outliers in the covariate dimensions, $\boldsymbol{x}_k^{(l)} = [x_1^{(l)}, x_2^{(l)}, \ldots, x_d]$.

Our approach first addresses covariate outliers $\boldsymbol{x}_k^{(l)}$ by introducing projection pursuit weights $w(\boldsymbol{x}_k)$. These weights are then applied to scale the residuals r, ensuring that the influence of an outlier is adjusted based on the presence of extreme covariate outliers $\boldsymbol{x}_k^{(l)}$. This method enables the model to transform contaminated data points $\{y_i^{(l)}, y_j^{(c)}, \boldsymbol{x}_k^{(l)}\}$ into a more reliable dataset. Notably, the projection pursuit weighting operates independently and can be applied to various likelihoods, as shown in our experiments.

To further handle extreme outliers in output response $y_i^{(l)}$, we employ a Huber density function—derived from the exponential of the Huber loss- giving robust L_1 norm treatment for the residuals having over-limit magnitude. The combination of projection pursuit weighting and Huber likelihood can handle cases where the locations i, j, and k coincide. Additionally, when extreme outliers are detected in the covariate dimensions $\boldsymbol{x}_k^{(l)}$, the model selectively retains the corresponding output $y_k^{(l)}$ if it improves the regression fit.

4 The Model

Let us consider a regression setting $y_i = f(\boldsymbol{x}_i) + \epsilon_i$, where $\epsilon_i \sim \mathcal{N}(0, \sigma^2)$ is a homoscedastic i.i.d. random variable with constant variance. In GP models, the systematic dependency between the covariates $\boldsymbol{x} \in \mathcal{X}$, where $\mathcal{X} \subseteq \mathbb{R}^d$, and the response $y \in \mathcal{Y}$ is given by a latent function, $f(\boldsymbol{x}) : \mathbb{R}^d \to \mathbb{R}$. In a truly non-parametric sense, the latent vector function at n covariates, $\mathbf{f} = [f(\mathbf{x}_1), \ldots, f(\boldsymbol{x}_n)]^\top$, is assumed to have a priori probability distribution. This distribution is a joint multivariate normal distribution with zero mean vector and covariance matrix, $\mathbf{K}$, that is,

$$\mathbf{f}|\mathbf{X}, \boldsymbol{\theta} \sim \mathcal{N}(\mathbf{f}|\mathbf{0}, \mathbf{K}). \tag{1}$$

The covariance matrix, $\mathbf{K}$, is a positive semi-definite matrix that captures residual spatial association with elements $K_{i,j} = k(\boldsymbol{x}_i, \boldsymbol{x}_j)$, $i, j = 1, \ldots, n$. The function $k(\cdot, \cdot)$, chosen from a parametric kernel family such as the Gaussian or the Matérn kernel, is characterized by hyperparameters denoted by $\boldsymbol{\theta}$. The likelihood of the data is expressed as $\mathbf{y}|\mathbf{f}, \sigma \sim \mathcal{N}(\mathbf{y}|\mathbf{f}, \boldsymbol{\Sigma})$, and the resulting posterior distribution on $\mathbf{f}$ as where $\boldsymbol{\Sigma} = \text{diag}(\sigma_1^2, \ldots, \sigma_n^2)$.

Next, we develop three aspects of the proposed GP-Huber model: Huber likelihood, projection pursuit weights, and the resulting unimodal posterior distribution. Following that, we discuss the hyperparametric settings of the GP-Huber.

4.1 Huber Likelihood

We propose to use the Huber density function based on the Huber loss proposed by [12] to model the likelihood of the observed data. The Huber loss function $\rho(\cdot)$ is a truncated mixture of two commonly used loss functions: squared loss, $l(r) = r^2$ for residuals below threshold b, and absolute loss, $l(r) = |r|$ for residuals $r_i = y_i - f(\mathbf{x}_i)$ below threshold b, given by

$$\rho(r) = \begin{cases} \frac{1}{2}r^2, & \text{if } |r| \leq b \\ b|r| - \frac{1}{2}b^2, & \text{otherwise} \end{cases} \qquad (2)$$

[12] considered the contamination model $(1 - \varepsilon)G(r) + \varepsilon H(r)$, where $G(r)$ is the Gaussian cumulative density function and $H(r)$ is the unknown cumulative density function. The associated least favorable Huber density function with a fraction of contamination ε is defined as

$$p_H(\mathbf{y}|\mathbf{f}, \phi) = \prod_{i=1}^{n} \frac{1-\varepsilon}{\sqrt{2\pi}\sigma} \exp\left(-\rho(r_i)\right). \qquad (3)$$

The parameter ε, symbolizing the fraction of the dataset presumed to deviate from the underlying model, can be computed utilizing the minimum covariance determinant estimator [13]. The threshold b is selected to protect estimation of the model parameters and hyperparameters against the fraction of contamination ε. The Huber likelihood provides a balance between sensitivity to inliers and robustness to outliers, controlled by the threshold b, which has a theoretical interpretation and can be set based on domain knowledge or easily tuned empirically. Student's-t likelihood, while also robust to outliers, may give undue influence to extreme observations because of its heavy tails. The Laplace likelihood's uniform linear loss may underweight small residuals—potentially leading to less efficient estimates when the data contains mostly inliers.

4.2 Projection Pursuit Weighting

The idea is to scale the residual r_i associated with the ith data point with projection pursuit weight $w(\boldsymbol{x}_i)$ based on robust variant of Mahalanobis distances, called projection statistics $\text{PS}(\boldsymbol{x}_i) : \mathbb{R}^d \to \mathbb{R}^d$. This scaling highlights the impact of outliers in single or multiple dimensions masking each other in the covariate space. Residual larger than the threshold b gets robust $L1$ norm treatment, while those smaller than b are treated with an efficient $L2$ norm within the Huber loss $\rho(r)$.

We obtain standardized the residual $r_{S_i} = r_i/(w_i \sigma s)$ by scaling r_i by its corresponding projection pursuit weight w_i and using a scaling factor $s = b_d \, \text{med}|\boldsymbol{r}|$, where $b_d = 1 + 5/(n-d)$ is the dimensionality correction factor. When the error distribution is unknown, s accounts for its spread parameter. The projection pursuit weights $\boldsymbol{w}$ limit the influence of outliers simultaneously arising in multiple covariate dimensions at multiple locations on the loss function, are based on projection statistics PS_i, calculated as

$$w_i = \begin{cases} 1, & \text{for } \text{PS}_i^2 \leq c_i, \\ \frac{c_i}{\text{PS}_i^2}, & \text{for } \text{PS}_i^2 > c_i. \end{cases} \qquad (4)$$

The projection statistics [8,28] are a robust version of Mahalanobis distances based on the median absolute distance from the median. Formally defined as the maxima of the standardized projection distances obtained by projecting the point cloud in the directions that originate from the co-ordinate wise median and that pass through each of the data points, $\boldsymbol{x}_i$ [20]. They're easy to calculate:

$$\text{PS}_i = \max_{||\boldsymbol{u}_j||=1} \frac{|\boldsymbol{x}_i^T \boldsymbol{u}_j - \underset{k}{\text{median}}(\boldsymbol{x}_k^T \boldsymbol{u}_j)|}{1.4826 \underset{i}{\text{median}} |\boldsymbol{x}_i^T \boldsymbol{u}_j - \underset{k}{\text{median}}(\boldsymbol{x}_k^T \boldsymbol{u}_j)|}, \qquad (5)$$

where $\boldsymbol{u}_j = \frac{\boldsymbol{x}_j - \mathbf{M}}{||\boldsymbol{x}_j - \mathbf{M}||}$; $j, k = 1, \ldots, n$. The co-ordinate wise median $\mathbf{M}$ is given by $\mathbf{M} = \{\underset{j=1,\ldots,n}{\text{med}} \, x_{j1}, \ldots, \underset{j=1,\ldots,n}{\text{med}} \, x_{jd}\}$. The projection statistics attain the maximum breakdown point given by $[(n - d - 1)/2]/n$ [19].

[27] and [20] showed that, when $n > 5d$, the squared projection statistics PS_i^2 roughly follow a χ^2 distribution with a degree of freedom equal to the number of non-zero elements ν_i in the row vector of the associated regressor, $\mathbf{x}_i$, i.e., $\text{PS}_i^2 \sim \chi^2_{\nu_i}$. However, when $n \leq 5d$, it is the PS that roughly follow a χ^2 distribution, that is, $\text{PS}_i \sim \chi^2_{\nu_i}$. Consequently, the threshold c_i is chosen as the 97.5 percentile of the chi-square distribution with ν_i degrees of freedom while defining weights in (4). Throughout the inference process (as detailed in Sect. 5), we use standardized residuals r_{S_i} within the Huber likelihood.

$$p_H(\mathbf{y}|\mathbf{f}, \phi) = \prod_{i=1}^{n} \frac{1-\varepsilon}{\sqrt{2\pi}\sigma} \exp\left(-\rho(r_{S_i})\right). \qquad (6)$$

4.3 GP-Huber Posterior

The posterior distribution resulting from our model, which incorporates a non-conjugate prior, is given as:

$$p(\mathbf{f}|\mathcal{D}, \boldsymbol{\theta}, \sigma) = \frac{p_G(\mathbf{f}|\mathbf{0}, \mathbf{K})}{p(\mathcal{D}|\boldsymbol{\theta}, \sigma)} p_H(\mathbf{y}|\mathbf{f}, \sigma), \qquad (7)$$

where where $p_G(\mathbf{f}|\mathbf{0}, \mathbf{K})$ is the Gaussian prior $\mathcal{N}(\mathbf{f}|\mathbf{0}, \mathbf{K})$ and $p_H(\mathbf{y}|\mathbf{f}, \sigma)$ is the likelihood modeled using the Huber density. This formulation leads to a posterior that does not have a closed-form expression due to the non-conjugate nature of the Huber likelihood. The marginal likelihood (or evidence) of the data, which plays a crucial role in model selection and hyperparameter optimization, is expressed as:

$$p(\mathcal{D}|\sigma, \boldsymbol{\theta}) = \int p_G(\mathbf{f}|\mathbf{0}, \mathbf{K}) p_H(\mathbf{y}|\mathbf{f}, \sigma) d\mathbf{f}. \qquad (8)$$

Theorem 1. *Let $\mathcal{D} = (\boldsymbol{x}_i, y_i)_{i=1}^n$ be a dataset with distinct covariates $\boldsymbol{x}_i \in \mathcal{X}$ and response $y_i \in \mathcal{Y}$, where $n < \infty$. The kernel matrix $\mathbf{K} \in \mathbb{R}^{n \times n}$ is positive definite, with elements $K_{ij} = k(\boldsymbol{x}_i, \boldsymbol{x}_j)$ defined by a continuous kernel function $k : \mathcal{X} \times \mathcal{X} \to \mathbb{R}$. Assume the Huber likelihood function $p_H(\mathbf{y}|\mathbf{f}, \boldsymbol{\sigma})$ based on strictly convex and continuous Huber loss $\rho(r_i) : \mathbb{R} \to \mathbb{R}$. Then the posterior distribution $p(\mathbf{f}|\mathcal{D}, \boldsymbol{\theta}, \sigma)$ is unimodal.*

The proof is presented in appendix 2.1. This theorem shows that despite the non-Gaussian and potentially complex nature of the Huber likelihood, the posterior retains a single peak. This simplifies both parameter inference and hyperparameter optimization.

We can set the threshold $b = 1.5$ to achieve high efficiency at the Gaussian distribution (see appendix 2.3). This would make our model robust to 10% outliers (since fraction of contamination is $\varepsilon = 0.1$). Note that, in the context of our work, "efficiency" refers to the estimator's ability to achieve low variance when the noise follows a Gaussian distribution. Specifically, a highly efficient estimator can make the best use of data that is predominantly Gaussian, leading to more accurate parameter estimation. The contamination fraction ε defines the model's tolerance to deviations from the Gaussian assumption, allowing it to handle a proportion of outlier points without being overly influenced by them. The parameter b controls the threshold for identifying outliers and thus influences the transition between $L2$ and $L1$ norm treatment. By setting $b = 0.45$, we get $\varepsilon = 0.45$ for heavy-tailed and Gaussian error distributions, we aim to accommodate up to 45% outliers while maintaining reasonable efficiency. The only hyperparameter of the likelihood function requiring estimation is $\phi = \sigma^2$.

5 Approximate Bayesian Inference

By retaining the optimization-friendly properties of convex problems ensured by to unimodality (see Theorem 1), our method enables the use of the Laplace approximation [29] for the posterior. To facilitate predictions f^*, we develop Gibbs sampling and Laplace's method. The key requirement for the latter is the continuity of the Huber density function. In Gibbs sampling, the joint posterior distribution $p(\mathbf{f}, \boldsymbol{\theta}, \sigma^2)$ can be simplified using the scale mixture model of the Laplace distribution for data points with residuals $r \geq b$: this representation expresses the likelihood of these points as a normal distribution—making the sampling process more efficient.

5.1 Gibbs Sampling

The Huber density function is a mixture of a truncated normal and a Laplace density function for an absolute standardized residual respectively lying within and outside the threshold b. This yields

$$p_H(y|f,\boldsymbol{\sigma}) = \begin{cases} \frac{C_1}{\sqrt{2\pi}w_i\sigma_g s}\exp\left(-\frac{r_i^2}{2w_i^2\sigma_g^2 s^2}\right) & |r_{S_i}| \leq b, \\ \frac{C_2}{2w_i as}\exp\left(-\frac{b|r_i|}{w_i as}\right) & |r_{S_i}| > b, \end{cases} \qquad (9)$$

where C_1 and C_2 are the constants respectively, defined as $C_1 = 1 - \varepsilon$ and $C_2 = \sqrt{\frac{\pi}{2}}\exp(b^2/2)$. The Laplace distribution $p_L(y_i|f(\mathbf{x}_i), a)$ with location parameter a can be represented as a scale mixture of normal distributions $\mathcal{N}(y_i|f(\mathbf{x}_i), \sigma_i^2)$ where σ_i^2 follows an exponential distribution $p_E(\sigma_i^2|\beta)$ [3] and $i = 1, \ldots, n_l$ are the indices of the points associated with the standardized residuals larger than the threshold b hereafter referred to as outlying points. Formally, we have

$$p_L(y_i|f(\mathbf{x}_i), a) = \int p_G(y_i|f(\mathbf{x}_i), \sigma_i^2) p_E(\sigma_i^2|\beta) d\sigma_i^2. \tag{10}$$

Using this property, we represent the individual standard deviations corresponding to n_l outlying training points as $\{\sigma_{l_1}, \ldots, \sigma_{l_{n_l}}\}$, which are elements of the vector $\boldsymbol{\sigma}_l$. The variance associated with n_g inlying points is denoted as σ_g^2. Conclusively, the Huber probability density function takes the form

$$\mathbf{y}|\mathbf{f}, \sigma_g^2, \boldsymbol{\sigma}_l^2, \beta \sim \begin{cases} \prod_{i=1}^{n_g} C_1 \mathcal{N}(y_i|f(\mathbf{x}_i), \sigma_g^2) & |r_{S_i}| \leq b, \\ \prod_{i=1}^{n_l} C_2 \mathcal{N}(y_i|f(\mathbf{x}_i), \sigma_{l_i}^2) \text{Exponential}(\sigma_{l_i}^2, \beta) & |r_{S_i}| > b, \end{cases} \tag{11}$$

where $n_g + n_l = n$ is the total number of points in the training dataset. An alternative representation of the likelihood function is given by

$$\mathbf{y}_g, \mathbf{y}_l|\mathbf{f}_g, \mathbf{f}_l, \sigma_g^2, \boldsymbol{\sigma}_l^2 \sim \mathcal{N}\left(\begin{bmatrix} \mathbf{y}_g|\mathbf{f}_g \\ \mathbf{y}_l|\mathbf{f}_l \end{bmatrix}, \begin{bmatrix} \boldsymbol{\Sigma}_{gg} & \mathbf{0} \\ \mathbf{0} & \boldsymbol{\Sigma}_{ll} \end{bmatrix}\right), \tag{12}$$

where $\boldsymbol{\Sigma}_{gg}$ and $\boldsymbol{\Sigma}_{ll}$ both are diagonal matrices, the former with constant diagonal elements equal to σ_g^2 and the latter with diagonal entries $\{\sigma_{l_1}^2, \ldots, \sigma_{l_{n_l}}^2\}$. Let the hyperparameter vector $\boldsymbol{\sigma}^2$ consist of the diagonal entries of the matrix $\boldsymbol{\Sigma}_{gg}$, which are σ_g^2 and $\boldsymbol{\sigma}_l^2$. The joint posterior probability density function of $\mathbf{f}$, $\boldsymbol{\sigma}^2$, and $\boldsymbol{\theta}$ is given by

$$p(\mathbf{f}, \boldsymbol{\sigma}^2, \boldsymbol{\theta}) \propto p(\mathbf{y}|\mathbf{f}, \boldsymbol{\sigma}^2) p_G(\mathbf{f}|\mathbf{0}, \mathbf{K}) p(\boldsymbol{\sigma}^2|\beta) p(\beta|\boldsymbol{\zeta}) p(\boldsymbol{\theta}|\boldsymbol{\zeta}). \tag{13}$$

We assume that the hyper-hyperparameter vector β and the hyperparameter vector $\boldsymbol{\theta}$ follow the log-uniform distribution with parameters contained in $\boldsymbol{\zeta}$. Since the distribution of the variance parameter σ_g^2 of n_g inlying training points is degenerate, the hyper-hyperparameter vector $\beta = [\beta_g, \beta_l]^T$ corresponding to the n_g points follows a degenerate distribution as well. Therefore, $p(\sigma_g^2|\beta_g)$ is a Dirac impulse while $\sigma_l^2|\beta_l \sim \text{Exponential}(\sigma_l^2|\beta_l)$. The samples generated from this distribution are highly correlated. Therefore, in order to better mix the Monte Carlo chains, we follow the trick used by [16] as follows:

$$p(\boldsymbol{\sigma}^2, \beta, \boldsymbol{\theta}) \propto \left[\int p_G(\mathbf{y}|\mathbf{f}, \boldsymbol{\Sigma}) p_G(\mathbf{f}|\mathbf{0}, \mathbf{K}) d\mathbf{f}\right] p(\boldsymbol{\sigma}^2|\beta) p(\beta|\boldsymbol{\zeta}) p(\boldsymbol{\theta}|\boldsymbol{\zeta}), \tag{14}$$

where the covariance matrix of the n_g inlying samples and the n_l outlying samples is given by $\boldsymbol{\Sigma} = \begin{bmatrix} \boldsymbol{\Sigma}_{gg} & \mathbf{0} \\ \mathbf{0} & \boldsymbol{\Sigma}_{ll} \end{bmatrix}$. The samples can be used to obtain the approximated probability density functions of the latent vector function, $p(\mathbf{f}^*|\mathcal{D}, \mathbf{X}^*)$, at the new test covariates contained in $\mathbf{X}^*$ by averaging over all unknowns. Formally, we have

$$p(\mathbf{f}^*|\mathcal{D}, \mathbf{X}^*) = \int p(\mathbf{f}^*|\mathbf{f}, \boldsymbol{\sigma}^2, \boldsymbol{\theta}, \mathbf{X}^*, \mathcal{D}) p(\mathbf{f}, \boldsymbol{\sigma}^2, \boldsymbol{\theta}|\mathcal{D}) d\mathbf{f} d\boldsymbol{\sigma}^2 d\boldsymbol{\theta}. \tag{15}$$

For T samples, it can be evaluated as

$$p(\mathbf{f}^*|\mathcal{D}, \mathbf{X}^*, \boldsymbol{\zeta}) = \tfrac{1}{T}\sum_{t=1}^{T} \int p(\mathbf{f}^*|\mathbf{f}, \mathbf{X}, \mathbf{X}^*, \boldsymbol{\theta}_t) p(\mathbf{f}|\mathcal{D}, \sigma_t^2, \boldsymbol{\theta}_t) d\mathbf{f}. \tag{16}$$

Table 1. RMSE and MAE values on the Neal dataset for the Case 1. Values in parentheses represent the performance for Case 3. Bold values highlight the best performance with the lowest RMSE and MAE.

	SCtMCMC	tLA	HuberMCMC$^{+\text{pw}}$	HuberLA$^{+\text{pw}}$	RCGP	GP	LaplaceMCMC
$\varepsilon \sim \mathcal{N}(0.01, 0.08)$							
RMSE	0.74 (0.52)	0.75 (1.31)	0.37 (0.42)	**0.25** (**0.25**)	1.84 (0.82)	1.44 (0.90)	0.43 (0.46)
MAE	0.47 (0.25)	0.48 (0.61)	0.31 (0.25)	**0.14** (**0.14**)	1.28 (0.54)	1.24 (0.68)	0.33 (0.26)
$\varepsilon \sim$ Student-$t(10)$							
RMSE	4.86 (11.56)	1.22 (1.31)	**0.50** (0.81)	1.17 (**0.37**)	1.89 (0.88)	1.52 (0.98)	0.59 (0.93)
MAE	1.67 (1.25)	0.77 (0.65)	**0.41** (0.39)	0.79 (**0.18**)	1.71 (0.85)	1.34 (0.22)	0.43 (0.35)
$\varepsilon \sim$ Laplace$(0, 0.1)$							
RMSE	4.76 (0.48)	1.23 (1.31)	**0.58** (0.42)	1.17 (**0.35**)	1.95 (0.86)	1.51 (0.89)	1.06 (0.82)
MAE	1.64 (0.23)	0.76 (0.61)	**0.41** (0.24)	0.68 (**0.18**)	1.27 (0.46)	1.23 (0.41)	0.75 (0.34)
$\varepsilon \sim$ Student-$t(1)$ (Cauchy)							
RMSE	4.75 (0.57)	1.25 (1.32)	0.61 (0.49)	1.20 (**0.17**)	1.97 (0.62)	1.50 (0.89)	**0.42** (0.75)
MAE	1.65 (0.27)	0.78 (0.67)	**0.47** (0.27)	0.81 (**0.11**)	1.78 (0.42)	1.32 (0.66)	0.66 (0.38)

5.2 Laplace Approximation

To ensure the continuity of the derivative of the Huber density function with respect to the latent vector function **f**, we utilize the pseudo-Huber loss function [4], which is defined as

$$\rho(r_S) = b^2 \left(\sqrt{1 + \left(\frac{r_S}{b}\right)^2} - 1 \right). \tag{17}$$

Laplace approximation of the posterior requires the likelihood to be log-concave in order for it to be represented by a unimodal multivariate normal distribution. It is executed by approximating the posterior distribution of **f** with a normal distribution [26], that is,

$$\mathbf{f} | \mathcal{D}, \sigma, \boldsymbol{\theta} \sim \mathcal{N}(\hat{\mathbf{f}} | \mathbf{f}, \mathbf{A}). \tag{18}$$

The remainder of the method is detailed in appendix 1. Finally, we present the following theorem which guarantees the robustness of GP-Huber to outliers.

Theorem 2. *Under the same assumptions as Theorem 1, the influence of an individual observation y on the posterior mean $\mathbb{E}[f \mid y]$ is bounded:*

$$\left| \frac{\partial}{\partial y} \mathbb{E}[f \mid y] \right| \leq \frac{b}{\sigma}.$$

Proof is provided in appendix 2.2

6 Experiments

Through our experiments, we aim to address the following questions:
(*Q*1) When is HuberLA$^{+\text{pw}}$ (GP-Huber with Laplace's method with pursuit weights) preferable, and under which outlier scenarios is HuberMCMC$^{+\text{pw}}$ (GP-Huber with Gibbs sampling with pursuit weights) more suitable?

(*Q*2) Does GP-Huber show a significant performance improvement over standard GP regression and the RCGP method proposed by [1] under their experimental settings?
(*Q*3) Does projection pursuit weighting give GP-Huber an edge over baselines with the same weighting?
(*Q*4) Does GP-Huber provide more accurate estimates of the planet-to-star radius ratio compared to the standard GP method used by [10] in the transmission spectroscopy experiment?

We conducted experiments on benchmark datasets with extreme outliers in location, magnitude, and error distribution. The threshold b was 1.5 for Gaussian errors and 0.45 for Student's-t, Laplace, and Cauchy errors. An anisotropic squared exponential kernel was used, with a zero mean function except in the spectroscopy experiment. Performance was measured using RMSE and MAE. Our implementation is available online[1].

6.1 Neal Dataset

We evaluate the proposed GP-Huber on the Neal dataset [23] for the following cases of extreme outliers:

Case 1: Extreme outliers $y_i^{(l)}, x_k^{(l)}$ in added in output and covariate dimensions, respectively.
Case 2: Only output dimensions $y_i^{(l)}$ were contaminated with extreme data points.
Case 3: Bad data points $y_j^{(c)}, x_k^{(l)}$ in added to both output and covariate dimensions, respectively, with the former being relatively close to the main data cluster compared to Case 1.
Case 4: Only output dimensions were contaminated with data points $y_j^{(c)}$ relatively close to the data cloud compared to Case 1.

In all the cases above, the locations i, j and k may differ or coincide (refer to appendix 3.1 for the location and magnitude details on outliers). For each case, we considered four different error distributions: $\mathcal{N}(0.01, 0.08)$, Student-t(10), Laplace(0, 0.1), Student's-t(1).

The baseline models considered for comparison on the Neal dataset, along with RCGP, include: GP with a Student's t error model solved using MCMC integration (SCtMCMC), GP with a Student's t error model using Laplace approximation (tLA), and GP with a Laplace likelihood solved via MCMC integration (LaplaceMCMC). Table 1 presents the RMSE and MAE values comparing GP-Huber against these baselines for Cases 1 and 3. Refer to appendix 3.1 for the Tables A3, A4 for the Cases 2, 4 and appendix 2.4 for the implementation details of the baselines. Furthermore, pursuit weighting is incorporated into all baseline models, and their performances are compared in Tables A5 to A8 (provided in appendix 3.2). Now, we are in position to answer $\mathcal{Q}1$.

---
[1] https://anonymous.4open.science/r/GpHuber-C9D6.

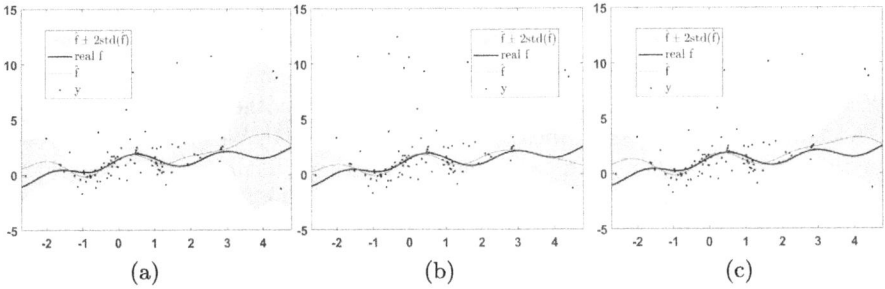

Fig. 2. Predicted values for the Case 1 of the Student's t-error distribution for the Neal dataset obtained from the eight considered GP regression models: (a) HuberMCMC; (b) HuberLA; (c) RCGP.

When is HuberMCMC better?
In scenarios with $y^{(l)}, x^{(l)}$ (Case 1), HuberMCMC performed better than HuberLA (see, Tables 1 and A3). HuberMCMC also outperformed tLA in predictive accuracy, demonstrating a more robust fit that is less influenced by $x^{(l)}$ (Fig. 2). HuberLA generally provided better uncertainty quantification compared to HuberMCMC (see Figs. 2 and A3), while maintaining competitive predictive performance. In outlier scenarios with $y^{(l)}$ (Case 2), HuberMCMC exhibited superior performance across Student's-t, Laplace, and Cauchy error distributions (see, Table A3). This suggests that HuberMCMC is a robust choice for datasets containing extreme output outliers i.e. outlier scenarios similar to Cases 1 and 2.

When is HuberLA better?
HuberLA exhibited superior performance in handling closer output outliers $y^{(c)}$ compared to HuberMCMC (values in parenthesis in the Table 1 and Table A4). Figure A4 highlights HuberLA's robustness to $x^{(l)}$, in contrast to tLA which is influenced by such points. While HuberLA generally provided more accurate predictions and reliable uncertainty quantification than both HuberMCMC and tLA, HuberMCMC performed competitively for the Cases 3 and 4.

From Tables A5 and A6 in appendix 3.2 (Cases 1 and 3), where projection pursuit weights were added to other baselines, we observe that HuberLA and HuberMCMC benefit the most from these weights. While Student's-t likelihood also scales residuals by pursuit weights, its logarithmic penalty $\propto \log(1 + r^2/\nu)$ (with ν controlling tail heaviness) is less sensitive to large residuals than Huber likelihood's linearized penalty $\propto |r|$. Laplace likelihood similarly penalizes $|r|$ but lacks a quadratic center, making Huber likelihood the optimal balance of robustness and efficiency. Tables A7 and A8 show the results for outlier Cases 2 and 4, where projection pursuit weighting is added to other baselines. The weights equal 1 for all data points due to the absence of covariate outliers $x^{(l)}$. GP-Huber performs comparably to other baselines in these cases. This demonstrates that the weighting mechanism enhances GP-Huber's accuracy, addressing $Q3$.

6.2 UCI Datasets

In this set of experiments, we compared the performance of GP-Huber on the UCI datasets, Energy and Yacht, against RCGP and other baselines: t-GP, m-GP, and standard GP, using the outlier settings from [1]. We specifically focused on the "focused outlier" and "asymmetrical outlier" scenarios, as they closely resemble our extreme and close outlier cases. MAE values of the comparison are presented in Table 2. As expected, HuberLA demonstrates to be more robust than HuberMCMC since the asymmetrical and focused outliers cases considered in the study of [1] broadly fall under the Cases 3 and 4 in our study. On the Energy dataset, HuberLA outperformed both tLA and RCGP.

Table 2. MAE values for energy and yacht. Bold values indicate the best performance for each row.

	GP	RCGP	t-GP	m-GP	HuberMCMC	HuberLA
Focused Outliers						
Energy	0.03 (0.04)	**0.02 (0.00)**	0.03 (0.05)	0.24 (0.00)	0.12 (0.01)	0.04 (0.01)
Yacht	0.26 (0.15)	**0.10 (0.14)**	0.20 (0.04)	0.24 (0.00)	0.24 (0.02)	0.18 (0.00)
Asymmetric Outliers						
Energy	0.54 (0.02)	0.44 (0.04)	0.42 (0.02)	0.41 (0.00)	0.47 (0.02)	**0.11 (0.00)**
Yacht	0.54 (0.06)	0.35 (0.02)	0.41 (0.00)	0.40 (0.00)	0.51 (0.01)	**0.12 (0.00)**

In our experiments, HuberLA outperformed RCGP and other baselines significantly in asymmetric outlier case and also showing the good computational efficiency, thus answering $Q2$. Note that the outliers are present only in the response and not in the covariate dimensions, the projection pursuit weights are equal to 1 for these datasets.

Computational costs for the experiments on Neal and UCI datasets are presented in Table A10 and A11 in appendix 4. HuberLA—similar to RCGP and tLA—requires less computational time than HuberMCMC, as expected. The models converge faster for unidimensional data: HuberMCMC performs comparably to MCMC techniques with Student-t likelihood. For multidimensional cases, HuberMCMC, as expected for sampling-based methods, requires more time to converge, while HuberLA achieves faster convergence (between 5 to 10 s).

6.3 Transmission Spectroscopy

Transmission spectroscopy records the relative change in the stellar flux, which is the incident photons per unit area, as a planet travels in front of the star. The sources of error, such as photon noise and instrumental and astrophysical systematics, raise many potential challenges for precise planet's atmosphere characterization. The goal is to infer the planet to star radius ratio ρ_{radius} from the observed flux as the planet passes in front of the star. The optical state parameters are metered via auxiliary measurements of the spectral trace such as position, width, angle, or other parameters, indicating the state of the detector and optics, which are thought to be the cause of instrumental systematics. Instead of modeling the latter as a linear function of the optical state parameters, [10] proposed a non-parametric model by leveraging GPs.

The observation set obtained from HST-NICMOS includes the light curves for 18 wavelength channels extracted from $n = 638$ spectra of the planetary system HD-189733. The flux measurements contained in the vector, $\boldsymbol{f} = [f_1, f_2, \ldots, f_n]^T$, are recorded at n time instants, $\{t_1, t_2, \ldots, t_n\}$ and the optical state parameters $\mathbf{x}_{t_i}$ collected in the matrix $\mathbf{X} \in \mathbb{R}^{n \times d}$ constitute the training dataset. We extend the work of [10] by using the GP-Huber model to estimate the planet-to-star radius ratio ρ_{radius}. As demonstrated earlier, the robustness to outliers of GP-Huber allows us to utilize 517 measurements associated with four out-of-transit orbits, namely orbit numbers, $\{2, 3, 4, 5\}$, and 137 measurements associated with one in-transit orbit, namely orbit number 1. The latter was excluded from the analysis performed by [10] as it constitutes much larger systematics effects attributed to the spacecraft settling. The observed transit flux modeled in the GP framework follows a normal distribution, that is,

$$\boldsymbol{f}(t, \mathbf{X}) \sim \mathcal{N}(\boldsymbol{T}(t, \boldsymbol{\phi}), \mathbf{K}), \tag{19}$$

where the parameter vector, $\boldsymbol{\phi}$, include the parameter of interest, ρ_{radius}, and other parameters. We consider the analytical quadratic limb darkening transit function proposed by [18]. Analogous with (11), we assume that the observed transit flux vector, $\boldsymbol{f} = \boldsymbol{f}(t, \mathbf{X})$, in the GP-Huber framework follows a normal distribution, that is,

$$\boldsymbol{f} | \boldsymbol{T}(t, \boldsymbol{\phi}), \mathbf{X}, \boldsymbol{\phi}, \boldsymbol{\theta}, \sigma^2 \sim \mathcal{N}\left(\boldsymbol{T}(t, \mathbf{X}), \boldsymbol{\Sigma} + \mathbf{K}\right). \tag{20}$$

The joint un-normalized log-posterior function of $\boldsymbol{\phi}$, $\boldsymbol{\beta}$, and $\boldsymbol{\theta}$ with the gamma aprior probability density function, $p(\boldsymbol{\theta}) = \frac{1}{l_\tau} \exp\left(\frac{-\boldsymbol{\theta}}{l_\tau}\right)$, over the covariance function hyperparameters is given by

$$\log P(\boldsymbol{\phi}, \boldsymbol{\theta}, \sigma^2, \boldsymbol{\beta} | \boldsymbol{f}, \mathbf{X}, \boldsymbol{\zeta}) = \log\left(\mathcal{L}(\mathbf{r}_S | \mathbf{X}, \boldsymbol{\phi}, \boldsymbol{\theta}, \sigma^2)\right)$$

$$- \frac{\tau}{l_\tau} - \sum_{i=1}^{d} \left(\frac{1}{s_i l_i}\right) + \log(\boldsymbol{\beta}) - \boldsymbol{\beta}^T \sigma^2 + \log(p(\boldsymbol{\beta} | \boldsymbol{\zeta})) + \mathrm{C}. \tag{21}$$

The challenging task now is to infer the parameter ρ_{radius} from the joint posterior distribution of $(\boldsymbol{\phi}, \boldsymbol{\theta}, \sigma^2, \boldsymbol{\beta})$. The log-likelihood $\mathcal{L}$ term is expressed as

$$\log \mathcal{L}(\mathbf{r}_S | \mathbf{X}, \boldsymbol{\phi}, \boldsymbol{\theta}, \sigma^2) = \tfrac{-1}{2} \mathbf{r}_S^T (\boldsymbol{\Sigma} + \mathbf{K})^{-1} \mathbf{r} - \tfrac{1}{2} \log|\boldsymbol{\Sigma} + \mathbf{K}| - \tfrac{n}{2} \log(2\pi) + \log(1 - \varepsilon), \tag{22}$$

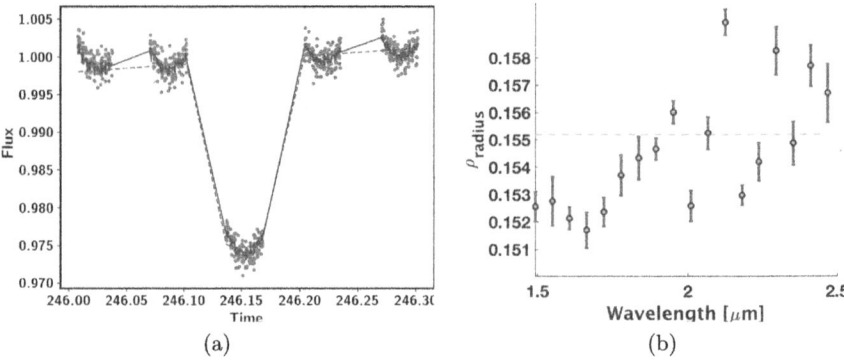

Fig. 3. Transit curve fit and estimated ρ_{radius}. (a) Transit curve mean function $T(t,\boldsymbol{\theta})$ (in red dotted line) and GP-Huber model fit (in blue solid line); (b) results of planet-to-star radius ratios (ρ_{radius}) obtained from GP-Huber with error-bars. The dashed grey line represents the sanity check values.

where $\mathbf{r} = \boldsymbol{f} - \boldsymbol{T}(\boldsymbol{t}, \mathbf{X})$. One of the approaches is to use the Bayesian method that seeks the posterior distribution of ρ_{radius} by marginalizing over the other parameters of the mean function parameters $\boldsymbol{\phi}$ and the covariance function hyperparameters, $\boldsymbol{\theta}$ using MCMC methods. The other method proposed as the type-II maximum likelihood method by [10], where the hyperparameters, $\boldsymbol{\theta}$ and σ^2. Formally, we have

$$(\hat{\boldsymbol{\phi}}, \hat{\boldsymbol{\theta}}, \hat{\sigma}^2, \hat{\boldsymbol{\beta}}) = \underset{\boldsymbol{\phi}, \boldsymbol{\theta}, \sigma^2, \boldsymbol{\beta}}{\arg \max} \log P(\boldsymbol{\phi}, \boldsymbol{\theta}, \sigma^2, \boldsymbol{\beta} | \boldsymbol{f}, \mathbf{X}, \boldsymbol{\zeta}). \qquad (23)$$

And the posterior distribution of the parameter of interest ρ_{radius} is obtained by marginalizing the joint posterior distribution $p(\boldsymbol{\phi}, \boldsymbol{\theta}, \sigma^2, \boldsymbol{\beta})$ over the hyperparameters and the rest of the mean function parameters. In the standard type II maximum likelihood method, the hyperparameters are fixed to their maximum likelihood estimates i.e. by maximizing the evidence $p(\mathcal{D}|\boldsymbol{\phi}, \boldsymbol{\theta}, \sigma^2)$.

Figure 3(a) shows the transit fit obtained for one wavelength channel. Figure 3(b) shows the estimated ρ_{radius} obtained using MCMC integration over the rest of the mean function parameters $\boldsymbol{\phi}$ and hyperparameters $\boldsymbol{\theta}$ along with the values estimated from the white light curve represented as the white dashed line. Note that the estimated ρ_{radius} values are very close to the white light curve value of 0.155. Most of our results agree with the results obtained from the Gibson model except for wavelength channels 1.665μm and 2.124μm (see, appendix 3.3), which effectively answers Q4. We retain the noisy orbit-1 observations—and still, GP-Huber delivers estimates on par with, or better than, existing methods. This highlights its robustness and accuracy in the face of outliers in both the flux and the optical state parameters, data that spectroscopy models typically discard.

7 Conclusions

The proposed GP-Huber model shows promise for handling a variety of heavy-tailed and Gaussian error distributions with extreme outliers in both covariate and output dimensions. Notably, it introduces additional parameters, b and ε, which can be heuristically set prior to parameter inference. The model's unimodal posterior simplifies Gibbs sampling and allows for an efficient Laplace approximation. We prove the bounded influence of observations on the posterior mean. From our experiments on the Neal and UCI datasets, we found that HuberMCMC^{+pw} shows superior robustness against extreme outliers, while HuberLA^{+pw} performs better with near outliers, compared to RCGP^{+pw} and other baselines^{+pw}. Additionally, the transmission spectroscopy experiment demonstrates their potential in real-world applications.

Future work involves extending the scalability of GP-Huber to handle large datasets by implementing sparse inference techniques.

Acknowledgments. I gratefully acknowledge Virginia Tech for laying the foundation of this research during my PhD studies. I also thank Argonne National Laboratory for its ongoing support and access to cutting-edge facilities.

Disclosure of Interests. The authors have no competing interests to declare that are relevant to the content of this article.

References

1. Altamirano, M., Briol, F.X., Knoblauch, J.: Robust and conjugate gaussian process regression. In: Forty-First International Conference on Machine Learning (2024)
2. Andrade, D., Takeda, A.: Robust gaussian process regression with the trimmed marginal likelihood. In: Uncertainty in Artificial Intelligence, pp. 67–76. PMLR (2023)
3. Andrews, D.F., Mallows, C.L.: Scale mixtures of normal distributions. J. Roy. Stat. Soc.: Ser. B (Methodol.) **36**(1), 99–102 (1974)
4. Charbonnier, P., Blanc-Féraud, L., Aubert, G., Barlaud, M.: Deterministic edge-preserving regularization in computed imaging. IEEE Trans. Image Process. **6**(2), 298–311 (1997)
5. Daemi, A., Alipouri, Y., Huang, B.: Identification of robust gaussian process regression with noisy input using em algorithm. Chemom. Intell. Lab. Syst. **191**, 1–11 (2019)
6. De Finetti, B.: The bayesian approach to the rejection of outliers. In: Proceedings of the fourth Berkeley Symposium on Probability and Statistics, vol. 1, pp. 199–210. University Press Berkeley, California (1961)
7. Desgagné, A., Gagnon, P.: Bayesian robustness to outliers in linear regression and ratio estimation. Braz. J. Probabil. Stat. **33**(2), 205–221 (2019)
8. Donoho, D.L.: Breakdown properties of multivariate location estimators. Technical report, Harvard University, Boston (1982). https://projecteuclid.org/journals/annals-of-statistics/volume-20/issue-4/Breakdown-Properties-of-Location-Estimates-Based-on-Halfspace-Depth-and/10.1214/aos/1176348890.full

9. Ghahramani, Z., Beal, M.: Propagation algorithms for variational bayesian learning. Adv. Neural Inf. Process. Syst. **13** (2000)
10. Gibson, N., Aigrain, S., Roberts, S., Evans, T., Osborne, M., Pont, F.: A gaussian process framework for modelling instrumental systematics: application to transmission spectroscopy. Mon. Not. R. Astron. Soc. **419**(3), 2683–2694 (2012)
11. Goldberg, P., Williams, C., Bishop, C.: Regression with input-dependent noise: a gaussian process treatment. Adv. Neural Inf. Process. Syst. **10** (1997)
12. Huber, P.J.: Robust estimation of a location parameter. In: Breakthroughs in Statistics: Methodology and Distribution, pp. 492–518. Springer, Heidelberg (1992). https://doi.org/10.1007/978-1-4612-4380-9_35
13. Hubert, M., Debruyne, M.: Minimum covariance determinant. Wiley Interdisc. Rev. Comput. Stat. **2**(1), 36–43 (2010)
14. Jylänki, P., Vanhatalo, J., Vehtari, A.: Robust gaussian process regression with a student-t likelihood. J. Mach. Learn. Res. **12**(11) (2011)
15. Kreidberg, L.: Exoplanet atmosphere measurements from transmission spectroscopy and other planet-star combined light observations. arXiv preprint arXiv:1709.05941 (2017)
16. Kuss, M.: Gaussian process models for robust regression, classification, and reinforcement learning. Ph.D. thesis, echnische Universität Darmstadt Darmstadt, Germany (2006)
17. Li, Z.Z., Li, L., Shao, Z.: Robust gaussian process regression based on iterative trimming. Astron. Comput. **36**, 100483 (2021)
18. Mandel, K., Agol, E.: Analytic light curves for planetary transit searches. Astrophys. J. **580**(2), L171 (2002)
19. Maronna, R.A., Yohai, V.J.: The behavior of the stahel-donoho robust multivariate estimator. J. Am. Stat. Assoc. **90**(429), 330–341 (1995)
20. Mili, L., Cheniae, M., Vichare, N., Rousseeuw, P.J.: Robust state estimation based on projection statistics [of power systems]. IEEE Trans. Power Syst. **11**(2), 1118–1127 (1996)
21. Minka, T.P.: Expectation propagation for approximate bayesian inference. arXiv preprint arXiv:1301.2294 (2013)
22. Naish-Guzman, A., Holden, S.: Robust regression with twinned gaussian processes. Adv. Neural Inf. Process. Syst. **20** (2007)
23. Neal, R.M.: Monte carlo implementation of gaussian process models for bayesian regression and classification. arXiv preprint physics/9701026 (1997)
24. Ramsey, J., Novick, M.: Plu robust bayesian decision theory: point estimation. J. Amer. Statist. Assoc. **75**, 401–407 (1980)
25. Ranjan, R., Huang, B., Fatehi, A.: Robust gaussian process modeling using em algorithm. J. Process Control **42**, 125–136 (2016)
26. Rue, H., Martino, S., Chopin, N.: Approximate bayesian inference for latent gaussian models by using integrated nested laplace approximations. J. R. Stat. Soc. Ser. B Stat Methodol. **71**(2), 319–392 (2009)
27. Stahel, W., Weisberg, S., Rousseeuw, P.J., van Zomeren, B.C.: Robust distances: simulations and cutoff values. In: Directions in Robust Statistics and Diagnostics: Part II, pp. 195–203. Springer, Heidelberg (1991). https://doi.org/10.1007/978-1-4612-4444-8_11
28. Stahel, W.A.: Robuste schätzungen: infinitesimale optimalität und schätzungen von kovarianzmatrizen. Ph.D. thesis, ETH Zurich (1981)
29. Tierney, L., Kadane, J.B.: Accurate approximations for posterior moments and marginal densities. J. Am. Stat. Assoc. **81**(393), 82–86 (1986)

30. Vanhatalo, J., Jylänki, P., Vehtari, A.: Gaussian process regression with student-t likelihood. Adv. Neural Inf. Process. Syst. **22** (2009)
31. West, M.: Outlier models and prior distributions in bayesian linear regression. J. R. Stat. Soc. Ser. B Stat Methodol. **46**(3), 431–439 (1984)
32. Williams, C.: Computing with infinite networks. Adv. Neural Inf. Process. Syst. **9** (1996)

Enriching Category Representations with LLMs Towards Robust Zero-Shot OOD Detection

Dian Chao[1], Yuxuan Zhang[1], Luping Zhou[2], and Yang Yang[1(✉)]

[1] Nanjing University of Science and Technology, Nanjing 210000, China
{chaodian,xuan_yuzhang,yyang}@njust.edu.cn
[2] University of Sydney, Sydney 2006, Australia
luping.zhou@sydney.edu.au

Abstract. Recent advancements in foundation models, particularly Visual-Language Models (VLMs), have enabled effective zero-shot Out-of-distribution (OOD) detection. Existing methods attempt to generate the names of OOD classes similar to in-distribution (ID) classes to explore the textual space of VLMs. However, they fail to integrate relevant ID information to reveal specific OOD features, thus limiting the distinction between ID and OOD classes. To address this issue, we propose a simple yet effective zero-shot OOD detection approach incorporating a specific semantic text generation strategy and a new regionally enhanced semantic OOD scoring function. In detail, we employ meticulously designed prompts to generate challenging OOD label texts using Large Language Models (LLMs). Subsequently, the specific semantic text generation strategy leverages LLMs to capture fine-grained textual representations of both ID and OOD classes. Additionally, the regionally enhanced semantic OOD score is formulated by adjusting the confidence of ID classes to improve OOD detection. Experiments demonstrate that our method achieves state-of-the-art (SOTA) performance on multiple OOD detection benchmarks. The code is available at repository.

Keywords: Out-of-distribution Detection · Zero-shot Learning · Visual-Language Models

1 Introduction

With the continuous development of deep learning and foundation models, the research community has shifted from traditional i.i.d. assumptions towards open-world scenarios. Consequently, traditional models exhibit performance degradation on OOD data [1–5,29,30,52]. In response, OOD detection has become essential for identifying and rejecting invalid inputs and ensuring safety. This capability is particularly crucial in high-stakes domains such as autonomous driving [6,7] and medical diagnostics [8].

Supplementary Information The online version contains supplementary material available at https://doi.org/10.1007/978-3-032-05962-8_2.

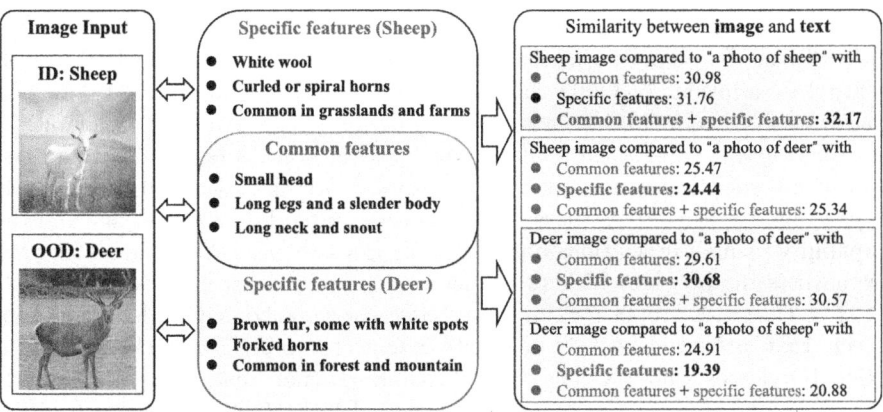

Fig. 1. Image-Text Similarity of Sheep and Deer: Comparing Common and Specific Features. Specific features refer to the unique characteristics of sheep or deer, while common features represent the shared traits. The right side shows the similarity scores between images of sheep/deer and text descriptions that include 'common', 'specific', or 'common+specific' features. For each image, we aim to maximize similarity with the corresponding class description while minimizing similarity with descriptions of unrelated classes.

To address these challenges, existing methods can be categorized into two historical stages: 1) vision-only methods [9–13,31]. and 2) vision-language methods. The vision-only approaches primarily focus on utilizing external OOD images to enhance model robustness or exploring uncertainty in visual representations across varying distributions, without taking into account the potential benefits introduced by textual information [14,15]. With the development of foundation models, VLMs [16] exhibit strong generalization capabilities after being trained on large-scale image-text pairs. In recent years, an increasing number of works [17,18] focus on leveraging textual modality features for OOD detection using VLMs. These approaches demonstrate superior performance compared to previous OOD detection methods. However, these methods primarily utilize ID class names and lack comprehensive exploitation of the textual modality. Recent works have begun to explore more extensive information from the textual modality. Several approaches [14,15] endeavor to generate OOD class names using resources such as WordNet [19], while others [20] leverage LLMs [21] to generate semantic descriptions of ID classes for zero-shot OOD detection.

However, existing methods tend to overlook the integration of ID information necessary for capturing distinctive OOD textual features. We argue that relying solely on textual features derived from OOD names or ID class descriptors is insufficient for effectively distinguishing hard OOD instances. Leveraging VLMs' ability to align textual and visual features, we can guide the model to focus on regions unique to hard OOD instances. To verify the intention, we first analyze the influence of common and specific features, as depicted in Fig. 1. Possibly, here give an example of a common feature and an example of a specific feature by combining descriptive terms (e.g., "a photo of a sheep with white wool, commonly found in grasslands and farms") and computing similarity with both sheep and deer images, we observe that common features lead to misclassification. In contrast, more specific features help reduce it. Acquiring such fine-grained textual descriptions of OOD classes can significantly enhance OOD detection performance. Unfortunately, large lexical databases like WordNet, while useful for constructing categorical relationships, lack the contextual specificity needed to capture specific features for each category. With the advancement of LLMs trained on extensive text, these models have acquired broad knowledge and the capability to analyze relationships and distinctions between categories. This work we harness the power of LLMs to generate fine-grained textual descriptions.

Therefore, we propose a simple yet effective zero-shot OOD detection approach that utilizes LLMs to generate names for hard OOD classes resembling ID classes while systematically excluding synonyms and near-synonyms through similarity calculations. To enhance VLMs' OOD detection capacities, fine-grained descriptions are generated by simultaneously considering both ID and OOD class names. Specifically, this work uses LLMs to generate descriptions for ID classes. Subsequently, LLMs are also employed to generate OOD classes that are prone to be misclassified as the given ID classes, along with specific features that distinguish these hard OOD classes from their ID counterparts. This approach aims to maximize the separation of textual feature spaces between hard OOD and ID classes. Furthermore, the impact of shared features between OOD and ID classes on OOD detection performance is analyzed using information entropy, demonstrating that common features adversely affect OOD detection. To address this, we propose a novel scoring method that adjusts the confidence of ID samples based on their similarity to hard OOD classes. Extensive experiments demonstrate that our method achieves SOTA performance across multiple datasets. This approach enhances the model's performance in hard OOD detection tasks and exhibits strong generalization capabilities. In summary, our key contributions are as follows:

- We further explore the textual space at the regional feature level using semantic texts generated by LLMs, aiming to identify discriminative regional features between ID and OOD counterparts and maximize their separation.

- We analyze the influence of common and specific features on OOD detection. Moreover, we propose a regionally enhanced semantic OOD score, adjusting ID confidence based on similarity to synthesized OOD classes.

- The effectiveness of the proposed method is validated across diverse settings, encompassing both simple and challenging OOD tasks. Experimental results indicate that this approach achieves SOTA performance across multiple OOD detection benchmarks.

2 Related Work

Traditional OOD Detection is typically categorized into two types: training-time regularization [22–26,28] and post hoc methods [2,12,13,27,32,33,51].

Training-time regularization methods assume that a subset of OOD data is accessible during model training. CSI [22] enhances the OOD detector through the application of contrastive learning. MOS [23] pre-groups all categories and introduces an additional class to each group, redesigning the loss function for training. VOS [24] improves energy scores by generating virtual anomalies. LogitNorm [25] offers an alternative to cross-entropy loss by separating the influence of the logit norm from the training process. CIDER [26] improves OOD detection performance by optimizing contrastive loss.

Post hoc methods do not alter the model's parameters; instead, they typically focus on designing an OOD score. MSP [2] utilizes the highest predicted softmax probability as the OOD score. ODIN [27] refines MSP by applying input perturbations and rescaling the logits. Energy [13] introduces the use of an energy function [34] to quantify OOD. Mahalanobis [12] calculates the OOD score based on the minimum Mahalanobis distance between the feature and the centroids of each class. GradNorm [32] develops the OOD score by utilizing the gradient space. ViM [35] integrates the norm of feature residuals with the principal space created by training features and the original logits to determine the degree of OOD-ness. KNN [33] explores the effectiveness of non-parametric nearest-neighbor distances for identifying OOD samples.

OOD Detection based on VLMs has been developed using CLIP [16] as the foundation, leveraging its powerful vision-language alignment capabilities. MCM [17] introduced this approach by utilizing maximum softmax probabilities to assess the similarity of images to known classes, thereby identifying OOD images. ZOC [36] train image decoders for extracting textual information from images. CLIPN [18] proposes constructing negative sample pairs and conducting pre-training to learn a 'no' concept for each class. MMOOD [20] propose using LLMs to generate additional descriptive terms for ID classes to enrich textual semantic information. Recent studies [14,15] have explored methods to leverage VLMs' zero-shot inference capability by generating OOD categories through various approaches, aiming to represent potential OOD scenarios. Specifically, EOE [14] utilizes LLMs to generate potential outlier class and designs an outlier penalty function to detect OOD samples. NegLabel [15] acquisition utilizes WordNet to gather a diverse set of OOD category names, complemented by a scoring function to identify the OOD class with low similarity to current IDs.

Large Language Models such as GPT-3 [37], LLaMA-3 [38], GPT-4 [39], are leading advancements in natural language processing. These models are trained on massive datasets with parameters ranging from hundreds of billions to trillions. LLMs represent significant advancements in natural language processing, pushing boundaries in language understanding, generation, and adaptation across various domains. Given LLMs' broad knowledge base, they are instrumental in providing similarities and differences among categories akin to ID.

3 Methodology

This section details the proposed approach. Section 3.1 defines the notation and outlines the problem. Section 3.2 introduces a method for generating outliers and fine-grained features by leveraging LLMs to augment class descriptions. The complete framework is depicted in Fig. 3. In Sect. 3.3, a novel OOD detection scoring function is presented, which clusters ID and OOD categories.

3.1 Notation and Preliminary

Without loss of generality, assume that we have n images which are denoted as $\boldsymbol{X} = \{x_1, \cdots, x_n\}$. The ID class names set $\boldsymbol{Y}^{(\text{id})} = \{y_1^{(\text{id})}, \cdots, y_c^{(\text{id})}\}$ is also available, where c denotes the number of class names. The goal of OOD detection is to determine whether an image $x \in \boldsymbol{X}$ belongs to the ID class $\boldsymbol{Y}^{(\text{id})}$ or not.

We prompt LLMs to generate OOD class names set to assist the OOD detection task. Additionally, extra information for both ID and OOD classes is generated to better align text and images. The descriptions for ID classes are denoted by $\boldsymbol{D}^{(\text{id})}$, and the OOD class names set and their descriptions are denoted by $\boldsymbol{Y}^{(\text{ood})}$ and $\boldsymbol{D}^{(\text{ood})}$, respectively. Furthermore, a pre-trained model is used to encode text including class name and description and image as feature, and then decide whether an image belongs to the ID class names set. Specifically, we use $\phi(\cdot)$ and $\psi(\cdot)$ to denote the image and text encoder, respectively. For an image $\boldsymbol{x}$ and a text $\boldsymbol{t}$, their features can be calculated by:

$$\boldsymbol{u} = \phi(\boldsymbol{x}), \ \boldsymbol{v} = \psi(\boldsymbol{t}), \tag{1}$$

where $\boldsymbol{u}, \boldsymbol{v} \in \mathcal{R}^d$ denote the image and text features, d denotes the feature dimension, respectively. The text input can be a class name or description.

Based on the features of the given image and text information, we can design an evaluation function to decide whether the image belongs to the ID class or not. For a comprehensive list of notations, refer to the Appendix A.1.

3.2 Specific Semantic Text Generation Strategy

Ask for OOD names
Instruction: Please directly tell me the category names without explanations and additional information.

Question: Which classes and {ID_CLASS} are similar in terms of size/pattern/environment?

Answer: Sure! Here are some examples: {OOD_CLASS1} {OOD_CLASS2} {OOD_CLASS3}

(a) OOD class generation.

Ask for description
Instruction: Please describe the visual characteristics in twenty words or fewer.

Question: Please describe the visual characteristics of {ID_CLASS}. The description should be precise.

Answer: Here are some characteristics: {ID_Description}

Question: What are the unique characteristics that distinguish {OOD_CLASS} from {ID_CLASS}?

Answer: Here are the characteristics that distinguish {OOD_CLASS} from {ID_CLASS}: {OOD_Description}

(b) Description generation.

Fig. 2. (a) The prompt queries to obtain OOD class names similar to ID classes, including instruction, question, and model response examples. (b) The prompt queries to obtain descriptive words for ID and OOD classes, including instruction, question, and model response examples.

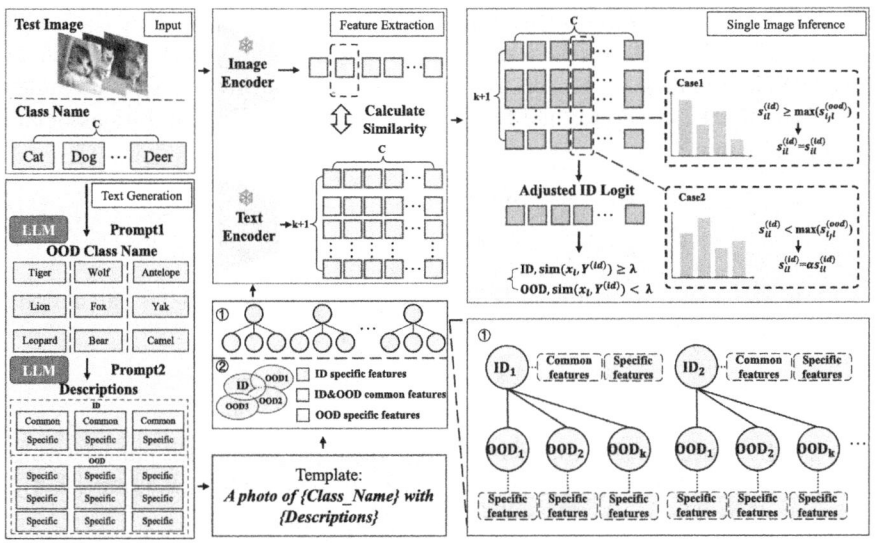

Fig. 3. The main framework of our model. LLMs are employed to generate OOD class names and descriptions for ID samples, following a fixed template. Feature vectors are then extracted using frozen encoders. Finally, the OOD detection process for a single image is demonstrated. In the enlarged section labeled ①, a detailed depiction is provided of how the relationship between an ID class and its corresponding hard OOD is constructed, along with their associated textual descriptions.

LLMs are adopted to generate additional textual information to support the OOD detection task. Beyond generating OOD class names, LLMs are also used to create nuanced textual descriptions for both ID and OOD class names.

LLMs are first utilized to generate OOD class names. To enhance the discriminative ability of the model, the generated OOD classes are required to closely resemble the ID classes. For example, if the ID class name is "cat", an OOD class name like "tiger" is preferred over unrelated options such as "book". To achieve this goal, prompts are refined to drive LLMs to generate target OOD class names by exploring the pivotal properties including size, pattern, and environment. The interaction process with LLMs is shown in Fig. 2 (a).

Formally, k OOD class names are generated for each ID class name, i.e., $\forall y_i^{(id)} \in Y^{(id)}$, we generate OOD class names set $\{y_{i1}^{(ood)}, \cdots, y_{iK_i}^{(ood)}\}$. $Y^{(ood)}$ are utilized to denote the whole OOD class names set, which is defined as follows:

$$Y^{(ood)} = \bigcup_{i=1}^{c} \{y_{i1}^{(ood)}, \cdots, y_{iK_i}^{(ood)}\}, \tag{2}$$

where K_i denotes the number of generated OOD class names and its value is dependent on the output of LLMs.

Since the strong knowledge capacity of the LLMs, it is necessary to filter out some OOD classes [15] that are too similar to ensure the distinguishability of the subsequent description generation. For a detailed explanation, please refer to Appendix B.1. To achieve this, features for both ID classes and their corresponding OOD class names are first extracted. Specifically, a pre-trained CLIP model is utilized to extract the textual features for a given ID class and its associated OOD class names:

$$\boldsymbol{v}_i^{(\text{id})} = \psi(\boldsymbol{y}_i^{(\text{id})}), \tag{3}$$

$$\forall j \in \{1, \cdots, k\}, \boldsymbol{v}_{ij}^{(\text{ood})} = \psi(\boldsymbol{y}_{ij}^{(\text{ood})}). \tag{4}$$

Then, the similarity between ID class and OOD class names is calculated

$$\forall j \in \{1, \cdots, k\}, s_{ij} = \frac{[\boldsymbol{v}_i^{(\text{id})}]^\top \boldsymbol{v}_{ij}^{(\text{ood})}}{\|\boldsymbol{v}_i^{(\text{id})}\| \|\boldsymbol{v}_{ij}^{(\text{ood})}\|}. \tag{5}$$

According to similarity, for each ID class, the top-k OOD class names with the lowest similarity scores are selected to construct pairs, where $k \leq \min\{K_i\}_{i=1}^c$. This process results in the filtered OOD class name set:

$$\hat{\boldsymbol{Y}}^{(\text{ood})} = \bigcup_{i=1}^c \{\boldsymbol{y}_{il_1}^{(\text{ood})}, \cdots, \boldsymbol{y}_{il_k}^{(\text{ood})}\}, \tag{6}$$

where $|\hat{\boldsymbol{Y}}^{(\text{ood})}| = ck$.

After obtaining the ID class name $\boldsymbol{Y}^{(\text{id})}$ and the filtered OOD class names $\hat{\boldsymbol{Y}}^{(\text{ood})}$, descriptions for each class are generated. Given the high similarity between an ID class name and its corresponding OOD class names, a novel strategy is devised to generate distinctive descriptions for each ID and OOD class.

For each ID class name and its paired similar OOD class names, we prompt LLMs to generate the description $\boldsymbol{D}^{(\text{id})} = \{\boldsymbol{d}_1^{(\text{id})}, \cdots, \boldsymbol{d}_c^{(\text{id})}\}$ that characterizes the ID class name concisely and precisely. For example, for the ID class name "sheep", the generated descriptions might include "white wool", "long neck and snout". These descriptions may overlap with features of similar OOD classes, for example, the OOD class "deer" similar to ID class "sheep", could also be described as "long neck and snout". Next, we prompt LLMs to generate concise and precise descriptions for paired OOD class names. In Appendix B.2, we analyze the impact of common and specific features on OOD detection, demonstrating that only specific features can enhance OOD detection. To ensure these descriptions highlight unique properties and avoid overlapping with the ID class, the LLMs are explicitly instructed to focus on distinguishing features in their generated descriptions $\boldsymbol{D}^{(\text{ood})} = \bigcup_{i=1}^c \{\boldsymbol{d}_{i1}^{(\text{ood})}, \cdots, \boldsymbol{d}_{ik}^{(\text{ood})}\}$. The prompt for description generation is given in Fig. 2 (b).

3.3 Regionally Enhanced Semantic OOD Score

A novel method is proposed to compute the ID similarity score to complete the OOD detection task.

For any image x_l and ID class name $y_i^{(\text{id})}$, we utilize the OOD class names $\{\hat{y}_{i1}^{(\text{ood})}, \cdots, \hat{y}_{ik}^{(\text{ood})}\}$ corresponding to $y_i^{(\text{id})}$, the ID description $d_i^{(\text{id})}$ corresponding to $y_i^{(\text{id})}$, and the OOD descriptions $\{d_{i1}^{(\text{ood})}, \cdots, d_{ik}^{(\text{ood})}\}$ to obtain the confidence score of image and ID class. Since there is a one-to-one correspondence between the class name and their descriptions, we first combine them using the following prompt to obtain an input text:

$$t = \text{"A photo of \{CLASS\_NAME\} with \{DESCRIPTION\}."}$$

By respectively substituting $CLASS\_NAME$ and $DESCRIPTION$ with the ID class name and its description, we obtain $t_i^{(\text{id})}$. Similar operations are used to obtain $\{t_{i1}^{(\text{ood})}, \cdots, t_{ik}^{(\text{ood})}\}$. Then, according to image x_l, text $t_i^{(\text{id})}$ and $\{t_{i1}^{(\text{ood})}, \cdots, t_{ik}^{(\text{ood})}\}$, we can calculate features by using:

$$u_l = \phi(x_l), \tag{7}$$

$$v_i^{(\text{id})} = \psi(t_i^{(\text{id})}), \tag{8}$$

$$\forall j \in \{1, \cdots, k\}, v_{ij}^{(\text{ood})} = \psi(t_{ij}^{(\text{ood})}). \tag{9}$$

Then, we can calculate the similarity by:

$$s_{il}^{(\text{id})} = \frac{u_l^\top v_i^{(\text{id})}}{\|u_l\| \|v_i^{(\text{id})}\|}, \tag{10}$$

$$\forall j \in \{1, \cdots, k\}, s_{i,j l}^{(\text{ood})} = \frac{u_l^\top v_{ij}^{(\text{ood})}}{\|u_l\| \|v_{ij}^{(\text{ood})}\|}. \tag{11}$$

Based on the similarity $s_{il}^{(\text{id})}$ and $\{s_{i,j l}^{(\text{ood})}\}_{j=1}^k$, a similarity strategy is proposed based on the rectification degree α. Intuitively, when the model is more inclined to classify an image as belonging to an OOD class, the confidence in the ID class should decrease. Formally, an amended similarity is defined as:

$$\hat{s}_{il}^{(\text{id})} = \begin{cases} \alpha s_{il}^{(\text{id})} & \text{if } s_{il}^{(\text{id})} \leq \max_{j=1}^k \{s_{i,j l}^{(\text{ood})}\}, \\ s_{il}^{(\text{id})} & \text{otherwise,} \end{cases} \tag{12}$$

where $0 < \alpha < 1$.

For now, we obtain the amended similarity score between an image and all ID class names. Similar to MCM [17], normalized confidence is used to determine whether an image belongs to an ID class. Specifically, the confidence is calculated using the following formula:

$$\texttt{sim}(x_l, t^{(\text{id})}) = \max_{i=1}^c \frac{e^{s_{il}^{(\text{id})}/\tau}}{\sum_{j=1}^c e^{s_{jl}^{(\text{id})}/\tau}}, \tag{13}$$

where τ is the temperature coefficient. Then, if the confidence score is larger than a threshold parameter λ, x_l is predicted as belonging to ID classes. Otherwise, x_l belongs to OOD classes. The detailed algorithm is provided in Appendix A.2.

Table 1. The OOD performance (%) ImageNet-1k as the ID dataset. The best results are highlighted in **bold**, and the second-best results are in underlined.

Methods	iNaturalist		SUN		Places		Textures		Average	
	AUROC↑	FPR95↓	AUROC↑	FPR95↓	AUROC↑	FPR95↓	AUROC↑	FPR95↓	AUROC↑	FPR95↓
Requires training (w. fine-tuning)										
MSP	87.44	58.36	79.73	73.72	79.67	74.41	79.69	71.93	81.63	69.61
ODIN	94.64	30.22	87.17	54.04	85.54	55.06	87.85	57.61	88.80	47.75
Energy	95.33	26.12	92.66	35.97	91.41	39.87	86.76	57.61	91.54	39.89
GradNorm	72.56	81.50	72.86	82.00	73.70	80.41	70.26	79.36	72.35	80.82
ViM	93.16	32.19	87.19	54.01	83.75	60.67	87.18	53.94	87.82	50.20
KNN	94.52	29.17	92.67	35.62	91.02	39.61	85.67	64.35	90.97	42.19
VOS	94.62	28.99	92.57	36.88	91.23	38.39	86.33	61.02	91.19	41.32
NPOS	96.19	16.58	90.44	43.77	89.44	45.27	88.80	46.12	91.22	37.93
ZOC	86.09	87.30	81.20	81.51	83.39	73.06	76.46	98.90	81.79	85.19
CLIPN	95.27	23.94	93.93	26.17	92.28	33.45	90.93	<u>40.83</u>	93.10	31.10
Zero-shot (w/o. fine-tuning)										
Mahalanobis	55.89	99.33	59.94	99.41	65.96	98.54	64.23	98.46	61.50	98.94
Energy	85.09	81.08	84.24	79.02	83.38	75.08	65.56	93.65	79.57	82.21
MCM	94.59	32.20	92.25	38.80	90.31	46.20	86.12	58.50	90.82	43.93
MMOOD	95.54	22.88	92.60	34.29	89.87	41.63	87.71	52.02	91.43	37.71
EOE	97.52	12.29	<u>95.73</u>	<u>20.40</u>	<u>92.95</u>	<u>30.16</u>	85.64	57.53	92.96	30.09
NegLabel	**99.49**	**1.91**	95.49	20.53	91.64	35.59	<u>90.22</u>	43.56	<u>94.21</u>	<u>25.40</u>
Ours	<u>98.59</u>	<u>6.03</u>	**96.52**	**18.72**	**93.13**	**28.86**	**92.22**	**39.15**	**95.12**	**23.19**

4 Experiments

4.1 Datasets and Metrics

Datasets. In this paper, we evaluate the effectiveness of the proposed methods under two different settings. First, we consider ImageNet-1K [40] as the ID dataset and use iNaturalist [41], SUN [42], Places [43], and Texture [44] as the OOD datasets, following the MCM [17]. Simultaneously, consistent with the settings of works, we use a subset of ImageNet-1k and the Waterbirds dataset [45] as ID datasets. Moreover, We further utilize a distinct subset of ImageNet-1K along with the Spurious OOD dataset [46] as out-of-distribution datasets to evaluate hard OOD detection.

Metrics. Following the setting of prior researches [14,15,17,18], we utilize two metrics: (1) the area under the ROC curve (AUROC), and (2) the false positive rate at 95% true positive rate (FPR95) for OOD samples.

4.2 Compared Methods

We compare our approach with the current SOTA OOD detection methods, encompassing both zero-shot and fine-tuned models. Among fine-tuned models, we evaluate MSP [2], ODIN [27], Energy [13], GradNorm [32], ViM [35], KNN [33], VOS [24], NPOS [47], CLIPN [18], and ZOC [36]. For zero-shot models, we consider MCM [17] along with post-hoc methods applied to the CLIP architecture, including Mahalanobis [12] and Energy [13] as additional baselines, and MMOOD [20], NegLabel [15], and EOE [14], which enhance category representations by incorporating textual descriptions. Notably, CLIPN [18] utilizes the large-scale CC-3M dataset [48] for additional pre-training of the text encoder.

4.3 Implementation Details

We utilize CLIP [16] as the backbone of our framework, incorporating ViT-B/16 as the image encoder and a masked self-attention transformer as the text encoder. Pre-trained weights for CLIP are adopted from OpenAI. Additionally, for LLMs, we employ LLaMA-3-8B [38], using pre-trained weights provided by Meta. In the experiments, unless otherwise specified, we use $k = 3$ to generate OOD classes corresponding to each ID class and set certification degree α to 0.8. We select the threshold value of λ when 95% of the ID samples are correctly classified and $T = 1$ as the temperature, following the standard practice [17,49]. The configuration of the experimental environment is provided in the Appendix A.3.

4.4 Performance Comparison

OOD Detection on Large-Scale Datasets. We use ImageNet-1k as the ID dataset and iNaturalist, SUN, Places, and Texture as the OOD datasets. Table 1 compares our approach with the latest SOTA methods, including both training-based and zero-shot inference methods. Our method achieves SOTA performance on the ImageNet-1k benchmark and surpasses a range of methods that employ fine-tuning for OOD detection, demonstrating the robust zero-shot OOD detection capabilities of CLIP. Furthermore, compared with traditional zero-shot OOD methods including Mahalanobis, Energy, and MCM, approaches like MMOOE, EOE, and NegLabel, which further explore textual features, achieve superior performance. Building upon these methods, our approach delves deeper into the specific textual features of OOD classes, resulting in outstanding performance across multiple datasets. Additionally, the OOD classes constructed for each ID, even if they do not include the exact class names of the OOD samples encountered, provide an expanded feature space that facilitates matching OOD samples. It is noteworthy that our method is slightly outperformed by NegLabel on the iNaturalist dataset. This is because NegLabel generates a large number of OOD class names, and the iNaturalist dataset contains a substantial number of plant species, among which these generated OOD class names are included. The performance results obtained using various VLMs backbones are included in the Appendix C.1.

OOD Detection on Hard OOD Datasets. To further demonstrate the effectiveness of the proposed approach, we conduct additional evaluations under two hard OOD conditions: 1) semantically hard OOD and 2) spurious OOD, as shown in Table 2. In detail, semantically hard OOD refers to OOD samples that are semantically similar to the ID samples; for this, we use ImageNet-10 and ImageNet-20 as the ID and OOD datasets, respectively, and vice versa. Spurious OOD refers to OOD samples that have false correlations with the ID samples,

Table 2. Zero-shot OOD detection performance on hard OOD detection tasks.

Methods	ID:ImageNet-10 OOD:ImageNet-20		ID:ImageNet-20 OOD:ImageNet-10		ID:Waterbirds OOD:Spurious OOD		Average	
	AUROC↑	FPR95↓	AUROC↑	FPR95↓	AUROC↑	FPR95↓	AUROC↑	FPR95↓
Mahalanobis	90.71	51.46	90.41	37.50	**99.55**	**2.21**	93.56	30.39
Energy	97.94	10.30	97.37	16.40	97.16	7.76	97.49	11.49
MCM	98.71	5.00	98.09	12.91	93.30	14.45	96.70	11.12
MMOOD	98.77	4.20	98.26	9.24	98.62	4.56	98.55	6.00
EOE	99.09	4.20	98.10	13.93	97.69	6.18	98.29	8.10
NegLabel	98.86	5.10	98.81	4.60	94.67	9.50	97.45	6.40
Ours	**99.32**	**1.10**	**99.23**	**1.40**	99.09	4.30	**99.21**	**2.27**

such as the spurious correlation between habitats and bird species. The results indicate that even under more challenging conditions, the proposed method consistently enhances OOD detection performance, achieving an average improvement of 3.73% in FPR95 and 0.66% in AUROC compared to the current SOTA methods. Specifically, on the task where ImageNet-10 serves as the ID dataset and ImageNet-20 as OOD, our method improves FPR95 by 3.10% and AUROC by 0.29%. When the roles are reversed, we observe improvements of 3.20% in FPR95 and 0.42% in AUROC. These results highlight the superior performance of our method in semantically hard OOD detection.

4.5 Ablation Studies

Score Functions. To verify our method on various OOD detection score functions, we have considered several zero-shot OOD methods, as shown in Table 3. We denote the scores before applying our method as MCM, Energy, and MaxLogit, and the scores after applying our method as MCM_{our}, $Energy_{our}$, and $MaxLogit_{our}$. This approach allows us to validate the impact of MCM scores on the experimental results in the ablation study of our main method. Specifically, after adjusting the ID confidence using our method, we perform OOD detection using the MCM, Energy, and MaxLogit methods. The results across three datasets indicate that our approach improves performance with different OOD detection scores. Using the MCM score, AUROC and FPR95 improved by 2.46% and 8.29%, respectively. This improvement is attributed to our scaling factor α being set to 0.8, which, when using MCM, amplifies the difference between ID and OOD scores, thus enhancing our method's effectiveness.

The Choice of LLMs. To verify our method on different LLMs, we have considered several LLMs with varying parameter sizes, as shown in Table 4. We conduct experiments using various LLMs to comprehensively assess the effectiveness of descriptors generated by different LLMs. Specifically, we utilize LLaMA-3-8b, ChatGPT-4, and Claude 2 for descriptor generation. The average results across three datasets indicate that using different LLMs achieved better performance compared to the baseline MCM. Additionally, LLaMA-3-8b outperforms

Table 3. Results after integrating our method with various scoring functions as baselines. The ID datasets are ImageNet-10, ImageNet-20, and Waterbirds, with corresponding OOD datasets being ImageNet-20, ImageNet-10, and Spurious OOD, respectively. "Average" represents the mean performance across these three datasets, and "Improvement" indicates the enhancement relative to the baseline.

Methods	Average		Improvement	
	AUROC↑	FPR95↓	AUROC↑	FPR95↓
MCM	96.70	11.12	/	/
MCM$_{ours}$	99.16	2.50	+2.46	-8.62
Energy	97.49	11.49	/	/
Energy$_{ours}$	97.83	8.92	+0.34	-2.57
MaxLogit	97.67	10.84	/	/
MaxLogit$_{ours}$	98.01	8.82	+0.34	-2.02

Claude2 and GPT-4.0 in both AUROC and FPR95 metrics, demonstrating the generalizability and robustness of our method. This can be attributed to the fact that LLaMA-3-8b excels at generating short, task-specific text, which benefits OOD detection by providing focused descriptions [50]. In contrast, GPT-4, while powerful in broader tasks, may produce more verbose responses that could introduce noise into similarity comparisons. Therefore, the performance differences between the two are likely due to factors such as the relevance and specificity of generated OOD class names, the precision of descriptive terms, and prompt interpretation.

Table 4. Impact of using different LLMs on results, consistent dataset settings as in Table 3. "A" represents the AUROC, "F" represents the FPR95.

Methods	Average		Improve	
	A↑	F↓	A↑	F↓
MCM	96.70	11.12	/	/
LLaMA-3-8b	99.16	2.50	+2.46	-8.62
Claude2	99.03	3.21	+2.33	-7.91
GPT-4.0	99.06	3.00	+2.36	-8.12

Table 5. Impact of number of OOD classes on results, consistent dataset settings as in Table 3. k denotes the number of selected OOD classes.

Number	Average		Improve	
	A↑	F↓	A↑	F↓
MCM	96.70	11.12	/	/
$k=1$	98.99	2.92	+2.29	-8.20
$k=2$	99.00	2.53	+2.30	-8.59
$k=3$	99.27	2.20	+2.57	-8.92
$k=4$	99.06	2.43	+2.36	-8.69
$k=5$	99.08	2.74	+2.38	-8.38

Fine-Grained Textual Features. To verify the effectiveness of generating specific descriptive terms for OOD classes, we created various types of descriptive information to evaluate performance, as shown in Table 4. We conduct experiment where descriptors are simplified to only use generated hard OOD classes for inference, altering the template to "A photo of {Class_Name}" to assess the

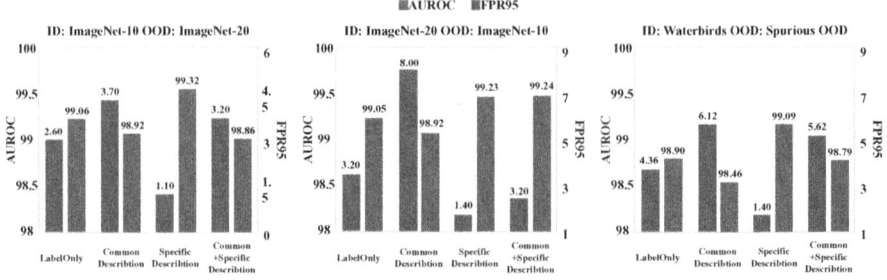

Fig. 4. Impact of prompt variation on LLM-generated descriptors.

efficacy of textual features. We refer to this as "Label only" in Fig. 4. Additionally, to validate the effectiveness of our descriptors in distinguishing OOD from current ID samples, we designed different prompts for verification. Specifically, we modify the question in Fig. 2 (b) to directly ask, "Please describe the visual characteristics of {OOD_CLASS}", "What are the visual features similar to {OOD_CLASS} and {ID_CLASS}?" to obtain descriptions that include both common and specific OOD features, as well as descriptions with only specific OOD features. In Fig. 4, these are represented as "Common+Specific description" and "Common description", respectively. "Specific description" represents the primary method of this paper, obtaining unique features that distinguish OOD classes from ID classes.

The results indicate that even when only category names are used to provide textual information ("Label only"), our method still outperforms the baseline MCM. However, when the textual description includes a significant amount of ID features ("Common description"), the performance of OOD detection significantly decreases, with the most notable decline observed on the ImageNet-20 dataset, where FPR95 and AUROC drop by 4.80% and 0.52%, respectively. When the OOD descriptors include only the unique features that distinguish OOD classes from ID classes ("Specific description"), our method achieves the best performance across all three datasets. When descriptors include both types of features ("Common+Specific description"), the results on various datasets are better than those with only the common description, but still inferior to those with only the specific description. This validates that common features shared between OOD and ID classes are detrimental to OOD detection.

4.6 Hyperparameter Sensitivity Analysis

Number of OOD Class Labels. Investigating the impact of the number of generated OOD classes on performance, we set k with different values, i.e., $\{1, 2, 3, 4, 5\}$. As shown in Table 5, performance improves initially and then declines as k increases, with the best results at $k = 3$. The initial gain stems from the expanded textual space, enhancing the model's capacity to separate ID and OOD samples. However, larger k increases the likelihood of generating semantically

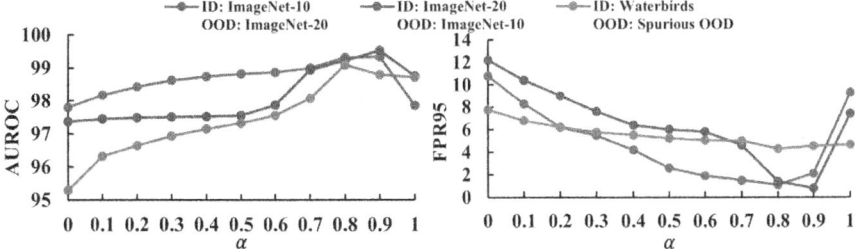

Fig. 5. Evaluation of hyperparameter α's effect on ID confidence correction, with FPR95 and AUROC trends in the left and right graphs.

similar OOD descriptions, causing feature overlap with ID or existing OOD classes. This overlap can be attributed to the inherent characteristics of LLMs, which may generate similar descriptions for semantically related concepts. For example, OOD descriptions for "cat" may include "kitty" and "kitten", blurring decision boundaries and impairing performance when $k > 3$.

ID Confidence Calibration. We investigate the influence of the ID confidence calibration coefficient on the performance, adjusting the rectification degree α across the range $\{0, 0.1, ..., 1\}$. We conduct experiments on the ImageNet-10, ImageNet-20, and Waterbirds datasets, and the results are shown in Fig. 5. We observe that when α is set to extreme values of 0 and 1, and the performance of OOD detection significantly decreases. When α is 0, setting the confidence directly to 0 leads to some ID samples being incorrectly classified as OOD, reducing robustness. Conversely, when α is 1, not adjusting the confidence negates the model's effectiveness. However, when α is between 0.7 and 0.9, the model performs well across all three datasets, indicating that our model is not sensitive to the α parameter.

5 Conclusion

In this paper, we propose a simple yet effective zero-shot OOD detection approach that leverages LLMs to enhance textual feature extraction for both ID and OOD classes. Specifically, we design prompts to generate specific semantic text, integrating ID class information to improve OOD distinction. We calibrate ID confidence based on generated OOD scores and propose a regionally enhanced semantic OOD score for detection. Our approach guides VLMs to focus on relevant image regions, leading to significant performance gains. Extensive experiments show our method outperforms SOTA approaches across multiple benchmarks and VLM architectures.

Acknowledgments. This work is supported by the National Key RD Program of China (2022YFF0712100), NSFC (62276131), Natural Science Foundation of Jiangsu Province of China under Grant (BK20240081).

References

1. Bendale, A., Boult, T.E.: Towards open world recognition. In: CVPR (2015)
2. Hendrycks, D., Gimpel, K.: A baseline for detecting misclassified and out-of-distribution examples in neural networks. In: ICLR (2017)
3. Yang, J., et al.: Generalized out-of-distribution detection: a survey. Int. J. Comput. Vis. (2024)
4. Zhang, J., et al.: OpenOOD v1.5: enhanced benchmark for out-of-distribution detection. arXiv:2306.09301 (2023)
5. Huang, G., et al., Densely connected convolutional networks. In: CVPR (2017)
6. Feng, D., Harakeh, A., Waslander, S.L..: A review and comparative study on probabilistic object detection in autonomous driving. Trans. Intell. Transp. Syst. (2022)
7. Chen, L., et al.: End-to-end autonomous driving: challenges and frontiers. Trans. Pattern Anal. Mach. Intell. (2024)
8. Kononenko, I.: Machine learning for medical diagnosis: history, state of the art and perspective. Artif. Intell. Med. (2001)
9. Hsu, Y.C., Shen, Y., Jin, H., et al.: Generalized ODIN: detecting out-of-distribution image without learning from out-of-distribution data. In: CVPR (2020)
10. Wang, H., Liu, W., Bocchieri, A., et al.: Can multi-label classification networks know what they don't know? In: NIPS (2021)
11. Sehwag, V., Chiang, M., Mittal, P., et al.: SSD: a unified framework for self-supervised outlier detection. In: ICLR (2021)
12. Lee, K., Lee, K., Lee, H., et al.: A simple unified framework for detecting out-of-distribution samples and adversarial attacks. In: NIPS (2018)
13. Liu, W., Wang, X., Owens, J.D., et al.: Energy-based out-of-distribution detection. In: NIPS (2020)
14. Cao, C., Zhong, Z., Zhou, Z., et al.: Envisioning outlier exposure by large language models for out-of-distribution detection. In: ICML (2024)
15. Jiang, X., Liu, F., Fang, Z., et al.: Negative label guided OOD detection with pretrained vision-language models. In: ICLR (2024)
16. Radford, A., Wook Kim, J., Hallacy, C., et al.: Learning transferable visual models from natural language supervision. In: ICML (2021)
17. Ming, Y., Cai, Z., Gu, J., et al.: Delving into out-of-distribution detection with vision-language representations. In: NIPS (2022)
18. Wang, H., Li, Y., Yao, H., et al.: CLIPN for zero-shot OOD detection: teaching CLIP to say no. In: ICCV (2023)
19. Fellbaum, C.: WordNet: An Electronic Lexical Database. In: MIT press (1998)
20. Dai, Y., Lang, H., Zeng, K., et al.: Exploring large language models for multi-modal out-of-distribution detection. In: EMNLP (2023)
21. Petroni, F., Rockt Aschel, T., Riedel, S., et al.: Language models as knowledge bases? In: EMNLP (2019)
22. Tack, J., Mo, S., Jeong, J., et al.: CSI: novelty detection via contrastive learning on distributionally shifted instances. In: NIPS (2020)
23. Huang, R., Li, Y.: MOS: towards scaling out-of-distribution detection for large semantic space. In: CVPR (2021)

24. Du, X., Wang, X., Gozum, G. et al.: Unknown-aware object detection: learning what you don't know from videos in the wild. In: CVPR (2022)
25. Wei, H., Xie, R., Cheng, H., et al.: Mitigating neural network overconfidence with logit normalization. In: ICML (2022)
26. Ming, Y., Sun, Y., Dia, O., et al.: CIDER: exploiting hyperspherical embeddings for out-of-distribution detection. In: arXiv, abs/2203.04450 (2022)
27. Jiang, X., Liu, F., Fang, Z., et al.: Enhancing the reliability of out-of-distribution image detection in neural networks. In: ICLR (2018)
28. Yang, Y., Zhang, Y., Song, X., et al.: Not all out-of-distribution data are harmful to open-set active learning. In: NIPS (2023)
29. Xi, W., Song, X., Guo, W., et al.: Robust semi-supervised learning for self-learning open-world classes. In: ICDM (2023)
30. Yang, Y., Jiang, N., Yi, X., et al.: Robust semi-supervised learning by wisely leveraging open-set data. Trans. Pattern Anal. Mach. Intell. **46**, 8334–8347 (2024)
31. Yang, Yang, Wei, Hongchen, Sun, Zhen-Qiang., et al.: S2OSC: a holistic semi-supervised approach for open set classification. ACM Trans. Knowl. Discov. Data. **16**, 1–27 (2022)
32. Huang, R., Geng, A., Li, Y., et al.: On the importance of gradients for detecting distributional shifts in the wild. In: NIPS (2021)
33. Sun, Y., Ming, Y., Zhu, X., et al.: Out-of-distribution detection with deep nearest neighbors. In: ICML (2022)
34. LeCun, Y., Chopra, S., et al.: A tutorial on energy-based learning. In: Predicting Structured Data (2006)
35. Wang, H., Li, Z., Feng, L., et al.: ViM: out-of-distribution with virtual-logit matching. In: CVPR (2022)
36. Esmaeilpour, S., Liu, B., Robertson, E., et al.: Zero-shot out-of-distribution detection based on the pre-trained model CLIP. In: AAAI (2022)
37. Brown, T.B., Mann, B., Ryder, N., et al.: Language models are few-shot learners. In: NIPS (2020)
38. Touvron, H., Martin, L., Stone, K., et al.: Llama 2: open foundation and fine-tuned chat models. In: arXiv, abs/2307.09288 (2023)
39. OpenAI: GPT-4 Technical Report. In: arXiv, abs/2303.08774 (2023)
40. Deng, J., Dong, W., Socher, R., et al.: ImageNet: a large-scale hierarchical image database. In: CVPR (2009)
41. Horn, G.V., Aodha, O.M., Song, Y., et al.: The INaturalist species classification and detection dataset. In: CVPR (2018)
42. Xiao, J., Hays, J., Ehinger, K.A., et al.: SUN database: large-scale scene recognition from abbey to zoo. In: CVPR (2010)
43. Zhou, Bolei, Lapedriza, Àgata., Khosla, Aditya, et al.: Places: a 10 million image database for scene recognition. Trans. Pattern Anal. Mach. Intell. **40**, 1452–1464 (2018)
44. Cimpoi, M., Maji, S., Kokkinos, I., et al.: Describing textures in the wild. In: CVPR (2014)
45. Sagawa, S., Wei Koh, P., Hashimoto, T.B., et al.: Distributionally robust neural networks for group shifts: on the importance of regularization for worst-case generalization. In: arXiv, abs/1911.08731 (2019)
46. Ming, Y., Yin, H., Li, Y., et al.: On the impact of spurious correlation for out-of-distribution detection. In: AAAI (2022)
47. Tao, L., Du, X., Zhu, J., et al.: Non-parametric outlier synthesis. In: ICLR (2023)
48. Sharma, P., Ding, N., Goodman, S., et al.: Conceptual Captions: A Cleaned, Hypernymed, Image Alt-text Dataset for Automatic Image Captioning (2018)

49. Bai, Y., Han, Z., Cao, B., et al.: ID-like prompt learning for few-shot out-of-distribution detection. In: CVPR (2024)
50. Li, Z., Li, X., Liu, Y., et al.: Label supervised LLaMA finetuning. In: arXiv, abs/2310.01208 (2023)
51. Xu, H., Yang, Y.: ITP: instance-aware test pruning for out-of-distribution detection. In: AAAI (2025)
52. Yang, Y., Xu, H.: Strengthen out-of-distribution detection capability with progressive self-knowledge distillation. In: ICML (2025)

GLADMamba: Unsupervised Graph-Level Anomaly Detection Powered by Selective State Space Model

Yali Fu[1], Jindong Li[2], Qi Wang[1,4(✉)], and Qianli Xing[3]

[1] School of Artificial Intelligence, Jilin University, Changchun, China
fuy123@mails.jlu.edu.cn, qiwang@jlu.edu.cn
[2] Hong Kong University of Science and Technology (Guangzhou), Guangzhou, China
jli839@connect.hkust-gz.edu.cn
[3] College of Computer Science and Technology, Jilin University, Changchun, China
qianlixing@jlu.edu.cn
[4] Engineering Research Center of Knowledge-Driven Human-Machine Intelligence, Ministry of Education, Changchun, China

Abstract. Unsupervised graph-level anomaly detection (UGLAD) is a critical and challenging task across various domains, such as social network analysis, anti-cancer drug discovery, and toxic molecule identification. However, existing methods often struggle to capture long-range dependencies efficiently and neglect the spectral information. Recently, selective state space models, particularly Mamba, have demonstrated remarkable advantages in capturing long-range dependencies with linear complexity and a selection mechanism. Motivated by their success across various domains, we propose GLADMamba, a novel framework that adapts the selective state space model into UGLAD field. We design a View-Fused Mamba (VFM) module with a Mamba-Transformer-style architecture to efficiently fuse information from different graph views with a selective state mechanism. We also design a Spectrum-Guided Mamba (SGM) module with a Mamba-Transformer-style architecture to leverage the Rayleigh quotient to guide the embedding refinement process, considering the spectral information for UGLAD. GLADMamba can dynamically focus on anomaly-related information while discarding irrelevant information for anomaly detection. To the best of our knowledge, this is the first work to introduce Mamba and explicit spectral information to UGLAD. Extensive experiments on 12 real-world datasets demonstrate that GLADMamba outperforms existing state-of-the-art methods, achieving superior performance in UGLAD. The code is available at https://github.com/Yali-Fu/GLADMamba.

Keywords: Unsupervised Graph-Level Anomaly Detection · Selective State Space Model · Graph Spectrum · Graph Neural Networks

---

Y. Fu and J. Li—Equal contribution.

1 Introduction

Unsupervised graph-level anomaly detection (UGLAD) is a prevalent task in numerous real-world scenarios, including social network analysis, drug discovery, and toxic molecule identification [17,24,25]. Its goal is to identify graphs that exhibit significantly different patterns from the majority, which often represent unexpected events or behaviors [22–24]. Unlike supervised approaches, unsupervised methods don't require labeled data, making them more adaptable to real-world scenarios where labeled anomalies are scarce or costly to obtain. Despite the existence of many excellent methods, several challenges still exist in this field.

Most GNN-based methods are inherently limited by the over-squashing issue, which restricts their ability to effectively model long-range dependencies between nodes [1,12,31]. This limitation hampers the information propagation across distant nodes, making it challenging to capture anomaly-related patterns and ultimately weakening detection performance. Although some studies [17,40,47] have incorporated Transformer into graph anomaly detection to mitigate this issue, the quadratic computational complexity of the attention mechanism significantly restricts the scalability of these methods, particularly for large-scale graphs. Additionally, as depicted in Fig. 1(a), relying solely on a single characteristic is insufficient for comprehensively capturing anomalies [17,22]. Thus, how to efficiently integrate information from multiple aspects (e.g., attributes and topologies) poses a critical challenge.

Furthermore, we observe spectral differences between normal and abnormal graphs in Fig. 1(b). And as demonstrated in [4,35,37,43], the energy distribution in the spectral domain shifts from low-frequency to high-frequency regions as the anomaly degree increases. However, most existing methods primarily focus on anomaly information in the spatial domain, neglecting the interaction with the spectral domain and failing to account for spectral differences between normal and anomalous graphs. Although a few works have explored the use of spectral information for graph-level anomaly detection, they rely on labeled data during training [4]. In the context of UGLAD, this remains an unexplored area, underscoring the need for further research and innovation.

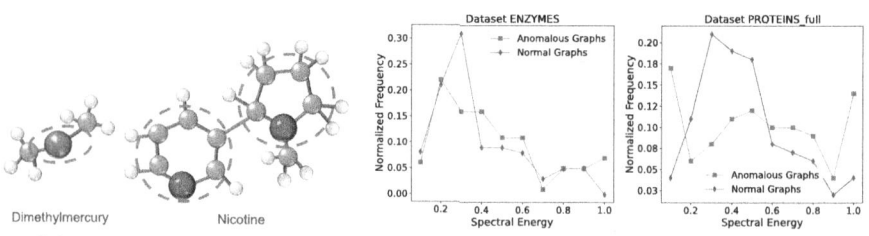

(a) Feature and structure.   (b) The normalized spectral energy distributions.

Fig. 1. The key factors related to graph anomalies.

Recently, selective state space models, especially Mamba [7], originally designed for sequence modeling, have demonstrated remarkable advantages in capturing long-range dependencies with linear computational complexity and a selection mechanism. These advantages have been extensively validated across various domains [1,5,29,39,44], making Mamba a strong candidate for addressing the challenges in UGLAD. Building on these strengths, we take the first step in integrating Mamba into UGLAD, unlocking its potential for more effective graph modeling while significantly improving computational efficiency and anomaly detection performance.

We propose a novel unsupervised graph-level anomaly detection framework that is powered by selective state space model (Mamba), named GLADMamba. We firstly design a View-Fused Mamba (VFM) module, which is a Mamba-Transformer-style architecture and can efficiently fuse different graph views by Mamba's selective state transition mechanism. Benefiting from the architecture and advantages of Mamba, VFM excels at integrating multi-view information and capturing long-range dependencies, showcasing powerful embedding capabilities while maintaining linear time complexity. Furthermore, we design a Spectrum-Guided Mamba (SGM) module, which is also a Mamba-Transformer-style architecture and leverages explicit spectral information to guide the embedding refinement process for UGLAD. By the intrinsic relationship between spectral energy and graph anomalies, SGM establishes interactions between the spatial and spectral domains. Concretely, it employs the Rayleigh quotient to discretize the continuous state space of SGM, making system parameters spectrum-dependent. Therefore, the Rayleigh quotient can guide the update of latent states in SGM, enabling the model to selectively focus on anomaly-related information and filter redundant information to enhance detection performance.

By the selection mechanism, GLADMamba can dynamically adjust its learning strategy based on specific characteristics of different input graphs, adaptively capturing anomaly patterns. Extensive experiments on 12 real-world datasets demonstrate the effectiveness of GLADMamba. And GLADMamba consistently outperforms state-of-the-art methods in the unsupervised graph-level anomaly detection task. Our key contributions are summarized as follows:

- We propose a novel model, named GLADMamba, which adapts the selective state space model (Mamba) for unsupervised graph-level anomaly detection. To the best of our knowledge, this is the first work to introduce Mamba to UGLAD.
- We design a View-Fused Mamba (VFM) module for efficient multi-view fusion, boosting detection accuracy. In addition, we design a Spectrum-Guided Mamba (SGM) module, the first spectrum-guided method in this field to preserve anomaly-related patterns via selective state updates. This work pioneers spectrum-guided Mamba architecture for UGLAD.
- We conduct extensive experiments on 12 real-world datasets, demonstrating that GLADMamba achieves state-of-the-art performance in the unsupervised graph-level anomaly detection task.

2 Related Work

2.1 Graph-Level Anomaly Detection

Graph-level anomaly detection aims to identify anomalous graphs within a graph set, where anomalies typically represent rare but critical patterns compared to normal graphs [6,25,45]. Conventional methods generally involve two main steps: first, a graph kernel, such as the Weisfeiler-Lehman kernel (WL) [32] or propagation kernel (PK) [28], is used to learn representations; second, an anomaly detection algorithm, such as isolation forest (iF) [18], one-class support vector machine (OCSVM) [26], or local outlier factor (LOF) [3], is applied to detect anomalous graphs based on the extracted graph representations.

In addition, graph neural networks (GNNs) [11,14,36,38] have attracted significant attention due to their remarkable performance in dealing with various graph data and tasks [16,19–21]. Thus, various types of GNNs are employed as the backbone to conduct graph-level anomaly detection [6,22–24,45]. For example, GOOD-D [22] designs a novel graph data augmentation method and employs contrastive learning at different levels for graph-level anomaly detection. CVT-GAD [17] employs a lightweight Transformer with an attention mechanism to model intra-graph and inter-graph node relationships, improving detection performance.

2.2 State Space Models

State Space Models (SSMs) [13] are classical frameworks for dynamic systems, while Structured SSMs (S4) [10] enhance SSMs with efficient long-sequence modeling. Mamba [7,30] builds on S4 by introducing a selection mechanism, enabling dynamic adaptation and improved efficiency. Together, they represent an evolution from traditional SSMs to modern, high-performance sequence modeling architectures. Beyond its core advancements, Mamba has demonstrated promising applications in various domains. It has been explored in computer vision [39], multimodal learning [29], audio [5], and natural language processing [44], showcasing its versatility across different modalities. Mamba has also shown preliminary and promising applications in graph representation learning [1]. For example, DG-Mamba [42] introduces a kernelized dynamic message-passing operator and a self-supervised regularization based on the principle of relevant information to improve efficiency, expressiveness, and robustness in dynamic graph learning. MOL-Mamba [12] enhances molecular representations by integrating hierarchical structural reasoning and electronic correlation learning, designing a hybrid Mamba-Graph and Mamba-Transformer framework supported by collaborative training strategies.

3 Preliminaries

3.1 Problem Statement

A graph is represented as $G = (\mathcal{V}, \mathcal{E}, \mathbf{A})$, where $\mathcal{V}$ denotes the set of nodes, $\mathcal{E}$ represents the set of edges, $\mathbf{A} \in \mathbb{R}^{|\mathcal{V}| \times |\mathcal{V}|}$ denotes the adjacency matrix, and $|\mathcal{V}|$

is the number of nodes. The entry $\mathbf{A}_{i,j}$ of $\mathbf{A}$ is set to 1 if an edge exists between node v_i and node v_j; otherwise, $\mathbf{A}_{i,j} = 0$. An attributed graph is defined as $G = (\mathcal{V}, \mathcal{E}, \mathbf{A}, \mathbf{F})$, where $\mathbf{F} \in \mathbb{R}^{|\mathcal{V}| \times d_f}$ is the feature matrix containing node attributes. Each row $\mathbf{f}$ of $\mathbf{F}$ corresponds to a feature vector of a node with d_f dimensions. The collection of graphs is denoted as $\mathcal{G} = \{G_1, G_2, ..., G_m\}$, where m is the total number of graphs. This work addresses the GLAD problem under an unsupervised setting, where no labels are available for model training.

3.2 State Space Models and Mamba

State Space Models (SSMs) [7,10,30] model the dynamic evolution of continuous systems via latent state $h(t) \in \mathbb{R}^{N \times \tilde{L}}$, mapping input $x(t) \in \mathbb{R}^{\tilde{L}}$ to output $y(t) \in \mathbb{R}^{\tilde{L}}$ through the following state transition equation and observation equation:

$$h'(t) = \mathcal{A}h(t) + \mathcal{B}x(t), \quad y(t) = \mathcal{C}h(t), \tag{1}$$

where $\mathcal{A} \in \mathbb{R}^{N \times N}$ is the state transition matrix, $\mathcal{B} \in \mathbb{R}^{N \times 1}$ is the input matrix, $\mathcal{C} \in \mathbb{R}^{1 \times N}$ is the output matrix, N denotes the state size, and $\tilde{L}$ denotes the sequence length.

By the step size Δ, continuous parameters $(\mathcal{A}, \mathcal{B})$ are discretized into discrete forms $(\overline{\mathcal{A}}, \overline{\mathcal{B}})$ for practical application of SSMs. Discrete SSMs are described as follows:

$$h_t = \overline{\mathcal{A}}h_{t-1} + \overline{\mathcal{B}}x_t, \quad y_t = \mathcal{C}h_t. \tag{2}$$

The selective SSM (Mamba) [7] focuses on relevant information selectively by making parameters $(\mathcal{B}, \mathcal{C}, \Delta)$ input-dependent.

3.3 Rayleigh Quotient

For a graph $G = (\mathcal{V}, \mathcal{E}, \mathbf{A})$, let $\mathbf{D}$ be the diagonal degree matrix with $\mathbf{D}_{ii} = \sum_j \mathbf{A}_{ij}$. Its Laplacian matrix $\mathbf{L}$ is defined as $\mathbf{L} = \mathbf{D} - \mathbf{A}$ (unnormalized) or $\mathbf{L} = \mathbf{I} - \mathbf{D}^{-1/2}\mathbf{A}\mathbf{D}^{-1/2}$ (normalized), where $\mathbf{I}$ is the identity matrix. The symmetric matrix $\mathbf{L}$ can be decomposed as $\mathbf{L} = \mathbf{U}\mathbf{\Lambda}\mathbf{U}^T$, where $\mathbf{\Lambda} = \text{diag}(\lambda_1, \lambda_2, \ldots, \lambda_{|\mathcal{V}|})$ contains the corresponding eigenvalues sorted in ascending order, i.e., $0 \leq \lambda_1 \leq \lambda_2 \leq \cdots \leq \lambda_{|\mathcal{V}|}$, and $\mathbf{U} = (\mathbf{u}_1, \mathbf{u}_2, \ldots, \mathbf{u}_{|\mathcal{V}|})$ represents the orthonormal eigenvectors. Let $\mathbf{X} = (x_1, x_2, \ldots, x_{|\mathcal{V}|})^T$ be the signal of G, and its graph Fourier transform is given by $\hat{\mathbf{X}} = (\hat{x}_1, \hat{x}_2, \ldots, \hat{x}_{|\mathcal{V}|})^T = \mathbf{U}^T\mathbf{X}$. As demonstrated in [4,35,37], the Rayleigh quotient $R(\mathbf{L}, \mathbf{X})$ can represent the accumulated spectral energy, with a higher quotient value indicating more high-frequency components. We employ the following Rayleigh quotient without explicit eigenvalue decomposition for computational efficiency:

$$R(\mathbf{L}, \mathbf{X}) = \frac{\mathbf{X}^T \mathbf{L} \mathbf{X}}{\mathbf{X}^T \mathbf{X}} = \frac{\sum_{k=1}^{|\mathcal{V}|} \lambda_k \hat{x}_k^2}{\sum_{k=1}^{|\mathcal{V}|} \hat{x}_k^2} = \frac{\sum_{(i,j) \in \mathcal{E}} (x_i - x_j)^2}{2 \sum_{i \in \mathcal{V}} x_i^2}. \tag{3}$$

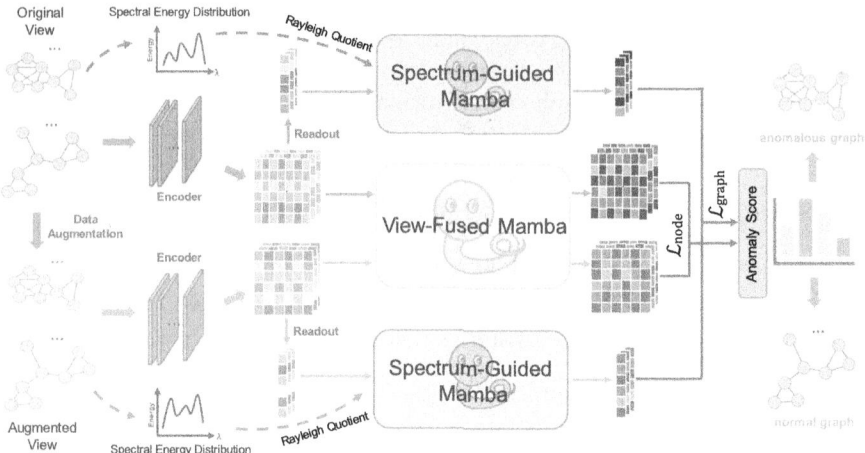

(a) The overall pipeline of the proposed GLADMamba.

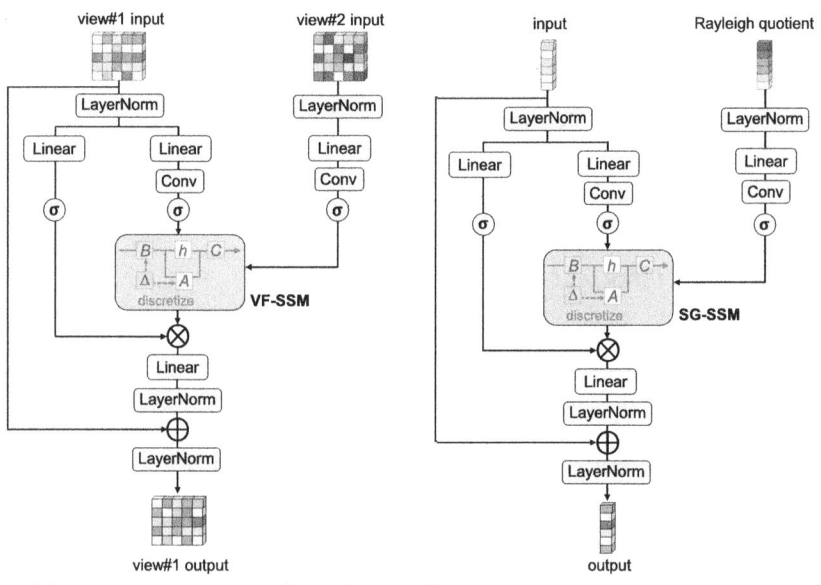

(b) View-Fused Mamba (VFM).   (c) Spectrum-Guided Mamba (SGM).

Fig. 2. Overview of the proposed GLADMamba model: (a) illustrates the overall pipeline of the framework; (b) depicts the View-Fused Mamba (VFM) module, which efficiently integrates multi-view information; (c) shows the Spectrum-Guided Mamba (SGM) module, which is designed to guide embedding refinement process by Rayleigh quotient.

4 Methodology

4.1 Data Augmentation and Encoding

For data augmentation, we obtain the original view o and augmented view a by a perturbation-free graph augmentation strategy [17,22,34], which is tailored for anomaly detection. And the view o and a focus on feature and structure characteristics of the graph, respectively. After data augmentation, we employ two independent GNN encoders on two views to obtain node and graph embeddings. Taking the original view o as an example, the GNN encoder updates node embeddings in the l-th layer according to the following message passing rule:

$$\mathbf{h}_v^{(o,l)} = \text{UPDATE}^{(l-1)}\left(\mathbf{h}_v^{(o,l-1)}, \text{AGG}^{(l-1)}\left(\{\mathbf{h}_u^{(o,l-1)} : u \in \mathcal{N}(v)\}\right)\right), \quad (4)$$

where $\mathbf{h}_v^{(o,l)}$ denotes the representation of node v on the view o at the l-th layer, $\mathcal{N}(v)$ represents the set of neighboring nodes of v, AGG is the aggregation function to combine information from neighboring nodes, and UPDATE is the update function to generate a new node representation. And we have $\mathbf{h}_v^{(o,0)} = \mathbf{f}_v$. After the L-layer GNN encoder, we obtain the representation $\mathbf{h}_v^o$ of node v by concatenation operation and the representation $\mathbf{h}_G^o$ of graph G on the view o by the readout function:

$$\mathbf{h}_v^o = [\mathbf{h}_v^{(o,1)}||\cdots||\mathbf{h}_v^{(o,L)}], \quad \mathbf{h}_G^o = \frac{1}{|\mathcal{V}_G|}\sum_{u \in \mathcal{V}_G}\mathbf{h}_u^o, \quad (5)$$

where $\mathcal{V}_G$ is the set of nodes in graph G. Let $\mathbf{H}^o$ denote the node representation matrix encoded from the original view o in the training/testing batch, where each row corresponds to the representation of a node. In the same manner, we obtain the representation $\mathbf{h}_v^a$ of node v, the representation $\mathbf{h}_G^a$ of graph G, and the node representation matrix $\mathbf{H}^a$ for view a.

4.2 View-Fused Mamba (VFM)

In the View-Fused Mamba (VFM) module, we propose a novel view fusion mechanism. Specifically, we deeply fuse different aspects of graph data (i.e., feature and structure information) captured by the original view o and augmented view a. Designed in a Mamba-Transformer-style architecture, the VFM efficiently captures and processes multi-view information for UGLAD. The detailed architecture of the View-Fused Mamba is depicted in Fig. 2(b).

Selective Parameterization in VF-SSM. For the parameter $\mathcal{A}$, we adopt HiPPO-LegS [8] for parameterization [7,9]. Before obtaining the input-dependent parameters ($\mathcal{B}$, $\mathcal{C}$, Δ), we sequentially process the node representations $\mathbf{H}^o$ and $\mathbf{H}^a$ from two views through the following operations: a layer normalization [2], a linear projection layer, a 1D convolutional layer, and a SiLU activation function. The formulas are as follows:

$$\mathbf{H}^o_{input} = \text{SiLU}(\text{Conv1D}(\text{Linear}(\text{LayerNorm}(\mathbf{H}^o)))), \quad (6)$$

$$\mathbf{H}^a_{input} = \text{SiLU}(\text{Conv1D}(\text{Linear}(\text{LayerNorm}(\mathbf{H}^a)))). \quad (7)$$

When parameterizing input-dependent parameters $\mathcal{B}, \mathcal{C}$ and Δ, the two views are fused through the following formulas:

$$\mathcal{B}^o = \mathbf{W}_{\mathcal{B}^o}\mathbf{H}^a_{input}, \quad \mathcal{C}^o = \mathbf{W}_{\mathcal{C}^o}\mathbf{H}^a_{input}, \quad \Delta^o = \text{softplus}(\mathbf{W}_{\Delta^o}\mathbf{H}^a_{input}), \quad (8)$$

$$\mathcal{B}^a = \mathbf{W}_{\mathcal{B}^a}\mathbf{H}^o_{input}, \quad \mathcal{C}^a = \mathbf{W}_{\mathcal{C}^a}\mathbf{H}^o_{input}, \quad \Delta^a = \text{softplus}(\mathbf{W}_{\Delta^a}\mathbf{H}^o_{input}), \quad (9)$$

where $\mathbf{W}$ denotes the corresponding learnable matrix.

Selective Discretization in VF-SSM. To discretize the parameters $\mathcal{A}$ and $\mathcal{B}$ into $\overline{\mathcal{A}}$ and $\overline{\mathcal{B}}$, we adopt the zero-order hold (ZOH) discretization rule, following [7,15].

$$\overline{\mathcal{A}}^o = \exp(\Delta^o \mathcal{A}^o), \quad \overline{\mathcal{B}}^o = (\Delta^o \mathcal{A}^o)^{-1}(\exp(\Delta^o \mathcal{A}^o) - I)(\Delta^o \mathcal{B}^o), \quad (10)$$

$$\overline{\mathcal{A}}^a = \exp(\Delta^a \mathcal{A}^a), \quad \overline{\mathcal{B}}^a = (\Delta^a \mathcal{A}^a)^{-1}(\exp(\Delta^a \mathcal{A}^a) - I)(\Delta^a \mathcal{B}^a). \quad (11)$$

After the discretization of system parameters, the VF-SSM in VFM performs $\text{SSM}(\overline{\mathcal{A}}^o, \overline{\mathcal{B}}^o, \mathbf{H}^o)$ and $\text{SSM}(\overline{\mathcal{A}}^a, \overline{\mathcal{B}}^a, \mathbf{H}^a)$ to update state selectively following Eq. (2). The output of VF-SSM is as follows:

$$\begin{aligned}\mathbf{y}^o_{ssm} &= \text{SSM}(\overline{\mathcal{A}}^o, \overline{\mathcal{B}}^o, \mathbf{H}^o_{input}), \\ \mathbf{y}^a_{ssm} &= \text{SSM}(\overline{\mathcal{A}}^a, \overline{\mathcal{B}}^a, \mathbf{H}^a_{input}).\end{aligned} \quad (12)$$

After VFM, we obtain the final node representations $\mathbf{Z}^o$ and $\mathbf{Z}^a$ for the original and augmented views, respectively, as follows:

$$\begin{aligned}\mathbf{u}^o &= \text{SiLU}(\text{Linear}(\text{LayerNorm}(\mathbf{H}^o))), \\ \mathbf{Z}^o &= \text{LayerNorm}(\text{LayerNorm}(\text{Linear}(\mathbf{y}^o_{ssm} \odot \mathbf{u}^o)) + \mathbf{H}^o), \\ \mathbf{u}^a &= \text{SiLU}(\text{Linear}(\text{LayerNorm}(\mathbf{H}^a))), \\ \mathbf{Z}^a &= \text{LayerNorm}(\text{LayerNorm}(\text{Linear}(\mathbf{y}^a_{ssm} \odot \mathbf{u}^a)) + \mathbf{H}^a),\end{aligned} \quad (13)$$

where $\odot$ denotes element-wise multiplication.

4.3 Spectrum-Guided Mamba (SGM)

To consider spectral differences between normal and anomalous graphs for the UGLAD task, we design a specialized Spectrum-Guided Mamba (SGM) module, as illustrated in Fig. 2(c). The SGM module adopts the Rayleigh quotient as a measure of spectral characteristics, which is closely related to anomalies as described in Sect. 3.3. Specifically, the SGM module utilizes the Rayleigh quotient to parameterize system parameters, making them spectrum-dependent and enabling spectrum-guided updates of latent states. Designed in a Mamba-Transformer-style architecture, the SGM effectively refines graph embeddings by selectively focusing on anomaly-relevant spectral information to enhance anomaly detection performance.

Selective Parameterization in SG-SSM. Let $\mathbf{h}_G$ denote the graph representations encoded in Sect. 4.1. Firstly, we utilize the MLP to obtain the Rayleigh quotient representation $\mathbf{h}_{RQ}$, as follows:

$$\mathbf{h}_{RQ} = \text{MLP}(diag(R(\mathbf{L}, \mathbf{X}))), \tag{14}$$

where $diag(\cdot)$ extracts the diagonal elements of Rayleigh quotient $R(\mathbf{L}, \mathbf{X})$.

The inputs $\mathbf{h}_G$ and $\mathbf{h}_{RQ}$ are passed through a series of operations, including a layer normalization [2], a linear projection, a 1D convolutional operation, and a SiLU activation function, as follows:

$$\mathbf{h}_{input} = \text{SiLU}(\text{Conv1D}(\text{Linear}(\text{LayerNorm}(\mathbf{h}_G)))), \tag{15}$$

$$\mathbf{h}_{RQ} = \text{SiLU}(\text{Conv1D}(\text{Linear}(\text{LayerNorm}(\mathbf{h}_{RQ})))). \tag{16}$$

We then utilize the obtained $\mathbf{h}_{RQ}$ to parameterize $\mathcal{B}$, $\mathcal{C}$ and Δ, making system parameters $(\mathcal{B}, \mathcal{C}, \Delta)$ spectrum-dependent, as follows:

$$\mathcal{B} = \mathbf{W}_\mathcal{B}\mathbf{h}_{RQ}, \quad \mathcal{C} = \mathbf{W}_\mathcal{C}\mathbf{h}_{RQ}, \quad \Delta = \text{softplus}(\mathbf{W}_\Delta\mathbf{h}_{RQ}), \tag{17}$$

where $\mathbf{W}$ is the corresponding learnable matrix. For the parameter $\mathcal{A}$, we still adopt HiPPO-LegS [8] for parameterization [7,9].

Selective Discretization in SG-SSM. According to the ZOH rule, we discretize the parameters $\mathcal{A}$ and $\mathcal{B}$:

$$\overline{\mathcal{A}} = \exp(\Delta\mathcal{A}), \quad \overline{\mathcal{B}} = (\Delta\mathcal{A})^{-1}(\exp(\Delta\mathcal{A}) - I)(\Delta\mathcal{B}). \tag{18}$$

The SG-SSM in SGM performs $\text{SSM}(\overline{\mathcal{A}}, \overline{\mathcal{B}}, \mathbf{h}_{input})$ following Eq. (2), yielding the output $\mathbf{y}_{ssm}$:

$$\mathbf{y}_{ssm} = \text{SSM}(\overline{\mathcal{A}}, \overline{\mathcal{B}}, \mathbf{h}_{input}). \tag{19}$$

After the Spectrum-Guided Mamba, we obtain the final output $\mathbf{z}_G$ as follows:

$$\begin{aligned}\mathbf{u} &= \text{SiLU}(\text{Linear}(\text{LayerNorm}(\mathbf{h}_G))), \\ \mathbf{z}_G &= \text{LayerNorm}(\text{LayerNorm}(\text{Linear}(y_{ssm} \odot \mathbf{u})) + \mathbf{h}_G).\end{aligned} \tag{20}$$

According to Eqs. (14)–(20), we obtain graph representations $\mathbf{z}_G^o$ and $\mathbf{z}_G^a$ for the original and augmented views, respectively.

4.4 Training and Inference

Training. We adopt the InfoNCE loss [46] as contrastive objective to maximize the agreement between the representations from two views at node and graph scales:

$$\begin{aligned}\mathcal{L}'_{node} &= \frac{1}{|B|} \sum_{G_j \in B} \frac{1}{2|V_{G_j}|} \sum_{v_i \in V_{G_j}} \left[\ell(\mathbf{z}_i^o, \mathbf{z}_i^a) + \ell(\mathbf{z}_i^a, \mathbf{z}_i^o)\right], \\ \ell(\mathbf{z}_i^o, \mathbf{z}_i^a) &= -\log \frac{e^{(cos(\mathbf{z}_i^o, \mathbf{z}_i^a)/\tau)}}{\sum_{v_k \in V_{G_j} \setminus v_i} e^{(cos(\mathbf{z}_i^o, \mathbf{z}_k^a)/\tau)}},\end{aligned} \tag{21}$$

where B is the training batch, $\mathbf{z}_i^o$ and $\mathbf{z}_i^a$ are the embeddings of node v_i on two views, $cos(,)$ is the cosine similarity function, and τ is the temperature parameter.

$$\mathcal{L}'_{graph} = \frac{1}{2|B|} \sum_{G_i \in B} \left[\ell(\mathbf{z}_{G_i}^o, \mathbf{z}_{G_i}^a) + \ell(\mathbf{z}_{G_i}^a, \mathbf{z}_{G_i}^o) \right],$$

$$\ell(\mathbf{z}_{G_i}^o, \mathbf{z}_{G_i}^a) = -\log \frac{e^{cos(\mathbf{z}_{G_i}^o, \mathbf{z}_{G_i}^a)/\tau}}{\sum_{G_j \in B \setminus G_i} e^{cos(\mathbf{z}_{G_i}^o, \mathbf{z}_{G_j}^a)/\tau}}, \quad (22)$$

where $\mathbf{z}_{G_i}^o$ and $\mathbf{z}_{G_i}^a$ are the embeddings of graph G_i on two views, and other notations are analogous to those in Eq. (21).

During the training phase, we adopt an adaptive loss to consider different sensitivities of node and graph scales for different datasets [17,22], as follows:

$$\mathcal{L}_{node} = (\sigma_{node})^\alpha \mathcal{L}'_{node}, \quad \mathcal{L}_{graph} = (\sigma_{graph})^\alpha \mathcal{L}'_{graph},$$
$$\mathcal{L} = \mathcal{L}_{node} + \mathcal{L}_{graph}, \quad (23)$$

where α is the hyper-parameter and σ is the standard deviation of predicted errors on the corresponding scale.

Inference. By minimizing $\mathcal{L}$ in Eq. (23) during the training, the model learns common patterns of normal graphs. When testing an anomalous graph, the loss $\mathcal{L}$ tends to be significantly higher; therefore, we utilize $\mathcal{L}$ as the anomaly score. Additionally, the z-score standardization is adopted to balance anomaly scores from different scales. The final anomaly score is formulated as:

$$S = \text{Std}(\mathcal{L}_{node}) + \text{Std}(\mathcal{L}_{graph}), \quad (24)$$

where $\text{Std}(\mathcal{L}) = (\mathcal{L} - \mu)/\sigma$, and μ is the mean value of predicted errors of training samples at the corresponding scale.

5 Experiments

5.1 Experiment Settings

Datasets. We conduct experiments on 12 public real-world datasets from TuDataset benchmark [27], which involve small molecules, bioinformatics, and social networks. The statistics of the datasets are presented in Table 1. Following the setting in [17,22,24], the samples in the minority class or real anomalous class are viewed as anomalies, while the rest are viewed as normal data. And only normal samples are used during training under the unsupervised setting.

Baselines. To evaluate the effectiveness of GLADMamba, we compare it with 9 competitive baselines, spanning both earlier and recent approaches. These include the two-stage methods PK-iF [18,28], WL-OCSVM [26,32], WL-iF [18,32], InfoGraph-iF [18,33] and GraphCL-iF [18,41], as well as end-to-end methods OCGIN [45], GLocalKD [24], GOOD-D [22] and CVTGAD [17].

Table 1. Statistics of the datasets [27] used in our experiments.

Category	Dataset	Graphs	Avg. Nodes	Avg. Edges	Node Attr.
Bioinformatics	ENZYMES	600	32.63	62.14	18
Small molecules	AIDS	2000	15.69	16.20	4
	DHFR	467	42.43	44.54	3
	BZR	405	35.75	38.36	3
	COX2	467	41.22	43.45	3
	NCI1	4110	29.87	32.30	–
	HSE	8417	16.89	17.23	–
	MMP	7558	17.62	17.98	–
	p53	8903	17.92	18.34	–
	PPAR-gamma	8451	17.38	17.72	–
Social networks	IMDB-B	1000	19.77	96.53	–
	REDDIT-B	2000	429.63	497.75	–

- **Two-stage methods:** These methods first generate graph embeddings by graph kernels (e.g., propagation kernel (PK) [28] or Weisfeiler-Lehman kernel (WL) [32]) or graph representation learning methods (e.g., InfoGraph [33] or GraphCL [41]), and then apply traditional algorithms (e.g., isolation forest (iF) [18] or one-class SVM (OCSVM) [26]) to identify anomalies.
- **End-to-end methods:** These approaches integrate graph representation learning and anomaly detection into a unified framework, enabling joint optimization. OCGIN [45] adapts GIN for end-to-end graph anomaly detection by one-class classification objective. GLocalKD [24] employs random distillation to learn normal patterns by training one GNN to predict another randomly-initialized GNN. GOOD-D [22] uses hierarchical contrastive learning to detect anomalies through semantic inconsistency. CVTGAD [17] employs a simplified Transformer for UGLAD.

Evaluation Metrics. Following [17,22,24], we use the area under the receiver operating characteristic curve (AUC) as the evaluation metric for UGLAD, where a higher AUC reflects better performance.

Implementation Details. For the baselines, we report their public results from [17,22]. We implement GLADMamba by PyTorch[1] on NVIDIA L40 and A40 GPUs, and ensure reproducibility by explicitly setting random seeds following [17,22]. We employ GCN as the default GNN encoder. For AIDS, DHFR, HSE, and MMP datasets, the encoder employs GIN.

---

[1] https://pytorch.org/.

Table 2. Overall performance comparison in terms of AUC (%, mean±std). The best and second-best results are highlighted in **bold** and underlined, respectively.

Method	PK-iF	WL-OCSVM	WL-iF	InfoGraph-iF	GraphCL-iF
ENZYMES	51.30±2.01	55.24±2.66	51.60±3.81	53.80±4.50	53.60±4.88
AIDS	51.84±2.87	50.12±3.43	61.13±0.71	70.19±5.03	79.72±3.98
DHFR	52.11±3.96	50.24±3.13	50.29±2.77	52.68±3.21	51.10±2.35
BZR	55.32±6.18	50.56±5.87	52.46±3.30	63.31±8.52	60.24±5.37
COX2	50.05±2.06	49.86±7.43	50.27±0.34	53.36±8.86	52.01±3.17
NCI1	50.58±1.38	50.63±1.22	50.74±1.70	50.10±0.87	49.88±0.53
IMDB-B	50.80±3.17	54.08±5.19	50.20±0.40	56.50±3.58	56.50±4.90
REDDIT-B	46.72±3.42	49.31±2.33	48.26±0.32	68.50±5.56	71.80±4.38
HSE	56.87±10.51	62.72±10.13	53.02±5.12	53.56±3.98	51.18±2.71
MMP	50.06±3.73	55.24±3.26	52.68±3.34	54.59±2.01	54.54±1.86
p53	50.69±2.02	54.59±4.46	50.85±2.16	52.66±1.95	53.29±2.32
PPAR-gamma	45.51±2.58	57.91±6.13	49.60±0.22	51.40±2.53	50.30±1.56
Avg.Rank	8.83	7.50	8.58	6.83	7.42

Method	OCGIN	GLocalKD	GOOD-D	CVTGAD	GLADMamba
ENZYMES	58.75±5.98	61.39±8.81	63.90±3.69	<u>67.79±5.43</u>	**68.39±4.55**
AIDS	78.16±3.05	93.27±4.19	97.28±0.69	**99.39±0.55**	<u>99.29±0.47</u>
DHFR	49.23±3.05	56.71±3.57	62.67±3.11	<u>62.95±3.03</u>	**63.79±4.16**
BZR	65.91±1.47	69.42±7.78	75.16±5.15	<u>75.92±7.09</u>	**77.25±4.62**
COX2	53.58±5.05	59.37±12.67	62.65±8.14	<u>64.11±3.22</u>	**66.38±1.40**
NCI1	<u>71.98±1.21</u>	68.48±2.39	61.12±2.21	69.07±1.15	**73.06±1.87**
IMDB-B	60.19±8.90	52.09±3.41	65.88±0.75	**70.97±1.35**	<u>69.63±2.70</u>
REDDIT-B	75.93±8.65	77.85±2.62	**88.67±1.24**	84.97±2.41	<u>86.12±0.41</u>
HSE	64.84±4.70	59.48±1.44	69.65±2.14	<u>70.30±2.90</u>	**71.19±2.68**
MMP	<u>71.23±0.16</u>	67.84±0.59	70.57±1.56	70.96±1.01	**73.19±3.22**
p53	58.50±0.37	64.20±0.81	62.99±1.55	<u>67.58±3.31</u>	**68.38±1.62**
PPAR-gamma	**71.19±4.28**	64.59±0.67	67.34±1.71	68.25±4.66	<u>69.21±3.46</u>
Avg.Rank	4.50	4.58	3.25	<u>2.17</u>	**1.33**

5.2 Overall Performance Comparison

We evaluate the performance of GLADMamba against several baselines in terms of AUC across 12 datasets. As summarized in Table 2, GLADMamba achieves the highest average rank, outperforming all baselines on 8 datasets and ranking second on the remaining datasets. The results also show that unified models surpass two-stage methods, highlighting the advantages of end-to-end optimization for representation learning and anomaly detection. These results underscore the effectiveness of GLADMamba in the UGLAD task across diverse domains.

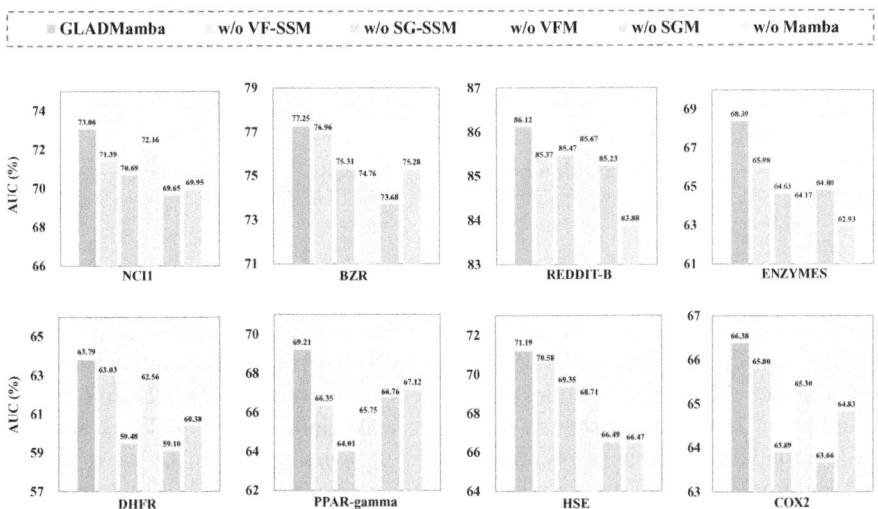

Fig. 3. Ablation study on key components across representative datasets.

5.3 Ablation Study

To validate the effectiveness of key components of GLADMamba, we conduct extensive ablation experiments on 8 representative datasets in Fig. 3. The variant w/o VF-SSM modifies the selective parameterization process in the VF-SSM using corresponding single-view inputs. The variant w/o SG-SSM replaces the Rayleigh quotient with corresponding graph-level representations. The variants w/o VFM, w/o SGM, and w/o Mamba denote the removal of the View-Fused Mamba, the Spectrum-Guided Mamba, and both, respectively.

The results show that GLADMamba consistently outperforms all variants. The variants w/o VFM, w/o SGM, and w/o Mamba significantly degrade performance, validating the effectiveness of Mamba in the UGLAD task and its superiority in capturing long-range dependencies. And the w/o VF-SSM variant, which relies solely on single-view information, suffers a performance decline due to its limited ability to identify complex anomalies. Furthermore, the significant performance drop in the w/o SG-SSM variant demonstrates the importance of spectral differences between normal and anomalous graphs for guiding GLADMamba's latent state updates. This also underscores that the SG-SSM component enhances GLADMamba's sensitivity to anomaly-related information by introducing Rayleigh quotient.

Table 3. Efficiency comparison on FLOPs, parameter size, and GPU memory usage.

Dataset	Model	FLOPs (M)↓	Params (MB)↓	GPU (GB)↓
AIDS	CVTGAD	33.27	1.88	8.58
	GLADMamba	48.97	0.07	5.12
REDDIT-B	CVTGAD	602.46	13.19	30.70
	GLADMamba	431.59	0.11	23.79
p53	CVTGAD	701.31	20.61	4.98
	GLADMamba	226.19	0.08	3.96

5.4 Efficiency Analysis

We assess the efficiency of GLADMamba on representative datasets in terms of FLOPs, parameter size, and GPU usage in Table 3. On the small-scale molecular dataset AIDS, the complexity differences between CVTGAD and GLADMamba are tolerable. However, on larger-scale datasets REDDIT-B and p53, the complexity differences become significant, particularly in terms of FLOPs and parameter size. This demonstrates the superiority of GLADMamba over Transformer-based approaches in scaling to large-scale graph anomaly detection.

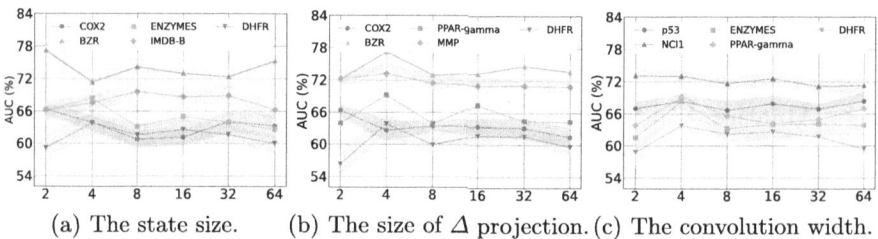

(a) The state size.　(b) The size of Δ projection. (c) The convolution width.

Fig. 4. The hyper-parameter analysis on representative datasets.

5.5 Hyper-parameter Analysis

The State Size of VFM and SGM. To investigate the impact of state size in Mamba, we conduct hyper-parameter analysis experiments in Fig. 4(a). The results indicate that performance variations with state size are not entirely consistent across datasets, likely due to the dependency of state size on dataset scale. Overall, the model can achieve satisfactory performance at smaller values (e.g., 4, 8).

The Size of Δ projection of VFM and SGM. The parameter Δ is constructed by linear projection of the input, controlling the strength of state updates. To investigate the impact of Δ projection size, we conduct experiments in Fig. 4(b). The results show that the model generally performs worst when the size is 2, except for the COX2 dataset. In general, the model can achieve respectable performance when the size is 4. As the projection size increases further, the performance remains relatively stable overall. These findings indicate that a moderate projection size (e.g., 4) is sufficient for optimal performance, avoiding suboptimal performance or unnecessary resource overhead.

The Local Convolution Width of VFM and SGM. The local convolution width refers to the kernel size of the Conv1D layer, controlling the model's receptive field. We conduct experiments to investigate its impact in Fig. 4(c). We observe that when the width is 2, the performance degrades due to limited expressiveness of the Conv1D. In most cases, the model achieves optimal performance when the width is 4. Overall, GLADMamba remains relatively insensitive to this parameter, demonstrating robust performance.

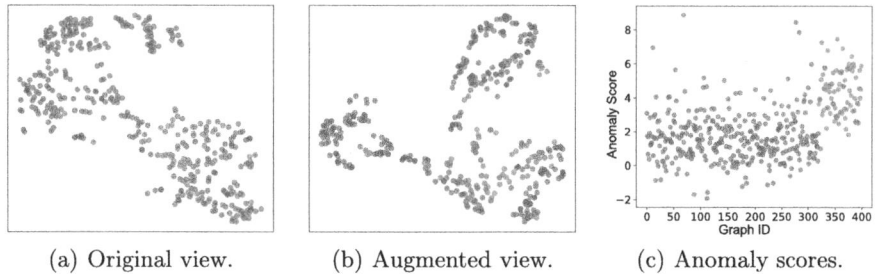

(a) Original view. (b) Augmented view. (c) Anomaly scores.

Fig. 5. Visualization analysis on AIDS dataset. (• normal graph, • anomalous graph.)

5.6 Visualization Analysis

We utilize t-SNE to visualize the graph embeddings from two views and anomaly scores learned by GLADMamba in Fig. 5. It can be observed that normal and anomalous graphs are not well-separated under a single view, as their distributions exhibit considerable overlap. However, when multiple views are integrated, normal and anomalous graphs exhibit a clear boundary in terms of anomaly scores, demonstrating the effectiveness of GLADMamba in UGLAD.

6 Conclusion

In this work, we introduce GLADMamba, a novel framework for UGLAD that effectively integrates the selective state space model and explicit spectral information. By leveraging the proposed View-Fused Mamba (VFM) and Spectrum-Guided Mamba (SGM) modules, GLADMamba dynamically selects and refines anomaly-related information, significantly improving detection performance. As far as we know, this is the first work to introduce Mamba and explicit spectral information to UGLAD. Experimental results on 12 real-world datasets demonstrate that GLADMamba outperforms existing state-of-the-art methods, highlighting its potential for advancing the UGLAD field. This fundamental architecture advancement establishes new possibilities for both graph learning and anomaly detection research.

Acknowledgments. This work is supported by the Youth Fund of the National Natural Science Foundation of China (No. 62206107).

Disclosure of Interests. We declare that our research adheres to ethical guidelines, ensuring no harm or misuse of data and respecting privacy and confidentiality. We have conducted the study with integrity and disclosed any potential conflicts of interest.

References

1. Atitallah, S.B., Rabah, C.B., Driss, M., Boulila, W., Koubaa, A.: Exploring graph mamba: a comprehensive survey on state-space models for graph learning. arXiv preprint arXiv:2412.18322 (2024)
2. Ba, J.L., Kiros, J.R., Hinton, G.E.: Layer normalization. arXiv preprint arXiv:1607.06450 (2016)
3. Breunig, M.M., Kriegel, H.P., Ng, R.T., Sander, J.: Lof: identifying density-based local outliers. In: Proceedings of the 2000 ACM SIGMOD International Conference on Management of Data, pp. 93–104 (2000)
4. Dong, X., Zhang, X., Wang, S.: Rayleigh quotient graph neural networks for graph-level anomaly detection. arXiv preprint arXiv:2310.02861 (2023)
5. Erol, M.H., Senocak, A., Feng, J., Chung, J.S.: Audio mamba: bidirectional state space model for audio representation learning. IEEE Sign. Process. Lett. (2024)
6. Fu, Y., Li, J., Liu, J., Xing, Q., Wang, Q., King, I.: HC-GLAD: dual hyperbolic contrastive learning for unsupervised graph-level anomaly detection. arXiv preprint arXiv:2407.02057 (2024)
7. Gu, A., Dao, T.: Mamba: linear-time sequence modeling with selective state spaces. arXiv preprint arXiv:2312.00752 (2023)
8. Gu, A., Dao, T., Ermon, S., Rudra, A., Ré, C.: Hippo: recurrent memory with optimal polynomial projections. In: Advances in Neural Information Processing Systems, vol. 33, pp. 1474–1487 (2020)
9. Gu, A., Goel, K., Gupta, A., Ré, C.: On the parameterization and initialization of diagonal state space models. In: Advances in Neural Information Processing Systems, vol. 35, pp. 35971–35983 (2022)
10. Gu, A., Goel, K., Re, C.: Efficiently modeling long sequences with structured state spaces. In: International Conference on Learning Representations (2022)
11. Hamilton, W., Ying, Z., Leskovec, J.: Inductive representation learning on large graphs. In: Advances in Neural Information Processing Systems, vol. 30 (2017)
12. Hu, J., et al.: Mol-mamba: enhancing molecular representation with structural & electronic insights. arXiv preprint arXiv:2412.16483 (2024)
13. Kalman, R.E.: A new approach to linear filtering and prediction problems (1960)
14. Kipf, T.N., Welling, M.: Semi-supervised classification with graph convolutional networks. arXiv preprint arXiv:1609.02907 (2016)

15. Li, D., et al.: Dyg-mamba: continuous state space modeling on dynamic graphs. arXiv preprint arXiv:2408.06966 (2024)
16. Li, J., Liu, Y., Xing, Q., Wang, Q., Pan, S.: No fear of representation bias graph contrastive learning with calibration and fusion. Available at SSRN 4774833 (2024)
17. Li, J., Xing, Q., Wang, Q., Chang, Y.: CVTGAD: simplified transformer with cross-view attention for unsupervised graph-level anomaly detection. In: Joint European Conference on Machine Learning and Knowledge Discovery in Databases, pp. 185–200. Springer (2023)
18. Liu, F.T., Ting, K.M., Zhou, Z.H.: Isolation forest. In: 2008 Eighth IEEE International Conference on Data Mining, pp. 413–422. IEEE (2008)
19. Liu, J., Fournier-Viger, P., Zhou, M., He, G., Nouioua, M.: CSPM: discovering compressing stars in attributed graphs. Inf. Sci. **611**, 126–158 (2022)
20. Liu, J., Yang, M., Zhou, M., Feng, S., Fournier-Viger, P.: Enhancing hyperbolic graph embeddings via contrastive learning. arXiv preprint arXiv:2201.08554 (2022)
21. Liu, J., Zhou, M., Fournier-Viger, P., Yang, M., Pan, L., Nouioua, M.: Discovering representative attribute-stars via minimum description length. In: 2022 IEEE 38th International Conference on Data Engineering (ICDE), pp. 68–80. IEEE (2022)
22. Liu, Y., Ding, K., Liu, H., Pan, S.: Good-d: on unsupervised graph out-of-distribution detection. In: Proceedings of the Sixteenth ACM International Conference on Web Search and Data Mining, pp. 339–347 (2023)
23. Luo, X., et al.: Deep graph level anomaly detection with contrastive learning. Sci. Rep. **12**(1), 19867 (2022)
24. Ma, R., Pang, G., Chen, L., van den Hengel, A.: Deep graph-level anomaly detection by glocal knowledge distillation. In: Proceedings of the Fifteenth ACM International Conference on Web Search and Data Mining, pp. 704–714 (2022)
25. Ma, X., et al.: A comprehensive survey on graph anomaly detection with deep learning. IEEE Trans. Knowl. Data Eng. **35**(12), 12012–12038 (2021)
26. Manevitz, L.M., Yousef, M.: One-class SVMs for document classification. J. Mach. Learn. Res. **2**(Dec), 139–154 (2001)
27. Morris, C., Kriege, N.M., Bause, F., Kersting, K., Mutzel, P., Neumann, M.: Tudataset: a collection of benchmark datasets for learning with graphs. arXiv preprint arXiv:2007.08663 (2020)
28. Neumann, M., Garnett, R., Bauckhage, C., Kersting, K.: Propagation kernels: efficient graph kernels from propagated information. Mach. Learn. **102**, 209–245 (2016)
29. Qiao, Y., et al.: Vl-mamba: exploring state space models for multimodal learning. arXiv preprint arXiv:2403.13600 (2024)
30. Qu, H., et al.: A survey of mamba. arXiv preprint arXiv:2408.01129 (2024)
31. Qureshi, S., et al.: Limits of depth: over-smoothing and over-squashing in gnns. Big Data Min. Analytics **7**(1), 205–216 (2023)
32. Shervashidze, N., Schweitzer, P., Van Leeuwen, E.J., Mehlhorn, K., Borgwardt, K.M.: Weisfeiler-lehman graph kernels. J. Mach. Learn. Res. **12**(9) (2011)
33. Sun, F.Y., Hoffman, J., Verma, V., Tang, J.: Infograph: unsupervised and semi-supervised graph-level representation learning via mutual information maximization. In: International Conference on Learning Representations (2020)
34. Tan, Y., Liu, Y., Long, G., Jiang, J., Lu, Q., Zhang, C.: Federated learning on non-IID graphs via structural knowledge sharing. In: Proceedings of the AAAI Conference on Artificial Intelligence, vol. 37, pp. 9953–9961 (2023)
35. Tang, J., Li, J., Gao, Z., Li, J.: Rethinking graph neural networks for anomaly detection. In: International Conference on Machine Learning, pp. 21076–21089. PMLR (2022)

36. Veličković, P., Cucurull, G., Casanova, A., Romero, A., Lio, P., Bengio, Y.: Graph attention networks. arXiv preprint arXiv:1710.10903 (2017)
37. Xu, F., Wang, N., Wu, H., Wen, X., Zhao, X., Wan, H.: Revisiting graph-based fraud detection in sight of heterophily and spectrum. In: Proceedings of the AAAI Conference on Artificial Intelligence, vol. 38, pp. 9214–9222 (2024)
38. Xu, K., Hu, W., Leskovec, J., Jegelka, S.: How powerful are graph neural networks? arXiv preprint arXiv:1810.00826 (2018)
39. Xu, R., Yang, S., Wang, Y., Du, B., Chen, H.: A survey on vision mamba: models, applications and challenges. arXiv e-prints (2024)
40. Yang, X., Zhao, X., Shen, Z.: A generalizable anomaly detection method in dynamic graphs. In: Proceedings of the AAAI Conference on Artificial Intelligence, vol. 39, pp. 22001–22009 (2025)
41. You, Y., Chen, T., Sui, Y., Chen, T., Wang, Z., Shen, Y.: Graph contrastive learning with augmentations. In: Advances in Neural Information Processing Systems, vol. 33, pp. 5812–5823 (2020)
42. Yuan, H., et al.: Dg-mamba: robust and efficient dynamic graph structure learning with selective state space models. arXiv preprint arXiv:2412.08160 (2024)
43. Zang, Y., et al.: Rethinking cancer gene identification through graph anomaly analysis. arXiv preprint arXiv:2412.17240 (2024)
44. Zhao, H., Zhang, M., Zhao, W., Ding, P., Huang, S., Wang, D.: Cobra: extending mamba to multi-modal large language model for efficient inference. arXiv preprint arXiv:2403.14520 (2024)
45. Zhao, L., Akoglu, L.: On using classification datasets to evaluate graph outlier detection: peculiar observations and new insights. Big Data **11**(3), 151–180 (2023)
46. Zhu, Y., Xu, Y., Yu, F., Liu, Q., Wu, S., Wang, L.: Graph contrastive learning with adaptive augmentation. In: Proceedings of the Web Conference 2021, pp. 2069–2080 (2021)
47. Zou, D., Peng, H., Liu, C.: A structural information guided hierarchical reconstruction for graph anomaly detection. In: Proceedings of the 33rd ACM International Conference on Information and Knowledge Management, pp. 4318–4323 (2024)

SODA: Out-of-Distribution Detection in Domain-Shifted Point Clouds via Neighborhood Propagation

Adam Goodge[1], Bryan Hooi[2], Jingyi Liao[1,2], Yongyi Su[1], Wee Siong Ng[1], Xun Xu[1(✉)], and Xulei Yang[1]

[1] Institute for Infocomm Research, Agency for Science, Technology and Research (A*STAR), Singapore, Singapore
xu_xun@i2r.a-star.edu.sg
[2] School of Computing, National University of Singapore, Singapore, Singapore

Abstract. As point cloud data increases in prevalence in a variety of applications, the ability to detect out-of-distribution (OOD) point cloud objects becomes critical for ensuring model safety and reliability. However, this problem remains under-explored in existing research. Inspired by success in the image domain, we propose to exploit advances in 3D vision-language models (3D VLMs) for OOD detection in point cloud objects. However, a major challenge is that point cloud datasets used to pre-train 3D VLMs are drastically smaller in size and object diversity than their image-based counterparts. Critically, they often contain exclusively computer-designed synthetic objects. This leads to a substantial domain shift when the model is transferred to practical tasks involving real objects scanned from the physical environment. In this paper, our empirical experiments show that synthetic-to-real domain shift significantly degrades the alignment of point cloud with their associated text embeddings in the 3D VLM latent space, hindering downstream performance. To address this, we propose a novel methodology called SODA which improves the detection of OOD point clouds through a neighborhood-based score propagation scheme. SODA is inference-based, requires no additional model training, and achieves state-of-the-art performance over existing approaches across datasets and problem settings.

Keywords: out-of-distribution detection · point clouds · vision-language models

1 Introduction

Out-of-distribution (OOD) detection is crucial for ensuring the safe and reliable deployment of models in practical applications. It has received significant research attention for 2D images, but remains largely unexplored in the context of 3D point clouds. The detection of unknown 3D objects poses a critical

---

Supplementary Information The online version contains supplementary material available at https://doi.org/10.1007/978-3-032-05962-8_4.

challenge in important applications including robotics, autonomous driving, and healthcare.

Vision-language models (VLMs), such as CLIP [25], have proven effective at OOD detection in image data. OOD inputs are detected by their low cosine similarity to the text embeddings of in-distribution (ID) class labels. Recently, several 3D VLMs incorporating point clouds into this multi-modal latent space have emerged. These models demonstrate strong performance in point cloud classification, but have yet to be evaluated for OOD detection.

A major advantage of VLMs is that they only require ID class labels, not labeled examples of ID data, due to their extensive pre-training on broad data. This is particularly useful in the context of point cloud data, which are typically more expensive to collect and annotate than images. However, point cloud datasets used to pre-train 3D VLMs are also much more limited in size and object diversity than their image counterparts. Moreover, they typically contain only synthetic, computer-designed objects. This results in domain shift when the model is transferred to practical downstream tasks that involve real objects scanned from the physical environment. Figure 1 shows a synthetic chair from ShapeNet [3] and a real chair from ScanObjectNN [28]. Real data can diverge from synthetic data due to several phenomena, such as: non-uniform point density, sensor noise, occlusion, background objects and physical imperfections. As most practical tasks involve real data, it is crucial that models are robust to this domain shift if they are to be deployed in practice.

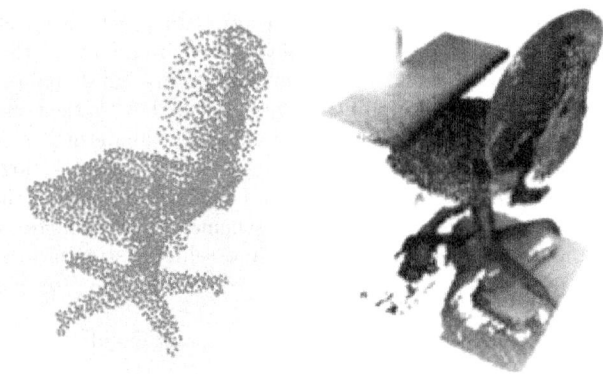

Fig. 1. Example of a synthetic chair sample (left) and real chair sample (right).

In this paper, we show through empirical experiments that "*synthetic-to-real*" domain shift hinders the alignment of the embeddings of real point clouds with their text labels in the latent space of 3D VLMs, evidenced by the degradation in classification performance of real objects. Moreover, we observe that the severity of this degradation has a strong correlation with the severity of the domain shift. However, we also observe that the model is effective at clustering real data by class in the latent space, suggesting that the model maintains an ability to distinguish between different classes of real objects. These observations motivate our proposed methodology for point cloud OOD detection, called **S**coring for **O**ut-of-**D**istribution Detection through **A**ggregation (**SODA**). We use the similarity of point clouds to ID class labels to initialize OOD scores, followed by an important score refinement step based on a neighborhood-based score propagation scheme which accounts for the severity of domain shift through dynamic 'source-similarity' weighting. We conduct comprehensive experimentation to evaluate our approach and find that it significantly improves OOD detection without additional fine-tuning of the backbone model.

In summary, our contributions are as follows:

- We investigate the effect of synthetic-to-real domain shift on 3D VLMs and find a degradation in the alignment of point cloud and text embeddings.
- We propose SODA, a novel methodology to improve OOD detection in domain shifted point-clouds via domain shift-aware neighborhood propagation.
- We show that this approach achieves state-of-the-art performance through rigorous experiments and ablation study.

The code to reproduce our experiments is available online.

2 Related Work

Numerous methods have been proposed for OOD detection in image data. Notably, MSP [11] uses the maximum softmax probability assigned to a sample by a classification model trained on ID classes, and subsequent methods adopt a similar approach using different confidence measures [14,19,20,27]. However, neural networks are known to make overly confident predictions even for OOD data [10]. OOD point cloud detection remains comparatively under-explored, and existing studies mostly focus on adapting established methods to point-cloud feature extraction models such as PointNet++ [23] and DGCNN [31] in [1], and PointPillars [17] in [13], VAEs [21], and teacher-student models [2]. OpenPatch [24] measures the distance of test sample patches to a memory bank containing patches of ID samples.

Recently, strong performance has been achieved in image-based OOD detection with vision-language models [6,8,9,30]. VLMs are typically trained on massive-scale image datasets that encompass a diverse range of classes, domains, and environments. This extensive exposure enables the model to learn rich visual representations, enhancing its ability to generalize across domains. In the 3D VLM space, two approaches have emerged. One approach is to project point cloud data into image inputs for existing 2D VLMs, examples of which include PointCLIP [37] and CLIP2Point [15]. Another approach is to introduce an additional point cloud encoder and train it to align point cloud embeddings with their paired image and text inputs extracted from a fixed 2D VLM. ULIP [34] and ULIP-2 [35] are notable examples, and the latter achieves state-of-the-art performance in downstream tasks.

As mentioned, point cloud datasets used to pre-train 3D VLMs are relatively limited in size and object diversity, limiting their generalization. Significant research attention has focused on domain adaptation to real point cloud data [16]. Common approaches include domain-invariant training or fine-tuning with task-specific data. In an OOD setting, this means adapting to ID data for each task individually, which is cumbersome or even infeasible in data-scarce scenarios. It also risks worsening performance through catastrophic forgetting [24]. As such, we focus on leveraging the pre-trained embedding space for training-free adaptation to synthetic-to-real domain shift, without adjusting model parameters.

3 Motivation

In this section, we investigate the effect of synthetic-to-real domain shift on the embeddings learnt by 3D VLMs. In our analysis, we use synthetic samples from ModelNet40 [33] and real samples from ScanObjectNN [28]. We focus on only the classes which are common to both datasets (listed under SR1 and SR2 in Table 1) in order to focus on the effect of domain shift and not the semantic differences between classes. We use ULIP-2 [35] as our fixed backbone VLM due to its superior performance. ULIP-2 trains a PointBERT point cloud encoder to align point cloud embeddings with paired image and text caption embeddings learnt by a 2D VLM. We extract the embeddings of both synthetic and real point clouds and make several observations:

Table 1. Class splits for experiments with ScanObjectNN. Classes under SR1 and SR2 overlap with classes of the same name in ModelNet40, but classes under SR3 classes do not.

SR1	SR2	SR3
chair	bed	bag
shelf	toilet	bin
door	desk	box
sink	table	pillow
sofa	display	cabinet

Observation 1: Degraded Text-Point Cloud Alignment. Following [35], we obtain text embeddings for each class label by creating class-based text prompts from a set of templates (more details in Sect. 4.2). We classify each sample according to their maximum cosine similarity to these text embeddings. With this setup, we observe that **classification accuracy drops from 94.27% on synthetic data to 73.83% on real data**. This suggests a significant degradation in the alignment of real data with their associated text labels in the latent space compared with synthetic data. This is detrimental to OOD detection, as

OOD data may be inappropriately matched to ID class labels, resulting in false negative errors, and vice versa. However, this degradation is not uniform. We take the average similarity of real samples to their 10 nearest synthetic samples as a measure of how 'close' they are to the source domain. In Figure 2, we see that this 'source similarity' has a direct, linear relationship with classification accuracy. In other words, **real samples that are closer to the source domain are better aligned with the text labels**.

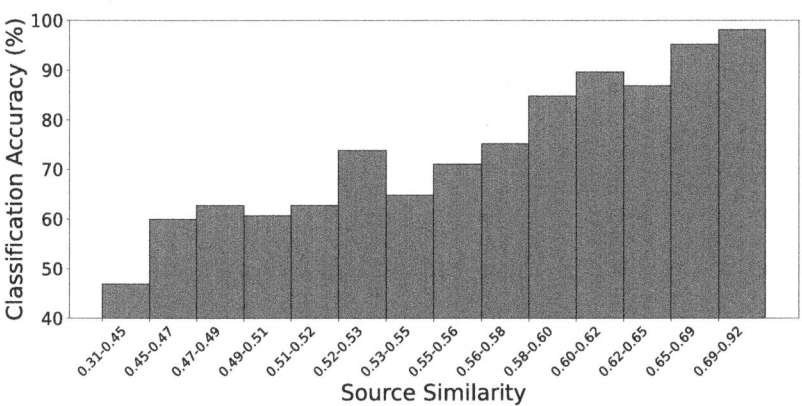

Fig. 2. Classification accuracy (%) of real ScanObjectNN point clouds sorted by cosine similarity to synthetic ModelNet40 samples.

Observation 2: Strong Class-Based Clustering. Our second observation is that real samples are strongly clustered by class. Figure 3 visualises the UMAP projections [22] of real point samples, with their colour corresponding to their class label. We see that the vast majority of samples are well clustered according to class. This suggests that, despite a weakened alignment with the text embeddings, the model retains an ability to distinguish between examples of different classes of real objects. This is promising for OOD detection, as it means that we can expect a real sample from an ID class to be mostly neighbored by other samples of the same ID class, and vice versa for OOD samples. These observations provide motivation for our proposed methodology.

4 Methodology

Our work most closely relates to [36], which exploits neighborhood structure within the test set for classification. However, a major difference in OOD detection is that we do not know the label space of OOD samples, which can belong to any unknown class, therefore it is a more challenging open-set problem.

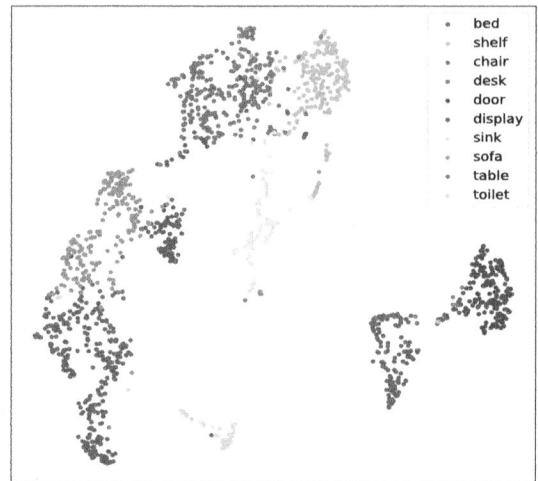

Fig. 3. UMAP projections of real domain test point clouds colored by their class.

Our methodology is inspired by the label propagation algorithm [39], a semi-supervised approach to classification which propagates class information from labeled to unlabeled data. However, as all test data is unlabeled in our setting, we have no ground truth information to propagate. [32] boosts the detection of OOD nodes within a graph by propagating energy-based scores between neighboring nodes. We explore the potential of this framework beyond graph data, particularly for addressing the challenges of domain shift in non-structured data, exploiting the strong class-based latent clustering of 3D VLMs to improve OOD detection performance in a transductive setting. Our methodology is illustrated in Fig. 4.

4.1 Problem Statement

We have a set of N ID class labels $\mathcal{C} = \{C_1, C_2, ..., C_N\}$, and an unlabeled test set $\mathbf{X}$, consisting of both ID and OOD real data. A sample is ID if it belongs to any ID class $C_i \in \mathcal{C}$ and OOD otherwise. We aim to distinguish between ID and OOD samples by devising a scoring function which assigns higher scores to ID samples than OOD samples in $\mathbf{X}$.

4.2 SODA

We begin by describing the source-free, zero-shot version of SODA (ZS-SODA), and then explain how source domain samples are incorporated to enhance performance in our full SODA methodology.

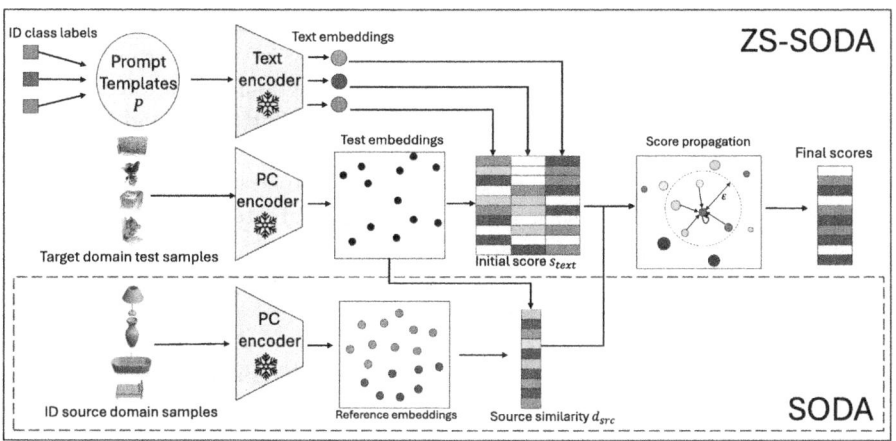

Fig. 4. An overview of SODA. Test samples are assigned initial scores based on their similarity to the ID class text embeddings. If available, these scores are multiplied by their source similarity, and refined via neighborhood propagation within an ε-similarity radius. Target domain images are ScanObjectNN and source domain images are ModelNet40.

Initial Scoring. We use a fixed, pre-trained 3D VLM with text encoder g_t and point cloud encoder g_{pc}. Following convention, we use a set of templates $\mathcal{P}$, which are shared between all classes, combined with each class label C_i to create a set of class-specific text prompts $\mathcal{P}_i$. An example template is "*a point cloud model of a CLS*" where *CLS* is replaced with C_i, and the other templates can be found in the supplementary material. These text prompts are encoded and l2-normalized, and we take the mean of these embeddings as the text prototype of class C_i:

$$\mathbf{P}_i = \frac{1}{|\mathcal{P}_i|} \sum_{p \in \mathcal{P}_i} g_t(p), \quad i \in 1,..,N. \qquad (1)$$

Similarly, we obtain the embedding of a query test sample $\mathbf{x}_i$ via the fixed point cloud encoder: $\mathbf{z}_i = g_{pc}(\mathbf{x}_i)$. With this, we assign the initial score of $\mathbf{x}_i$ as the maximum of its cosine similarities to the text prototypes:

$$s_{text}(\mathbf{x}_i) = \max_{i=1,...,N} \left(sim(\mathbf{z}_i, \mathbf{P}_i) \right) \qquad (2)$$

ID samples are assumed to have higher similarity to their correct class label, resulting in a high score, compared with OOD samples. However, as we observed, the alignment of point cloud embeddings with their text embeddings is degraded by synthetic-to-real domain shift, which challenges this assumption. To address this, we introduce a score refinement step through neighborhood-based score propagation.

Score Propagation. The misalignment of real point cloud embeddings with the text embeddings means that the initial scores are prone to substantial uncertainty or noise. However, we also observed that nearby samples are likely to belong to the same class. Based on this, we refine initial scores using the scores of nearby samples. For example, an ID sample may have an erroneously low score, but by adjusting its score in line with its neighbors, this uncertainty is reduced, the score landscape is smoothened over the latent space, and the overall robustness of OOD scores of individual samples is improved. We achieve this by constructing a *similarity graph*, with a node for each test sample and an edge connecting nodes i and j if their cosine similarity is greater than ε:

$$e_{i,j} = \begin{cases} 1, & \text{if } sim(\mathbf{z_i}, \mathbf{z_j}) \geq \varepsilon \\ 0, & \text{otherwise} \end{cases} \quad (3)$$

We set $\varepsilon = \text{percentile}(\mathbf{S}, 100(1-\eta))$, where $\mathbf{S}$ is the similarities between all pair-wise test samples and η is a hyper-parameter. A smaller η results in a higher ε threshold and a sparser similarity graph, i.e. fewer neighbors per sample on average. This formulation is adaptive to the local density of each sample; densely packed samples will have more neighbors within an ε-similarity radius and therefore more neighbors in the similarity graph, compared to samples in sparse regions. This adaptive strategy is important to limit the propagation of information to only the most similar neighbors, rather than an inflexible k nearest neighbor strategy. We set $\eta = 0.02$ in our main experiments and our ablation study shows that performance is robust within a reasonable range of η.

We update the score of a sample $\mathbf{x}_i$ as follows:

$$s^{(t)}(\mathbf{x}_i) = \alpha s^{(0)}(\mathbf{x}_i) + \frac{1-\alpha}{|\mathcal{N}_i|} \sum_{j \in \mathcal{N}_i} s^{(t-1)}(\mathbf{x}_j), \quad (4)$$

where t is the current iteration, $s^{(0)}(\mathbf{x}_i) = s_{text}(\mathbf{x}_i)$ and $\mathcal{N}_i$ is the set of neighbors to node i in the similarity graph. In other words, its updated score is a weighted sum of its initial score and the mean of its neighbors' current scores. Through this procedure, the score of an individual sample is moved closer to those of its neighbors, while anchored to its own initial score to avoid instability, which smoothens the scoring function over the local neighborhood. We allow self-loops in the graph so that every node has at least one neighbor ($|\mathcal{N}_i| > 0 \ \forall i$). We complete T iterations to obtain the final OOD scores. T is a hyper-parameter, and we experiment with different T settings in the ablation study.

4.3 Source Similarity

We observed that real samples that are closer to the source domain in cosine similarity are more likely to be correctly classified through text-based similarity matching. Based on this observation, we hypothesise that these samples are better aligned with the text labels, which means that their text-based OOD scores are more reliable. As such, in our full SODA methodology, we use this source similarity to re-weight the importance of different neighbors during score propagation. More formally, given a set of 'reference samples' from ID classes in the source domain, $\mathbf{X}^{ref}$, we extract the embeddings of each reference sample

$\mathbf{x}_i^{ref}$ from the same fixed point cloud encoder: $\mathbf{z}_i^{ref} = g_{pc}(\mathbf{x}_i^{ref})$. For a test sample $\mathbf{x}_i$, we take the mean of the cosine similarities of $\mathbf{z}_i$ to its top k ($k = 10$) closest reference sample embeddings to define its source similarity, denoted d_{src}:

$$d_{src}(\mathbf{x}_i) = \frac{1}{k} \sum_{j \in \text{top} k(\mathbf{z}_i)} (sim(\mathbf{z}_j^{ref}, \mathbf{z}_i)) \quad (5)$$

To further benefit from neighborhood propagation, we iteratively update d_{src} for each sample according to the same formula as Eq. 4, with $s^{(0)} = d_{src}$. With this, the updated OOD score at the tth iteration is given by:

$$s^{(t)}(\mathbf{x}_i) = d_{src}^{(t)}(\mathbf{x}_i) \cdot s_{text}^{(t)}(\mathbf{x}_i). \quad (6)$$

The effect of this is two-fold. Firstly, the OOD scores of samples with high d_{src} will increase. This is beneficial, as a test sample with greater closeness to source domain ID samples intuitively suggests it is more likely to be ID itself, despite the domain shift. Secondly, this score increase means that this sample has greater influence, or weighting, when its score is propagated to its neighbors in the next iteration, thereby increasing the scores of semantically similar samples in the latent space. After several iterations, score information from reliable ID test samples will flow to their more uncertain ID neighbors, and vice versa for OOD samples, resulting in more robust OOD scores.

5 Experiments

We conduct experiments to study the effectiveness of our methodology in point cloud OOD detection under domain shift. In practical settings, we would assign all test samples with a score below a user-defined threshold as OOD. However, the aim of this work is to improve the OOD scoring process, therefore we use evaluation metrics that do not require the setting of a specific threshold. Namely, AUC (higher is better) and FPR95 (lower is better), which is the false positive rate at 95% recall. We also conduct an ablation study to analyze the behavior of our methodology under different experimental settings.

5.1 Datasets

We follow the experimental framework of [1] in our main experiments, using the most popular benchmark point cloud datasets. In particular, we use real samples from ScanObjectNN [28] as our test data and ModelNet40 [33] as our reference data. We split the object classes into the three subsets shown in Table 1. All of the classes in SR1 and SR2 are also in ModelNet40, whereas SR3 classes are not. As such, we conduct one experiment with SR1 as ID and SR2∪SR3 as OOD classes, and another experiment with SR2 as ID and SR1∪SR3 as OOD classes. The number of reference samples in each class ranges from 109 to 889, and the details can be found in the supplementary material. Following [1], we randomly

Table 2. AUC (higher is better) and FPR95 (lower is better) scores. Best/second best scores are highlighted in bold/underlined. Baselines under '*Customized Model*' are taken from [1] and all train a model using ID source domain data. Baselines under '*Pre-trained Model*' use the pre-trained features from ULIP-2.

	SR1		SR2		Average	
	AUC ↑	FPR95 ↓	AUC ↑	FPR95 ↓	AUC ↑	FPR95 ↓
Customized Model						
MSP [11]	81.0	79.6	70.3	86.7	75.6	83.2
MLS [29]	82.1	76.6	67.6	86.8	74.8	81.7
ODIN [19]	81.7	77.3	70.2	84.4	76.0	80.8
Energy [20]	81.9	77.5	67.7	87.3	74.8	82.4
GradNorm [14]	77.6	80.1	68.4	86.3	73.0	83.2
ReAct [27]	81.7	75.6	67.6	87.2	74.6	81.4
NF [1]	78.0	84.4	74.7	84.2	76.4	84.3
OE+mixup [12]	71.2	89.7	60.3	93.5	65.7	91.6
ARPL+CS [4]	82.8	74.9	68.0	89.3	75.4	82.1
Cosine proto [7]	79.9	74.5	76.5	77.8	78.2	76.1
CE (L2) [1]	79.7	84.5	75.7	80.2	77.7	82.3
SubArcFace [5]	78.7	84.3	75.1	83.4	76.9	83.8
Pre-trained Model						
MSP* [11]	83.0	84.2	74.6	81.4	78.8	82.8
MLS* [29]	81.0	79.4	83.2	62.7	82.1	71.0
Cosine Proto [7]	80.7	70.2	73.6	83.3	77.1	76.8
Mahalanobis [18]	73.8	89.7	65.3	83.3	69.5	86.5
OpenPatch [24]	85.8	<u>54.4</u>	71.6	74.1	78.7	64.3
ZS-SODA* (*Ours*)	<u>85.9</u>	67.1	<u>87.1</u>	<u>50.4</u>	<u>86.5</u>	<u>58.7</u>
SODA (*Ours*)	**93.3**	**33.3**	**87.7**	**47.4**	**90.5**	**40.4**

*source-free methods

sample 1024 points from reference point clouds and 2048 points from test point clouds.

We also experiment with ModelNet-C [26], which contains corrupted versions of ModelNet40 data, with multiple types of corruptions which are commonly observed in real data, such as global and local noise and point dropout. In these experiments, we use the clean ModelNet40 ID samples as reference samples and the corrupted ModelNet-C samples as test samples. We use the strongest level of corruption in our experiments, as this represents the greatest degree of domain shift. We conduct two types of experiments, one with each of SR1 and SR2 from Table 1 as the ID/OOD samples respectively.

Table 3. AUC (higher is better) and FPR95 (lower is better) performance of all pre-trained methods for ScanObjectNN test samples. ZS-SODA and SODA without propagation are simply the initial scores. Avg. change shows the average change after propagation over all methods.

	S1		S2		Average	
	AUC ↑	FPR95 ↓	AUC ↑	FPR95 ↓	AUC ↑	FPR95 ↓
Without Propagation						
MSP	83.0	84.2	74.7	81.4	78.8	82.8
Source Similarity	86.6	58.5	79.2	71.1	82.9	64.8
Cosine Proto	80.7	70.2	73.6	83.3	77.1	76.8
ZS-SODA	81.0	79.4	83.2	62.7	82.1	71.0
SODA	88.6	63.0	84.8	58.0	86.7	60.5
With Propagation						
MSP	87.7	61.9	78.7	71.3	83.2	66.6
Source Similarity	90.1	43.2	84.5	55.2	87.3	49.2
Cosine Proto	82.5	56.8	74.2	76.2	78.3	66.5
ZS-SODA	85.9	67.1	87.1	50.4	86.5	58.7
SODA	**93.3**	**33.3**	**87.7**	**47.4**	**90.5**	**40.4**
Avg. change	4.0	−19.4	2.9	−10.0	3.5	−14.7

5.2 Baselines

Under *'Customized Model'*, we adopt the methods presented in [1] as baselines. All of these methods use models that have been trained on exclusively ID data from the source domain. We present their PointNet++ results due to its superior performance. Under, *'Pre-trained Model'*, we adopt methods that use pre-trained models. OpenPatch [24] and Mahalanobis [18], which measures the Mahanalobis distance to the reference samples, use a single modality PointBERT backbone. We also implement MSP, MLS and Cosine Proto, which measures the maximum similarity to ID reference sample prototypes, using the same features extracted from the 3D VLM ULIP-2 (PointBERT backbone) as ZS-SODA and SODA. For hyper-parameters, we use $T = 5$, $\alpha = 0.2$ and $\eta = 0.02$ by default without tuning. The effect of hyper-parameter settings is shown in the ablation study. We run our experiments in PyTorch on an Nvidia A5000 24G GPU.

5.3 Results

ScanObjectNN. Table 2 shows the average AUC and FPR95 scores over three random trials, for ID classes SR1 and SR2 separately, as well as their average. The standard deviations are shown in the supplementary material. We see that pre-trained methods mostly out-perform the customized model methods. This can be explained by the difference in model architecture as well as the superior representation learning that results from larger scale pre-training. We also see that our methodology significantly improves performance over all baselines. We see that ZS-SODA and SODA achieve an average of 3.9 and 8.5 percentage points improvement in AUC score over the next best-performing baseline, and a -13.4 and -31.4 point reduction in FPR95 respectively. SODA is also computationally efficient; we show in the supplementary material that similarity graph construction and score propagation contribute only a tiny portion of the overall runtime compared to the feature extraction phase. In the supplementary material, we also conduct experiments using both reference and test samples from ShapeNet [3] (i.e. all synthetic) and both reference and test samples from ScanObjectNN (i.e. all real), and find a similar improvement from our methodology.

We also measure the impact of score propagation using the other OOD methods as the initial scores, namely MSP, Cosine Proto and the source similarity d_{src} itself. Table 3 shows that score propagation greatly improves performance, with an average improvement of 3.5 points in AUC and -14.7 points in FPR95 across all methods, which demonstrates the positive effect of score propagation on OOD detection. We also see that SODA consistently outperforms the other methods, both with and without propagation, which demonstrates the complementary benefits of accounting for the similarity to the source domain alongside text similarity in detecting domain-shifted OOD inputs.

Table 4. Performance of ZS-SODA and SODA (and change in performance from initial scores before propagation) on corrupted ModelNet-C test samples.

Corruption	ZS-SODA		SODA	
	AUC ↑	FPR95 ↓	AUC ↑	FPR95 ↓
Add Global	89.7 (+2.7)	41.4 (−11.5)	97.1 (+1.5)	20.9 (−9.0)
Add Local	90.0 (+5.5)	52.4 (−11.8)	95.7 (+3.9)	23.3 (−26.9)
Dropout Global	76.9 (+3.9)	75.3 (−7.9)	88.4 (+5.7)	62.3 (−12.7)
Dropout Local	76.6 (+3.2)	74.9 (−6.6)	86.7 (+3.5)	58.9 (−11.8)
Jitter	48.6 (−0.6)	97.8 (+1.6)	60.5 (+1.5)	88.0 (−2.7)
Rotate	86.2 (+3.1)	55.5 (−6.8)	95.4 (+2.7)	35.9 (−8.4)
Scale	87.6 (+1.8)	35.4 (−13.2)	96.5 (+1.1)	23.5 (−0.4)
Average	79.4 (+2.8)	61.8 (−8.0)	88.6 (+2.8)	44.7 (−10.3)

ModelNet-C. Table 4 shows the average performance with ModelNet-C test samples. For brevity, we show the average results over both experimental setups for ZS-SODA and SODA, followed by the change in these metrics from the initial scores before score propagation (in parentheses). We see that our methodology consistently improves performance in both metrics across corruption types, except for ZS-SODA which declines slightly for the jitter corruption. On average, we see a 2.8 point improvement in AUC for both ZS-SODA and SODA, and a $-8.0/-10.3$ improvement in FPR95 scores for ZS-SODA/SODA. The full results are shown in the supplementary.

5.4 Ablation Study

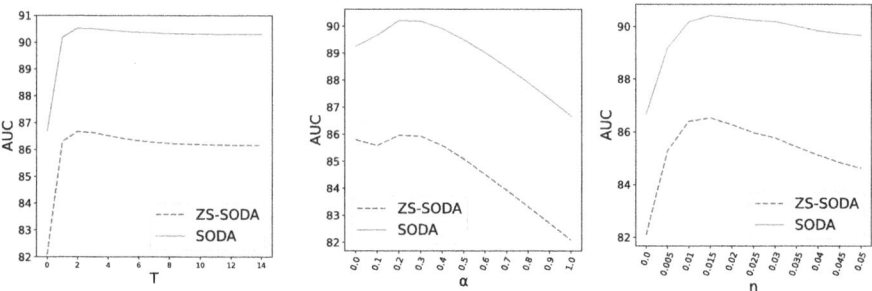

Fig. 5. Average AUC performance with different numbers of iterations, T (left), settings of α (middle), and settings of η (right).

Hyper-parameters. Figure 5 shows how performance varies with different settings of hyper-parameters. Firstly, the leftmost figure shows AUC performance after different numbers of propagation iterations. $T = 0$, gives the initial score, from which we see a large increase in performance after just one iteration. Performance slightly drops before converging at around $T = 6$ iterations, after which the OOD scores are fully converged and there is no more change in performance. In the middle figure, we see how performance changes as α in Eq. 4 varies. $\alpha = 1$ is equivalent to the initial scores, while a smaller α gives greater weight to the current score information from neighbors in score updates. We see that optimal performance is achieved around $\alpha \approx 0.25$, which signifies the importance of neighborhood information in refining the initial scores. The rightmost figure shows performance for different settings of η. A larger η corresponds to a lower ε threshold in Eq. 3, and consequently a denser similarity graph with more connecting edges between samples. We see peak performance is achieved at $\eta \approx 0.015$, and slowly declines from there. As η increases, there are more samples propagating score information to neighbors of lower cosine similarity, which eventually hinders performance as the propagated information becomes less relevant. In practice, the setting of these hyper-parameters are guided by the number of available samples and also the sensitivity of individual applications to the trade-off between false positive and negative errors.

Backbone Models. Table 5 shows the performance of SODA before and after score propagation using different backbone 3D VLMs: ULIP-2, ULIP [34] and PointCLIPv2 [38]. We see that score propagation consistently improves both

Table 5. AUC and FPR95 performance of SODA without propagation (the initial score) and with propagation for different backbone feature extraction models.

	Without Propagation		With Propagation		Avg. change	
	AUC ↑	FPR95 ↓	AUC ↑	FPR95 ↓	AUC ↑	FPR95 ↓
PointCLIPv2	63.7	91.4	65.3	86.5	1.6	−4.9
ULIP	78.5	76.7	82.4	64.4	3.9	−12.3
ULIP-2	**86.7**	**60.5**	**90.5**	**40.4**	**3.8**	**−20.1**

AUC and FPR95 metrics across all backbone models. Furthermore, we see that this improvement is most pronounced with ULIP-2, which also achieves the best performance overall. This aligns with its superior performance in other downstream tasks demonstrated in the original work. We can expect a better model to learn more meaningful latent representations, resulting in more semantically meaningful neighbors which are beneficial for score propagation.

In the supplementary material, we perform several additional experiments. Firstly, we test different formulations of text prompt templates and find that different prompts give better performance in different experimental setups. Overall, using the average of the embeddings from multiple prompt templates is more robust than any single template.

6 Conclusion

We investigate the effect of synthetic-to-real domain shift on the embeddings learnt by pre-trained 3D vision-language models and find that the alignment of real domain point clouds with their corresponding text labels is degraded compared with synthetic data. This has significant implications for OOD detection and other practical downstream tasks that concern real point cloud data. To address this, we propose a novel methodology called SODA which updates and refines the OOD scores assigned to test samples using score information propagated from similar, nearby points within their local neighborhood. This has a local smoothening effect on the scoring function which improves robustness and significantly enhances detection performance. We achieve state-of-the-art performance in both AUC and FPR95 metrics across different experimental settings.

Acknowledgments. This research work is supported by the Agency for Science, Technology and Research (A*STAR) under its MTC Programmatic Funds (Grant No. M23L7b0021).

References

1. Alliegro, A., Cappio Borlino, F., Tommasi, T.: 3DOS: towards 3D open set learning-benchmarking and understanding semantic novelty detection on point clouds. NeurIPS **35**, 21228–21240 (2022)

2. Bhardwaj, A., Pimpale, S., Kumar, S., Banerjee, B.: Empowering knowledge distillation via open set recognition for robust 3D point cloud classification. Pattern Recogn. Lett. **151**, 172–179 (2021)
3. Chang, A.X., et al.: Shapenet: an information-rich 3D model repository. arXiv preprint arXiv:1512.03012 (2015)
4. Chen, G., Peng, P., Wang, X., Tian, Y.: Adversarial reciprocal points learning for open set recognition. IEEE Trans. Pattern Anal. Mach. Intell. **44**(11), 8065–8081 (2021)
5. Deng, J., Guo, J., Liu, T., Gong, M., Zafeiriou, S.: Sub-center arcface: boosting face recognition by large-scale noisy web faces. In: Computer Vision–ECCV 2020: 16th European Conference, Glasgow, UK, August 23–28, 2020, Proceedings, Part XI 16, p. 741–757. Springer (2020)
6. Esmaeilpour, S., Liu, B., Robertson, E., Shu, L.: Zero-shot out-of-distribution detection based on the pre-trained model clip. In: AAAI, vol. 36, pp. 6568–6576 (2022)
7. Fontanel, D., Cermelli, F., Mancini, M., Caputo, B.: Detecting anomalies in semantic segmentation with prototypes. In: CVPR, pp. 113–121 (2021)
8. Fort, S., Ren, J., Lakshminarayanan, B.: Exploring the limits of out-of-distribution detection. In: NeurIPS, vol. 34, pp. 7068–7081 (2021)
9. Goodge, A., Hooi, B., Ng, W.S.: When text and images don't mix: Bias-correcting language-image similarity scores for anomaly detection. arXiv preprint arXiv:2407.17083 (2024)
10. Guo, C., Pleiss, G., Sun, Y., Weinberger, K.Q.: On calibration of modern neural networks. In: International Conference on Machine Learning, pp. 1321–1330. PMLR (2017)
11. Hendrycks, D., Gimpel, K.: A baseline for detecting misclassified and out-of-distribution examples in neural networks. arXiv preprint arXiv:1610.02136 (2016)
12. Hendrycks, D., Mazeika, M., Dietterich, T.: Deep anomaly detection with outlier exposure. arXiv preprint arXiv:1812.04606 (2018)
13. Huang, C., et al.: Out-of-distribution detection for lidar-based 3D object detection. In: 2022 IEEE 25th International Conference on Intelligent Transportation Systems (ITSC), pp. 4265–4271. IEEE (2022)
14. Huang, R., Geng, A., Li, Y.: On the importance of gradients for detecting distributional shifts in the wild. In: NeurIPS, vol. 34, pp. 677–689 (2021)
15. Huang, T., et al.: Clip2point: transfer clip to point cloud classification with image-depth pre-training. In: ICCV, pp. 22157–22167 (2023)
16. Huch, S., Lienkamp, M.: Towards minimizing the lidar sim-to-real domain shift: object-level local domain adaptation for 3D point clouds of autonomous vehicles. Sensors **23**(24), 9913 (2023)
17. Lang, A.H., Vora, S., Caesar, H., Zhou, L., Yang, J., Beijbom, O.: Pointpillars: fast encoders for object detection from point clouds. In: Proceedings of the IEEE/CVF Conference on Computer Vision and Pattern Recognition, pp. 12697–12705 (2019)
18. Lee, K., Lee, K., Lee, H., Shin, J.: A simple unified framework for detecting out-of-distribution samples and adversarial attacks. In: NeurIPS, vol. 31 (2018)
19. Liang, S., Li, Y., Srikant, R.: Enhancing the reliability of out-of-distribution image detection in neural networks. arXiv preprint arXiv:1706.02690 (2017)
20. Liu, W., Wang, X., Owens, J., Li, Y.: Energy-based out-of-distribution detection. In: NeurIPS, vol. 33, pp. 21464–21475 (2020)
21. Masuda, M., Hachiuma, R., Fujii, R., Saito, H., Sekikawa, Y.: Toward unsupervised 3D point cloud anomaly detection using variational autoencoder. In: ICIP, pp. 3118–3122. IEEE (2021)

22. McInnes, L., Healy, J., Melville, J.: Umap: uniform manifold approximation and projection for dimension reduction. arXiv preprint arXiv:1802.03426 (2018)
23. Qi, C.R., Yi, L., Su, H., Guibas, L.J.: PointNet++: deep hierarchical feature learning on point sets in a metric space. In: NeurIPS, vol. 30 (2017)
24. Rabino, P., Alliegro, A., Borlino, F.C., Tommasi, T.: Openpatch: a 3D patchwork for out-of-distribution detection. arXiv preprint arXiv:2310.03388 (2023)
25. Radford, A., et al.: Learning transferable visual models from natural language supervision. In: ICML, pp. 8748–8763. PMLR (2021)
26. Ren, J., Pan, L., Liu, Z.: Benchmarking and analyzing point cloud classification under corruptions. arXiv:2202.03377 (2022)
27. Sun, Y., Guo, C., Li, Y.: React: out-of-distribution detection with rectified activations. In: NeurIPS, vol. 34, pp. 144–157 (2021)
28. Uy, M.A., Pham, Q.H., Hua, B.S., Nguyen, D.T., Yeung, S.K.: Revisiting point cloud classification: a new benchmark dataset and classification model on real-world data. In: ICCV (2019)
29. Vaze, S., Han, K., Vedaldi, A., Zisserman, A.: Open-set recognition: a good closed-set classifier is all you need? arXiv preprint arXiv:2110.06207 (2021)
30. Wang, H., Li, Y., Yao, H., Li, X.: CLIPN for zero-shot OOD detection: teaching clip to say no. In: ICCV, pp. 1802–1812 (2023)
31. Wang, Y., Sun, Y., Liu, Z., Sarma, S.E., Bronstein, M.M., Solomon, J.M.: Dynamic graph CNN for learning on point clouds. ACM Trans. Graph. **38**(5), 1–12 (2019)
32. Wu, Q., Chen, Y., Yang, C., Yan, J.: Energy-based out-of-distribution detection for graph neural networks. arXiv preprint arXiv:2302.02914 (2023)
33. Wu, Z., Song, S., Khosla, A., Yu, F., Zhang, L., Tang, X., Xiao, J.: 3D shapenets: a deep representation for volumetric shapes. In: CVPR, pp. 1912–1920 (2015)
34. Xue, L., et al.: Ulip: learning a unified representation of language, images, and point clouds for 3D understanding. In: CVPR, pp. 1179–1189 (2023)
35. Xue, L., et al.: Ulip-2: towards scalable multimodal pre-training for 3D understanding. arXiv preprint arXiv:2305.08275 (2023)
36. Yang, S., et al.: Exploiting the intrinsic neighborhood structure for source-free domain adaptation. In: Advances in Neural Information Processing Systems, vol. 34, pp. 29393–29405 (2021)
37. Zhang, R., et al.: Pointclip: point cloud understanding by clip. In: CVPR, pp. 8552–8562 (2022)
38. Zhu, X., et al.: Pointclip v2: prompting clip and GPT for powerful 3D open-world learning. In: Proceedings of the IEEE/CVF International Conference on Computer Vision, pp. 2639–2650 (2023)
39. Zhu, X., Ghahramani, Z., Lafferty, J.D.: Semi-supervised learning using gaussian fields and harmonic functions. In: (ICML-03), pp. 912–919 (2003)

Unsupervised Surrogate Anomaly Detection

Simon Klüttermann[1,3], Tim Katzke[1,2(✉)], and Emmanuel Müller[1,2,3]

[1] TU Dortmund University, Dortmund, Germany
{simon.kluettermann,tim.katzke,emmanuel.mueller}@cs.tu-dortmund.de
[2] Research Center Trustworthy Data Science and Security, Dortmund, Germany
[3] Lamarr Institute for Machine Learning and Artificial Intelligence, Dortmund, Germany

Abstract. In this paper, we study unsupervised anomaly detection algorithms that learn a neural network representation, i.e., regular patterns of normal data, which anomalies are deviating from. Inspired by a similar concept in engineering, we refer to our methodology as surrogate anomaly detection. We formalize the concept of surrogate anomaly detection into a set of axioms required for optimal surrogate models and propose a new algorithm, named DEAN (Deep Ensemble ANomaly detection), designed to fulfill these criteria. We evaluate DEAN on 121 benchmark datasets, demonstrating its competitive performance against 19 existing methods, as well as the scalability and reliability of our method.

Keywords: Anomaly Detection · Ensemble Methods

1 Introduction

Anomaly detection (AD) is a crucial subdomain of data analytics with countless applications ranging from fraud detection [24] to health monitoring [10]. In all of these domains, anomalies are rare, exceptional or interesting objects that are highly deviating from the residual (regular) data [46]. Generally, anomaly detection can be approached in three primary ways: with extensive access to labeled anomalies (supervised), with access to a limited number of labeled anomalies (semi-supervised), or without labeled anomalies (unsupervised). In this paper, we focus on unsupervised anomaly detection. This setting poses the unique challenge of identifying a wide range of anomalies without any predefined anomalous patterns or examples to follow. At the same time, this approach is particularly valuable in real-world scenarios, where obtaining labeled data may be costly or impractical. Consequently, employing methods capable of detecting deviations from a purely data-driven inferred notion of normality becomes essential.

Supplementary Information The online version contains supplementary material available at https://doi.org/10.1007/978-3-032-05962-8_5.

© The Author(s), under exclusive license to Springer Nature Switzerland AG 2026
R. P. Ribeiro et al. (Eds.): ECML PKDD 2025, LNAI 16013, pp. 71–88, 2026.
https://doi.org/10.1007/978-3-032-05962-8_5

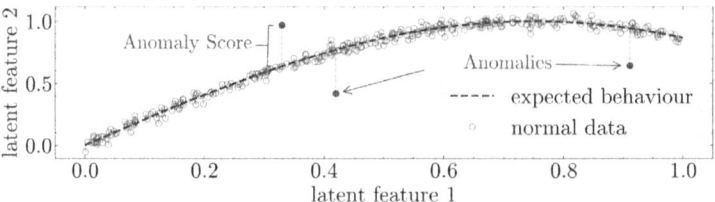

Fig. 1. Example of surrogate anomaly detection: Anomalies are detected by learning a representation that encodes the regular patterns of normal data and measuring deviations from the expected behavior.

To solve the task of unsupervised anomaly detection, various anomaly detection algorithms have been proposed. Methods such as AnoGan [43] aim to model the probability density distribution of normal samples and consider samples in low-density regions as abnormal. Other algorithms, like KNN [14], consider samples that are further away in the variable space from other samples as more anomalous. Approaches like Isolation Forests [39] measure how easily samples can be separated. Still, it can be shown that both of these alternative approaches effectively model densities too [7,20].

While density estimation is an intuitive solution to anomaly detection, any method based on this approach has two fundamental drawbacks. First, they do not scale well to high-dimensional data, which is known as the curse of dimensionality [3]. Second, there is usually no explicit modeling of the data-generating process involved, which limits how well the method generalizes to new data.

In contrast to modeling complex density distributions for high dimensional input data, we consider in this paper algorithms that learn low dimensional representations as approximations of the underlying regular patterns in the data. More specifically, we are inspired by surrogate models in engineering applications [33], where simple surrogate models are used to approximate more complex or expensive processes. Similarly, we search for models that capture a pattern of the underlying data-generating process instead of modeling the whole distribution, which we will subsequently refer to as surrogate anomaly detection models. An illustrative toy example of such a model is shown in Fig. 1.

Some existing algorithms can be considered instantiations of such surrogate anomaly detection models. Autoencoder [53] and PCA-based anomaly detection [9] learns an identity function to compress regular data and measure the deviation of anomalies as the reconstruction error. DeepSVDD [51] learns a representation in which regular data can be modeled by mapping it to a lower dimensional constant, where anomalies deviate highly from this constant value. Because these algorithms don't need to model the entire density distribution in its original input space, they scale more effectively to high dimensional data [13].

However, these methods are not without limitations either. Unlike density estimation methods, the objective of training a surrogate is much less well-defined, leading to an unlimited amount of options on how to create such a surrogate, each with its own drawbacks. We exploit this variability to formalize the idea of surrogate models into a blueprint for creating arbitrary surrogates. Within this framework, we propose five axioms that an ideal surrogate model should satisfy. Based on these, we suggest a new surrogate AD algorithm called DEAN, which, to the best of our knowledge, is the first algorithm adhering to all of them.

We evaluate our algorithm by following the procedure outlined in a recent benchmark survey paper [21], comparing it against 19 competitors across 121 datasets. Our algorithm performs highly competitively, showing only minor performance differences with the best non-surrogate competitors and outperforming all other surrogate-based methods.

Our main contributions are: (1) the formulation of a general framework for surrogate anomaly detection; (2) the establishment of guiding axioms for designing optimal surrogate algorithms; and (3) the development and comprehensive evaluation of a novel algorithm based on these principles.

To ensure the reproducibility of our results, our implementation, as well as our appendices containing further details about our experiments, are publicly available at github.com/KDD-OpenSource/DEAN.

2 Related Work

This section reviews related work with a focus on three key aspects: unsupervised anomaly detection, emphasizing approaches that extract meaningful patterns, ensemble methods, which, as discussed later, may enable the extraction of diverse patterns, and surrogate models in a more general context.

2.1 Unsupervised Anomaly Detection

Anomaly detection in an unsupervised setting inherently faces the challenge of defining a suitable objective without ground truth labels. A common suggestion is to model the densities of normal, expected samples [46], under the assumption that samples in low-density regions are less likely to be generated by the same process as normal data, and are therefore more likely to be anomalies. However, density estimation fundamentally suffers from the so called curse of dimensionality [3], which limits how well these algorithms work on high-dimensional data.

Instead of modeling the densities of normal samples, certain anomaly detection methods extract a characteristic pattern that normal samples typically satisfy and test, whether new samples conform to this pattern. Examples of this are DeepSVDD [51], which tries to learn a representation in which every sample is mapped close to a certain point, or reconstruction-based methods like Autoencoder [53] and PCA [9], which try to learn a lower dimensional latent representation, that captures all necessary information to reconstruct (only) normal samples.

These anomaly detection algorithms are less affected by the curse of dimensionality, because latent patterns typically do not increase significantly in complexity with additional features [13]. Still, these algorithms also have flaws.

DeepSVDD requires careful training or will simply not perform well [21], and using reconstruction-based algorithms requires choosing a suitable size of the latent space, which is difficult without feedback through labeled anomalies [42]. Thus, in this paper, we generalize such models and suggest an optimal approach based on axioms that outline essential properties.

2.2 Ensemble Methods

Ensembles are a powerful method in machine learning [2]; techniques such as bagging, boosting, and stacking are well-established for combining multiple submodels into a superior model. In supervised tasks, the availability of labels facilitates the coordination of submodels [11]. While there exist approaches to mitigate this, for example with synthetic ground truth anomalies [18], in unsupervised settings, the absence of labels complicates this process. Thus, many unsupervised anomaly detection approaches simply aggregate the anomaly scores produced by various algorithms [30]. This strategy takes advantage of the fact, that errors made by diverse submodels tend not to be repeated across the entire ensemble [8].

One effective approach is the use of homogeneous ensembles, which merge many similar and simple submodels that, although weak individually, collectively yield robust performance through a combination of specialization and diversity [12,39]. Moreover, model-independent methods such as feature bagging [36] can further enhance diversity by ensuring that submodels specialize in different subsets of data dimensions, which can also improve explainability [29].

2.3 Surrogate Models

Surrogate models are simplified abstractions of more complex or computationally expensive models [33]. In engineering, they are commonly employed when, for example, physical simulations are too costly [45]. In machine learning, surrogates have been used to approximate, accelerate, or explain other machine learning models. This has been applied to uncertainty estimation [54], explainability (both globally [44], and locally [50]), surrogate task-based models [57], and to accelerate anomaly detection [16].

In contrast, we propose surrogate anomaly detection to directly learn an approximation of the regular patterns in the input data. This approach enables a more reliable measurement of deviations compared to traditional density estimation methods, particularly for complex, high-dimensional data.

3 Theory of Surrogate Anomaly Detection

In engineering applications, surrogate models are frequently employed when the underlying processes are too complex to model directly. Similarly, when it comes to anomaly detection, it may be impractical to model a complex distribution directly. Here, we define a *surrogate* as a model that approximately learns characteristic patterns of normal samples and identifies anomalies through deviations from these patterns.

This idea can be formalized by requiring that a learnable function $f : \mathbb{R}^d \to \mathbb{R}^k$ approximates a target pattern $g : \mathbb{R}^d \to \mathbb{R}^k$ over the set $X \subset \mathbb{R}^d$ of normal data samples:

$$f(x) \approx g(x), \quad \forall x \in X \quad (1)$$

For example, consider a dataset where each normal sample satisfies $x_0 = x_1$. In this case, if we set $f(x) = x_0$ and $g(x) = x_1$, any significant discrepancy between x_0 and x_1 would indicate an anomaly. In practice, f may be realized by training a neural network to map high-dimensional input data to a lower-dimensional latent space (with $k \ll d$), where the underlying structure of normality is more apparent.

The target pattern g may be chosen in various ways. For instance, in an autoencoder g is the identity function, i.e., $g_{AE}(x) = x$. However, since sufficiently expressive neural networks are universal function approximators [41], there are no inherent restrictions on the choice of g; the only requirement is that it represents a pattern that is largely invariant across normal samples.

To quantify the extent to which a sample x deviates from the learned pattern, we can measure the difference between $f(x)$ and $g(x)$:

$$score(x) = \|f(x) - g(x)\| \quad (2)$$

Since the goal is to ensure that normal samples conform to the learned pattern, we can minimize the aggregate deviation over the training data X_{train} by employing the loss function

$$\mathcal{L} = \sum_{x \in X_{train}} score(x) \quad (3)$$

A critical observation is that while minimizing this loss drives $f(x)$ closer to $g(x)$ for normal samples, it does not directly enforce a high anomaly score for abnormal ones. Consequently, surrogate models may require additional mechanisms to avoid trivial solutions, as discussed in [25].

In summary, Eqs. 2 and 3 provide a general framework for developing surrogate anomaly detection algorithms. Although any function g consistent with the definition may be used, its effectiveness in yielding a well-performing anomaly detector may vary considerably.

3.1 Surrogate Axioms

To guide the selection of the pattern function g in our surrogate model, we propose five axioms that an optimal surrogate algorithm should satisfy. We assume that a performance measure $m(f)$ (e.g., AUC-ROC) exists, which evaluates how well a model separates anomalies from normal samples.

First, note that the comparison in Eq. 2 depends not only on the relative deviation of $f(x)$ from $g(x)$, but also on the magnitude of $\|g(x)\|$. If $\|g(x)\|$ varies significantly across samples, this may unfairly bias their anomaly score assignments.

Axiom 1 (Scale Consistency). *The pattern function g should produce outputs of similar scale for all inputs:* $\forall x_1, x_2 \in \mathbb{R}^d$ *it holds that* $\|g(x_1)\| \approx \|g(x_2)\|$.

An optimal surrogate must also yield similar results under identical training conditions, ensuring that any observed performance is not a mere artifact of random initialization.

Axiom 2 (Reliable Training Procedure). *When learning to approximate g multiple times under identical training conditions, the variance in performance should be small. For learned instances* $f_1, ..., f_n$ *it holds that* $Var(m(f_i)) \leq \delta^2$, *where the constant* $\delta > 0$ *is as small as possible.*

It is also crucial to be robust against trivial solutions – functions that (locally) minimize the loss $\mathcal{L}$, yet have no ability to discern between normal and anomalous samples – since such solutions render the model useless for anomaly detection.

Axiom 3 (Robustness to Trivial Solutions). *There should be no trivial solution* $f_{trivial}$ *such that* $\nabla \mathcal{L}(f_{trivial}) = 0$ *and* $f_{trivial}(x) \approx c$ *for all* $x \in \mathbb{R}^d$ *and some constant* $c \in \mathbb{R}^k$.

Hyperparameter selection poses a significant challenge in anomaly detection [15,59]. Thus, an optimal surrogate should exhibit stability under reasonable variations in hyperparameters, that do not fundamentally alter the model's methodological design or learning dynamics.

Axiom 4 (Hyperparameter Invariance). *For any two reasonable hyperparameter sets* H_A *and* H_B, *let* f_{H_A} *and* f_{H_B} *be the corresponding learned models. Then the performance difference should be bounded as* $|m(f_{H_A}) - m(f_{H_B})| \leq \eta$, *where* $\eta > 0$ *is chosen to be as small as possible.*

Finally, because anomalies can be both complex and subtle, it is imperative that the surrogate model possesses sufficient expressive power. The model must be able to capture intricate patterns in the data, allowing it to accurately distinguish between normal and anomalous behavior.

Axiom 5 (Complex Pattern Learning). *The learnable function f needs to be represented by a universal function approximator, capable of approximating any continuous function* $g : \mathbb{R}^d \to \mathbb{R}^k$ *to arbitrary precision on subsets of* $\mathbb{R}^d$.

3.2 Axiom Compliance

Both of the most established deep anomaly detection paradigms that conform to our surrogate definition exhibit significant deviations from the proposed axioms, highlighting inherent limitations in their design.

Autoencoder: An Autoencoder [53] defines its surrogate usually via the identity function $g_{AE}(x) = x$, training a neural network to reconstruct its input while enforcing a compression step to prevent the trivial layer-by-layer identity mapping. However, this approach violates Axiom 4 because the latent dimensionality must be carefully chosen, which critically affects performance. Moreover, autoencoders can converge to local minima – such as outputting the mean of the training samples (violating Axiom 3) – and the lack of consistent scaling in g results in biased anomaly scores (violating Axiom 1).

DeepSVDD: DeepSVDD [51] constructs its surrogate model using a constant pattern function $g_{SVDD}(x) = c$, where c is a predetermined constant, usually chosen as the mean output of the initialized network. To mitigate the risk of learning a trivial constant prediction, the method suggests avoiding bounded activation functions and removing the learnable shifts[1] from each network layer. Unfortunately, the latter restriction limits the network's capacity to learn complex patterns, thereby breaching either Axiom 3 or Axiom 5.

4 A Minimal Surrogate: The DEAN Model

Given that no surrogate known to us adheres to all aforementioned axioms, we propose a novel deep learning-based approach. We observe that increased complexity in the pattern function g often leads to arbitrary weighting of different samples (Axiom 1) and intensifies challenges during training for the function f that needs to be learned (Axioms 2 and 3). Thus, we advocate for selecting the simplest possible function g that adequately identifies the essential data patterns.

Depending on the measure of complexity, one might consider $g_0(x) = 0$ as the simplest option. However, this surrogate violates Axiom 3 by introducing a local minimum where every weight in the last layer becomes zero [51]. Although such a minimum might not always be reached [27] or could be avoided using regularization, these strategies would, in turn, compromise our remaining axioms. Instead, we propose $g_{DEAN}(x) = 1$ and the surrogate generated by it. While a local minimum may still occur via the learnable shifts in the final layer, it is more manageable, as we demonstrate later (Sect. 4.2).

Thus, we train a neural network to output a constant value of 1. In accordance with our framework, the loss and score functions are defined as

$$\mathcal{L} = \sum_{x \in X_{train}} \|f(x) - 1\|, \qquad score(x) = \|f(x) - q\| \qquad (4)$$

where

$$q = \frac{1}{\|X_{\text{train}}\|} \sum_{x_T \in X_{\text{train}}} f(x_T) \approx 1$$

This choice of q ensures that the distribution of normal samples is centered, thereby improving the robustness of the anomaly score.

---
[1] We refer to the bias term of a neural network as "learnable shift" to reduce confusion.

Since we only learn a one-dimensional pattern with this approach, the model may, in the worst case, fix only one feature as a function of the remaining ones, which can lead to an increased number of false negatives. While one might extend g to a higher-dimensional constant vector $g(x) = (1, 1, \ldots, 1)^T$, this typically results in significantly correlated outputs across the network's features and may violate Axiom 4. To address these challenges, we propose using an ensemble of surrogates. Specifically, we combine many independently trained submodels with g_{DEAN} into a more effective model F. An integer constant, denoted by *power*, guides the aggregation of these models:

$$score_F(x) = \frac{1}{\|F\|} \sum_{f_i \in F} \|f_i(x) - q_i\|^{power} \qquad (5)$$

where each q_i is computed analogously to q. Owing to the simplicity of our surrogate, training each neural network takes only seconds, thus allowing us to combine a large number of submodels. The use of fully independent networks facilitates parallelization, reduces the correlation among learned patterns, and permits the application of ensemble methods such as feature bagging [36] to further improve diversity and runtime consistency in high-dimensional settings. Feature bagging additionally can ensure a constant number of features for each submodel, resulting in a close-to-constant runtime for higher dimensional data.

We refer to this overall setup as *DEAN* (Deep Ensemble ANomaly detection).

4.1 DEAN Parameterization

In our instantiation of DEAN, we advocate for a diverse ensemble of simple and efficient feedforward networks.

Network Architecture: We use a basic Multi-Layer Perceptron (MLP) with only a few hidden layers. Hidden layers are constructed with bias terms and use ReLU activations, while the output layer excludes a bias term and employs a SELU activation to mitigate the risk of dead neurons.

Ensemble Structure: A large ensemble size allows specialization in a variety of different patterns. For high-dimensional datasets, feature bagging is used to promote the diversity of submodels by training each on a random subset of the available features. For datasets with few features, all of them may be used to ensure critical correlations are captured.

Power Parameter: The *power* parameter allows controlling the sensitivity of the aggregated anomaly score. A higher value accentuates significant deviations in one model over multiple smaller deviations across models.

Training Configuration: A lower-than-standard learning rate is paired with a relatively high batch size. This configuration not only stabilizes training but also encourages the network to converge towards local minima, which is beneficial for ensemble diversity.

4.2 Axiom Compliance of DEAN

DEAN is designed to fulfill all of our surrogate axioms. Since $g(x) = 1$ for all x, Axiom 1 (Scale Consistency) is satisfied. The compliance with Axioms 2 (Reliable Training Procedure) and 4 (Hyperparameter Invariance) is best evaluated via experimental comparisons (see Sect. 5.4). We now discuss the more challenging Axioms 3 (Robustness to Trivial Solutions) and 5 (Complex Pattern Learning). These are non-trivial because the meaningless function $f_{trivial}(x) = 0 \cdot x + 1$ perfectly minimizes the DEAN loss and is independent of its input.

Axiom 3: Given its ensemble structure, DEAN inherently mitigates trivial solutions. In the event that they occur, their contribution to the ensemble anomaly score is zero since $f_{trivial}(x) = 1$ for all x implies that $\|f_{trivial}(x) - q\| = 0$. Thus, with a sufficient number of submodels, the overall performance of DEAN remains unaffected by any individual trivial solution.

Axiom 5: DeepSVDD addresses a similar issue of trivial solutions by removing learnable shifts entirely [51]; however, this approach limits the network's capacity and violates Axiom 5. To still mitigate this risk, while preserving expressiveness, we remove learnable shifts only from the final layer. This adjustment increases the complexity required to achieve a trivial solution, making it less likely to be reached during training, while ensuring that the network retains the ability to approximate any function (see Appendix B).

5 Experimental Evaluation

To experimentally evaluate our method, we refer to the protocol outlined in the survey paper ADBench [21]. ADBench recommends 121 datasets (57 of which are entirely uncorrelated) for benchmarking unsupervised anomaly detection algorithms, as well as a set of baseline algorithms to compare against.

5.1 Experimental Setup

Following the approach of ADBench, we compare DEAN against a total of 19 state-of-the-art algorithms. This includes KNN [14], LOF [6], CBLOF [22], Isolation Forest [39], PCA [9], DeepSVDD [51], OCSVM [5], LODA [47], HBOS [19], COPOD [37], ECOD [38], SOD [34] and DAGMM [60]. In addition, we consider a regular Autoencoder [53], as it is also a surrogate algorithm, as well as a variational autoencoder [28] and a normalizing flow [49] as deep learning density-based competitors. To further capture recent advances not originally considered in ADBench, we also compare against NeuTral-AD [48] (which leverages contrastive learning), DTE [40] (based on diffusion models), and GOAD [4] (which employs geometric transformations). In contrast to ADBench, all models are trained on uncontaminated data (one-class setting).

For the parameterization of DEAN, we adhere to the guidelines proposed in Sect. 4.1 in order to train an ensemble of 100 submodels for 50 epochs each, using early stopping with a patience of 10 epochs. We adopt the following specific hyperparameter choices: A feedforward neural network with three hidden layers of 255 neurons each. A lower-than-standard learning rate of 0.0001 and a rather high batch size of 512. Feature bagging with 200 random features per model for datasets containing at least 200 features. A power parameter set to 9, emphasizing pronounced deviations in anomaly detection. We consider variations in ensemble size and other hyperparameters in Sects. 5.3 and 5.4. Detailed information regarding the implementation and parameterization of the compared methods can be found in our code repository.

5.2 Anomaly Detection Performance

Table 1. Distribution of AUC-ROC performance for all evaluated algorithms. Deep learning models (blue) and shallow models (yellow) are differentiated by surrogate status (squares for surrogates, triangles for non-surrogates). Mean and median values are shown in green and purple, respectively.

Algorithm	AUC-ROC (all)	AUC-ROC (larger half of datasets)
■ DEAN		
■ Autoencoder [53]		
■ DeepSVDD [51]		
■ PCA [9]		
▼ NF [49]		
▼ DTE [40]		
▼ GOAD [4]		
▼ DAGMM [60]		
▼ NeuTral [48]		
▼ VAE [28]		
▼ SOD [34]		
▼ OCSVM [5]		
▼ LOF [6]		
▼ LODA [47]		
▼ KNN [14]		
▼ IForest [39]		
▼ HBOS [19]		
▼ ECOD [38]		
▼ COPOD [37]		
▼ CBLOF [22]		

Our primary performance evaluation metric is the Area Under the Receiver Operating Characteristic (AUC-ROC). For additional insight, we provide a complementary evaluation based on the Area Under the Precision-Recall Curve (AUC-PR), alongside individual results for each dataset, in Appendix E and F.

A summarization of the observed AUC-ROC performance is given in Table 1. Consistent with the results from ADBench, our analysis shows that no method outperforms all others in a statistically significant manner across all datasets. Our algorithm performs highly competitively when averaged across all datasets and is only slightly outperformed by KNN and LOF. These competitors do not scale well to the more challenging datasets. Thus, when only considering the larger half of the datasets studied here, the median performance of DEAN is higher than all competitors considered.

To further illustrate our findings and provide a concise ranking of performance, we provide the critical difference diagrams in Fig. 2. In these diagrams, a Friedman test [17] is used to determine if significant differences exist between algorithm performances (measured in AUC-ROC), and algorithms with no significant differences are connected using a Wilcoxon test [56]. We consider p-values below $p \leq 5\%$ after Bonferroni-Holm correction [26] to be significant.

Notably, DEAN performs significantly stronger than every other surrogate or deep learning algorithm, with the exception of NeuTral (see Fig. 2a). Similar to ADBench, widely recognized shallow algorithms such as KNN, LOF, and CBLOF remain strong competitors. Our algorithm outperforms CBLOF, but does not quite achieve the same average rank as KNN and LOF. We attribute this outcome to the fact that benchmark datasets are often low-dimensional, contain a large number of samples, and exhibit anomalies that are relatively simple in nature. This combination favors distance-based methods, as differences in local densities are more pronounced; however, they may not capture the complexity encountered in real-world applications. Moreover, the lazy learning paradigm intrinsic to KNN and LOF, which necessitates the retention of training instances during inference, is well known to scale badly to large, high-dimensional datasets [1].

For instance, when considering only the larger half of the datasets, DEAN emerges as the best fit, outperforming every competitor (see Fig. 2b). This performance advantage, coupled with its scalability and robust learning framework, makes DEAN particularly well suited for advanced tasks where the expressive power of neural networks is needed without introducing unnecessary complexity.

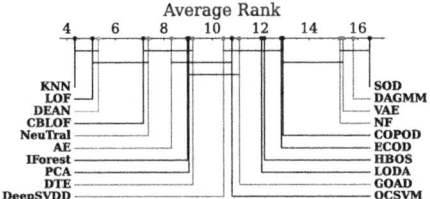
(a) Using all ADBench datasets.

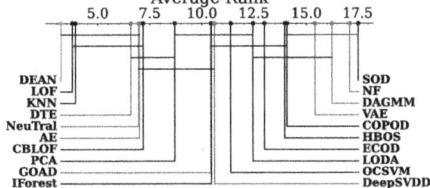
(b) Using only the larger half of datasets.

Fig. 2. Critical difference diagrams comparing the AUC-ROC performance. A lower rank indicates better performance, while algorithms with no statistically significant differences are connected by a horizontal line. DEAN is depicted in green, other deep learning algorithms in blue. (Color figure online)

5.3 Runtime and Ensemble Analysis

Figure 3 provides an overview of our runtime measurements and the impact of using (larger) ensembles on the performance of deep learning-based surrogate models. To this end, Fig. 3a reports both the median and maximum runtimes across datasets to account for the substantial variability in dataset sizes. All experiments were conducted on a system running Ubuntu 22.04.3 LTS, powered by an Intel® Xeon® w9-3495X processor with a base clock of approximately 3400 MHz and turbo boost frequencies up to around 4500 MHz and with 495 GB of RAM available. The runtime measurements were obtained using single-core execution for each algorithm to ensure a fair comparison.

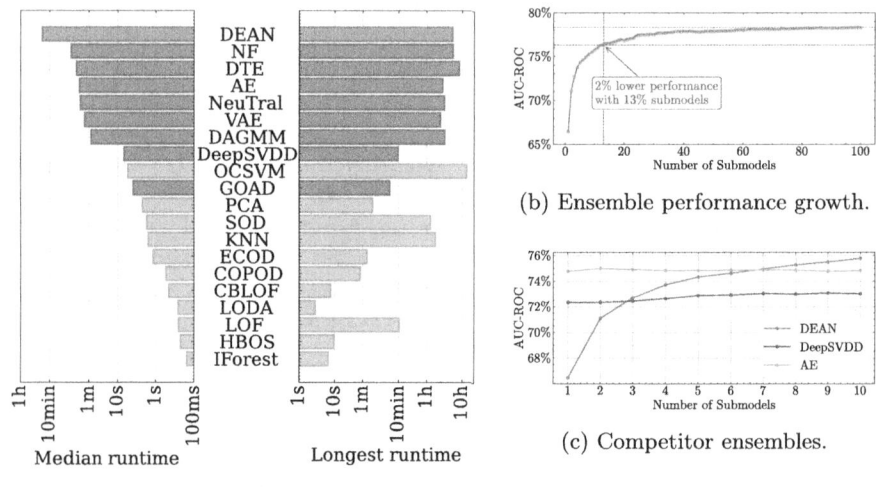

Fig. 3. (a) Overall runtime overview across all datasets; DEAN is depicted in green, other deep learning algorithms in blue, and shallow algorithms in yellow. (b) and (c) average AUC-ROC performance changes with varying ensemble size. (Color figure online)

As expected, deep learning methods generally exhibit longer runtimes, with the DEAN ensemble showing a median runtime of approximately 15 min per dataset. Notably, for a DEAN ensemble comprising 100 submodels, this corresponds to an average training time of less than 9 sec per submodel. However, it is important to emphasize that deep learning methods are particularly well-suited for GPU acceleration, and DEAN, as an ensemble method of independently optimized submodels, can be almost perfectly parallelized. Furthermore, due to the use of feature bagging, the worst-case runtime scenario is significantly mitigated, with most deep learning approaches requiring comparable or even longer runtimes.

Naturally, the runtime is also rather sensitive to the number of submodels. As illustrated in Fig. 3b, while increasing the number of submodels improves performance, the relationship is non-linear. Using only 13 submodels results in an average performance that is merely 2% lower than that achieved with 100 submodels, yet it requires approximately 87% less training time. At the same time, the continued performance improvement with additional submodels reflects the high variance of the individual models used in DEAN, incentivized by the simplicity of the submodels. In contrast, Fig. 3c shows that ensembles based on Autoencoder or DeepSVDD methods exhibit nearly constant performance, likely due to their complex, less diverse submodel characteristics.

5.4 Evaluation of Axiom Compliance

Compliance with Axioms 2 and 4 is difficult to assess theoretically, therefore we evaluate these properties experimentally on the same datasets. For Axiom 2, Fig. 4 demonstrates that the repetition uncertainty of DEAN – calculated as the standard deviation across 10 runs per datasets and then averaged – is lower than that observed for other surrogate deep learning algorithms under identical training conditions. For Axiom 4, we present DEAN's performance when evaluated with modified hyperparameter sets. Since the average performances are nearly equal, one may argue that the influence of such modifications is negligible. This is also in stark contrast to DeepSVDD [21] and Autoencoder [35] behavior.

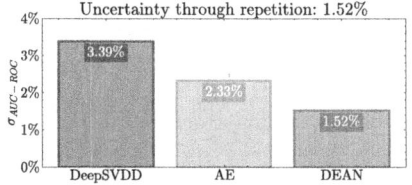
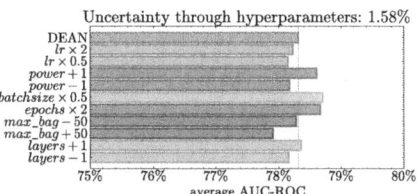

Fig. 4. Left: Repetition uncertainty for various surrogate algorithms, Right: DEAN performance with varied hyperparameters and the resulting uncertainty.

6 Anomaly Detection Beyond Benchmarks

While DEAN reliably achieves competitive performance with an easy-to-configure parameterization, real-world applications often demand flexibility beyond standard benchmarks. The simplicity of our submodels and the inherent ensemble structure render DEAN highly adaptable.

For instance, the ensemble structure facilitates explainability via Shapley values [29]; feature bagging helps mitigate the high computational cost of such methods. In addition, the ensemble character natively supports a distributed implementation through federated learning [55]. The ensemble also enables the incorporation of secondary requirements, such as robustness against adversarial attacks by pruning or reweighting less robust submodels [8]. The simplicity of each submodel also permits modifications in the training procedure to incorporate additional information [31], such as in semi-supervised anomaly detection [52] or outlier exposure [23]. Moreover, employing different machine learning models within the DEAN framework can yield lightweight variants suitable for resource-constrained devices such as IoT systems [32].

To summarize, we see three major ways DEAN can be adapted: (1) altering the selection of submodels, (2) adjusting the ensemble weighting, and (3) modifying the submodel training procedure. As a proof-of-concept, we apply all three adaptations for the task of fair anomaly detection [58] (see Appendix B).

7 Conclusion

In this paper, we present the first systematic study of surrogate models for anomaly detection and establish a comprehensive framework for constructing such models from mathematical functions. We propose five axioms that any optimal surrogate anomaly detection algorithm should satisfy and employ these axioms to develop DEAN, a novel algorithm that meets all of them.

An extensive evaluation demonstrates that it not only performs competitively – particularly excelling over other deep learning-based methods and alternative surrogates – but also offers exceptional adaptability. In the future, we believe that the axiomatic design of DEAN, based on an ensemble of simple submodels, can furthermore facilitate straightforward modifications to enhance secondary anomaly detection goals, like explainability, adversarial robustness, or fairness.

Acknowledgements. This work was supported by the Lamarr-Institute for ML and AI, the Research Center Trustworthy Data Science and Security, the Federal Ministry of Education and Research of Germany and the German federal state of NRW. The Linux HPC cluster at TU Dortmund University, a project of the German Research Foundation, provided the computing power.

References

1. Aggarwal, C.C.: Outlier Analysis. Springer (2013). https://doi.org/10.1007/978-1-4614-6396-2
2. Aggarwal, C.C., Sathe, S.: Theoretical foundations and algorithms for outlier ensembles. SIGKDD Explor. Newsl. **17**(1), 24–47 (2015). https://doi.org/10.1145/2830544.2830549
3. Bellman, R.: Dynamic programming. Science **153**(3731), 34–37 (1966)
4. Bergman, L., Hoshen, Y.: Classification-based anomaly detection for general data. In: International Conference on Learning Representations (ICLR) 2020 (2020). https://openreview.net/forum?id=H1lK_lBtvS

5. Bounsiar, A., Madden, M.G.: One-class support vector machines revisited. In: 2014 International Conference on Information Science Applications (ICISA), pp. 1–4 (2014). https://doi.org/10.1109/ICISA.2014.6847442
6. Breunig, M., Kröger, P., Ng, R., Sander, J.: LOF: identifying density-based local outliers, vol. 29, pp. 93–104 (2000). https://doi.org/10.1145/342009.335388
7. Buschjäger, S., Honysz, P.J., Morik, K.: Randomized outlier detection with trees. Int. J. Data Sci. Analytics **13**(2), 91–104 (2022). https://doi.org/10.1007/s41060-020-00238-w
8. Böing, B., Klüttermann, S., Müller, E.: Post-robustifying deep anomaly detection ensembles by model selection. In: 2022 IEEE International Conference on Data Mining (ICDM), pp. 861–866 (2022). https://doi.org/10.1109/ICDM54844.2022.00098
9. Callegari, C., Gazzarrini, L., Giordano, S., Pagano, M., Pepe, T.: A novel PCA-based network anomaly detection, pp. 1 – 5 (2011). https://doi.org/10.1109/icc.2011.5962595
10. Castro, C.M.R.I.I.P.M.: Detecting falls as novelties in acceleration patterns acquired with smartphones. PLoS ONE **9**, None (2014). https://doi.org/10.1371/journal.pone.0094811
11. Chakraborty, D., Narayanan, V., Ghosh, A.: Integration of deep feature extraction and ensemble learning for outlier detection. Pattern Recogn. **89**, 161–171 (2019). https://doi.org/10.1016/j.patcog.2019.01.002
12. Chen, J., Sathe, S., Aggarwal, C., Turaga, D.: Outlier detection with autoencoder ensembles, pp. 90–98 (2017). https://doi.org/10.1137/1.9781611974973.11
13. Chen, W., Li, H., Li, J., Arshad, A.: Autoencoder-based outlier detection for sparse, high dimensional data, pp. 2735–2742 (2020). https://doi.org/10.1109/BigData50022.2020.9378325
14. Cunningham, P., Delany, S.: k-nearest neighbour classifiers. Mult. Classif. Syst. **54** (2007). https://doi.org/10.1145/3459665
15. Ding, X., Zhao, L., Akoglu, L.: Hyperparameter sensitivity in deep outlier detection: analysis and a scalable hyper-ensemble solution. In: Advances in Neural Information Processing Systems, vol. 35, pp. 9603–9616. Curran Associates, Inc. (2022). https://proceedings.neurips.cc/paper_files/paper/2022/file/3e9113e2bc2e700baa7d765470f140e1-Paper-Conference.pdf
16. Flusser, M., Somol, P.: Efficient anomaly detection through surrogate neural networks. Neural Comput. Appl. **34**, 1–15 (2022). https://doi.org/10.1007/s00521-022-07506-9
17. Friedman, M.: A comparison of alternative tests of significance for the problem of m rankings. Ann. Math. Stat. **11**, 86–92 (1940)
18. Fung, C., Qiu, C., Li, A., Rudolph, M.: Model selection of anomaly detectors in the absence of labeled validation data. IEEE Trans. Artif. Intell. (2025). https://doi.org/10.1109/TAI.2025.3562505
19. Goldstein, M., Dengel, A.R.: Histogram-based outlier score (HBOS): a fast unsupervised anomaly detection algorithm (2012). https://api.semanticscholar.org/CorpusID:3590788
20. Gu, X., Akoglu, L., Rinaldo, A.: Statistical analysis of nearest neighbor methods for anomaly detection. In: Neural Information Processing Systems (NeurIPS), pp. 10921–10931 (2019). http://dblp.uni-trier.de/db/conf/nips/nips2019.html#GuAR19
21. Han, S., Hu, X., Huang, H., Jiang, M., Zhao, Y.: Adbench: anomaly detection benchmark. In: Neural Information Processing Systems (NeurIPS) (2022).

https://proceedings.neurips.cc/paper_files/paper/2022/file/cf93972b116ca5268827d575f2cc226b-Paper-Datasets_and_Benchmarks.pdf
22. He, Z., Xu, X., Deng, S.: Discovering cluster-based local outliers. Pattern Recogn. Lett. **24**(9), 1641–1650 (2003). https://doi.org/10.1016/S0167-8655(03)00003-5
23. Hendrycks, D., Mazeika, M., Dietterich, T.: Deep anomaly detection with outlier exposure. arXiv:1812.04606 (2019)
24. Hilal, W., Gadsden, S.A., Yawney, J.: Financial fraud: a review of anomaly detection techniques and recent advances. Exp. Syst. Appl. **193** (2022). https://doi.org/10.1016/j.eswa.2021.116429
25. Hoffer, E., Ailon, N.: Deep metric learning using triplet network. In: Similarity-Based Pattern Recognition (2015). https://api.semanticscholar.org/CorpusID:2784676
26. Holm, S.: A simple sequentially rejective multiple test procedure. Scand. J. Stat. **6**(2), 65–70 (1979). http://www.jstor.org/stable/4615733
27. Karr, N., Nachman, B., Shih, D.: One-class dense networks for anomaly detection. In: Proceedings of the Machine Learning and the Physical Sciences Workshop at NeurIPS 2022 (2022). https://ml4physicalsciences.github.io/2022/files/NeurIPS_ML4PS_2022_130.pdf
28. Kingma, D., Welling, M.: Auto-encoding variational bayes (2014). https://doi.org/10.61603/ceas.v2i1.33
29. Klüttermann, S., Balestra, C., Müller, E.: On the efficient explanation of outlier detection ensembles through shapley values. In: Advances in Knowledge Discovery and Data Mining, pp. 43–55 (2024). https://doi.org/10.1007/978-981-97-2259-4_4
30. Klüttermann, S., Müller, E.: Evaluating and comparing heterogeneous ensemble methods for unsupervised anomaly detection (2023). https://doi.org/10.1109/IJCNN54540.2023.10191405
31. Klüttermann, S., Müller, E.: About test-time training for outlier detection. arXiv:2404.03495 (2024)
32. Klüttermann, S., Peka, V., Doebler, P., Müller, E.: Towards highly efficient anomaly detection for predictive maintenance. In: 2024 International Conference on Machine Learning and Applications (ICMLA), pp. 1691–1696 (2024). https://doi.org/10.1109/ICMLA61862.2024.00261
33. Koziel, S., Ciaurri, D.E., Leifsson, L.: Surrogate-Based Methods, pp. 33–59. Springer Berlin Heidelberg, Berlin, Heidelberg (2011). https://doi.org/10.1007/978-3-642-20859-1_3
34. Kriegel, H.P., Kröger, P., Schubert, E., Zimek, A.: Outlier detection in axis-parallel subspaces of high dimensional data. In: Advances in Knowledge Discovery and Data Mining, pp. 831–838 (2009). https://doi.org/10.1007/978-3-642-01307-2_86
35. Kumar, V., Srivastava, V., Mahjabin, S., Pal, A., Klüttermann, S., Müller, E.: Autoencoder optimization for anomaly detection: a comparative study with shallow algorithms. In: International Joint Conference on Neural Networks (IJCNN). https://psorus.github.io/papers/vikas.pdf
36. Lazarevic, A., Kumar, V.: Feature bagging for outlier detection. In: KDD 2005, Proceedings of the Eleventh ACM SIGKDD International Conference on Knowledge Discovery in Data Mining, p. 157–166 (2005). https://doi.org/10.1145/1081870.1081891
37. Li, Z., Zhao, Y., Botta, N., Ionescu, C., Hu, X.: Copod: copula-based outlier detection. In: 2020 IEEE International Conference on Data Mining (ICDM) (2020). https://doi.org/10.1109/ICDM50108.2020.00135

38. Li, Z., Zhao, Y., Hu, X., Botta, N., Ionescu, C., Chen, G.H.: ECOD: unsupervised outlier detection using empirical cumulative distribution functions. IEEE Trans. Knowl. Data Eng. **35**(12), 12181–12193 (2023). https://doi.org/10.1109/TKDE.2022.3159580
39. Liu, F.T., Ting, K.M., Zhou, Z.H.: Isolation forest. In: International Conference on Data Mining (ICDM) (2008). https://doi.org/10.1109/ICDM.2008.17
40. Livernoche, V., Jain, V., Hezaveh, Y., Ravanbakhsh, S.: On diffusion modeling for anomaly detection. In: International Conference on Learning Representations (ICLR) 2024 (2024). https://openreview.net/forum?id=lR3rk7ysXz
41. Lu, Z., Pu, H., Wang, F., Hu, Z., Wang, L.: The expressive power of neural networks: a view from the width. In: NIPS 2017, Proceedings of the 31st International Conference on Neural Information Processing Systems, pp. 6232–6240. Curran Associates Inc., Red Hook, NY, USA (2017). https://doi.org/10.5555/3295222.3295371
42. Ma, M.Q., Zhao, Y., Zhang, X., Akoglu, L.: The need for unsupervised outlier model selection: a review and evaluation of internal evaluation strategies. ACM SIGKDD Explor. Newsl. **25**(1) (2023). https://doi.org/10.1145/3606274.3606277
43. Mattia, F.D., Galeone, P., Simoni, M.D., Ghelfi, E.: A survey on GANs for anomaly detection. arXiv:1906.11632 (2021)
44. Monteiro, W.R., Reynoso-Meza, G.: A multi-objective optimization design to generate surrogate machine learning models in explainable artificial intelligence applications. EURO J. Decisi. Processes **11**, 100040 (2023). https://doi.org/10.1016/j.ejdp.2023.100040
45. Mora-Mariano, D., Flores-Tlacuahuac, A.: A machine learning approach for the surrogate modeling of uncertain distributed process engineering models. Chem. Eng. Res. Des. **186**, 433–450 (2022). https://doi.org/10.1016/j.cherd.2022.07.050
46. Olteanu, M., Rossi, F., Yger, F.: Meta-survey on outlier and anomaly detection. Neurocomputing **555**, 126634 (2023). https://doi.org/10.1016/j.neucom.2023.126634
47. Pevný, T.: Loda: lightweight on-line detector of anomalies. Mach. Learn. **102**(2), 275–304 (2015). https://doi.org/10.1007/s10994-015-5521-0
48. Qiu, C., Pfrommer, T., Kloft, M., Mandt, S., Rudolph, M.: Neural transformation learning for deep anomaly detection beyond images. In: International Conference on Machine Learning, pp. 8703–8714. PMLR (2021). https://proceedings.mlr.press/v139/qiu21a.html
49. Rezende, D.J., Mohamed, S.: Variational inference with normalizing flows. In: ICML 2015, Proceedings of the 32nd International Conference on International Conference on Machine Learning - Volume 37, pp. 1530–1538. JMLR.org (2015). https://dl.acm.org/doi/10.5555/3045118.3045281
50. Ribeiro, M.T., Singh, S., Guestrin, C.: "why should i trust you?": explaining the predictions of any classifier. In: Proceedings of the 22nd ACM SIGKDD International Conference on Knowledge Discovery and Data Mining, pp. 1135–1144 (2016). https://doi.org/10.1145/2939672.2939778
51. Ruff, L., et al.: Deep one-class classification. In: Proceedings of the 35th International Conference on Machine Learning, pp. 4393–4402 (2018). https://proceedings.mlr.press/v80/ruff18a.html
52. Ruff, L., et al.: Deep semi-supervised anomaly detection. In: 8th International Conference on Learning Representations, ICLR 2020, Addis Abeba, Ethiopia, April 26–30, 2020. OpenReview.net (2020). https://openreview.net/forum?id=HkgH0TEYwH

53. Sakurada, M., Yairi, T.: Anomaly detection using autoencoders with nonlinear dimensionality reduction. In: MLSDA 2014, Proceedings of the MLSDA 2014 2nd Workshop on Machine Learning for Sensory Data Analysis, pp. 4–11 (2014). https://doi.org/10.1145/2689746.2689747
54. Sudret, B., Marelli, S., Wiart, J.: Surrogate models for uncertainty quantification: an overview. In: 2017 11th European Conference on Antennas and Propagation (2017). https://doi.org/10.23919/EuCAP.2017.7928679
55. Wang, X., Wang, Y., Javaheri, Z., Almutairi, L., Moghadamnejad, N., Younes, O.S.: Federated deep learning for anomaly detection in the internet of things. Comput. Electr. Eng. **108**, 108651 (2023). https://doi.org/10.1016/j.compeleceng.2023.108651
56. Wilcoxon, F.: Individual Comparisons by Ranking Methods, pp. 196–202. Springer, New York (1992). https://doi.org/10.1007/978-1-4612-4380-9_16
57. Ye, F., Zheng, H., Huang, C., Zhang, Y.: Deep unsupervised image anomaly detection: an information theoretic framework. In: 2021 IEEE International Conference on Image Processing (ICIP), pp. 1609–1613 (2021). https://doi.org/10.1109/ICIP42928.2021.9506079
58. Zhang, H., Davidson, I.: Towards fair deep anomaly detection. In: FAccT 2021, Proceedings of the 2021 ACM Conference on Fairness, Accountability, and Transparency, pp. 138–148. Association for Computing Machinery, New York (2021). https://doi.org/10.1145/3442188.3445878
59. Zhao, Y., Rossi, R., Akoglu, L.: Automatic unsupervised outlier model selection. In: Advances in Neural Information Processing Systems, vol. 34, pp. 4489–4502 (2021). https://proceedings.neurips.cc/paper_files/paper/2021/file/23c894276a2c5a16470e6a31f4618d73-Paper.pdf
60. Zong, B., Song, Q., Min, M.R., Cheng, W., Lumezanu, C., ki Cho, D., Chen, H.: Deep autoencoding gaussian mixture model for unsupervised anomaly detection. In: International Conference on Learning Representations (2018). https://api.semanticscholar.org/CorpusID:51805340

Multivariate Time Series Anomaly Prediction Based on Forecasting and Reconstruction Using Transformer with Temporal and Feature-Wise Attention

Chihiro Maru[1]([✉]), Masato Oguchi[2], and Ichiro Kobayashi[2]

[1] Faculty of Science and Engineering, Chuo University, Tokyo, Japan
cmaru671@g.chuo-u.ac.jp
[2] Graduate School of Humanities and Sciences, Ochanomizu University, Tokyo, Japan
{oguchi,koba}@is.ocha.ac.jp

Abstract. Anomaly detection has been actively studied, enabling the high-accuracy detection of anomalies. However, because anomaly detection assumes that an anomaly has already occurred, detecting future anomalies before they occur and preventing them from happening is impossible. Therefore, we develop a Transformer-based Anomaly Prediction (TranAP) method, which is designed to detect future anomalies. TranAP predicts future values from previous time series and uses reconstruction techniques to detect signs of anomalies using the predicted results. Detecting these precursors requires a correct understanding of the temporal characteristics of the multivariate time series (MTS). Because the timing of behavior leading to an anomaly may differ for each feature, we apply multi-head attention (ATTN) in the time dimension for each feature. Additionally, TranAP captures the dependencies between different features that the conventional ATTN could not. Because the effect of ATTN is partially diminished within the attention block, even after improvement to capture detailed information in MTS, we modify the operation of the block to preserve this effect. We demonstrate the effectiveness of TranAP by comparing it with state-of-the-art models. This improved attention mechanism of TranAP allows for a better understanding of behavior that leads to anomalies.

Keywords: anomaly prediction · multivariate time series forecasting · reconstruction · Transformer · attention block · multi-head attention

1 Introduction

Anomaly detection has been extensively studied and has demonstrated high performance. An anomaly, also known as an outlier or novelty, refers to an unusual, irregular, inconsistent, unexpected, rare, faulty, or simply a strange observation,

---

Supplementary Information The online version contains supplementary material available at https://doi.org/10.1007/978-3-032-05962-8_6.

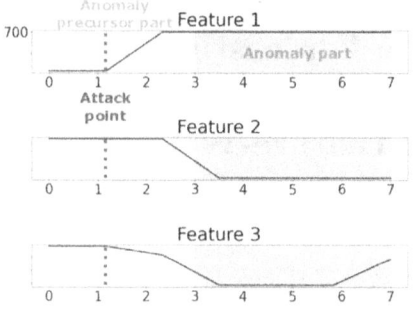
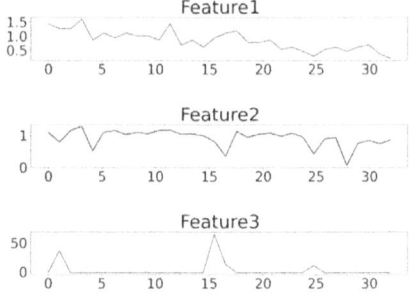

Fig. 1. Example of an anomaly precursor.

Fig. 2. Univariate time series for each feature.

depending on the context. Anomaly detection aims at identifying unexpected patterns or data points in real-world applications. Anomaly detection for multivariate time series (MTS) requires handling time series with several features, and numerous deep learning (DL)-based models have been proposed to address this task [16,26]. Most of these models focus on accurately detecting anomalies that have already occurred, whereas detecting future anomalies before they manifest is increasingly expected. Anomaly prediction is the process of identifying current patterns or signs that may indicate upcoming abnormal events [12]. The goal is to detect these precursors before the occurrence of anomalies, thereby enabling proactive preventive actions.

Figure 1 illustrates the transition of data points for each feature of an MTS obtained from a real-world system. An abnormal event occurs in the anomaly part owing to an external attack that sets the value of feature 1 to 700. However, this anomaly does not occur immediately after the attack. A time lag (the anomaly precursor part in Fig. 1) exists between the attack and the actual occurrence of a critical abnormal event, which is recognized as an anomaly. During this period, the effects of the attack spill over to features other than feature 1, which was initially attacked, and signs triggering an abnormal event can be observed in several features.

PAD proposed an anomaly prediction model that requires anomalous data and an anomaly detection model for training [12]. We propose a Transformer-based Anomaly Prediction (TranAP) method that uses only normal data for training and does not require an anomaly detection model. TranAP uses MTS forecasting, which predicts future values from previous values and determines whether an anomaly will occur in the future by reconstructing the prediction results.

Anomaly prediction requires an accurate understanding of the temporal characteristics of the MTS. The behavior leading to an anomaly may occur at different times for each feature, as shown in Fig. 2. However, general multi-head attention (ATTN) cannot capture each characteristic. Furthermore, because MTS anomaly prediction targets data with several features, more detailed MTS characteristics can be extracted by capturing the dependencies between the features.

Therefore, we enhance ATTN to better capture the different temporal dependencies for each feature as well as the dependencies between features.

In addition, the attention block comprises ATTN, residual connection (RES) [9], and layer normalization (LN) [5], which contribute to the Transformer performance [32]. Previous studies on natural language processing (NLP) revealed that other components cancel the effects of ATTN [13]. To the best of our knowledge, studies on the attention block of the MTS are yet to be conducted. Further research is needed to confirm whether the same observations can be made in MTS as in natural language.

The contributions of this study are as follows:

- We proposed a novel framework specialized for anomaly prediction tasks by utilizing MTS forecasting and reconstruction. Unlike the conventional anomaly prediction model that requires anomalous data and an anomaly detection model for training, the proposed framework does not need them.
- We applied ATTN in the time direction for each feature and also in the feature direction to focus on the behavior leading to anomalies in MTS.
- We found that RES partially cancels the effect of ATTN in the attention block. Based on this finding, we modified the attention block to preserve the strong effect of the improved attention mechanism.
- We evaluated TranAP on five real-world datasets, demonstrating that anomaly prediction using MTS forecasting and reconstruction is effective. Various experiments showed that improving attention mechanisms helps capture the detailed characteristics of MTS.

2 Related Work

Anomaly Detection in MTS. Because anomaly detection requires handling time series with multiple features, numerous anomaly detection models using DL have been proposed [31,34,35,38]. Most of these models focus on detecting anomalies that have already occurred, and cannot detect future anomalies.

Some anomaly detection models use techniques such as autoregression and reconstruction. These models detect anomalies by predicting or reconstructing data points within a given input and comparing them with actual values. TranAP is similar to the aforementioned models because it performs anomaly predictions based on forecasting and reconstruction. However, TranAP predicts future unseen MTS whose actual values are unknown from the given input, and thus cannot perform comparisons during anomaly prediction. Therefore, we adopt a framework to evaluate the results of MTS forecasting by reconstruction (see Sect. 3.2).

Anomaly Prediction. The currently proposed anomaly prediction model called PAD [12] uses training data consisting of normal and pseudo-anomalous data. In the training phase, PAD requires anomaly detection and prediction models; the latter model is trained to imitate the results of the former. Specifically, the anomaly prediction model receives the MTS at timestep $t = T - 1$ to predict whether an anomaly will occur at $t = T$. It is trained to predict the same outcome as the anomaly detection result at $t = T$ obtained by the anomaly detection model. However, it is difficult to prepare all combinations of anomalies

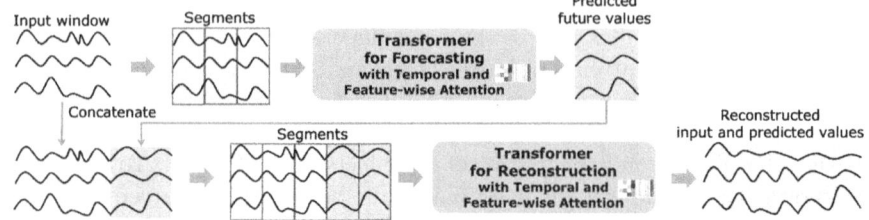

Fig. 3. TranAP architecture. The proposed model consists of Transformer-based forecasting and reconstruction.

and their precursors, and the trained anomaly prediction model has difficulty detecting precursors correctly for unknown anomalies that are not included in the training data [6,36]. Furthermore, the anomaly prediction model requires an anomaly detection model for training, which makes it difficult to train them efficiently.

Transformer Attention Block Analysis. The ATTN, a key component of Transformer, has been analyzed in several studies on NLP [2,10,14,19,21,27]. Transformer is composed of not only ATTN but also these components such as RES and LN. Previous studies have shown that other components cancel the effect of ATTN [13]. However, most Transformer-based models have only improved the ATTN and have not considered the operation of the entire attention block, e.g., [25,31,34,35,37].

MTS Forecasting Using Transformer. MTS forecasting is the task of predicting future MTS values from previous values [18,22,30]. Transformer-based forecasting models have been proposed [7,20,25,33,39,40]. These models improve ATTN and focus on efficiently extracting long-term time dependencies with less computational complexity. Because the MTS has several features, more detailed information about the data can be extracted by capturing the dependencies between features. Crossformer [37] is a Transformer-based model for MTS forecasting that improves ATTN to capture the dependencies between features.

3 Methodology

3.1 Problem Statement

Consider the MTS $\mathcal{X}$ consisting of M data points $\{\mathbf{x}_1, \mathbf{x}_2, \ldots, \mathbf{x}_M\}$, where each data point $\mathbf{x}_t \in \mathbb{R}^D$ is collected at a certain timestep t. $D(D > 1)$ is the number of features in the MTS. We adopt a window-based approach in the anomaly prediction task, similar to [12]. That is, $\mathcal{X}$ is divided into a set of windows of input length T such as $\{\mathbf{x}_{1:T}, \mathbf{x}_{1+step\_size:T+step\_size}, \ldots, \mathbf{x}_{M-T+1:M}\}$, and the input to the model is in window units.

The problem with anomaly prediction is that, given an input window of input length T, we predict whether an anomaly will occur during the next τ timesteps. For example, given an input window $\mathbf{x}_{1:T} \in \mathbb{R}^{T \times D}$ from timestep 1 to T, we predict whether anomalies may occur between timestep $T+1$ and $T+\tau$; that is, whether an unseen $\mathbf{x}_{T+1:T+\tau} \in \mathbb{R}^{\tau \times D}$ contains anomalies. Here, τ denotes the prediction length. In this case, we output $y^{pred}_{T+1:T+\tau} \in \{0,1\}$ (where 1 denotes an anomalous window) for each given window $\mathbf{x}_{1:T}$ as the anomaly prediction result for $\mathbf{x}_{T+1:T+\tau}$. This problem is evaluated for each testing window as in [12]. Given the MTS $\hat{\mathcal{X}}$ for testing, it is divided into a set of windows of input length T as in training. For example, given $\hat{\mathbf{x}}_{1:T}$, we can predict whether an unseen future $\hat{\mathbf{x}}_{T+1:T+\tau}$ is an anomalous window using the trained model. The correct label used for the evaluation is $\hat{y}_{T+1:T+\tau} \in \{0,1\}$, and if $\{\hat{y}_{T+1}, \hat{y}_{T+2}, \ldots, \hat{y}_{T+\tau}\}$ contains one or more abnormal labels, we denote $\hat{y}_{T+1:T+\tau}$ as one.

In the following, we denote an input window as $\mathbf{x}_{1:T}$ and a predicted window as $\mathbf{x}_{T+1:T+\tau}$ for simplicity.

3.2 Model Structure

TranAP mainly consists of Transformer-based MTS forecasting and reconstruction, as illustrated in Fig. 3. We use only normal data for training [3,8]. TranAP enables the detection of any combination of anomalies and their precursors not included in the training dataset. Because the model has already been trained with normal data, it can successfully predict future values when a normal window is given. However, given a window that deviates from normality, the results will not be correct predictions of future trends. Such deviations can be detected as precursors of an anomaly. Similar to TranAP, some anomaly detection models use prediction techniques. However, while these models predict values within an input window, allowing for comparison with actual values, TranAP predicts a future unseen window and thus cannot be compared with actual values. Therefore, we utilize the Transformer for reconstruction to evaluate the results of MTS forecasting. The MTS, which concatenates the input and predicted values, is reconstructed. It is also trained using only normal data, enabling successful reconstruction when it receives a predicted MTS with normality. However, when it receives a predicted MTS that deviates from normality, the reconstruction fails, and the window is determined as a precursor of an anomaly.

3.3 Segmentation of Time Series

In MTS tasks, the segmentation of the input time series contributes to the accuracy of each task [25, 37]. Figure 4 shows the interactions between data points when a window is given to the trained TranAP. The (i,j) cell indicates the extent to which the jth data point on the key side contributes to the computation of the output corresponding to the ith data point on the query side. From Fig. 4, we observe that the interactions

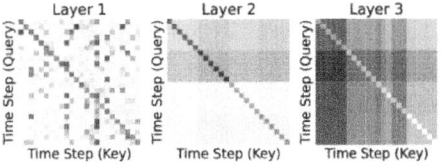

Fig. 4. Interactions between data points in each layer.

tend to be divided into segments, particularly after the second layer. As the characteristics of temporally close data points in the time series are similar, they have similar interactions. Moreover, aggregating information from multiple data points into segments reduces the computational complexity while maintaining the accuracy of the anomaly prediction (see Sect. 5.1). We divide the input window into segments when performing MTS forecasting and reconstruction.

3.4 Temporal and Feature-Wise ATTN

We perform ATTN in the time dimension (temporal ATTN) and feature dimension (feature-wise ATTN) in Transformer-based MTS forecasting and reconstruction.

Temporal ATTN. General Transformer-based models capture the temporal dependencies between input representations by performing ATTN in the time dimension. This computation fails to capture the temporal characteristics of each feature because all features of each input representation share the same attention map and the information of all features at a timestep is aggregated into a single embedding.

Because the timing of behaviors leading to an anomaly differs for each feature, capturing each temporal characteristic is essential for anomaly prediction. Therefore, we perform ATTN on each feature separately in the univariate time series.

Temporal ATTN receives $\mathbf{H} \in \mathbb{R}^{N \times D \times d_{\text{model}}}$ as input, where N is the number of segments. Note that $\mathbf{H}$ is a vector after trainable linear projection added with a positional embedding. We define $\mathbf{H}_{:,d}$ as a vector of all segments with feature $d (1 \leq d \leq D)$. After temporal ATTN (ATTN^{time}), we obtain the output $\mathbf{H}^{\text{time}}$:

$$\hat{\mathbf{H}}^{\text{time}}_{:,d} = \text{LN}\left(\text{ATTN}^{\text{time}}\left(\mathbf{H}_{:,d}, \mathbf{H}_{:,d}, \mathbf{H}_{:,d}\right) + \mathbf{H}_{:,d}\right), \tag{1}$$
$$\mathbf{H}^{\text{time}} = \text{LN}\left(\text{FF}\left(\hat{\mathbf{H}}^{\text{time}}\right) + \hat{\mathbf{H}}^{\text{time}}\right),$$

where FF denotes the feedforward network.

Feature-wise ATTN. Temporal ATTN alone does not capture feature-wise dependencies. We apply ATTN in the feature dimension (ATTN^{feature}) after performing temporal ATTN:

$$\hat{\mathbf{H}}^{\text{feature}}_{i,:} = \text{LN}\left(\text{ATTN}^{\text{feature}}\left(\mathbf{H}^{\text{time}}_{i,:}, \mathbf{H}^{\text{time}}_{i,:}, \mathbf{H}^{\text{time}}_{i,:}\right) + \mathbf{H}^{\text{time}}_{i,:}\right), \tag{2}$$
$$\mathbf{H}^{\text{feature}} = \text{LN}\left(\hat{\mathbf{H}}^{\text{feature}} + \text{FF}\left(\hat{\mathbf{H}}^{\text{feature}}\right)\right),$$

where $\mathbf{H}_{i,:}$ is a vector of all features of the ith $(1 \leq i \leq N)$ segment.

3.5 Effect of ATTN

Although many Transformer-based models have improved the attention mechanism, [13] reported that RES cancels the effect of ATTN in NLP. Therefore, we investigate the operation in the attention block when dealing with the MTS.

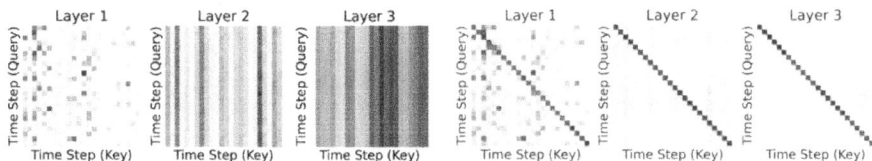

(a) ATTN mixes input representations other than its own. (b) RES preserves the original information.

Fig. 5. Interactions between representations in each layer.

Transformer consists of layers with an attention block. The attention block comprises three components: ATTN, RES, and LN.

$$\widetilde{\mathbf{H}} = \mathrm{LN} \underbrace{(\mathrm{ATTN}\,(\mathbf{H},\mathbf{H},\mathbf{H}) + \mathbf{H})}_{\mathrm{RES}}, \qquad (3)$$

where $\mathbf{H} := [\mathbf{h}_1, \mathbf{h}_2, \ldots, \mathbf{h}_L] \in \mathbb{R}^{L \times d_{\mathrm{model}}}$ is the sequence of input representations, and $\mathbf{h}_i \in \mathbb{R}^{d_{\mathrm{model}}}$ is the ith input representation. $\widetilde{\mathbf{H}} := [\widetilde{\mathbf{h}}_1, \widetilde{\mathbf{h}}_2, \ldots, \widetilde{\mathbf{h}}_L] \in \mathbb{R}^{L \times d_{\mathrm{model}}}$ is the sequence of output representations, and $\widetilde{\mathbf{h}}_i \in \mathbb{R}^{d_{\mathrm{model}}}$ is the output corresponding to $\mathbf{h}_i$.

Among these components, ATTN and RES have contrasting effects on the computation of output representations. While ATTN mixes the input representations, RES preserves the original input representations.

We can visualize the interactions between the representations after ATTN and RES in each layer when a window is provided to the trained TranAP in Fig. 5. The (i, j) cell indicates how strongly the key input $\mathbf{h}_j \in \{\mathbf{h}_1, \mathbf{h}_2, \ldots, \mathbf{h}_L\}$ contributes to computing the query output $\widetilde{\mathbf{h}}_i$. The diagonal elements correspond to the effect of preserving the original input information, that is, preserving $\mathbf{h}_{j=i}$ when computing $\widetilde{\mathbf{h}}_i$. ATTN in Fig. 5a mixes information from input representations other than its own. On the other hand, RES in Fig. 5b loses the mixing effect of ATTN and strongly preserves the information from the original input representation. These results indicate that RES cancels the effect of ATTN on the MTS.

We modify Eq. (3) to adjust for the mixing effect of ATTN and the preservation effect of RES:

$$\widetilde{\mathbf{H}} = \mathrm{LN}\,(\mathrm{ATTN}\,(\mathbf{H},\mathbf{H},\mathbf{H}) + \lambda \mathbf{H}), \qquad (4)$$

where $\lambda(0 \leq \lambda \leq 1)$ is a parameter that adjusts each effect. The lower λ, the stronger the influence of ATTN.

We calculate the mixing ratio r_i for ATTN, RES, and LN, which represents the ratio of the mixing effect to the sum of the mixing and preservation effects. A higher mixing ratio indicates that the mixing effect is stronger than the preservation effect. Table 1 shows the mixing ratio after performing ATTN, RES, and

Table 1. Mean value of the mixing ratio for each component.

Components	$\lambda = 0$	$\lambda = 0.25$	$\lambda = 1$
Multi-head attention	95.8	96.0	95.9
Residual connection	91.7	84.5	74.2
Layer normalization	91.8	84.5	74.2

LN with $\lambda = 0, 0.25, 1$. The values in Table 1 represent the mean ratios of the heads and layers.

These results demonstrate that, while general Transformer-based models (i.e., $\lambda = 1$) lose the mixing effect of ATTN after RES, increasing the influence of ATTN in the attention block can preserve the mixing effect even after RES. We set λ to preserve a strong mixing effect.

3.6 Anomaly Prediction Flow

Here, we define the Transformer for forecasting operations as TF^{pred} and the Transformer for reconstruction operations as $\text{TF}^{\text{reconst}}$.

Training. TranAP is trained using only normal data. Given an input window $\mathbf{x}_{1:T}$, the Transformer for forecasting predicts the following future τ timesteps $\mathbf{x}_{T+1:T+\tau}$:

$$\mathbf{x}^{\text{pred}}_{T+1:T+\tau} = \text{TF}^{\text{pred}}(\mathbf{x}_{1:T}), \tag{5}$$

where $\mathbf{x}^{\text{pred}}_{T+1:T+\tau}$ denotes the predicted values. We utilize the mean squared error (MSE) to compute the difference between the predicted values and ground truth during the training phase of the Transformer for forecasting. The Transformer is trained to minimize the following objective function:

$$\mathcal{L}^{\text{pred}} = \left\| \mathbf{x}^{\text{pred}}_{T+1:T+\tau} - \mathbf{x}_{T+1:T+\tau} \right\|_2^2. \tag{6}$$

The Transformer for reconstruction reconstructs a vector $\mathbf{x}_{1:T} \oplus \mathbf{x}^{\text{pred}}_{T+1:T+\tau} \in \mathbb{R}^{(T+\tau) \times D}$ that combines the original input $\mathbf{x}_{1:T}$ and the predicted $\mathbf{x}^{\text{pred}}_{T+1:T+\tau}$:

$$\mathbf{x}^{\text{reconst}}_{1:T+\tau} = \text{TF}^{\text{reconst}}(\mathbf{x}_{1:T} \oplus \mathbf{x}^{\text{pred}}_{T+1:T+\tau}), \tag{7}$$

where $\oplus$ is the operation of the concatenation of two vectors, and $\mathbf{x}^{\text{reconst}}_{1:T+\tau}$ represents the reconstructed values. The Transformer for reconstruction is trained to minimize the following objective function to reconstruct values similar to the input:

$$\mathcal{L}^{\text{reconst}} = \left\| \mathbf{x}^{\text{reconst}}_{1:T+\tau} - \mathbf{x}_{1:T+\tau} \right\|_2^2. \tag{8}$$

Anomaly Prediction. The trained Transformer for forecasting receives an input window $\hat{\mathbf{x}}_{1:T}$ and predicts the future $\hat{\mathbf{x}}^{\text{pred}}_{T+1:T+\tau}$. Subsequently, the trained Transformer for reconstruction reconstructs $\hat{\mathbf{x}}_{1:T} \oplus \hat{\mathbf{x}}^{\text{pred}}_{T+1:T+\tau}$:

$$\begin{aligned}\hat{\mathbf{x}}^{\text{pred}}_{T+1:T+\tau} &= \text{TF}^{\text{pred}}(\hat{\mathbf{x}}_{1:T}), \\ \hat{\mathbf{x}}^{\text{reconst}}_{1:T+\tau} &= \text{TF}^{\text{reconst}}(\hat{\mathbf{x}}_{1:T} \oplus \hat{\mathbf{x}}^{\text{pred}}_{T+1:T+\tau}),\end{aligned} \tag{9}$$

where $\hat{\mathbf{x}}_{1:T+\tau}^{\text{reconst}}$ denotes the reconstructed values. The anomaly prediction score $\mathcal{A}_{\text{AP}}(\hat{\mathbf{x}}_{T+1:T+\tau}|\hat{\mathbf{x}}_{1:T})$ is defined as

$$\mathcal{A}_{\text{AP}}(\hat{\mathbf{x}}_{T+1:T+\tau}|\hat{\mathbf{x}}_{1:T}) = \left\| \hat{\mathbf{x}}_{1:T+\tau}^{\text{reconst}} - \hat{\mathbf{x}}_{1:T} \oplus \hat{\mathbf{x}}_{T+1:T+\tau}^{\text{pred}} \right\|_2^2. \tag{10}$$

$\mathcal{A}_{\text{AP}}(\hat{\mathbf{x}}_{T+1:T+\tau}|\hat{\mathbf{x}}_{1:T})$ means the degree to which an anomaly can occur in future $\hat{\mathbf{x}}_{T+1:T+\tau}$ (i.e., $\hat{\mathbf{x}}_{1:T}$ can be a precursor of an anomaly) given an input window $\hat{\mathbf{x}}_{1:T}$. A window $\hat{\mathbf{x}}_{1:T}$ with an anomaly prediction score $\mathcal{A}_{\text{AP}}(\hat{\mathbf{x}}_{T+1:T+\tau}|\hat{\mathbf{x}}_{1:T})$ that exceeds a predefined threshold is determined to be a precursor of an anomaly (i.e., $y_{T+1:T+\tau}^{\text{pred}} = 1$). Then, the result of the anomaly prediction $y_{T+1:T+\tau}^{\text{pred}} \in \{0,1\}$ is compared with the correct label $y_{T+1:T+\tau} \in \{0,1\}$ to evaluate the success or failure of the anomaly prediction.

4 Experiments

4.1 Anomaly Prediction in MTS

Datasets. We assess the performance of the proposed TranAP on five real-world datasets: SWaT [23], PSM [1], SMD [29], SMAP [11], and NIPS-TS-GECCO [15,24].

Baselines. We compare TranAP with nine anomaly detection models and one anomaly prediction model **PAD**.

Anomaly detection models consist of reconstruction-based models: **LSTM-AE** [28], **MAD-GAN** [17], **USAD** [4], **CAE-M** [38], **TranAD** [31], **Anomaly Transformer** [34], and **DCdetector** [35]; the autoregression-based model **LSTM** [11]; and the density-estimation model **DAGMM** [41]. Anomaly detection models can be applied to anomaly prediction tasks by considering the precursors of anomalies as an anomaly (see Appendix A.3).

Experimental Settings. All models follow the experimental setup with an input length $T = 48$ and prediction lengths $\tau \in \{24, 36, 48, 72, 96\}$. The attention ratio λ is set to 0.5 for the SMD and SMAP datasets and 0.25 for the other datasets. The segment length L_{seg} is set to 24 for the SMD and NIPS-TS-GECCO datasets and 12 for the other datasets. We choose the F1-score as evaluation metrics to compare the performance of TranAP with those of the other models. All experiments are repeated five times and the mean of the metrics is reported.

4.2 Main Results

We first evaluate the anomaly prediction performance, as shown in Table 2. Overall, we achieve state-of-the-art results for almost all datasets. The mean F1-score over all the datasets is 8.1 points higher than that of the baselines. The F1-score is 2.5–6.8 points higher than that of the baselines for datasets with relatively clear precursors of anomalies, such as the SWaT and PSM datasets. On the other hand, for datasets with small anomaly precursors, such as the SMD and SMAP datasets, the F1-score is comparable to that of the baselines. The NIPS-TS-GECCO dataset is a challenging dataset with several types of anomalies.

However, TranAP is successful, whereas the baselines fail to predict anomalies. The standard deviations of the F1-score of TranAP in the five repetitions of the experiments are within 0.14%–4.09% for all datasets.

Despite a fixed input length and different prediction lengths, the F1-score does not change significantly. In actual operations, it is desirable to detect the precursors of anomalies further into the future. Therefore, the prediction length should be increased to the extent that the evaluation metrics, such as the F1-score, do not change significantly.

5 Analysis

5.1 Ablation Study

Input Length.
We investigate the effect of input length by changing the input lengths $T \in \{12, 24, 48, 96, 168\}$ with a fixed prediction length $\tau = 96$ in Fig. 6. The F1-score is the highest when $T = 12$ for the SWaT dataset and $T = 24$ for the PSM dataset. In these datasets, the behav-

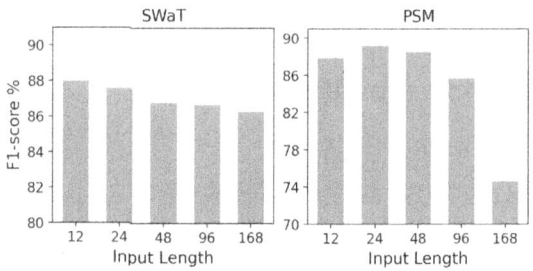

Fig. 6. F1-score when changing input lengths.

ior leading to anomalies is likely to have occurred at slightly earlier time steps when the prediction length is 96. The longer the input length, the lower the value of the F1-score. If the input length is too long, the input contains information that is irrelevant to anomaly prediction.

Effect of Segment.
We investigate the average running time per iteration and F1-score for different segment lengths in the SWaT and PSM datasets in Fig. 7. We set an input length $T = 48$, prediction length $\tau = 48$, and segment lengths $L_{seg} \in \{1, 3, 6, 12, 24, 48\}$. The average running time per iteration is reduced by 55.4%–81.5% without decreasing the F1-score. Note that the F1-score is the highest with $L_{seg} = 24$ for the SWaT dataset and $L_{seg} = 6$ for the PSM dataset. In the PSM dataset with $L_{seg} = 48$, the F1-score decreases because the time steps with different temporal characteristics are grouped into a single segment.

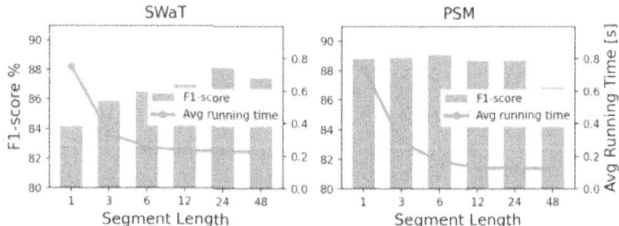

Fig. 7. Running time and F1-score when changing segment lengths.

Table 2. MTS anomaly prediction results. We use an input length $T = 48$ and prediction lengths $\tau \in \{24, 36, 48, 72, 96\}$. The evaluation metrics are the precision (P), recall (R), and F1-score (F1). The best results are in **bold**, and the second best are underlined. All values are in percentages.

Models											Anomaly Detection Models for Anomaly Prediction Tasks																Anomaly Prediction Models					
	LSTM			LSTM-AE			DAGMM			MAD-GAN			USAD			CAE-M			TranAD			Ano Trans			DCdetector			PAD			TranAP		
Metric	P	R	F1	P	R	F1	P	R	F1	P	R	F1	P	R	F1	P	R	F1	P	R	F1	P	R	F1	P	R	F1	P	R	F1	P	R	F1
SWaT 24	15.2	92.8	26.1	96.4	70.9	81.7	67.1	82.7	74.0	92.3	75.2	82.9	78.2	81.7	79.8	66.2	80.2	70.1	90.7	76.2	82.8	18.1	91.6	30.2	98.6	68.6	80.9	69.2	58.3	56.1	92.8	81.7	86.9
36	15.2	91.0	26.1	96.7	74.0	83.8	76.8	79.3	77.1	84.2	73.9	77.1	84.2	73.3	77.1	78.4	81.3	79.8	74.6	24.7	73.9	77.1	84.6	81.8	71.1	85.3	77.6	82.5	76.4	79.4	73.5	81.8	87.1
48	15.4	91.1	26.4	97.0	74.8	84.5	76.9	79.8	77.4	92.8	74.0	82.4	82.3	76.4	82.1	78.8	62.7	80.2	70.4	89.7	77.7	82.8	18.4	91.2	30.7	99.8	76.5	84.3	93.3	93.4	81.4	87.0
72	15.5	90.7	26.5	97.0	75.2	84.8	83.2	78.6	80.1	81.6	77.6	78.5	77.4	81.6	79.1	63.1	79.7	70.4	90.1	78.1	83.6	18.6	92.0	31.0	99.2	67.2	80.1	65.6	68.4	48.8	92.9	82.3	87.3
96	15.8	90.6	26.9	97.1	74.4	84.3	81.8	78.2	79.0	91.5	76.9	83.5	82.0	79.9	80.7	63.4	79.2	70.4	91.4	77.6	83.9	18.9	91.0	31.2	97.2	52.6	64.6	32.1	89.0	33.8	93.4	81.0	86.8
PSM 24	60.5	89.1	72.0	67.9	83.2	74.6	78.2	87.4	82.6	77.3	87.2	81.9	81.7	86.8	84.1	70.9	88.2	78.6	85.9	85.2	85.3	40.1	56.4	46.8	86.9	83.0	78.9	39.0	87.0	45.9	92.7	86.4	89.2
36	64.0	84.2	72.4	67.3	85.2	75.1	69.8	87.6	77.7	76.8	68.7	97.7	73.5	87.5	79.9	71.4	87.3	78.6	75.3	86.8	80.5	51.4	78.0	61.9	83.6	81.5	82.5	35.1	83.9	48.9	96.4	82.4	88.8
48	60.6	87.5	71.6	67.3	77.4	72.0	78.8	85.8	82.1	80.0	84.0	82.0	74.6	86.5	79.9	71.9	86.3	78.5	86.5	80.9	83.6	63.4	69.4	45.4	54.5	63.7	60.5	29.4	97.5	81.4	88.7
72	62.2	88.5	87.2	74.6	80.7	60.7	71.8	71.9	85.2	77.8	82.7	07.5	86.7	81.5	79.9	72.8	84.8	78.4	85.8	46.8	14.3	96.8	54.6	75.6	46.7	56.6	54.1	55.3	32.2	99.4	87.9	88.2
96	66.4	58.4	07.2	96.9	75.8	72.2	80.3	82.9	81.6	80.4	82.5	81.3	76.4	83.4	79.9	72.8	77.8	83.5	78.2	92.5	77.3	84.0	55.0	63.0	47.6	56.0	86.4	94.2	28.0	64.1	97.0	81.4	88.5
SMD 24	46.5	55.8	50.4	41.2	56.1	47.2	41.2	76.1	53.4	34.7	77.4	77.8	84.0	37.7	76.9	50.6	43.5	74.0	54.8	83.7	64.5	09.4	54.2	91.3	51.3	33.4	85.3	46.3	65.4	71.3	45.0	73.9	55.9
36	47.7	52.8	50.1	47.2	51.5	49.0	41.1	87.5	55.3	84.3	73.1	54.2	42.3	72.3	53.4	44.5	37.2	6.5	59.5	43.8	69.6	53.7	72.9	84.3	03.2	44.4	97.7	15.2	58.6	10.0	46.9	68.8	55.8
48	46.3	51.5	48.5	48.1	50.2	48.9	44.2	72.9	55.0	41.4	73.6	52.9	42.3	73.3	53.6	47.1	69.9	56.3	43.1	71.3	53.7	79.9	42.8	55.1	41.6	79.0	48.0	55.6	76.1	05.4	26.2	62.1	57.7
72	49.1	46.5	47.5	52.0	47.1	49.4	44.7	87.1	25.7	24.8	56.9	55.7	14.8	66.9	0.0	57.0	50.8	68.5	58.1	14.7	56.9	25.6	26.9	02.4	63.6	23.6	29.0	24.8	0.7	39.9	13.6	56.0	55.4	55.7
96	49.6	47.9	48.3	53.6	46.5	49.6	52.1	70.9	60.1	14.6	97.3	85.7	34.8	97.2	58.3	54.5	68.0	60.5	46.2	73.7	56.8	60.6	33.1	42.7	43.5	92.2	57.1	74.1	34.1	34.8	48.9	69.5	57.0
SMAP 24	74.8	53.1	62.1	78.5	52.4	62.9	85.6	49.1	62.3	88.8	54.8	64.9	62.8	88.5	49.6	62.8	89.7	48.4	62.9	57.0	42.9	48.9	77.1	49.8	45.3	10.8	56.4	17.5	77.7	62.1	68.9
36	74.9	53.0	62.1	78.5	52.1	62.7	85.5	48.8	96.2	28.6	84.9	62.8	88.6	48.6	62.8	88.5	49.6	62.8	88.6	48.6	62.8	57.6	42.3	48.7	64.6	33.8	71.1	07.6	71.9	38.8	25.2	3.6	65.7
48	74.3	52.7	61.7	78.9	52.2	62.8	25.6	48.7	62.1	87.0	48.9	62.6	88.9	48.3	62.6	85.8	49.4	62.7	88.7	48.4	62.6	71.4	53.9	61.4	69.8	47.7	48.7	13.6	60.1	14.4	79.4	51.9	62.8
72	74.5	52.6	61.7	79.3	51.9	62.8	87.0	49.0	62.7	88.9	49.5	63.6	89.6	49.6	63.9	86.1	49.1	62.5	89.0	48.7	62.7	88.0	48.6	76.2	97.3	05.4	26.2	68.0	59.6	61.5	56.4	09.8	83.6	51.6	64.0
96	76.0	52.6	21.7	98.5	17.9	85.1	76.2	88.6	65.1	66.4	78.8	85.1	86.5	90.4	51.1	86.5	90.4	51.5	88.7	15.1	26.4	58.8	55.0	86.4	54.3	73.1	53.6	67.7	04.9	35.6	01.1	48.0	02.0	08.0	65.2	63.3
GECCO 24	83.0	22.3	35.2	83.2	62.2	3	35.2	40.2	85.1	72.6	2	40.2	85.7	26.2	40.3	85.7	26.2	40.3	85.7	26.2	40.3	85.7	26.2	40.2	44.1	14.9	21.7	14.3	31.5	19.3	47.2	31.5	15.9	38.3	77.5	51.3
36	82.1	20.0	32.1	84.7	20.0	32.4	37.4	87.1	18.4	30.2	84.4	37.0	24.0	87.7	23.1	45.1	12.2	17.5	46.2	23.3	15.1	45.3	10.3	42.4	74.4	54.0
48	84.9	18.4	30.2	87.1	18.4	30.3	88.8	22.2	35.5	88.8	22.5	35.9	88.8	22.5	29.7	8.8	13.6	19.7	52.3	27.8	13.1	41.0	3.9	45.8	74.1	56.6
72	93.4	16.2	27.7	89.7	20.4	33.3	33.3	89.7	20.4	33.3	89.7	20.4	33.3	89.7	20.4	33.7	01.1	41.4	5.2	8.0	65.0	35.2	23.4	51.0	12.9	53.7	73.8	62.1
96	94.0	14.9	25.7	98.6	14.9	25.9	90.9	19.2	31.6	90.9	19.2	31.6	90.9	19.2	31.6	90.9	19.2	31.7	90.9	19.2	31.6	50.2	13.5	20.5	42.2	46.9	43.5	4.7	60.6	6.2	55.6	73.6	63.2
Average	57.6	59.9	47.9	76.4	54.8	54.7	70.7	67.1	61.6	74.3	64.1	61.1	75.2	62.4	62.8	71.7	61.7	61.4	79.1	60.7	59.9	45.3	50.2	38.8	60.9	62.2	59.7	25.7	42.4	73.6	71.9	70.9

Effect of ATTN. We examine the impact of the mixing effect of ATTN and the preservation effect of RES on the anomaly prediction performance by adjusting the attention ratio λ in Eq. (4). Table 3 denotes the F1-score with an input length $T = 48$, prediction length $\tau = \{24, 96\}$, and attention ratio $\lambda = \{0, 0.25, 1\}$ in the SWaT and PSM datasets. Although increasing the mixing effect improves the F1-score, completely eliminating the preservation effect (i.e., $\lambda = 0$) tends to degrade the performance of anomaly prediction. Therefore, the increased mixing effect of ATTN leads to improved performance, and the preservation effect of RES also contributes to anomaly prediction in the attention block.

Table 3. F1-score when changing attention ratios.

Attention ratio		0	0.25	1
SWaT	24	86.8	**86.9**	86.6
	96	86.5	**86.8**	86.6
PSM	24	88.0	**89.2**	87.3
	96	87.2	**88.5**	88.0

Effect of Temporal and Feature-Wise ATTN. We perform anomaly prediction on all datasets using four different attention mechanisms: general (**Original**), feature-wise (**F-ATTN**), temporal (**T-ATTN**), and temporal and feature-wise ATTN (**TF-ATTN**).

Table 4 denotes the F1-score with an input length $T = 48$ and prediction lengths $\tau \in \{24, 96\}$. In all cases, the F1-score is higher than that of the other attention mechanisms for **Original**. **F-ATTN** achieves a higher F1-score than **Original** for all prediction lengths, indicating that it is important to reflect the dependencies between features in the final computed representations. The longer the prediction length, the more **T-ATTN**, which treats each feature independently, functions. Therefore, each feature has a different temporal dependency, which is important for anomaly prediction. This indicates that performing **TF-ATTN** enables detailed extraction of the MTS characteristics and contributes to improving anomaly prediction.

Table 4. F1-score when changing attention mechanisms.

Attention mechanism		Original	F-ATTN	T-ATTN	TF-ATTN
SWaT	24	83.2	86.3	85.4	**86.9**
	96	85.3	86.4	86.6	**86.8**
PSM	24	88.4	88.7	**90.2**	89.2
	96	87.3	87.3	**88.7**	88.5
SMD	24	38.6	53.6	53.3	**55.9**
	96	44.1	51.4	53.1	**54.7**
SMAP	24	59.3	62.5	61.9	**63.1**
	96	61.0	62.6	**63.3**	63.0
GECCO	24	50.0	50.5	50.7	**51.3**
	96	57.3	58.9	63.0	**63.2**

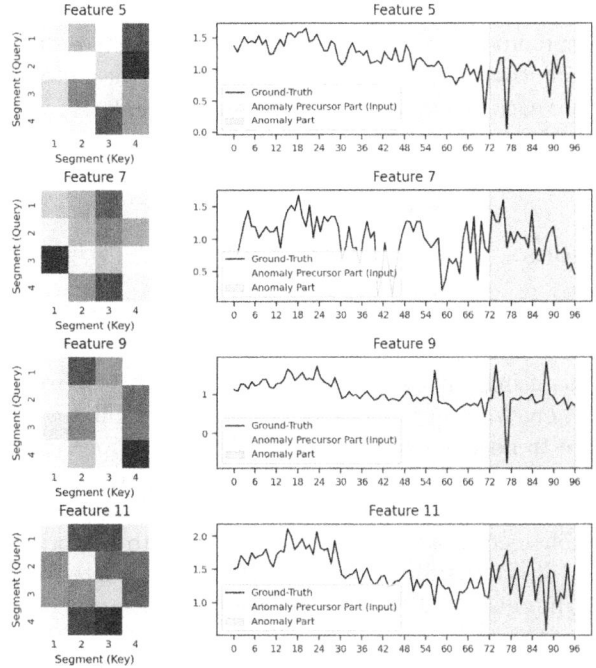

Fig. 8. Attention maps after temporal ATTN.

5.2 Visualization of Attention Maps

We visualize the interactions between representations after temporal and feature-wise ATTN to confirm the effectiveness of the improved attention mechanism. A window $\hat{x}_{48:71}$ from the PSM dataset with an input length $T = 24$ and segment length $L_{\text{seg}} = 6$ which contains the precursors of the anomalies (yellow highlighted area of Fig. 8 to the right) is fed to the trained encoder. An anomaly occurs in $\hat{x}_{72:95}$ (red highlighted area of Fig. 8 to the right).

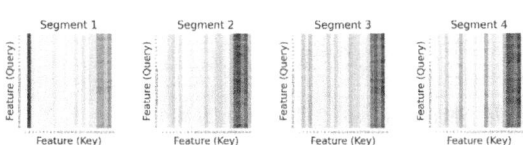

Fig. 9. Attention maps after feature-wise ATTN.

Figure 8 shows the attention maps of $\hat{x}_{48:71}$ for each feature after performing temporal ATTN. The attention maps of each feature differ in time direction, indicating that each feature has different temporal characteristics. In the attention maps, the attention weights of the segments (keys) that contain behaviors leading to anomalies tends to be higher for each segment (query). This indicates that temporal ATTN can focus on the behaviors leading to the anomaly.

Figure 9 shows the attention maps between features when performing feature-wise ATTN after temporal ATTN. The dependencies between features are captured, and this information is essential for capturing the MTS characteristics. When we compare each attention map of the segments, all segments exhibit similar dependencies between features. These segments are close in time and thus capture similar feature-wise dependencies.

6 Conclusions

In this paper, we proposed an anomaly prediction framework based on MTS forecasting and reconstruction using Transformer. Our model is trained to predict future trends using only normal data. Therefore, when given a time series exhibiting deviations from normal features, the results will not be accurate predictions of future trends, which can then be detected as precursors to anomaly occurrences through reconstruction. Detecting precursors of anomalies requires an accurate understanding of the temporal characteristics of the MTS. We modified the attention mechanism of each Transformer to perform ATTN in the time and feature directions. However, an NLP study reported that the effect of the ATTN was diminished after applying RES, despite using improved attention mechanisms. Therefore, we confirmed the same phenomenon in the context of MTS. We successfully preserved the strong effects of the improved attention mechanism by modifying the operation of the attention block. We enhanced the anomaly prediction performance by introducing these improvements.

Acknowledgements. This work was supported by the 4th Research Grant from the Hagiwara Foundation of Japan and by JSPS KAKENHI Grant Number JP24999361 (Grant-in-Aid for Early-Career Scientists).

References

1. Abdulaal, A., Liu, Z., Lancewicki, T.: Practical approach to asynchronous multivariate time series anomaly detection and localization. Proceedings of the 27th ACM SIGKDD Conference on Knowledge Discovery & Data Mining, pp. 2485–2494 (2021)
2. Abnar, S., Zuidema, W.: Quantifying attention flow in transformers. In: Proceedings of the 58th Annual Meeting of the Association for Computational Linguistics, pp. 4190–4197 (Jul 2020)
3. Ahmad, S., Lavin, A., Purdy, S., Agha, Z.: Unsupervised real-time anomaly detection for streaming data. Neurocomputing **262**, 134–147 (2017)
4. Audibert, J., Michiardi, P., Guyard, F., Marti, S., Zuluaga, M.A.: Usad: unsupervised anomaly detection on multivariate time series. In:Proceedings of the 26th ACM SIGKDD International Conference on Knowledge Discovery & Data Mining, pp. 3395–3404 (2020)
5. Ba, J.L., Kiros, J.R., Hinton, G.E.: Layer normalization. arXiv preprint arXiv:1607.06450 (2016)

6. Chen, Z., Chen, D., Zhang, X., Yuan, Z., Cheng, X.: Learning graph structures with transformer for multivariate time-series anomaly detection in iot. IEEE Internet Things J. **9**(12), 9179–9189 (2021)
7. Du, D., Su, B., Wei, Z.: Preformer: predictive transformer with multi-scale segment-wise correlations for long-term time series forecasting. ICASSP 2023-2023 IEEE International Conference on Acoustics, Speech and Signal Processing (ICASSP), pp. 1–5 (2023)
8. Goldstein, M., Uchida, S.: A comparative evaluation of unsupervised anomaly detection algorithms for multivariate data. PLoS ONE **11**(4), e0152173 (2016)
9. He, K., Zhang, X., Ren, S., Sun, J.: Deep residual learning for image recognition. In: Proceedings of the IEEE Conference on Computer Vision and Pattern Recognition, pp. 770–778 (2016)
10. Htut, P.M., Phang, J., Bordia, S., Bowman, S.R.: Do attention heads in bert track syntactic dependencies? arXiv preprint arXiv:1911.12246 (2019)
11. Hundman, K., Constantinou, V., Laporte, C., Colwell, I., Soderstrom, T.: Detecting spacecraft anomalies using lstms and nonparametric dynamic thresholding. In: Proceedings of the 24th ACM SIGKDD International Conference on Knowledge Discovery & Data Mining, pp. 387–395 (2018)
12. Jhin, S.Y., Lee, J., Park, N.: Precursor-of-anomaly detection for irregular time series. Proceedings of the 29th ACM SIGKDD Conference on Knowledge Discovery and Data Mining, pp. 917–929 (2023)
13. Kobayashi, G., Kuribayashi, T., Yokoi, S., Inui, K.: Incorporating residual and normalization layers into analysis of masked language models. In: Proceedings of the 2021 Conference on Empirical Methods in Natural Language Processing, pp. 4547–4568, November 2021
14. Kovaleva, O., Romanov, A., Rogers, A., Rumshisky, A.: Revealing the dark secrets of BERT. In: Proceedings of the 2019 Conference on Empirical Methods in Natural Language Processing and the 9th International Joint Conference on Natural Language Processing (EMNLP-IJCNLP), pp. 4365–4374, November 2019
15. Lai, K.H., Zha, D., Xu, J., Zhao, Y.: Revisiting time series outlier detection: Definitions and benchmarks. NeurIPS Datasets and Benchmarks (2021)
16. Landauer, M., Onder, S., Skopik, F., Wurzenberger, M.: Deep learning for anomaly detection in log data: a survey. Mach. Learn. Appl. **12**, 100470 (2023)
17. Li, D., Chen, D., Jin, B., Shi, L., Goh, J., Ng, S.K.: Mad-gan: Multivariate anomaly detection for time series data with generative adversarial networks. In: International Conference on Artificial Neural Networks, pp. 703–716 (2019)
18. Lim, B., Zohren, S.: Time-series forecasting with deep learning: a survey. Phil. Trans. R. Soc. A **379**(2194), 20200209 (2021)
19. Lin, Y., Tan, Y.C., Frank, R.: Open sesame: getting inside BERT's linguistic knowledge. Proceedings of the 2019 ACL Workshop BlackboxNLP: Analyzing and Interpreting Neural Networks for NLP pp. 241–253, August 2019
20. Liu, S., Yu, H., Liao, C., Li, J., Lin, W., Liu, A.X., Dustdar, S.: Pyraformer: Low-complexity pyramidal attention for long-range time series modeling and forecasting. In: International Conference on Learning Representations (2021)
21. Mareček, D., Rosa, R.: From balustrades to pierre vinken: Looking for syntax in transformer self-attentions. In: Proceedings of the 2019 ACL Workshop BlackboxNLP: Analyzing and Interpreting Neural Networks for NLP, August 2019
22. Masini, R.P., Medeiros, M.C., Mendes, E.F.: Machine learning advances for time series forecasting. J. Econ. Surv. **37**(1), 76–111 (2023)

23. Mathur, A.P., Tippenhauer, N.O.: Swat: A water treatment testbed for research and training on ics security. In: 2016 International Workshop on Cyber-Physical Systems for Smart Water Networks (CySWater), pp. 31–36 (2016)
24. Moritz, S., Rehbach, F., Chandrasekaran, S., Rebolledo, M., Bartz-Beielstein, T.: Gecco industrial challenge 2018 dataset: A water quality dataset for the'internet of things: Online anomaly detection for drinking water quality'competition at the genetic and evolutionary computation conference 2018, kyoto, japan. Kyoto, Japan (2018)
25. Nie, Y., H. Nguyen, N., Sinthong, P., Kalagnanam, J.: A time series is worth 64 words: Long-term forecasting with transformers. In: International Conference on Learning Representations (2023)
26. Pang, G., Shen, C., Cao, L., Hengel, A.V.D.: Deep learning for anomaly detection: a review. ACM Comput. Surv. (CSUR) **54**(2), 1–38 (2021)
27. Reif, E., Yuan, A., Wattenberg, M., Viegas, F.B., Coenen, A., Pearce, A., Kim, B.: Visualizing and measuring the geometry of bert. Advances in Neural Information Processing Systems **32** (2019)
28. Said Elsayed, M., Le-Khac, N.A., Dev, S., Jurcut, A.D.: Network anomaly detection using lstm based autoencoder. In: Proceedings of the 16th ACM Symposium on QoS and Security for Wireless and Mobile Networks, pp. 37–45 (2020)
29. Su, Y., Zhao, Y., Niu, C., Liu, R., Sun, W., Pei, D.: Robust anomaly detection for multivariate time series through stochastic recurrent neural network. In: Proceedings of the 25th ACM SIGKDD International Conference on Knowledge Discovery & Data Mining, pp. 2828–2837 (2019)
30. Torres, J.F., Hadjout, D., Sebaa, A., Martínez-Álvarez, F., Troncoso, A.: Deep learning for time series forecasting: a survey. Big Data **9**(1), 3–21 (2021)
31. Tuli, S., Casale, G., Jennings, N.R.: TranAD: deep transformer networks for anomaly detection in multivariate time series data. Proc. VLDB **15**(6), 1201–1214 (2022)
32. Vaswani, A., Shazeer, N., Parmar, N., Uszkoreit, J., Jones, L., Gomez, A.N., Kaiser, Ł., Polosukhin, I.: Attention is all you need. Advances in neural information processing systems **30** (2017)
33. Wu, H., Xu, J., Wang, J., Long, M.: Autoformer: decomposition transformers with auto-correlation for long-term series forecasting. Adv. Neural. Inf. Process. Syst. **34**, 22419–22430 (2021)
34. Xu, J., Wu, H., Wang, J., Long, M.: Anomaly transformer: Time series anomaly detection with association discrepancy. arXiv preprint arXiv:2110.02642 (2021)
35. Yang, Y., Zhang, C., Zhou, T., Wen, Q., Sun, L.: Dcdetector: Dual attention contrastive representation learning for time series anomaly detection. In: Proceedings of the 29th ACM SIGKDD Conference on Knowledge Discovery and Data Mining, pp. 3033–3045 (2023)
36. Zhang, C., Zhou, T., Wen, Q., Sun, L.: Tfad: A decomposition time series anomaly detection architecture with time-frequency analysis. In: Proceedings of the 31st ACM International Conference on Information & Knowledge Management, pp. 2497–2507 (2022)
37. Zhang, Y., Yan, J.: Crossformer: transformer utilizing cross-dimension dependency for multivariate time series forecasting. In: International Conference on Learning Representations (2023)
38. Zhang, Y., Chen, Y., Wang, J., Pan, Z.: Unsupervised deep anomaly detection for multi-sensor time-series signals. IEEE Trans. Knowl. Data Eng. (2021)

39. Zhou, H., Zhang, S., Peng, J., Zhang, S., Li, J., Xiong, H., Zhang, W.: Informer: Beyond efficient transformer for long sequence time-series forecasting. Proceedings of the AAAI conference on artificial intelligence **35**(12), 11106–11115 (2021)
40. Zhou, T., Ma, Z., Wen, Q., Wang, X., Sun, L., Jin, R.: Fedformer: frequency enhanced decomposed transformer for long-term series forecasting. International Conference on Machine Learning, pp. 27268–27286 (2022)
41. Zong, B., Song, Q., Min, M.R., Cheng, W., Lumezanu, C., Cho, D., Chen, H.: Deep autoencoding gaussian mixture model for unsupervised anomaly detection. In: International Conference on Learning Representations (2018)

Improving Novel Anomaly Detection with Domain-Invariant Latent Representations

Padmaksha Roy[1](✉), Ming Jin[1], Himanshu Singhal[1], Tyler Cody[1], and Kevin Choi[2]

[1] Virginia Tech, Blacksburg, VA, USA
{padmaksha,jinming,himanshusinghal,tcody}@vt.edu
[2] AI Center of Excellence, Deloitte, Mclean, VA, USA
kevchoi@deloitte.com

Abstract. Zero-day anomaly detection is critical in industrial applications where novel, unforeseen threats can compromise system integrity and safety. Traditional detection systems often fail to identify these unseen anomalies due to their reliance on in-distribution data. Domain generalization addresses this gap by leveraging knowledge from multiple known domains to detect out-of-distribution events. In this work, we introduce a multi-task representation learning technique that fuses information across related domains into a unified latent space. By jointly optimizing classification, reconstruction, and mutual information regularization losses, our method learns a minimal(bottleneck), domain-invariant representation that discards spurious correlations. This latent space decorrelation enhances generalization, enabling the detection of anomalies in unseen domains. Our experimental results demonstrate significant improvements in zero-day or novel anomaly detection across diverse anomaly detection datasets.

Keywords: Representation Learning · OOD Detection · Multi-task Learning

1 Introduction

Anomaly detection is a fundamental task in various applications, enabling the early identification of unusual patterns in network traffic, system logs, or user behavior that may signal intrusions or malicious activities [20,23]. As cyber threats evolve and novel attacks—such as zero-day vulnerabilities—emerge, traditional defenses often fall short, leading to severe disruptions and data breaches. In many real-world applications, training and test data stem from different distributions, making out-of-distribution (OOD) generalization a critical challenge. Standard deep neural networks excel when the training and testing data are drawn from the same distribution; however, their performance degrades when confronted with unseen domains. Existing approaches such as few-shot learning and meta-learning [14,15,17,19,21] attempt to bridge this gap but often require target domain data during training or otherwise risk embedding biases from specific domains. Our approach addresses these challenges by targeting a latent space that embodies a minimal sufficient representation for the downstream task of OOD classification. We consider a scenario where the samples from different domains or datasets have distinct feature correlation structures. High-dimensional data poses unique challenges due to the curse of dimensionality. In such spaces, conventional distance measures lose their discriminative power because the relative contrast between the nearest and farthest neighbors diminishes—a phenomenon highlighted by the principle of concentration of distance. Inspired by the principle of relevant information(PRI) preservation [31], we design a latent space classification loss that aims to regularize the latent space by minimizing the mutual information content between the input and latent space, effectively decorrelating class-specific feature correlation information of the original data. To guarantee that the latent space preserves sufficient input information, we incorporate a reconstruction loss that compels the model to accurately reconstruct the input data from its latent embedding. This prevents over-compression and ensures that the latent space retains the necessary structure for the task. These two losses guide the cross-entropy loss to preserve only the relevant information required for accurate classification. Multi-task learning facilitates learning representations from multiple diverse domains and the joint optimization help improve generalization to unseen domains. By integrating these objectives, our framework works as a zero-shot multi-task learning system. We mix data from multiple source domains with cross-domain samples and also attempt to decorrelate dataset specific spurious correlation information with the mutual information (MI) penalty. This strategy ensures that the learned latent space is invariant to domain-specific correlation information, thereby enhancing generalization to unseen OOD classes without requiring any target domain data during training. Our main contributions can be summarized as follows:

- We propose a novel classification framework that leverages mutual information regularization and reconstruction loss to guide the latent space toward retaining only the most relevant features for out-of-distribution (OOD) classification. The result is a *compressed, invariant* representation that effectively discards *spurious* domain-specific information.
- We demonstrate that integrating data from multiple sources and cross-domains with varying *correlation* patterns enhances *coverage*, improving generalization to unseen domains.
- Our domain-invariant latent space analysis mitigates the adverse effects of *high-dimensionality*. Experiments demonstrate an 8%-15% increase in average precision, and recall and a 4%-9% improvement in average AUC-ROC across all source/IN, cross-domain, and OOD datasets.

2 Related Work

Domain generalization techniques can be grouped into the following primary categories: domain invariant representation learning, meta-learning, latent dimension regularization, and metric learning. *1) Domain Invariant Representation*

Learning: This method aims to identify domain invariant representations that can be extended to unseen domains. The crux of these strategies, as seen in works such as [29], is to filter out domain-specific insights while maintaining cross-domain information. Notable studies employing autoencoders, such as [1], amalgamate multiple domains during training, augmented by data enhancement techniques, to extract domain-invariant characteristics. These features then demonstrate superior generalization to out-of-distribution data. Another study, Maximum Mean Discrepancy Adversarial Autoencoder (MMD-AAE) [11], in the context of few-shot learning, emphasizes aligning varied domain distributions to a generic prior distribution while engaging in adversarial feature learning. An innovative approach is suggested in [12], where a domain-centric masking technique is applied to learn both domain-specific and domain-invariant features. This will facilitate efficient source domain classification and sufficient generalization to target domains. In [13], a noise-enhanced supervised autoencoder reconstructs and classifies both inputs and their reconstructions, using intra-class correlation to show improved feature discrimination and generalization. Moreover, the authors [25] propose domain generalization through domain-invariant representation that uniformly distributes across multiple source domains. Their approach employs moment alignment of distributions and enforces feature disentanglement via an entropy loss. The DIFEX [16] paper employs knowledge distillation to capture internally-invariant Fourier phase features and aligns cross-domain correlations to extract mutually-invariant representations.

2) Meta-learning: This approach employs learning from several related tasks for domain generalization, as observed in works such as [19,24,28]. The study in [26] introduces a technique to discern a domain interdependent projection leading to a latent space. This space minimizes biases in the data while preserving the inherent relationship across multiple domains. Model Agnostic Meta-Learning (MAML) has also been extended to latent dimension settings by performing the gradient-based adaptation in the low dimensional space instead of the higher dimensional space of model parameters [27]. Zero-shot learning [8] aims at learning models from seen classes and inferring on samples whose categories were unseen during the training process.

3) Information Bottleneck Principle and Metric Learning: In contrast to the aforementioned methodologies, our strategy propels direct disentanglement or decorrelation between multiple training domains. An information-theoretic perspective on variance-invariance-covariance has been provided here [3] in the context of self-supervised learning which helps to achieve generalization guarantees for downstream supervised learning tasks. Adversarial learning-based domain adaptation methods are prone to negative transfer which hurts the generalization performance [4]. Metric learning aims to learn a representation function that can map higher-dimensional data to a latent embedded space. The authors [5] propose mixing target labels with training samples to improve the quality of representations or embeddings for classification purposes.

4) Other Related Works: The authors [6] suggest using the statistics of softmax outputs to estimate both the probability of error and the likelihood of a test sample being out-of-domain. They compare the performance of this approach by directly using the raw softmax output probabilities as a measure of confidence. The paper [7] addresses the problem of domain shift when a learned model tends to degrade heavily on a target domain via unsupervised domain adaptation by learning a common feature map from multiple source domains by minimizing the domain distribution discrepancy between those multiple source domains. The authors in [9] use nearest-neighbor distance for flexible OOD detection without strict assumptions, while [10] address spurious correlations by developing causal tools to distinguish invariant features, thereby improving generalization.

Our approach is inspired by the principle of relevant information (PRI) [31], aiming to learn a compressed latent space that retains only the relevant information for downstream tasks. By combining data from multiple domains and decorrelating their spurious correlations, we encourage the network to learn invariant representations. This multi-task representation learning method ensures that the latent space captures minimal, sufficient information for classification while discarding irrelevant, domain-specific details.

3 Problem Formulation

In our domain generalization problem, let $\mathcal{C} = \{0, 1, \ldots, K\}$ denote the complete set of class labels, which we partition into three disjoint subsets; $\mathcal{C} = \mathcal{C}_s \cup \mathcal{C}_c \cup \mathcal{C}_o$, $\mathcal{C}_s \cap \mathcal{C}_c = \mathcal{C}_s \cap \mathcal{C}_o = \mathcal{C}_c \cap \mathcal{C}_o = \emptyset$. For example, if $\mathcal{C}_s = \{1, 3, 5\}$ (source domain), then $\mathcal{C}_c = \{2, 4, 6\}$ (cross-domains) and $\mathcal{C}_o = \{9, 10, 11\}$ (OOD). During training, we have access only to samples from the source and cross-domains. Formally, the training set is defined as $\mathcal{S}_{\text{train}} = \bigcup_{i=1}^{M} \{(x_j^i, y_j^i) \mid y_j^i \in \mathcal{C}_s \cup \mathcal{C}_c,\ j = 1, \ldots, N_i\}$, where M is the total number of tasks and N_i is the number of samples in task i. Our objective is to learn a model that generalizes to unseen OOD classes $y \in \mathcal{C}_o$ by leveraging multi-task representation learning. We enforce domain-invariant feature extraction through joint optimization over classification, reconstruction, and mutual information regularization losses, thereby encouraging a disentangled latent space that tends to forget spurious correlations. The extension to multiple domains necessitates the definition of a multi-task learning objective over all the M source and cross domains which can be given as

$$\mathcal{L}_{rec}(\mathcal{S}_{train}; \theta, \phi) = \sum_{i=1}^{M} \left\| f_\theta^{(i)} \left(g_\phi^{(i)}(X^i) \right) - X^i \right\|_2^2 \tag{1}$$

In this expression, $g_\phi^{(i)}$ and $f_\theta^{(i)}$ denote the encoder and decoder functions respectively for each of the M sources and cross domains, X^i is the input training data from a particular domain. We aggregate the reconstruction loss across different source and cross-domain datasets, ensuring that the total loss accounts for all input domains. Basically, the reconstruction error is computed separately for each domain and then summed to form the overall reconstruction loss.

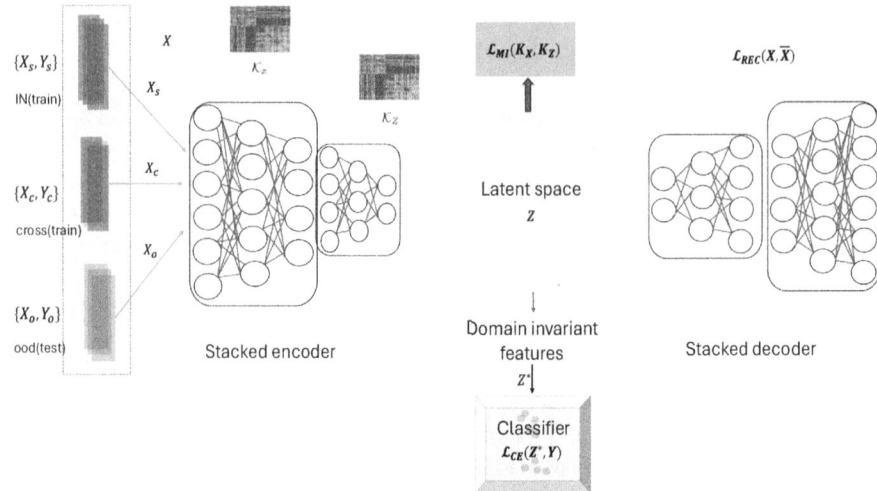

Fig. 1. Training the Multi-task Latent Space Regularized Encoder-Decoder Model (MTLS-RED). During testing, the trained latent space is directly used to classify new samples. (Color figure online)

3.1 Mutual Invariance Regularization

In information theory, the dependence measure or the total correlation between the feature variables is measured as the statistical independence in each dimension and is expressed as the Kullback Leibler(KL) divergence between the joint probability distribution and the marginal distribution of the features [22]. We enforce de-correlation between the input and the latent kernel space—spanning multiple source and cross-domains—by introducing a mutual information minimization penalty that explicitly reduces dependencies between input and latent space kernels in the form of decorrelation. The matrix-based Renyi's second-order entropy [22] of a normalized positive definite(NPD) matrix $\mathcal{K}_x$, estimated on $l \times l$ samples in the input space, where l is the batch size, can be given as

$$\hat{H}_2(\mathcal{K}_x) = \frac{1}{1-\alpha} \log_2 \left(\sum_{k=1}^{l} \lambda_k(\mathcal{K}_x)^\alpha \right), \qquad (2)$$

where the Gram matrix $\mathcal{K}_x$ is obtained by evaluating the positive definite (PSD) kernel on all l pairs of training samples in a batch of training data, that is, and $\lambda_k(X)$ denotes the kth eigenvalue of the input kernel matrix $\mathcal{K}_x$ of the l_{th} batch, Here, $\alpha = 2$ considering Renyi's second-order entropy.

Similarly, Renyi's quadratic entropy of the latent space kernel $\mathcal{K}_Z$ of size $l \times l$ is estimated as

$$\hat{H}_2(\mathcal{K}_z) = \frac{1}{1-\alpha} \log_2 \left(\sum_{k=1}^{l} \lambda_k(\mathcal{K}_z)^\alpha \right), \qquad (3)$$

The argument in Eq. (3) is called the information potential. In the above section, we use the matrix-based second-order Renyi's entropy ($\alpha = 2$) [22] to evaluate the entropy or the uncertainty of the latent and the input space in terms of the normalized eigenspectrum of the Hermitian matrix of the projected data in the Hilbert space. Now, we can estimate the matrix-based second-order joint entropy between the latent space kernel Z and the input space kernel X as

$$\hat{H}_2\left(\mathcal{K}_x, \mathcal{K}_z\right) = H_2 \left(\frac{\mathcal{K}_x \circ \mathcal{K}_z}{tr\left(\mathcal{K}_x \circ \mathcal{K}_z\right)} \right), \tag{4}$$

where $\circ$ represents the Hadamard product. Based on the above definitions, we calculate the joint entropy of the latent and the input space with the help of the matrix-based normalized Renyi's entropy of the latent space and the input space kernels. The joint entropy is used to derive the mutual information between the input and the latent space.

The Mutual Information Divergence. We use the matrix-based mutual information divergence to estimate the mutual information between the latent and input space kernels. Minimizing the mutual information indirectly results in de-correlating the feature correlation that exists in the original input space which helps in improving the generalization performance. The mutual information during each batch of the training can be estimated as

$$\hat{MI}(\mathcal{K}_x; \mathcal{K}_z) = \hat{H}_2\left(\mathcal{K}_x\right) + \hat{H}_2\left(\mathcal{K}_z\right) - \hat{H}_2\left(\mathcal{K}_x, \mathcal{K}_z\right), \tag{5}$$

where $\hat{H}_2\left(\mathcal{K}_X, \mathcal{K}_Z\right)$, is the second-order joint entropy between the latent and the input kernel space. Minimizing this divergence as a regularization penalty in the final loss objective will aid in preserving useful disentangled information in the latent space during each iteration of the training process.

3.2 The Multi-task Learning Objective

In our latent space multi-task learning approach, we leverage the label information of the multiple source and cross-domain encoded data in the latent space during the training process. In our approach, we do a joint optimization of the classification and the reconstruction loss along with the mutual information penalty in the latent space. The total loss calculated over all the M tasks can be written as

$$\mathcal{L}\left(\mathcal{S}_{train}, Z; \phi, \theta, \sigma\right) = \min_{\phi, \theta, \sigma} \sum_{i=1}^{M} \Big\{ \mathcal{L}_{ce}\left(g_\phi\left(X^i\right), y^i\right) \\ + \beta \cdot \mathcal{L}_{MI}\left(X^i; Z^i, \sigma\right) + \lambda \cdot \mathcal{L}_{rec}\left(X^i; \phi, \theta\right) \Big\}, \tag{6}$$

where, $\mathcal{L}_{ce}$ is the cross-entropy loss calculated on the latent space encoding considering the binary classification problem, given as,

$$\mathcal{L}_{ce}\left(g_\phi\left(X^i\right), y^i\right) = -\left(y^i \log\left(\mathcal{S}_y^i\left(g_\phi\left(X^i\right)\right)\right) + \left(1 - y^i\right) \log\left(1 - \left(\mathcal{S}_y\left(g_\phi\left(X^i\right)\right)\right)\right)\right)$$

Algorithm 1. The Multi-task Latent Space Regularized Encoder-Decoder Model (MTLS-RED)

Input:
Source domain data $\{X_{s1}, X_{s2}, ..., X_{sm}\}$, $X_s \in \mathbf{R}^d$, $\forall m \in \{1, 2, 3, ..\}$
Cross-domain data $\{X_{c1}, X_{c2}, ..., X_{cn}\}$, $X_c \in \mathbf{R}^d$, $\forall n \in \{4, 5, 6, ..., \}$
Out-of-distribution (OOD) datasets $\{X_{o_1}, X_{o_2}, ..., X_{o_k}\}$, $X_o \in \mathbf{R}^d$, $\forall k \in \{7, 8, 9, .., \}$
(used for testing only)
Source and cross-domain labels $\{y_i^m\}_{i=1}^n$, $\forall m \in \{1, 2, 3, 4, 5, 6, ..., M\}$
Initialize encoder (E) and decoder (D) weights:
 $\mathbf{W}_\phi \in \mathbf{R}^{d_x \times d_z}$, $\mathbf{W}_\theta \in \mathbf{R}^{d_z \times d_x}$
Initialize kernel bandwidths: σ_x, σ_y (learnable)
Set learning rates $\alpha_1, \alpha_2, \alpha_\sigma$
while not end of epochs **do**:
  for batch = 1 to total batches N **do**:
    Sample mini-batch data $\{X_i\}_1^l \in \mathbf{R}^d$, where l is batch-size
    Compute RBF kernels for input space $\mathcal{K}_{x_l}$ and latent space $\mathcal{K}_{z_l}$ of size $l \times l$
    Compute mutual information between input space X_l and latent space Z_l
using matrix-based Rényi's entropy:

$$MI(\mathcal{K}_{X_l}; \mathcal{K}_{Z_l})$$

    Perform a forward pass on encoder $E(X_{\phi_i})$
    Compute total batch loss:

$$\mathcal{L}_l = \mathcal{L}_{ce}\left(X^l, y^l\right) + \lambda \mathcal{L}_{rec}\left(X^l, X^{l'}\right) + \beta \mathcal{L}_{\mathcal{MI}}\left(X^l \| Z^l\right)$$

    Update $\mathbf{W}_\phi, \mathbf{W}_\theta$, and σ_x, σ_z
    $\mathbf{W}_{\phi_{l+1}} \leftarrow \mathbf{W}_{\phi_l} - \alpha_1 \nabla_\phi \mathcal{L}_l(\theta, \phi, \sigma)$
    $\mathbf{W}_{\theta_{l+1}} \leftarrow \mathbf{W}_{\theta_l} - \alpha_2 \nabla_\theta \mathcal{L}_l(\theta, \phi, \sigma)$
    $\sigma_{x_{l+1}}, \sigma_{z_{l+1}} \leftarrow \sigma_{x_l}, \sigma_{z_l} - \alpha_\sigma \nabla_\sigma \mathcal{L}_l(\theta, \phi, \sigma)$
  end for
end while
Output: Trained MTLS-RED model with optimized encoder-decoder weights $\mathbf{W}_\phi, \mathbf{W}_\theta$ and learned kernel bandwidths σ_x, σ_y

---

$\mathcal{L}_{MI}$ is the disentanglement or de-correlation loss between the latent space and the input space expressed in the form of mutual information divergence measured in their kernel space, given in Eq. 5, $\mathcal{S}_y$ is the softmax function applied on the encoded data $g_\phi(x)$, $\mathcal{L}_{rec}$ is the reconstruction loss, ϕ, θ are the encoder and decoder parameters. The σ represents the kernel bandwidth, a crucial parameter for estimating mutual information between the input and latent space.

We guide the cross-entropy loss by incorporating mutual information regularization between the latent and input spaces. This regularization discourages the retention of irrelevant information in the latent representation, with its strength governed by the hyperparameter β The parameter β regulates the trade-off between reducing dependencies in the latent space and maintaining classification performance. During joint optimization, we aim to balance the reconstruction loss and mutual information regularization. The parameter λ controls the reconstruction weight, determining the extent of compression we want to enforce in the latent space.

4 Experiments

In this section, we demonstrate the performance of our proposed model on benchmark cybersecurity and healthcare datasets.

4.1 Dataset

- **CSE-CIC-IDS2018** [18] This is a publicly available cybersecurity dataset that is made available by the Canadian Cybersecurity Institute (CIC). It consists of 7 major kinds of intrusion datasets. We use SOLARIS, GOLDENEYE as source domain data, INFILTRATION, BOTNET as cross-domain data, and RARE, SLOWHTTPS, HOIC and a BENIGN dataset of a different day as the OOD test classes.
- **CICIoT 2023** [18] This is a state-of-the-art dataset for profiling, behavioral analysis, and vulnerability testing of different IoT devices with different protocols from the network traffic, consisting of 7 major attack classes. We use BENIGN, DoS, and DDoS as source data, RECON, as cross-domain data and WEB, MIRAI as OOD test data.
- **CICIoMT 2024** [18] This is a benchmark dataset to enable the development and evaluation of Internet of Medical Things (IoMT) security solutions. The attacks are categorized into five classes. We use BENIGN, DDoS, DoS as source-domain, RECON, and SPOOFING as cross-domain, and MQTT as OOD data.
- **Arrythmia** This dataset is about atrial fibrillation (also called AFib or AF) which is a quivering or irregular heartbeat (arrhythmia) that can lead to blood clots, stroke, heart failure, and other heart-related complications. The dataset contains five classes/categories: N (Normal), S (Supraventricular ectopic beat), V (Ventricular ectopic beat), F (Fusion beat), and Q (Unknown beat).

4.2 Baselines

We consider the following models related to multi-task representation learning and few-shot learning as baselines.

- **Correlation Alignment for Deep Domain Adaptation (CORAL)** [30] This work has been employed for supervised domain adaptation, aligning source and target covariances to enhance OOD generalization.
- **Multi-task Autoencoder (MTAE)** [1] This encoder-decoder model optimizes reconstruction error across multiple domains in a supervised manner, jointly training sources and cross-domain data with label information in a two-stage process.

- **Minimum Mean Discrepancy-Autoencoder(MMD-AE)** [2,11] This paper uses the MMD measure as regularization for domain generalization between multiple cross-domain data. We use it as a few-shot learning method where the cross-domain data are added to improve the OOD generalization.
- **Noise Enhanced Supervised Autoencoder (NSAE)** [13]This model jointly predicts input labels, reconstructs inputs as noisy samples, and refines them through an additional fine-tuning step using a supervised classifier.
- **Domain-invariant Feature Exploration for Domain Generalization (DIFEX)** [16] This paper utilizes mutual invariance to extract cross-domain features for OOD classification, capturing domain-specific semantics through internal invariance while preserving shared information, and extends CORAL with an additional regularization term.

4.3 Training Strategy

To achieve robust generalization, we arbitrarily categorize the datasets into three groups: source domain datasets, cross-domain datasets, and out-of-distribution (OOD) datasets. The OOD datasets are reserved exclusively for testing purposes, serving as an evaluation benchmark for assessing model generalization. Our training strategy focuses on enhancing OOD performance by leveraging source domain data to improve learning on cross-domain datasets. To accomplish this, we systematically mix different proportions of source domain data with cross-domain data, integrating them into the benign dataset to construct the final training set. Additionally, we experiment with different combinations of source and cross-domain datasets to identify the most effective configurations for improving coverage across all three dataset categories—source, cross-domain, and OOD. Our training strategy is detailed in MTLS-RED Algorithm 1.

Selecting the Cross-Domains, Source and OOD Domains. In [32], the authors argue that learning a model that generalizes to unseen data can be facilitated when the *covariance* (or correlation structure) among features is well-conditioned and sufficiently diverse. In other words, if the training data exhibit meaningful variations or "patterns of dependencies" across features, then a function that captures those variations can more reliably extrapolate beyond the training distribution. Hence, by adding source domain data (with one correlation structure) to cross-domain data (with a different correlation structure), we produce a more *varied* training distribution—one that exposes the learner to multiple ways in which features can co-vary. The learner, in turn, is incentivized to find a representation that extracts the stable, non-spurious relationships across these distributions.

This approach is inspired by the paper's emphasis on the role of well-conditioned covariances for successful extrapolation, suggesting that diverse training correlations expand the set of feature configurations on which the model is trained, thus boosting generalization performance in truly novel test domains.

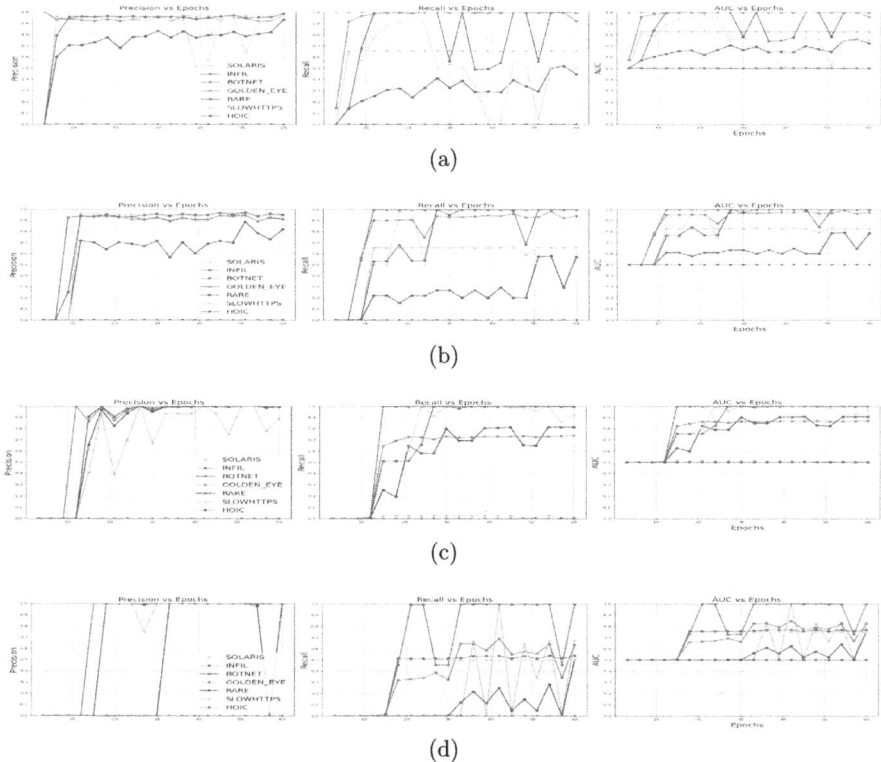

Fig. 2. Precision, recall, and accuracy plots for the rarest class (RARE, in blue), which has only 525 samples in the CIC-IDS dataset using training data from GOLDENEYE (source) and BOTNET (cross) domains. Figures (a) show precision, recall, and AUC over epochs without regularization on validation data; (b) apply MI = 0.01, reconstruction = 0.99; (c) apply MI = 0.99, reconstruction = 0.01, (d) use equal weights of 0.5. High MI regularization (case (c)) leads to over 10–20% improvement and stability across all metrics. Higher MI penalty helps in achieving better classification of the RARE class. (Color figure online)

DOS and DDOS share similar feature correlations, while MIRAI and WEB differ, and GOLDEN and SOLARIS exhibit distinct correlations from INFIL and BOTNET. We aim to enhance generalization by training on datasets with varying feature correlation structures while ensuring overlapping marginal distributions for effective extrapolation.[1]

---

[1] https://github.com/padmaksha18/MTRAE/blob/main/mtrae/mtl-reg-cse-cic-ids-V333333-noisy-equal-cross.ipynb.

Table 1. We report **accuracy** (with standard deviation) of the proposed and baseline methods on the CIC-CSE-IDS dataset, where cross-domain data is gradually added to the source domain during training in the range (0âĂŞ50%). Best test accuracies for each model are highlighted. The OOD domains are used only for test/evaluation purposes. During train, each anomaly dataset has equal amount (50%) of BENIGN samples added to it, i.e., the train and test datasets are balanced (equal normal and anomaly samples).

Model	Percent	SOURCE DOMAIN		CROSS DOMAIN		OOD DOMAIN			
		SOLARIS	GOLDEYE	INFIL	BOTNET	RARE	HOIC	HTTPS	BENIGN
MTAE	0%	**99.97 (2.5)**	92.70 (1.3)	04.00 (0.1)	09.50 (0.2)	00.30 (0.0)	00.38 (0.0)	02.30 (0.1)	97.98 (2.4)
	20%	99.50 (2.5)	**99.70 (2.5)**	69.40 (2.5)	79.50 (2.5)	61.30 (1.5)	27.38 (0.7)	32.30 (0.8)	**98.11 (2.5)**
	30%	81.60 (2.0)	79.60 (2.0)	69.70 (1.7)	78.50 (2.0)	65.40 (1.6)	**50.00 (1.3)**	42.40 (1.1)	62.00 (1.6)
	50%	61.61 (1.5)	61.30 (1.5)	31.30 (0.8)	61.60 (1.5)	**72.60 (1.8)**	48.50 (1.2)	**69.80 (1.7)**	83.32 (2.1)
MMD-AE	0%	**99.99 (2.5)**	**99.29 (2.5)**	00.53 (0.0)	**99.98 (2.5)**	55.47 (1.4)	**99.98 (2.5)**	**99.69 (2.5)**	**99.71 (2.5)**
	20%	99.98 (2.5)	92.55 (0.1)	**22.55 (0.6)**	99.83 (2.5)	12.19 (0.3)	41.34 (1.0)	98.77 (2.5)	98.67 (2.5)
	30%	99.78 (2.5)	02.52 (0.1)	15.35 (0.4)	99.83 (2.5)	12.19 (0.3)	41.27 (1.0)	99.69 (2.5)	98.61 (2.5)
	50%	99.96 (2.5)	01.88 (0.1)	12.30 (0.3)	99.83 (2.5)	14.13 (0.4)	41.12 (1.0)	56.21 (1.4)	99.14 (2.5)
NSAE	0%	99.99 (2.5)	99.98 (2.5)	00.09 (0.0)	99.99 (2.5)	77.03 (1.9)	**99.90 (2.5)**	**97.02 (2.4)**	99.58 (2.5)
	20%	99.80 (2.5)	**99.99 (2.5)**	04.82 (0.1)	34.92 (0.9)	36.04 (0.9)	00.00 (0.0)	05.16 (0.1)	**99.80 (2.5)**
	30%	**99.99 (2.5)**	03.16 (0.1)	00.32 (0.0)	**99.83 (2.5)**	59.36 (1.5)	15.90 (0.4)	00.35 (0.0)	99.69 (2.5)
	50%	99.98 (2.5)	34.36 (0.9)	**53.66 (1.3)**	99.83 (2.5)	12.36 (0.3)	00.00 (0.0)	19.33 (0.5)	99.40 (2.5)
CORAL	0%	59.18 (1.5)	90.61 (2.3)	30.45 (0.8)	00.80 (0.0)	08.40 (0.2)	55.06 (1.4)	03.40 (0.1)	69.94 (1.7)
	20%	61.53 (1.5)	12.64 (0.3)	**31.79 (0.8)**	50.43 (1.3)	**33.74 (0.9)**	41.31 (1.0)	**50.38 (1.3)**	67.54 (1.7)
	30%	38.85 (1.0)	**99.99 (2.5)**	0.00 (0.0)	0.01 (0.0)	22.96 (0.6)	82.21 (2.1)	0.00 (0.0)	95.01 (2.4)
	50%	**99.99 (2.5)**	38.85 (1.0)	00.01 (0.0)	00.00 (0.0)	22.96 (0.6)	**82.21 (2.1)**	00.01 (0.0)	**99.19 (2.5)**
MTLS-RED	0%	**98.83 (2.2)**	96.08 (2.2)	72.41 (2.1)	**96.12 (2.4)**	28.01 (0.7)	80.99 (2.0)	73.93 (1.8)	73.23 (1.8)
	20%	79.00 (2.0)	78.85 (2.0)	78.71 (2.0)	78.68 (2.0)	78.88 (2.0)	79.13 (2.0)	78.82 (2.0)	79.01 (2.0)
	30%	83.90 (2.1)	80.70 (2.0)	70.70 (2.0)	83.80 (2.1)	76.50 (1.9)	81.96 (2.0)	**85.00 (2.1)**	77.10 (1.9)
	50%	86.46 (2.0)	**89.33 (2.0)**	**79.20 (2.0)**	89.12 (2.0)	**78.99 (2.0)**	**89.33 (2.0)**	79.25 (2.0)	**79.64 (2.0)**

4.4 Hyperparameter Sensitivity

In the joint optimization framework, achieving an optimal balance between the compression regularization (λ) and the mutual information regularization (β) is crucial for ensuring strong generalization across all classes. The reconstruction loss, weighted by λ, governs the degree of compression in the latent space—excessive compression may lead to the loss of essential features, while insufficient compression can result in overfitting to the input distribution. Meanwhile, the mutual information regularization, controlled by β, acts as a de-correlation penalty, reducing redundant dependencies between the latent and input spaces. Properly tuning β ensures that the latent representation retains only the most discriminative information for classification. Our findings indicate that prioritizing entropy regularization (higher β) while reducing the emphasis on reconstruction loss (lower λ) yields the best overall model performance across diverse scenarios, reinforcing the importance of controlled compression and structured disentanglement in the latent space.

Importance of Kernel Bandwidth. In a non-parametric estimation method such as our mutual information penalty, the kernel bandwidth σ plays a crucial

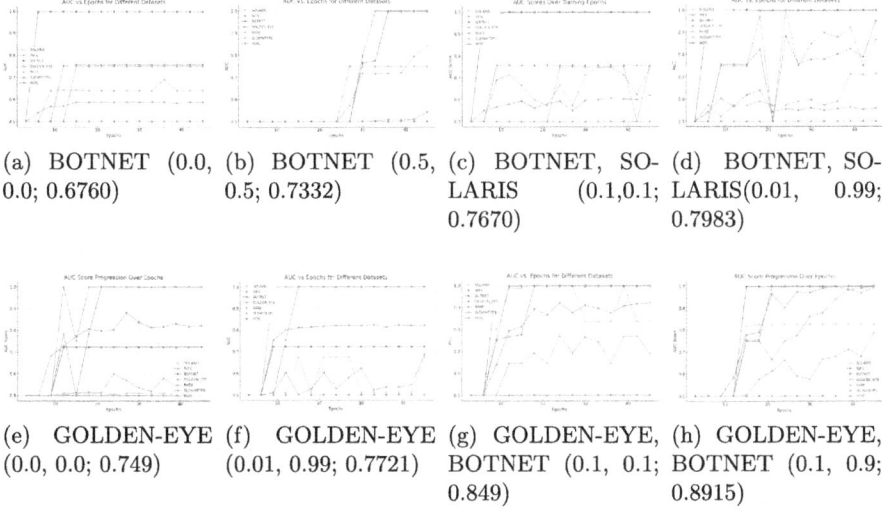

(a) BOTNET (0.0, 0.0; 0.6760) (b) BOTNET (0.5, 0.5; 0.7332) (c) BOTNET, SOLARIS (0.1,0.1; 0.7670) (d) BOTNET, SOLARIS (0.01, 0.99; 0.7983)

(e) GOLDEN-EYE (0.0, 0.0; 0.749) (f) GOLDEN-EYE (0.01, 0.99; 0.7721) (g) GOLDEN-EYE, BOTNET (0.1, 0.1; 0.849) (h) GOLDEN-EYE, BOTNET (0.1, 0.9; 0.8915)

Fig. 3. From left to right, the plots show improved average AUC-ROC as datasets are combined and regularization is applied, enhancing generalization to unseen domains. We evaluate this using seven CIC-CSE-IDS attack datasets with equal benign samples, reporting results as (reconstruction weight, MI penalty, Average AUC on all datasets).

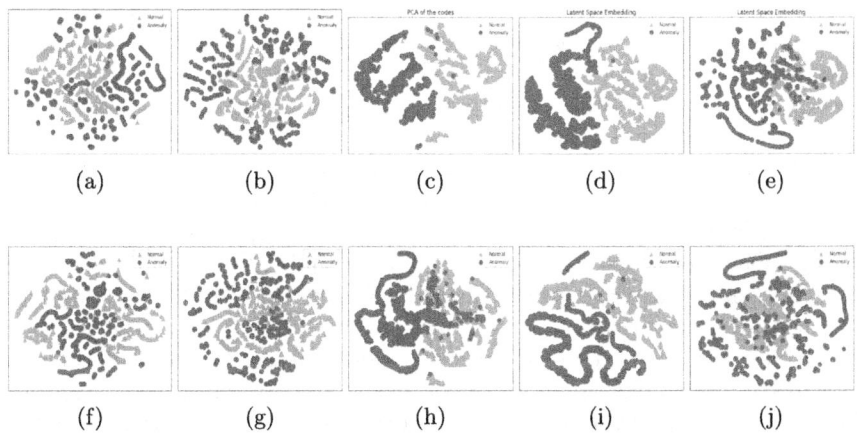

(a)　(b)　(c)　(d)　(e)

(f)　(g)　(h)　(i)　(j)

Fig. 4. T-SNE projection of the latent space of without regularization case (bottom row) and MTL-RED (top row) for some of the attacks in CIC-IDS and CIC-IOMT/IOT: SOLARIS, RARE, DOS, DDOS, and RECONAISSANCE. Subfigures (a)–(e) correspond to MTL-RED, and (f)–(j) to no regularization case. (Color figure online)

role. By learning σ jointly with the encoder and decoder, we adapt the kernel scale to match the data distribution's complexity. We vary the proportion of cross-domain data in training, ranging from 0%-50% of the source data, to ana-

Table 2. We report **accuracy** (with std deviation) of the proposed and baseline methods on the CIC-IOMT/IOT dataset Other details are similar as Table 1.

Model	Percent	SOURCE DOMAINS		CROSS DOMAINS		OOD DOMAINS			
		DDOS	DOS	RECON	SPOOF	MQTT	MIRAI	WEB	BENIGN
MTAE	0%	99.96 (2.5)	99.99 (2.6)	54.07 (1.5)	46.98 (1.3)	78.43 (2.1)	**99.97 (2.8)**	30.55 (0.8)	97.53 (2.8)
	20%	99.99 (2.8)	99.99 (2.7)	98.66 (2.3)	71.84 (1.4)	78.43 (2.0)	79.38 (1.8)	**30.55 (0.7)**	97.53 (2.2)
	30%	99.99 (2.4)	99.99 (2.5)	**99.99 (2.5)**	75.55 (1.9)	**99.93 (2.9)**	80.07 (2.3)	21.38 (0.6)	98.63 (2.3)
	50%	**99.99 (2.4)**	**99.99 (2.7)**	98.53 (2.1)	74.43 (2.2)	89.42 (2.2)	80.83 (2.2)	29.02 (0.7)	97.78 (2.7)
MMD-AE	0%	99.96 (3.0)	99.96 (2.5)	49.95 (1.3)	41.32 (0.9)	**95.87 (2.7)**	84.01 (1.8)	21.15 (0.6)	**98.56 (2.9)**
	20%	**99.99 (2.8)**	**99.99 (2.7)**	98.47 (2.9)	70.54 (1.9)	90.54 (2.7)	**84.01 (2.2)**	42.53 (0.9)	96.49 (2.1)
	30%	99.99 (2.4)	99.99 (2.8)	99.11 (2.1)	73.60 (1.7)	89.42 (2.5)	77.60 (2.2)	58.04 (1.4)	93.48 (2.4)
	50%	99.61 (2.4)	99.46 (2.4)	**99.30 (2.5)**	**78.23 (2.2)**	94.84 (2.4)	72.08 (2.1)	**67.21 (1.5)**	92.41 (2.3)
NSAE	0%	**99.99 (2.5)**	99.99 (2.0)	46.90 (1.1)	32.42 (0.8)	69.11 (1.7)	**99.90 (2.7)**	56.05 (1.1)	94.68 (2.0)
	20%	99.99 (3.0)	**99.99 (2.9)**	97.77 (2.8)	69.11 (1.9)	**99.90 (2.6)**	99.87 (2.1)	36.66 (0.9)	**97.71 (2.3)**
	30%	99.99 (2.6)	99.99 (2.9)	**98.70 (2.5)**	**71.29 (1.9)**	99.71 (2.7)	99.90 (2.1)	43.83 (1.2)	96.11 (2.0)
	50%	99.99 (2.4)	99.99 (2.7)	98.62 (2.1)	70.64 (2.0)	99.89 (2.3)	99.90 (2.6)	49.70 (1.1)	95.78 (2.4)
CORAL	0%	**99.99 (2.6)**	99.99 (3.0)	98.53 (2.4)	74.43 (2.2)	89.42 (2.0)	**81.13 (2.3)**	30.53 (0.8)	98.73 (2.7)
	20%	99.99 (2.2)	**99.99 (2.8)**	98.53 (2.8)	74.43 (2.2)	89.42 (2.1)	81.13 (2.1)	**42.30 (1.0)**	98.73 (2.2)
	30%	99.99 (2.4)	99.99 (2.9)	**98.86 (2.5)**	75.55 (1.9)	**99.90 (2.9)**	80.08 (2.3)	42.03 (0.9)	**98.73 (2.5)**
	50%	99.99 (2.5)	99.99 (2.7)	99.11 (2.3)	**77.21 (2.0)**	99.57 (2.7)	80.51 (2.2)	42.30 (1.0)	98.73 (2.4)
MTLS-RED	0%	99.99 (2.7)	99.99 (2.8)	98.41 (2.4)	78.92 (2.0)	78.21 (1.9)	76.04 (1.8)	73.91 (1.7)	87.67 (2.5)
	20%	99.99 (2.6)	99.99 (2.7)	98.41 (2.3)	78.92 (1.9)	78.21 (1.8)	99.75 (2.5)	68.03 (1.6)	91.83 (2.4)
	30%	99.99 (2.8)	99.99 (2.5)	98.41 (2.8)	78.21 (1.9)	53.19 (1.5)	99.87 (2.6)	73.67 (1.8)	**93.05 (2.3)**
	50%	**99.99 (2.5)**	**99.99 (2.8)**	**98.98 (2.5)**	**81.17 (2.3)**	**95.87 (2.7)**	**99.88 (2.3)**	**75.91 (1.6)**	91.20 (2.4)

lyze the effects of the de-correlation penalty and reconstruction regularization under different scenarios. In Tables 1 and 2, we observe that as the proportion of cross-domain data in training increases, the performance of most baseline models deteriorates on the IN distribution. In particular, OOD domain data remain completely unseen throughout the training process. Table 1 reveals an intriguing trend: as cross-domain data increases to 40% – 50%, adjusting the kernel bandwidth and hyperparameters β and λ allows us to train a model that achieves comprehensive generalization across all training and test datasets.

Figure 3 illustrates the improvement in average AUC-ROC as datasets are combined and regularization is introduced. Both strategies—dataset combination and regularization—enhance generalization to unseen domains. The datasets are added strategically to improve coverage of unseen domains, ensuring a broader representation. In most cases, assigning *higher weight to the MI penalty* while keeping the *reconstruction weight minimal* leads to the best generalization performance. Figure 2 demonstrates the impact of the regularization penalty on the RARE dataset. Our results indicate that incorporating regularization—and particularly increasing the weight on the mutual information (decorrelation) penalty—leads to improved and more stable precision, recall, and AUC when training on the combined GOLDEN-EYE and SOLARIS dataset.

In Fig. 4, we visualize the latent space representations of a standard multi-task encoder-decoder model without regularization and our proposed model incorporating the MI penalty. We observe improved clustering of source, cross-domain, and target domain classes when regularization is applied, demonstrating

Table 3. We report **accuracy** (with std deviation) of the proposed and baseline methods on the Arrythmia dataset. For each case, the dataset contains equal amount of normal and anomaly samples.

Model	Percent (%)	SOURCE DOMAINS		CROSS DOMAINS		OOD DOMAINS
		VEB	BENIGN	SVEB	Q	F
MTAE	50%	99.17 (2.48)	62.94 (1.57)	60.53 (1.51)	90.41 (2.26)	60.00 (2.50)
MMD-AE	50%	98.58 (2.46)	63.63 (1.59)	44.90 (1.12)	93.33 (2.33)	89.66 (2.24)
NSAE	50%	97.18 (2.43)	72.71 (1.82)	41.70 (1.04)	80.00 (2.00)	90.17 (2.25)
CORAL	50%	97.87 (2.45)	58.24 (1.46)	69.70 (1.74)	95.26 (2.38)	73.33 (1.83)
MTLS-RED	50%	**99.34 (2.48)**	**77.49 (1.94)**	**73.48 (1.84)**	**95.52 (2.39)**	**93.33** (2.33)

its effectiveness in structuring the latent space. As shown in Table 2, increasing the proportion of cross-domain data during training significantly enhances classification performance across OOD datasets, such as WEB and SPOOFING attacks. Likewise, Table 3 presents the evaluation of our method on the Arrhythmia dataset, where the model is trained on the normal and VEB classes while considering all other anomaly classes—SVEB, Q as cross-domain, and F—as OOD test class. In Table 4, we evaluate our approach on a time-series dataset (EMG Gesture Recognition) and compare with the baselines.

Table 4. Performance (accuracy %) of MTL-RED, DIFEX, CORAL with EMG time series dataset divided into 4 domains each consisting of 6 classes for all the 9 persons.

MODEL	Domain1	Domain2	Domain3	Domain4
DIFEX	65.02 ± 2.00	66.15 ± 2.50	**64.06 ± 2.00**	62.98 ± 2.00
CORAL	52.39 ± 2.00	52.51 ± 2.50	53.89 ± 2.00	57.06 ± 2.00
MTL-RED	**66.41 ± 3.40**	**66.30 ± 2.50**	55.92 ± 2.00	**65.82 ± 2.50**

5 Conclusion

Our paper addresses the challenge of detecting novel and out-of-distribution (OOD) anomalies through domain generalization techniques. By training on multiple source and cross-domain datasets with distinct correlation structures, we aim to increase the coverage to generalize to unseen anomaly classes. Subsequently, guided by the principle of relevant information preservation (PRI), our regularization steers the cross-entropy loss in latent space to retain essential features to achieve domain generalization. Real-world cybersecurity and healthcare datasets often exhibit different correlation patterns among the different classes, which can be exploited to increase the coverage for extrapolation to new, unseen domains. Future work will further explore methods for latent space anomaly detection.

Acknowledgment. We gratefully acknowledge the support of the Virginia Tech National Security Institute (VTNSI) and the Deloitte & Touche LLP, USA, for supporting this research. We also extend our sincere thanks to our collaborators at Deloitte—Ajay Kumar, Alison Hu, Sanmitra Bhattacharya, and Edward Bowen for their insightful contributions.

A Joint Optimization and the Principle of Relevant Information Preservation (PRI)

Our approach is motivated by Tishby's Principle of Relevant Information (PRI), which states that an optimal representation should preserve only the information in the input that is necessary for the task at hand, while discarding irrelevant details. In our context, the goal is to learn a latent representation Z from the input X that is both predictive of the target Y and minimally influenced by spurious correlations present in X. To achieve this, we jointly optimize a loss function that combines three key components:

1. **Cross-Entropy Loss** ($\mathcal{L}_{\text{CE}}$): This term ensures that the latent representation Z is discriminative enough to accurately predict the target Y.
2. **Reconstruction Loss** ($\mathcal{L}_{\text{recon}}$): This term (e.g., mean squared error) forces Z to retain sufficient information to reconstruct the input X, thereby preventing excessive compression.
3. **Mutual Information Penalty** ($\mathcal{L}_{\text{MI}}$): By penalizing the mutual information between X and Z, this term encourages the model to discard spurious and domain-specific correlations, leading to a more invariant and disentangled latent space.

The overall objective can be written as:

$$\mathcal{L} = \mathcal{L}_{\text{CE}} + \lambda_{\text{recon}} \mathcal{L}_{\text{recon}} + \lambda_{\text{MI}} \mathcal{L}_{\text{MI}}, \tag{7}$$

where λ_{recon} and λ_{MI} are hyperparameters that balance the trade-off between reconstruction fidelity and the strength of the decorrelation (compression) penalty.

In the framework of PRI (proposed by Tishby and later on implemented in various contexts), we aim to minimize the mutual information between X and Z while maintaining high mutual information between Z and Y. This idea is often expressed as:

$$\mathcal{L}_{\text{PRI}} = I(X;Z) - \beta\, I(Y;Z), \tag{8}$$

where:

- $I(X;Z)$ quantifies the total information that the latent representation Z retains about X.
- $I(Y;Z)$ measures the information in Z that is useful for predicting Y.
- β is a parameter controlling the trade-off between compression (minimizing $I(X;Z)$) and predictive power (maximizing $I(Y;Z)$).

In practice, our joint loss in Eq. (7) serves as a proxy for the PRI objective in Eq. (8):

- The $\mathcal{L}_{\text{CE}}$ term drives Z to retain information relevant to Y (i.e., maximizing $I(Y; Z)$).
- The combination of $\mathcal{L}_{\text{recon}}$ and $\mathcal{L}_{\text{MI}}$ encourages Z to compress X by preserving only the necessary information and discarding spurious correlations, effectively minimizing $I(X; Z)$.

Moreover, our implementation of the mutual information penalty is based on the Renyi entropy of kernel matrices computed from X and Z, with kernel bandwidths s_x and s_y that are adjusted during training. This enables the model to learn an optimal level of decorrelation, ensuring that the latent space does not overfit to domain-specific artifacts while still preserving the relevant structure needed for accurate classification and reconstruction. In summary, our joint optimization framework, which integrates classification, reconstruction, and decorrelation, is a practical instantiation of the PRI principle. By carefully balancing these objectives, our model is guided to learn a compressed yet task-relevant latent representation that generalizes effectively across domains.

References

1. Ghifary, M., Kleijn, W.B., Zhang, M., Balduzzi, D.: Domain generalization for object recognition with multi-task autoencoders. In: Proceedings of the IEEE International Conference on Computer Vision, pp. 2551–2559 (2015)
2. Sathya, R., Sekar, K., Ananthi, S., Dheepa, T.: Adversarially trained variational auto-encoders with maximum mean discrepancy based regularization. In: 2022 International Conference on Knowledge Engineering and Communication Systems (ICKES), pp. 1–6. IEEE (2022)
3. Shwartz-Ziv, R., Balestriero, R., Kawaguchi, K., Rudner, T.G.J., LeCun, Y.: An information-theoretic perspective on variance-invariance-covariance regularization. arXiv preprint arXiv:2303.00633 (2023)
4. Jeon, E., Ko, W., Yoon, J.S., Suk, H.I.: Mutual information-driven subject-invariant and class-relevant deep representation learning in bci. IEEE Trans. Neural Netw. Learn. Syst. **34**(2), 739–749 (2021)
5. Venkataramanan, S., Psomas, B., Kijak, E., Amsaleg, L., Karantzalos, K., Avrithis, Y.: It takes two to tango: mixup for deep metric learning. arXiv preprint arXiv:2106.04990 (2021)
6. Hendrycks, D., Gimpel, K.: A baseline for detecting misclassified and out-of-distribution examples in neural networks. arXiv preprint arXiv:1610.02136 (2016)
7. Xu, R., Chen, Z., Zuo, W., Yan, J., Lin, L.: Deep cocktail network: multi-source unsupervised domain adaptation with category shift. In: Proceedings of the IEEE Conference on Computer Vision and Pattern Recognition, pp. 3964–3973 (2018)
8. Wang, W., Zheng, V.W., Han, Yu., Miao, C.: A survey of zero-shot learning: settings, methods, and applications. ACM Trans. Intell. Syst. Technol. (TIST) **10**(2), 1–37 (2019)
9. Sun, Y., Ming, Y., Zhu, X., Li, Y.: Out-of-distribution detection with deep nearest neighbors. In: International Conference on Machine Learning, pp. 20827–20840. PMLR (2022)

10. Arjovsky, M., Bottou, L., Gulrajani, I., Lopez-Paz, D.: Invariant risk minimization. arXiv preprint arXiv:1907.02893 (2019)
11. Li, H., Pan, S.J., Wang, S., Kot, A.C.: Domain generalization with adversarial feature learning. In: Proceedings of the IEEE Conference on Computer Vision and Pattern Recognition, pp. 5400–5409 (2018)
12. Chattopadhyay, P., Balaji, Y., Hoffman, J.: Learning to balance specificity and invariance for in and out of domain generalization. In: Vedaldi, A., Bischof, H., Brox, T., Frahm, J.-M. (eds.) ECCV 2020. LNCS, vol. 12354, pp. 301–318. Springer, Cham (2020). https://doi.org/10.1007/978-3-030-58545-7_18
13. Liang, H., Zhang, Q., Dai, P., Lu, J.: Boosting the generalization capability in cross-domain few-shot learning via noise-enhanced supervised autoencoder. In: Proceedings of the IEEE/CVF International Conference on Computer Vision, pp. 9424–9434 (2021)
14. Vinyals, O., Blundell, C., Lillicrap, T., Wierstra, D.: Matching networks for one shot learning. Adv. Neural Inf. Process. Syst. **29** (2016)
15. Snell, J., Swersky, K., Zemel, R.: Prototypical networks for few-shot learning. Adv. Neural Inf. Process. Syst. **30** (2017)
16. Lu, W., Wang, J., Li, H., Chen, Y., Xie, X.: Domain-invariant feature exploration for domain generalization. arXiv preprint arXiv:2207.12020 (2022)
17. Vuorio, R., Sun, S.H., Hu, H., Lim, J.J.: Multimodal model-agnostic meta-learning via task-aware modulation. Adv. Neural Inf. Process. Syst. **32** (2019)
18. Canadian Institute for Cybersecurity: Public datasets for intrusion detection and anomaly detection, including CSE-CIC-IDS2018, IoT Dataset, IoMT Dataset, and Arrhythmia Dataset. https://www.unb.ca/cic/datasets/. Accessed 14 Feb 2025
19. Finn, C., Abbeel, P., Levine, S.: Model-agnostic meta-learning for fast adaptation of deep networks. In: International Conference on Machine Learning, pp. 1126–1135. PMLR (2017)
20. Zhou, K., Liu, Z., Qiao, Y., Xiang, T., Loy, C.C.: Domain generalization: a survey. IEEE Trans. Pattern Anal. Mach. Intell. (2022)
21. Sung, F., Yang, Y., Zhang, L., Xiang, T., Torr, P.H.S., Hospedales, T.M.: Learning to compare: relation network for few-shot learning. In: Proceedings of the IEEE Conference on Computer Vision and Pattern Recognition, pp. 1199–1208 (2018)
22. Yu, S., Alesiani, F., Xi, Yu., Jenssen, R., Principe, J.: Measuring dependence with matrix-based entropy functional. In: Proceedings of the AAAI Conference on Artificial Intelligence, vol. 35, no. 12, pp. 10781–10789 (2021)
23. Wang, J., et al.: Generalizing to unseen domains: a survey on domain generalization. IEEE Trans. Knowl. Data Eng. (2022)
24. Li, Y., et al.: Deep domain generalization via conditional invariant adversarial networks. In: Proceedings of the European Conference on Computer Vision (ECCV), pp. 624–639 (2018)
25. Jin, X., Lan, C., Zeng, W., Chen, Z.: Feature alignment and restoration for domain generalization and adaptation. arXiv preprint arXiv:2006.12009 (2020)
26. Erfani, S., et al.: Robust domain generalisation by enforcing distribution invariance. In: Proceedings of the Twenty-Fifth International Joint Conference on Artificial Intelligence (IJCAI-16), pp. 1455–1461. AAAI Press (2016)
27. Rusu, A.A., et al.: Meta-learning with latent embedding optimization. arXiv preprint arXiv:1807.05960 (2018)
28. Li, D., Yang, Y., Song, Y.Z., Hospedales, T.: Learning to generalize: meta-learning for domain generalization. In Proceedings of the AAAI Conference on Artificial Intelligence, vol. 32, no. 1 (2018)

29. Seo, S., Suh, Y., Kim, D., Kim, G., Han, J., Han, B.: Learning to optimize domain specific normalization for domain generalization. In: Vedaldi, A., Bischof, H., Brox, T., Frahm, J.-M. (eds.) ECCV 2020. LNCS, vol. 12367, pp. 68–83. Springer, Cham (2020). https://doi.org/10.1007/978-3-030-58542-6_5
30. Sun, B., Saenko, K.: Deep coral: correlation alignment for deep domain adaptation. In: Hua, G., Jégou, H. (eds.) ECCV 2016. LNCS, vol. 9915, pp. 443–450. Springer, Cham (2016). https://doi.org/10.1007/978-3-319-49409-8_35
31. Tishby, N., Pereira, F. C., Bialek, W.: The information bottleneck method (2000). arXiv preprint physics/0004057
32. Dong, K., Ma, T.: First steps toward understanding the extrapolation of nonlinear models to unseen domains. arXiv preprint arXiv:2211.11719 (2022)

Evidential Spectrum-Aware Contrastive Learning for OOD Detection in Dynamic Graphs

Nan Sun[1,2], Xixun Lin[1,2(✉)], Zhiheng Zhou[3], Yanmin Shang[1,2], Zhenlin Cheng[4(✉)], and Yanan Cao[1,2]

[1] Institute of Information Engineering, Chinese Academy of Sciences, Beijing, China
{sunnan,linxixun,shangyanmin,caoyanan}@iie.ac.cn
[2] School of Cyber Security, University of Chinese Academy of Sciences, Beijing, China
[3] Academy of Mathematics and Systems Science, Chinese Academy of Sciences, Beijing, China
zhouzhiheng@amss.ac.cn
[4] Beijing Wuzi University, Beijing, China
chengzhenlin@bwu.edu.cn

Abstract. Recently, Out-of-distribution (OOD) detection in dynamic graphs, which aims to identify whether incoming data deviates from the distribution of the in-distribution (ID) training set, has garnered considerable attention in security-sensitive fields. Current OOD detection paradigms primarily focus on static graphs and confront two critical challenges: i) high bias and high variance caused by single-point estimation, which makes the predictions sensitive to randomness in the data; ii) score homogenization resulting from the lack of OOD training data, where the model only learns ID-specific patterns, resulting in overall low OOD scores and a narrow score gap between ID and OOD data. To tackle these issues, we first investigate OOD detection in dynamic graphs through the lens of Evidential Deep Learning (EDL). Specifically, we propose **EviSEC**, an innovative and effective OOD detector via **Evi**dential **S**pectrum-awar**E** **C**ontrastive Learning. We design an evidential neural network to redefine the output as the posterior Dirichlet distribution, explaining the randomness of inputs through the uncertainty of distribution, which is overlooked by single-point estimation. Moreover, spectrum-aware augmentation module generates OOD approximations to identify patterns with high OOD scores, thereby widening the score gap between ID and OOD data and mitigating score homogenization. Extensive experiments on real-world datasets demonstrate that EviSAC effectively detects OOD samples in dynamic graphs. Our source code is available at https://github.com/Sunnan191/EviSEC

Keywords: Dynamic graph · Out-of-distribution detection · Evidential deep learning · Graph spectrum

1 Introduction

Real-world graph data often evolves temporally, allowing dynamic graphs to be ubiquitously applied across non-Euclidean domains such as citation networks [1],

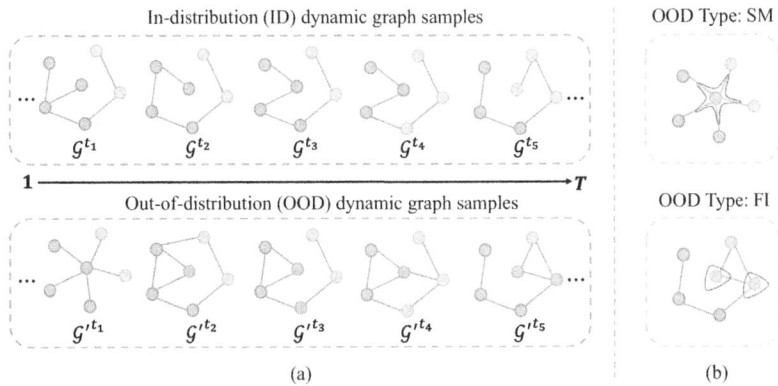

Fig. 1. Dynamic graph examples of (a) ID samples maintain consistent structures, while OOD samples exhibit deviations. (b) Examples include cases such as SM (Structure Manipulation) and FI (Feature Interpolation), highlighting structural changes and feature variations, respectively.

social communities [2], and transaction records [3]. Recently, studies on dynamic graphs have gained increasing popularity, among which Dynamic Graph Neural Networks (DGNNs) [4] have rapidly emerged as powerful approaches for dynamic graph representation learning [5]. These models primarily leverage Graph Neural Networks (GNNs) and sequence-based architectures to capture temporal variations in dynamic graphs.

Most existing models on dynamic graphs are predominantly trained with the closed-world assumption that the training and test data share the same data distribution, with such data termed In-Distribution (ID) data. Nevertheless, real-world scenarios frequently deviate from this ideal assumption, often involving Out-of-Distribution (OOD) dynamic graphs, which are unobserved during the training process. Figure 1 provides examples illustrating the behavior of ID and OOD dynamic graph with two OOD types. During the inference stage, performing predictions blindly without recognizing OOD samples can render the output unreliable and pose serious risks. Such cases are especially unacceptable in safety-critical domains, such as medical diagnostics [6] and autonomous driving [7]. An ideal model should effectively handle both ID test performance and OOD detection performance. Therefore, OOD detection in dynamic graphs has seen a growing demand, which aims to identify whether incoming data deviate from the distribution of the training set.

Early works in OOD detection primarily focus on static graphs. Liu et al. [8] propose a hierarchical contrastive learning method that captures common patterns of ID graphs across different granularities (node, graph, and group levels), so that OOD graphs that deviate from these patterns can be effectively identified. GNNSAFE [9] extends energy-based models [10] to static graphs and develops an energy function that classifies nodes with high energies as OOD samples. In parallel, research on anomaly detection [11] in dynamic graphs has also gained attraction. Netwalk [12] uses random walks and autoencoders to generate similar node representations for ID data, thereby identifying anomalous interactions between nodes with distinct representations. TADDY [13] employs transformers to capture both global and local structural anomalies in node representations. *Although the above approaches perform fairly well, they are confronted with two critical limitations:*

i) **High bias and high variance caused by single-point estimation.** Most of the aforementioned methods follow a manner of single-point estimation, which overlook the inherent randomness presented in the data, so that their OOD detection results are sensitive to natural noise, resulting in high bias and high variance in the output.

ii) **Score homogenization resulting from the lack of OOD training data.** During the training stage, only ID data is available whereas OOD data remains unseen. This will cause the problem of score homogenization, i.e., the model only learns the ID-specific patterns, making it tend to assign overall lower OOD scores, regardless of whether the sample is ID or OOD. The small score gap between ID and OOD data makes it challenging to effectively distinguish OOD samples.

To address these limitations, we thoroughly investigate OOD detection in dynamic graphs from a novel perspective drawing on Evidential Deep Learning (EDL)—a theoretically grounded framework for uncertainty quantification through Dirichlet distributions. Specifically, we propose **EviSEC**, an innovative and effective OOD detector via **Evi**dential **S**pectrum-awar**E** **C**ontrastive Learning. We design an evidential neural network to reshape the output class probability of single-point estimation into a probability Dirichlet distribution, allowing us to describe the variability and randomness of the data through the uncertainty of distribution. Furthermore, we develop two loss functions to guide the model to output sharper Dirichlet distributions with low uncertainty scores for ID samples while preserve the ID performance. To tackle the issue of missing OOD samples, we propose a spectral-aware data augmentation module that generates OOD approximations of dynamic graphs. Based on this, the contrastive loss can enable the model to learn and assign higher uncertainty scores, thereby mitigating the problem of score homogenization. Finally, our OOD detector computes the learned uncertainty as the OOD score, which efficiently distinguishes OOD samples with higher uncertainty. The main contributions of this study are summarized as follows:

1. EviSEC is the first to establish a direct link between EDL and OOD detection in dynamic graphs. We propose an evidential neural network that uses the uncertainty of posterior distribution to describe the randomness of the input, addressing the problem of single-point estimation. Our method effectively improves OOD detection while maintaining ID testing performance.
2. We propose a spectral-aware data augmentation module to generate OOD approximations for dynamic graphs, alleviating the lack of OOD training samples. Based on this, our contrastive learning module enlarges the score

gap, mitigating the issue of score homogenization and effectively enhancing the OOD detection performance.
3. Experimental results on multiple real-world datasets validate the claimed advantages of our approach, which achieves consistent performance gains over multiple powerful competitors with an average AUROC improvement of 24.32%.

2 Related Works

2.1 Dynamic Graph Representation Learning

Early attempts in dynamic graph representation learning [5,14] employ traditional methods including random walks [15], matrix factorization [16], and temporal point processes [17,18] to model graph information over time. However, compared to these methods, DGNNs outperform in expressive power, since they combine message passing and temporal modeling to better capture topological and temporal dynamics. For instance, EvolveGCN [19] employs RNNs to dynamically adapt the weights of GNNs across temporal steps. DEFT [20] utilizes transformers to model temporal dependencies through self-attention mechanisms. Instead of using RNNs, LEDG [21] applies gradient-based meta learning to learn updating strategies. While these methods excel in predictive tasks, they largely focus on ID data, often neglecting OOD detection in dynamic graphs.

2.2 Graph Out-of-Distribution Detection

Graph OOD detection primarily focuses on static graphs and can be broadly categorized into the following three approaches:

Post-processing Methods. These model-agnostic methods directly process outputs of pretrained models to estimate OOD scores. For instance, Lee et al. [22] use Mahalanobis distance to measure the deviation of input data. Similarly, maximum softmax probabilities (MSP) [23] can be utilized as confidence scores, with lower values signaling OOD samples. ODIN [24] enhances MSP by incorporating temperature scaling and input perturbation to increase the score gap. Yet, these methods typically follow single-point estimation, which is prone to high variance and bias, thereby hindering their ability to recognize the OOD patterns.

Energy-Based Methods. These approaches are based on the framework of energy-based models, where energy scores measure the discrepancy between input data and the model's learned distribution. Specifically, energy scores [25] effectively separate OOD samples from ID data, as OOD samples typically yield higher values. GNNSAFE [9] develops an energy function directly extracted from GNNs trained with energy propagation on static graphs. Nevertheless, directly adapting these approaches to dynamic settings is challenging since they require a fundamental redesign of the energy propagation mechanism over time.

Uncertainty-Based Methods. Uncertainty [26] measures the unreliability of a model's predictive distribution. A previous study [27] adopts the graph neural stochastic diffusion framework to model uncertainty in node classification tasks. Zhao et al. [28] propose a graph-based kernel estimation method to predict node-level Dirichlet distributions within the EDL framework. DAEDL [29] promotes EDL performance through a density estimation algorithm. In addition, several studies [30,31] utilize the uncertainty measurement framework of conformal prediction to provide statistical guarantees for the detection results. However, the absence of OOD samples can cause severe score homogenization in detection.

3 Preliminary

3.1 Problem Definition

The dynamic graphs are interpreted as a sequence of graphs $\mathcal{G}^{1:T} = \{\mathcal{G}^t\}_{t=1}^T$, where T specifies the total number of timesteps. Each discrete graph snapshot $\mathcal{G}^t = (\mathcal{V}^t, \mathcal{E}^t, \mathbf{X}^t, \mathbf{A}^t)$ contains node set $\mathcal{V}^t$, edge set $\mathcal{E}^t$, adjacency matrix $\mathbf{A}^t \in \{0,1\}^{N^t \times N^t}$, and feature matrix $\mathbf{X}^t \in \mathbb{R}^{N^t \times d}$, where $N^t = |\mathcal{V}^t|$ and d respectively denote the node count and the feature dimension at timestep t. Dynamic graph representation learning aims to develop a powerful encoder $f_\theta(\cdot, \cdot)$ to capture the temporal dependency. To achieve this, the graph snapshots $\mathcal{G}^{t:t+\Delta t}$ are commonly employed as input to model the dynamics within the temporal window Δt. Based on such input settings, we formulate OOD detection in dynamic graphs as the task of ascertaining whether $\mathcal{G}^{t:t+\Delta t}$ follow the same distribution as ID data:

Definition 1 (OOD detection in Dynamic Graphs). *Let the ID dataset $\mathcal{D}_{\text{in}}$ (resp. OOD dataset $\mathcal{D}_{\text{out}}$) consist of graph sequences drawn from the distributions $\mathbb{P}_{\text{in}}$ (resp. $\mathbb{P}_{\text{out}}$). The training dataset $\mathcal{D}^{tr} = \{\mathcal{G}_{\text{in}}^t\}_{t=1}^T$ is a subset of $\mathcal{D}_{\text{in}}$, containing ID graphs at different timesteps. The test dataset $\mathcal{D}^{te}$ is constituted by two disjoint subsets, $\mathcal{D}_{\text{in}}^{te} \subset \mathcal{D}_{\text{in}}$ and $\mathcal{D}_{\text{out}}^{te} \subset \mathcal{D}_{\text{out}}$, i.e., $\mathcal{D}^{te} = \mathcal{D}_{\text{in}}^{te} \cup \mathcal{D}_{\text{out}}^{te}$, such that $\mathcal{D}^{tr} \cap \mathcal{D}_{\text{in}}^{te} = \emptyset$. For arbitrary input snapshots $\mathcal{G}^{t:t+\Delta t} \in \mathcal{D}^{te}$, the goal of OOD detection in dynamic graphs is to design a discriminant function $G(\cdot, \cdot)$ to determine whether $\mathcal{G}^{t:t+\Delta t}$ follow $\mathbb{P}_{\text{in}}$ or $\mathbb{P}_{\text{out}}$ based on the OOD detection score:*

$$\text{detect}(\mathcal{G}^{t:t+\Delta t}) = \begin{cases} 1 & G\left(f_\theta(\mathcal{G}^{t:t+\Delta t}, \mathcal{W}), \mathcal{D}^{tr}\right) \geq \gamma, \\ 0 & G\left(f_\theta(\mathcal{G}^{t:t+\Delta t}, \mathcal{W}), \mathcal{D}^{tr}\right) < \gamma, \end{cases} \quad (1)$$

where γ is the detection threshold, $\mathcal{W}$ represents the parameters of the encoder.

3.2 Evidential Deep Learning

EDL is grounded in Subjective Logic (SL) theory [32], which represents subjective multinomial opinion as a non-negative triplet $\boldsymbol{\tau} = (\boldsymbol{b}, u, \boldsymbol{\beta})$. In a K-class classification problem, $\boldsymbol{b} = [b_1, b_2, \ldots, b_K]$ assigns belief mass b_i to each class; u quantifies the overall uncertainty across classes, satisfying $u + \sum_{i=1}^K b_i = 1$; and $\boldsymbol{\beta} = [\beta_1, \beta_2, \ldots, \beta_K]$ is a predefined base rate vector. Based on $\boldsymbol{\tau}$, the projected probability distribution for each class is defined as $p_i = b_i + \beta_i u$, where $i = 1, 2, \ldots, K$. EDL adopts the K-dimensional Dirichlet distribution $\text{Dir}^{pr}(p; w\beta)$ as the prior distribution, where w is the prior weight. The conjugate posterior of EDL, i.e., $\text{Dir}^{po}(p; \alpha)$ with concentration (parameter) $\alpha = [\alpha_1, \alpha_2, \cdots, \alpha_K]$ is defined as:

$$\text{Dir}^{po}(p; \alpha) = \frac{\Gamma\left(\sum_{i=1}^{K}\alpha_i\right)}{\prod_{i=1}^{K}\Gamma(\alpha_i)} \prod_{i=1}^{K} p_i^{\alpha_i - 1}, \tag{2}$$

where Γ denotes the Gamma function, $\alpha_i \geq 0$, and $p_i \neq 0$ if $\alpha_i < 1$. To obtain the posterior distribution in Eq. 2, EDL first designs a post-processing module to capture the evidence vector $e = [e_1, e_2, \cdots, e_K]$, which represents the observation evidences for K classes. Then EDL combines the observed evidence with the prior to update the posterior concentration $\alpha = [\alpha_1, \alpha_2, \cdots, \alpha_K]$ as

$$\alpha_i = e_i + \beta_i w, \text{where } i = 1, 2, \ldots, K. \tag{3}$$

Thereby the multinomial opinion $\tau = (b, u, \beta)$ in SL can be equivalently represented by EDL through the bijection mapping F between τ and $\text{Dir}^{po}(p; \alpha)$:

$$F: \tau \longleftrightarrow \text{Dir}^{po}(p; \alpha), \text{where } b_i = \frac{\alpha_i - \beta_i w}{\alpha_{\text{sum}}}, u = \frac{w\sum_{i=1}^{K}\beta_i}{\alpha_{\text{sum}}}, \alpha_{\text{sum}} = \sum_{i=1}^{K}\alpha_i. \tag{4}$$

EDL treats the predictive uncertainty u in Eq. 4 as a discriminative metric for OOD detection. Specifically, for ID samples shown in Fig. 2(a), the model assigns relatively high evidence to at least one class, resulting in a sharp Dirichlet distribution (large α_{sum}) with lower uncertainty ($u \to 0$). Conversely, for OOD samples shown in Fig. 2(b), the evidence allocated across all classes is relatively low, leading to a flat Dirichlet distribution (small α_{sum}) with high uncertainty ($u \to 1$). This difference in uncertainty values clearly shows how the model can tell apart ID and OOD samples. A predefined threshold γ (e.g., $\gamma = 0.5$) can thus be applied to trigger OOD detection.

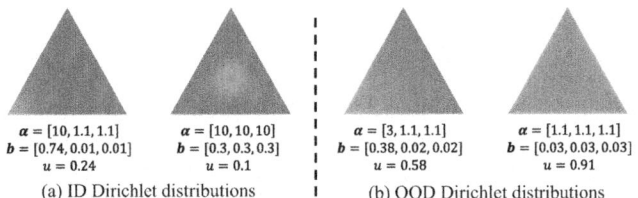

Fig. 2. Heatmaps of Dirichlet distributions in 3-class classification with four groups of concentration parameters and corresponding subjective opinions. Warm (resp. cool) colors represent relatively high (resp. low) probability density values in the distribution.

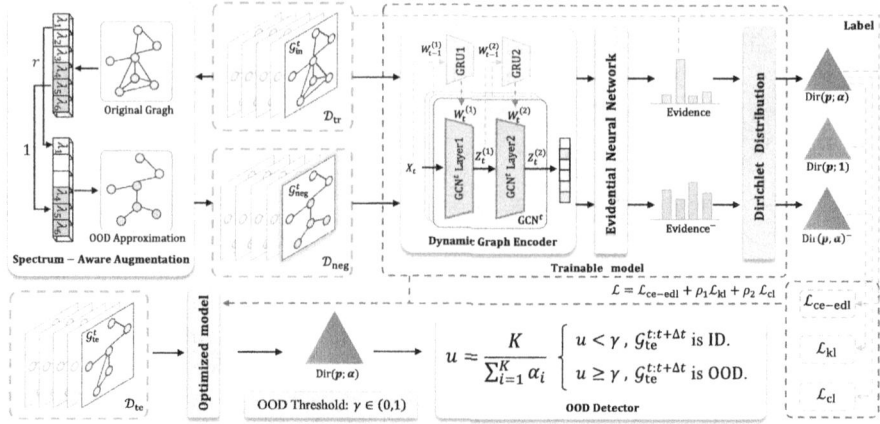

Fig. 3. An overall illustration of the proposed method, EviSEC, which follows a two-stage paradigm: (1) During training, original dynamic graph samples and OOD approximations generated via spectrum-aware augmentation are assigned different Dirichlet distributions by the dynamic graph encoder and the EDL module—sharper for ID samples and flatter for OOD approximations. The loss function enlarges the gap in their uncertainty scores. (2) During inference, the trained model accurately identifies OOD samples using a learned uncertainty threshold.

4 Methodology

In this section, we present a novel EDL framework for OOD detection in dynamic graphs. Our proposed model, i.e., **EviSEC** combines a flexible dynamic graph encoder (Sect. 4.1) with an evidential neural network (Sect. 4.2) to address the limitations of single-point estimation without sacrificing ID performance. Furthermore, to mitigate score homogenization, we introduce a new spectrum-aware contrastive learning strategy (Sect. 4.3). Finally, we design an OOD detector (Sect. 4.4) based on the uncertainty scores. The overall architecture is illustrated in Fig. 3.

4.1 Dynamic Graph Encoder

EviSEC adopts a dynamic graph encoder [19] to efficiently capture the topological structure and temporal dependencies in dynamic graphs through the evolution of GCN parameters. Specifically, we employ a GCN with weight matrix set $\mathcal{W}_t = \{\mathbf{W}_t^{(1)}, \mathbf{W}_t^{(2)}, \ldots, \mathbf{W}_t^{(L)}\}$, where $\mathbf{W}_t^{(l)}$ denotes the weight matrix at l-th layer, to learn the node embedding matrix $\mathbf{Z}_t^{(l)}$ at each timestep t:

$$\mathbf{Z}_t^{(l)} = \begin{cases} \mathbf{X}^t, & \text{if } l = 0, \\ \sigma\left(\tilde{\mathbf{D}}^{t-\frac{1}{2}} \tilde{\mathbf{A}}^t \tilde{\mathbf{D}}^{t-\frac{1}{2}} \mathbf{Z}_t^{(l-1)} \mathbf{W}_t^{(l)}\right), & \text{if } l > 0, \end{cases} \quad (5)$$

where σ is a non-linear activation function, $\tilde{\mathbf{A}}^t$ is the adjacency matrix augmented with self-loops, and $\tilde{\mathbf{D}}^t$ denotes the diagonal degree matrix of $\tilde{\mathbf{A}}^t$.

To naturally store historical dependencies, $\mathbf{W}_t^{(l)}$ is regarded as a hidden state of the dynamical system. We utilize gated recurrent units (GRUs) to incorporate the layer input $\mathbf{Z}_t^{(l-1)}$ into the update of $\mathbf{W}_t^{(l)}$ over time:

$$\underbrace{\mathbf{W}_t^{(l)}}_{\text{GCN weights}} = \text{GRU}(\underbrace{\mathbf{Z}_t^{(l-1)}}_{\text{embeddings}}, \underbrace{\mathbf{W}_{t-1}^{(l)}}_{\text{GCN weights}}). \tag{6}$$

By iteratively updating the weight matrix set from $\mathcal{W}_t$ to $\mathcal{W}_{t+\Delta t}$, our dynamic graph encoder can aggregate the evolutionary patterns of the input $\mathcal{G}^{t:t+\Delta t}$ to generate the final output $f_\theta(\mathcal{G}^{t:t+\Delta t}, \mathcal{W}_{t+\Delta t}) = \mathbf{Z}_{t+\Delta t}^{(L)}$. To perform a specific classification task, the output of our encoder is passed through a classifier $g_\phi(\cdot)$ to generate the final prediction $\hat{\mathbf{y}} = \text{softmax}\left(g_\phi\left(f_\theta\left(\mathcal{G}^{t:t+\Delta t}, \mathcal{W}_{t+\Delta t}\right)\right)\right)$.

4.2 Evidential Neural Network

EviSEC proposes an evidential neural network to reshape the prediction $\mathbf{p} = [p_1, p_2, \ldots, p_K]$ into a Dirichlet distribution. Thus, we can leverage the uncertainty of distribution to describe the randomness of the input, addressing the high bias and high variance issues in single-point estimation. Specifically, two loss functions are developed to guide the network to assign a sharper posterior distribution with lower uncertainty to the ID data, allowing for a robust OOD detection process. Notably, our method maintains the highest probability assigned to the target class, which preserves ID performance.

In a K-class classification task, since there is no prior information, we can simply assume the uniform Dirichlet distribution $\text{Dir}^{pr}(\mathbf{p}; \mathbf{1})$ as the prior distribution $\text{Dir}^{pr}(\mathbf{p}; w\boldsymbol{\beta})$, where the base rate $\boldsymbol{\beta} = \left[\frac{1}{K}, \frac{1}{K}, \ldots, \frac{1}{K}\right]$ and the prior weight $w = K$. Based on the preliminary mentioned in Sect. 3.2, the posterior concentration $\boldsymbol{\alpha} = [\alpha_1, \alpha_2, \cdots, \alpha_K]$ and the class probability $\mathbf{p} = [p_1, p_2, \ldots, p_K]$ are derived as follows,

$$\alpha_i = e_i + \beta_i w \overset{\text{Dir}^{pr}(\mathbf{p};\mathbf{1})}{=} e_i + 1, \text{where } i = 1, 2, \ldots, K. \tag{7}$$

$$p_i = \mathbb{E}_{\mathbf{p} \sim \text{Dir}^{po}(\mathbf{p};\boldsymbol{\alpha})}[p_i] = \int p_i \text{Dir}^{po}(\mathbf{p};\boldsymbol{\alpha}) d\mathbf{p} = \frac{\alpha_i}{\alpha_{\text{sum}}}, \text{where } i = 1, 2, \ldots, K. \tag{8}$$

To update the posterior concentration $\boldsymbol{\alpha}$, our evidential neural network includes an evidence collector $\mathbf{e}_{\theta,\phi}(\cdot)$ to construct the corresponding evidence vector $\mathbf{e} = [e_1, e_2, \ldots, e_K]$:

$$\mathbf{e}_{\theta,\phi}\left(\mathcal{G}^{t:t+\Delta t}\right) = \exp\left(g_\phi\left(f_\theta\left(\mathcal{G}^{t:t+\Delta t}, \mathcal{W}_{t+\Delta t}\right)\right)\right) - \mathbf{1}. \tag{9}$$

By subtracting all-ones vector $\mathbf{1}$ from exponentiated logits, our method ensures negative logits to yield negative evidences. To ensure that $\mathbf{e}_{\theta,\phi}(\cdot)$ produces sharp distributions with low uncertainty scores for ID samples, our network comprises two key losses: the evidential learning cross-entropy loss $\mathcal{L}_{\text{ce-edl}}$

and the Kullback-Leibler divergence loss $\mathcal{L}_{\text{kl}}$ following traditional EDL framework [33]. $\mathcal{L}_{\text{ce-edl}}$ can be calculated as the negative log-likelihood of the predicted class probability $\boldsymbol{p}$ with respect to the one-hot label $\boldsymbol{y} = [y_1, y_2, \ldots, y_K]$:

$$\begin{aligned}\mathcal{L}_{\text{ce-edl}} &= \frac{1}{|\mathcal{D}^{\text{tr}}|} \sum_{(\mathcal{G}^{l:t+\Delta t},\boldsymbol{y})\in\mathcal{D}^{\text{tr}}} \mathbb{E}_{\boldsymbol{p}\sim\text{Dir}^{po}(\boldsymbol{p};\boldsymbol{\alpha})}\left[-\sum_{i=1}^{K} y_i \log(p_i)\right] \\ &= \frac{1}{|\mathcal{D}^{\text{tr}}|} \sum_{(\mathcal{G}^{l:t+\Delta t},\boldsymbol{y})\in\mathcal{D}^{\text{tr}}} \sum_{i=1}^{K} y_i \mathbb{E}_{p_i\sim\text{Dir}^{po}(\boldsymbol{\alpha})}\left[-\log(p_i)\right] \\ &= \frac{1}{|\mathcal{D}^{\text{tr}}|} \sum_{(\mathcal{G}^{l:t+\Delta t},\boldsymbol{y})\in\mathcal{D}^{\text{tr}}} \sum_{i=1}^{K} y_i \left(\psi(\alpha_{\text{sum}}) - \psi(\alpha_i)\right).\end{aligned} \quad (10)$$

The digamma function $\psi(\cdot)$ is the logarithmic derivative of the Gamma function. We can see that Eq. 10 ensures the preservation of the original ID testing performance and guides the model to assign the highest concentration to the target class. However, it may still allow $e_{\theta,\phi}(\cdot)$ to allocate relatively high evidence to non-target classes, thereby increasing the uncertainty u of ID data. To address this, we introduce $\mathcal{L}_{\text{kl}}$ to further penalize the model if it provides excessive evidence for non-target categories:

$$\mathcal{L}_{\text{kl}} = \frac{1}{|\mathcal{D}^{\text{tr}}|} \sum_{(\mathcal{G}^{l:t+\Delta t},\boldsymbol{y})\in\mathcal{D}^{\text{tr}}} \text{KL}\left(\text{Dir}^{po}(\boldsymbol{p};\hat{\boldsymbol{\alpha}}), \text{Dir}^{po}(\boldsymbol{p};\boldsymbol{1})\right). \quad (11)$$

Here $\hat{\boldsymbol{\alpha}} = \boldsymbol{y} + (\boldsymbol{1}-\boldsymbol{y})\odot\boldsymbol{\alpha}$, and $\odot$ represents the Hadamard product. $\hat{\boldsymbol{\alpha}}$ signifies the adjusted concentration parameter, which reserves correct predictions while damping the contribution from irrelevant classes.

4.3 Spectrum-Aware Contrastive Learning

In the above computational process, since only ID data is available, the model tends to assign generally lower uncertainty scores. The absence of OOD data hinders the model's ability to learn and predict higher uncertainty scores, leading to a severe score homogenization issue and further compromising its effectiveness in distinguishing OOD data. To mitigate this, we propose a graph spectrum-aware augmentation technique to generate negative samples as OOD approximations for dynamic graphs. Through contrastive loss, we further widen the gap in uncertainty scores between ID and OOD data.

Spectrum-Aware Augmentation. Previous work [34] demonstrates that low-frequency components in the graph spectrum capture global features (e.g., graph connectivity), while high-frequency components often reflect noise. Therefore, our technique changes the low-frequency components in the graph spectrum to generate negative samples.

Let the symmetric normalized Laplacian matrix of the adjacency matrix with self-loops $\tilde{\mathbf{A}}$ represented as $\mathbf{L} = \mathbf{I} - \tilde{\mathbf{D}}^{-1/2}\tilde{\mathbf{A}}\tilde{\mathbf{D}}^{-1/2}$, which can be eigendecomposed as follows,

$$\mathbf{L} = \mathbf{U}\mathbf{\Lambda}\mathbf{U}^\top = \sum_{i=1}^{N} \lambda_i \mathbf{u}_i \mathbf{u}_i^\top, \quad (12)$$

where $\mathbf{\Lambda} = \text{diag}(\lambda_1, \lambda_2, \ldots, \lambda_N)$ is the eigenvalue diagonal matrix and $\mathbf{U} = [\mathbf{u}_1^\top, \mathbf{u}_2^\top, \ldots, \mathbf{u}_N^\top]$ is the corresponding orthogonal eigenvector matrix. For simplicity's sake, we assume $0 \leq \lambda_1 \leq \lambda_2 \leq \cdots \leq \lambda_N < 2$. Then the graph spectrum can be partitioned into two parts: low-frequency components with eigenvalues $\lambda_{low} = \{\lambda_1, \lambda_2, \ldots, \lambda_{\lfloor N/2 \rfloor}\}$ and high-frequency components with eigenvalues $\lambda_{high} = \{\lambda_{\lfloor N/2 \rfloor+1}, \lambda_{\lfloor N/2 \rfloor+2}, \ldots, \lambda_N\}$.

Our method generates OOD approximations by perturbing the low-frequency information with a preservation ratio r, where $0 \leq r < 1$. For the low-frequency eigenspaces $\{\mathbf{u}_i \mathbf{u}_i^\top\}_{i=1}^{\lfloor N/2 \rfloor}$ of λ_{low}, we only preserve the first r portion and discard the remaining part. For the high-frequency eigenspaces $\{\mathbf{u}_j \mathbf{u}_j^\top\}_{j=\lfloor N/2 \rfloor+1}^{N}$ of λ_{high}, we keep them intact. Based on this, the negative sample $\mathbf{L}_r^-$ is generated as follows,

$$\mathbf{L}_r^- = \sum_{i=1}^{\lfloor rN/2 \rfloor} \mathbf{u}_i \mathbf{u}_i^\top + \sum_{j=\lfloor N/2 \rfloor+1}^{N} \mathbf{u}_j \mathbf{u}_j^\top. \quad (13)$$

Contrastive Loss. With the above negative samples, we seek to enable the model to learn and assign higher uncertainty scores for OOD approximations, which correspond to smoother posterior distributions. To increase the gap in uncertainty scores between the sample pairs, our contrastive loss is formed as the log-likelihood between the class probability $\mathbf{p}^- = [p_1^-, p_2^-, \ldots, p_K^-]$ of the negative sample and the class probability $\mathbf{p}$ of the original input:

$$\mathcal{L}_{\text{cl}} = \frac{1}{|\mathcal{D}^{\text{tr}}|} \sum_{(\mathcal{G}^{t:t+\Delta t}, y) \in \mathcal{D}^{\text{tr}}} \mathbb{E}_{\mathbf{p}^-}\left[\sum_{i=1}^{K} p_i \log(p_i^-)\right]. \quad (14)$$

With two balancing factors ρ_1 and ρ_2, the overall loss function of EviSEC is formulated as:

$$\mathcal{L} = \mathcal{L}_{\text{ce-edl}} + \rho_1 \mathcal{L}_{\text{kl}} + \rho_2 \mathcal{L}_{\text{cl}}. \quad (15)$$

4.4 OOD Detector

After our model has been optimized by Eq. 15, EviSEC includes an OOD detector to compute the uncertainty of posterior distribution $\text{Dir}^{po}(\mathbf{p}; \boldsymbol{\alpha})$ as the OOD score. In specific, the uncertainty u is derived from the Dirichlet concentration $\boldsymbol{\alpha}$ through Eq. 4:

$$u = \frac{K}{\alpha_{\text{sum}}}, \text{ where } \alpha_{\text{sum}} = \sum_{i=1}^{K} \alpha_i. \quad (16)$$

On the one hand, a lower u corresponds to a sharper and more confident output distribution, suggesting the sample is from the ID class. On the other hand, a higher u corresponds to a smoother output distribution, indicating that the sample is likely an OOD instance. Then the OOD detector can select a threshold γ to determine whether the input is OOD according to the learned u.

5 Experiment

This section empirically validates the effectiveness of EviSEC by addressing four key research questions: **RQ1**, how does EviSEC perform compared with competitive methods? **RQ2**, how do the evidential neural network and the spectrum-aware contrastive learning enhance OOD detection in dynamic graphs? **RQ3**, how effective is our method in staying compatible with ID tasks? **RQ4**, how do key parameters affect EviSEC's performance?

Table 1. Dataset details. "Time Splits" shows the data division (train/val/test).

	#Nodes	#Edges	#Time Splits	Task
BC-OTC [3]	5,881	35,588	95/14/28	Edge Classification
BC-Alpha [3]	3,777	24,173	95/13/28	Edge Classification
UCI [2]	1,899	59,835	62/9/17	Link Prediction
AS [35]	6,474	13,895	70/10/20	Link Prediction
Elliptic [36]	203,769	234,355	31/5/13	Node Classification
Brain [37]	5,000	1,955,488	10/1/1	Node Classification

5.1 Experimental Setup

Datasets. As summarized in Table 1, we adopt the datasets and preprocessing steps used in previous dynamic graph representation works [19–21]. These include: i) **BC-OTC**, a trust-based bitcoin transaction network; ii) **BC-Alpha**, a similar bitcoin transaction network from another platform; iii) **UCI**, a student community network; iv) **AS**, a router traffic flow network; v) **Elliptic**, bitcoin transactions from the Elliptic network; and vi) **Brain**, a region connectivity network in the brain.

OOD Data. We extend the OOD data generation framework from recent work [9] on static graphs to generate OOD dynamic graphs through two strategies: i) Structure Manipulation (**SM**), which utilizes a stochastic block model to generate graphs as OOD samples, and ii) Feature Interpolation (**FI**), which applies random interpolation to create node features for OOD data.

Baselines. Beyond the three OOD detection families outlined in our Related Works, we also utilize several dynamic graph anomaly detection methods as baselines. These include: i) post-processing methods (MSP [23], ODIN [24], Mahalanobis [22]), ii) energy-based methods (Energy [25], GNNSAFE [9]), iii) uncertainty-based methods (Entropy [38], EDL [39], DAEDL [29]) and iv) anomaly detection methods(NetWalk [12], TADDY [13], SLADE [40]).

Metrics. We adopt the commonly used evaluation metrics [41] for OOD detection, including: i) **AUROC**, the area under the receiver operating characteristic curve; ii) **AUPR**, area under the precision-recall curve; and iii) **FPR95**, false positive rate at 95% true positive rate. Additionally, **F1**, the harmonic mean of precision and recall, is employed to evaluate ID performance.

Implementation. We employ grid search to determine the optimal values of three key hyper-parameters in our model: the balancing factors ρ_1 and ρ_2, and the preservation rate r in augmentation. The remaining parameters, including the training epochs, the number of layers L, hidden dimension and temporal window size Δt, are adopted from prior studies [19,20]. To ensure a fair comparison, both the baselines and EviSEC are configured with identical settings. All experiments were conducted on Python 3.6.13 and NVIDIA A800 80 GB GPU.

5.2 OOD Detection Performance(RQ1)

In Table 2 and Table 3, we present the key results of EviSEC in comparison with eleven competitive models from four families for the SM and FI OOD types, respectively. These experiments are conducted across six real-world scenarios, measured by AUROC, AUPR, and FPR95. For the OOD type of SM, EviSEC consistently surpasses all baselines across all six datasets, boosting the average AUROC by 24.57%, increasing the average AUPR by 25.64%, and reducing the average FPR95 by 34.65%. For the OOD type of FI, the corresponding changes are 24.08%, 25.22%, and 37.39%, respectively. These results demonstrate that our model exhibits strong adaptability to different OOD types. In both OOD types, we are pleased to observe exceptionally satisfactory performance on the BTC-OTC and BC-Alpha datasets. Specifically, we achieved nearly perfect AUROC and AUPR scores, as well as extremely low FPR95, significantly surpassing the performance of other models. These results reinforce the superiority of EviSEC for OOD detection in dynamic graphs.

5.3 Ablation Study(RQ2)

To systematically evaluate the contribution of core components ($\mathcal{L}_{\text{ce-edl}}$, $\mathcal{L}_{\text{kl}}$ and $\mathcal{L}_{\text{cl}}$) in our framework, we conducted comprehensive ablation studies across six benchmark datasets. Through progressive removal of individual loss components from the complete EviSEC architecture, we quantitatively assessed their respective impacts on OOD detection capability measured by **AUROC**. As presented in Table 4, the full configuration demonstrates significant superiority over all ablated variants, with particular note to the Elliptic dataset where we observe

Table 2. OOD detection results for the OOD type of structure manipulation (**SM**) evaluated by AUROC/AUPR/FPR95 on six datasets. The best performance is **bolded**, with the runner-up underlined.

Dataset\Baseline	BC-OTC	BC-Alpha	UCI	AS	Elliptic	Brain
	AUROC ↑	AUPR ↑	FPR95 ↓			
NetWalk	52.38 48.06 92.80	48.62 52.70 98.40	48.67 46.02 98.68	52.71 56.31 94.20	38.97 46.58 91.30	54.38 52.60 100.0
TADDY	77.20 65.38 98.07	64.28 59.05 95.20	54.80 58.69 95.18	56.89 55.73 88.67	52.61 54.98 93.20	56.80 59.08 100.0
SLADE	74.35 64.30 94.26	66.40 60.50 92.80	59.80 50.20 94.19	51.20 56.98 89.20	48.80 54.70 95.20	51.30 55.47 <u>95.58</u>
MSP	48.65 52.82 92.55	45.79 48.63 91.50	54.38 46.01 97.20	52.76 47.39 94.20	48.64 40.43 90.25	44.87 42.15 99.80
ODIN	55.15 42.63 88.88	55.26 49.07 100.0	41.68 39.92 96.68	56.08 45.25 98.34	48.77 50.62 92.57	48.83 42.39 100.0
Mahalanobis	61.44 34.88 96.80	43.21 39.34 92.34	40.68 38.72 94.29	57.26 49.77 97.04	49.56 52.03 98.62	36.20 32.17 98.65
Energy	58.80 31.88 88.11	50.33 52.68 99.19	50.68 55.48 92.70	57.21 54.23 95.46	50.69 52.70 98.37	34.67 48.94 99.27
GNNSAFE	87.02 85.57 85.32	<u>89.66</u> <u>86.34</u> <u>78.20</u>	62.41 <u>66.34</u> <u>90.04</u>	67.08 59.71 <u>87.62</u>	64.58 60.22 96.55	72.12 <u>71.17</u> 98.87
Entropy	45.15 23.48 99.09	50.55 55.18 100.0	60.27 50.66 99.21	55.39 60.22 92.44	52.66 55.71 98.06	61.62 52.33 99.80
EDL	61.83 28.35 98.40	55.33 54.08 100.0	55.18 47.02 96.55	58.77 62.72 90.58	54.87 50.68 97.54	65.99 66.60 99.40
DAEDL	<u>90.12</u> <u>88.33</u> <u>69.88</u>	85.34 80.20 90.68	<u>70.22</u> 64.09 90.27	<u>74.48</u> <u>69.85</u> 88.36	<u>66.53</u> <u>68.97</u> <u>80.65</u>	<u>74.39</u> 70.17 96.31
EviSEC	**96.39 94.52 13.47**	**97.14 92.30 13.86**	**72.09 68.84 82.77**	**78.39 76.50 80.46**	**70.61 72.35 74.68**	**76.73 73.51 92.64**

Table 3. OOD detection results for the OOD type of feature interpolation (**FI**) evaluated by AUROC/AUPR/FPR95 on six datasets. The best performance is **bolded**, with the runner-up underlined.

Dataset\Baseline	BC-OTC	BC-Alpha	UCI	AS	Elliptic	Brain
	AUROC ↑	AUPR ↑	FPR95 ↓			
NetWalk	57.06 58.54 91.78	60.45 65.12 99.20	50.86 48.34 90.60	56.27 50.20 88.71	42.08 45.32 99.80	42.48 37.08 100.0
TADDY	79.68 64.43 94.07	68.31 64.81 96.08	56.76 52.63 94.71	55.16 51.20 85.64	50.65 55.08 96.20	52.99 57.04 100.0
SLADE	76.81 64.09 93.26	65.86 58.06 94.52	54.32 49.06 90.35	50.34 55.98 90.70	52.74 58.62 94.64	47.03 55.93 98.40
MSP	43.04 38.80 94.38	46.28 38.98 94.31	33.74 42.58 98.77	51.20 48.29 99.25	44.28 39.38 88.64	34.18 33.66 100.0
ODIN	50.26 47.87 90.32	54.20 50.84 99.80	46.20 48.07 98.82	58.91 47.30 96.53	50.24 59.26 94.40	50.07 56.30 99.25
Mahalanobis	45.20 51.35 98.20	45.84 42.09 95.63	43.82 44.24 93.29	56.98 51.28 95.77	48.53 54.08 89.60	44.31 42.07 98.65
Energy	60.28 59.60 72.37	51.20 59.61 95.44	55.21 56.38 90.52	54.30 52.27 91.70	58.89 60.58 94.20	48.67 50.38 97.27
GNNSAFE	70.05 <u>86.79</u> 68.30	<u>87.25</u> <u>88.37</u> 68.46	64.00 <u>68.27</u> <u>89.42</u>	66.57 64.35 **80.29**	66.80 58.92 94.38	63.44 60.18 <u>90.43</u>
Entropy	42.95 26.83 100.0	47.23 50.35 100.0	55.69 54.31 98.70	52.17 48.69 88.64	59.07 62.18 96.50	70.02 71.17 96.56
EDL	53.81 38.03 95.42	59.30 52.18 100.0	48.67 49.72 94.21	64.38 64.80 <u>82.50</u>	61.20 64.52 90.20	64.20 68.17 93.57
DAEDL	<u>80.54</u> 86.28 <u>54.31</u>	80.14 74.58 <u>65.31</u>	<u>65.28</u> 64.97 91.25	<u>70.07</u> <u>69.57</u> 86.25	<u>68.34</u> <u>66.30</u> <u>78.57</u>	<u>72.18</u> <u>73.15</u> 96.51
EviSEC	**97.29 98.51 5.22**	**96.40 94.44 10.27**	**70.91 72.08 80.16**	**72.58 74.25** 84.20	**72.15 70.25 58.68**	**74.21 76.47 89.40**

a substantial absolute performance improvement of 17.41%. This empirical validation confirms that the synergistic combination significantly enhances OOD detection performance.

5.4 ID Performance(RQ3)

As mentioned in Sect. 4.2, EviSEC does not alter the value of the maximum component in the predictive distribution. Therefore, when comparing ID performance measured by **F1** scores with representation learning methods such as EvolveGCN [19], LEDG [21], DEFT-MLP, DEFT-GAT and DEFT-T [20], our approach still achieves performance close to (or even surpassing) state-of-the-art levels (see Fig. 4). This demonstrates that our method does not sacrifice ID task performance while enhancing OOD detection capabilities.

Table 4. Ablation study results for the SM OOD type across six datasets. ✓́ means the variant with random negative edge sampling augmentation.

$\mathcal{L}_{\text{ce-edl}}$	$\mathcal{L}_{\text{kl}}$	$\mathcal{L}_{\text{cl}}$	BC-OTC	BC-Alpha	UCI	AS	Elliptic	Brain
-	✓	✓	86.24	85.14	66.28	65.80	58.32	68.45
✓	-	✓	95.58	95.28	70.60	72.87	68.24	73.12
✓	✓	-	90.17	93.69	68.07	74.10	65.78	69.56
✓	✓	✓́	91.08	92.26	69.31	73.54	67.92	70.27
✓	✓	✓	**96.39**	**97.14**	**72.09**	**78.39**	**70.61**	**76.73**

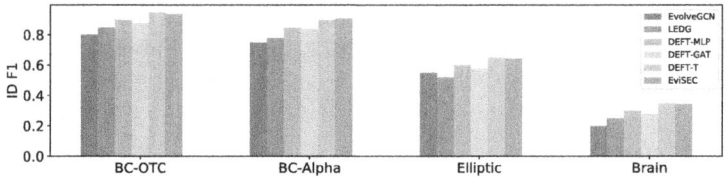

Fig. 4. In-Distribution performance of classification tasks with **F1** scores on the y-axis.

5.5 Parameter Sensitivity(RQ4)

Figure 5 shows the hyper-parameter sensitivity of EviSEC measured by AUROC in terms of the balancing factors ρ_1 and ρ_2, and the preservation rate r in augmentation. Specifically, ρ_1, ρ_2 range from 0.2 to 2.0 with a step size of 0.2 on the AS dataset, and $r \in \{0, 0.2, 0.4, 0.6, 0.8\}$ on six datasets. We observe that setting them to moderate values (e.g., $\rho_1 \in \{0.4, 0.6, 0.8\}$, $\rho_2 \in \{0.6, 0.8, 1.0\}$, $r \in [0.2, 0.4]$) usually achieves optimal performance. We can conclude that: i) $\mathcal{L}_{\text{ce-edl}}$ and $\mathcal{L}_{\text{cl}}$ have a greater impact than $\mathcal{L}_{\text{kl}}$; and ii) a smaller r, i.e., retaining less low-frequency information, tends to generate more effective OOD approximations.

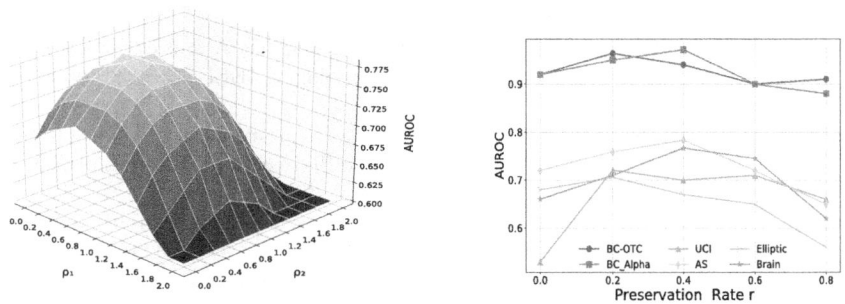

Fig. 5. Hyper-parameter sensitivity of EviSEC.

6 Conclusion

In this work, we propose EviSEC, an innovative and effective OOD detection framework comprising two key modules. Specifically, we propose an evidential neural network that uses the uncertainty of posterior distribution to explain the randomness of the input, thereby mitigating the high bias and high variance issues associated with single-point estimation. Moreover, we design a spectral-aware contrastive learning module to generate OOD approximations for enlarging the score gap between the ID and OOD data, effectively mitigating the issue of score homogenization. Empirical evaluation demonstrates that our model outperforms others across various datasets for OOD detection in dynamic graphs.

Acknowledgments. This work is supported by the National Key Research and Development Program of China (NO. 2022YFB3102200) and the National Natural Science Foundation of China (No. 62402491).

References

1. Tang, J., Zhang, J., Yao, L., Li, J., Zhang, L., Su, Z.: Arnetminer: extraction and mining of academic social networks. In: Proceedings of the 14th ACM SIGKDD International Conference on Knowledge Discovery and Data Mining, pp. 990–998 (2008)
2. Rossi, R.A., Ahmed, N.K.: The network data repository with interactive graph analytics and visualization. In: AAAI (2015). https://networkrepository.com
3. Kumar, S., Hooi, B., Makhija, D., Kumar, M., Faloutsos, C., Subrahmanian, V.: Rev2: Fraudulent user prediction in rating platforms. In: Proceedings of the Eleventh ACM International Conference on Web Search and Data Mining, pp. 333–341 (2018)
4. Zhang, S., Chen, L., Wang, C., Li, S., Xiong, H.: Temporal graph contrastive learning for sequential recommendation. In: Proceedings of the AAAI Conference on Artificial Intelligence, vol. 38, pp. 9359–9367 (2024)
5. Khoshraftar, S., An, A.: A survey on graph representation learning methods. ACM Trans. Intell. Syst. Technol. **15**(1), 1–55 (2024)
6. Kononenko, I.: Machine learning for medical diagnosis: history, state of the art and perspective. Artif. Intell. Med. **23**(1), 89–109 (2001)
7. Yurtsever, E., Lambert, J., Carballo, A., Takeda, K.: A survey of autonomous driving: common practices and emerging technologies. IEEE access **8**, 58443–58469 (2020)
8. Liu, Y., Ding, K., Liu, H., Pan, S.: Good-d: On unsupervised graph out-of-distribution detection. In: Proceedings of the Sixteenth ACM International Conference on Web Search and Data Mining, pp. 339–347 (2023)
9. Wu, Q., Chen, Y., Yang, C., Yan, J.: Energy-based out-of-distribution detection for graph neural networks. arXiv preprint arXiv:2302.02914 (2023)
10. Ranzato, M., Boureau, Y.L., Chopra, S., LeCun, Y.: A unified energy-based framework for unsupervised learning. In: Artificial Intelligence and Statistics, pp. 371–379. PMLR (2007)

11. Song, C., Lin, X., Shen, H., Shang, Y., Cao, Y.: Uniform: towards unified framework for anomaly detection on graphs. In: Proceedings of the AAAI Conference on Artificial Intelligence, vol. 39, pp. 12559–12567 (2025)
12. Yu, W., Cheng, W., Aggarwal, C.C., Zhang, K., Chen, H., Wang, W.: Netwalk: A flexible deep embedding approach for anomaly detection in dynamic networks. In: Proceedings of the 24th ACM SIGKDD International Conference on Knowledge Discovery & Data Mining, pp. 2672–2681 (2018)
13. Liu, Y., Pan, S., Wang, Y.G., Xiong, F., Wang, L., Chen, Q., Lee, V.C.: Anomaly detection in dynamic graphs via transformer. IEEE Trans. Knowl. Data Eng. **35**(12), 12081–12094 (2021)
14. Lin, X., Cao, J., Zhang, P., Zhou, C., Li, Z., Wu, J., Wang, B.: Disentangled deep multivariate hawkes process for learning event sequences. In: 2021 IEEE International Conference on Data Mining (ICDM), pp. 360–369. IEEE (2021)
15. Grover, A., Leskovec, J.: node2vec: Scalable feature learning for networks. In: Proceedings of the 22nd ACM SIGKDD International Conference on Knowledge Discovery and Data Mining, pp. 855–864 (2016)
16. Li, J., Dani, H., Hu, X., Tang, J., Chang, Y., Liu, H.: Attributed network embedding for learning in a dynamic environment. In: Proceedings of the 2017 ACM on Conference on Information and Knowledge Management, pp. 387–396 (2017)
17. Zuo, Y., Liu, G., Lin, H., Guo, J., Hu, X., Wu, J.: Embedding temporal network via neighborhood formation. In: Proceedings of the 24th ACM SIGKDD International Conference on Knowledge Discovery & Data Mining, pp. 2857–2866 (2018)
18. Zhang, S., Zhou, C., Liu, Y., Zhang, P., Lin, X., Ma, Z.M.: Neural jump-diffusion temporal point processes. In: International Conference on Machine Learning (2024)
19. Pareja, A., et al.: Evolvegcn: evolving graph convolutional networks for dynamic graphs. In: Proceedings of the AAAI conference on artificial intelligence, vol. 34, pp. 5363–5370 (2020)
20. Bastos, A., Nadgeri, A., Singh, K., Suzumura, T., Singh, M.: Learnable spectral wavelets on dynamic graphs to capture global interactions. In: Proceedings of the AAAI Conference on Artificial Intelligence, vol. 37, pp. 6779–6787 (2023)
21. Xiang, X., Huang, T., Wang, D.: Learning to evolve on dynamic graphs (student abstract). In: Proceedings of the AAAI Conference on Artificial Intelligence, vol. 36, pp. 13091–13092 (2022)
22. Lee, K., Lee, K., Lee, H., Shin, J.: A simple unified framework for detecting out-of-distribution samples and adversarial attacks. Advances in neural information processing systems **31** (2018)
23. Hendrycks, D., Gimpel, K.: A baseline for detecting misclassified and out-of-distribution examples in neural networks. arXiv preprint arXiv:1610.02136 (2016)
24. Liang, S., Li, Y., Srikant, R.: Enhancing the reliability of out-of-distribution image detection in neural networks. arXiv preprint arXiv:1706.02690 (2017)
25. Liu, W., Wang, X., Owens, J., Li, Y.: Energy-based out-of-distribution detection. Adv. Neural. Inf. Process. Syst. **33**, 21464–21475 (2020)
26. Abdar, M., et al.: A review of uncertainty quantification in deep learning: techniques, applications and challenges. Inf. Fusion **76**, 243–297 (2021)
27. Lin, X., et al.: Graph neural stochastic diffusion for estimating uncertainty in node classification. In: Forty-First International Conference on Machine Learning (2024)
28. Zhao, X., Chen, F., Hu, S., Cho, J.H.: Uncertainty aware semi-supervised learning on graph data. Adv. Neural. Inf. Process. Syst. **33**, 12827–12836 (2020)
29. Yoon, T., Kim, H.: Uncertainty estimation by density aware evidential deep learning. In: International Conference on Machine Learning, pp. 57217–57243. PMLR (2024)

30. Zhang, S., Zhou, C., Liu, Y., Zhang, P., Lin, X., Pan, S.: Conformal anomaly detection in event sequences. In: International Conference on Machine Learning (2025)
31. Lin, X., et al.: Conformal graph-level out-of-distribution detection with adaptive data augmentation. In: Proceedings of the ACM on Web Conference 2025, pp. 4755–4765 (2025)
32. Jøsang, A.: Subjective logic, vol. 3. Springer (2016)
33. Sensoy, M., Kaplan, L., Kandemir, M.: Evidential deep learning to quantify classification uncertainty. Advances in neural information processing systems **31** (2018)
34. Liu, N., Wang, X., Bo, D., Shi, C., Pei, J.: Revisiting graph contrastive learning from the perspective of graph spectrum. Adv. Neural. Inf. Process. Syst. **35**, 2972–2983 (2022)
35. Leskovec, J., Kleinberg, J., Faloutsos, C.: Graphs over time: densification laws, shrinking diameters and possible explanations. In: Proceedings of the Eleventh ACM SIGKDD International Conference on Knowledge Discovery in Data Mining, pp. 177–187 (2005)
36. Weber, M., et al.: Anti-money laundering in bitcoin: experimenting with graph convolutional networks for financial forensics. arXiv preprint arXiv:1908.02591 (2019)
37. Xu, D., et al.: Adaptive neural network for node classification in dynamic networks. In: 2019 IEEE International Conference on Data Mining (ICDM), pp. 1402–1407. IEEE (2019)
38. Shannon, C.E.: Communication theory of secrecy systems. Bell Syst. Tech. J. **28**(4), 656–715 (1949)
39. Deng, D., Chen, G., Yu, Y., Liu, F., Heng, P.A.: Uncertainty estimation by fisher information-based evidential deep learning. In: International Conference on Machine Learning, pp. 7596–7616. PMLR (2023)
40. Lee, J., Kim, S., Shin, K.: Slade: Detecting dynamic anomalies in edge streams without labels via self-supervised learning. In: Proceedings of the 30th ACM SIGKDD Conference on Knowledge Discovery and Data Mining, pp. 1506–1517 (2024)
41. Guo, Y., Yang, C., Chen, Y., Liu, J., Shi, C., Du, J.: A data-centric framework to endow graph neural networks with out-of-distribution detection ability. In: Proceedings of the 29th ACM SIGKDD Conference on Knowledge Discovery and Data Mining, pp. 638–648 (2023)

HAGAN: Homophily-Aware Generative Adversarial Network for Graph Anomaly Detection

Wenkai Wang, Fan Gao, and Meihong Wang(✉)

School of Informatics, Xiamen University, Xiamen 361102, China
{30920231154336,gaofan}@stu.xmu.edu.cn, wangmh@xmu.edu.cn

Abstract. With the increasing prevalence of graph-structured data, graph anomaly detection has emerged as a crucial research domain. Motivated by the realistic challenge that many practical problems are constrained by limited sample data, this study proposes a semi-supervised setting, unlike conventional unsupervised and supervised learning methods, where only a subset of normal samples is available. A key challenge in this context is the absence of anomalous samples, which can lead to model bias and compromise detection performance. To address this issue, we introduce a novel model, Homophily-Aware Generative Adversarial Network (HAGAN), which leverages a generative adversarial network to generate high-quality anomalous nodes. These generated nodes are seamlessly integrated into the real graph using a transformer-based graph autoencoder. Furthermore, the discriminator employs a GNN architecture enhanced with an edge homogeneity identification mechanism to improve anomaly detection. The proposed model is evaluated on four large-scale real-world benchmark datasets, and experimental results demonstrate that HAGAN consistently achieves state-of-the-art performance across multiple evaluation metrics.

Keywords: Machine Learning · Anomaly Detection · GNN

1 Introduction

In the context of the growing prevalence of graph-structured data, graph anomaly detection (GAD) has emerged as a significant research focus [16]. Unlike traditional anomaly detection [25], graph anomaly detection seeks to identify anomalous patterns within complex relationships and structures. It has been widely applied in various fields, including social networks [18], network security [3], and financial systems [6].

In recent years, a wide array of research has emerged in the field of GAD, primarily focusing on two key approaches: unsupervised and supervised methods.

Supplementary Information The online version contains supplementary material available at https://doi.org/10.1007/978-3-032-05962-8_9.

Although these researches have demonstrated promising results, they overlook a critical challenge: the inherent imbalance between normal and anomalous samples in real-world datasets [15]. Unsupervised methods assume that the labels of all nodes are unknown. However, the overwhelming prevalence of normal samples makes it relatively easy to identify normal nodes, which results in unsupervised methods not fully leveraging these normal samples. Supervised methods typically rely on a subset of nodes labeled as anomalous. However, anomalous patterns in real-world data are both diverse and scarce, making the labeling process costly. Furthermore, this rarity may not offer enough information for the model to effectively learn discriminative features.

Based on the above discussion, we assume a semi-supervised setting in which labels for only a subset of normal samples are available. In this context, an important issue arises from the lack of anomalous samples. Anomalous samples often exhibit significant differences in features or connectivity structures compared to normal samples, and relying solely on normal samples may not provide sufficient information to accurately identify anomalies. In order to address the above problem, this paper proposes **H**omophily-**A**ware **G**enerative **A**dversarial **N**etwork (**HAGAN**) for GAD. Our objective is trying to alleviate the lack of anomalous samples by generating high-quality anomaly nodes.

However, some challenges arise here: **1. How to ensure the high-quality of the generated anomaly nodes?** A common approach is random generation; however, this often leads to suboptimal node quality. To address this limitation, we employ a generative adversarial network (GAN) [14] to generate anomalous nodes, leveraging adversarial training to produce realistic and high-quality results. **2. How to integrate the generated nodes with the original graph?** Since the generated nodes are isolated, it is imperative to establish structural relationships between the generated nodes and the original nodes. A simple random connection approach may disrupt the inherent characteristics of the original graph structure. Therefore, we utilize a pre-trained graph autoencoder (GAE) to reconstruct the graph structure and seamlessly achieve integration. **3. How to alleviate the problem that generated nodes will introduce noise?** GNN is chosen as the discriminator due to its effectiveness. However, in GAD tasks, GNNs are vulnerable to noise from heterophilic edges [19], where information from normal and anomalous nodes interferes during aggregation. To address this, we integrate an edge homophily identification module that reduces noise from generated nodes and helps the model better capture heterophilic edges inherent in the graph.

To sum up, the main contributions of this paper are as follows:

- We propose HAGAN, a novel framework that accomplishes the semi-supervised GAD task by generating high-quality anomaly nodes.
- We propose a Transformer-based GAE to integrate the generator-produced nodes into the original graph, thereby preserving its inherent structural integrity.
- We integrate an edge homophily identification method into the GNN discriminator to enhance its discriminative ability.

- We evaluate the effectiveness of HAGAN on four real-world benchmark datasets. The experiments demonstrate that our approach delivers state-of-the-art performance.

2 Related Work

Traditional methods such as LOF [2] and isForest [25] struggle to effectively capture both local and global structural information. With the increasing prevalence of graph-structured data, several shallow methods based on graph structures have emerged, such as Radar [23] and ANOMALOUS [30]. However, these shallow techniques typically lack the expressive power that deep learning possesses. In recent years, the rapid advancement of GNN has positioned deep learning methods based on graph structures at the forefront of research.

2.1 Unsupervised Methods

DOMINANT [8] uses GNN to capture both structural and attribute information for anomaly detection in attributed networks. DONE [1] employs deep one-class classification to detect anomalies via distributional deviation. OCNNN [37] optimizes a one-class objective function to distinguish normal and anomalous instances. TAM [31] leverages the stronger affinity among normal nodes compared to anomalous ones. CoCo [36] introduces a method based on the correlation discrepancy between local and global contextual information of nodes.

Besides, Self-supervised methods based on contrastive learning have also emerged as a key research focus in recent years. Notable examples include CoLA [26], ANEMONE [17], SL-GAD [41], Sub-CR [39], CONAD [38] and GRADATE [10]. The core principle of these methods is to enhance the model's discriminative ability by performing contrastive learning at various scales, bringing similar node representations closer together while pushing dissimilar ones further apart.

2.2 Supervised Methods

Current research on supervised methods primarily focuses on edge homophily. Edges between nodes can be classified into two types: homophilic (connecting nodes with the same labels) and heterophilic (connecting nodes with different labels). By identifying edge homophily, these methods optimize the graph structure or design novel aggregation strategies, thereby reducing noise during model training. H^2-FDetector [33] enhances fraud detection by transmitting similar information over homophilic edges and dissimilar information over heterophilic edges. GDN [11] mitigates structural distribution shift in GAD by isolating and constraining key anomalous features. SpareGAD [13] simplifies graph structure through sparsification, removing task-irrelevant edges and employing a heterophilic-aware aggregation scheme. HedGe [40] reduces excessive distributional differences by generating homogeneous edges, modifying the loss function to suppress heterogeneous edge formation.

2.3 Generative Anomaly Detection

Early methods, such as AnoGAN [32] and GAN-AD [22], achieve notable success in their respective domains. However, these methods are not designed for graph data. AdONE [1] is the first approach to use adversarial training for this task, helping to further minimize the influence of outliers while generating the embeddings. GAAN [5] and AEGIS [7] both employ GAN architectures for graph anomaly detection. GAAN generates fake graph nodes from Gaussian noise and learns latent representations via an encoder, while its discriminator determines whether connected node pairs originate from the real graph. AEGIS, on the other hand, enhances generalization by generating information-rich potential anomalies and training a discriminator to distinguish them from normal data.

3 Preliminaries

3.1 Definition 1. Graph

In this paper, we focus on anomaly detection in attributed graphs with labeled normal nodes, while the number of anomalous labels is extremely sparse. An attributed graph is denoted by $\mathcal{G} = (\mathcal{V}, \mathcal{E}, \mathbf{X})$, where $\mathcal{V} = \{v_1, v_2, ..., v_N\}$ denotes the node set, $N = |\mathcal{V}|$, $\mathcal{E} \subseteq \mathcal{V} \times \mathcal{V}$ with $e \in \mathcal{E}$ denotes the edge set, $\mathbf{X}_{origin} \in \mathcal{R}^{N \times d}$ denotes the node features with $\mathbf{x}_{origin}(v_i) \in \mathcal{R}^d$ being the attribute vector of v_i and d denotes the attribute dimension in the original data. The adjacency matrix of $\mathcal{G}$ is denoted as $\mathbf{A} \in \{0,1\}^{N \times N}$ and $\mathbf{A}_{ij} = 1$ if and only if $e_{ij} \in \mathcal{E}$.

3.2 Definition 2. Graph Anomaly Detection

Given a graph $\mathcal{G}$ mentioned above, the objective of anomaly detection is to calculate an anomaly score $f(v) \in (0,1)$, where f is an anomaly score function and $v \in \mathcal{V}$. The anomaly score reflects the extent of the abnormality of the node, which means that a higher $f(v)$ indicates a higher probability of anomalous of the node v.

4 Method

In this section, we introduce the details of HAGAN, as presented in Fig. 1. HAGAN consists of two stages: the first stage involves pretraining a Transformer-based Graph Autoencoder, while the second stage focuses on training GAN.

4.1 Transformer-Based GAE

GAE demonstrates significant advantages in reconstructing graph structures [24]. However, their effectiveness typically relies on the assumption that the input data inherently exhibit a graph structure, while generated nodes are typically isolated, posing a challenge for integration.

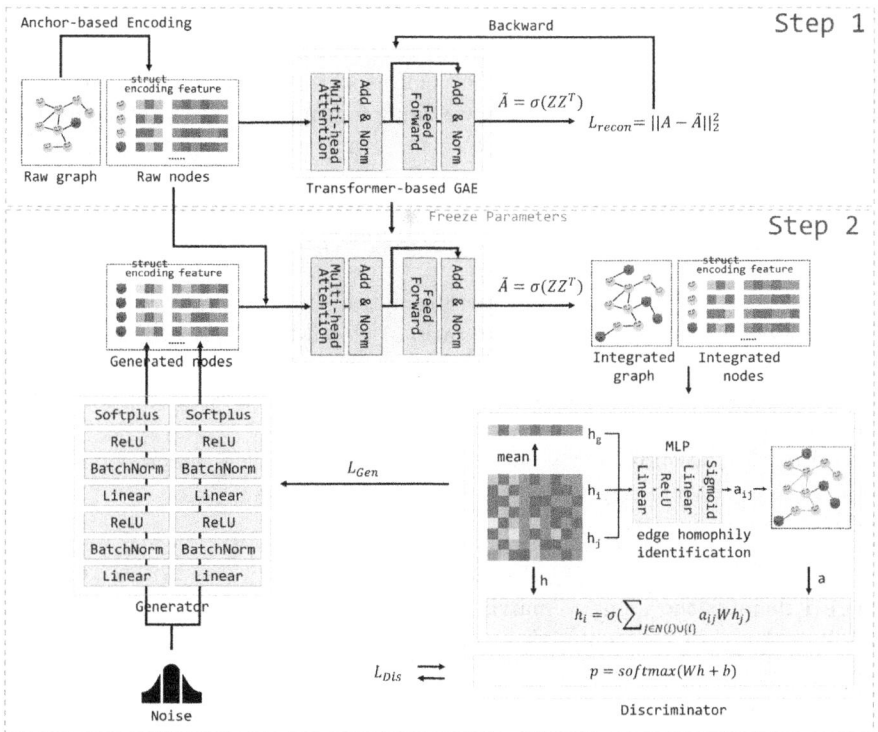

Fig. 1. The overall architecture of HAGAN, which consists of two stages. In Stage 1, a Transformer-based GAE is pretrained on real data. In Stage 2, the generator synthesizes anomalous nodes, which are integrated with the original graph via the pretrained GAE. The integrated graph is then processed by the discriminator, a GNN equipped with an edge homogeneity identification mechanism. Specifically, for each edge (i, j), their features along with the global average feature are fed into an MLP to compute a homophily probability, which is then used to guide the attention coefficient computation.

To overcome this limitation, we introduce anchor-based encoding, which plays a role similar to positional encoding [35] by injecting structural information into the generated isolated nodes. The real and generated nodes are treated as a unified sequence. Leveraging the Transformer's powerful sequence modeling capability along with the encoded structural information, we propose a Transformer-based GAE to obtain expressive node embeddings.

Anchor-Based Encoding. Given a graph $\mathcal{G} = (\mathcal{V}, \mathcal{E}, \mathbf{X})$, we select k anchor points, denoted as $\mathcal{V}_{Anchor} = \{a_1, a_2, ..., a_k\} \subset \mathcal{V}$. For node $v \in \mathcal{V}$, we define its anchor-based encoding (structural features) $\mathbf{X}_{struct}$ as:

$$\mathbf{X}_{struct} = [d(v, a_1), d(v, a_1), ...d(v, a_k)] \tag{1}$$

where $d(v, a_i)$ represents the shortest path distance between node v and anchor point a_i.

Based on the above definition, a crucial aspect of anchor-based encoding is the selection of anchor points. Here, we employ graph diffusion techniques [12]. Formally, given an adjacency matrix $\mathbf{A}$, the graph diffusion matrix $\mathbf{S} \in \mathcal{R}^{N \times N}$ is defined by:

$$\mathbf{S} = \sum_{k=0}^{\infty} \theta_k \mathbf{T}^k \ (\theta_k \in [0,1] \ and \ \sum_{k=0}^{\infty} \theta_k = 1) \tag{2}$$

where $\mathbf{T} \in \mathcal{R}^{N \times N}$ denotes the generalized transition matrix, θ_k denotes the weighting coefficient determining the ratio of global-local information. The row $\mathbf{s}_i$ in $\mathbf{S}$ represents the connectivity of node v_i, and its row sum is used to determine each node's connectivity strength, allowing us to select the top k nodes as anchors.

In practice, we use Personalized PageRank (PPR) [28] which choose $\mathbf{T} = \mathbf{AD}^{-1}$ and $\theta_k = \alpha(1-\alpha)^k$:

$$\mathbf{S}^{PPR} = \alpha(\mathbf{I} - (1-\alpha)\mathbf{D}^{-1/2}\mathbf{AD}^{-1/2}) \tag{3}$$

where $\mathbf{I}$ denotes the identity matrix, $\mathbf{D} \in \mathcal{R}^{N \times N}$ denotes the diagonal degree matrix and $\alpha \in (0,1)$ denotes the teleport probability.

Autoencoder. We concatenate $\mathbf{X}_{struct}$ and $\mathbf{X}_{origin}$ to leverage their complementary information. Furthermore, linear transformation are applied to obtain the fusion representation $\mathbf{H}_{fusion}$:

$$\mathbf{H}_{fusion} = \mathbf{W}_r[\mathbf{W}_s\mathbf{X}_{struct} \| \mathbf{W}_o\mathbf{X}_{origin}] \tag{4}$$

where $\|$ is the concatenation operation and $\mathbf{W}_r, \mathbf{W}_s, \mathbf{W}_o$ denotes three distinct learnable parameter matrices.

For encoder, we consider the set of nodes as a sequence and input it into the Transformer's encoder to obtain the node embeddings:

$$\mathbf{H}'^{(l)} = LayerNorm(\mathbf{H}^{(l-1)} + MultiHeadAttention(\mathbf{H}^{(l-1)})) \tag{5}$$

$$\mathbf{H}^{(l)} = LayerNorm(\mathbf{H}'^{(l)} + FFN(\mathbf{H}'^{(l)})) \tag{6}$$

where $\mathbf{H}^{(l)}$ and $\mathbf{H}^{(l-1)}$ respectively denotes the output of the l-th layer and $(l\text{-}1)$-th attention layer. The input $\mathbf{H}^{(0)}$ is $\mathbf{H}_{fusion}$ and the output of the final attention layer $\mathbf{H}^{(L)}$ is denoted as the output node embeddings $\mathbf{Z}$.

For decoder, we choose the widely used inner product method due to its simplicity and effectiveness:

$$\tilde{\mathbf{Z}} = g(\mathbf{Z}) \tag{7}$$

$$\tilde{\mathbf{A}} = \sigma(\tilde{\mathbf{Z}}\tilde{\mathbf{Z}}^T) \tag{8}$$

where g denotes a normalization function to prevent gradient explosion and vanishing and $\tilde{\mathbf{A}}$ denotes the reconstructed adjacency matrix.

To facilitate the subsequent use of the generator, we pre-train TGAE using reconstruction loss function:

$$\mathcal{L}_{recon} = \|\mathbf{A} - \tilde{\mathbf{A}}\|_2^2 \tag{9}$$

4.2 GAN Architecture

Fence [27] demonstrated that GAN can achieve superior performance in anomaly detection by modifying the traditional loss function to encourage the generator to produce data at the edges of the normal data distribution. Inspired by this work, we adopt a similar architecture.

Generator. In our generator, we utilize gaussian noise as the standard input and employ a dual-branch architecture to produce structural features and original features. We define the model as follows:

$$G_{struct}(z_i) = g(\sigma(f_{struct}(z_i))) \tag{10}$$

$$G_{origin}(z_i) = g(\sigma(f_{origin}(z_i))) \tag{11}$$

where f_{struct} and f_{origin} denote different 3-layer feedforward neural networks, σ denotes the activation function, g denotes a normalization function, $G_{struct}(z_i) \in \mathcal{R}^k$ denotes the generated structural features and $G_{origin}(z_i) \in \mathcal{R}^d$ denotes the generated original features.

The loss function $\mathcal{L}_{gen}$ is designed to comprise three components. $\mathcal{L}_{dist}$ guides the generator to produce samples with a discriminator score of α, positioning them at the boundary of normal nodes to enhance high-quality. $\mathcal{L}_{divr}$ enhances diversity in generated nodes, addressing GANs' susceptibility to mode collapse by maximizing their average distance from the mean. $\mathcal{L}_{kl}$ promotes the dispersion of generated data in a multidimensional space, preventing the generator from concentrating samples in specific dimensions during training. Formally, the loss function is defined as:

$$\mathcal{L}_{gen} = \beta_1 \mathcal{L}_{dist} + \beta_2 \mathcal{L}_{divr} + \mathcal{L}_{kl} \tag{12}$$

$$\mathcal{L}_{dist} = -\frac{1}{M} \sum_{i=1}^{M} log(1 - (|\alpha - D(G(z_i))|)) \tag{13}$$

$$\mathcal{L}_{divr} = \frac{1}{\frac{1}{M}\sum_{i=1}^{M}(\|G(z_i) - \mu\|_2)}, \quad \mu = \frac{1}{C}\sum_{i=1}^{C} G(z_i) \tag{14}$$

$$\mathcal{L}_{kl} = KL(G_{struct}(z_i) \| \frac{1}{C}) + KL(G_{origin}(z_i) \| \frac{1}{C}) \tag{15}$$

where $\alpha \in [0,1]$ is a hyperparameter, β_1 and β_2 are weight hyperparameters, $D(\cdot)$ denotes the discriminator, M denotes the number of generated nodes, $G(z_i) = [G_{struct}(z_i) \| G_{origin}(z_i)]$ denotes the output of the generator, $C = k + d$ and $KL(P\|Q)$ denotes the KL divergence.

After obtaining the output from the generator, we employ the pre-trained TGAE to integrate the generated nodes into the original graph:

$$\tilde{\mathbf{X}}_{struct} = \begin{bmatrix} \mathbf{X}_{struct} \\ G_{struct}(z_i) \end{bmatrix}, \quad \tilde{\mathbf{X}}_{origin} = \begin{bmatrix} \mathbf{X}_{origin} \\ G_{origin}(z_i) \end{bmatrix} \tag{16}$$

$$\tilde{\mathbf{A}} = TGAE(\tilde{\mathbf{X}}_{struct}, \tilde{\mathbf{X}}_{origin}) \tag{17}$$

Next, we select the edges in $\tilde{\mathbf{A}}$ that are related to the generated nodes and add them to the original graph, while preserving the inherent edges. The resulting graph serves as the input to the discriminator.

Notably, we denote the ratio of generated nodes to real nodes as $p_G = \frac{M}{N}$. As a hyperparameter, p_G will be explored further in our experiments.

Discriminator. In our discriminator, we utilize a GNN architecture due to its superior capability in processing graph-structured data. However, traditional GNNs indiscriminately aggregate features from all neighboring nodes, which can lead to undesirable feature smoothing: the features of anomalous nodes may be overwhelmed by dominant normal nodes, and normal nodes may also incorporate noisy information from anomalous neighbors.

GraphCAD [4] suggests that normal and anomalous nodes can be effectively distinguished by leveraging the global context of the graph. Inspired by this insight, we introduce an edge homophily identification mechanism based on global context to address this issue.

First, we obtain the fusion representation $\tilde{\mathbf{H}}_{fusion}$:

$$\tilde{\mathbf{H}}_{fusion} = \mathbf{W}_r[\mathbf{W}_s \tilde{\mathbf{X}}_{struct} \parallel \mathbf{W}_o \tilde{\mathbf{X}}_{origin}] \tag{18}$$

where $\parallel$ is the concatenation operation and $\mathbf{W}_r, \mathbf{W}_s, \mathbf{W}_o$ denotes three distinct learnable parameter matrices.

Next, we employ a multilayer GNN to process the graph structure. Specifically, at the l-th layer of GNN, the global context $\mathbf{h}_g^{(l)}$ is computed to aggregate information from all nodes within the graph. In this context, to identify the edge e_{ij}, we leverage nodes v_i, v_j and $\mathbf{h}_g^{(l)}$ to estimate the homophily probability $c_{ij}^{(l)}$:

$$\mathbf{h}_g^{(l)} = \sum_{i=1}^{\tilde{N}} \mathbf{W}^{(l)} \mathbf{h}_i^{(l-1)} \tag{19}$$

$$d_{ij}^{(l)} = \mathbf{W}^{(l)} \mathbf{h}_i^{(l-1)} - \mathbf{W}^{(l)} \mathbf{h}_j^{(l-1)} \tag{20}$$

$$d_{ig}^{(l)} = \mathbf{W}^{(l)} \mathbf{h}_i^{(l-1)} - \mathbf{h}_g^{(l)} \tag{21}$$

$$d_{jg}^{(l)} = \mathbf{W}^{(l)} \mathbf{h}_j^{(l-1)} - \mathbf{h}_g^{(l)} \tag{22}$$

$$c_{ij}^{(l)} = MLP([d_{ij}^{(l)} \parallel d_{ig}^{(l)} \parallel d_{jg}^{(l)}]) \tag{23}$$

where $\tilde{N} = N + M$, $\mathbf{W}^{(l)}$ is learnable parameter matrices of the l-th and MLP is a two-layer multilayer perceptron with a *sigmoid* activation function, ensuring that $c_{ij}^{(l)}$ is constrained within the range $(0, 1)$.

We incorporate $c_{ij}^{(l)}$ into the computation of attention coefficients, with the intention that $c_{ij}^{(l)}$ approaches 0 for heterogeneous edges. This enables a pruning-like effect during message passing, effectively preventing information exchange between normal and anomalous nodes. The attention coefficient $a_{ij}^{(l)}$ and the message aggregation process of the GNN are designed as follows:

$$a_{ij}^{(l)} = \frac{c_{ij}^{(l)}}{\sum_{k=1}^{\tilde{N}} c_{ik}^{(l)}} \quad (24)$$

$$\mathbf{h}_i^{(l)} = \sigma(\sum_{j \in \mathcal{N}(i) \cup \{i\}} a_{ij}^{(l)} \mathbf{W}^{(l)} \mathbf{h}_j^{(l-1)}) \quad (25)$$

where $\mathcal{N}(v)$ denotes the neighbors of i and σ denotes an activation function. The input $\mathbf{H}^{(0)}$ is $\tilde{\mathbf{H}}_{fusion}$ and the output of the final attention layer $\mathbf{H}^{(L)}$ is denoted as the output node embeddings $\mathbf{Z}$.

Finally, we employ a simple detector to obtain the anomaly probability p_v of node v:

$$p_v = sigmoid(\mathbf{W}_p \mathbf{z}_v + \mathbf{b}) \quad (26)$$

where $\mathbf{W}_p$ and $\mathbf{b}$ denote the weight and bias parameters respectively.

The loss function $\mathcal{L}_{dis}$ is designed to comprise two components. $\mathcal{L}_{node}$ is node discrimination loss. $\mathcal{L}_{edge}$ is edge discrimination loss. Formally, the loss function is defined as:

$$\mathcal{L}_{dis} = \mathcal{L}_{node} + \sum_{l=1}^{L} \mathcal{L}_{edge}^{(l)} \quad (27)$$

$$\mathcal{L}_{node} = -\frac{1}{N_t} \sum_{i=1}^{N_t} (\gamma_1 log(1 - D(\mathbf{x}_i)) + \gamma_2 log(D(G(z_i)))) \quad (28)$$

$$\mathcal{L}_{edge}^{(l)} = -\frac{1}{|\mathcal{E}_t|} \sum_{e_{ij} \in \mathcal{E}_t} (y_{ij} log(c_{ij}^{(l)}) + (1 - y_{ij}) log(1 - c_{ij}^{(l)})) \quad (29)$$

where γ_1 and γ_2 are weight hyperparameters, N_t denotes the number of training nodes and $\mathcal{E}_t$ denotes the edges whose both endpoints are within the set of training nodes. For each $e_{ij} \in \mathcal{E}_t$, if node i and node j have the same label (e_{ij} is homophilic), $y_{ij} = 1$, otherwise (e_{ij} is heterophilic) $y_{ij} = 0$.

5 Experiments

5.1 Experiment Setup

Datasets. We conduct comprehensive evaluations of HAGAN on four large-scale real-world benchmark datasets, including Amazon [9], Reddit [21], YelpChi [21] and TFinance [34], covering four domains: e-commerce, social media, business reviews, and finance. The key statistics are presented in the appendix.

Table 1. The AUC and AP results across four real-world GAD datasets are presented. The best performance in each row is boldfaced, with the second-best underlined.

Dataset	Amazon		Reddit		YelpChi		TFinance	
Metric	AUC	AP	AUC	AP	AUC	AP	AUC	AP
Radar	0.5684	0.1701	0.5826	0.0858	0.5557	0.2906	0.0587	0.0458
ANOMALOUS	0.5205	0.1788	0.5900	0.0883	0.5824	0.3195	0.0579	0.0459
DOMINANT	0.2662	0.0839	0.5722	0.0743	0.4799	0.2549	0.8077	0.4715
DONE	0.7302	0.3653	0.6102	0.0859	0.5188	0.2737	0.8962	0.6910
AdONE	0.7746	0.5003	0.6178	0.0849	0.5199	0.2828	0.8960	0.6035
GAAN	0.6558	0.1672	0.5589	0.0822	0.5319	0.2711	0.6481	0.1579
AEGIS	0.8022	0.4998	0.5474	0.0950	0.4785	0.2557	0.8424	0.6036
CoLA	0.5803	0.1931	0.5488	0.0508	0.4619	0.1718	0.6148	0.2263
OCGNN	0.8602	0.7647	0.5247	0.0655	**0.5973**	0.3131	0.9049	0.7645
CONAD	0.2646	0.0838	0.5714	0.0744	0.4801	0.2545	0.8072	0.4555
TAM	0.8699	0.7454	0.5927	0.0871	0.5819	0.2916	**0.9314**	0.4612
CoCo	0.8620	0.8048	0.5724	0.0747	0.5836	0.3211	0.8790	0.5411
HAGAN (Ours)	**0.9038**	**0.8238**	**0.6223**	**0.0994**	0.5940	**0.3638**	0.9193	**0.7838**

Baselines. HAGAN is compared with two shallow methods, Radar [23] and ANOMALOUS [30], as well as ten GNN-based deep methods, including DOMINANT [8], DONE [1], AdONE [1], GAAN [7], AEGIS [5], CoLA [26], OCGNN [37], TAM [31], and CoCo [36].

Notably, many methods are originally unsupervised. To ensure fairness, we modify these methods according to our semi-supervised setup. For supervised methods, which require anomalous labels, we exclude them from our baseline.

Metrics. Following previous studies [31], we employ two widely recognized and complementary evaluation metrics for anomaly detection: Area Under the Receiver Operating Characteristic Curve (AUC) and Area Under the Precision-Recall Curve (AP). Higher AUC/AP indicates better performance.

Implementation Details. Our semi-supervised setting use a portion of nodes labeled (50%) as normal for training, while the remaining nodes are used for validation and testing. HAGAN is implemented using pytorch 2.2.0+cu118 with Python 3.10, running on two NVIDIA GeForce RTX 3090 (24GB). All datasets are optimized using the Adam optimizer. The number of anchor nodes k is set to 64, the dimensions of each feature in the hidden layers are set to 64, and the number of layers of GNN is set to 2. Besides, the settings for other hyperparameters are presented in the appendix.

5.2 Performance Comparison

The results are presented in Table 1. HAGAN demonstrates consistently strong performance across all datasets, maintaining stable results, whereas many other models exhibit significant fluctuations in certain datasets. For instance, OCGNN performs poorly on the Reddit dataset, and DONE struggles with the Amazon dataset. Notably, HAGAN excels in the AP metric, achieving the best performance across all datasets. In particular, on the YelpChi dataset, it outperforms the second-best model, CoCo, by a significant margin of 13.29%. While HAGAN does not achieve the highest AUC scores on the YelpChi and TFinance datasets, it still ranks second, further highlighting its robustness. These results suggest that HAGAN demonstrates strong generalizability and robustness in GAD tasks.

5.3 Transformer-Based GAE Analysis

In this analysis, we focus on evaluating the performance of TGAE. Specifically, we implement a GCN-based GAE and a GCN-based VGAE, and modify the TGAE model to separately utilize only the original features ($TGAE_{origin}$) and only the structural features ($TGAE_{struct}$) for evaluation. The reconstruction loss $\mathcal{L}_{recon}$ is used as the evaluation metric.

As presented in Table 2, TGAE performs similarly to other common graph autoencoders on most datasets, achieving the best results on the YelpChi dataset. Moreover, $TGAE_{struct}$ outperforms $TGAE_{origin}$. These experimental results demonstrate the effectiveness of both the anchor-based encoding and TGAE in graph reconstruction tasks.

Table 2. Reconstruction loss of GAEs.

Model	Amazon	Reddit	YelpChi	TFinance
GAE	**0.2134**	**0.2499**	0.2429	0.2459
VGAE	0.2512	0.2508	0.2515	0.2717
$TGAE_{struct}$	0.2382	0.2509	0.2192	**0.2257**
$TGAE_{origin}$	0.2540	0.2509	0.2613	0.2614
TGAE	0.2312	0.2504	**0.2147**	0.2466

5.4 Ablation Analysis

In this analysis, we focus on the necessity of three modules. Specifically, we modify HAGAN as follows: 1. **NoGEN** that replace the generator with a random feature generation approach. 2. **NoGAE** that randomly establish connections between generated nodes and real nodes. 3. **NoEHI** that remove the edge homophily identification from the discriminator and replace with GCN.

As presented in Table 3, NoGEN exhibits the poorest performance, which can be attributed to the inability of the random feature generation method to ensure the quality of the generated samples. This further underscores the necessity of our motivation to generate high-quality samples. NoGAE achieves relatively better results, suggesting that the removal of TGAE's influence has a limited effect. However, it still fails to match the full model, likely due to the disruption of the original graph structure caused by the random connection establishment method. NoEHI performs poorly, which aligns with the Challenge 3 discussed in Sect. 1, and further validates the rationale behind our proposed edge homogeneity identification mechanism.

Table 3. The AUC and AP of variants.

Metric	Variants	Dataset			
		Amazon	Reddit	YelpChi	TFinance
AUC	NoGEN	0.6477	0.4275	0.5253	0.8726
	NoGAE	0.7859	0.5935	0.5548	0.9090
	NoEHI	0.7525	0.4345	0.5365	0.8893
	HAGAN	**0.9038**	**0.6223**	**0.5940**	**0.9193**
AP	NoGEN	0.3191	0.0518	0.2675	0.6441
	NoGAE	0.5230	0.0943	0.3096	0.7559
	NoEHI	0.3545	0.0547	0.2775	0.7077
	HAGAN	**0.8238**	**0.0994**	**0.3638**	**0.7838**

5.5 Generated Sample Analysis

In this analysis, we focus on the performance with respect to α and p_G. We evaluated the performance of HAGAN across various values of α, specifically: 0.3, 0.35, 0.4, 0.45, 0.5, 0.55, 0.6, 0.65, and 0.7. As presented in Fig. 2, both metrics exhibit an initial increase followed by a decrease, with the extrema occurring around $\alpha = 0.5$. This is because α represents the probability that a generated sample is classified as anomalous by the discriminator, and a value of 0.5 indicates a state where normal and anomalous instances are difficult to distinguish, aligning with our definition of high-quality anomalies. Furthermore, after reaching the peak, the performance significantly declines, as the generated anomalies become overly distinct, limiting the discriminator's learning efficiency.

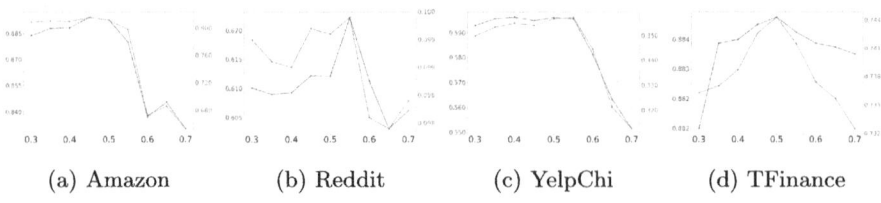

(a) Amazon (b) Reddit (c) YelpChi (d) TFinance

Fig. 2. The AUC (blue) and AP (green) with respect to α. (Color figure online)

We evaluated the performance of HAGAN across various values of p_G, testing values within the 0% to 50% range and visualizing the values near the extrema. As presented in Fig. 3, both metrics exhibit an initial increase followed by a decrease, and the optimal p_G values vary significantly across different datasets. We believe that an excessively high proportion of anomalous nodes may disrupt the underlying graph structure, deviating from real-world scenarios, while a proportion that is too low may lead the model to overly focus on learning from normal nodes.

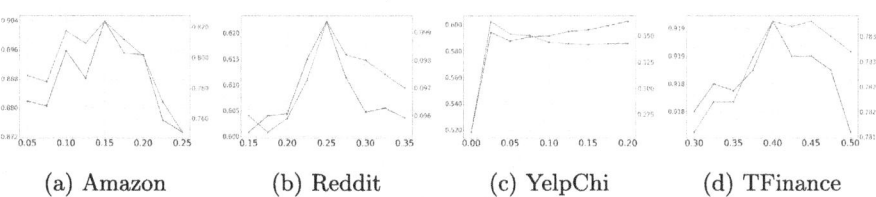

(a) Amazon (b) Reddit (c) YelpChi (d) TFinance

Fig. 3. The AUC (blue) and AP (green) with respect to p_G. (Color figure online)

5.6 GAN Adversarial Analysis

In practice, we observe that as training progresses, the generator's performance lags behind the discriminator, leading to a decline in the quality of generated samples. This issue has been addressed in prior research [20,29], where a common solution is to train the discriminator multiple times within a single epoch. However, while conventional GANs focus on optimizing the generator, our goal is to enhance the discriminator. To this end, we adopt a training strategy (**Strategy 1**) that involves training the generator multiple times within a single epoch. Figure 4 presents the results of training the generator and discriminator at different ratios on the Amazon dataset, specifically 1:3, 1:1, 2:1, 3:1, 4:1, and 5:1. Figure 4(c) presents the variation in the anomaly probability of discriminator outputs for the generated samples at each epoch, under different training ratios. It is evident that when the training ratio is set to 1:3 or 1:1, the anomaly probability rapidly approaches 1.0, indicating that the generator is unable to keep pace with the discriminator, resulting in the generation of low-quality samples. This observation is also reflected in Fig. 4(a) and (b), where the AUC and AP metrics quickly reach their peaks and then begin to decline. In contrast, when the generator undergoes multiple training iterations, overall performance improves, with the best results observed at a 3:1 training ratio. Furthermore, as illustrated in Fig. 4 (c), the average predicted probability of abnormality for the generated samples by the discriminator hovers around 0.7, with the minimum reaching 0.5. This observation aligns with the objective of the generator in HAGAN to produce samples that are difficult for the discriminator to distinguish from real

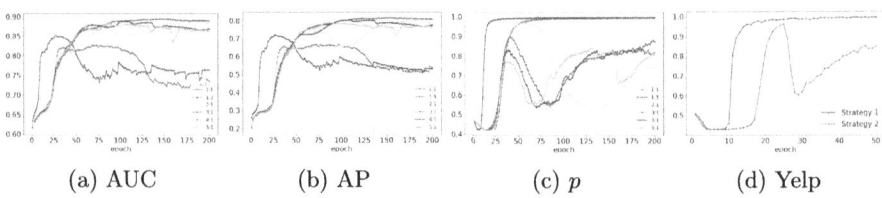

(a) AUC (b) AP (c) p (d) Yelp

Fig. 4. The results of training the generator and discriminator at ratios 1:3 (blue), 1:1 (red), 2:1 (pink), 3:1 (green), 4:1 (purple) and 5:1 (orange). (Color figure online)

anomalies, thereby demonstrating the reliability of the samples generated by the generator.

Unfortunately, when we applied Strategy 1 to the YelpChi dataset, the results were suboptimal. We hypothesize that this result can be attributed to the discriminator initially making random predictions that prevented it from providing meaningful feedback to the generator. To address this issue, we propose an alternative training strategy (**Strategy 2**), in which the discriminator is first trained independently, without training the generator, and the generator is subsequently trained multiple times within each epoch. Figure 4 (d) presents the anomaly probability of generated samples on the YelpChi dataset under different training strategies. As presented, Strategy 2 effectively mitigates the rapid degradation in the quality of generated samples. The performance of HAGAN across four datasets under different training strategies is presented in Table 4.

Table 4. The AUC and AP of Strategies.

Metric	Strategy	Dataset			
		Amazon	Reddit	YelpChi	TFinance
AUC	1	**0.9038**	**0.6123**	0.5316	0.9174
	2	0.8533	0.5941	**0.5940**	**0.9188**
AP	1	**0.8238**	**0.0994**	0.2728	0.7784
	2	0.7168	0.0931	**0.3638**	**0.7839**

5.7 Anchor Nodes Analysis

In this analysis, we focus on the performance with respect to k. Table 5 presents the reconstruction loss under different numbers of anchor points. It can be observed that the performance is relatively poor when the number of anchors k is small. This aligns with our hypothesis, as a limited number of anchors increases the likelihood that many nodes will have identical or similar distances to the anchors, even if these nodes are structurally dissimilar in the graph. Such cases hinder the ability to effectively capture structural characteristics.

Intuitively, increasing the number of anchors should provide richer and more fine-grained structural representations. However, the experimental results show that the performance does not continuously improve with more anchors. Instead, it begins to decline after a certain point. We speculate that as k increases, newly added anchors may be located close to existing ones or concentrated in densely connected regions, leading to redundant structural information. This redundancy can introduce noise and interfere with the model's ability to make accurate structural distinctions.

Table 5. Reconstruction loss of k.

k	Amazon	Reddit	YelpChi	TFinance
8	0.2358	0.2507	0.2221	0.2346
16	0.2344	0.2508	0.2201	0.2415
32	0.2322	0.2505	0.2156	**0.2252**
64	0.2312	**0.2504**	0.2147	0.2466
96	**0.2308**	0.2508	0.2134	0.2465
128	0.2329	0.2509	**0.2117**	0.2422

5.8 Complexity Analysis

Anchor-Based Encoding Complexity. The dominant computational cost arises from performing BFS traversals to compute shortest path lengths. Specifically, for each of the k selected anchor nodes, a single-source shortest path is computed. The total complexity of the BFS step across all anchors is $\mathcal{O}(k(n+m))$, where n is the number of nodes and m is the number of edges.

GAE Complexity. The computational complexity of the GAE model is mainly determined by the Transformer encoder and the inner product decoder. For a graph with n nodes and embedding dimension d, the encoder requires $\mathcal{O}(Ln^2d)$, and the decoder plus loss computation costs $\mathcal{O}(n^2d)$. Thus, the total complexity per subgraph is $\mathcal{O}(n^2d)$.

GAN Complexity. Generator consists of multiple fully connected layers, where the computation primarily involves feature transformation with a time complexity of $\mathcal{O}(N)$, where N is the number of generated nodes. The discriminator employs a GNN, in which each layer models pairwise feature relationships and computes attention weights. The overall time complexity is approximately $\mathcal{O}(N^2d)$, where d is the feature dimension. As the graph size increases, the discriminator tends to become the computational bottleneck.

6 Conclusion

This paper presents a semi-supervised approach for graph anomaly detection and introduces HAGAN, a novel framework that generates high-quality anomaly nodes using a GAN. By incorporating a pre-trained Transformer-based GAE, HAGAN ensures seamless integration of the generated nodes while maintaining structural integrity. The framework also uses a GNN discriminator with edge homophily identification to reduce noise. Experimental results on benchmark datasets show that HAGAN achieves state-of-the-art performance. Future work will explore more effective anchor point selection strategies and investigate the application of generative approaches to dynamic or heterogeneous graphs.

References

1. Bandyopadhyay, S., N, L., Vivek, S.V., Murty, M.N.: Outlier resistant unsupervised deep architectures for attributed network embedding. In: Proceedings of the 13th International Conference on Web Search and Data Mining, pp. 25–33 (2020)
2. Breunig, M.M., Kriegel, H.P., Ng, R.T., Sander, J.: Lof: identifying density-based local outliers. In: Proceedings of the 2000 ACM SIGMOD International Conference on Management of Data, pp. 93–104 (2000)
3. Caville, E., Lo, W.W., Layeghy, S., Portmann, M.: Anomal-e: a self-supervised network intrusion detection system based on graph neural networks. Knowl.-Based Syst. **258**, 110030 (2022)
4. Chen, B., et al.: Graph contrastive learning for anomaly detection (2021). https://api.semanticscholar.org/CorpusID:251799764
5. Chen, Z., Liu, B., Wang, M., Dai, P., Lv, J., Bo, L.: Generative adversarial attributed network anomaly detection. In: Proceedings of the 29th ACM International Conference on Information & Knowledge Management, pp. 1989–1992 (2020)
6. Cheng, D., Ye, Y., Xiang, S., Ma, Z., Zhang, Y., Jiang, C.: Anti-money laundering by group-aware deep graph learning. IEEE Trans. Knowl. Data Eng. **35**(12), 12444–12457 (2023)
7. Ding, K., Li, J., Agarwal, N., Liu, H.: Inductive anomaly detection on attributed networks. In: Proceedings of the Twenty-Ninth International Conference on International Joint Conferences on Artificial Intelligence, pp. 1288–1294 (2021)
8. Ding, K., Li, J., Bhanushali, R., Liu, H.: Deep anomaly detection on attributed networks. In: Proceedings of the 2019 SIAM international conference on data mining. pp. 594–602. SIAM (2019)
9. Dou, Y., Liu, Z., Sun, L., Deng, Y., Peng, H., Yu, P.S.: Enhancing graph neural network-based fraud detectors against camouflaged fraudsters. In: Proceedings of the 29th ACM International Conference on Information & Knowledge Management, pp. 315–324 (2020)
10. Duan, J., Wang, S., Zhang, P., Zhu, E., Hu, J., Jin, H., Liu, Y., Dong, Z.: Graph anomaly detection via multi-scale contrastive learning networks with augmented view. In: Proceedings of the AAAI Conference on Artificial Intelligence, vol. 37, pp. 7459–7467 (2023)
11. Gao, Y., Wang, X., He, X., Liu, Z., Feng, H., Zhang, Y.: Alleviating structural distribution shift in graph anomaly detection. In: Proceedings of the Sixteenth ACM International Conference on Web Search and Data Mining, pp. 357–365 (2023)

12. Gasteiger, J., Weißenberger, S., Günnemann, S.: Diffusion improves graph learning. Advances in neural information processing systems **32** (2019)
13. Gong, Z., Wang, G., Sun, Y., Liu, Q., Ning, Y., Xiong, H., Peng, J.: Beyond homophily: Robust graph anomaly detection via neural sparsification. In: IJCAI, pp. 2104–2113 (2023)
14. Goodfellow, I.J., et al.: Generative adversarial networks. Commun. ACM **63**, 139–144 (2014). https://api.semanticscholar.org/CorpusID:1033682
15. Haixiang, G., Yijing, L., Shang, J., Mingyun, G., Yuanyue, H., Bing, G.: Learning from class-imbalanced data: review of methods and applications. Expert Syst. Appl. **73**, 220–239 (2017)
16. Huang, M., et al.: Auc-oriented graph neural network for fraud detection. In: Proceedings of the ACM Web Conference 2022, pp. 1311–1321 (2022)
17. Jin, M., Liu, Y., Zheng, Y., Chi, L., Li, Y.F., Pan, S.: Anemone: graph anomaly detection with multi-scale contrastive learning. In: Proceedings of the 30th ACM International Conference on Information & Knowledge Management, pp. 3122–3126 (2021)
18. Khan, W., Haroon, M.: An efficient framework for anomaly detection in attributed social networks. Int. J. Inf. Technol. **14**(6), 3069–3076 (2022)
19. Kim, H., Lee, B.S., Shin, W.Y., Lim, S.: Graph anomaly detection with graph neural networks: current status and challenges. IEEE Access **10**, 111820–111829 (2022)
20. Kotha, P., Janardhan Babu, V., Ankam, S.: Generative adversarial networks: a comprehensive review. In: International Conference on Computer & Communication Technologies, pp. 105–114. Springer (2023)
21. Kumar, S., Zhang, X., Leskovec, J.: Predicting dynamic embedding trajectory in temporal interaction networks. In: Proceedings of the 25th ACM SIGKDD International Conference on Knowledge Discovery & Data Mining, pp. 1269–1278 (2019)
22. Li, D.: Anomaly detection with generative adversarial networks for multivariate time series. arXiv preprint arXiv:1809.04758 (2018)
23. Li, J., Dani, H., Hu, X., Liu, H.: Radar: Residual analysis for anomaly detection in attributed networks. In: IJCAI, vol. 17, pp. 2152–2158 (2017)
24. Lin, M., Wen, K., Zhu, X., Zhao, H., Sun, X.: Graph autoencoder with preserving node attribute similarity. Entropy **25** (2023), https://api.semanticscholar.org/CorpusID:257790352
25. Liu, F.T., Ting, K.M., Zhou, Z.H.: Isolation-based anomaly detection. ACM Trans. Knowl. Discovery Data (TKDD) **6**(1), 1–39 (2012)
26. Liu, Y., et al.: Anomaly detection in dynamic graphs via transformer. IEEE Trans. Knowl. Data Eng. **35**(12), 12081–12094 (2021)
27. Ngo, P.C., Winarto, A.A., Kou, C.K.L., Park, S., Akram, F., Lee, H.K.: Fence gan: towards better anomaly detection. In: 2019 IEEE 31St International Conference on tools with artificial intelligence (ICTAI), pp. 141–148. IEEE (2019)
28. Page, L., Brin, S., Motwani, R., Winograd, T.: The pagerank citation ranking: Bringing order to the web. Tech. rep, Stanford infolab (1999)
29. Pawar, D.: Advancements and applications of generative adversarial networks: a comprehensive review. Int. J. Res. Appl. Sci. Eng. Technol. (2024). https://api.semanticscholar.org/CorpusID:269903498
30. Peng, Z., Luo, M., Li, J., Liu, H., Zheng, Q., et al.: Anomalous: a joint modeling approach for anomaly detection on attributed networks. In: IJCAI, vol. 18, pp. 3513–3519 (2018)

31. Qiao, H., Pang, G.: Truncated affinity maximization: One-class homophily modeling for graph anomaly detection. Advances in Neural Information Processing Systems **36** (2024)
32. Schlegl, T., Seeböck, P., Waldstein, S.M., Schmidt-Erfurth, U., Langs, G.: Unsupervised anomaly detection with generative adversarial networks to guide marker discovery. In: International Conference on Information Processing in Medical Imaging, pp. 146–157. Springer (2017)
33. Shi, F., Cao, Y., Shang, Y., Zhou, Y., Zhou, C., Wu, J.: H2-fdetector: a gnn-based fraud detector with homophilic and heterophilic connections. In: Proceedings of the ACM Web Conference 2022, pp. 1486–1494 (2022)
34. Tang, J., Li, J., Gao, Z., Li, J.: Rethinking graph neural networks for anomaly detection. In: International Conference on Machine Learning, pp. 21076–21089. PMLR (2022)
35. Vaswani, A., et al.: Attention is all you need. Advances in neural information processing systems **30** (2017)
36. Wang, R., Xi, L., Zhang, F., Fan, H., Yu, X., Liu, L., Yu, S., Leung, V.C.M.: Context correlation discrepancy analysis for graph anomaly detection. IEEE Trans. Knowl. Data Eng. **37**(1), 174–187 (2025). https://doi.org/10.1109/TKDE.2024.3488375
37. Wang, X., Jin, B., Du, Y., Cui, P., Tan, Y., Yang, Y.: One-class graph neural networks for anomaly detection in attributed networks. Neural Comput. Appl. **33**(18), 12073–12085 (2021). https://doi.org/10.1007/s00521-021-05924-9
38. Xu, Z., Huang, X., Zhao, Y., Dong, Y., Li, J.: Contrastive attributed network anomaly detection with data augmentation. In: Pacific-Asia Conference on Knowledge Discovery and Data Mining, pp. 444–457. Springer (2022)
39. Zhang, J., Wang, S., Chen, S.: Reconstruction enhanced multi-view contrastive learning for anomaly detection on attributed networks. arXiv preprint arXiv:2205.04816 (2022)
40. Zhang, R., et al.: Generation is better than modification: combating high class homophily variance in graph anomaly detection. arXiv preprint arXiv:2403.10339 (2024)
41. Zheng, Y., Jin, M., Liu, Y., Chi, L., Phan, K.T., Chen, Y.P.P.: Generative and contrastive self-supervised learning for graph anomaly detection. IEEE Trans. Knowl. Data Eng. **35**(12), 12220–12233 (2021)

RandomAD: A Random Kernel-Based Anomaly Detector for Time Series

Wenjie Xi[✉] and Jessica Lin

George Mason University, Fairfax, VA 22033, USA
{wxi,jessica}@gmu.edu

Abstract. Time series anomaly detection is a critical task with a wide range of applications including industrial monitoring, financial fraud detection, and medical diagnostics. Among existing methods, $C^{22}MP$ represents the state-of-the-art by combining Matrix Profile with catch22, a hand-crafted feature set, to enhance anomaly detection performance. However, catch22 features are limited in their ability to capture a full range of temporal characteristics in time series data. Recent advances in random convolutional kernel methods, such as the ROCKET family, have demonstrated strong performance in time series classification and clustering tasks. In this work, we propose RandomAD, a semi-supervised anomaly detection approach that leverages thousands of random convolutional kernels to extract a rich set of features. Our method adopts MiniRocket's random kernel generation strategy to produce a large pool of kernels with randomly initialized weights based on the training data. To address the lack of labeled anomalies in the semi-supervised setting, we introduce a kernel selection mechanism to retain only the most informative kernels. Additionally, we incorporate a multi-window selection strategy with an anomaly filtering module to optimize both window size and detection results. Through extensive experiments on the benchmark datasets, we demonstrate that RandomAD consistently outperforms existing state-of-the-art methods.

Keywords: Random convolutional kernel · Anomaly detection · Time series

1 Introduction

Time series anomaly detection (TSAD) focuses on detecting unusual subsequences (often referred to as *discords* when they represent the most anomalous patterns) or time points within long data streams. Due to its significance in wide-ranging applications including industrial monitoring, fraud detection and medical diagnostics [10], it has attracted considerable attention from researchers [19]. One remarkable approach for finding discords is the Matrix Profile (MP) [27], a data structure that stores each subsequence's Euclidean distance to its nearest neighbor. MP-based methods [14,27] are effective at finding anomalies that stand out due to their distinctive shapes.

However, relying solely on shape-based comparisons has limitations. In many real-world applications, anomalies may not manifest as distinct shapes but instead as subtle deviations in statistical characteristics or underlying dynamics. Incorporating features such as variance, entropy, or autocorrelation can capture these subtle changes, thereby improving the performance. To address this problem, $C^{22}MP$ [21] is introduced as an extension of the traditional MP framework by integrating catch22 [15], a collection of 22 domain-independent time series features. By using catch22 to extract features from each subsequence and with an early-abandoning mechanism, $C^{22}MP$ can detect anomalies efficiently and accurately. While this fusion is able to detect feature-based anomalies and improve TSAD performance, it also brings two challenges since it relies on a fixed set of handcrafted features: (1) it cannot capture complex anomalies outside the predefined feature space, and (2) it requires domain knowledge or labeled data when selecting the most relevant features for a specific dataset.

Inspired by recent success of random convolutional kernel techniques in time series classification [6,7,22] and clustering [12], we propose RandomAD, which extracts a rich set of features using random convolutional kernels. Specifically, we adopt the random kernel generation mechanism in MiniRocket [7] to generate thousands of different convolutional kernels with randomly initialized weights based on the training set. Unlike MiniRocket, which is a supervised method that leverages class labels to guide kernel selection, the semi-supervised anomaly detection does not have access to labeled anomalies. Therefore, we propose a kernel selection mechanism to retain only the most informative kernels capable of effectively capturing underlying patterns under semi-supervised setting. Each selected kernel is then applied to extract features from subsequences, transforming each subsequence into a feature representation.

Additionally, we introduce a multi-window selection strategy to adaptively determine the window sizes used in the framework. Existing methods typically rely on fixed window lengths or manually tuned "magic numbers", which are often suboptimal when handling different types of anomalies with varying characteristics [13]. Several approaches have been proposed to address this problem. For example, MADRID [13] efficiently computes time series discords across all subsequence lengths by leveraging shared computations, iterative doubling, and forward pruning. Similarly, MERLIN [17] iteratively compares subsequences of varying lengths with their immediate neighbors in a parameter-free manner to detect discords. However, both methods rely on raw distance comparisons between subsequences and still require a large search space for window selection.

In contrast, our approach adopts a large number of random convolutional kernels to extract a diverse set of features from subsequences. These random kernels highlight specific local regions of interest and therefore are less sensitive to small changes in window size. This property enables us to restrict the search to a small set of candidate window sizes within a predefined range, rather than exhaustively testing every possible value. We will discuss this in more detail in Sect. 4.6. Furthermore, by integrating the anomaly filtering mechanism, which selects the most effective window size based on anomaly scores, RandomAD can automatically identify an appropriate window size and produce reliable final anomaly detection results.

In summary, our contributions are as follows:

- We introduce random convolutional kernel feature extraction for time series anomaly detection and propose a novel kernel selection mechanism to identify effective kernels in a semi-supervised setting.
- We propose a multi-window selection strategy combined with an anomaly filtering mechanism that automatically determines the optimal window size and final anomaly detection result based on the anomaly scores.
- Extensive experiments on 250 datasets demonstrate that our proposed method outperforms all tested state-of-the-art approaches.

2 Related Work

2.1 Time Series Anomaly Detection

Time series anomaly detection has been extensively studied, with hundreds of methods proposed in recent decades [19]. Due to space constraint, we refer readers to the comprehensive survey [19] for a broader overview and focus here on key approaches that serve as baselines in our work.

Matrix Profile (MP) [27], a data structure that stores the Euclidean distance of each subsequence to its nearest neighbor, is a widely used method for time series anomaly detection. Intuitively, the matrix profile can be used to detect discord—the most unusual subsequence in the time series—by identifying the subsequence with the largest nearest neighbor distance. Since its initial introduction, many variants and follow-up works have been proposed to enhance its capabilities. SCRIMP [28] efficiently computes exact MPs in an anytime fashion, while MERLIN [17] eliminates the need to predefine subsequence lengths. DAMP [14] extends MP to real-time detection in streaming data, and $C^{22}MP$ [21] integrates catch22 [15] features with MP to detect anomalies by using time series characteristics instead of shapes.

Deep learning methods are popular in recent years. Autoencoder-based models such as LSTM-VAE [18] and USAD [2] learn to reconstruct normal sequences and detect anomalies based on the reconstruction error. Telemanom [9] trains LSTMs to predict future values, and then applies a dynamic threshold to the prediction error to detect anomalies. Transformer-based approaches like TranAD [24] use attention mechanisms to capture long-term dependencies, while adversarial training enhances anomaly detection stability.

Some methods detect anomalies based on density and distribution. RRCF [8] maintains an ensemble of random binary trees, assigning anomaly scores based on data perturbation effects. MDI [3] detects anomalies by identifying subsequences whose distributions differ significantly from the rest of the series using divergence measures. GANF [5] combines normalizing flows with Bayesian networks to model joint probability distributions and detect anomalies as low-density observations. NormA [4] builds a model of normal behavior and detects anomalies by measuring (dis)similarity to this reference model.

These methods offer a strong foundation for time series anomaly detection and demonstrate competitive performance, making them well-suited for inclusion as baseline comparisons in our evaluation.

2.2 Random Convolutional Kernel

Random convolutional kernel methods have played an important role in time series classification and clustering in recent years. The first such method, ROCKET [6], was proposed by Dempster et al. It applies tens of thousands of convolutional kernels with random weights to input data, calculates two aggregated features, and forms a high-dimensional feature vector. The feature vector is then used for classification using a linear model. MiniRocket [7] streamlines the process by using a small fixed set of kernels with predetermined weights, which reduces variability and significantly improves efficiency while maintaining classification accuracy. MultiRocket [22] further extends MiniRocket by incorporating additional pooling strategies and combining features from multiple kernel sets to capture a richer representation. In time series clustering, Li et al. proposed RandomNet [12], a CNN-LSTM framework with random weights and an ensemble mechanism to filter out irrelevant representations for clustering.

ROCKET has also been adopted for anomaly detection with classical detectors such as One-Class SVM [16], Isolation Forest [29], and kNN variants [23]. We extend this direction by using MiniRocket and introducing kernel selection and multi-window selection with an anomaly filtering mechanism for semi-supervised TSAD.

3 Methodology

3.1 Problem Formulation

We investigate the problem of semi-supervised time series anomaly detection. Specifically, we consider a univariate time series as the training set, represented as a sequence of observations of size T:

$$\mathcal{T} = \{a_1, \ldots, a_T\}, \tag{1}$$

where each data point a_t is collected at a specific timestamp t and $a_t \in \mathbb{R}$. The training dataset consists of historical normal data without anomalies.

Given an unseen test time series $\hat{\mathcal{T}}$ of length $\hat{T}$ with an anomaly, we compute anomaly score sequence $\mathcal{S} = \{s_1, \ldots, s_{\hat{T}}\}$, where each $s_t \in \mathbb{R}^+$ represents the degree of anomaly at timestamp t. The final anomaly location is determined based on the anomaly score sequence.

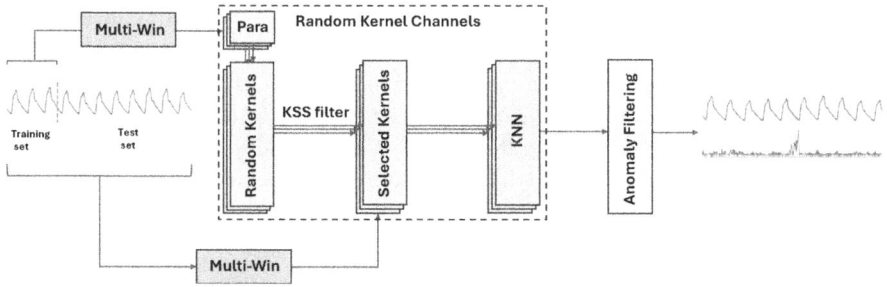

Fig. 1. Overview of RandomAD.

3.2 Overview of RandomAD

Next, we present a novel anomaly detection framework that leverages random convolutional kernels with adaptive selection mechanisms to select the best kernels and window sizes. As illustrated in Fig. 1, our framework preprocesses time series under **multi-window selection strategy** using multiple sliding windows of different sizes. The preprocessed data are then fed into multiple random kernel channels, each corresponding to a specific window size. Each channel consists of three key components: (1) a **random kernel module** that generates various convolutional kernels, (2) an **adaptive kernel selection mechanism** that filters the kernels to extract the most informative features, and (3) a **kNN-based anomaly scoring mechanism** that calculates anomaly scores based on deviations in the feature space. Each channel independently produces an anomaly score sequence, and finally the **anomaly filtering module** selects the final result based on these scores. In the following subsections, we provide a detailed explanation of each component.

3.3 Multi-window Selection Strategy

In time series analysis, selecting an appropriate window size is crucial, as different time series—or even different segments within the same series—can exhibit varying temporal dynamics, making some anomalies detectable only at specific window sizes [13]. Therefore, relying on a fixed window size, as is common in many existing methods [14,19,21,24], can lead to suboptimal performance. To address this problem, we introduce a multi-window selection strategy that adapts to the intrinsic temporal scales present in the time series data.

Our window size selection strategy defines appropriate lower and upper bounds, within which candidate window sizes are generated uniformly. The lower bound is set to a fixed value to ensure a minimum context length for capturing subtle local patterns. To determine the upper bound m, we perform an autocorrelation analysis on time series. Specifically, we compute the autocorrelation function for non-negative lags and, within a predefined lag interval (from 10 to 1000), we identify the first significant peak. The peak reflects the dominant periodicity of the series and is selected as the upper bound.

Once the lower and upper bounds are determined, we generate multiple candidate window sizes by evenly dividing the interval. For example, if the upper bound $m = 40$ and we select four candidate window sizes, the resulting candidate window sizes would be 10, 20, 30, and 40.

Through the integration of multi-window selection strategy, our framework is able to dynamically adapt to the diverse temporal characteristics present in time series data. With the anomaly filtering module, our method provides robust and accurate performance across diverse time series applications. We will discuss the anomaly filtering module in the following subsection.

3.4 Random Kernel-Based Feature Extractor

Although $C^{22}MP$ [21] demonstrates strong performance, it relies on a handcrafted feature extraction method catch22 [15] to capture time series characteristics, which may miss important features unique to different time series datasets. Inspired by the random convolutional kernel methods [6,7,12,22], we adopt random kernel feature extraction to provide a richer data representation that is capable of capturing a broader range of features. Specifically, we use the random kernel generation mechanism in MiniRocket [7], which has been shown to produce a smaller yet effective feature representations in a fraction of time.

Length and Weights. MiniRocket's kernel generation mechanism uses convolutional kernels of length 9. The weights of each kernel are restricted to two values, -1 and 2, and the sum of the weights equals zero. This zero-sum property ensures that the kernels only focus on relative magnitude in the input rather than absolute values, making them invariant to constant offsets in the data.

Bias. The bias of each kernel is directly obtained from the convolution output by sampling quantiles from randomly selected training examples.

Dilation. To capture patterns at multiple scales, each kernel is applied with various dilation factors, which spread the kernel across the input sequence. Specifically, a kernel with dilation d processes every d^{th} element of the input. The dilation values are selected from a fixed range $D = \{\lfloor 2^0 \rfloor, \ldots, \lfloor 2^{\max} \rfloor\}$, where the exponents are uniformly spaced between 0 and $\max = \log_2 \left(\frac{l_{\text{input}}-1}{l_{\text{kernel}}-1} \right)$, where l_{input} and l_{kernel} are length of input and kernel, respectively.

Padding. Padding is alternated across kernel/dilation combinations so that half use padding and half do not. Zero padding is added at the start and end of the time series, which ensures the convolution operation begins and ends with the kernel centered on the first and last elements of the sequence.

Feature Extraction. Finally, the extracted features are summarized using Proportion of Positive Values (PPV), which effectively captures the essential characteristics of the convolution output.

3.5 Kernel Selection Through Kernel Selection Score

The previous module generates a large number of random kernels to extract diverse features from all subsequences. Unlike classification task, where random kernel methods [6,7,22] can leverage class labels to learn weights for features through classifier training, semi-supervised anomaly detection relies only on normal data. Without access to labeled anomalies, it requires an effective mechanism to identify informative kernels based on the distribution of normal patterns. To that end, we propose a kernel selection scoring function, which we describe below.

Let $\mathbf{X} \in \mathbb{R}^{N \times M}$ denote the feature matrix, where N represents the number of subsequences extracted via a sliding window, and M is the total number of random kernels. The i-th column, $\mathbf{X}_i$, corresponds to the feature values produced by kernel i across all subsequences.

To address the kernel selection challenge, we introduce Kernel Selection Score (KSS) based on entropy and mutual information. For each kernel i, we first compute its entropy, denoted as:

$$H(\mathbf{X}_i) = - \sum_{x \in \mathcal{V}_i} p_i(x) \log p_i(x), \tag{2}$$

where $\mathcal{V}_i$ is the set of feature values from kernel i and $p_i(x)$ is the empirical probability of output x. A lower entropy indicates that the kernel's output is more stable and less noisy.

Next, we quantify the similarity between the outputs of different kernels by computing the mutual information. For any two kernels i and j, the mutual information is defined as:

$$I(\mathbf{X}_i, \mathbf{X}_j) = \sum_{(x,y) \in \mathcal{V}_i \times \mathcal{V}_j} p_{i,j}(x,y) \log \frac{p_{i,j}(x,y)}{p_i(x) p_j(y)}, \tag{3}$$

where $p_{i,j}(x,y)$ is the joint probability that kernel i outputs x and kernel j outputs y simultaneously. High mutual information implies that kernel i shares commonality with another kernel, suggesting that it captures underlying patterns within the data.

To integrate these two aspects, we define KSS for kernel i as follows:

$$KSS(\mathbf{X}_i) = \alpha \left(\frac{1}{|\mathcal{N}(i)|} \sum_{j \in \mathcal{N}(i)} I(\mathbf{X}_i, \mathbf{X}_j) \right) - \beta H(\mathbf{X}_i), \tag{4}$$

where $\mathcal{N}(i)$ denotes the set of all kernels excluding i. α and β are positive scaling factors that balance the contributions of mutual information and entropy, respectively. Entropy and mutual information are closely related: entropy measures the stability of features generated by a single kernel, while mutual information evaluates the relationships between different kernels. Integrating both metrics enables the selection of kernels that are both stable and share meaningful commonalities. Setting either parameter to 0 eliminates its corresponding effect. We evaluate the impact of each in the following section. The kernels are then ranked in descending order based on their KSS values, and the top γ fraction are selected.

By selecting kernels with high KSS values, we can identify random kernels that have both strong mutual information with others and low entropy, thereby extracting stable and meaningful patterns from the data. Such a method is particularly beneficial in semi-supervised anomaly detection, where the algorithm must rely on the inherent structure of the data.

3.6 kNN-Based Anomaly Scoring

After selecting the kernel, each channel undergoes feature extraction and anomaly scoring. For each channel, we apply the selected kernel to both the training and test sets, and generate feature vectors to capture the characteristics of each subsequence in the time series.

The anomaly scoring mechanism employs the k-nearest-neighbor (kNN) algorithm to quantify the anomaly level of each test subsequence. Specifically, for each test subsequence, we compute its Euclidean distance to all training subsequences in the feature space and identify the k nearest neighbors. The anomaly score assigned to the last timestamp of the test subsequence is the average Euclidean distance to these top-k neighbors.

Using random kernels, the distance calculation focuses on the difference of the features rather than raw time series values. As a result, each channel produces its own sequence of anomaly scores.

3.7 Anomaly Filtering

To determine the best result from multiple channels, each corresponding to a different candidate window size, we introduce an anomaly filtering mechanism that utilizes the detection index Δ to quantify the difference between anomalous subsequences. For each channel, we obtain a sequence of anomaly scores, $\mathcal{S} = \{s_1, s_2, \ldots, s_{\hat{T}}\}$, computed with a candidate window size w. The filtering process is performed as follows:

1. **Identifying the Primary Anomaly:**
   We first locate the highest anomaly score s_{h1} in $\mathcal{S}$ and its corresponding index i_{h1}.
2. **Defining an Exclusion Range:**
   To avoid selecting nearby points that may belong to the same anomaly, we define an exclusion range centered around i_{h1}. Specifically, we set:

$$EX_{start} = \max\{0, i_{h1} - w\}, \tag{5}$$

$$EX_{end} = \min\{\hat{T}, i_{h1} + w\}. \tag{6}$$

Within the interval $[EX_{start}, EX_{end}]$, none of the scores can be further considered.

3. **Computing the Detection Index:**
   Next, we search for the highest anomaly score outside the exclusion range, denoted as s_{h2}. The detection index is then calculated by:

   $$\Delta = s_{h1} - s_{h2}. \tag{7}$$

   A larger Δ indicates a more obvious difference between the most anomalous subsequence and the rest of the data, which indicates that the corresponding window size is more effective in capturing anomalies.

4. **Channel Selection:**
   By comparing the detection index of all channels, we select the channel with the largest Δ as the final result. With this mechanism, our framework is able to dynamically adapt to the most appropriate window size, therefore enhancing the robustness and accuracy of the anomaly detection.

4 Experiments

4.1 Experimental Settings

In this section, we describe the details of our experimental setup.

Dataset. To evaluate our proposed method, we conduct experiments on various public time series datasets. Given the concerns raised by Wu and Keogh [26] regarding flaws in existing anomaly detection benchmarks, we select datasets that provide realistic and meaningful challenges for anomaly detection. Specifically, we use all 250 datasets from the Hexagon ML/UCR Time Series Anomaly Archive [25], which was introduced to address the problems from other benchmark datasets [1,9,11,20] such as trivial anomaly patterns, unrealistic anomaly densities, and mislabeled ground truth. The datasets span diverse domains, including medicine, sports, biology, industry, etc. [21,26]. Each dataset is split into a training set which contains no anomalies, and a test set which contains exactly one labeled anomaly. The sequence lengths and anomaly lengths vary greatly across datasets, with sequence length ranging from 6674 to 900000 data points and anomaly length ranging from 1 to 1701 data points. In addition to this archive, we also use 10 datasets from [21] to intuitively visualize our results.

Evaluation Metrics. To ensure fair and meaningful evaluation, we follow the accuracy metric recommended by the dataset creators and previous works [14, 21,26]. Specifically, let L be the length of the labeled anomaly, the prediction is considered correct if the location of the highest anomaly score predicted by the algorithm falls within $\pm L$ data points of the ground truth anomaly location. If $L < 100$, we set $L = 100$. The final accuracy score we present is computed as the *ratio of correctly detected anomalies* across all datasets.

Equipment. The experiments are run on a machine with AMD Ryzen 9 5900X and 64 GB RAM. Since the method does not involve neural network training, there is no need to use a GPU.

Table 1. Comparison of our method against 13 baseline methods on 250 UCR Time Series Anomaly Archive datasets.

Method	Score	Method	Score
RandomAD (Full)	**0.704**	DAMP	0.556
RandomAD ($\alpha = 0$)	0.688	C^{22}MP	0.568
RandomAD ($\beta = 0$)	0.688	USAD	0.276
AutoEncoder	0.236	Telemanom	0.468
LSTM-VAE	0.198	SCRIMP	0.416
RRCF	0.030	MERLIN	0.440
MDI	0.470	NormA	0.474
TranAD	0.190	GANF	0.240

Hyper-parameters. To balance the contributions of entropy and mutual information, we set both α and β to 1 in Eq. 4. Each channel uses 1000 random kernels, with a total of 4 channels. We set $\gamma = 0.5$ for the kernel selection rate and for kNN anomaly scoring, we set $k = 3$.

Baseline Methods. We compare our method against 13 state-of-the-art methods: TranAD [24], MDI [3], RRCF [8], LSTM-VAE [18], AutoEncoder [2], USAD [2], Telemanom [9], SCRIMP [28], MERLIN [17], NormA [4], GANF [5], DAMP [14] and C^{22}MP [21]. See Sect. 2 for more details. Our source code is publicly available[1].

4.2 Experimental Results

Table 1 shows the accuracy scores of our proposed approach and 13 baseline methods on 250 datasets from the UCR Anomaly Archive. All results of baseline methods are from [21]. Due to space constraint, we are unable to show the selected window size and anomaly detection result of our method on each dataset. Interested readers can refer to our GitHub repository[1] for the full results.

From Table 1, we can observe that our proposed work, RandomAD, achieves an accuracy score of 0.704, which outperforms all baseline methods and has around a 24% performance improvement over the second-best method, C^{22}MP (0.568). Additionally, we include results where the impact of mutual information (RandomAD, $\alpha = 0$) and entropy (RandomAD, $\beta = 0$) are individually removed in Eq. 4. Both have anomaly score of 0.688 which shows the importance of combining both in kernel selection.

It is worth noting that in the C^{22}MP paper [21], the authors also presented an ensemble of DAMP and C^{22}MP with an accuracy score of 0.692. However, this approach is not a true algorithm; it is a post-hoc ensemble that selects the better algorithm after manually observing the labels. Our method achieves higher accuracy without relying on any manual selection processes, as all modules are automatically adapted to the data.

These results demonstrate the superiority of RandomAD, which leverages random kernel feature extraction, over approaches based on shape comparison

---

[1] https://github.com/Jackxiini/RandomAD

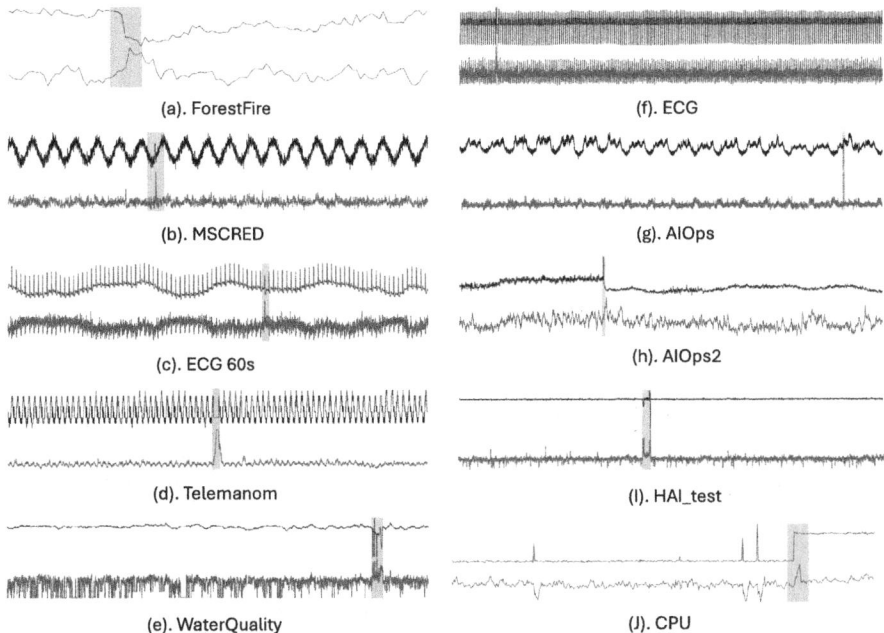

Fig. 2. The performance of RandomAD on 10 datasets outside the UCR Anomaly Archive. The top portion (black) is the original test data, and the bottom portion (blue) is the corresponding anomaly score computed by RandomAD. Ground-truth anomalies are marked by red boxes. (Color figure online)

and fixed features. The superiority reflects the ability of our random kernel module to effectively capture the underlying patterns in the data, as well as the effectiveness of the multi-window selection and anomaly filtering mechanisms.

4.3 Visualization

To demonstrate the effectiveness of our method, Fig. 2 presents the visualization of anomalies detected by RandomAD across ten datasets used in previous studies [21], none of which are part of the UCR Anomaly Archive [25]. Each dataset is divided into training set and test set, with the test set containing a single anomaly. The upper portion of each subfigure (shown in black) represents the original test data, while the lower portion (in blue) shows the anomaly scores calculated by our model. The ground-truth anomalies are highlighted with red boxes. Our method effectively detects anomalies and their correct locations in all datasets. It is worth noting that even in datasets without clear patterns, such as subfigures (a) and (j), our method can correctly locate the anomalies.

Table 2. Ablation study results show the impact of each module on the performance.

Method Variant	Score
RandomAD (Full)	**0.704**
w/ fixed window size (10)	0.548
w/ fixed window size (AT)	0.668
w/o kernel selection	0.688
w/o random kernels	0.580

4.4 Ablation Study

To verify the effectiveness of each component in our framework, we conduct an ablation study by removing or replacing individual modules and evaluating the resulting performance. Table 2 summarizes the accuracy scores under various configurations.

As shown in Table 2, the full model achieves the highest score of 0.704. Replacing the multi-window selection strategy with a fixed window size leads to a significant performance drop: with a fixed window size of 10, the score decreases to 0.548, while using a fixed window size based on autocorrelation (AT, equivalent to setting the upper bound as the window size) results in a score of 0.668. This demonstrates the importance of the multi-window selection strategy and the anomaly filtering module in adapting to the varying characteristics of different datasets.

In addition, removing the kernel selection mechanism leads to a slight drop in performance (to 0.688). It is worth noting that since removing this mechanism significantly increases the feature length, it significantly increases the total running time (from 3.8 h to 7.3 h). The result highlights the effectiveness of this mechanism in selecting more informative kernels.

Finally, removing random kernels and applying kNN directly on the raw subsequences for anomaly detection reduces the accuracy score to 0.580, illustrating the effectiveness of random convolutional kernels in capturing meaningful features.

4.5 Sensitivity Analysis

To investigate the sensitivity of our method's performance to hyperparameters, we evaluated five hyperparameters: number of kernels, kernel selection rate γ, number of channels and the scaling factors in Eq. 4, α and β. Fig. 3 shows the results for the first three hyperparameters, along with a linear regression curve fit demonstrating how the running time differs from the linear trend.

Number of Kernels. The number of generated kernels directly affects the ability of our method to extract features. Figure 3a demonstrates that increasing the number of kernels generally improves accuracy; however, this improvement

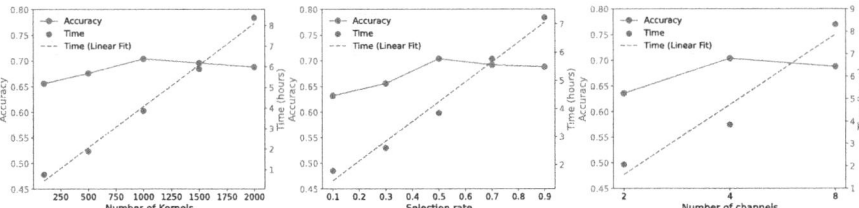

(a) Effect of the number of kernels on accuracy and running time.

(b) Effect of the kernel selection rate on accuracy and running time.

(c) Effect of the number of channels on accuracy and running time.

Fig. 3. Sensitivity analysis illustrating the trade-offs between accuracy and computational cost under different configurations.

stops after reaching a certain value. Specifically, the accuracy score increases from 0.652 at 100 kernels to a peak of 0.704 at 1000 kernels, and then decreases slightly to 0.688 at 2000 kernels. This suggests that exceeding a certain number of kernels may generate too many irrelevant kernels, which can hurt performance.

In contrast, the running time increases almost linearly with the number of kernels, from 0.76 h with 100 kernels to 8.38 h with 2000 kernels. While using more kernels (e.g., 1000 kernels) can improve performance, choosing fewer kernels can significantly reduce the computational cost. Notably, choosing only 100 kernels reduces the running time by about one-tenth compared to 1000 kernels, while still maintaining competitive accuracy. It is also worth mentioning that even with only 100 kernels, the accuracy score of 0.652 is still significantly higher than other compared methods. This demonstrates the superiority of using random convolutional kernels.

Kernel Selection Rate. Choosing an appropriate kernel selection rate is critical to performance. A selection rate that is too low may discard many informative kernels, while a selection rate that is too high may introduce irrelevant kernels, both of which have a negative impact on accuracy. Figure 3b shows that as the kernel selection rate increases, the accuracy improves until about 0.5, after which the accuracy decreases slightly. In addition, the computation time increases nearly linearly with the increase in the selection rate. Therefore, we suggest using 0.5 as the kernel selection rate to balance accuracy and computational efficiency.

Number of Channels. Increasing the number of window size candidates in the Multi-Window Selection Strategy directly corresponds to an increased number of channels, with each window size corresponding to a separate channel. Figure 3c demonstrates the impact of varying the number of channels on performance. The accuracy score improves significantly when the number of channels increases from 2 to 4, but additional channels (from 4 to 8) do not continue to improve

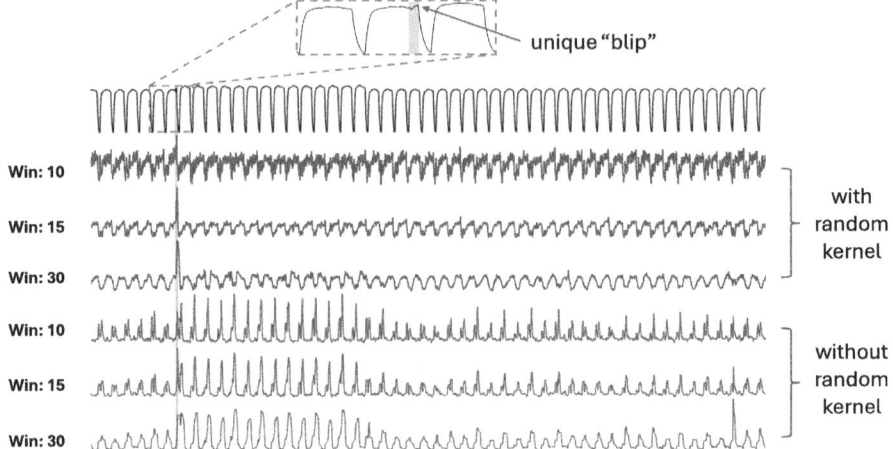

Fig. 4. Anomaly detection results with (blue) and without (green) random kernels across different window sizes (10, 15, 30) on the NASA spacecraft dataset. The black line shows a test segment with an anomaly ("blip" in red box). (Color figure online)

the accuracy score. This demonstrates the effectiveness of our proposed multi-window selection strategy and anomaly filtering mechanism, and also shows that our method is insensitive to small changes in the window size, which allows our method to provide good performance with a small set of window size candidates. We further analyze this in the following section.

Scaling Factor. We further analyze the sensitivity of the accuracy score to α and β. We have highlighted the importance of balancing these two factors, as demonstrated in Table 1, where setting either α or β to 0 leads to performance degradation. To further investigate their influence, we conduct additional experiments by setting $\alpha = 0.2$ and $\beta = 0.8$, which obtain an accuracy score of 0.672. Reversing these values ($\alpha = 0.8$, $\beta = 0.2$) achieves a similar accuracy score of 0.66. These results indicate that both factors significantly affect performance. Given that assigning equal values produces the best result, we recommend setting α and β equally to balance their contributions.

4.6 Effectiveness Analysis

To further illustrate the advantages of using random kernels and demonstrate that our method is less sensitive to small changes in window size, we conduct experiments on a real dataset from NASA spacecraft. The top part of Fig. 4 (black line) represents a segment of the test set, where we highlight the anomaly, a small unique "blip" of length 15, within the red dashed box. The blue line in the figure shows the anomaly scores produced by our method under three different window sizes: 10, 15, and 30. The green line represents the results when removing the random kernel feature extraction and relying on raw subsequences for kNN-based anomaly scoring.

The results clearly demonstrate that with random kernels, all three window sizes successfully detect the anomaly. In contrast, when using raw values, only the window size of 15 correctly detects the anomaly, while the others fail. Moreover, without random kernels, the anomaly score struggles to differentiate abnormal subsequences from normal ones. For instance, with a window size of 30, some normal subsequences on the right side exhibit high anomaly scores. In comparison, the random kernel method maintains clear separation between normal and abnormal subsequences across all window sizes and the normal regions do not experience abrupt changes in anomaly scores due to changes in window size.

The comparison highlights two advantages of our method. First, the random kernels selected by the kernel selection mechanism can effectively extract meaningful features that can capture the underlying patterns. Second, this method is less sensitive to the window size, allowing us to search the appropriate window size in a small search space.

5 Conclusion

In this work, we introduce RandomAD, a random convolutional kernel method for time series anomaly detection. While the idea of using convolutional kernels with random weights to generate diverse features is not new, the main contribution of our work lies in the kernel selection mechanism to select informative kernels that capture meaningful pattern in the sequence. In addition, since the random kernel module is robust to small variations in window size, we introduce an efficient multi-window selection strategy with a small search space. Incorporated with the anomaly filtering mechanism, our method effectively determines the appropriate window size and final anomalies. Extensive experiments on 250 datasets from the UCR Anomaly Archive demonstrate that RandomAD outperforms state-of-the-art methods.

References

1. Ahmad, S., Lavin, A., Purdy, S., Agha, Z.: Unsupervised real-time anomaly detection for streaming data. Neurocomputing **262**, 134–147 (2017)
2. Audibert, J., Marti, S., Guyard, F., Zuluaga, M.A.: From univariate to multivariate time series anomaly detection with non-local information. In: Lemaire, V., Malinowski, S., Bagnall, A., Guyet, T., Tavenard, R., Ifrim, G. (eds.) AALTD 2021. LNCS (LNAI), vol. 13114, pp. 186–194. Springer, Cham (2021). https://doi.org/10.1007/978-3-030-91445-5_12
3. Barz, B., Rodner, E., Garcia, Y.G., Denzler, J.: Detecting regions of maximal divergence for spatio-temporal anomaly detection. IEEE Trans. Pattern Anal. Mach. Intell. **41**(5), 1088–1101 (2018)
4. Bhatnagar, A., et al.: Merlion: a machine learning library for time series. arXiv preprint arXiv:2109.09265 (2021)

5. Dai, E., Chen, J.: Graph-augmented normalizing flows for anomaly detection of multiple time series. arXiv preprint arXiv:2202.07857 (2022)
6. Dempster, A., Petitjean, F., Webb, G.I.: Rocket: exceptionally fast and accurate time series classification using random convolutional kernels. Data Min. Knowl. Disc. **34**(5), 1454–1495 (2020)
7. Dempster, A., Schmidt, D.F., Webb, G.I.: MINIROCKET: a very fast (almost) deterministic transform for time series classification. In: Proceedings of the 27th ACM SIGKDD Conference on Knowledge Discovery & Data Mining, pp. 248–257 (2021)
8. Guha, S., Mishra, N., Roy, G., Schrijvers, O.: Robust random cut forest based anomaly detection on streams. In: International Conference on Machine Learning, pp. 2712–2721. PMLR (2016)
9. Hundman, K., Constantinou, V., Laporte, C., Colwell, I., Soderstrom, T.: Detecting spacecraft anomalies using LSTMs and nonparametric dynamic thresholding. In: Proceedings of the 24th ACM SIGKDD International Conference on Knowledge Discovery & Data Mining, pp. 387–395 (2018)
10. Jacob, V., Song, F., Stiegler, A., Rad, B., Diao, Y., Tatbul, N.: Exathlon: a benchmark for explainable anomaly detection over time series. arXiv preprint arXiv:2010.05073 (2020)
11. Laptev, N., Amizadeh, S., Billawala, Y.: S5-a labeled anomaly detection dataset, version 1.0 (16m) (2015)
12. Li, X., Xi, W., Lin, J.: RandomNet: clustering time series using untrained deep neural networks. Data Min. Knowl. Disc. **38**(6), 3473–3502 (2024)
13. Lu, Y., Srinivas, T.V.A., Nakamura, T., Imamura, M., Keogh, E.: Matrix profile XXX: MADRID: a hyper-anytime and parameter-free algorithm to find time series anomalies of all lengths. In: 2023 IEEE International Conference on Data Mining (ICDM), pp. 1199–1204. IEEE (2023)
14. Lu, Y., Wu, R., Mueen, A., Zuluaga, M.A., Keogh, E.: DAMP: accurate time series anomaly detection on trillions of datapoints and ultra-fast arriving data streams. Data Min. Knowl. Disc. **37**(2), 627–669 (2023)
15. Lubba, C.H., Sethi, S.S., Knaute, P., Schultz, S.R., Fulcher, B.D., Jones, N.S.: Catch22: canonical time-series characteristics: selected through highly comparative time series analysis. Data Min. Knowl. Disc. **33**(6), 1821–1852 (2019)
16. Melakhsou, A.A., Batton-Hubert, M.: Explainable abnormal time series subsequence detection using random convolutional kernels. In: International Conference on Deep Learning Theory and Applications, pp. 280–294. Springer (2023)
17. Nakamura, T., Imamura, M., Mercer, R., Keogh, E.: MERLIN: parameter-free discovery of arbitrary length anomalies in massive time series archives. In: 2020 IEEE International Conference on Data Mining (ICDM), pp. 1190–1195. IEEE (2020)
18. Park, D., Hoshi, Y., Kemp, C.C.: A multimodal anomaly detector for robot-assisted feeding using an LSTM-based variational autoencoder. IEEE Robot. Autom. Lett. **3**(3), 1544–1551 (2018)
19. Schmidl, S., Wenig, P., Papenbrock, T.: Anomaly detection in time series: a comprehensive evaluation. Proc. VLDB Endow. **15**(9), 1779–1797 (2022)
20. Shu, X., Zhang, S., Li, Y., Chen, M.: An anomaly detection method based on random convolutional kernel and isolation forest for equipment state monitoring. Eksploatacja i Niezawodność **24**(4), 758–770 (2022)
21. Su, Y., Zhao, Y., Niu, C., Liu, R., Sun, W., Pei, D.: Robust anomaly detection for multivariate time series through stochastic recurrent neural network. In: Proceed-

ings of the 25th ACM SIGKDD International Conference on Knowledge Discovery & Data Mining, pp. 2828–2837 (2019)
22. Tafazoli, S., et al.: Matrix profile XXIX: C 22 MP, fusing catch 22 and the matrix profile to produce an efficient and interpretable anomaly detector. In: 2023 IEEE International Conference on Data Mining (ICDM), pp. 568–577. IEEE (2023)
23. Tan, C.W., Dempster, A., Bergmeir, C., Webb, G.I.: MultiRocket: multiple pooling operators and transformations for fast and effective time series classification. Data Min. Knowl. Disc. **36**(5), 1623–1646 (2022)
24. Theissler, A., Wengert, M., Gerschner, F.: Rockad: transferring rocket to whole time series anomaly detection. In: International Symposium on Intelligent Data Analysis, pp. 419–432. Springer (2023)
25. Tuli, S., Casale, G., Jennings, N.R.: TranAD: deep transformer networks for anomaly detection in multivariate time series data. Proc. VLDB Endow. **15**(6), 1201–1214 (2022)
26. Wu, R., Keogh, E.J.: Supporting page for current time series anomaly detection benchmarks are flawed and are creating the illusion of progress (2020). https://wu.renjie.im/research/anomaly-benchmarks-are-flawed/tkde/
27. Wu, R., Keogh, E.J.: Current time series anomaly detection benchmarks are flawed and are creating the illusion of progress. IEEE Trans. Knowl. Data Eng. **35**(3), 2421–2429 (2021)
28. Yeh, C.C.M., et al.: Matrix profile I: all pairs similarity joins for time series: a unifying view that includes motifs, discords and shapelets. In: 2016 IEEE 16th International Conference on Data Mining (ICDM), pp. 1317–1322. IEEE (2016)
29. Zhu, Y., Yeh, C.C.M., Zimmerman, Z., Kamgar, K., Keogh, E.: Matrix profile XI: SCRIMP++: time series motif discovery at interactive speeds. In: 2018 IEEE International Conference on Data Mining (ICDM), pp. 837–846. IEEE (2018)

HCT: A Hierarchical Contrastive Learning Framework for Transferable Graph Anomaly Detection

Jiawei Ye, Hongyi Li, Qinlin Xie, Sicheng Liang, Yu Liu, and Jie Wu[✉]

Fudan University, Shanghai 200433, China
{jwye,jwu}@fudan.edu.cn,
{hyli24,xieqinlin00,scliang23,yuliu24}@m.fudan.edu.cn

Abstract. Graph anomaly detection (GAD) aims to identify abnormal nodes that differ from the majority within a graph and has been widely applied in real-world applications, where solutions based on graph neural network (GNN) have recently achieved remarkable success. However, GNN struggles to adapt to variations in the underlying data distributions, limiting its practical applicability. Existing efforts either train separate models for each dataset, rely heavily on source data, or overlook graph heterogeneity in GAD tasks, leading to challenges in transferability and generality. Therefore, how to effectively establish the underlying normal patterns and enable anomaly detection across graphs with varying feature and structure distributions remains an under-explored problem. To tackle these challenges, this paper proposes HCT, a general GAD framework for cross-graph transfer learning. Specifically, we first introduce node-feature disparity-based ranking and feature mapping to align anomaly features across graphs. Moreover, we employ a hierarchical contrastive learning framework to capture and transfer anomaly patterns effectively. HCT extracts deep structure information from the source graph at the node, subgraph, and view levels while employing a lightweight, trainable network module in the target graph to minimize cross-graph structure differences via contrastive learning. Besides, we design a structure-enhanced regularization objective to improve model adaptation in label-scarce scenarios. Extensive experiments on four real-world datasets demonstrate the effectiveness of HCT against state-of-the-art baselines with 1.63%–8.05% average performance improvement across both settings, showcasing its strong generality and adaptability.

Keywords: Graph Anomaly Detection · Transfer Learning · Contrastive Learning

1 Introduction

Graph anomaly detection (GAD) aims at identifying abnormal nodes that show significant deviations from the majority of nodes in a graph. It has garnered considerable research attention due to its broad real-world applications, such as fraud detection [1], spam review identification [2] and rumor detection [3]. Thanks to exceptional performance in handing high-dimensional features and complex interdependent relations on graphs, the Graph Neural Network (GNN) has recently been introduced into GAD with promising progress [4]. However, since graphs are non-Euclidean, with diverse structures and node attributes across different graphs, GNN-based GAD faces challenges when confronted with substantial variations in the underlying data distributions [5]. Hence, how to effectively model normal patterns and distinguish anomaly nodes in different graphs has become an urgent problem.

Existing GNN-based GAD explorations can be divided into supervised and unsupervised approaches. Supervised GAD methods detect anomaly node patterns through message passing/aggregation optimization [1,6] or distribution correlation between graph and high frequency spectral [7,8], assuming the availability of sufficient labeled data. In contrast, unsupervised GAD methods rely on non-label capture graph anomaly patterns through unsupervised learning techniques such as graph reconstruction [9] and contrastive learning [10,11]. Unfortunately, existing mainstream solutions require training separate detection models for each dataset, leading to high training costs and challenges in adapting to new graphs, which might be impractical for large-scale real-world scenarios.

Recently, the pretrain-finetune paradigm has shown great potential in graph-based tasks with GNN [12-14]. It leverages unsupervised pre-training to inject generalizable graph knowledge into GNNs, which can then be fine-tuned for effective generalization across different graphs without training from scratch. However, current studies [15] focus on the neighborhood homophily assumption that a node and its neighborhood nodes share similar labels while graphs typically exhibit neighborhood heterogeneity in GAD tasks, which may degrade GAD performance.

How to effectively establish the underlying normal patterns and enable anomaly detection over different distribution graphs is an under-explored problem, which is non-trivial due to three main challenges: (1) Cross-graph Feature Alignment: Different graphs exhibit significant variations in semantic space and feature dimensions. Current methods [11,16] rely on source graphs to provide signals, but in real-world scenarios, these signals may be inaccessible due to regulatory and privacy constraints. (2) Anomaly Pattern Learning: Existing transfer learning methods [12,17] often neglect the detailed exploration of generic anomaly patterns. Moreover, the structure differences between graphs make it challenging to effectively mine and transfer these patterns across diverse graphs. (3) Graph Label Scarcity: GNN-based GAD typically focuses on single-dataset settings, achieving outstanding performance by relying on sufficient labels in the graphs, which are not always available in real-world scenarios.

To tackle these challenges, we present HCT, a novel general GAD framework based on hierarchical contrastive learning, which enables effective transfer across cross-graph domains. For cross-graph feature alignment, we introduce the node-feature disparity to align feature anomaly semantics and dimensions across different graphs, enabling transfer without reliance on source graph signals. For anomaly detection, hierarchical contrastive learning is employed to deeply mine and transfer anomaly information. During pre-training, we construct a multi-level contrastive learning network based on graph augmentation, capturing anomaly information at the node, subgraph, and view levels to enhance normal patterns modeling and anomaly patterns understanding. During fine-tuning, we leverage low-rank adaptation (LoRA) [18] due to its success in large language model adaptability to transfer anomaly detection by adding a lightweight and trainable network, while using contrastive learning to shorten structure differences in different graphs. Additionally, we propose a structure-enhanced regularization objective that exploits graph neighborhood heterogeneity to enhance the model's adaptability on graphs with scarce labels. Consequently, we find that HCT demonstrates strong detection performance compared to baselines, with 1.63%–8.05% average performance improvement across public and 10-shot settings. Furthermore, it surpasses training-from-scratch methods over 10% absolute improvement on some datasets. Generally, the contributions are as follows:

– We introduce a novel general GAD framework HCT, which leverages node-feature disparity for feature alignment, enabling migration without relying on source graph signals. In addition, it employs a hierarchical contrastive strategy to capture deep anomaly patterns.
– We propose an efficient transfer strategy that employs LoRA for anomaly pattern transfer, with contrastive learning to reduce cross-graph structural differences, and incorporates structure-enhanced regularization to improve adaptability in label-scarce scenarios.
– Extensive experiments on four large-scale real-world datasets demonstrate the superiority of HCT over state-of-the-art methods, showing significant performance in generality and adaptability.

2 Related Work

Graph Anomaly Detection. In this paper, we focus on anomaly detection on undirected attributed graphs, where anomalies involve either feature differences from neighboring nodes or dissimilar nodes being tightly connected. With the significant improvements of GNNs in graph data mining, GNN-based GAD [19] has garnered widespread attention. Existing mainstream solutions train separate detection models for each dataset. Supervised GNNs utilize message passing and aggregation or graph-high frequency distribution correlation to uncover anomaly patterns, such as BWGNN [20] applies localized band-pass filters to manage higher frequency anomalies, while AMNet [8] captures both low-frequency and high-frequency signals. Unsupervised GNNs leverage contrastive learning [10,11], graph reconstruction [9], or auxiliary objectives [21] to train models without any labeled data. In real-world large-scale graph data scenarios, training separate models for each dataset leads to high training costs and difficulties in quickly adapting to new domains. While some GAD methods [9,16] attempt to apply cross-domain transfer, their reliance on source graph limits their generalizability. Unlike existing methods, our proposed HCT enables fine-tuning on target datasets without needing joint fine-tuning with the source graph, allowing for rapid adaptation in data-scarce scenarios.

Graph Contrastive Learning. (GCL) focuses on uncovering the inherent similarities and differences between objects in graphs, aiming to extract universal graph knowledge. Recently, GCL has emphasized mining graph information from different levels. GraphCL [22] leverages view augmentation strategies to enhance node representations by contrasting augmented subgraphs. GRADATE [23] further explores subgraph representation learning by designing cross-view contrastive losses to capture local features and structure information. Unlike previous works, we consider hierarchical anomaly feature mining, and innovatively introduce view-level contrastive learning during the pre-training phase.

Graph Transfer Learning aims to pre-train a GNN and apply it to various datasets. The pretrain-finetune paradigm [12,24], which involves pre-training a GNN on a source graph and then fine-tuning it on a target graph, has attracted significant attention due to its ability to transfer knowledge without requiring direct relationships between the source and target graphs. For instance, GCC [15] focuses on pre-training to develop a more general GNN. Besides, GraphControl [17] and GraphLoRA [13] emphasize fine-tuning to adapt the pre-trained GNN to different graphs. Most relevant to our work is GraphLoRA, which freezes the pre-trained GNN and utilizes LoRA-based contrastive learning to facilitate knowledge transfer. In contrast to GraphLoRA, our approach further considers graph neighborhood heterogeneity during the fine-tuning stage and incorporates a structure-enhanced objective to improve adaptability for cross-graph anomaly detection.

3 Methodology

3.1 Problem Formulation

Notations. In the following section, we formalize the GAD task. For the input, the notation $G = (V, E)$ denotes the given undirected graph, where $V = \{v_1, v_2, \ldots, v_n\}$ represent the node set with n nodes and $E = \{(v_i, v_j) | v_i, v_j \in V\}$ is the edge set. In addition, the node feature matrix $X \in \mathbb{R}^{n \times d}$ represents the node attributes, where each node in V has a feature vector of d-dimensional attributes. The adjacency matrix $A \in \{0, 1\}^{n \times n}$ encodes the graph structure, where $A_{ij} = 1$ indicates the presence of an edge between nodes v_i and v_j. D denotes the degree matrix of A.

Graph Neural Networks. Major GNNs adopt message-passing networks, where neighboring nodes exchange and aggregate information to share and update node features, capturing both local relationships and global information in the graph. In this paper, we use GCN [25] as the basic module, where the hidden representation at the $\ell + 1$-th layer can be defined as:

$$h_i^{(\ell+1)} = \sigma\left(h_i^{(\ell)} W^{(\ell)}\right). \tag{1}$$

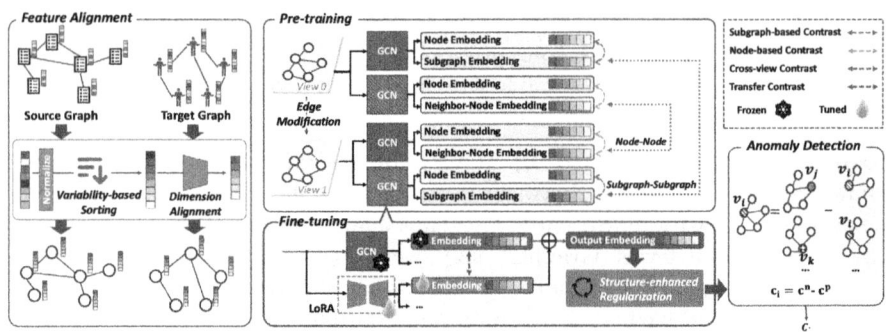

Fig. 1. The overall framework of HCT. Notably, networks under two views use the same architecture and share parameters.

$$H_i^{(\ell+1)} = \sigma \left(D_i^{-\frac{1}{2}} A_i D_i^{-\frac{1}{2}} H_i^{(\ell)} W^{(\ell)} \right). \tag{2}$$

where $h_i^{(\ell)}$ and $H_i^{(\ell)}$ represent the node hidden-layer representation and the subgraph hidden-layer representation, respectively. $\sigma(\cdot)$ is nonlinear transformation, $D_i^{-\frac{1}{2}} A_i D_i^{-\frac{1}{2}}$ indicates the normalization of the adjacency matrix, $W^{(\ell)}$ denotes the network parameters.

Problem Statement. The GAD model aims to learn an anomaly scoring function $f : G \to C$ that differentiates abnormal nodes V_a from normal nodes V_n within a given graph G, where V_a and V_n satisfy $V_a \cup V_n = V$, $V_a \cap V_n = \emptyset$. C is the anomaly score, with higher values indicating a higher likelihood of anomaly. In this paper, we focus on transferable GAD, which leverages anomaly knowledge from a pre-trained model on the source graph G_s and applies it to the target graph G_t with different data distributions. Assuming the source graph is unlabeled and the target graph has limited labeled nodes, HCT aims to transfer the pre-trained model from G_s and fine-tune it on G_t for anomaly detection. The optimization objective using target training nodes can be expressed as follows:

$$f_\phi^* = \arg\min_\phi \mathcal{L}\left(f_\phi\left(X_t, A_t\right), Y_t\right). \tag{3}$$

where $\mathcal{L}$ is the fine-tuning loss function, X_t and A_t represent the node feature matrix and adjacency matrix in G_t, and Y_t denotes training labels available for G_t. The function $f_\phi(\cdot) = p_\phi \circ g_\theta(\cdot)$, where p_ϕ is the tunable module and g_θ is the frozen pre-trained model.

3.2 HCT Overview

The overall framework of HCT is illustrated in Fig. 1. First, we design a feature alignment module to map features between the source and target graphs. In this module, node-feature disparity is introduced to capture anomaly semantics, aligning the feature anomaly semantics and dimensions across different graphs through anomaly-based ranking and weighted mapping, reducing the distribution discrepancy between the source and target graphs. Next, we propose a hierarchical graph contrastive network to train a pre-trained model on the source graph, which innovatively employs cross-view contrastive learning on node and subgraph to uncover more local anomaly information for detection. Subsequently, we introduce a structure-aware transfer learning strategy for transferring anomaly information to the target graph. Inspired by LoRA [18], we apply low-rank adaptation to the pre-trained contrastive learning network with contrastive learning to minimize the structure differences between the source and target graphs. In this process, structure-enhanced regularization leverages label and graph neighborhood heterogeneity to enhance adaptability in scenarios with limited labels on the target graph. Finally, we combine the various anomaly information to calculate the anomaly score for each node in the target graph.

3.3 Feature Alignment

The graph from different domains typically exhibits significant differences in features when performing anomaly detection. For example, in social reviews, features may include user profiles and comment content, while in financial transactions, features might represent customer transaction behaviors. Therefore, the primary task in GAD transfer learning is to align the features into a common feature space. Feature alignment generally includes two main parts: semantic and dimension alignment. Previous work [13] aligns features by designing specialized function to minimize difference in node feature distributions with the data requirement for both the source graph and the target graph. However, it is not always feasible when source graph data is unavailable. To this end, we introduce a discrepancy-based feature alignment module, which achieves feature alignment by abstracting anomaly semantics without requiring joint training with the source graph. It consists of two phases: discrepancy-based feature ranking that aligns anomaly semantics, and feature mapping that aligns dimensionality.

Discrepancy-Based Feature Ranking. The goal of GAD is to identify anomaly nodes within the graph, which exhibit significant feature disparity compared to normal nodes. In GAD, high-frequency graph signals tend to play a more crucial role in detection [7,20,26], showing that features with greater disparity across nodes are more important for distinguishing anomaly patterns. Therefore, node-feature disparity is introduced to measure the importance of each feature for GAD. Given a graph G with a feature matrix X, the node-feature disparity of its features can be defined as:

$$dis_k(\mathcal{N}(X)) = \frac{1}{|E|} \sum_{(v_i, v_j) \in E} (\mathcal{N}(X_{ik}) - \mathcal{N}(X_{jk}))^2. \tag{4}$$

where $\mathcal{N}(\cdot)$ denotes the normalization. A larger dis_k indicates that the k-th feature exhibits greater variation between connected nodes, which suggests a stronger association with high-frequency graph signals.

To align feature anomaly semantics, we reorder the features based on node-feature disparity. Specifically, rather than joint training, we rank the features of all input graphs in descending order of disparity, thereby achieving anomaly semantic alignment.

Feature Mapping. To unify the feature dimensions across multiple graphs, combined with the varying importance of different features in GAD, we employ weighted feature projection to map features from different dimensions into a common feature space. For a given feature matrix X, we first normalize the features and then apply a fully connected layer for weighted mapping. The feature mapping is defined as follows:

$$Z = map(X) = \mathcal{N}(X) \cdot (w_m dis)^T. \tag{5}$$

where w_m represents the parameters of the mapping function.

3.4 Hierarchical Graph Contrastive Network

To effectively extract anomaly patterns, we employ a hierarchical contrastive learning network for unsupervised training on the source graph. Inspired by GRADATE [23], we first apply view augmentation through graph enhancement techniques. In each view, subgraphs are generated using random walks and paired with target nodes. Subsequently, node-level and subgraph-level contrastive learning are utilized to capture both global and local anomaly patterns. Throughout this process, cross-view subgraph-subgraph and novelly introduced node-node contrasts optimize the model's embeddings across views. A joint-balanced optimization objective is then introduced to guide the training process.

Graph Augmentation. Edge modification [27] is employed to perform view augmentation, helping the model uncover deeper semantic information. Specifically, given the source graph $G_s = (V_s, E_s)$ with edge set E_s including m edges, we construct a second view $\hat{G}_s = (V_s, \hat{E}_s)$ by randomly dropping $\frac{pm}{2}$ edges from the adjacency matrix and adding an equal number of edges, where p represents the proportion (with $p = 0.2$ in our experiments). This approach allows the model to learn more anomaly knowledge without depending on the specific structure of the graph, thus improving its generalization.

To improve scalability on large-scale graphs, we use a random walk with restart strategy, as proposed in previous work [15], to sample subgraphs and construct node pairs targeting specific nodes. Subgraphs G_i and G'_i, sampled from the same central node, are considered positive pairs, while subgraphs from different central nodes are treated as negative pairs.

Node-Level Anomaly Knowledge Learning. Node-level contrastive learning focuses on the relationships between nodes and their neighboring nodes within each view. In each view, the node representations from its own subgraphs' neighboring nodes form positive pairs, while those from neighboring nodes of subgraphs with different central nodes form negative pairs. As shown in Eq. (2), the GCN layer maps node information from the subgraph into the embedding space.

To obtain the neighboring node representations, we employ an MLP to project the node features into the same embedding space, resulting in the neighboring node representation $u_i = H_i^{(\ell+1)}[1,:]$. Subsequently, following Eq. (1), the target node representation e_i^0 is computed.

As anomaly nodes tend to have lower feature similarity with their neighboring nodes, we leverage a bilinear function to measure the node-level correlation between the target node and its neighboring nodes:

$$c_i^0 = f_b(u_i, e_i) = \sigma\left(u_i W_b e_i^\top\right). \tag{6}$$

where W_b represents the learnable parameter. Given the graph neighborhood heterogeneity, in positive pairs, the target node is expected to have a high correlation with its neighbors, resulting in c_i^0 approaching 1. In contrast, negative pairs exhibit low correlation, causing c_i^0 to approach 0. Therefore, the node-level contrastive loss is calculated as follows:

$$\mathcal{L}_\mathcal{N} = -\sum_{i=1}^n \left(p_i \log c_i^0 + (1-p_i)\log(1-c_i^0)\right). \tag{7}$$

where p_i is equal to 0 for positive pairs and 1 for negative pairs.

Correspondingly, the node-level correlation in the another view, denoted as $\hat{c}_i^0$, and the node-level contrastive loss $\hat{\mathcal{L}}_\mathcal{N}$ can be computed analogously.

Subgraph-Level Anomaly Knowledge Learning. Importantly, a new GCN layer operates independently at the subgraph level from the GCN at the node level and does not share the weight parameters. The Readout function is then applied to aggregate the node features within the subgraph G_i, computing its representation as follows:

$$s_i = \text{Readout}(Z_i) = \frac{1}{n_i}\sum_{j=1}^{n_i}(Z_i)_j. \tag{8}$$

where Z_i represents the feature representations of all nodes in G_i, n_i is the number of nodes in G_i, and $(Z_i)_j$ is the feature of the j-th node in G_i.

Using an MLP to map the node features into the same embedding space as the subgraph representation, we obtain the target node representation e_i^1, as defined in Eq. (1). Similarly, the subgraph-level correlation c_i^1 between the target node representation e_i^1 and the subgraph representation z_i can be calculated from the bilinear function. The optimization of subgraph-level contrast is as follows:

$$\mathcal{L}_\mathcal{S} = -\sum_{i=1}^n \left(p_i \log(c_i^1) + (1-p_i)\log(1-c_i^1)\right). \tag{9}$$

Likewise, subgraph-level correlation $\hat{c}_i^1$ and loss $\hat{\mathcal{L}}_\mathcal{S}$ can also be computed for another view.

View-Level Anomaly Knowledge Learning. Building on the advantages of graph augmentation techniques, view-level contrastive learning considers node-node and subgraph-subgraph contrastive learning across different views.

For cross-view node-node contrast, the node forms a positive pair with the neighboring node representations from its own subgraph in another view and forms a negative pair with neighboring node representations from subgraphs centered around different nodes in the two views. Based on prior work [28], we design the following loss function:

$$\mathcal{L}_{\mathcal{NN}} = -\sum_{i=1}^{n} \log\left(\frac{\exp(u_i \cdot \hat{u}_i)}{\exp(u_i \cdot u_j) + \exp(u_i \cdot \hat{u}_j)}\right). \tag{10}$$

where u_i and $\hat{u}_i$ are the neighboring node representations of node v_i in the two views, while u_j and $\hat{u}_j$ are those of another node v_j in the two views.

For cross-view subgraph-level contrast, a target node v_i forms positive pairs with its own subgraph in another view, and negative pairs with subgraphs centered around different nodes in both views. The loss function is:

$$\mathcal{L}_{\mathcal{SS}} = -\sum_{i=1}^{n} \log\left(\frac{\exp(z_i \cdot \hat{z}_i)}{\exp(z_i \cdot z_j) + \exp(z_i \cdot \hat{z}_j)}\right). \tag{11}$$

where z_i and $\hat{z}_i$ represent the subgraph representations of node v_i in the two views, while z_j and $\hat{z}_j$ represent those of another node v_j in the two views.

Joint-Balanced Optimization. During the pre-training phase, we propose a joint-balanced optimization objective to integrate information from different contrastive learning. To effectively balance node-level, subgraph-level, and view-level information, we introduce trade-off parameters that facilitate this process:

$$\begin{aligned}\mathcal{L}'_{\mathcal{N}} &= \alpha \mathcal{L}_{\mathcal{N}} + (1-\alpha)\hat{\mathcal{L}}_{\mathcal{N}} \\ \mathcal{L}'_{\mathcal{S}} &= \alpha \mathcal{L}_{\mathcal{S}} + (1-\alpha)\hat{\mathcal{L}}_{\mathcal{S}} \\ \mathcal{L}_{\mathcal{CR}} &= \beta \mathcal{L}_{\mathcal{NN}} + (1-\beta)\mathcal{L}_{\mathcal{SS}}.\end{aligned} \tag{12}$$

where $\alpha \in (0,1)$ is used to balance the two views, and $\beta \in (0,1)$ is used to balance node and subgraph representations.

To leverage the advantages of hierarchical contrast, the overall joint objective function during pre-training is defined as follows:

$$\mathcal{L}_{\text{pretrain}} = \beta \mathcal{L}'_{\mathcal{N}} + (1-\beta)\mathcal{L}'_{\mathcal{S}} + \mathcal{L}_{\mathcal{CR}}. \tag{13}$$

Through the above steps, we obtain a pre-trained GAD model g_θ via unsupervised learning on the source graph G_s.

3.5 Structure-Aware Transfer Learning

During fine-tuning, structure differences between the source and target graphs hinder the transferability of pre-trained GAD models. To bridge this gap, we propose a structure-aware transfer learning strategy which comprises two key components: (1) LoRA-based fine-tuning, which alleviates structural differences between graphs, and (2) structure-enhanced regularization, which exploits graph neighborhood heterogeneity to enhance adaptation in label-scarce scenarios.

LoRA-Based Fine-Tuning. During fine-tuning, we freeze the weights of the pre-trained model g_θ while adding a lightweight, trainable GCN layer with the same architecture to capture structure information from the target graph. This setup allows the pre-trained model to retain structural knowledge from the source graph while the newly added module effectively integrates structural patterns from the target graph. Moreover, LoRA significantly reduces the number of parameters updated during fine-tuning, mitigating potential issues such as overfitting and catastrophic forgetting.

For each GCN layer at the node and subgraph levels with weight matrix W, LoRA introduces an additional GCN layer with parameter matrix ΔW. The hidden representation at $l+1$-th layer is defined as follows:

$$h_i^{(\ell+1)} = \sigma\left(h_i^{(\ell)} W^{(\ell)}\right) + \sigma'\left(h_i^{(\ell)} \Delta W^{(\ell)}\right). \tag{14}$$

where $\Delta W^{(\ell)} = W_B^l W_A^l$, $\sigma\prime$ represents add nonlinear transformation. $W_B^l \in \mathbb{R}^{d_l \times r}$, $W_A^l \in \mathbb{R}^{r \times d_{l+1}}$, and the rank $r \ll \min(d_l, d_{l+1})$.

To enhance the transfer of graph-structured knowledge, we incorporate contrastive learning into each newly added GCN layer. Specifically, the representation h_i of the same node in the original GCN, and its counterpart h'_i in the newly added GCN layer are treated as a positive pair, while representations of different nodes across the two GCN layers are considered negative pairs. The fine-tuning contrastive loss is thus defined as:

$$\mathcal{L} = -\sum_{i=1}^{n} \log\left(\frac{\exp(h_i \cdot h'_i)}{\exp(h_i \cdot h_j) + \exp(h_i \cdot h'_j)}\right). \tag{15}$$

Based on the above equations, we can obtain the contrastive losses $\mathcal{L}_{C\mathcal{L}\mathcal{N}}$, $\hat{\mathcal{L}}_{C\mathcal{L}\mathcal{N}}$, $\mathcal{L}_{C\mathcal{L}S}$ and $\hat{\mathcal{L}}_{C\mathcal{L}S}$ for node-level and subgraph-level fine-tuning in both views. Considering the integrated optimization of multi-level contrastive learning information, the fine-tuning contrastive loss is as follows:

$$\begin{aligned}\mathcal{L}'_{C\mathcal{L}\mathcal{N}} &= \alpha \mathcal{L}_{C\mathcal{L}\mathcal{N}} + (1-\alpha)\hat{\mathcal{L}}_{C\mathcal{L}\mathcal{N}} \\ \mathcal{L}'_{C\mathcal{L}S} &= \alpha \mathcal{L}_{C\mathcal{L}S} + (1-\alpha)\hat{\mathcal{L}}_{C\mathcal{L}S} \\ \mathcal{L}_{C\mathcal{L}} &= \beta \mathcal{L}'_{C\mathcal{L}\mathcal{N}} + (1-\beta)\mathcal{L}'_{C\mathcal{L}S}.\end{aligned} \tag{16}$$

where α and β take the same values as optimization parameters in pre-training.

Structure-Enhanced Regularization. In GAD, anomaly nodes exhibit dissimilarity with their neighboring node features, whereas normal nodes are more similar to their neighbors. To this end, we leverage the principle of structure heterogeneity to enhance transferability in scenarios with limited labels.

Building on the correlation calculation in Eq. (6), we introduce a structure-enhanced regularization objective. Normal nodes demonstrate high correlation with their neighbors/subgraphs, while anomaly nodes show low correlation. The regularization objectives at the node-level and subgraph-level are as follows:

$$\begin{aligned}\mathcal{L}_{RN} &= -\sum_i y_i \log(1 - c_i^0) + (1 - y_i) \log(c_i^0) \\ \mathcal{L}_{RS} &= -\sum_i y_i \log(1 - c_i^1) + (1 - y_i) \log(c_i^1).\end{aligned} \quad (17)$$

Here, y represents the label information in the target graph. The regularization objectives for the other view can be defined as $\hat{\mathcal{L}}_{RN}$ and $\hat{\mathcal{L}}_{RS}$. Similar to Eq. (16), we introduce the trade-off parameter to derive the final structure-enhanced optimization objective $\mathcal{L}_R$.

Fine-Tuning Objective Optimization. During the fine-tuning phase, we employ multi-task learning to jointly optimize multiple objective functions. The overall objective function is defined as follows:

$$\mathcal{L}_{\text{finetune}} = \lambda_1 \mathcal{L}_\mathcal{R} + \lambda_2 \mathcal{L}_{\mathcal{CL}} + \lambda_3 \mathcal{L}_{\mathcal{CR}}. \quad (18)$$

where λ_i represents the importance of each objective function, which is set to 1 in our experiments.

3.6 Anomaly Detection

In anomaly detection, normal nodes exhibit high similarity with their own subgraph and neighbor node representations, while showing low similarity with the subgraph and neighboring node representations of other nodes. On the other hand, anomaly nodes are dissimilar to both their own subgraph and the subgraphs and neighboring nodes of other nodes. Thus, we define the anomaly score using the correlation as follows:

$$c_i = c^n - c^p. \quad (19)$$

where c^n represents the correlation in negative pair and c^p represents the correlation in positive pair. Leveraging the trade-off parameter in Eq. (12), we integrate node-level, subgraph-level, and view-level anomaly information, with the anomaly score further represented as:

$$\begin{aligned}c_i^{node} &= \alpha c_i^0 + (1 - \alpha)\hat{c}_i^0 \\ c_i^{sub} &= \alpha c_i^1 + (1 - \alpha)\hat{c}_i^1 \\ C_i &= \beta c_i^{node} + (1 - \beta) c_i^{sub}.\end{aligned} \quad (20)$$

As a single-round detection may not always capture the relevant semantics, we perform multi-round anomaly detection and compute the average across these rounds as the final detection result.

Table 1. Statistics of datasets including the number of nodes and edges, the node feature dimension, the ratio of anomaly nodes in graph.

	Nodes	Edges	Features	Anomaly
Questions	48,921	153,540	301	3.00%
T-Finance	39,357	21,222,543	10	4.60%
Weibo	8,405	407,963	400	10.30%
Reddit	10,984	168,016	64	3.30%
Tolokers	11,758	519,000	10	21.80%

4 Experimental Evaluation

4.1 Experiments Settings

Datasets. For pre-training, we use the Questions [29] dataset which focuses on social media as source graph. For comprehensive evaluations, we consider four large-scale real-world datasets as target graphs that span a variety of domains, including finance (T-Finance [20]), crowd-sourcing (Toloker [29]), and social media (Weibo, Reddit) [30]. The statistics of datasets are provided in Table 1.

Baselines. We compare HCT with eight methods. For training-from-scratch methods, we choose two conventional GNNs, GIN [31] and GraphSAGE [32], along with AMNET [8] and BWGNN [20], which are specifically designed for the GAD task. For cross-graph transfer, we include three SOTA methods GCC [15]+finetuning, GraphControl [17], GraphLoRA [13], and the GAD-specific baselines ARC [5]. Notably, we add a classifier to GCC during finetuning, as it is originally an unsupervised contrastive learning model.

Metrics and Evaluation. We introduce two main metrics that match those of previous empirical studies [4,5], including the Area Under the Receiver Operating Characteristic Curve (AUROC) and the Area Under the Prevision Recall Curve (AUPRC). For all metrics, anomalies are considered as the positive class, and higher scores indicate better model performance. Experiments are conducted in two distinct settings: public and 10-shot. The public setting assumes sufficient labels, with 10% of the target graph dataset randomly sampled for training. The 10-shot setting represents a low-label scenario, where only 10 labeled instances per class are available in the target graph. In both cases, 80% of the target graph dataset is used for testing. For all methods, we report the average AUROC/AUPRC with standard deviations over 5 trials.

Settings. In HCT, both GCN consist of a single layer with ReLU activation. The subgraph size is fixed at 4, and both node and subgraph features are projected into a 64-dimensional hidden space. The model is trained for up to 400 epochs, followed by 100 rounds anomaly score calculation. Our implementation builds on prior work [23], with all experiments conducted on a single A800 GPU.

Table 2. Comparison of GAD performance in AUROC (%, mean ± std), where highlighted results indicate the first and second rankings. OM indicates 'Out of Memory' in our experimental settings.

Model	T-Finance Public	T-Finance 10-shot	Reddit Public	Reddit 10-shot	Weibo Public	Weibo 10-shot	tolokers Public	tolokers 10-shot
GIN	76.70±9.26	69.91±4.14	53.87±0.88	52.71±2.76	82.83±2.78	63.99±2.90	52.85±0.43	55.51±1.41
GraphSAGE	57.61±6.67	59.93±5.05	46.69±1.98	44.58±2.14	21.01±5.61	16.01±3.87	58.88±0.93	54.49±2.87
AMNet	83.38±1.82	80.51±3.96	50.68±0.21	57.56±0.51	80.52±1.51	71.50±2.79	59.31±0.35	53.01±1.96
BWGNN	83.57±2.84	79.92±4.31	50.90±2.83	55.58±3.90	67.37±2.70	59.68±1.31	60.25±0.18	56.03±2.65
GCC+finetuning	50.34±0.26	47.13±9.34	50.02±0.07	51.04±2.61	84.05±3.86	77.91±5.25	50.97±2.18	49.96±0.25
GraphControl	85.71±1.59	71.27±0.58	50.06±0.13	54.45±1.17	90.05±6.56	75.63±2.69	60.18±2.47	53.92±2.37
GraphLoRA	OM	OM	50.00±2.18	54.18±0.61	77.30±2.95	69.51±0.68	50.36±0.43	49.58±0.01
ARC	75.25±0.69	68.84±4.75	58.90±0.29	57.58±1.99	88.45±0.30	77.43±0.21	48.31±0.75	49.64±2.96
HCT	88.99±0.23	81.17±3.01	55.39±0.19	54.99±1.12	91.63±0.30	80.65±3.07	61.61±0.73	59.81±0.69

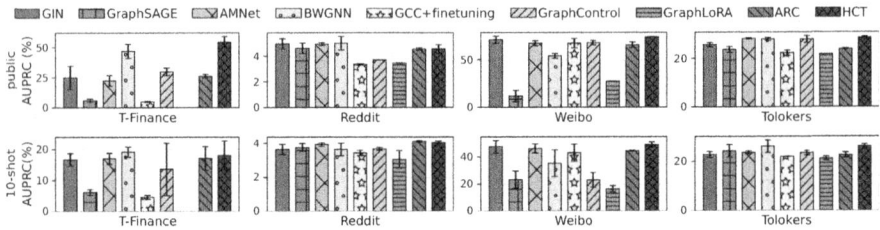

Fig. 2. GAD performance in terms of AUPRC.

4.2 Main Results

We evaluate the GAD performance by comparing HCT with eight baselines. Table 2 shows the comparison results of AUROC in both settings, while Fig. 2 illustrates the AUPRC comparison. The observations are as follows:

Overall Performance. HCT demonstrates strong anomaly detection capability in the transferable GAD scenario across various datasets. Specifically, HCT achieves state-of-the-art results on three out of four datasets and approaches the optimal performance on the remaining one. Compared to the best-performing baseline, GraphControl, HCT improves AUROC by 2.91% and AUPRC by 8.05% in the public setting. In the 10-shot setting, it surpasses the strongest baseline, AMNet, by 3.51% in AUROC and 1.63% in AUPRC.

Effectiveness of Cross-graph Transferability. HCT presents robust stability in cross-domain transfer, even when dealing with disparate graph domains. Compared to training-from-scratch methods, HCT leverages anomaly knowledge from the source graph to enhance performance on the target graph, achieving over a 10% AUROC improvement on the Reddit dataset. Moreover, we observe that transfer learning baselines show minimal improvements or even adverse effects when fine-tuned on specific datasets. In contrast, HCT not only enhances performance on datasets from similar domains but also improves AUROC by 1.85% in the public setting and 7.89% in the 10-shot setting on the cross-domain T-finance and Tolokers datasets, surpassing other transfer learning methods.

Table 3. Ablation study with AUROC(%, mean ± std) in public and 10-shot settings.

Model	T-Finance Public	10-shot	Reddit Public	10-shot	Weibo Public	10-shot	tolokers Public	10-shot
HCT	**88.99±0.23**	**81.17±3.01**	**55.39±0.49**	**54.99±1.12**	**91.63±0.03**	**80.65±3.07**	**61.61±0.73**	**59.81±0.69**
w/o dfs	85.16±0.12	65.19±2.01	52.75±0.99	49.59±4.30	43.29±8.90	78.32±0.72	60.08±1.32	49.07±3.76
w/o view	83.20±0.39	59.26±8.66	51.21±0.44	50.74±1.75	62.72±4.78	65.15±3.79	59.78±0.44	59.23±0.87
w/o aug	80.01±0.10	28.27±6.48	53.39±0.68	50.58±1.60	14.16±0.88	66.01±8.57	61.02±0.32	59.20±0.94
w/ node	54.51±0.36	25.60±10.39	53.88±0.79	49.79±3.30	16.12±0.42	62.80±6.96	61.46±0.28	58.72±1.36
w/ subgraph	83.19±0.17	37.35±9.35	52.17±0.80	51.12±3.71	22.78±8.90	66.53±4.56	59.71±0.11	59.08±0.83
w/ finetuning	88.23±2.75	81.05±2.04	55.04±0.36	50.09±0.82	89.40±0.65	72.62±9.15	60.49±0.10	59.69±2.02
w/o ser	60.99±5.21	53.36±2.51	43.75±1.48	46.89±5.33	66.24±1.29	65.02±5.16	56.12±1.42	49.89±3.97

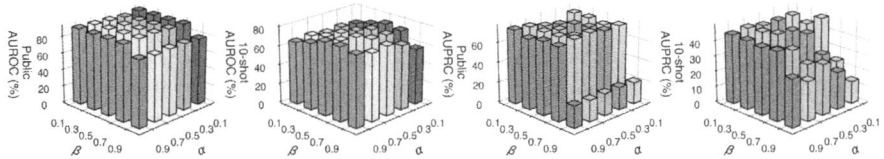

Fig. 3. Sensitivity analysis for the trade-off parameters α and β on Weibo.

Effectiveness of Heterogeneity Consideration. It is curial to consider heterogeneity in GAD. Compared to GraphLoRA, which assumes homogeneity, HCT demonstrates an average improvement of 10.32% in AUROC and 18.21% in AUPRC in the public setting, and 7.36% in AUROC and 12.69% in AUPRC in the few-shot setting, all under the same LoRA-based fine-tuning conditions. Moreover, general transfer learning methods based on homogeneity assumption are less effective than specialized approaches that account for graph neighborhood heterogeneity in GAD, which is evidenced by the strong AUROC and AUPRC performance of AMNet, BWGNN, and ARC.

4.3 Further Validation and Analysis

Ablation Studies. We evaluate the importance of our purposed modules in HCT, including feature alignment, hierarchical contrastive learning, and structure-enhanced objectives. To this end, several variants are designed: For feature alignment, **w/o dfs** replaces feature alignment with a simple dimensional mapping module, without ranking and weighting mechanism based on node-feature disparity. For hierarchical contrastive learning, **w/node** and **w/subgraph** denote using only node-level or subgraph-level contrast, respectively. **w/o aug** represents the performance without graph augmentation, and **w/o view** indicates the exclusion of view-level contrast. To evaluate LoRA-based contrast effectiveness, **w/finetuning** refers to full fine-tuning on the training dataset for comparison. For objective optimization, **w/o ser** evaluates the impact of removing structure-aware regularization. The results, as shown in Table 3, show that the fully equipped HCT consistently achieves the best performance, thus demonstrating the effectiveness of each component.

Convergence Analysis. We discuss the important trade-off parameters, α and β, involved in our methods. As shown in Fig. 3, these parameters effectively enhance GAD performance on the Weibo dataset, demonstrating the effectiveness of view balancing and node-subgraph balancing. Notably, we observe a significant drop in AUROC and AUPRC when $\beta = 0.9$, indicating that subgraph-level information plays a crucial role in capturing graph anomalies.

5 Conclusion

In this paper, we investigate the challenge of cross-graph anomaly detection in GNNs. To address the differences in feature and structure distributions across graphs, we introduce HCT, a novel general GAD framework that enables effective cross-graph transfer on undirected attributed graphs. To achieve this, HCT integrates a disparity-based mapping mechanism for cross-graph feature alignment alongside hierarchical contrastive learning to facilitate anomaly pattern capture and transfer. Additionally, a structure-aware regularization objective is proposed to enhance adaptability in label-scarce scenarios. Extensive experiments on four large-scale real-world datasets confirm the effectiveness and generalizability of HCT, significantly outperforming baselines while maintaining stable transferability across disparate graph domains. In the future, we will continue to explore the graph heterogeneity and efficient detection on large-scale graphs for the task.

Acknowledgments. This study was funded by Joint Innovation Initiative of the Yangtze River Delta Science and Technology Innovation Community (Jiangsu, Zhejiang, Shanghai)(grant number YDZX20223100004022-3).

Disclosure of Interests. The authors have no competing interests to declare that are relevant to the content of this article.

References

1. Duan, M., Zheng, T., Gao, Y., Wang, G., Feng, Z., Wang, X.: DGA-GNN: dynamic grouping aggregation GNN for fraud detection. In: Proceedings of the AAAI Conference on Artificial Intelligence, vol. 38, pp. 11820–11828 (2024)
2. McAuley, J.J., Leskovec, J.: From amateurs to connoisseurs: modeling the evolution of user expertise through online reviews. In: Proceedings of the 22nd International Conference on World Wide Web, pp. 897–908 (2013)
3. Bian, T., et al.: Rumor detection on social media with bi-directional graph convolutional networks. In: Proceedings of the AAAI Conference on Artificial Intelligence, vol. 34, pp. 549–556 (2020)
4. Tang, J., Hua, F., Gao, Z., Zhao, P., Li, J.: Gadbench: revisiting and benchmarking supervised graph anomaly detection. Adv. Neural. Inf. Process. Syst. **36**, 29628–29653 (2023)
5. Liu, Y., Li, S., Zheng, Y., Chen, Q., Zhang, C., Pan, S.: ARC: a generalist graph anomaly detector with in-context learning. In: Advances in Neural Information Processing Systems (2024)

6. Zhu, J., Yan, Y., Zhao, L., Heimann, M., Akoglu, L., Koutra, D.: Beyond homophily in graph neural networks: current limitations and effective designs. Adv. Neural. Inf. Process. Syst. **33**, 7793–7804 (2020)
7. Gao, Y., Wang, X., He, X., Liu, Z., Feng, H., Zhang, Y.: Addressing heterophily in graph anomaly detection: a perspective of graph spectrum. In: Proceedings of the ACM Web Conference 2023, pp. 1528–1538 (2023)
8. Chai, Z., et al.: Can abnormality be detected by graph neural networks? In: IJCAI, pp. 1945–1951 (2022)
9. Ding, K., Li, J., Bhanushali, R., Liu, H.: Deep anomaly detection on attributed networks. In: Proceedings of the 2019 SIAM International Conference on Data Mining, pp. 594–602. SIAM (2019)
10. Zheng, Y., Jin, M., Liu, Y., Chi, L., Phan, K.T., Chen, Y.P.P.: Generative and contrastive self-supervised learning for graph anomaly detection. IEEE Trans. Knowl. Data Eng. **35**(12), 12220–12233 (2021)
11. Liu, Y., Li, Z., Pan, S., Gong, C., Zhou, C., Karypis, G.: Anomaly detection on attributed networks via contrastive self-supervised learning. IEEE Trans. Neural Netw. Learn. Syst. **33**(6), 2378–2392 (2021)
12. Zhao, H., Chen, A., Sun, X., Cheng, H., Li, J.: All in one and one for all: a simple yet effective method towards cross-domain graph pretraining. In: Proceedings of the 30th ACM SIGKDD Conference on Knowledge Discovery and Data Mining, pp. 4443–4454 (2024)
13. Yang, Z.R., Han, J., Wang, C.D., Liu, H.: GraphLoRA: structure-aware contrastive low-rank adaptation for cross-graph transfer learning. arXiv preprint arXiv:2409.16670 (2024)
14. Gui, A., Ye, J., Xiao, H.: G-Adapter: towards structure-aware parameter-efficient transfer learning for graph transformer networks. In: Proceedings of the AAAI Conference on Artificial Intelligence, vol. 38, pp. 12226–12234 (2024)
15. Qiu, J., et al.: GCC: graph contrastive coding for graph neural network pretraining. In: Proceedings of the 26th ACM SIGKDD International Conference on Knowledge Discovery & Data Mining, pp. 1150–1160 (2020)
16. Qiao, H., Pang, G.: Truncated affinity maximization: one-class homophily modeling for graph anomaly detection. Adv. Neural. Inf. Process. Syst. **36**, 49490–49512 (2023)
17. Zhu, Y., Wang, Y., Shi, H., Zhang, Z., Jiao, D., Tang, S.: GraphControl: adding conditional control to universal graph pre-trained models for graph domain transfer learning. In: Proceedings of the ACM Web Conference 2024, pp. 539–550 (2024)
18. Hu, E.J., et al.: LoRA: low-rank adaptation of large language models. ICLR **1**(2), 3 (2022)
19. Ma, X., et al.: A comprehensive survey on graph anomaly detection with deep learning. IEEE Trans. Knowl. Data Eng. **35**(12), 12012–12038 (2021)
20. Tang, J., Li, J., Gao, Z., Li, J.: Rethinking graph neural networks for anomaly detection. In: International Conference on Machine Learning, pp. 21076–21089. PMLR (2022)
21. Huang, T., Pei, Y., Menkovski, V., Pechenizkiy, M.: Hop-count based self-supervised anomaly detection on attributed networks. In: Joint European Conference on Machine Learning and Knowledge Discovery in Databases, pp. 225–241. Springer (2022)
22. Hafidi, H., Ghogho, M., Ciblat, P., Swami, A.: Negative sampling strategies for contrastive self-supervised learning of graph representations. Signal Process. **190**, 108310 (2022)

23. Duan, J., et al.: Graph anomaly detection via multi-scale contrastive learning networks with augmented view. In: Proceedings of the AAAI Conference on Artificial Intelligence, vol. 37, pp. 7459–7467 (2023)
24. Li, S., Han, X., Bai, J.: AdapterGNN: parameter-efficient fine-tuning improves generalization in GNNs. In: Proceedings of the AAAI Conference on Artificial Intelligence, vol. 38, pp. 13600–13608 (2024)
25. Wu, F., Souza, A., Zhang, T., Fifty, C., Yu, T., Weinberger, K.: Simplifying graph convolutional networks. In: International Conference on Machine Learning, pp. 6861–6871. PMLR (2019)
26. Gao, Y., Wang, X., He, X., Liu, Z., Feng, H., Zhang, Y.: Alleviating structural distribution shift in graph anomaly detection. In: Proceedings of the Sixteenth ACM International Conference on Web Search and Data Mining, pp. 357–365 (2023)
27. Jin, M., Liu, Y., Zheng, Y., Chi, L., Li, Y.F., Pan, S.: ANEMONE: graph anomaly detection with multi-scale contrastive learning. In: Proceedings of the 30th ACM International Conference on Information & Knowledge Management, pp. 3122–3126
28. Oord, A.v.d., Li, Y., Vinyals, O.: Representation learning with contrastive predictive coding. arXiv preprint arXiv:1807.03748 (2018)
29. Platonov, O., Kuznedelev, D., Diskin, M., Babenko, A., Prokhorenkova, L.: A critical look at the evaluation of GNNs under heterophily: are we really making progress? arXiv preprint arXiv:2302.11640 (2023)
30. Kumar, S., Zhang, X., Leskovec, J.: Predicting dynamic embedding trajectory in temporal interaction networks. In: Proceedings of the 25th ACM SIGKDD International Conference on Knowledge Discovery & Data Mining, pp. 1269–1278 (2019)
31. Xu, K., Hu, W., Leskovec, J., Jegelka, S.: How powerful are graph neural networks? arXiv preprint arXiv:1810.00826 (2018)
32. Hamilton, W., Ying, Z., Leskovec, J.: Inductive representation learning on large graphs. Adv. Neural Inf. Process. Syst. **30** (2017)

Bias and Fairness

Fair and Privacy-Preserving Synthetic Data Generation via Clustering-Based Variational Autoencoder and Adversarially Debiased Wasserstein Generative Adversarial Networks with Gradient Penalty

Malek Adouani[✉] and Zaineb Chelly Dagdia

Université Paris-Saclay, UVSQ, DAVID, Versailles, France
{malek.adouani,zaineb.chelly-dagdia}@uvsq.fr

Abstract. The increasing reliance on machine learning in sensitive domains, such as healthcare, has amplified concerns about bias and privacy in data-driven decision-making. While fairness-aware generative models aim to mitigate bias, they often depend on labeled data, limiting their applicability in unsupervised settings. Conversely, differentially private generative models ensure privacy but may still encode hidden biases. Existing methods fail to jointly optimize fairness and privacy without explicit supervision. To address this gap, we propose a hybrid generative framework that integrates clustering-based Variational Autoencoder (VAE) with Wasserstein Generative Adversarial Networks with Gradient Penalty (WGAN-GP) to generate fair and privacy-preserving synthetic data. The VAE structures latent representations under zero-Concentrated Differential Privacy (zCDP) while incorporating K-Means clustering directly in the latent space. The clustering serves as a factor to influence the generative process into producing samples that resemble real data in unsupervised settings. These structured representations along with cluster labels then guide WGAN-GP's generator toward sample generation and enhance adversarial debiasing through the Fairness Critic, which penalizes correlations between synthetic data and sensitive attributes to ensure fairness. By integrating clustering-based VAEs with WGAN-GP, our framework enforces fairness while maintaining strong privacy guarantees. Experimental results demonstrate that it outperforms existing generative models by effectively reducing bias, preserving privacy, and ensuring high data utility across multiple fairness and privacy metrics.

Keywords: Generative Adversarial Networks · Unsupervised learning · Bias mitigation · Privacy preservation

1 Introduction

Machine learning models are increasingly deployed in critical applications such as healthcare and finance, where biased and privacy-compromising decisions can have serious societal consequences. Models trained on biased datasets risk reinforcing societal disparities, leading to discriminatory outcomes that disproportionately affect marginalized groups [10]. While fairness-aware machine learning methods attempt to mitigate bias, many rely on labeled data, which are often scarce, costly to obtain, and may not fully capture the diversity of real-world populations [15]. When labels are incomplete or unavailable, fairness assessment becomes more challenging, as bias can manifest in hidden ways within latent representations and sampling distributions [12]. At the same time, privacy concerns in sensitive domains necessitate mechanisms that protect individual data while enabling meaningful analysis. Differential Privacy [9] has emerged as a strong privacy-preserving solution, ensuring that synthetic datasets do not reveal information about specific individuals. However, privacy-preserving generative models often fail to address hidden biases in data, as differential privacy constraints can obscure fairness-related information rather than eliminate it [11]. This tradeoff between fairness and privacy presents a fundamental challenge in generative modeling, particularly when working with unlabeled data. Generative models, especially Generative Adversarial Networks (GANs), offer a promising approach to producing realistic synthetic data that preserves statistical properties of the original dataset. Fairness-aware GANs introduce debiasing constraints [10], but their reliance on labeled data limits their utility in unsupervised scenarios. Conversely, differentially private GANs prioritize privacy but often fail to mitigate bias, potentially encoding and perpetuating hidden disparities in generated samples [11]. This raises a crucial open problem: How can we jointly enforce fairness and privacy in generative modeling without requiring labeled data?

To address this challenge, we propose a hybrid generative framework that integrates fairness-aware latent space structuring with privacy-preserving mechanisms, enabling the generation of fair and privacy-preserving synthetic data in an unsupervised setting. Our approach combines:

– Clustering-based Variational Autoencoder (VAE) with zero-Concentrated Differential Privacy (zCDP): The clustering based VAE plays a pivotal role in structuring the latent space while preserving privacy. By incorporating K-Means clustering directly into the latent representation, the model enforces the grouping of similar data points, ensuring that downstream generative processes capture the structured distributions of real data in unsupervised settings. The cluster labels serve as guiding signals for the subsequent adversarial training phase, enabling controlled sample generation that aligns with the underlying data structure. The variational inference framework further enhances the model's ability to learn meaningful data representations, improving the quality of generated representations [21]. To ensure strong privacy guarantees, we enforce zCDP, which bounds the moments of privacy loss random variable rather than imposing a fixed limit, making it a more refined and mathematically rigorous privacy mechanism. This approach avoids the infinite loss scenarios associated with traditional (ϵ, δ)-DP (Differential Privacy) while offering tighter privacy guarantees [9]. By structuring the latent space through clustering-based enforcement and mathematically rigorous pri-

vacy constraints, our VAE component provides a strong foundation for generating high-quality, fair, and privacy-compliant synthetic data.
- Adversarially Debiased Wasserstein GAN with Gradient Penaty (WGAN-GP): While VAE ensures fairness in latent representations and enforces privacy, it does not directly control fairness at the synthetic data level. To achieve this, we deploy WGAN-GP which stabilizes training and mitigates mode collapse challenges that often arises in GANs trained on biased data [10]. Crucially, the cluster-aware latent representations obtained from the VAE serve as conditional inputs to the GAN, ensuring that the generator produces samples that align with the structured distributions discovered in an unsupervised manner. Additionally, we introduce an adversarial debiasing mechanism via the fairness critic, which penalizes unwanted correlations between generated data and sensitive attributes. This technique has been shown to be effective in reducing bias in generative models by directly enforcing fairness constraints through adversarial optimization [7]. The training process ensures a tradeoff between data realism and fairness, where the clustering-based VAE conditions the generator while the fairness critic refines the final output to achieve unbiased data generation.

By explicitly addressing bias in the generative process and incorporating zCDP, our framework named "Clust-VAE-WGAN-GP" bridges the gap between fairness-aware and privacy-preserving generative modeling in unsupervised settings. This advancement is valuable for applications where explicit labels are unavailable, enabling more ethical and reliable synthetic data generation.

2 Related Work

Ensuring fairness in synthetic data generation remains a critical challenge in machine learning where models trained on biased data can exacerbate societal inequalities. Bias arises from sources such as covariate shift, selection bias, and class imbalance, leading to discriminatory outcomes that disproportionately affect certain demographic groups [1]. A major challenge lies in labeled data, as machine learning models often assume datasets are representative of the population—an assumption that rarely holds in real-world applications [15]. Generative models, such as VAEs and GANs, offer promising solutions for bias mitigation by learning complex data distributions. However, fairness-aware generative modeling remains challenging, particularly in unsupervised settings where bias can propagate through latent representations and sampling distributions [3]. FairGAN [7] and its improved version FairGAN+ [8] introduced fairness constraints to enforce statistical parity across sensitive attributes, ensuring that generated samples do not disproportionately favor specific demographic groups. TabFairGAN [2] extends these techniques to tabular data, leveraging Wasserstein GAN (WGAN) to create demographically balanced datasets by adjusting sample distributions. Similarly, conditional GANs (cGANs) [16] aim to reduce bias by conditioning on fairness-related constraints, thereby promoting balanced representations in generated samples. However, these methods rely on explicit class labels, making them unsuitable for unsupervised generative modeling, where such labels are unavailable. Furthermore, fairness evaluation in generative models is inherently challenging, as even highly accurate sensitive attribute classifiers introduce measurement errors that can distort fairness assessments [3]. Given the limitations of labeled data, semi-supervised learning has emerged as a promising approach to enhance fairness by leveraging unlabeled data. [20], for instance, demonstrated its effectiveness in mitigating class imbalance in fault detection diagnosis, while in medical AI, it has been shown to improve fairness by capturing broader data distributions and reducing bias in predictive models [6]. By compensating for biased labeled datasets, semi-supervised methods lead to more generalizable and fairer models [15]. Another emerging approach is Positive-Unlabeled Learning, where models learn from datasets containing only positive samples and unlabeled data [14]. Observer-GAN [13] introduced an observer network to generate pseudo-negative samples, allowing the model to differentiate between groups without explicit labels, thereby improving fairness and generalization in synthetic data generation. In parallel to fairness-aware methods, researchers have focused on privacy-preserving generative models to ensure that synthetic data does not expose sensitive individual information. Differentially Private GANs (DPGANs) [4] and PATEGAN [19] integrate differential privacy (DP) mechanisms to prevent data leakage by injecting noise into the model's gradients or outputs. Meanwhile, RDPCGAN [5] leverages Rényi Differential Privacy (RDP) to achieve even stronger privacy guarantees while preserving data utility. However, a key limitation of most differentially private GANs is their exclusive focus on privacy, often neglecting fairness constraints. As a result, bias can persist in privacy-preserving synthetic datasets, potentially exacerbating disparities if left unaddressed. Despite progress in fairness-aware generative modeling, unsupervised approaches remain underexplored. Existing methods either require labeled data to enforce fairness or focus solely on privacy, overlooking bias mitigation. This gap highlights the need for a hybrid generative model that ensures fairness without explicit class labels while preserving privacy, enabling ethical and reliable synthetic data generation in sensitive domains.

3 Proposed Method

This section introduces our Clust-VAE-WGAN-GP hybrid generative framework, which integrates a Cluster-Based VAE with zCDP and a WGAN-GP enhanced by a Fairness Critic.

3.1 Overall Architecture

As illustrated in Fig. 1, the model operates in two interconnected stages. In the first stage, the Cluster-Based VAE encodes input data into a continuous latent space, where K-Means clustering is applied to structure the latent representations. This clustering mechanism generates cluster embeddings that influence the generative process, guiding it to produce synthetic samples that closely resemble real ones in an unsupervised setting. This is achieved by conditioning the generator in the second stage on the clustering information, ensuring that the generated data aligns with the learned latent structure. To enforce privacy, zCDP regulates information leakage through Gaussian noise injection. WGAN-GP utilizes the resulting clustered latent encodings (i.e., continuous private samples), along with their assigned cluster labels outputted from the Cluster-Based VAE with zCDP. The generator is explicitly conditioned on these cluster labels, ensuring that generated samples preserve the latent structure learned in the unsupervised setting. This conditioning mechanism helps maintain distributional consistency across clusters, enhancing data realism. The Fairness Critic further enforces fairness by evaluating correlations between generated samples and predefined sensitive attributes, guiding the generator to reduce statistical dependence on these attributes via adversarial debiasing. The discriminator randomly receives samples from the generator and the continuous private samples to determine and tries to distinguish real from fake samples. Its output is regulated through Wasserstein loss and Gradient penalty for smoother update to the generator. By integrating structured latent encodings from the VAE with adversarial fairness constraints in WGAN-GP, our model generates high-fidelity, privacy-preserving, and bias-free synthetic data, making it suitable for fairness-aware applications in privacy-sensitive domains. Algorithm 1 presents the Clust-VAE-WGAN-GP functioning.

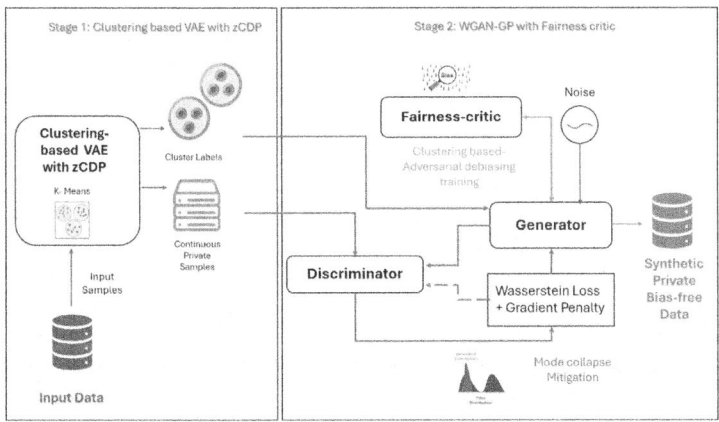

Fig. 1. Overall architecture of Clust-VAE-WGAN-GP.

3.2 Detailed Architecture

Let $\mathcal{X}$ be the input data space, where each sample $\mathbf{x} \in \mathcal{X}$ is drawn from a biased dataset. The objective is to learn a synthetic data generator that satisfies the following conditions: (i) The generated data preserves privacy by adhering to differential privacy constraints, preventing individual re-identification. (ii)

The generative process mitigates bias by minimizing correlations between generated data and predefined sensitive attributes, ensuring fair and representative sample distributions using fairness critic. (iii) The model learns cluster-aware latent representations and promotes data realism, making it suitable for unsupervised learning tasks. To ensure these conditions, the components of Clust-VAE-WGAN-GP are structured as follows.

Clustering-Based VAE with zCDP. Figure 2 illustrates the VAE component, which integrates probabilistic encoding, clustering, and zCDP to generate structured, private latent encodings. Given an input sample x, the encoder maps it to a latent representation z by approximating the posterior distribution [21]:

$$q_\phi(z|x) = \mathcal{N}(\mu_\phi(x), \sigma_\phi^2(x)) \tag{1}$$

where $\mu_\phi(x)$ and $\sigma_\phi(x)$ are the mean and standard deviation parameters, respectively, learned by the encoder network. The reparameterization trick ensures continuous and differentiable latent representations. The training objective minimizes the KL-divergence (KL-loss) between $q_\phi(z|x)$ and the prior $p(z)$, structuring the latent space to align with the original data distribution. $p(z)$ is used to generate deterministic points $\hat{x}$ using KL-loss regularization. The decoder reconstructs the input $\hat{x}$ into $\hat{x}_c$, while minimizing the reconstruction loss, preserving essential data properties. To resemble real data in the unsupervised setting, K cluster centroids $c_k{}_{k=1}^K$ are initialized in the latent space $\hat{x}$, and proximity constraints are enforced via K-Means clustering. These will be next given as an input to the WGAN-GP. For privacy preservation, zCDP is integrated into the VAE by adding Gaussian noise to gradients during backpropagation, mitigating the risk of sensitive information leakage. The privacy loss ρ is given by the following equation, where q is the sampling probability, σ is the noise multiplier, and T is the total number of training iterations [9]:

$$\rho = \frac{q^2 \sigma^{-2} T}{2} \tag{2}$$

The structured latent encodings $\hat{x}_c$ and their corresponding cluster labels c_k form the basis for training the second stage of the model, ensuring that the WGAN-GP component adheres to fairness and privacy constraints.

WGAN-GP with Adversarial Fairness Critic. Figure 3 presents the second stage of the framework, where a WGAN-GP learns to generate structured synthetic data while enforcing fairness constraints.

The latent encodings $\bar{x}_c$ and cluster labels generated by the VAE serve as input to the WGAN-GP component, where the labels constitute a condition for the generator during GAN training. The generator G_θ receives as input a combination of structured latent noise $\bar{z} \sim p(z)$ and cluster label embeddings c_k, producing synthetic samples $\bar{x}_f$ that tend to resemble real data and their assignment to the same cluster. The discriminator D_ψ is trained to differentiate

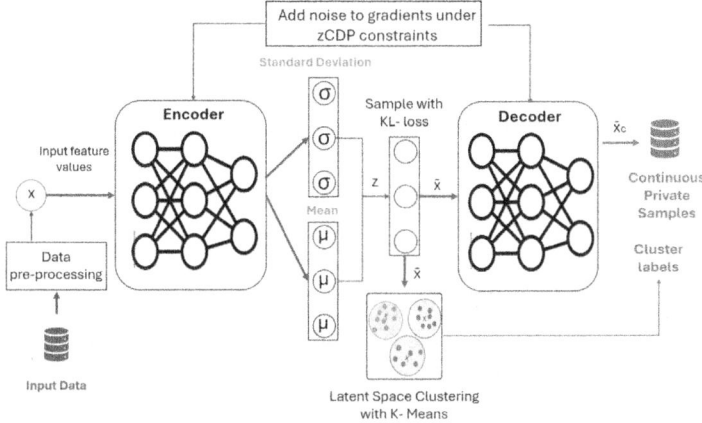

Fig. 2. Overview of Clustering-Based VAE with zCDP mechanism.

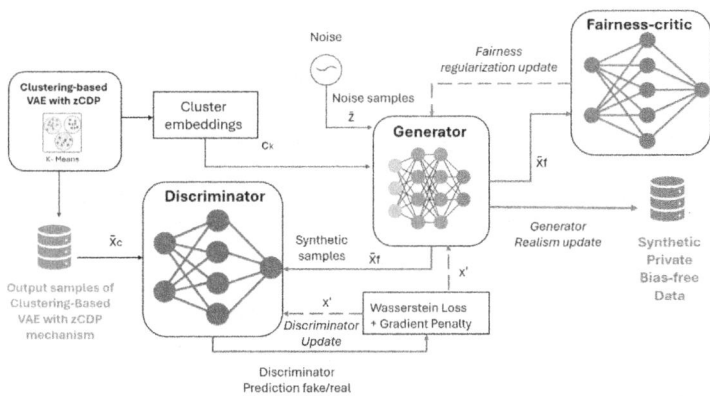

Fig. 3. Overview of WGAN-GP with a Fairness Critic.

between real samples $\bar{x}_c$ and synthetic samples $\bar{x}_f$ while optimizing the revised WGAN-GP loss:

$$\mathcal{L}_{\text{WGAN-GP}} = \mathbb{E}[D_\psi(\bar{x}_f)] - \mathbb{E}[D_\psi(\bar{x}_c)] + \lambda \mathbb{E}[(\|\nabla_{x'} D_\psi(x')\| - 1)^2] \quad (3)$$

where x' represents interpolated samples between real and generated data, stabilizing training. The fairness critic C_φ enforces fairness by penalizing dependence to sensitive attributes s from generated samples. Since the generator is conditioned on structured cluster labels, the Fairness Critic can detect and penalize correlations between synthetic samples and sensitive attributes, minimizing bias. The generator is updated to reduce statistical dependence on these attributes via the fairness loss:

$$\mathcal{L}\text{fair} = \mathbb{E}[|C_\varphi(G_\theta(\bar{z}, c_k)) - s|^2] \quad (4)$$

To ensure trade-off between data realism and fairness constraints, the synthetic samples $\bar{x}_f$ are assigned cluster labels based on precomputed cluster embeddings. These embeddings, obtained from the Clustering-based VAE, remain fixed during WGAN-GP training. This conditioning reinforces both bias mitigation and structured generation while ensuring consistency in cluster-based representation.

Algorithm 1. The Clust-VAE-WGAN-GP algorithm

Require: Dataset $\mathcal{X}$, learning rates η_1, η_2, η_3, batch size B, number of clusters K, privacy noise σ, Wasserstein loss weight λ
1: **Initialize:** Clustering-based VAE V_ϕ, WGAN-GP (G_θ, D_ψ), Fairness Critic C_φ
2: Compute zCDP privacy parameters (ϵ, δ) using Gaussian mechanism
3: Pre-train VAE: Encode input $\mathcal{X}$ into latent space, compute mean and variance, and apply KL loss
4: Initialize cluster centroids using K-Means on VAE latent representations
5: **for** each training epoch **do**
6:    **for** each batch $\mathcal{B} \subset \mathcal{X}$ **do**
7:       Encode $\mathcal{B}$ using VAE, inject Gaussian noise $\mathcal{N}(0, \sigma^2)$, sample latent representations
8:       Assign cluster labels based on precomputed cluster embeddings
9:       Train WGAN-GP:
10:          Sample noise **z** and cluster embeddings to generate synthetic data
11:          Compute Wasserstein loss with gradient penalty
12:          Update generator G_θ and discriminator D_ψ
13:       Train Fairness Critic C_φ:
14:          Predict sensitive attributes from generated samples
15:          Compute fairness loss and update G_θ to remove bias
16:    **end for**
17: **end for**
18: **Return:** Trained models V_ϕ, G_θ, D_ψ, and C_φ

---

4 Experimental Setup

We investigate the following Research Questions (RQ) using the datasets detailed in Table 1: (1) RQ1: How can we generate synthetic data that closely resembles real data while maintaining high fidelity? (RQ2): How can we balance the trade-off between privacy and utility in synthetic data generation? (3) RQ3: How can synthetic data generation effectively mitigate bias? (4) RQ4: How can we guarantee the trade-off between privacy and fairness? (RQ5): How can we ensure that synthetic data preserves privacy?

For hyperparameter tuning, the VAE with clustering uses 4 layers in both the encoder and decoder, while the discriminator and fairness critic use 3 layers, and

Table 1. Overview of Benchmark Datasets Characteristics.

Dataset	# Instances	# Features	Labels	# Numerical	# Categorical
HIV	8916	22	Unlabeled	3	19
Corporate Stress	3000	45	Binary	37	8
Obesity	2111	17	Binary	8	9
Heart Failure	299	13	Binary	12	1
Diabetes Dataset	253680	22	Binary	21	1
Pediatric	782	58	Binary	19	39

the generator uses 4 layers. The LeakyReLU activation function is applied. We chose a batch size of 100. The noise multiplier ranges from 0.1 to 0.5. The learning rate is set to 0.0001. Sensitive attributes, such as Age, Gender, and Ethnicity, are manually identified for each dataset. A privacy accountant is used to convert ρ, the privacy loss parameter of zCDP, into (ϵ, δ)-DP for a fair comparison with baseline methods using (ϵ, δ)-DP. The number of clusters for K-Means is varied from 10 to 25. Kindly refer to our method's source code at the following link: Unsupervised Cluster-based VAE WGAN GP.

To assess *synthetic data realism*, the quality of synthetic data and its similarity to real data, we used the following metrics [16]:

- **Maximum Mean Discrepancy (MMD)**: Measures the distributional distance between real and synthetic data, with lower values indicating higher realism.
- **Kolmogorov-Smirnov (KS) Test**: The KS test assesses whether real and synthetic data follow the same distribution by measuring the maximum difference between their cumulative distribution functions. A lower KS value indicates stronger similarity. If the p-value is greater than 0.05, the difference is not statistically significant, suggesting that the synthetic data may follow the same distribution as the real data.
- **Wasserstein Distance (WD)**: Measures the optimal transport cost required to match the synthetic data distribution to the real data distribution, where lower values indicate better alignment.
- **Dimension-Wise Probability (DWP) Score**: Evaluates the per-feature distribution similarity between real and synthetic datasets. A score closer to 1 indicates greater similarity, meaning the synthetic data closely follows the real data's feature distributions.
- **Alpha-Precision**: Measures how many synthetic samples lie within the support of the real data distributions. A value closer to 1 indicates better utility.
- **Beta-Recall**: Measures how much of the real data distribution is covered by the synthetic data. A value closer to 1 indicates better utility.

Since explicit labels are unavailable, *fairness* is evaluated based on how sensitive attributes are represented within clusters in the generated data:

- **Statistical Parity in Clusters (SP)** [18]: Ensures that sensitive attributes do not influence cluster assignments, promoting fairness.
- **Mutual Information (MI) Between Clusters and Sensitive Attributes** [18]: Quantifies the dependency between synthetic cluster assignments and sensitive attributes. Lower MI values indicate better fairness.
- **Cluster Quality and Bias Impact** [17]:
  - **Silhouette Score (SS)**: Measures how well data points fit within their assigned clusters, with values closer to 1 indicating well-defined, unbiased clusters.
  - **Davies-Bouldin Index (DBI)**: Evaluates intra-cluster cohesion and inter-cluster separation, where lower values indicate better clustering performance.

To evaluate the privacy risks associated with synthetic data, we utilized the following metrics [16]:

- **Epsilon Identifiability Risk:** Quantifies the probability that an individual record can be uniquely identified in synthetic data. A higher epsilon risk suggests potential re-identification threats.
- **Nearest Neighbour Distance Ratio (NNDR):** Evaluates how distinguishable real data points are from synthetic ones based on nearest-neighbour distances. A lower NNDR means better privacy preservation.

We compared our Clust-VAE-WGAN-GP method with the following baseline approaches to assess its potential in mitigating bias and preserving privacy.

- **FairGAN** [7]: Introduces fairness constraints to enforce statistical parity across sensitive attributes in generated data.
- **TabFairGAN** [2]: Extends FairGAN to tabular data using Wasserstein GAN (WGAN) for demographically balanced datasets.
- **DPGAN** [4]: Ensures privacy in synthetic data generation by incorporating differential privacy mechanisms.
- **RDPCGAN** [5]: Utilizes Rényi Differential Privacy (RDP) to achieve strong privacy guarantees while maintaining data utility.

5 Results and Discussion

5.1 Data Realism Evaluation

Evaluation Under No Privacy Constraints. To address RQ1, Table 2 compares the utility of synthetic data generated by our method against baseline approaches. The results show that our model consistently outperforms baseline methods across most datasets and remains highly competitive with TabFairGAN. Specifically, it achieves the best performance in four out of six realism metrics for the Heart and Pediatric datasets. In three other datasets (HIV, Stress, and Diabetes), our method shares top-performing metrics with TabFairGAN. For instance, in the Pediatric dataset, our method achieved the lowest MMD and

WD values (0.0010, 0.238), outperforming TabFairGAN (0.1890, 0.25), FairGAN (0.2011, 0.49), DPGAN (0.2154, 0.55), and RDP-CGAN (0.7801, 0.30). It also attained the highest DWP score (0.5977), α-precision (0.741), and β-recall (0.712), clearly surpassing all baselines. In the Heart dataset, our method leads across all six metrics, with a DWP score of 0.675, α-precision of 0.715, and β-recall of 0.712. In the HIV dataset, it achieved the best DWP score (0.63) and β-recall (0.749), while remaining competitive on the other metrics. In Stress and Diabetes, it shared top performance: achieving the highest DWP scores (0.501, 0.5018) and the highest α-precision and β-recall in both datasets (Stress: 0.770, 0.509; Diabetes: 0.678, 0.888). The superior performance of our method stems from the integration of variational autoencoders with variational inference, enabling it to effectively capture feature correlations. Additionally, the novel conditioning mechanism introduced by K-Means clustering within the latent space guides the generative process, ensuring that synthetic samples closely resemble real data in an unsupervised setting. However, TabFairGAN remains a strong competitor, sharing several top-performing metrics with our method in the HIV, Stress, and Diabetes datasets and outperforming it in the Obesity dataset. This advantage can be attributed to its generator architecture, which incorporates ReLU activation for numerical attributes and Gumbel-softmax for categorical features, enhancing its ability to generate mixed-type data—particularly beneficial for the Obesity dataset.

Evaluation Under Privacy Constraints. To answer RQ2, Fig. 4 illustrates MMD trends under varying privacy budgets. Our method, in almost all datasets, consistently achieves lower MMD values at higher privacy budgets (e.g., 1000 and ∞), demonstrating a strong tradeoff between privacy and utility. However, at lower privacy budgets, RDP-CGAN shows competitive performance with lower MMD values. This can be attributed to the stronger privacy bound imposed by zCDP in our approach, which can introduce more noise at lower privacy budgets. Meanwhile, standard DP mechanisms, used in DP-GAN are vulnerable to exponential privacy loss accumulation causing decreased utility. Additionally, we observe instability in MMD values at higher privacy budgets for all models in the case of the Stress and Diabetes datasets, where MMD values do not exhibit a descending pattern as the privacy budget increases. This instability arises from dataset characteristics: the Diabetes dataset's large size and moderate feature count make it difficult to balance privacy and utility, as reduced noise can cause the generator to focus on irrelevant patterns, leading to less reliable results. The Stress dataset has a moderate size and includes a mix of binary and categorical

Table 2. Data Realism Metrics Across Methods under no privacy constraints.

Dataset	Method	MMD	KS-test	WD	DWP score	α-precision	β-recall
HIV	Our Method	0.07	**0.09**	0.43	**0.63**	0.567	**0.749**
	TabFairGAN	**0.0398**	0.07	**0.057**	0.4418	**0.692**	0.690
	FairGAN	0.1461	0.03	0.57	0.4294	0.680	0.680
	DPGAN	0.1452	3.50e−46	0.58	0.3481	0.600	0.650
	RDP-CGAN	0.9646	1.65e−6	0.30	0.3830	0.510	0.580
Stress	Our Method	0.035	**0.28**	0.28	**0.501**	**0.770**	0.509
	TabFairGAN	**0.0011**	0.51	**0.036**	0.4571	0.690	**0.690**
	FairGAN	0.0030	2.14e−68	0.480	0.3124	0.650	0.670
	DPGAN	0.0028	2.17e−56	0.51	0.3578	0.610	0.630
	RDP-CGAN	0.8488	3.380e−2	0.35	0.2304	0.530	0.550
Obesity	Our Method	0.2013	**0.05**	0.56	0.43	0.439	0.487
	TabFairGAN	**0.0213**	0.087	**0.083**	**0.4948**	**0.697**	**0.581**
	FairGAN	0.5609	1.19e−86	0.97	0.2457	0.600	0.590
	DPGAN	0.0876	1.237e−9	0.97	0.3159	0.570	0.610
	RDP-CGAN	1.0431	5.41e−2	0.80	0.1551	0.480	0.520
Heart	Our Method	0.227	**0.1701**	0.227	**0.675**	**0.715**	**0.712**
	TabFairGAN	**0.2674**	0.07	0.19	0.3194	0.690	0.690
	FairGAN	0.2300	6.55e−12	0.37	0.2760	0.680	0.690
	DPGAN	0.2387	9.34e−5	0.531	0.3576	0.630	0.660
	RDP-CGAN	0.7563	7.14e−1	0.34	0.1941	0.500	0.550
Diabetes	Our Method	**0.0352**	0.035	0.285	**0.5018**	**0.678**	**0.888**
	TabFairGAN	0.1782	**0.09**	0.22	0.3750	0.612	0.690
	FairGAN	0.1942	5.87e−9	0.51	0.3014	0.620	0.650
	DPGAN	0.2083	3.22e−7	0.57	0.2998	0.580	0.600
	RDP-CGAN	0.7999	7.22e−4	0.28	0.2554	0.490	0.500
Pediatric	Our Method	**0.0010**	0.03	**0.238**	**0.5977**	**0.741**	**0.712**
	TabFairGAN	0.1890	**0.05**	0.25	0.3950	0.690	0.690
	FairGAN	0.2011	3.21e−8	0.49	0.3198	0.670	0.690
	DPGAN	0.2154	2.98e−6	0.55	0.3120	0.630	0.640
	RDP-CGAN	0.7801	6.11e−3	0.30	0.2679	0.520	0.560

workplace stress indicators, contributing to the observed instability in MMD values. This combination of mixed data types and weakly structured patterns makes it challenging for the generator to capture meaningful relationships. This results to the vulnerability of the generator to overfitting noise rather than learning useful representations increasing instability.

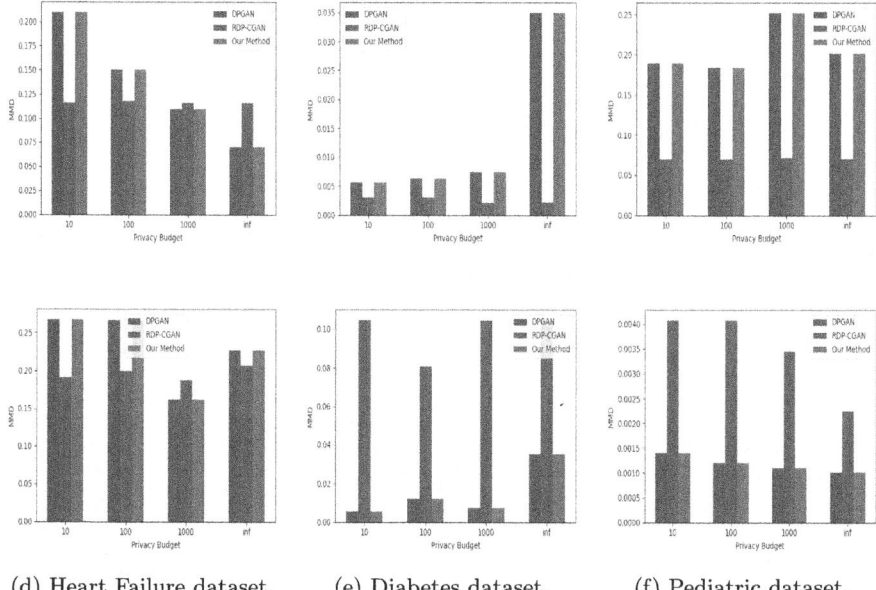

(d) Heart Failure dataset.   (e) Diabetes dataset.   (f) Pediatric dataset.

Fig. 4. Mean Maximum Discrepancy (MMD) comparison across different methods (DPGAN, RDP-CGAN, and our approach) under varying privacy budgets.

5.2 Data Fairness Evaluation

To investigate RQ3, Table 3 presents the fairness evaluation of our method in comparison with FairGAN and TabFairGAN, two state-of-the-art generative models explicitly designed to incorporate fairness mechanisms. The results demonstrate that our approach consistently achieves superior fairness outcomes. For instance, in the Pediatric dataset, our method outperformed baseline models by ensuring evenly spread statistical parity across sensitive attributes and achieving the lowest MI values (MI-Gender: 0.0010, MI-Age: 0.0006), the highest Silhouette Score (0.5297), and the lowest DBI score (0.5025) – FairGAN exhibited higher MI values (MI-Gender: 0.1341, MI-Age: 0.1428), lower Silhouette Score (0.0153), and a higher DBI Score (2.0988). Across all datasets, our method consistently attained balanced and evenly spread statistical parity, the lowest DBI scores, and the highest Silhouette Scores in 5 out of 6 datasets. These results highlight the effectiveness of the fairness critic, which dynamically guides the generator to produce bias-free synthetic data by actively penalizing dependencies between sensitive attributes and the generative process.

5.3 Data Privacy Evaluation

To respond to RQ(5), we report in Table 4 results of privacy, our method consistently yielded low identifiability risk values, ranging from 0.0100 to 0.0221,

Table 3. Comprehensive Analysis of Fairness Metrics Across Baseline Methods.

Dataset	Method	SP (Age)	SP (Gender)	SP (Ethnicity)	MI (Gender)	MI (Age)	MI (Ethnicity)	SS	DBI
HIV	TabFairGAN	-	Balanced	Unbalanced	**0.0000**	-	0.0495	**0.5778**	0.6034
	FairGAN	-	Unbalanced	Unbalanced	0.0517	-	0.0948	0.0926	2.2951
	Our Method	-	Balanced	Balanced	0.0360	-	**0.0656**	0.5527	**0.5349**
Stress	TabFairGAN	Evenly Spread	Balanced	-	0.0102	**0.0000**	-	0.0332	3.8059
	FairGAN	Evenly Spread	Evenly Spread	-	0.0922	0.0000	-	0.1531	2.1520
	Our Method	Balanced	Balanced	-	**0.0009**	0.0040	-	**0.4508**	**1.5409**
Obesity	TabFairGAN	Unbalanced	Balanced	-	**0.0039**	0.0604	-	0.1974	1.5800
	FairGAN	Unbalanced	Unbalanced	-	0.0209	0.0128	-	0.3211	1.7665
	Our Method	Balanced	Balanced	-	0.0346	**0.2027**	-	**0.4166**	**1.1452**
Heart Failure	TabFairGAN	Balanced	Balanced	-	0.0481	0.2340	-	0.3276	0.6575
	FairGAN	Balanced	Unbalanced	-	0.1463	0.4619	-	0.0987	1.4818
	Our Method	Balanced	Balanced	-	**0.0526**	**0.0000**	-	**0.6266**	**0.5150**
Pediatric	TabFairGAN	Evenly Spread	Evenly Spread	-	0.0166	0.0492	-	0.0766	2.0979
	FairGAN	Unbalanced	Balanced	-	0.1341	0.1428	-	0.0153	2.0988
	Our Method	Evenly Spread	Evenly Spread	-	**0.0010**	**0.0006**	-	**0.5297**	**0.5025**
Diabetes	TabFairGAN	Evenly Spread	Balanced	-	0.0601	**0.0000**	-	0.3320	1.2595
	FairGAN	Evenly Spread	Evenly Spread	-	0.1282	0.0000	-	0.0525	2.1114
	Our Method	Evenly Spread	Evenly Spread	-	**0.0005**	0.0028	-	**0.5276**	**0.5003**

indicating strong privacy guarantees across all datasets. Additionally, NNDR scores exceeded 1.0 in five out of six datasets, with higher values (e.g., 3.64 for Obesity) reflecting that synthetic samples were typically more distant from real data points, further supporting privacy preservation.

Table 4. Privacy Risk Metrics Across Datasets

Dataset	EIR	NNDR
HIV	0.0101	2.0998
Stress	0.0102	1.1012
Obesity	0.0101	3.6430
Heart	0.0100	1.0564
Diabetes	0.0221	1.5492
Pediatric	0.0101	0.0561

5.4 The Effect of Adversarial Debiasing Training

Table 5 presents a comparative analysis of our full architecture, which integrates adversarial debiasing (Adv. Deb.), against a variant that excludes this component (No Adv. Deb.), allowing us to isolate its impact on fairness. The results demonstrate that adversarial debiasing consistently improves fairness metrics, particularly statistical parity and mutual information (MI), as reflected in higher Silhouette Scores and lower DBI values. For instance, in the HIV dataset, our method achieves balanced gender parity and a significantly lower MI of 0.0360, whereas removing adversarial debiasing results in unbalanced parity and a much higher MI of 0.0739. These improvements stem from the dynamic fairness enforcement of the adversarial debiasing critic, which actively penalizes statistical dependencies between sensitive attributes and generated data during training. This ensures that fairness is not a byproduct of data representation but an explicitly optimized objective, effectively preventing demographic biases from being learned and propagated.

Table 5. Ablation Study: Impact of Adversarial Debiasing on Fairness.

Dataset	Our Method	SP (Age)	SP (Gender)	SP (Ethnicity)	MI (Gender)	MI (Age)	MI (Ethnicity)	SS	DBI
HIV	Adv. Deb.	-	**Balanced**	**Balanced**	**0.0360**	-	**0.0453**	**0.5527**	**0.5349**
	No Adv. Deb.	-	Unbalanced	Unbalanced	0.0739	-	0.0587	0.4009	1.2117
Stress	Adv. Deb.	**Balanced**	Balanced	-	**0.0020**	**0.0031**	-	**0.4318**	3.2728
	No Adv. Deb.	Unbalanced	Balanced	-	0.0077	0.0320	-	0.0410	**3.1810**
Obesity	Adv. Deb.	Balanced	Balanced	-	**0.0346**	**0.2027**	-	**0.4166**	**1.1452**
	No Adv. Deb.	Unbalanced	Balanced	-	0.0570	0.1591	-	0.1591	1.7886
Heart Failure	Adv. Deb.	Balanced	Balanced	-	**0.0526**	**0.0000**	-	**0.6266**	**0.5150**
	No Adv. Deb.	Balanced	Balanced	-	0.0900	0.3022	-	0.3022	1.0797
Pediatric	Adv. Deb.	Evenly Spread	Evenly Spread	-	**0.0010**	**0.0006**	-	**0.5297**	**0.5025**
	No Adv. Deb.	Evenly Spread	Evenly Spread	-	0.0186	0.4161	-	0.4161	0.6323
Diabetes	Adv. Deb.	Evenly Spread	Evenly Spread	-	**0.0008**	0.3185	-	0.3185	**0.5000**
	No Adv. Deb.	Evenly Spread	Evenly Spread	-	0.0839	0.3185	-	0.3185	0.7777

5.5 The Effect of Privacy on Fairness

To answer RQ4, we assess the tradeoff between fairness and privacy. We analyzed the evolution of Silhouette Scores and Davies-Bouldin Index values under varying privacy budgets and present them in Fig. 5. Our results indicate that as the privacy budget increases, Silhouette Scores improve, reflecting enhanced cohesion, while DBI values decrease, signifying enhanced fairness. For instance, in the HIV dataset, the Silhouette Score rises from 0.3953 at $\varepsilon = 0.1$ to 0.7143 at $\varepsilon = 100$, while DBI decreases from 1.3341 to 0.5900, demonstrating improved fairness level with relaxed privacy constraints. However, certain anomalies suggest that excessive noise can introduce instability in clustering quality. Notably, in the Stress dataset, DBI spikes from 1.5409 at $\varepsilon = 10$ to 3.2728 at $\varepsilon = 100$, while the Silhouette Score drops from 0.4508 to 0.4318. Despite leveraging zCDP for tighter privacy bounds via Rényi divergence, these results highlight the nuanced sensitivity of tuning the zCDP privacy budget. While zCDP reduces instability compared to traditional DP, the relationship between privacy strength (ρ) and fairness remains irregular, highlighting the delicacy of calibrating zCDP. This behavior is partly influenced by the fairness critic, which guides the model to generate balanced representations across subgroups. As zCDP introduces noise, the fairness critic retains more signal to enforce equitable data generation. However, when the privacy budget is too tight (low ρ), the added noise limits the critic's ability to discern and correct subgroup disparities, weakening fairness enforcement. Conversely, with a looser budget, the critic can more effectively align distributions across sensitive attributes, leading to lower DBI scores.

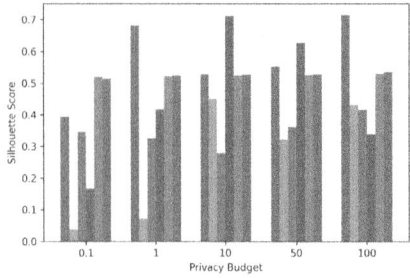
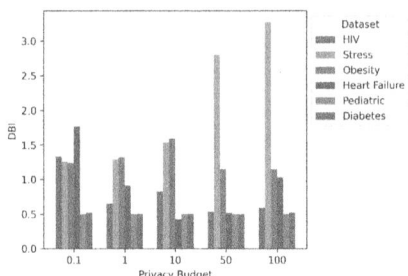

(a) Silhouette Scores across different privacy budgets. Higher values indicate better-defined clusters, showing the trade-off between privacy and clustering quality.

(b) Davies-Bouldin Index (DBI) under different privacy budgets. Lower values indicate better clustering structure and separation, highlighting the fairness-privacy trade-off.

Fig. 5. Comparison of clustering performance under different privacy budgets using Silhouette Score and Davies-Bouldin Index (DBI). The results illustrate the impact of privacy constraints on clustering structure and fairness.

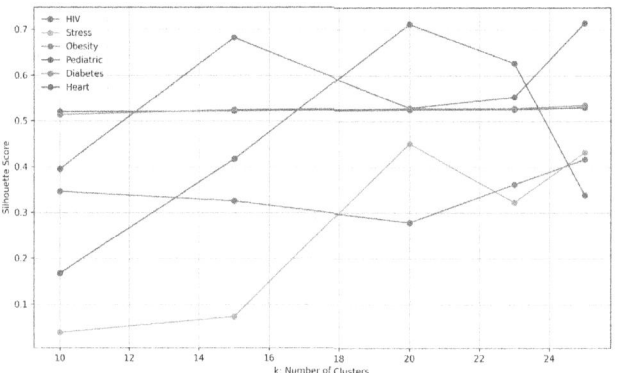

Fig. 6. Silhouette Score Across Six Datasets.

5.6 The Effect of Clustering on Data Quality

Figure 6 shows that clustering sensitivity to the number of clusters (k) depends on dataset characteristics. HIV, with many categorical features, improves steadily with k, peaking at 25 clusters, suggesting complex subgroup structures. Heart, being small and mostly numerical, is highly sensitive—peaking at $k = 20$ then dropping—indicating the risk of excessive cluster formation, leading to the loss of meaningful patterns. Stress dataset starts with poor clustering at $k = 10$ (0.04), but improves significantly by $k = 20$, suggesting that more clusters are needed to meaningfully separate complex patterns in the data. The drop in performance at $k = 23$ and 25 indicates over-segmentation, where noise may be mistaken for distinct groups. In contrast, Pediatric and Diabetes, both high-dimensional and largely numerical, show stable scores across k, indicating consistent group patterns. Obesity shows moderate improvement. Overall, smaller or more categorical datasets are more sensitive to k, while large numerical datasets are more robust.

6 Conclusion

We proposed a novel hybrid generative framework that enforces fairness and privacy in unsupervised synthetic data generation. By integrating a clustering-based Variational Autoencoder with a Wasserstein GAN with Gradient Penalty, our approach structures latent representations while ensuring privacy through zero-Concentrated Differential Privacy. Adversarial debiasing via the Fairness Critic mitigates bias without requiring explicit labels. Extensive experiments across multiple healthcare datasets demonstrate our method's superiority over existing fairness-aware and privacy-preserving generative models. By leveraging various data realism and fairness metrics, we provided a rigorous and interpretable evaluation of generative quality, bias mitigation, and privacy preservation. Our results highlight the effectiveness of our approach in generating high-quality, fair, and privacy-compliant synthetic data across varying privacy budgets in unsupervised settings. As future work, we aim to explore adaptive clustering techniques to dynamically adjust cluster formation and contrastive learning to further enhance bias mitigation.

Acknowledgments. This work was supported by the France 2030 grants RHU RECORDS (ANR-18-RHUS-0004) and IHU PROMETHEUS (ANR-23-IAHU-0004) and the iRECORDS project, funded by ERA PerMed (JTC_2021).

References

1. Ferrara, E.: Fairness and bias in artificial intelligence: a brief survey of sources, impacts, and mitigation strategies. Science **6**(1), 3 (2024). https://doi.org/10.3390/sci6010003
2. Rajabi, A., Garibay, O.O.: TabFairGAN: fair tabular data generation with generative adversarial networks (2021). arXiv preprint arXiv:2109.00666
3. Teo, C., Abdollahzadeh, M., Cheung, N.M.M.: On measuring fairness in generative models. In: Advances in Neural Information Processing Systems, vol. 36, pp. 10644–10656 (2023)
4. Xie, L., Lin, K., Wang, S., Wang, F., Zhou, J.: Differentially private generative adversarial network (2018). arXiv preprint arXiv:1802.06739
5. Torfi, A., Fox, E.A., Reddy, C.K.: Differentially private synthetic medical data generation using convolutional GANs. Inf. Sci. **586**, 485–500 (2022)
6. Movva, R., Koh, P.W., Pierson, E.: Using unlabeled data to enhance fairness of medical AI. Nat. Med. **30**, 944–945 (2024). https://doi.org/10.1038/s41591-024-02892-0

7. Xu, D., Yuan, S., Zhang, L., Wu, X.: FairGAN: fairness-aware generative adversarial networks. In: 2018 IEEE International Conference on Big Data (Big Data), pp. 570–575. IEEE (2018)
8. Xu, D., Yuan, S., Zhang, L., Wu, X.: FairGAN+: achieving fair data generation and classification through generative adversarial nets. In: 2019 IEEE International Conference on Big Data (Big Data), pp. 1401–1406. IEEE (2019)
9. Bun, M., Steinke, T.: Concentrated differential privacy: simplifications, extensions, and lower bounds (2016). arXiv preprint arXiv:1605.02065
10. Deshmukh, G., Naik, A.: Biases and fairness in deep learning models: a survey on inculcating fairness in generative models. In: 2023 7th International Conference On Computing, Communication, Control And Automation (ICCUBEA), pp. 1–39 (2023). https://doi.org/10.1109/ICCUBEA58933.2023.10391962
11. Chen, I.Y., Szolovits, P., Ghassemi, M.: Can AI help reduce disparities in general medical and mental health care? AMA J. Ethics **21**(2), 167–179 (2019)
12. Corbett-Davies, S., Goel, S.: The measure and mismeasure of fairness: a critical review of fair machine learning (2018). arXiv preprint arXiv:1808.00023
13. Zamzam, O., Akrami, H., Leahy, R.M.: Learning from positive and unlabeled data using observer-GAN (2022). arXiv preprint arXiv:2208.12477v2
14. Zhao, Y., Xu, Q., Wen, P., Jiang, Y., Huang, Q.: Dist-PU: positive-unlabeled learning from a label distribution perspective (2022). arXiv preprint arXiv:2212.02801
15. Paolis Kaluza, M.C., Jain, S., Radivojac, P.: An approach to identifying and quantifying bias in biomedical data. Pac. Symp. Biocomput. **28**, 311–322 (2023)
16. Ghosheh, G.O., Li, J., Zhu, T.: A survey of generative adversarial networks for synthesizing structured electronic health records. ACM Comput. Surv. **55**(8) (2023). https://doi.org/10.1145/3636424
17. Ros, F., Riad, R., Guillaume, S.: PDBI: a partitioning Davies-Bouldin index for clustering evaluation. Neurocomputing **528**, 178–199 (2023). https://doi.org/10.1016/j.neucom.2023.01.043
18. Kang, J., Xie, T., Wu, X., Maciejewski, R., Tong, H.: InfoFair: information-theoretic intersectional fairness. In: 2022 IEEE International Conference on Big Data (Big Data), pp. 1455–1464 (2022). https://doi.org/10.1109/BigData55660.2022.10020588
19. Jordon, J., Yoon, J., Van Der Schaar, M.: PATE-GAN: generating synthetic data with differential privacy guarantees. In: International Conference on Learning Representations. openreview.net (2018)
20. Wang, H., Bi, J., Hua, M., Yan, K., Afshari, A.: Semi-supervised CWGAN-GP modeling for AHU AFDD with high-quality synthetic data filtering mechanism. Build. Environ. (2025). https://doi.org/10.1016/j.buildenv.2024.112265
21. Ma, C., et al.: CAD-VAE: leveraging correlation-aware latents for comprehensive fair disentanglement (2025). arXiv preprint arXiv:2503.07938

Optimizing and Tuning Fairness in Machine Learning: An Augmented Lagrangian Method with a Performance Budget

Michele Fontana[1,2](✉), Francesca Naretto[1], and Anna Monreale[1]

[1] University of Pisa, Pisa, Italy
michele.fontana@phd.unipi.it, {francesca.naretto,anna.monreale}@unipi.it
[2] ISTI-CNR, Pisa, Italy

Abstract. Fairness in Machine Learning has become a concern, particularly if models are deployed in high-stakes decision-making. Most existing approaches aim to enforce fairness during training, but they face significant challenges for the scalability and the effectiveness of fairness enforcement. To address these limitations, we propose a method for training fair classifiers under multiple group and intersectional fairness constraints with high predictive performance. We combine an Augmented Lagrangian learning procedure with a tunable *performance budget*, which regulates the trade-off between fairness and utility. Experiments demonstrate that our method mitigates bias while scaling efficiently with increasing problem complexity. By adjusting the performance budget, we provide a flexible mechanism to balance fairness enforcement and predictive performance, offering a solution for real-world applications.

Keywords: Fairness · Machine Learning · Ethical AI

1 Introduction

In recent years, Machine Learning (ML) models have been developed and widely applied across various domains without posing any particular attention on the model trustworthiness but only optimizing the model utility for the specific task to be addressed. However, with the advent of new EU AI legislation[1], there is now an increased emphasis on the legal and ethical requirements of ML models, including, but not limited to, fairness, privacy and transparency [20–22]. Fairness seeks to reduce biases in model predictions. Although achieving fairness and model utility simultaneously is ideal, practitioners often face challenges in balancing the two, as improving one aspect can often undermine the other. In the literature, to prevent the amplification of unfair behavior of ML models Multi-Objective Optimization approaches have been proposed considering that fair ML has the goal of simultaneously minimizing classification error while also

---
[1] The AI Act.

Supplementary Information The online version contains supplementary material available at https://doi.org/10.1007/978-3-032-05962-8_13.

optimizing for one or more fairness criteria [24]. Nevertheless, the state-of-the-art approaches present some limits related to their scalability and their ability to find an acceptable trade-off between fairness and model performance, especially when addressing intersectional fairness.

In this paper, we propose `FairLAB` (Fairness via Lagrangian Augmented and performance Budget), a method for learning a neural network (`NN`) model that balances predictive performance while satisfying a collection of fairness constraints, including intersectional ones. Our method integrates fairness directly into the learning process by ensuring that fairness violations are addressed dynamically while optimizing the predictive objective. It exploits a *performance budget*, which enables control over the performance-fairness trade-off. Intersectional fairness further increases the complexity of this task, as multiple sensitive attributes combine to form a large number of subgroups, making fairness enforcement computationally challenging. To overcome the scalability issue, `FairLAB` exploits a *divide-et-impera* strategy which splits the fairness problem in subtasks addressed by multiple learners. A wide experimentation on three datasets demonstrates that `FairLAB` successfully mitigates fairness requirements also in case of challenging settings while maintaining under control the model utility and outperforms the state-of-the-art methods.

2 Related Work

Group Fairness. Several studies have explored the group fairness problem, proposing different mitigation strategies: pre-processing, in-processing, and post-processing methods [3]. Among them we focus on the *in-processing* approaches, which incorporate fairness requirements directly into the model's training. A common tactic involves regularization schemes that penalize correlations between predicted outcomes and sensitive attributes, balancing fairness against predictive performance [14]. Constraint-based optimization methods similarly aim to enforce fairness while maintaining overall accuracy, by coupling a performance metric with fairness constraints [4]. Cotter et al. [5] propose a primal-dual Lagrangian approach that can incorporate multiple, potentially non-differentiable constraints. Lokhande et al. [17] exploit the Augmented Lagrangian Method (ALM), though their approach is limited to a single fairness constraint and one binary sensitive attribute. Agarwal et al. [1] introduce Exponentiated Gradient (`ExpGrad`), which reduces fair classification to a sequence of cost-sensitive subproblems. Another category is adversarial debiasing, where an adversarial network tries to predict sensitive attributes from the model's outputs. The main model is trained to defeat the adversary, thus mitigating bias [6,27]. Another research direction addresses fairness under a Multi-Objective Optimization (MOO) framework, which aims to jointly optimize multiple fairness metrics along with predictive performance. MOO approaches capture various trade-offs by constructing a *Pareto front* of equivalent models [7], either with gradient-based or evolutionary algorithms [26,28]. Among the gradient-based methods, Ruchte et al. [24] introduce `COSMOS`, an efficient algorithm to approximate the Pareto front in high-dimensional settings, reducing the computational costs often associated with naive MOO approaches.

Intersectional Fairness. These algorithms must address two key challenges: *data sparsity*, where certain demographic subgroups contain very few instances, and *computational complexity*, which grows exponentially with the number of protected attributes. As a result, standard fairness metrics may become computationally intractable [11]. Hence, alternative approaches have been developed, including *subgroup fairness* [15] and *differential fairness* [10], that handle numerous subgroups more efficiently. A prominent line of work adopts an *auditing* paradigm: an auditor identifies subgroups exhibiting high unfairness under a given metric, and a learner then reduces prediction error subject to fairness constraints [16]. For instance, in [15], it is proposed a zero-sum game that leverages a cost-sensitive classification oracle. Another approach combines and extends group fairness methods, to incorporate *differential fairness* in intersectional settings, employing a tailored loss function to balance fairness and accuracy, relying on the correlations between protected and unprotected features [19].

To the best of our knowledge, in the literature there are no methods that can handle the performance-fairness trade-off directly in the learning process, addressing simultaneously group and intersectional fairness efficiently.

3 Background

Fairness Fundamentals. Here we describe the group and intersectional fairness metrics used throughout our work. Consider a dataset with a sensitive attribute a taking values in $\{v_1, v_2, \ldots, v_n\}$ and a binary classifier $\hat{Y} \in \{0,1\}$. The *Demographic Parity* (DP) [2] assesses whether the probability of receiving a positive prediction is independent of the sensitive attribute. Formally, the disparity in positive prediction rates across subgroups of the attribute a is quantified as $DP(\hat{Y}) = \max_{1 \leq i < j \leq n} |\Pr(\hat{Y} = 1 \mid a = v_i) - \Pr(\hat{Y} = 1 \mid a = v_j)|$. The *Equal Opportunity* metric [13] measures the maximum gap in true positive rates across subgroups, while *Predictive Equality* [13] measures the maximum gap in false positive rates. *Equalized Odds* (EOD) [13] enforces fairness simultaneously in both measures and is defined as the maximum between them. We say that a classifier $\hat{Y}$ is fair with respect to metric F if $F^a(\hat{Y}) \leq \tau$, where τ is a given threshold (often set to 0.2).

In practice, fairness concerns often involve not just single sensitive attributes (e.g., gender or race), but *intersections* of multiple attributes (e.g., race *and* gender). This is known as *intersectional fairness*, and it aims to protect subgroups that may be disadvantaged at the intersection of multiple identities [10]. To evaluate fairness in this setting, the same group fairness metrics (e.g., DP, EOD) are applied to the cross-product of sensitive attributes, treating each intersectional group (e.g., Black Woman, White Man, etc.) as a distinct subgroup. This allows for a more fine-grained assessment of disparities that may be hidden when attributes are considered in isolation. However, this also increases the number of groups to monitor, raising statistical and optimization challenges in both measurement and mitigation.

In the following, we use $F^a(m)$ to denote the value of fairness metric F evaluated on model m w.r.t. to attribute a.

Augmented Lagrangian Method. (ALM) [9] is a constrained optimization technique that extends the Lagrangian formulation. Consider a problem:

$$\min_{\mathbf{x} \in \mathbb{R}^d} f(\mathbf{x}) \quad \text{subject to} \quad g_i(\mathbf{x}) \leq 0 \, (i = 1, \ldots, r), \quad h_j(\mathbf{x}) = 0 \, (j = 1, \ldots, m)$$

ALM introduces a penalty parameter $\sigma > 0$ and Lagrange multipliers $\lambda \in \mathbb{R}^m$, $\mu \in \mathbb{R}^r$ to enforce equality and inequality constraints, respectively. The Augmented Lagrangian $\mathcal{L}_A(\mathbf{x}, \lambda, \mu, \sigma)$ is defined as:

$$f(\mathbf{x}) + \sum_{j=1}^{m} \lambda_j h_j(\mathbf{x}) + \frac{\sigma}{2} \sum_{j=1}^{m} h_j(\mathbf{x})^2 + \frac{1}{2\sigma} \sum_{i=1}^{r} \left(\max\{0, \mu_i + \sigma g_i(\mathbf{x})\}^2 - \mu_i^2 \right)$$

At each iteration e, the variable $\mathbf{x}$ is updated by minimizing $\mathcal{L}_A$, followed by multiplier updates that correct constraint violations. The multipliers for equality and inequality constraints are adjusted as

$$\lambda^{(e+1)} = \lambda^{(e)} + \rho h\big(\mathbf{x}^{(e+1)}\big), \quad \mu^{(e+1)} = \max\Big\{0, \mu^{(e)} + \rho g\big(\mathbf{x}^{(e+1)}\big)\Big\} \quad (1)$$

When applied to deep learning, $\mathcal{L}_A$ is treated as a loss function that accounts for both predictive objectives and constraints satisfaction. For classification tasks, the function to be minimized is usually the Cross Entropy. The model parameters are updated through gradient-based methods. The multipliers are refreshed via Eq. 1 after each epoch, reducing constraint violations as training proceeds [18].

4 FairLAB Method

Our objective is to train a neural network that balances predictive performance and fairness while satisfying a collection of fairness constraints, even intersectional ones. Our method integrates fairness directly into the learning process by ensuring that fairness violations are addressed dynamically while optimizing the predictive objective. We exploit a *performance budget* that controls the performance-fairness trade-off. Intersectional fairness increases the computational complexity, as multiple sensitive attributes create a large number of subgroups. To mitigate this issue, we adopt a *divide-et-impera* strategy, wherein a central orchestrator divides the fairness problem in sub-tasks among multiple learners by partitioning the fairness constraints, reducing the need to handle all intersectional subgroups simultaneously and improving scalability. Figure 1 provides a schematic representation of the process, which consists of two main phases: a *setup phase*, where constraints are assigned to the learners, and a *global learning phase*, where fairness violations are iteratively identified and mitigated.

Preliminaries. Before detailing the algorithmic process, we describe its inputs and we define the key concepts. The algorithm takes as input (i) a set of fairness

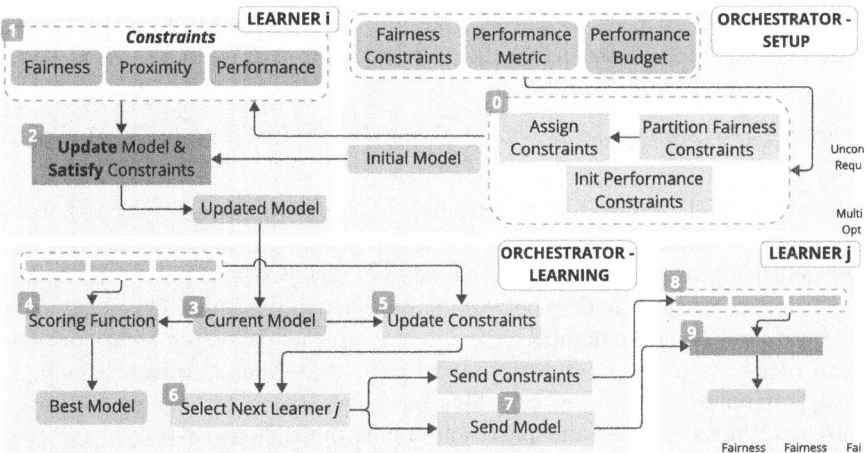

Fig. 1. Overview of FairLAB's main steps in the setup and global learning phases.

Algorithm 1: $\text{FairLAB}_{\text{Orchestrator}}(w^1, E, P, \mathcal{R}, \beta)$

Input: w^1, E : the initial parameters, the number of iterations.
Input: P, $\mathcal{R}$: the performance metric to optimize, the fairness requirements.
Input: β : the performance budget.
Output: w_{best}: the last best parameters.

1   $\tilde{\mathcal{R}} = BinarizeConstraints(\mathcal{R})$;
2   $L = InitLocalLearners(\tilde{\mathcal{R}})$;
3   $w_{\text{best}} = w^1; s_{\text{best}} = EvaluateModel(w^1, \mathbf{S}); p^* = P(w^1)$;
4   **for** $e \leftarrow 1$ **to** E **do**
5     $\mathcal{P}^e, \mathcal{D}^e = BuildPerformance\&ProximityConstraints(w^e, \beta, p^*)$;
6     $l^e = SelectLocalLearner(w^e, L)$;
7     $w^{e+1}, p^* = UpdateModel_{Local}(l^e, w^e, \mathcal{P}^e, \mathcal{D}^e)$;
8     $s^{e+1} = EvaluateModel(w^{e+1}, \mathbf{S})$;
9   **if** $s^{e+1} > s_{best}$ **then**
10       $w_{\text{best}} = w^{e+1}; s_{\text{best}} = s^{e+1}$

11 **return** w_{best}

---

requirements $\mathcal{R}$, (ii) a performance metric P (e.g. accuracy or F_1 score) to be maximized and (iii) a performance budget $\beta \geq 0$. The fairness requirement is defined as $\mathcal{R} = \{(F_i, a_i, \tau_i)\}_{i=1}^{|\mathcal{R}|}$, where F_i is a fairness metric (e.g. DP or EOD), $a_i \in \mathcal{A}$ is a sensitive attribute (either binary or non-binary) belonging to the set of sensitive attributes $\mathcal{A}$ involved in the fairness requirements $\mathcal{R}$, $\tau_i \geq 0$ is a threshold defining the maximum acceptable violation. Note that, in case of intersectional fairness an attribute a_i might be both a simple attribute e.g., race or gender, and a combined attribute, e.g., race and gender. Given a ML model m each constraint takes the form $F_i^{a_i}(m) \leq \tau_i$, and $F_i^{a_i}(m)$ denotes the evaluation of the fairness metric F_i on the attribute a_i for the ML model m. To quantify constraint satisfaction, we define the *scoring function* S, expressed as in Eq. 2:

$$\text{S}(m; \mathcal{R}, P) = \lambda_P P(m) - (1 - \lambda_P) \sum_{i=1}^{|\mathcal{R}|} \max\{0, F_i^{a_i}(m) - \tau_i\} \left(F_i^{a_i}(m) - \tau_i\right) \quad (2)$$

where $\lambda_P \in [0, 1]$ determines the trade-off between performance and fairness. Since fairness constraints are often defined over categorical attributes that may have multiple possible values, we introduce a *binary partition* process that allows us to compare fairness metrics between pairs of attribute values. Given a sensitive attribute a with domain $\text{dom}(a) = \{v_1, v_2, \ldots, v_n\}$, we define the binary partition on an attribute as an operator, that restricts the domain values to any pair $\{v_i, v_j\}$, denoted as $\pi(a \mid v_i, v_j)$. This binary partition process enables also a strategy of fairness constraint partition among multiple learners.

Method Description. To provide a clear understanding of the main steps performed by FairLAB, we present its pseudo-code in Algorithm 1. The proposed approach operates in a *setup phase* (lines 1–3) followed by a *global learning phase*. During *setup*, the orchestrator converts the fairness requirement $\mathcal{R}$ into a set of pairwise binary constraints, using the binary partition process, which we denote as $\tilde{\mathcal{R}}$ (line 1). Specifically, for each constraint $(F_i, a_i, \tau_i) \in \mathcal{R}$, the orchestrator generates a set of constraints of the form $\left(F_i, \pi(a_i \mid v_j, v_k), \tau_i\right)$ $\forall (v_j, v_k) \in \text{dom}(a_i)$. The resulting set $\tilde{\mathcal{R}}$ contains all the derived binary constraints and replaces the original multi-valued fairness constraints in the subsequent optimization process. This transformation ensures that fairness constraints are enforced, reducing the complexity of handling multi-valued sensitive attributes. Once $\tilde{\mathcal{R}}$ is constructed, the orchestrator initializes a set of learners $L = \{l_1, \ldots, l_{|\text{dom}(a)|}\}$ (line 2), where each learner is made responsible for enforcing the fairness constraints that involve a specific value v of attribute a, explicitly assigned by the orchestrator, i.e., $(F_i, \pi(a \mid v, v_j), \tau_i) \in \tilde{\mathcal{R}}$. As a consequence, we have a number of learners equal to the $|\text{dom}(a)|$.

After partitioning the fairness constraints, the orchestrator sets up the parameters for the next phase (line 3). Given the initial parameters of the network w^1 the orchestrator assigns it to w_{best}. Moreover, given the scoring function to evaluate the constraint satisfaction S, the orchestrator evaluates the current model to assign the initial scoring value to s_{best} and its performance as the best ones to p^*. Next, FairLAB starts the *global learning phase*, which is an optimization procedure consisting of a maximum of E iterations (line 4). A generic iteration e involves the following steps: (i) *constraint updates* (line 5), (ii) *learner selection* (line 6), (iii) *model updates* (line 7), and (iv) *model evaluation* (line 8). In the following, we detail each of these steps.

Constraints Updates. In each iteration e, given the model m characterized by the parameters w^e, the orchestrator updates two sets of constraints: (i) the *performance* constraints $\mathcal{P}^e$ and (ii) the *proximity* constraints $\mathcal{D}^e$.

The *performance* constraints $\mathcal{P}^e$ ensure that the model maintains high predictive performance throughout the training process, preventing excessive degradation due to fairness enforcement. However, for converging to acceptable balance between fairness and performance we introduce the *performance budget* β, a key factor that enables the control of how much performance can be sacrificed to satisfy fairness constraints. A larger β permits a greater reduction in utility, allowing stronger fairness enforcement, while a smaller β prioritizes performance at the possible expense of fairness improvements. As a consequence the constraints are defined as: $P(m) \geq p^* + \rho_{\text{step}}$ and $P(m) \geq p^* - \beta$. The first constraint incentivizes performance improvement at each iteration by requiring the model to exceed the best observed performance p^* by at least a small step size ρ_{step}. This helps prevent stagnation and ensures that fairness constraints do not lead to a complete neglect of predictive performance. The second constraint prevents excessive deterioration of predictive performance by ensuring that performance does not drop more than β units below the highest recorded performance p^*. The parameter β acts as a performance safeguard, allowing some flexibility for fairness improvements while preserving overall utility.

The *proximity* constraints $\mathcal{D}^e$ are designed to ensure that fairness properties already achieved at a given iteration are preserved in subsequent updates. Without such constraints, fairness improvements obtained in earlier iterations could be undone as the model continues to optimize for other objectives. To prevent this, given the subset of attributes for which we have the fairness constraints almost or fully satisfied, we propose to measure how much the model's prediction distribution shifts for each subgroup between different iterations using the *1-Wasserstein distance* (also known as the Earth Mover's Distance) [25]. This distance quantifies the minimal amount of probability mass that must be transferred to transform one distribution into another. The proximity constraints then enforce an upper bound on this shift, ensuring that the model's decision distribution remains stable across training updates:

$$\mathcal{D}^e = \{W_1(w^{e-1}, w^e \mid v) \leq \delta \mid \forall a_i \in \mathcal{A} \; \forall v \in \mathcal{AS}(a_i)\},$$

where $W_1(w^{e-1}, w^e \mid v)$ represents the 1-Wasserstein distance between the distribution of model outputs for subgroup v at iteration e and iteration $e-1$, while δ is a small tolerance threshold that controls the maximum allowed change in subgroup-level decision distributions. Note that, given a sensitive attribute a, such distance is conditioned to its values, named *active set* $\mathcal{AS}(a)$, which either satisfy or are close to satisfying fairness constraints. More formally, given a sensitive attribute $a \in \mathcal{A}$, the value v belongs to $\mathcal{AS}(a)$ if and only if there is no fairness violation or the violation between v and any $v_j \neq v$ does not exceed a given threshold, i.e., $\tau_i - F_i^{\pi(a|v,v_j)}(m) \leq \nu_{tot}$. We highlight that $\mathcal{D}^e$ constraints serve to (i) *reduce the risk of fairness violations re-emerging* by discouraging large shifts in subgroup-level decision distributions, which could lead to previously satisfied fairness constraints being violated in subsequent iterations; and (ii) *regularize subgroup-level decision changes*, preventing overfitting to specific fairness constraints while maintaining consistency in model predictions.

Learner Selection. At each iteration, the orchestrator selects a learner to perform the next model update. To make this selection, each learner $l_i \in L$ first reports its total fairness violation ν_i, which quantifies how much the fairness constraints assigned to l_i are currently being violated. The orchestrator then assigns a selection probability to each learner, ensuring that learners with higher fairness violations are more likely to be chosen for updates. The selection probability follows a softmax-like distribution, defined as $\frac{e^{-T\nu_i}}{\sum_j e^{-T\nu_j}}$, where $T > 0$ is a temperature parameter that controls the sharpness of the probability distribution. In particular, when T is small, the probability distribution is concentrated around the learners with the highest fairness violations, strongly prioritizing them for updates. This mechanism ensures that the optimization process dynamically focuses on the fairness constraints with higher violation, while still allowing occasional updates from other learners to maintain overall stability in the model training process.

Model Update. In this phase, the selected learner l^e receives the updated model parameters w^e along with the two sets of constraints $\mathcal{P}^e, \mathcal{D}^e$. The learner first constructs the full set of constraints that will be optimized in the current iteration: $\mathcal{K}_{l^e} = \mathcal{R}_{l^e} \cup \mathcal{P}^e \cup \mathcal{D}^e$, where $\mathcal{R}_{l^e}$ is the subset of fairness constraints assigned to the learner l^e during the setup phase. The learner then constructs its scoring function LS, which follows a similar formulation to the scoring function S defined in Eq. 2. The key difference is that, while S is computed over the initial set of fairness constraints $\mathcal{R}$, the local scoring function LS is defined specifically for the constraints $\mathcal{K}_{l^e}$ assigned to the selected learner l^e in the current iteration. At this point l^e proceeds with a learning process based on the ALM described in Sect. 3, to update the model parameters w^e. In this process, we employ a standard task-specific loss function (e.g., cross-entropy for classification tasks) as the primary objective function in ALM. We precise that, since all constraints in $\mathcal{K}_{l^e}$ are formulated as inequality constraints, the Augmented Lagrangian function is defined exclusively over this type of constraint, without including equality constraints. The goal of this optimization process is to refine the network parameters w^e and obtain a new set of parameters w^{e+1} that satisfies the constraints in $\mathcal{K}_{l^e}$, while maintaining predictive performance. Since fairness and performance metrics are often non-differentiable, the learner l^e approximates them using soft confusion-matrices. To achieve this, the learner queries the model m to obtain the logits, which are then processed through the *Entmax* function to produce a sparse probability distribution [23]. This probability distribution is subsequently used to construct soft confusion matrices, from which fairness and performance metrics are computed. These soft approximations allow for the application of gradient-based optimization techniques within the Augmented Lagrangian framework. To ensure numerical stability and prevent fairness constraints from dominating the optimization process, the learner employs an early-stopping criterion in ALM. Specifically, the Lagrangian multipliers are updated only if a constraint violation does not improve over multiple consecutive epochs. This prevents excessive growth of the multipliers relative to the primary optimization objective and mitigates numerical instability.

Model Evaluation. At the end of the model update, the learner l^e returns the updated model w^{e+1}, corresponding to the one that maximizes LS. If the new model achieves a higher performance than any previously recorded one, the learner also updates the reference performance value p^* that will be used in the next performance constraints $\mathcal{P}^{e+1}$. The orchestrator then evaluates w^{e+1} using its function S. If the new model w^{e+1} achieves a higher score than the best recorded so far, the orchestrator updates its reference model, marking w^{e+1} as the new best model.

This iterative process continues until a stopping criterion is met. Training stops either when the maximum number of iterations is reached or when an early-stopping condition is triggered based on S. At that point, the algorithm outputs the model that attains the highest value of S.

5 Experimental Settings

We present the experimental setup for validating FairLAB[2], considering three benchmarking datasets: FolkTables, Compas, and MEPS[3]. For each dataset we remove duplicates, standardize numerical features by removing the mean and scaling to unit variance, and encode categorical features using one-hot encoding.

FolkTables dataset contains census data from California in 2014, with age, education level and so on. The task is to classify whether an individual's income exceeds $50K$. We use $183,380$ samples with 20 features. The sensitive attributes considered are *Job*, *Race* and *MaritalStatus*.

Compas dataset contains criminal records from Broward County, Florida. It includes demographic information, criminal history, and risk scores for $6,172$ defendants. The task is to predict whether an arrested was convicted of violence within two years. After pre-processing, the dataset consists of 34 features. The sensitive attributes considered are *Gender*, *Race* and *Age*.

MEPS dataset contains information on healthcare expenditures, medical service utilization, and patient demographics from the United States in 2015. It contains $33,400$ records and over 200 features. After feature selection and one-hot encoding, we reduce to 132. The classification task is to predict whether an individual's total medical expenses exceed the third quantile. The sensitive attributes considered are *Gender*, *Race* and *MaritalStatus*.

For the hyper-parameters and the other implementation details, we refer the interested reader to the Supplementary Material.

Competitors. We compare FairLAB against: (i) Vanilla, a ML approach that optimizes only for predictive performance without incorporating fairness constraints, serving as a reference to estimate the initial algorithmic bias present in the data; (ii) FFVAE (Adversarial), an adversarial debiasing method designed to mitigate unfairness in scenarios involving non-binary sensitive attributes [6]; (iii) Exponentiated Gradient (ExpGrad), a constrained learning approach that dynamically adjusts constraint weights to balance fairness and accuracy, producing a final model by combining multiple reweighted classifiers [1]; and (iv)

---

[2] We performed the experiments on a server having an Intel(R) Xeon(R) Gold 5120 CPU @ 2.20 GHz, 16 cores and 64 GB of RAM. The code is available at: https://github.com/michelefontana92/FairLAB.
[3] Folk, Compas, Meps.

Table 1. Results of the 2-Ways Intersections. In F_1 we highlight in bold the best performance, while for DP and EOD we report in bold the values below the fairness threshold (0.20) and underline the lowest value.

	Debiasing results on FolkTables											
	Demographic Parity (DP)						Equalized Odds (EOD)					
Algorithm	JobRace		JobMarital		RaceMarital		JobRace		JobMarital		RaceMarital	
	F_1	DP	F_1	DP	F_1	DP	F_1	EOD	F_1	EOD	F_1	EOD
Vanilla	**0.77**	0.39	**0.77**	0.38	**0.77**	0.36	**0.77**	0.37	**0.77**	0.37	**0.77**	0.48
Adversarial	0.73	0.28	0.74	0.25	0.71	0.28	0.75	0.28	0.70	<u>**0.14**</u>	0.70	<u>**0.18**</u>
ExpGrad	0.75	0.34	0.70	**0.19**	0.67	**0.20**	0.73	0.25	0.75	0.24	0.74	0.28
COSMOS	0.70	0.23	0.73	0.29	0.73	0.32	0.74	0.28	0.73	**0.20**	0.73	0.33
FairLAB (0.05)	0.72	**0.20**	0.74	**0.19**	0.72	**0.20**	0.74	**0.20**	0.73	**0.20**	0.74	**0.19**

	Debiasing results on Compas											
	Demographic Parity (DP)						Equalized Odds (EOD)					
Algorithm	GenderRace		GenderAge		RaceAge		GenderRace		GenderAge		RaceAge	
	F_1	DP	F_1	DP	F_1	DP	F_1	EOD	F_1	EOD	F_1	EOD
Vanilla	**0.69**	0.49	**0.69**	0.62	**0.69**	0.56	**0.69**	0.45	**0.69**	0.64	**0.69**	0.53
Adversarial	0.65	0.27	0.67	0.30	0.60	0.22	0.65	**0.18**	0.55	<u>**0.09**</u>	0.61	**0.20**
ExpGrad	0.61	**0.12**	0.65	0.26	0.63	0.26	0.65	**0.20**	0.65	**0.11**	0.64	0.27
COSMOS	0.66	0.32	0.64	0.31	0.68	0.38	0.68	0.36	0.69	0.44	0.62	0.29
FairLAB (0.05)	0.66	**0.19**	0.65	**0.20**	0.64	**0.19**	0.66	**0.19**	0.65	**0.20**	0.65	**0.20**

	Debiasing results on MEPS											
	Demographic Parity (DP)						Equalized Odds (EOD)					
Algorithm	GenderRace		GenderMarital		RaceMarital		GenderRace		GenderMarital		RaceMarital	
	F_1	DP	F_1	DP	F_1	DP	F_1	EOD	F_1	EOD	F_1	EOD
Vanilla	**0.81**	0.29	**0.81**	0.45	**0.81**	0.53	**0.81**	0.34	**0.81**	0.57	**0.81**	0.62
Adversarial	0.78	0.22	0.70	**0.10**	0.78	0.40	0.78	0.35	0.80	0.42	0.75	0.45
ExpGrad	0.80	0.26	0.79	0.33	0.79	0.33	0.80	0.32	0.79	0.40	0.78	0.52
COSMOS	0.80	0.21	0.79	0.29	0.79	0.37	0.78	0.25	0.80	0.30	0.80	0.40
FairLAB (0.05)	0.80	<u>**0.14**</u>	0.79	0.18	0.79	**0.20**	0.75	**0.19**	0.78	<u>**0.15**</u>	0.76	**0.20**

COSMOS, a MOO method that efficiently learns a Pareto front of models with equivalent trade-offs between fairness and accuracy [24].

6 Experiments

In this section we provide our experimental evaluation of FairLAB, against the competitors across multiple fairness settings. In the evaluation we use DP and EOD as fairness metrics, and F_1 score for the predictive performance. Our analysis aims to assess (i) how effectively FairLAB balances fairness and predictive performance, studying key factors such as the performance budget β and the proximity threshold δ that influence its behavior, and (ii) its scalability.

In particular, we analyze from simpler to more complex fairness scenarios, exploring the intersectional fairness with two sensitive attributes in Sect. 6.1 and with three in Sect. 6.2, highlighting the increasing difficulty of enforcing fairness as dimensionality grows. Following, Sect. 6.3 examines cases where multiple fairness constraints are applied simultaneously, incorporating both group-level and intersectional constraints. Section 6.4 explores the impact of the proximity threshold δ on the trade-off between preserving the fairness properties and improving the performance. Finally, Sect. 6.5 proves that FairLAB is scalable.

6.1 Experiments with Two-Attribute Intersections

We evaluate fairness constraints by enforcing either DP or EOD individually, considering all intersections of two sensitive attributes for each dataset. We impose $F^{a_i}(m) \leq 0.2$ on subgroups defined by a_i which intersects two attributes. Here F is DP or EOD. Table 1 reports the results.

Demographic Parity. FairLAB is the only method that meets fairness objectives in all cases. While Adversarial often achieves a substantial bias reduction (as seen by comparing fairness values to Vanilla, the baseline), in some scenarios it fails (e.g., *JobRace* in FolkTables and *RaceMarital* in MEPS). Similarly, ExpGrad succeeds for certain intersections (e.g., *JobMarital* in FolkTables) but struggles elsewhere (e.g., *JobRace* in FolkTables). COSMOS has mixed outcomes, even exceeding fairness by more than 0.18 (e.g., *RaceAge* in Compas).

Equalized-Odds. FairLAB meets the fairness constraint in every configuration, demonstrating strong bias mitigation. For FolkTables, all competitors achieve acceptable fairness and F_1 score. For Compas and MEPS, results are mixed: while Adversarial performs well, the other methods mitigate bias only for certain attributes, often exceeding the desired bias threshold of 20 by at least 0.10.

Performance Analysis. All fairness-aware approaches have lower F_1 than the unconstrained Vanilla, which achieves the highest performance but significantly violates fairness. Among the debiasing methods, FairLAB strikes a strong balance between fairness and utility, maintaining competitive F_1 while meeting all fairness targets. For instance, on MEPS under EOD, FairLAB reduces bias below 0.20 with a slight decrease in F_1 (at most 0.06). By contrast, Adversarial sometimes suffers substantial utlity drops (e.g., $F_1 = 0.55$ on Compas, compared to 0.69 for Vanilla and 0.65 for FairLAB). Although ExpGrad and COSMOS often retain good F_1 scores, they do not always meet the fairness constraints.

6.2 Experiments with Three-Attribute Intersections

In this experiment, we evaluate FairLAB by creating attributes combining three sensitive factors to test its performance in a more complex setting. Specifically, we consider *JobRaceMarital* for FolkTables, *GenderRaceAge* for Compas, and *GenderRaceMarital* for MEPS. We enforce DP and EOD separately, each with a threshold of 0.20. In addition, given the more challenging setting, we evaluate FairLAB under three different values of β to analyze the trade-off between fairness and F_1 score. Table 2 reports the F_1 and fairness values for all methods.

Demographic Parity. None of the competitors reduce DP below 0.20 on any dataset. Adversarial shows significant violations (e.g., 0.65 in Compas), indicating that it becomes less effective as the dimensionality of the sensitive attribute increases. Although ExpGrad and COSMOS achieve moderate improvements, with DP between 0.33 and 0.43, these remain well above the threshold. By contrast, FairLAB achieves the fairness objectives with bigger values for the performance budget β. In addition, with β, it offers tunable trade-offs. For $\beta = 0.05$, it attains

Table 2. Results 3-Ways Intersections. The F_1 column highlights in bold the best predictive performance, while the DP and EOD columns highlight in bold the values below the fairness threshold (0.20) and underline the lowest value.

Algorithm	FolkTables				Compas				MEPS			
	DP		EOD		DP		EOD		DP		EOD	
	F_1	DP	F_1	EOD	F_1	DP	F_1	EOD	F_1	DP	F_1	EOD
Vanilla	**0.77**	0.50	**0.77**	0.84	**0.69**	0.75	**0.69**	0.82	**0.81**	0.59	**0.81**	0.69
Adversarial	0.76	0.45	0.75	0.80	0.67	0.65	0.63	0.67	0.79	0.56	0.80	0.60
ExpGrad	0.74	0.36	0.66	0.50	0.60	0.43	0.60	0.71	0.79	0.36	0.78	0.56
COSMOS	0.71	0.33	0.75	0.67	0.61	0.42	0.67	0.73	0.80	0.43	0.80	0.53
FairLAB (0.05)	0.72	0.30	0.70	0.35	0.64	0.31	0.66	0.42	0.76	**0.20**	0.75	0.25
FairLAB (0.10)	0.68	**0.20**	0.68	0.31	0.62	0.25	0.60	0.34	0.75	**0.17**	0.73	**0.20**
FairLAB (0.15)	0.65	**0.17**	0.65	0.28	0.58	**0.19**	0.56	0.24	0.71	**0.18**	0.71	**0.18**

$DP \leq 0.20$ only in MEPS, implying that a minimal sacrifice in F_1 is sufficient there but not in FolkTables or Compas (where DP remains around 0.30). Increasing β to 0.10 narrows this gap, dropping DP to 0.20 in FolkTables at the cost of an F_1 reduction from 0.72 to 0.68. Achieving $DP \leq 0.20$ in Compas requires $\beta = 0.15$, which drives F_1 as low as 0.58. This highlights the *data-dependent* nature of intersectional fairness: some datasets (e.g. Compas) demand a larger performance budget to meet the tighter fairness constraint.

Equalized Odds. A similar pattern emerges for EOD. While ExpGrad and COSMOS exceed 0.50 in every scenario, FairLAB lowers EOD below 0.20 in MEPS with $\beta \geq$ 0.10. However, FairLAB still registers EOD values of 0.28 and 0.24 in FolkTables and Compas, respectively, suggesting that meeting intersectional EOD thresholds for all subgroups may require even higher budgets.

Performance Analysis. In all three datasets, the unconstrained model Vanilla achieves the highest F_1 scores (e.g., 0.77 in FolkTables and 0.69 in Compas), albeit with severe fairness violations. Methods like Adversarial, ExpGrad, and COSMOS typically retain F_1 close to Vanilla, but their debiasing effect is insufficient for three-attribute intersections. The pivotal element of FairLAB's performance is the parameter β, which balances accuracy and fairness, explaining why FairLAB with $\beta = 0.05$ can satisfy DP in MEPS but not in FolkTables or Compas: the latter datasets require more significant adjustments to model predictions to mitigate intersectional biases. For EOD, the same reasoning applies, further amplified by the metric's dependence on both true and false positive rates, which increases data fragmentation when three sensitive attributes intersect. Another factor is the *data distribution* within each intersectional subgroup. With three attributes, certain subgroups may contain relatively few samples, so applying EOD constraints forces the model to adapt its decision boundary more drastically. As β grows, FairLAB can impose these constraints more effectively, albeit with a noticeable drop in F_1.

Table 3. Results of Multiple Constraints, with DP. For F_1, the best performance is in bold, while for DP we highlight the values below the fairness threshold (0.20 for the intersectional and 0.10 for the single attribute) and underline the lowest value.

		Debiasing results on FolkTables						
Algorithm	F_1	$J*R*M$ DP	$J*R$ DP	$J*M$ DP	$R*M$ DP	Job DP	$Race$ DP	$Marital$ DP
Vanilla	**0.77**	0.50	0.39	0.38	0.36	0.18	0.21	0.22
COSMOS	0.73	0.36	0.34	0.23	0.27	0.09	0.15	0.18
FairLAB (0.05)	0.72	0.32	**0.20**	**0.16**	0.28	**0.04**	**0.12**	**0.15**
FairLAB (0.10)	0.67	**0.20**	**0.14**	**0.14**	**0.17**	**0.03**	**0.10**	**0.09**
FairLAB (0.15)	0.67	**0.19**	**0.17**	**0.20**	**0.18**	**0.02**	**0.08**	**0.09**

		Debiasing results on Compas						
Algorithm	F_1	$G*R*A$ DP	$G*R$ DP	$G*A$ DP	$R*A$ DP	$Gender$ DP	$Race$ DP	Age DP
Vanilla	**0.69**	0.75	0.49	0.62	0.56	0.31	0.24	0.39
COSMOS	0.66	0.46	0.33	0.27	0.34	0.13	0.20	0.14
FairLAB (0.05)	0.62	0.32	**0.17**	**0.20**	**0.20**	**0.09**	**0.08**	**0.07**
FairLAB (0.10)	0.60	0.27	**0.16**	**0.18**	**0.18**	**0.07**	**0.10**	**0.08**
FairLAB (0.15)	0.61	**0.23**	**0.16**	**0.14**	**0.18**	**0.07**	**0.07**	**0.05**

		Debiasing results on MEPS						
Algorithm	F_1	$G*R*M$ DP	$G*R$ DP	$G*M$ DP	$R*M$ DP	$Gender$ DP	$Race$ DP	$Marital$ DP
Vanilla	**0.81**	0.59	0.29	0.45	0.53	**0.09**	0.22	0.39
COSMOS	0.76	0.29	0.25	**0.15**	0.28	**0.01**	**0.09**	**0.10**
FairLAB (0.05)	0.76	**0.17**	**0.09**	**0.12**	**0.14**	**0.01**	**0.07**	**0.09**
FairLAB (0.10)	0.76	**0.17**	**0.12**	**0.10**	**0.17**	**0.02**	**0.09**	**0.06**
FairLAB (0.15)	0.75	**0.12**	**0.08**	**0.07**	**0.19**	**0.01**	**0.05**	**0.07**

6.3 Experiments with Mixed Constraints

We also evaluate FairLAB in a scenario where multiple intersectional fairness constraints are enforced *simultaneously*. Specifically, each dataset is subject to seven constraints which express all the possible intersectional attributes (combining two or three attributes) and the single sensitive attributes (e.g., *Gender*, *Race*). We set the threshold to 0.20 for the intersectional attributes and to 0.10 for the single ones. We compare FairLAB exclusively to COSMOS because it is the only method capable of handling multiple fairness constraints simultaneously[4].

Demographic Parity. Table 3 shows that FairLAB successfully meets all DP constraints on both FolkTables and MEPS. As already mentioned, the trade-off between fairness and accuracy depends on the performance budget β, which value varies across datasets to achieve the required fairness level. On FolkTables, reducing DP below 0.20 at the three-way attribute *JobRaceMarital* requires $\beta \geq 0.10$, which lowers F_1 from 0.77 to 0.67. In contrast, MEPS requires a lower β, with FairLAB satisfying every constraint at $\beta = 0.05$ while maintaining a good F_1 of 0.76. The behavior on Compas is more challenging, as FairLAB meets six out of seven constraints with β in $[0.10, 0.15]$, while *GenderRaceAge* remains slightly above 0.20. However, we consider this result acceptable, as the deviation

---
[4] Columns with ∗ are intersectional attributes, where initials indicate their features.

Table 4. Results of Multiple Constraints, with EOD. For F_1 we highlight the best performance, for EOD we report in bold the values below the fairness threshold (0.20 for intersectional and 0.10 for single attributes) and underline the lowest value.

Algorithm	F_1	$J*R*M$ EOD	$J*R$ EOD	$J*M$ EOD	$R*M$ EOD	Job EOD	$Race$ EOD	$Marital$ EOD
Debiasing results on FolkTables								
Vanilla	0.77	0.84	0.37	0.37	0.48	0.18	0.27	0.36
COSMOS	0.75	0.80	0.34	0.33	0.21	0.12	0.19	**0.09**
FairLAB (0.05)	0.73	0.38	0.24	**0.18**	**0.19**	0.18	0.12	**0.09**
FairLAB (0.10)	0.60	0.29	**0.20**	**0.20**	**0.19**	**0.08**	<u>**0.07**</u>	**0.08**
FairLAB (0.15)	0.59	<u>0.24</u>	**0.15**	**0.10**	**0.16**	**0.06**	0.10	<u>**0.03**</u>

Algorithm	F_1	$G*R*A$ EOD	$G*R$ EOD	$G*A$ EOD	$R*A$ EOD	$Gender$ EOD	$Race$ EOD	Age EOD
Debiasing results on Compas								
Vanilla	0.69	0.82	0.45	0.64	0.53	0.30	0.22	0.30
COSMOS	0.67	0.71	0.26	0.39	0.43	0.11	0.19	0.16
FairLAB (0.05)	0.63	0.35	0.27	**0.20**	0.25	0.14	**0.07**	0.12
FairLAB (0.10)	0.59	0.26	**0.18**	**0.15**	**0.16**	**0.07**	**0.05**	**0.09**
FairLAB (0.15)	0.54	<u>0.22</u>	**0.14**	**0.10**	**0.12**	**0.02**	<u>**0.01**</u>	**0.06**

Algorithm	F_1	$G*R*M$ EOD	$G*R$ EOD	$G*M$ EOD	$R*M$ EOD	$Gender$ EOD	$Race$ EOD	$Marital$ EOD
Debiasing results on MEPS								
Vanilla	0.81	0.69	0.34	0.57	0.62	**0.10**	0.25	0.49
COSMOS	0.69	<u>0.15</u>	**0.10**	0.12	**0.13**	**0.02**	**0.08**	**0.07**
FairLAB (0.05)	0.77	0.29	**0.20**	**0.18**	**0.20**	**0.07**	**0.09**	**0.09**
FairLAB (0.10)	0.70	**0.19**	<u>**0.07**</u>	**0.09**	**0.17**	**0.03**	**0.05**	**0.05**
FairLAB (0.15)	0.69	**0.20**	0.12	0.14	**0.19**	**0.05**	<u>**0.02**</u>	<u>**0.04**</u>

is minimal given that it is very close to the target and occurs in a highly complex setting where all other constraints are successfully satisfied. Regarding the competitor, COSMOS generally preserves higher F_1 scores but fails most intersectional constraints. On FolkTables, for instance, it surpasses 0.30 for $JobRaceMarital$, indicating difficulty in handling finer demographic partitions.

Equalized Odds. Table 4 confirms a similar pattern when EOD constraints are imposed. FairLAB once again reduces the three-way attribute well below the unconstrained baseline in FolkTables and Compas, but cannot always push EOD under 0.20 for every subgroup, even at higher performance budgets (e.g., 0.24 on FolkTables and 0.22 on Compas). Nevertheless, these values are quite close to the target and represent notable improvements over COSMOS, which reaches 0.70 or 0.80 on the same intersectional group. On MEPS, FairLAB achieves or nears the threshold in all subgroups when $\beta \geq 0.10$. COSMOS exhibits partial success, meeting some constraints on MEPS's single attributes more easily, yet it remains less effective for the higher-dimensional partitions.

Performance Analysis. As observed in Sects. 6.1 and 6.2, the parameter β in FairLAB governs the balance between fairness and accuracy. Larger budgets allow the model to target smaller DP/EOD values but can reduce F_1 by up to 10–15 points relative to the unconstrained baseline Vanilla. On FolkTables, for instance, lowering EOD to around 0.24 at $JobRaceMarital$ requires $\beta = 0.15$,

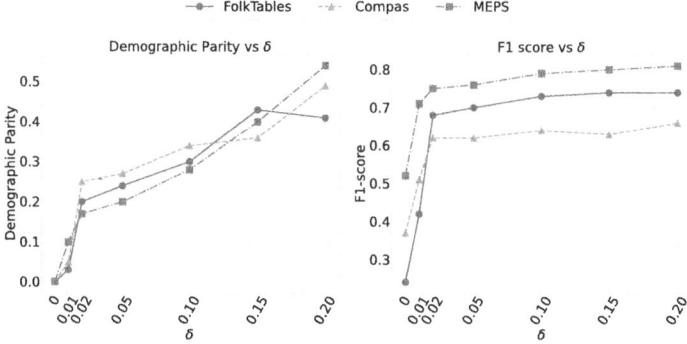

Fig. 2. Impact of the proximity parameter δ on the fairness and F_1 of the final model.

which yields an F_1 of 0.59 compared to 0.77 for Vanilla. However, COSMOS, while retaining a higher F_1, remains above 0.70 in EOD for the same attribute, indicating that the debiasing strategy is not working. On MEPS, FairLAB faces a more moderate trade-off and meets nearly all constraints with β as low as 0.05 or 0.10, incurring only a slight drop in F_1. Overall, these experiments demonstrate that meeting multiple constraints—especially at the intersectional level—can demand a significant performance budget in some datasets, but FairLAB consistently outperforms COSMOS in reducing unfairness across diverse subgroup partitions.

6.4 Impact of the Proximity Parameter

We also investigate how the *proximity threshold* δ influences the final model learned under the three-attribute scenario discussed in Sect. 6.2. By design, δ dictates how closely the new model must mimic the orchestrator's conditional distributions on specified subgroups, effectively limiting how much the updated model's predictions can deviate. We vary δ and record the resulting DP and F_1 scores, keeping the performance budget fixed at $\beta = 0.05$.

Figure 2 illustrates that increasing δ grants more freedom for the updated model to diverge from the orchestrator, yielding higher F_1 but at the expense of fairness. When δ becomes large, the new model no longer inherits the orchestrator's fairness properties from previous iterations and instead optimizes primarily for learner constraints. Consequently, once $\delta \geq 0.05$, DP surpasses the 0.20 threshold in FolkTables, Compas, and MEPS, indicating that intersectional fairness can no longer be maintained. In contrast, with smaller values (e.g., $\delta = 0.01$ or 0.02), the updated model remains sufficiently close to the orchestrator's distribution, keeping DP below 0.20 without incurring a pronounced performance penalty. This trade-off underscores the importance of calibrating δ to preserve the orchestrator's fairness characteristics while allowing for potential improvements in F_1.

Table 5. Average training times in: (1) INT2 (2-Ways Intersections) (2) INT3 (3-Ways Intersections) (3) MIXED (Multiple Constraints).

Algorithm	FolkTables			Compas			MEPS		
	INT2	INT3	MIXED	INT2	INT3	MIXED	INT2	INT3	MIXED
Vanilla	30.3 min	30.3 min	30.3 min	3.5 min	3.5 min	3.5 min	27.2 min	27.2 min	27.2 min
Adversarial	3.7 h	2 day	-	1.2 h	3.5 h	-	5.2 h	1.1 day	-
ExpGrad	20.8 min	1.2 h	-	5.4 min	7.1 min	-	14.6 min	40.3 min	-
COSMOS	10.7 h	2.2 day	4.5 day	3.3 h	1.5 day	2.8 day	13.4 h	1.7 day	3.9 day
FairLAB (0.05)	1.3 h	2.4 h	2.7 h	6.3 min	9.7 min	12.1 min	30.8 min	45.2 min	48.9 min

6.5 Runtime Analysis

We assess the scalability of FairLAB by measuring its training times in the experimental settings in Sect. 6.1, 6.2, and 6.3. Each setting involves an increasing number of fairness constraints and/or more complex intersectional attributes, allowing us to observe how computational costs scale with the problem complexity. Table 5 shows that FairLAB balances efficiency and fairness constraints, maintaining moderate training times even in complex settings. Compared to COSMOS, it achieves faster convergence, while ExpGrad, though faster, often fails to meet fairness requirements. Adversarial remains feasible in simpler cases but becomes impractical for larger-scale constraints. Overall, FairLAB offers a good trade-off between runtime and debiasing performance, making it suitable for real-world applications.

7 Conclusions

We introduced FairLAB, a method for training fair and high-performing NN under both group and intersectional fairness constraints, exploiting ALM. With the *performance budget*, we provide explicit control to the trade-off between fairness and performance, making FairLAB adaptive. It is also scalable thanks to a divide-et-impera strategy for decomposing the fairness problem, particularly when multiple sensitive attributes interact. Experimental results show that FairLAB mitigates bias across challenging real-world scenarios, where multiple fairness constraints, must be satisfied simultaneously. Also, our empirical evaluation shows that FairLAB outperforms state-of-the-art fairness mitigation methods, striking a balance between fairness and performance, even in high-dimensional settings. These results highlight the applicability of FairLAB for fairness-aware real-world applications. As future work, we plan to extend it to decentralized learning scenarios, such as Federated Learning [8,12], with the challenge of ensuring fairness across distributed nodes, while preserving user privacy and model performance.

Acknowledgments. This research was partially supported by: SoBigData.it – "Strengthening the Italian RI for Social Mining and Big Data Analytics" – Prot. IR0000013 - Avviso n. 3264 del 28/12/2021; Partenariato Esteso PE00000013 - "FAIR - Future Artificial Intelligence Research" - Spoke 1 "Human-centered AI"; The European

Union's Horizon Europe research and innovation programme for the project FINDHR (g.a. No. 101070212); The European Union Horizon 2020 program under grant agreement No. 101120763 *TANGO* and No. 101070416 *GREEN.DAT.AI*; Views and opinions expressed are however those of the author(s) only and do not necessarily reflect those of the European Union or the European Health and Digital Executive Agency (HaDEA). Neither the European Union nor the granting authority can be held responsible for them.

Disclosure of Interests. The authors have no competing interests to declare that are relevant to the content of this article.

References

1. Agarwal, A., Beygelzimer, A., Dudík, M., Langford, J., Wallach, H.M.: A reductions approach to fair classification. In: ICML, vol. 80, pp. 60–69. PMLR (2018)
2. Calders, T., Kamiran, F., Pechenizkiy, M.: Building classifiers with independency constraints. In: ICDM Workshops, pp. 13–18. IEEE Computer Society (2009)
3. Caton, S., Haas, C.: Fairness in machine learning: a survey. ACM Comput. Surv. **56**(7), 166:1–166:38 (2024)
4. Celis, L.E., Huang, L., Keswani, V., Vishnoi, N.K.: Classification with fairness constraints: a meta-algorithm with provable guarantees. In: FAT (2019)
5. Cotter, A., Jiang, H., Sridharan, K.: Two-player games for efficient non-convex constrained optimization. In: Algorithmic Learning Theory, pp. 300–332 (2019)
6. Creager, E., et al.: Flexibly fair representation learning by disentanglement. In: ICML (2019)
7. Désidéri, J.A.: Multiple-gradient descent algorithm (MGDA) for multiobjective optimization. C.R. Math. **350**(5–6), 313–318 (2012)
8. Fontana, M., Naretto, F., Monreale, A.: A new approach for cross-silo federated learning and its privacy risks. In: 18th International Conference on Privacy, Security and Trust, PST 2021, Auckland, New Zealand, 13–15 December 2021, pp. 1–10. IEEE (2021). https://doi.org/10.1109/PST52912.2021.9647753
9. Fortin, M., Glowinski, R.: Augmented Lagrangian Methods: Applications to the Numerical Solution of Boundary-Value Problems, vol. 15. Elsevier (2000)
10. Foulds, J.R., Islam, R., Keya, K.N., Pan, S.: An intersectional definition of fairness. In: ICDE, pp. 1918–1921 (2020)
11. Gohar, U., Cheng, L.: A survey on intersectional fairness in machine learning: notions, mitigation, and challenges. arXiv preprint arXiv:2305.06969 (2023)
12. Haffar, R., Naretto, F., Sánchez, D., Monreale, A., Domingo-Ferrer, J.: GLORFLEX: local to global rule-based explanations for federated learning. In: 2024 IEEE International Conference on Fuzzy Systems (FUZZ-IEEE), pp. 1–9 (2024). https://doi.org/10.1109/FUZZ-IEEE60900.2024.10611878
13. Hardt, M., Price, E., Srebro, N.: Equality of opportunity in supervised learning. In: NIPS, pp. 3315–3323 (2016)
14. Kamishima, T., Akaho, S., Sakuma, J.: Fairness-aware learning through regularization approach. In: Data Mining Workshops (ICDMW) (2011)
15. Kearns, M., Neel, S., Roth, A., Wu, Z.S.: Preventing fairness gerrymandering: auditing and learning for subgroup fairness. In: ICML, pp. 2564–2572 (2018)
16. Kim, M., Reingold, O., Rothblum, G.: Fairness through computationally-bounded awareness. Adv. Neural Inf. Process. Syst. **31** (2018)

17. Lokhande, V.S., Akash, A.K., Ravi, S.N., Singh, V.: FairALM: augmented Lagrangian method for training fair models with little regret. In: Vedaldi, A., Bischof, H., Brox, T., Frahm, J.-M. (eds.) ECCV 2020. LNCS, vol. 12357, pp. 365–381. Springer, Cham (2020). https://doi.org/10.1007/978-3-030-58610-2_22
18. Lu, S., et al.: A stochastic linearized augmented Lagrangian method for decentralized bilevel optimization. NeurIPS **35**, 30638–30650 (2022)
19. Martinez, N.L., Bertran, M.A., Papadaki, A., Rodrigues, M., Sapiro, G.: Blind pareto fairness and subgroup robustness. In: International Conference on Machine Learning, pp. 7492–7501. PMLR (2021)
20. Naretto, F., Monreale, A., Giannotti, F.: Evaluating the privacy exposure of interpretable global explainers. In: 2022 IEEE 4th International Conference on Cognitive Machine Intelligence (CogMI), pp. 13–19 (2022). https://doi.org/10.1109/CogMI56440.2022.00012
21. Naretto, F., Pellungrini, R., Fadda, D., Rinzivillo, S.: EXPHLOT: explainable privacy assessment for human location trajectories. In: Discovery Science. DS 2023. LNCS. Springer, Cham (2023). https://doi.org/10.1007/978-3-031-45275-8_22
22. Naretto, F., Pellungrini, R., Monreale, A., Nardini, F.M., Musolesi, M.: Predicting and explaining privacy risk exposure in mobility data. In: Appice, A., Tsoumakas, G., Manolopoulos, Y., Matwin, S. (eds.) DS 2020. LNCS (LNAI), vol. 12323, pp. 403–418. Springer, Cham (2020). https://doi.org/10.1007/978-3-030-61527-7_27
23. Peters, B., Niculae, V., Martins, A.F.: Sparse sequence-to-sequence models. In: Proceedings of the ACL (2019)
24. Ruchte, M., Grabocka, J.: Scalable pareto front approximation for deep multi-objective learning. In: ICDM, pp. 1306–1311 (2021)
25. Villani, C.: The Wasserstein Distances, pp. 93–111. Springer, Heidelberg (2009)
26. Yu, G., Ma, L., Wang, X., Du, W., Du, W., Jin, Y.: Towards fairness-aware multi-objective optimization. Complex Intell. Syst. **11**(1), 50 (2025)
27. Zhang, B.H., Lemoine, B., Mitchell, M.: Mitigating unwanted biases with adversarial learning. In: AAAI/ACM Conference on AI, Ethics, and Society (2018)
28. Zhang, Q., Liu, J., Yao, X.: Fairness-aware multiobjective evolutionary learning. IEEE Trans. Evol. Comput. (2024)

Open Access This chapter is licensed under the terms of the Creative Commons Attribution 4.0 International License (http://creativecommons.org/licenses/by/4.0/), which permits use, sharing, adaptation, distribution and reproduction in any medium or format, as long as you give appropriate credit to the original author(s) and the source, provide a link to the Creative Commons license and indicate if changes were made.

The images or other third party material in this chapter are included in the chapter's Creative Commons license, unless indicated otherwise in a credit line to the material. If material is not included in the chapter's Creative Commons license and your intended use is not permitted by statutory regulation or exceeds the permitted use, you will need to obtain permission directly from the copyright holder.

Better Features, Better Calibration: A Simple Fix for Overconfident Networks

Soumya Suvra Ghosal[1]([✉]), Ramya Hebbalaguppe[2], and Dinesh Manocha[2]

[1] University of Maryland, College Park, USA
sghosal@umd.edu
[2] TCS Research Labs, Chennai, India

Abstract. A model is considered perfectly calibrated when the predicted probabilities align accurately with the true likelihood of the associated classes being correct. Past studies have shown that Deep Neural Networks (DNNs) are susceptible to overfitting and generate miscalibrated predictions. In this paper, we identify that the miscalibration problem in DNNs can be traced back to the features learned by the network. To this end, we propose a new training approach called RelCal, which guides the model to focus on a subset of relevant features for each class. Our empirical analysis highlights that training with RelCal helps mitigate overconfidence in DNNs, leading to better-calibrated models in terms of Expected Calibration Error (ECE) and Adaptive Expected Calibration Error (AECE). We demonstrate the state-of-the-art results on a diverse range of 8 image classification datasets across architectures spanning CNNs to Transformer-based architectures in terms of network calibration without compromising discriminative performance. Compared to the current best calibration technique, RankMixup [32], RelCal reduces the ECE by 4.25% on the challenging imbalanced dataset CIFAR-100-LT. Additionally, on the large-scale ImageNet dataset, RelCal reduces the AECE from 9.45% to 3.08%— a 6.37% improvement over the baseline model trained with NLL loss.

Keywords: Confidence Calibration · Reliability · Uncertainty Quantification

1 Introduction

DNNs excel in tasks like object detection, classification, and segmentation but often produce miscalibrated, overconfident predictions. However, despite achieving impressive classification accuracy, they often produce miscalibrated and overconfident predictions [11,28,29]. Analysis by [11] revealed that due to large model

Supplementary Information The online version contains supplementary material available at https://doi.org/10.1007/978-3-032-05962-8_14.

capacity, neural networks typically become prone to overfitting the negative log-likelihood (NLL) loss during training, thereby essentially prioritizing higher accuracy at the expense of well-calibrated predictions.

The primary issue with miscalibrated predictions lies in providing a false sense of correctness, i.e., the prediction probability associated with a given class may overestimate the likelihood of the class being correct. This issue carries significant implications, especially in safety-critical domains like autonomous driving [10] and healthcare applications [8], where the model must not only be accurate but also correctly confident [11] (Fig. 1).

There have been numerous efforts to tackle the problem. [11] proposed Temperature Scaling, i.e., dividing the logit outputs by a scalar temperature constant $T > 0$ before performing the softmax operation. Other than temperature scaling, various post-hoc techniques [30,35,43] have been introduced to improve calibration during inference. To mitigate model overfitting and miscalibration, [29] suggested training with label-smoothing, and [28] proposed training with focal loss [26]. Recently, [15] argued that in contrast to post-hoc calibration methods that rely on a small set of parameters, train-time strategies leveraging the extensive array of learnable parameters within a DNN offer stronger calibration performance. While many studies propose new training losses for better calibration, we trace miscalibration to the features learned by the model and refine them during training for improved calibration.

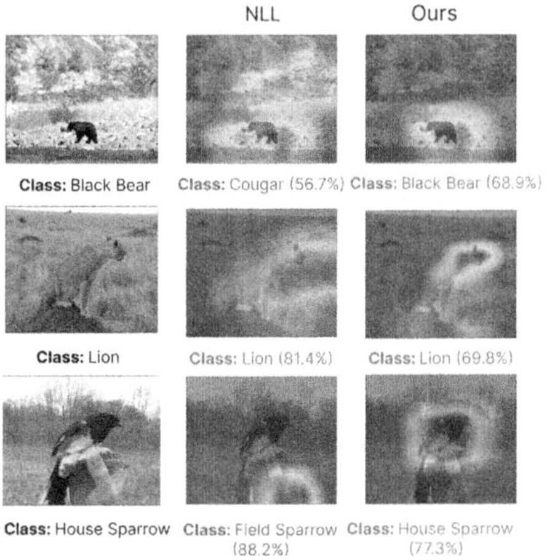

Fig. 1. We illustrate via Grad-CAM visualizations for `ResNet-50` feature extractor trained on `ImageNet` with and without using `RelCal`. Notice that training with `RelCal` allows the network to focus on relevant features of the category enabling better discrimination.

When processing an input image, DNNs typically learn a feature representation which is then passed through a dense linear layer to generate the logit output. Intuitively, each dimension within these feature embeddings can be associated to represent some semantic attribute present in the image [17,24]. Using a dense layer means that the prediction for a particular class is influenced by contributions from all feature dimensions. Our approach is based on the idea that not all feature dimensions carry equal significance for a particular class. Our approach prioritizes class-relevant features—for example, whiskers and fur matter for "Cat" class but not for "Snake" class.

Main Contributions. Building on this rationale, we propose RelCal, a simple and novel approach centered on training a model to prioritize a subset of features that are crucial for each class. To pinpoint critical features for a specific class, we introduce a **relevance score**, computed as the absolute value of the feature dimension's contribution to that class. Our analysis (see Sect. 4) suggests that RelCal introduces an implicit regularization on the model weights, thereby reducing the weight norm. Additionally, we noted that training with RelCal demonstrated an increase in NLL loss on accurately classified test samples (see Fig. 2), indicating decreased output confidence. Therefore, based on our observations, we infer that RelCal enhances model calibration by imposing regularization on the network weights, consequently mitigating overconfident predictions. These findings align with the analysis in [28] which identified increase in weight norm as a contributing factor to miscalibration. Further, our observations also highlight that training with RelCal not only enhances calibration but also improves test accuracy.

1. **A simple and novel approach, RelCal for improving model calibration.** During training, RelCal aims to alleviate overfitting by guiding the model to focus on a subset of relevant features that are crucial for each class. Training with RelCal leads to reduction in norm of model weights and prediction confidence thereby improving model calibration.
2. **We highlight the strong calibration performance of RelCal:** (a) on 5 standard image classification benchmarks (SVHN, CIFAR-10, CIFAR-100, TinyImageNet-200, and ImageNet-1k), (b) two imbalanced datasets (CIFAR-10-LT, and CIFAR-100-LT), (c) one fine-grained image classification dataset (CUB-200), and (d) one NLP dataset (20 Newsgroups). For example, on CUB-200 [42], a fine-grained image classification dataset, using ResNet-101 architecture, our approach reduces the Expected Calibration Error from 8.41% to 2.99%—a **5.42%** of improvement compared to focal loss [28].
3. **RelCal is architecture agnostic.** We conduct extensive experimentation using models of varying capacities from ResNet [14] (see Table 6), WideResNet [44] (see Table 7) and Vision Transformer (see Appendix) architectures. Our findings demonstrate that RelCal significantly improves model calibration regardless of the architectural choice.

2 Related Works

Calibration Techniques. In deep neural networks (DNNs), the issue of miscalibration was first brought to light by [11]. Their analysis unveiled that DNN models trained with NLL loss tend to exhibit unwarranted overconfidence, leading to a discrepancy between output confidence and actual accuracy. The severity of this issue has sparked considerable research into mitigating this problem. Broadly, approaches to calibrate DNNs can be categorized into two main strategies: train-time calibration and posthoc calibration.

Train-time Calibration approaches introduce additional loss terms/regularization during the training process to enhance model calibration. [34] proposed adding additional entropy loss; [21] proposed MMCE, an auxiliary loss term computed using a reproducing kernel in a Hilbert space; [29] used Label Smoothing (LS) on soft targets; [28] showed that using Focal loss (FL) [26] can be beneficial in preventing the model from becoming overconfident. [15] proposed training with an additional MDCA loss to explicitly minimize the difference in confidence and accuracy for all the classes. Other representative works are MbLS, MixUp, Confidence Ranking Calibration, ACLS [4,27–29,33,45]. Our approach on the contrary utilizes a relevance score for confidence calibration.

Post-hoc Calibration methods operate on models after they have been trained, typically utilizing a validation set. A widely-used post-hoc calibration technique is Temperature Scaling [11], which involves the division of logit outputs by a scalar temperature constant $T > 0$ before applying the softmax operation. Apart from temperature scaling, several other post-hoc approaches [30,35,43] have been proposed that transform the model output during inference to improve calibration. Dirichlet calibration [19] builds on Dirichlet distributions and extends the Beta-calibration [20] approach, which was originally designed for binary classification, to a multi-class setting. Posthoc calibration assumes the availability of a validation dataset to tune the hyperparameters on the test set and may not generalize well incase of distribution drift.

Pruning Approaches. Extensive research explores training-time pruning to enhance DNN sparsity [2,12,13,39]. The closest methods to our proposed approach include ReAct [40], DICE [41], LINe [1], and ASH [6] which explore *test-time* sparsification mechanism for OOD detection, lacking explicit learning of crucial features. RelCal differs from these studies as it serves as a *training-time* regularization technique focusing on learning relevant features to enhance model calibration.

3 Background

Notations. In this paper, we consider a supervised multi-class classification problem. Formally, we consider a training set $\mathcal{D}_{\text{train}}$ consisting of N training samples: $\{\mathbf{x}_i, y_i\}_{i=1}^N$. The samples are drawn *i.i.d.* from a probability distribution: $\mathcal{P}_{\mathcal{X},\mathcal{Y}}$. Here, $\mathbf{x} \in \mathcal{X}$ is a random variable defined in the image space, and $y \in \mathcal{Y} = \{1,\ldots,K\}$ represents its label. Traditionally, a parameterized model $f_\theta : \mathcal{X} \to \mathcal{Y}$ is trained on samples drawn from the marginal distribution $\mathcal{P}_{\text{in}}$ of $\mathcal{X}$. The standard aim is to minimize the expected loss $\mathbb{E}_{(\mathbf{x},y)\sim\mathcal{P}}[l(f_\theta(\mathbf{x}), y)]$ under the training distribution $\mathcal{P}$, for some loss function $l : \mathcal{Y} \times \mathcal{Y} \to \mathbb{R}_+$.

Calibration. Consider a sample $\mathbf{x} \in \mathcal{X}$ input to a classifier f_θ parameterized by θ. The logit output of the classifier is represented as $\mathbf{f}(\mathbf{x}, \theta) \in \mathbb{R}^K$. The confidence probabilities $\mathbf{p} \in \mathbb{R}^K$ are typically obtained by applying a softmax operation to the logit vector $\mathbf{f}(\mathbf{x}, \theta)$. Let $\hat{y} = \arg\max_{k\in\mathcal{Y}} \mathbf{f}(\mathbf{x}, \theta)[k]$ represent the class predicted by f. Correspondingly, the confidence for the predicted class is computed as $\hat{p} = \mathbf{p}[\hat{y}]$. A model is defined as perfectly calibrated [11] when:

$$\mathbb{P}\left(\hat{y}_i = y_i \mid \hat{p}_i = p_i\right) = p_i, \quad \forall p_i \in (0,1) \tag{1}$$

Intuitively, if a perfectly calibrated classifier predicts an output with confidence $\hat{p} = 0.8$, then the prediction is accurate 80% of time. The model is over-confident if the prediction accuracy is less than 80% and is under-confident if the prediction accuracy is more than 80%.

4 Our Approach: RelCal

Our proposed training approach is designed to enhance the model's focus on relevant features crucial for each class. To identify these important feature dimensions, we first define the notion of *relevance* (see Sect. 4.1). Next, given an input image, we select a subset of features by thresholding the calculated feature-wise relevance score. In what follows, we provide an in-depth overview of our proposed approach RelCal.

4.1 Learning the Relevant Features

For feature extraction, we consider a deep neural network f_θ parameterized by θ. Given an input $\mathbf{x} \in \mathcal{X}$, let $\mathbf{h}(\mathbf{x}) \in \mathbb{R}^L$ represent the features extracted from the penultimate layer of the model. The final output $\mathbf{f}(\mathbf{x})$ is obtained by passing $\mathbf{h}(\mathbf{x})$ through a dense linear layer with weight matrix $\mathbf{W} \in \mathbb{R}^{L \times K}$:

$$\mathbf{f}(\mathbf{x}, \theta) = \mathbf{W}^T \mathbf{h}(\mathbf{x}) + \mathbf{b} \tag{2}$$

where $\mathbf{b} \in \mathbb{R}^K$ is the bias vector. Typically, the penultimate layer embeddings $\mathbf{h}(\mathbf{x})$ serve as a proxy for the features learned by a neural net [38]. Hence, we calculate the feature-wise relevance score based on penultimate embeddings $\mathbf{h}(\mathbf{x})$.
Relevance Score. Our main idea is to define a notion of relevance for each feature dimension in $\mathbf{h}(\mathbf{x}) = [h^{(1)}, h^{(2)}, ..., h^{(L)}]$. This is primarily motivated by the observation that the classification of a specific example is dependent on a subset of pertinent attributes. Further, the significance of a particular feature dimension can fluctuate across various classes and instances. Revisiting the "Cat" vs "Snake" example, attributes like whiskers and fur hold significance for a "Cat" image, but may not be relevant for an image from the "Snake" class. To formulate the notion of significance between a feature dimension $h^{(l)}$, where $l \in \{1, \cdots, L\}$, and a class $c \in \{1, \cdots, K\}$, an intuitive relevance score can be defined as:

$$r(h^{(l)}, c) = |h^{(l)} \mathbf{W}_{l,c}|, \tag{3}$$

where $\mathbf{W}_{l,c}$ represents the weight connecting the feature dimension $h^{(l)}$ & the c-th class, and $|\cdot|$ is the absolute value operator. The term $h^{(l)} \mathbf{W}_{l,c}$ essentially quantifies the contribution of the feature $h^{(l)}$ to the c-th class. Finally, based on Eq. 3, we construct a relevance matrix $\mathbf{R} \in \mathbb{R}^{L \times K}$ such that $\mathbf{R}[i,j] = r(h^{(i)}, j) \; \forall \; i \in \{1, \cdots, L\}, j \in \{1, \cdots, K\}$.
Mask Matrix. Given a feature dimension $h^{(l)}$, its contribution for each class can be measured using the relevance score $r(h^{(l)}, \cdot)$. Based on these scores, we can

identify the classes for which $h^{(l)}$ is significant by thresholding on the calculated relevance scores. Specifically, for each feature dimension $h^{(l)}$ we generate a mask vector $\mathbf{m}^{(l)} \in \{0,1\}^K$ in which each element is 0/1 and is defined as:

$$\mathbf{m}^{(l)}[j] = \begin{cases} 1 & \text{if } r(h^{(l)}, j) \geq \delta^{(l)} \\ 0 & \text{if } r(h^{(l)}, j) < \delta^{(l)} \end{cases} \forall j \in \{1, \cdots, K\}, \quad (4)$$

where, $\delta^{(l)}$ represents the threshold constant for the feature dimension $h^{(l)}$. To modulate the threshold, we define a pruning percentile p. Specifically, the threshold $\delta^{(l)}$ is set as the p-th percentile of the scores in the vector $\mathbf{R}[l,:]$. Next, we define the mask matrix $\mathbf{M} \in \mathbb{R}^{L \times K}$ as: $\mathbf{M} = [\mathbf{m}^{(1)}; \mathbf{m}^{(2)}; \cdots ; \mathbf{m}^{(L)}]$.

4.2 Training

During training, given an input sample $\mathbf{x}$, we use the mask matrix to prune out any insignificant connection between a feature dimension and class. Specifically, after pruning, the logit output for the c-th class is given by:

$$\mathbf{f}_{\text{rel}}(\mathbf{x}, \theta)[c] = \sum_{l=1}^{L} (\mathbf{R} \odot \mathbf{M})^\top [c, l] + \mathbf{b}[c] , \quad (5)$$

where, $\odot$ indicates the Hadamard product. Note that, our formulation also flexibly allows each feature dimension to be used for multiple class predictions. As an example, a class "Laptop" might depend on the two most relevant feature dimensions: keyboard and screen. Similarly, the class prediction for "TV" might rely on two features telecontrol and screen. In both cases, the feature of screen is responsible for the classes "TV" and "Laptop". Finally, our training objective takes the form:

$$\min_{\theta} \mathbb{E}_{(\mathbf{x},y) \sim \mathcal{P}_{\mathcal{X}\mathcal{Y}}} \left[\mathcal{L} \left(\mathbf{f}_{\text{rel}}(\mathbf{x}; \theta), y \right) \right], \quad (6)$$

where $\mathcal{L}$ is any standard classification loss.

In Appendix, we provide a detailed algorithmic description and PyTorch-based pseudocode of our proposed method. Further, in Sect. 4.3, we show that training RelCal does not lead to any additional computational overhead. The complete code will be made available following paper's acceptance.

Understanding Why RelCal Improves Calibration. Existing studies [11, 28] have shown that a significant factor contributing to miscalibration lies in the tendency to overfit the training loss, leading to overconfident yet incorrect predictions. Furthermore, [28] have also pinpointed that the increase in logit magnitudes can be linked to an increase in the norm of the model weights $\|\mathbf{W}\|$. To understand, how RelCal improves model calibration, in Fig. 2 we visualize the evolution of different metrics during training the model.

1. **RelCal reduces overconfident predictions.** In Fig. 2(a), we compare the test NLL loss for the correctly classified samples throughout training for models trained with and without RelCal. We observe that the loss for the RelCal

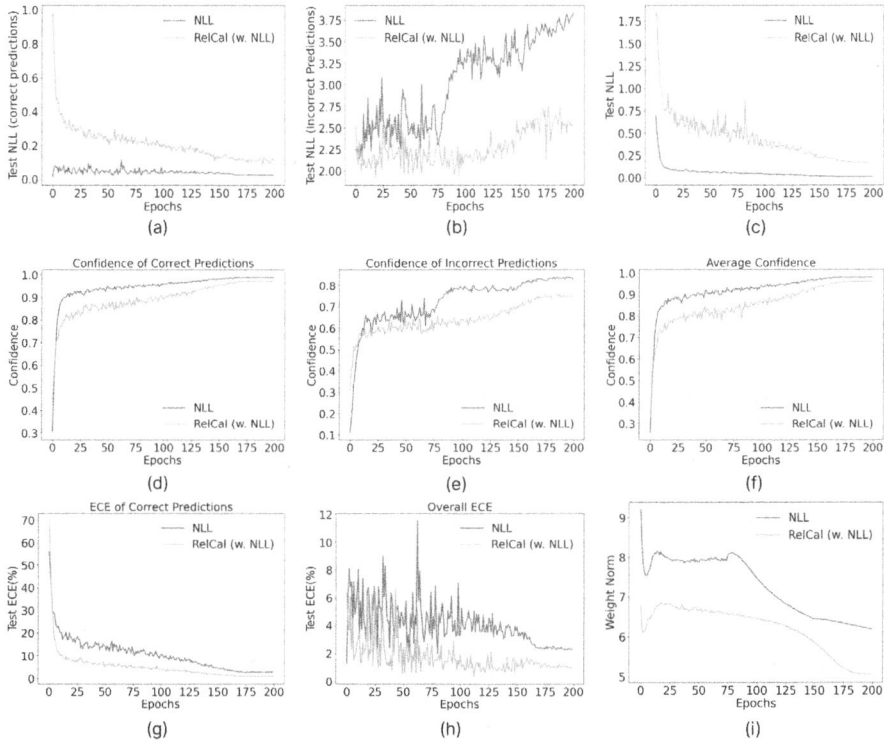

Fig. 2. We visualize ResNet-50's performance metrics on CIFAR-10 across training epochs.

trained model remains consistently higher, indicating relatively lower confidence in correctly predicted samples. This observation is further corroborated by Fig. 2(d), where we track the confidence of correctly predicted test samples. It is noteworthy that although RelCal reduces confidence in predictions, there is an enhancement in test accuracy (see Table 3). Additionally, Fig. 2(b) illustrates that the RelCal-trained model demonstrates a lower NLL loss for the misclassified samples. This indicates that for incorrect predictions, RelCal (w. NLL) generates relatively higher confidence for the correct class compared to the NLL-trained model, consequently resulting in: (a) reduced test NLL and, (b) decreased confidence for the misclassified class. This observation is also further verified in Fig. 2(e).

2. **RelCal acts as weight regularizer.** Recall that the relevance matrix is defined as $\mathbf{R}[i,j] = r(h^{(i)}, j) = |h^{(i)}\mathbf{W}_{i,j}|$. Let $\mathbf{H} \in \mathbb{R}^{L \times L} = \text{diag}(h^{(1)}, h^{(2)}, \cdots, h^{(L)})$, be a diagonal matrix with the entries set as the feature embeddings. Then, the relevance matrix can be expressed as $\mathbf{R} = |\mathbf{HW}| = |\mathbf{H}||\mathbf{W}|$, where $|\cdot|$ represents the absolute value of the elements of the matrix and $\mathbf{W} \in \mathbb{R}^{L \times K}$ is the weight of the last linear layer. Based on this formulation, the logit output for the c-th class can also be written as:

$$\mathbf{f}_{\text{rel}}(\mathbf{x}, \theta)[c] = \sum_{l=1}^{L} (\mathbf{R} \odot \mathbf{M})^{\top}[c, l] + \mathbf{b}[c], \quad (7)$$

$$= \sum_{l=1}^{L} (|\mathbf{H}||\mathbf{W}| \odot \mathbf{M})^{\top}[c, l] + \mathbf{b}[c], \quad (8)$$

$$= \sum_{l=1}^{L} ((|\mathbf{W}| \odot \mathbf{M})^{\top}|\mathbf{H}|)[c, l] + \mathbf{b}[c], \quad (9)$$

$$= \sum_{l=1}^{L} (\mathbf{W}_{\text{rel}}^{\top}|\mathbf{H}|)[c, l] + \mathbf{b}[c], \text{ where } \mathbf{W}_{\text{rel}} = |\mathbf{W}| \odot \mathbf{M} \quad (10)$$

From Eq. 2, model output based on standard training objective without RelCal can be written as:

$$\mathbf{f}(\mathbf{x}, \theta)[c] = \sum_{l=1}^{L} (\mathbf{W}^{\top} \mathbf{H})[c, l] + \mathbf{b}[c] \quad (11)$$

Comparing Eqs. 10 and 11, we observe that training with RelCal provides an additional implicit regularization on the network weight $\mathbf{W}$. This observation is further supported by Fig. 2(i), where we plot the norm of the weight matrix $\|\mathbf{W}\|$ across different training epochs. We see that the weight norm of the RelCal-trained model is always lower than the model trained using only NLL loss, further indicating that RelCal effectively regularizes the model weights.

4.3 Exploring the Properties of RelCal

In this section, we provide a comprehensive understanding of the advantages offered by RelCal as well as explore its properties.

RelCal Focuses on Relevant Cues. The core idea of our method is that learning class-relevant features can address the issue of overly confident predictions, leading to enhancement in model calibration. To examine our hypothesis, we analyse GradCAM [37] visualizations of few representative bird images from CUB-200-2011 [42] dataset in Fig. 4(b). To ensure a fair comparison, both models are trained using NLL loss. Our observations indicate that the model trained with RelCal exhibits a more precise focus on semantic attributes critical for accurate classification. For instance, the image of the "Winged Gull" in the last row has been misclassified by both models. However, it is noteworthy that the class predicted by the RelCal-trained model is much more relevant compared to the other model. Specifically, RelCal predicts the image as a "California Gull" which is closely related to the original image, whereas the other model outputs the class label as "Least Auklet" which is entirely unrelated to a Gull. This conclusion is further supported by the saliency maps, highlighting the enhanced discriminative capability of the RelCal-trained model.

RelCal Reduces Misclassification Confidence. Figure 3 shows distribution plots of confidence scores for correct and incorrect predictions made by a ResNet-50 model on the CIFAR-10 and CIFAR-10-LT dataset trained with and without

RelCal. The results highlight that RelCal significantly reduces the average confidence level of incorrect predictions. This indicates that RelCal not only results in a more calibrated model but also provides a more realistic confidence measure for each prediction, particularly misclassification. To further corroborate the observation in Fig. 3, we validate our findings through an analysis in Fig. 4(a).

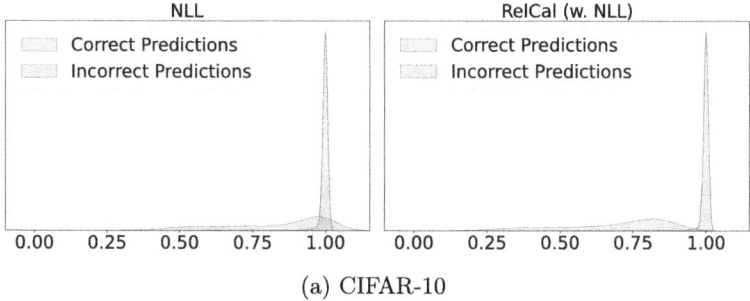

(a) CIFAR-10

Fig. 3. Confidence score distribution for correct and misclassified predictions on CIFAR-10.

RelCal is Model Agnostic. To assess the model-agnostic nature of RelCal, we conducted experiments employing different ResNet architectures with varying capacities, ranging from 11.2M to 42.5M parameters. Specifically, we trained two models for each architecture—one using standard technique and other using RelCal. For training both models, we used focal loss [28]. The experimental results are presented in Table 6. We observe that training with RelCal consistently enhances model calibration, irrespective of the underlying model architecture. In Appendix, we provide further analysis utilizing other standard architectures such as WideResNet [44], and Vision Transformers [7].

Analysis on Relevant Feature Selection. A key aspect of our algorithm is the strategic selection of the most relevant features for class predictions. In particular, the features are chosen based on the dimensions that contributed most to the class's output. In this analysis, we contrast our feature selection mechanism with a random feature selection method that depends on a stochastic process for randomly selecting elements within the feature vector. We report results of this analysis in Table 1. Empirical results highlight that randomly choosing feature dimensions is suboptimal for model calibration.

Table 1. Analysis on relevant feature selection. We compare different strategies for selecting the relevant features. All models are trained using focal loss [28]. Best performing results are marked in **bold**. Model is ResNet-50 and the dataset is CIFAR-100.

Method	ECE ↓	AECE ↓
Random features	8.74	8.97
Features with least relevance	11.73	12.90
RelCal (w. FL) (ours)	**2.45**	**2.43**

Training Time of `RelCal`. In Table 2, we compare the train time of `RelCal` against the standard training method using NLL loss for different datasets. We observe that training using `RelCal` incurs no additional computational overhead as compared to standard training procedures. Thus, our method not only alleviates miscalibration but also does not impose any extra training time.

Table 2. Computational cost for training. We train ResNet-50 with the same batch size for both setups, using the software configuration reported in Appendix.

Training Method	C-10	C-100	TIN-200
	(Train time in hours)		
NLL	3.27	3.11	7.30
RelCal (w. NLL) (Ours)	3.33	3.28	7.42

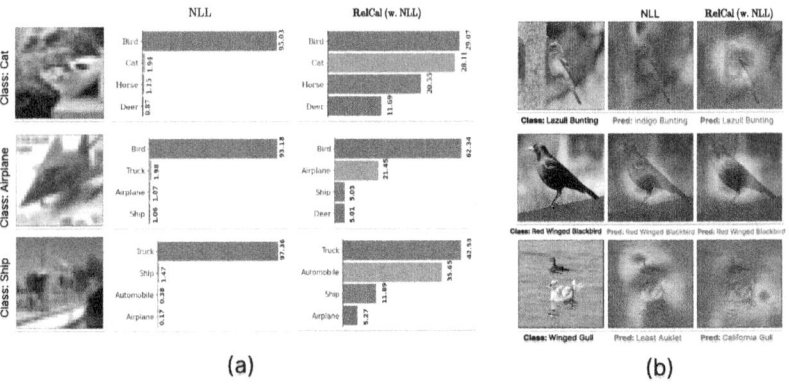

Fig. 4. (a) Training with `RelCal` reduces the confidence of the misclassifications. Images are from the CIFAR-10 dataset. (b) GradCAM visualization of models trained with and without `RelCal` using NLL loss. The model is ResNet-101 and the images are from CUB-200.

5 Experiments

In this section, we highlight the effectiveness of our proposed training approach `RelCal`. We present a set of experiments to evaluate `RelCal` against state-of-the-art train-time calibration methods on several benchmarks.

Datasets. To understand the effectiveness of `RelCal` for network calibration, we primarily evaluate `RelCal` on four standard image classification datasets - SVHN [31], CIFAR10 [18], CIFAR-100 [18], TinyImageNet-200 [23] (TIN-200) and one fine-grained image dataset CUB-200 [42]. We divide the training set into two distinct subsets: (a) a training subset comprising 90% of the samples, and (b) a validation subset with the remaining 10%, which is used for hyper-parameter optimization. Further, to analyse the generalization capability of our method, we also evaluate on the large-scale ImageNet [5] dataset. In addition, we also validate our technique on two imbalanced long-tailed datasets: CIFAR-10-LT [3], CIFAR-100-LT [3], and a standard natural language processing (NLP) dataset, Newsgroups [22]. Our choice of diverse datasets allows us to comprehensively assess the generalization capability of our proposed method, RelCal, for network calibration. For more detailed descriptions of each dataset, refer to the Appendix.

Evaluation Metrics. For evaluation, we report standard calibration metrics, including Expected Calibration Error (ECE), and Adaptive Expected Calibration Error (AECE), along with test accuracy to assess the calibration performance. For fair comparison, following previous studies [15,27,32], we use 15 bins to measure the ECE and AECE. Training with RelCal surpasses state-of-the-art calibration techniques, enhancing both calibration and test accuracy.

Training Details. For image-classification tasks, we used the ResNet [14] and WideResNet [44] architecture for primary experimentation. For the NLP classification task, following past studies [27], we train a Global Pooling CNN (GP-CNN) architecture [25]. The pruning percentile $p \in \{15, 25, 35, 55, 75, 85, 95\}$ is cross-validated as described in the Appendix. Following our validation strategy, we set $p = 85$ for the ResNet-50 model and $p = 95$ for the ResNet-101 and WideResNet-26-10 model across all datasets. We report ablation results for the effect of p in Sect. 7.2. We provide further training details in Appendix.

Table 3. Calibration performance with different loss functions. Comparison of calibration performance when using RelCal with three commonly used loss functions (NLL/LS/FL). We observe that for all classification loss, training with RelCal enhances model calibration. Results obtained using RelCal are highlighted in blue. R50 represents ResNet-50 [14] model and WRN-26-10 represents WideResNet-26-10 [44] architecture. The best results for each dataset are marked in **bold**.

Dataset	Model	NLL			RelCal (w. NLL)			LS [29]			RelCal (w. LS [29])			FL [28]			RelCal (w. FL [28])		
		Acc ↑	ECE ↓	AECE ↓	Acc ↑	ECE ↓	AECE ↓	Acc ↑	ECE ↓	AECE ↓	Acc ↑	ECE ↓	AECE ↓	Acc ↑	ECE ↓	AECE ↓	Acc ↑	ECE ↓	AECE ↓
CIFAR-10	R50	94.99	3.65	2.95	95.19	2.98	2.88	94.97	3.25	3.56	94.91	3.05	3.23	95.02	3.32	3.30	**95.32**	**0.97**	**1.02**
CIFAR-10	WRN-26-10	95.60	2.83	2.83	95.88	2.47	2.47	95.64	4.48	4.29	95.91	3.05	3.23	95.85	4.65	4.44	**96.08**	**0.60**	**0.80**
CIFAR-10-LT(IF=10)	R50	89.39	6.91	6.91	89.87	6.47	6.44	89.85	3.86	4.06	89.56	3.41	3.98	88.78	4.16	4.12	**89.95**	**3.21**	**3.21**
CIFAR-10-LT(IF=100)	R50	73.53	20.05	20.04	76.19	15.10	15.09	74.19	14.77	14.76	74.50	14.92	14.87	70.03	14.98	15.01	74.43	**14.71**	**14.67**
CIFAR-100	R50	78.13	12.54	12.39	**78.91**	9.34	9.23	77.27	6.87	6.84	78.54	3.92	3.83	77.69	5.51	5.40	78.32	**2.75**	**2.45**
CIFAR-100	WRN-26-10	80.21	8.29	8.34	**80.63**	6.50	6.44	79.27	2.94	2.93	80.32	3.12	3.59	80.42	4.62	4.73	80.10	**2.73**	**2.75**
CIFAR-100-LT(IF=10)	R50	60.53	13.23	13.14	**63.57**	12.57	12.43	62.31	6.73	6.75	61.88	6.18	6.12	62.09	6.16	6.19	62.40	**5.74**	**5.73**
CIFAR-100-LT(IF=100)	R50	39.00	32.13	32.12	40.60	28.39	28.38	39.26	19.98	19.94	**43.21**	20.91	20.93	36.20	20.76	20.75	41.52	**18.23**	**18.22**
TinyImagenet-200	R50	65.76	13.20	13.19	66.14	8.26	8.23	63.52	2.85	2.27	64.75	2.38	2.13	63.80	3.22	3.08	**66.48**	**2.17**	**2.19**
CUB-200	R101	72.57	18.19	18.18	72.85	8.46	8.38	73.25	12.51	12.52	**75.02**	3.45	3.46	72.87	8.41	8.39	73.11	**2.99**	**3.22**
SVHN	R50	96.15	2.41	2.40	**96.21**	2.10	2.05	95.83	4.35	4.18	96.20	4.60	4.38	96.14	4.16	4.21	96.10	**1.10**	**1.07**
20 Newsgroups	GP-CNN	66.89	22.74	22.78	65.07	22.06	22.47	66.55	6.67	6.36	66.78	5.44	5.89	67.03	13.32	13.30	**67.43**	10.88	10.86

Baselines. We compare our method against an array of competitive train-time calibration techniques including Negative Log Likelihood (NLL), Label Smoothing [29], MMCE [21], Focal Loss (FL) [28], FL+MDCA [15], CPC [4], MbLS [27] and RankMixup [32]. For detailed description of each method, refer Appendix.

Table 4. Comparison with state-of-art. We compare `RelCal` with an array of state-of-art train-time calibration techniques on CIFAR10/100 [18] and ImageNet [5] dataset. Best results are highlighted in **bold**. All values are in percentage (%). Mean and std of our method are estimated over 3 random runs.

Methods	CIFAR-10 [18]						CIFAR-100 [18]						ImageNet [5]		
	ResNet-50			ResNet-101			ResNet-50			ResNet-101			ResNet-50		
	Acc ↑	ECE ↓	AECE ↓	Acc ↑	ECE ↓	AECE ↓	Acc ↑	ECE ↓	AECE ↓	Acc ↑	ECE ↓	AECE ↓	Acc ↑	ECE ↓	AECE ↓
NLL	94.99	3.65	2.95	94.48	3.68	3.57	78.13	12.54	12.39	77.84	13.12	13.10	73.86	9.34	9.45
MMCE [21] (ICML 2018)	95.20	3.87	3.89	95.03	3.83	3.83	77.12	12.90	12.89	77.56	13.53	13.39	74.29	8.81	8.83
LS [29] (NeurIPS 2019)	94.97	3.25	3.56	94.10	3.21	3.21	77.27	6.87	6.84	76.98	8.54	8.58	75.14	3.31	3.23
FL [28] (NeurIPS 2020)	95.02	3.32	3.30	95.16	3.48	3.49	77.69	5.51	5.40	77.12	4.99	5.01	74.69	3.93	3.94
FL+MDCA [15] (CVPR 22)	95.16	1.84	1.78	95.18	2.01	2.15	75.46	5.71	5.71	77.21	3.74	3.79	75.05	6.95	6.33
CPC [4] (CVPR 22)	95.10	4.67	4.67	**95.38**	5.34	5.39	77.78	10.98	10.90	77.82	12.17	12.18	74.98	4.38	4.32
MbLS [27] (CVPR 22)	95.24	1.21	2.98	95.31	**1.39**	3.45	77.12	4.56	4.56	77.55	5.48	5.78	75.29	4.24	4.28
RankMixup [32] (ICCV 23)	94.88	2.59	2.58	94.25	3.24	3.21	77.11	3.46	3.45	76.46	3.49	3.49	74.86	3.93	3.92
`RelCal` (w. FL) (Ours)	**95.32**±0.49	**0.97**±0.18	**1.02**±0.14	**95.38**±0.36	1.41±0.20	**1.40**±0.17	**78.32**±0.36	**2.75**±0.40	**2.45**±0.37	**78.12**±0.44	**2.43**±0.28	**2.44**±0.30	**75.51**±0.75	**3.06**±0.43	**3.08**±0.38

6 Results

Investigating the Impact of Different Loss Functions with `RelCal`. Since `RelCal` is designed to learn features relevant to each class, it can be seamlessly integrated with standard classification and calibration losses such as Negative Log Likelihood (NLL), Label Smoothing (LS) [29], Focal Loss (FL) [28], MDCA [15], or MbLS [27]. Due to space constraints, we show comparative analysis of model calibration using NLL, LS, and FL in Table 3. We report additional results using MDCA and MbLS in Appendix. Our empirical evaluation reveals several key insights: (**1.**) Integrating `RelCal` with these loss functions substantially enhances calibration performance across various datasets and architectures. For instance, employing `RelCal` in conjunction with NLL loss on the TIN-200 dataset leads to a reduction in both ECE and AECE by 4.94% and 4.96% respectively, as compared to the standard NLL training. (**2.**) Beyond calibration improvements, `RelCal` also enhances test accuracy. Notably, when used in conjunction with FL, we see a 5.32% improvement in accuracy on the

Table 5. Results on Imbalanced Datasets. Comparison of calibration performances on two imbalanced datasets CIFAR-10-LT [3] and CIFAR-100-LT [3]. For imbalanced datasets, we use an imbalance factor (IF) of 10.

Methods	ResNet-50 [14]					
	CIFAR-10-LT (IF = 10)			CIFAR-100-LT (IF = 10)		
	Acc ↑	ECE ↓	AECE ↓	Acc ↑	ECE ↓	AECE ↓
NLL	89.39	6.91	6.91	60.53	13.23	13.14
LS [29]	89.85	3.86	4.06	62.31	6.73	6.75
FL [28]	88.78	4.16	4.12	62.09	6.16	6.19
FL+MDCA [15]	87.60	5.45	5.44	46.20	11.32	11.43
MbLS [27]	87.82	7.04	6.99	58.10	8.36	8.93
RankMixup [32]	89.80	5.80	5.84	**63.83**	10.01	9.98
`RelCal` (w. FL)(Ours)	**89.95**	**3.21**	**3.21**	62.40	**5.74**	**5.73**

Table 6. Exploring relationship between model capacity and pruning percentile p. We observe training with `RelCal` leads to more gains in calibration for models with larger capacities.

Model	Params	FLOPS	Optimal p	ECE (%) (↓)		
				FL	RelCal (w.FL)	Δ
R-18	11.2M	0.6G	15	1.11	0.63	+0.48
R-34	21.2M	1.1G	65	2.69	1.59	+1.10
R-50	23.5M	1.3G	85	3.32	0.97	+2.35
R-101	42.5M	2.5G	95	3.48	1.41	+2.07

CIFAR-100-LT dataset. (3.) Out of all configurations tested, the combination of RelCal and FL [28] demonstrates superior calibration performance across most datasets.

Based on these observations, for the subsequent sections of this paper, we primarily train RelCal in conjunction with Focal Loss [28] unless stated otherwise.

Comparison with State-of-the-Art. Table 4 compares our RelCal with an array of competitive train-time calibration techniques. We observe that RelCal consistently improves ECE and AECE on all the datasets and different architectures. Notably, on CIFAR-10 with ResNet-50 architecture, RelCal reduces the ECE to **0.97**% and AECE to **1.02**%, which are considerable improvements over state-of-art techniques such as RankMixup [32] and MbLS [27]. Further, we observe that RelCal also demonstrates superior performance on the large-scale ImageNet [5] dataset thereby highlighting the importance of learning class-relevant features. Further, we also note that RelCal is able to achieve the best calibration performance without sacrificing on the test accuracy.

Performance on Imbalanced Datasets. In Table 4, we highlighted the impressive performance of RelCal over various standard datasets. However, it is essential to recognize that these datasets are predominantly balanced, which may not fully capture the challenges that models face in real-world scenarios. When deployed in the wild, a model is more likely to encounter skewed and long-tailed distributions where few classes dominate over the rare classes [36]. To simulate this setup, following [3], we deliberately introduce class imbalance to the CIFAR dataset to create a long-tail (-LT) distribution. This type of evaluation is important for understanding how well the model can make confident and reliable predictions, especially for rare classes, where class distributions are often imbalanced. The results of this experiment are presented in Table 5, where it is noteworthy that RelCal achieves the highest calibration performance for both CIFAR-10-LT and CIFAR-100-LT datasets.

Performance on different architectures. In Table 4, we established the superiority of RelCal on ResNet [14]. Going beyond, in Table 7, we show that RelCal remains competitive and outperforms the state-of-the-art for other common architectures such as WideResNet [44]. From Table 7, we observe that on CIFAR-10 dataset using WideResNet-26-10 model, RelCal reduces the ECE to 0.60%– a 1.12% improvement over RankMixup [32].

Table 7. Results using WideResNet architecture.

Methods	WideResNet-26-10 [44]					
	CIFAR-10 [18]			CIFAR-100 [18]		
	Acc ↑	ECE ↓	AECE ↓	Acc ↑	ECE ↓	AECE ↓
NLL	95.60	2.83	2.83	80.21	8.29	8.34
LS [29]	95.64	4.48	4.29	79.27	2.94	2.93
FL [28]	95.85	4.65	4.44	**80.42**	4.62	4.73
FL+MDCA [15]	95.90	0.98	1.27	80.05	3.13	3.19
MbLS [27]	95.89	1.32	2.56	79.21	4.58	4.51
RankMixup [32]	95.88	1.72	1.49	78.56	3.13	3.24
RelCal (w. FL)(Ours)	**96.08**	**0.60**	**0.80**	80.10	**2.73**	**2.75**

7 Discussion

7.1 Exploring Relationship Model Capacity and p

In this section, we investigate the presence of any correlation between model capacity and the optimal pruning percentile p. To this end, we utilize a series of ResNet [14] models with varying capacities, specifically ResNet-18, ResNet-34, ResNet-50, and ResNet-101. We present the results of our experiments in Table 6. Our findings reveal two important insights: (1) We discern a positive correlation between the pruning percentile p and number of model parameters. This observation aligns with the analysis presented in [11], which demonstrated that models with larger capacities are more susceptible to overfitting. (2) The advantages gained from training with RelCal become notably more pronounced in models with larger capacities, such as ResNet-50 and ResNet-101.

7.2 Ablations on Pruning Percentile p

In this ablation, we aim to understand the effect of pruning percentile p on the calibration performance. The pruning percentile p plays a critical role in determining the threshold for selecting the relevant features during training. A higher value of p implies a more stringent criterion for feature relevance, potentially pruning more connections deemed less significant for each class. This ablation is based on a ResNet-50 model trained on CIFAR-10 dataset. Specifically, we train and compare multiple models by varying $p \in \{15, 25, 35, 55, 75, 85, 95\}$. Figure 5 reports the influence of p on the Expected Calibration Error (ECE). We observe that: (1) Setting $p = 85$ provides the optimal calibration performance, which is consistent with one chosen using our validation strategy (see Appendix). Further, irrespective of the pruning percentile used, RelCal is consistently better than FL [28]. (2) Lower p values significantly diminish the model's calibration performance, corroborating the necessity of pruning irrelevant features. (3) In the extreme case, when p is too high (e.g. $p = 95$), we observe a slight deterioration in the calibration performance.

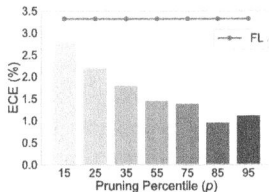

Fig. 5. Effect of varying the pruning percentile (p) on calibration performance of RelCal (w. FL).

Additional Comparison. In Appendix, we also compare RelCal with other common sparsification techniques like Unit Dropout [39], Targeted Dropout [9], DICE [41], Adaptive Dropout [2], and Guided Dropout [16]. Our findings show that RelCal consistently achieves the best ECE.

8 Conclusion

We propose RelCal, a simple and novel training approach designed to enhance network calibration by concentrating on class-relevant features. Our comprehensive experiments across various datasets and architectures demonstrate the effectiveness of `RelCal` in improving model calibration without much increase in training time. Notably, training `RelCal` in conjunction with focal loss consistently outperforms state-of-art train-time calibration methods, achieving significant reductions in both ECE and AECE metrics. Furthermore, our approach also exhibits promising results on challenging long-tailed datasets. Our mathematical analysis suggests that `RelCal` enhances model calibration by implicitly regularizing network weights, thereby mitigating overconfident predictions.

References

1. Ahn, Y.H., Park, G.M., Kim, S.T.: Line: out-of-distribution detection by leveraging important neurons (2023)
2. Ba, J., Frey, B.: Adaptive dropout for training deep neural networks. In: Advances in Neural Information Processing Systems, vol. 26 (2013)
3. Cao, K., Wei, C., Gaidon, A., Arechiga, N., Ma, T.: Learning imbalanced datasets with label-distribution-aware margin loss. In: Advances in Neural Information Processing Systems (2019)
4. Cheng, J., Vasconcelos, N.: Calibrating deep neural networks by pairwise constraints. In: 2022 IEEE/CVF Conference on Computer Vision and Pattern Recognition (CVPR), pp. 13699–13708 (2022). https://doi.org/10.1109/CVPR52688.2022.01334
5. Deng, J., Dong, W., Socher, R., Li, L.J., Li, K., Fei-Fei, L.: Imagenet: a large-scale hierarchical image database. In: 2009 IEEE Conference on Computer Vision and Pattern Recognition, pp. 248–255. IEEE (2009)
6. Djurisic, A., Bozanic, N., Ashok, A., Liu, R.: Extremely simple activation shaping for out-of-distribution detection. In: The Eleventh International Conference on Learning Representations (2023), https://openreview.net/forum?id=ndYXTEL6cZz
7. Dosovitskiy, A., et al.: An image is worth 16x16 words: transformers for image recognition at scale. In: International Conference on Learning Representations (2021)
8. Dusenberry, M.W., et al.: Analyzing the role of model uncertainty for electronic health records. In: Proceedings of the ACM Conference on Health, Inference, and Learning (2020)
9. Gomez, A.N., et al.: Learning sparse networks using targeted dropout. arXiv preprint arXiv:1905.13678 (2019)
10. Grigorescu, S., Trasnea, B., Cocias, T., Macesanu, G.: A survey of deep learning techniques for autonomous driving. J. Field Robot. **37**(3), 362–386 (2020)
11. Guo, C., Pleiss, G., Sun, Y., Weinberger, K.Q.: On calibration of modern neural networks. In: International Conference on Machine Learning, pp. 1321–1330. PMLR (2017)
12. Han, S., Mao, H., Dally, W.J.: Deep compression: compressing deep neural networks with pruning, trained quantization and huffman coding (2016)
13. Han, S., Pool, J., Tran, J., Dally, W.: Learning both weights and connections for efficient neural network. In: Advances in Neural Information Processing Systems, pp. 1135–1143 (2015)
14. He, K., Zhang, X., Ren, S., Sun, J.: Identity mappings in deep residual networks (2016)

15. Hebbalaguppe, R., Prakash, J., Madan, N., Arora, C.: A stitch in time saves nine: a train-time regularizing loss for improved neural network calibration. In: Proceedings of the IEEE/CVF Conference on Computer Vision and Pattern Recognition, pp. 16081–16090 (2022)
16. Keshari, R., Singh, R., Vatsa, M.: Guided dropout. In: Proceedings of the AAAI Conference on Artificial Intelligence, vol. 33, pp. 4065–4072 (2019)
17. Kriegeskorte, N.: Deep neural networks: a new framework for modeling biological vision and brain information processing. Ann. Rev. Vis. Sci. **1**, 417–446 (2015)
18. Krizhevsky, A., Hinton, G.: Learning multiple layers of features from tiny images. Technical Report, 0, University of Toronto, Toronto, Ontario (2009)
19. Kull, M., Perello-Nieto, M., Kängsepp, M., Song, H., Flach, P., et al.: Beyond temperature scaling: obtaining well-calibrated multiclass probabilities with dirichlet calibration. arXiv preprint arXiv:1910.12656 (2019)
20. Kull, M., Silva Filho, T., Flach, P.: Beta calibration: a well-founded and easily implemented improvement on logistic calibration for binary classifiers. In: Artificial Intelligence and Statistics, pp. 623–631. PMLR (2017)
21. Kumar, A., Sarawagi, S., Jain, U.: Trainable calibration measures for neural networks from kernel mean embeddings. In: International Conference on Machine Learning, pp. 2805–2814. PMLR (2018)
22. Lang, K.: Newsweeder: Learning to filter netnews. In: Machine Learning Proceedings 1995, pp. 331–339. Elsevier (1995)
23. Le, Y., Yang, X.: Tiny imagenet visual recognition challenge. CS 231N **7**(7), 3 (2015)
24. LeCun, Y., Bengio, Y., Hinton, G.: Deep learning. Nature **521**(7553), 436–444 (2015)
25. Lin, M., Chen, Q., Yan, S.: Network in network. arXiv preprint arXiv:1312.4400 (2013)
26. Lin, T.Y., Goyal, P., Girshick, R., He, K., Dollár, P.: Focal loss for dense object detection. In: Proceedings of the IEEE International Conference on Computer Vision, pp. 2980–2988 (2017)
27. Liu, B., Ben Ayed, I., Galdran, A., Dolz, J.: The devil is in the margin: margin-based label smoothing for network calibration. In: Proceedings of the IEEE/CVF Conference on Computer Vision and Pattern Recognition, pp. 80–88 (2022)
28. Mukhoti, J., Kulharia, V., Sanyal, A., Golodetz, S., Torr, P., Dokania, P.: Calibrating deep neural networks using focal loss. Adv. Neural. Inf. Process. Syst. **33**, 15288–15299 (2020)
29. Müller, R., Kornblith, S., Hinton, G.E.: When does label smoothing help? In: Advances in Neural Information Processing Systems, vol. 32 (2019)
30. Naeini, M.P., Cooper, G., Hauskrecht, M.: Obtaining well calibrated probabilities using bayesian binning. In: Twenty-Ninth AAAI Conference on Artificial Intelligence (2015)
31. Netzer, Y., Wang, T., Coates, A., Bissacco, A., Wu, B., Ng, A.Y.: Reading digits in natural images with unsupervised feature learning (2011)
32. Noh, J., Park, H., Lee, J., Ham, B.: Rankmixup: ranking-based mixup training for network calibration. In: Proceedings of the IEEE/CVF International Conference on Computer Vision, pp. 1358–1368 (2023)
33. Park, H., Noh, J., Oh, Y., Baek, D., Ham, B.: Acls: adaptive and conditional label smoothing for network calibration. In: Proceedings of the IEEE/CVF ICCV (2023)
34. Pereyra, G., Tucker, G., Chorowski, J., Kaiser, Ł., Hinton, G.: Regularizing neural networks by penalizing confident output distributions. arXiv preprint arXiv:1701.06548 (2017)

35. Platt, J., et al.: Probabilistic outputs for support vector machines and comparisons to regularized likelihood methods. Adv. Large Margin Classifiers **10**(3), 61–74 (1999)
36. Reed, W.J.: The pareto, zipf and other power laws. Econ. Lett. **74**(1), 15–19 (2001)
37. Selvaraju, R.R., Cogswell, M., Das, A., Vedantam, R., Parikh, D., Batra, D.: Gradcam: visual explanations from deep networks via gradient-based localization. In: 2017 IEEE International Conference on Computer Vision (ICCV), pp. 618–626 (2017)
38. Simonyan, K., Zisserman, A.: Very deep convolutional networks for large-scale image recognition. arXiv preprint arXiv:1409.1556 (2014)
39. Srivastava, N., Hinton, G., Krizhevsky, A., Sutskever, I., Salakhutdinov, R.: Dropout: a simple way to prevent neural networks from overfitting. J. Mach. Learn. Res. **15**(1), 1929–1958 (2014)
40. Sun, Y., Guo, C., Li, Y.: React: out-of-distribution detection with rectified activations. Adv. NeurIPS **34**, 144–157 (2021)
41. Sun, Y., Li, Y.: Dice: leveraging sparsification for out-of-distribution detection. In: Proceedings of European Conference on Computer Vision (2022)
42. Wah, C., Branson, S., Welinder, P., Perona, P., Belongie, S.: The caltech-ucsd birds-200-2011 dataset (2011)
43. Zadrozny, B., Elkan, C.: Obtaining calibrated probability estimates from decision trees and naive bayesian classifiers. In: Proceedings of the International Conference on Machine Learning, vol. 1, pp. 609–616 (2001)
44. Zagoruyko, S., Komodakis, N.: Wide residual networks. In: BMVC (2016)
45. Zhang, H., Cisse, M., Dauphin, Y.N., Lopez-Paz, D.: mixup: beyond empirical risk minimization. In: ICLR (2018)

Bias vs Bias Dawn of Justice: A Fair Fight in Recommendation Systems

Tahsin Alamgir Kheya[✉], Mohamed Reda Bouadjenek, and Sunil Aryal

Deakin University, Geelong, VIC, Australia
{t.kheya,reda.bouadjenek,sunil.aryal}@deakin.edu.au

Abstract. Recommendation systems play a crucial role in our daily lives by impacting user experience across various domains, including e-commerce, job advertisements, entertainment, etc. Given the vital role of such systems in our lives, practitioners must ensure they do not produce unfair and imbalanced recommendations. Previous work addressing bias in recommendations overlooked bias in certain item categories, potentially leaving some biases unaddressed. Additionally, most previous work on fair re-ranking focused on binary-sensitive attributes. In this paper, we address these issues by proposing a fairness-aware re-ranking approach that helps mitigate bias in different categories of items. This re-ranking approach leverages existing biases to correct disparities in recommendations across various demographic groups. We show how our approach can mitigate bias on multiple sensitive attributes, including gender, age, and occupation. We experimented on three real-world datasets to evaluate the effectiveness of our re-ranking scheme in mitigating bias in recommendations. Our results show how this approach helps mitigate social bias with little to no degradation in performance.

Keywords: Recommendation System · Fair re-ranking · Bias in Recommendations

1 Introduction

Recently, Recommendation Systems (RSs) have become an integral part of our lives by providing personalized suggestions to us. They play an important role in shaping our digital experience, contributing to our decisions for online purchases, movie recommendations, music playlists, news feeds, and more. RS spares us the trouble of sifting through vast amounts of data by curating customized and diverse content. Given their profound impact on our daily lives, it is essential to ensure they provide fair recommendations and do not perpetuate harmful biases. For instance, [58] highlights how top-ranked results for job roles favor one gender over the other and systematically disadvantage minority groups. While significant progress has been made in addressing fairness in recommendations [3,44,51], it is still an ongoing topic of research with new studies emerging continuously.

AI models are vulnerable to picking up biases that exist in the dataset used to train them [4,9,13,27,36]. For instance, [28] discusses how there is significant bias in movie recommendations for male and female users, across genres

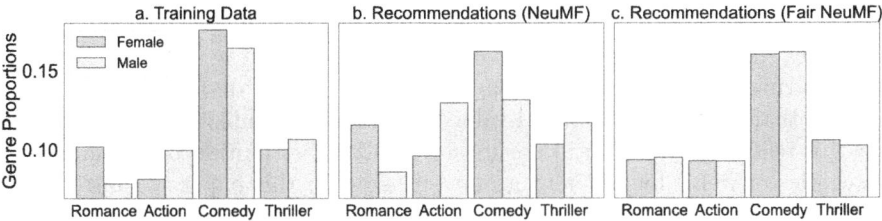

Fig. 1. Comparison of proportions of different movie genres for users of two genders in the training data, plain recommendations, and fairness-aware recommendations. There are disparities in the number of movies recommended to each gender for the four genres. This graph is based on the NeuMF [20] model for the ML100K dataset [19].

like romance and action. To mitigate such biases, researchers have used various fairness constraints to design re-ranking algorithms [15–17,58]. While there has been abundant work in the field of fair re-ranking in recommendations, existing approaches are deficient in two key ways: (i) they primarily focus on single or binary sensitive attributes and, (ii) they do not include the item categories when designing their approaches, which plays a vital role in users' end experience.

To illustrate the importance of mitigating bias on a granular scale by considering categories, we refer to Fig. 1. In this figure, we present how the proportions of movies from different genres vary for male and female users using the ML100K dataset across three stages: the training set, the top 20 plain recommendations provided by the NeuMF model, and the top 20 recommendations after fair re-ranking. From this figure, we can derive and explain several key insights: (i) The dataset used to train the model is not fair or neutral as shown in plot a. Certain genders tend to exhibit inherent biases towards specific categories, which societal stereotypes can influence. (ii) During the training process, the model can learn these biases and amplify them, intensifying their impact on the final output. We choose to demonstrate this using one popular recommendation model called NeuMF (plot b). The amplification of such biases by recommendation models is very common, as noted by [34,37]. While this helps visualize the discrepancy in movie recommendations for different genders, similar biases can exist in other domains, such as news recommendations, which can have far more profound consequences if not addressed. A similar concern is highlighted by [57], where YouTube recommender systems are found to facilitate pathways to extremist or radicalizing content. These kinds of content, when exposed to users, especially young generations, may have negative impacts on their well-being. (iii) The biases present in plots a and b, have similar trends of being oppositely skewed. As such, male users are more biased towards action and thrillers, while less towards romance and comedies. And female users are more biased towards romance and comedies while less towards action and thrillers. We take advantage of these opposing biases and use them as a corrective mechanism against social bias. After applying our fair category-aware re-ranking approach the discrepancy in the categories of movies recommended to the different groups of users decreases significantly as seen in plot c.

Ensuring the categories of items are considered when designing a re-ranking scheme that also caters to multi-valued sensitive attributes is thus vital. This kind of refined approach will ensure a balanced distribution of recommended categories of items for different groups of users. In this paper, we introduce a fairness-aware re-ranking scheme that allows us to produce fair recommendations by considering users' social attributes, accommodating both binary and multi-valued attributes. This strategy builds on the concept of counterfactual fairness by leveraging the bias in the training set to tackle/counteract social bias in a category-aware setting. Essentially, we use the category preferences of users with different sensitive attributes to adjust the recommendations, leveraging the opposing biases to promote fairness. We evaluate the effectiveness of this scheme on different recommendation algorithms (including traditional and deep approaches), experimenting on three real-world datasets.

2 Related Work

2.1 Consumer-Side Fairness in Recommendation Systems

Fairness in recommendation systems is a multi-sided concept, which is categorized into (i) Provider-Fairness: fairness for providers or sellers in terms of exposure; (ii) Consumer-Fairness: which focuses on the fairness of items being recommended to users from different protected classes and (iii) CP-Fairness which considers both [6]. Our work focuses on C-Fairness, with our goal of similar recommendations regardless of the user's sensitive attributes. It has been observed in prior research how recommendation systems are prone to bias influenced by demographic factors like gender [8,11,12,39,42], age [12,42], occupation [32,54], race [49] and more. To promote fairness for consumers, researchers have proposed a variety of mitigation strategies that span across the pre-processing, in-processing, and post-processing stages of the ML pipeline. For instance, [45] shows how small additions of augmented data can substantially improve both individual and group fairness in recommender systems. The authors in [52] propose a multi-task adversarial learning scheme that satisfies three different fairness criteria, including group, individual, and counterfactual. Optimizing a fairness-aware regularization term along with the main recommendation loss is also a popular approach to mitigating bias in recommendations [2,5,28,53,56].

2.2 Fair Re-ranking

Re-ranking is a popular post-processing strategy to mitigate bias in recommendations. This method focuses on rearranging the items recommended to users for the top-k list by considering both recommendation quality and a fairness constraint. For instance, [15] introduces a re-ranking approach that incorporates a fairness constraint to mitigate unfairness in explainable recommenders that use knowledge graphs. The authors in [31] introduce a fairness-constrained reranking method to ensure the utility disparity between different groups of users are below a certain threshold ϵ, while the optimization maximizes preference scores of items selected. Singh and Joachims [47] integrate common fairness concepts like demographic parity, disparate impact, and disparate treatment into their optimal ranking algorithm. The main idea behind the most relevant work is optimizing fairness and utility jointly by using a hyper-parameter to control the trade-off [51]. Although the current research community has not explored fair re-ranking for multi-valued attributes as much, there are a few works we wanted to highlight [22,38,50,55]. Unlike these, we are enforcing C-Fairness for multi-valued attributes in a category aware-setting. Most existing fair ranking schemes for recommendations focus on binary sensitive attributes and apply fairness definitions using the intuition of Equalized odds and Demographic parity to design their fairness constraint [2,31,40,47]. For demographic parity each sensitive group (like male and female) should receive the same proportions of positive predictions [18]. On the other hand, the concept of Equalized odds holds if the system has similar true positive rates and false positive rates across two different demographic groups [18]. In the current literature, these works would try to minimize the disparity between two groups of users or items based on popularity or user-sensitive attributes with binary values (like binary gender: [male, female], or age: [old, young]). While this approach is valuable in some way, it tends to oversimplify the complexity of user identities that are multi-dimensional.

Additionally, most re-ranking schemes don't consider the proportion of categories in the items recommended. Such schemes can fail to mitigate bias and disparities that exist across different types of items (like genres for movies). There are however some works that do consider different classes when designing ranking schemes [16,17,24,48]. For instance, [16] introduces algorithms to re-rank job candidates to achieve a desired distribution in the top results in regards to users' sensitive attributes like gender and age. The works by [16,17,24] aim for provider-side fairness. Our work is very close to that of [48], which re-ranks movies to ensure the recommendations align well with the historical interaction of the users by using genre distributions of previously played movies. Although this work is generating fair recommendations by ensuring users get recommendations following the proportions of genres that they previously watched, our work focuses on fairness in terms of users' sensitive attributes.

3 Proposed Re-ranking Scheme

3.1 Notation

We present all metrics for fairness assessment using the mathematical notation presented in Table 1.

We start with the two main distributions, both of which consider categories of the items.

Table 1. Notation Table

Notation	Description
$\mathcal{U}$ and $\mathcal{V}$	The set of users and items, respectively.
v_j	A single item, where j indexes the items.
c	An item category, such as Action, Sci-Fi, Romance, etc.
$\mathcal{C}$	The list of unique categories associated with all items.
C	A category matrix where $C_{v,c} = 1$ if item v belongs to category c, and 0 otherwise.
C_v	The list of categories associated with item v.
$\mathcal{V}_u$	The set of items the user u has interacted with in the past.
$t_{v,u}$	The timestamp of the interaction with item v by user u.
s_u	Represents the value of a sensitive attribute (male, female, engineer, etc.) for user u.
S	Represents a sensitive attribute like age, gender, occupation, etc.
$\text{score}_{u,v}$	The predicted score of item v by user u.

Definition 1 (Counterfactual Category Proportion (CCP)). *Let $o(c|s_u)$ return the average proportion of category c for all users who have a sensitive attribute that is not s_u, where $\mathcal{U}_{\neg s_u} = \{w \in \mathcal{U} \mid s_u \neq s_w\}$.*

$$o(c|s_u) = \frac{1}{|\mathcal{U}_{\neg s_u}|} \sum_{u \in \mathcal{U}_{\neg s_u}} m(c|u) \quad (1)$$

where

$$m(c|u) = \frac{\sum_{v \in \mathcal{V}_u} \frac{C_{v,c}}{|C_v|} \cdot t_{v,u}}{\sum_{v \in \mathcal{V}_u} t_{v,u}}$$

We use the timestamps of the interactions to apply more weight to interactions that took place recently. We follow [40], where they also employed the training set for their re-ranking algorithm.

Definition 2 (Recommended Category Proportion (RCP)). *Let $r(c|u)$ be the category proportion for user u relative to the items they are being recommended (represented by I) for category c.*

$$r(c|u, I) = \frac{\sum_{j=1}^{|I|} \frac{C_{v_j,c}}{|C_{v_j}|} \cdot \frac{1}{j^\gamma}}{\sum_{j=1}^{|I|} \frac{1}{j^\gamma}} \quad (2)$$

where we use $\gamma \in [0, 1]$ to help us weigh the item category contribution according to the rank (j) of the item in the recommended list I

3.2 Counterfactual Fairness

To design our category-aware fair re-ranking scheme, we use the concept of counterfactual fairness [30] that is formally defined as:

$$P(\hat{Y}_{A \leftarrow a}(U) = y \mid X = x, A = a) = P(\hat{Y}_{A \leftarrow a'}(U) = y \mid X = x, A = a)$$

Here, counterfactual fairness is achieved if the predicted outcome $\hat{Y}$ for an individual u (with latent variable U and non-sensitive features X) is the same when intervening to externally set the user's sensitive attribute from a to a'. This concept avoids discrimination by making sure that sensitive attributes do not influence the outcomes unfairly. Using this intuition, we extend it by not only considering individual-level outcomes but also including a group-level distribution of historical interactions for a fairness reference point.

3.3 Proposed Fair Re-ranking Idea

When designing our re-ranking approach, we want to adjust the recommendations based on how users of different sensitive groups interact with items of different categories. For this, we leverage the popularity of different categories among users with different sensitive attributes from their historical interactions. By doing so, we effectively simulate a counterfactual scenario, where we use category preferences of users who do not share the same sensitive attributes. To achieve this we want to ensure that the deviation between:

- the category distribution recommended to a user, where the proportion of a single category is defined by $r(c|u, I)$ (as shown in Eq. 2) and
- the average category distribution of users who don't share the same sensitive attribute as this user, where the proportion of a single category is defined by $o(c|s_u)$ (as shown in Eq. 1) is minimized.

Essentially, $o(c|s_u)$ acts as a counterfactual baseline for us that helps counteract the tendency of recommenders to reinforce existing biases from the data they are trained on. This intuition will help align users' recommendations and act as a defying mechanism for historical bias.

To quantify the disparity between the two distributions, we will use KL divergence. Using Kullback-Leibler (KL) divergence, in this case, has numerous advantages, such as sensitivity to subtle differences in the two category distributions, alignment with counterfactual definition, where we capture the difference in how recommended items differ when sensitive attributes are changed and ease of interpretation. The equation below helps quantify the disparity between the two distributions:

$$D_{KL}(o||r(I)|u) = \sum_{c \in \mathcal{C}} o(c|s_u) log \frac{o(c|s_u)}{\tilde{r}(c|u, I)} \quad (3)$$

where

$$\tilde{r}(c|u, I) = (1 - \alpha) \cdot r(c|u, I) + \alpha \cdot o(c|s_u)$$

To avoid getting any value of $r(c|u, I) = 0$, we use $\tilde{r}$ where α is a really small number between 0 and 1. Note that here, o and $r(I)$ represent the distribution of CCP and RCP across all categories for user u.

We use an adaptation of Maximum Marginal Relevance (MMR) [7] to determine the optimal set of items I^*, which can be formalized as:

$$I^* = \text{argmax}_{I \subseteq TopN, |I|=k}(1 - \beta) \cdot rel(I, u) - \beta \cdot D_{KL}(o, r(I), u) \quad (4)$$

where
$$rel(I, u) = \sum_{v \in I} score_{u,v}$$

We use a hyperparameter $\beta \in [0, 1]$ to calibrate the trade-off between relevance and fairness like some previous works, including [25,35,48]. This gives us a combinatorial optimization problem that is NP-hard. Following the works by [46,48], which demonstrated that the greedy optimization of an equation similar to Eq. 4 is equivalent to the greedy optimization of a surrogate submodular function, we adopt a similar approach condensing our equation to:

$$I^* = \operatorname{argmax}_{I \subseteq TopN, |I|=k} (1 - \beta) \cdot rel(I, u) + \beta \cdot \sum_c o(c|s_u) log \sum_{j=1}^{|I|} \frac{1}{j^\gamma} \tilde{r}(c|v_j) \quad (5)$$

where $\tilde{r}(c|v_j) = (1 - \alpha) \cdot r(c|v_j) + \alpha \cdot o(c|s_u)$, and represents the proportion of category c in movie v_j. The simplified submodular greedy optimization has an optimal guarantee of $1 - \frac{1}{e}$ [41]. The algorithm for this optimization is presented as Algorithm 1. Here we generate the top N items for each user (represented by $TopN$) and then re-rank to find the top k items (where $N \geq k$). Instead of using $o(c|s_u)$ directly, we add a small constant variation across all c values (the impact of which can be considered negligible) to ensure non-zero entries. Additionally, we normalize the relevance term and fairness term through the min-max normalization scheme to ensure they are on the same scale.

We want to mention that although we aim to provide fair recommendations to the users based on their sensitive attributes, we ensure this does not come at the expense of personalization. For our fair scheme, the goal is still prioritizing the preferences of users, but in a way that prevents the reinforcement of social stereotypes.

4 Experimental Methodology

4.1 Datasets

We evaluate the effectiveness of our scheme on three publicly available datasets from different domains as shown in Table 2. The datasets are all pre-processed to remove items and users by k-core filtering, which is a common practice adopted in prior research [1,10,28]. In our case, we use 5-core filtering. For the Yelp dataset, we follow Kheya et al. [28] and condense the number of categories from over 300 to 21.

4.2 Baselines

As suggested by [14], we evaluate our re-ranking scheme on several recommendation approaches, including traditional ones (Biased Matrix Factorization [29] and Weighted Matrix Factorization [21,43]) and deep learning-based ones (Neural Matrix Factorization [20] and Variational Auto Encoder Collaborative Filtering

Algorithm 1. The Counterfactually Fair Re-ranking Optimization

Input: $\mathcal{U}, TopN, \beta, k, scores, S$
Output: Matrix R of size $|\mathcal{U}| \times k$ which contains fair top-k recommendation lists for each user.

1: $scores \leftarrow$ train baseline model and store scores of candidate items.
2: $R \leftarrow$ empty matrix of size $|\mathcal{U}| \times k$
3: $H(u) \leftarrow$ store historical interactions of all users.
4: Compute o for all possible s_u values, following Equation 4 for chosen S
5: **for all** users $u \in \mathcal{U}$ **do**
6:    **for** index $= 0$ **to** k-1 **do**
7:       **for all** items $i \in TopN_u \setminus R(u)$ **do**
8:          Compute fairness-aware scores for i using:

$$(1-\beta) \cdot rel(I, u) + \beta \cdot \sum_c o(c|s_u) \log \sum_{j=1}^{|R(u) \cup i|} \frac{1}{j^\gamma} \tilde{r}(c|v_j)$$

9:       **end for**
10:      Select the item i^* with the highest fairness-aware score.
11:      Add i^* to $R(u)$.
12:    **end for**
13: **end for**
14: **return** R

Table 2. Details of the three datasets along with the sensitive attributes, where G=Gender, A=Age, and O=Occupation. The number after each sensitive attribute represents the number of classes for that sensitive attribute. For instance, G: 2 means gender has two classes-[male, female]. Note: in our experiments, we use binary gender, but our method can be applied to non-binary genders as well.

Name	Interactions	Users	Items	Sensitive Attribute	Categories
ML-100K [19]	99,278	943	1,348	G: 2, A: 7, O: 21	18
ML-1M [19]	999,611	6,040	3,416	G: 2, A: 7, O: 21	18
Yelp [37]	97,991	1,316	1,272	G: 2	21

[33]). For all the models, we choose the best one based on the HitRatio@20 and NDCG@20 values after running them over multiple epochs for different combinations of hyperparameters. We empirically discovered that for weighing ranked items, using a gamma value of 0.1 works best in both reducing bias and minimizing performance degradation (refer to Fig. 2). For the smaller datasets, we use N as the total number of items in the dataset. For the 1M datatset, N is chosen to be 1000, and $TopN_u$ for each user is the top 1,000 items for user u.

Bias. For calculating bias, we extend two metrics introduced by [28], which take into account the distribution of categories of items recommended. They were originally used to quantify gender bias in recommendations. We extend them and use them to find the sum of pair-wise differences between all user

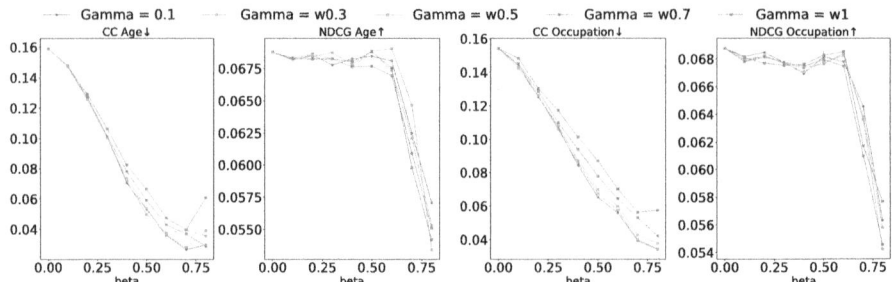

Fig. 2. Impact of γ across different β values on NDCG and CC values for VAE-CF model for ML100K.

groups, as suggested by the authors, to quantify bias in multi-valued sensitive attribute groups. The first metric calculates disparity in category distributions without considering the rank, like so:

$$CC(c,\mathcal{U}) = \frac{1}{|\mathcal{U}|} \sum_{u \in \mathcal{U}} \frac{1}{|TopK_u|} \sum_{v \in TopK_u} \frac{C_{v,c}}{|C_v|} \tag{6}$$

The second metric scores items by discounting them based on the rank of the items in the top k list. This equation is formalized as:

$$CDCG(c,\mathcal{U}) = \frac{1}{|\mathcal{U}|} \sum_{u \in \mathcal{U}} \frac{1}{|TopK_u|} \sum_{j=1}^{|TopK_u|} \frac{\frac{C_{v_j,c}}{|C_{v_j}|}}{\log(j+1)} \tag{7}$$

The sum of pairwise differences in CC and $CDCG$ values are then summed across all categories to represent the final bias values.

Performance. To evaluate the performance of the models, we use HitRatio@k, which measures the proportion of users who get at least one relevant item recommended to them. Additionally, we use a ranking-based metric called NDCG@k (Normalized Cumulative Gain) to measure the quality of the recommendations by giving higher importance to relevant items appearing higher in the list. For all our calculations, we use $k = 20$.

5 Results

We present the results of our experiments in Fig. 3, Fig. 5, Fig. 4 and Table 3.

5.1 Baseline Comparison

Out of all the models, NeuMF is more prone to capturing bias relating to sensitive attributes of users. The underlying architecture of this model uses Generalized

Table 3. Performance and bias values across all three datasets for sensitive attributes Age (A), Gender (G), and Occupation (O).

ML100K

	MF								WMF							
	NDCG↑		HitRatio↑		CC↓		CDCG↓		NDCG↑		HitRatio↑		CC↓		CDCG↓	
	Orig.	Fair	Orig.	Fair	Orig.	Fair	Orig.	Fair	Orig.	Fair	Orig.	Fair	Orig.	Fair	Orignal	Fair
A	0.0423		0.4210		0.1254	0.0297	0.0485	0.0107	0.0490		0.4708		0.2055	0.0302	0.0745	0.0109
G	0.0397	0.0405	0.3924	0.4019	0.1300	0.0624	0.0507	0.0166	0.0372	0.0405	0.3924	0.4210	0.1888	0.0409	0.0736	0.0131
O	0.0430		0.4231		0.1688	0.0335	0.0650	0.0121	0.0483		0.4719		0.2248	0.0331	0.0830	0.0112

	VAE-CF								NeuMF							
	NDCG↑		HitRatio↑		CC↓		CDCG↓		NDCG↑		HitRatio↑		CC↓		CDCG↓	
	Orig.	Fair	Orig.	Fair	Orig.	Fair	Orig.	Fair	Orig.	Fair	Orig.	Fair	Orig.	Fair	Orignal	Fair
A	0.0681		0.5451		0.1591	0.0362	0.0601	0.0135	0.0688		0.5758		0.2450	0.0295	0.0877	0.0107
G	0.0688	0.0682	0.5387	0.5419	0.0516	0.0371	0.0214	0.0177	0.0708	0.0688	0.5440	0.5567	0.2275	0.0253	0.0850	0.0099
O	0.0678		0.5355		0.1542	0.0561	0.0574	0.0200	0.0717		0.5769		0.2402	0.0358	0.0878	0.0136

ML1M

	MF								WMF							
	NDCG↑		HitRatio↑		CC↓		CDCG↓		NDCG↑		HitRatio↑		CC↓		CDCG↓	
	Orig.	Fair	Orig.	Fair	Orig.	Fair	Orig.	Fair	Orig.	Fair	Orig.	Fair	Orig.	Fair	Orignal	Fair
A	0.0378		0.3768		0.1392	0.0537	0.0509	0.0202	0.0465		0.4722		0.2228	0.0217	0.0802	0.0080
G	0.0363	0.0377	0.3474	0.3700	0.2016	0.0629	0.0708	0.0261	0.0428	0.0455	0.4394	0.4662	0.3643	0.0447	0.1334	0.0144
O	0.0376		0.3732		0.1286	0.0597	0.0476	0.0224	0.0464		0.4727		0.2374	0.0234	0.0867	0.0103

	VAE-CF								NeuMF							
	NDCG↑		HitRatio↑		CC↓		CDCG↓		NDCG↑		HitRatio↑		CC↓		CDCG↓	
	Orig.	Fair	Orig.	Fair	Orig.	Fair	Orig.	Fair	Orig.	Fair	Orig.	Fair	Orig.	Fair	Orignal	Fair
A	0.0510		0.4985		0.2076	0.0330	0.0758	0.0149	0.0470		0.4778		0.2554	0.0219	0.0928	0.0081
G	0.0515	0.0513	0.4616	0.4884	0.2603	0.0667	0.0969	0.0309	0.0478	0.0451	0.4389	0.4684	0.4101	0.0593	0.1484	0.0159
O	0.0519		0.4959		0.1514	0.0677	0.0542	0.0274	0.0468		0.4828		0.2562	0.0148	0.0928	0.0068

Yelp

	MF								WMF							
	NDCG↑		HitRatio↑		CC↓		CDCG↓		NDCG↑		HitRatio↑		CC↓		CDCG↓	
	Orig.	Fair	Orig.	Fair	Orig.	Fair	Orig.	Fair	Orig.	Fair	Orig.	Fair	Orig.	Fair	Orignal	Fair
G	0.0202	0.0203	0.2660	0.2690	0.0158	0.0202	0.0072	0.0062	0.0264	0.0258	0.3590	0.3389	0.0502	0.0247	0.0178	0.0088

	VAE-CF								NeuMF							
	NDCG↑		HitRatio↑		CC↓		CDCG↓		NDCG↑		HitRatio↑		CC		CDCG	
	Orig.	Fair	Orig.	Fair	Orig.	Fair	Orig.	Fair	Orig.	Fair	Orig.	Fair	Orig.	Fair	Orignal	Fair
G	0.0900	0.0840	0.7196	0.6877	0.0670	0.0261	0.0235	0.0080	0.0897	0.0837	0.7310	0.6960	0.0617	0.0245	0.0222	0.0065

Matrix Factorization (GMF) and Multi-Layer Perceptrons (MLP), that captures the relationships between users and the items they have interacted with. This can cause the model to capture intricate details about user preferences, which can reflect societal stereotypes [28]. VAE-CF uses probabilistic variational autoencoders to learn user-item interactions by encoding them in latent space. While it is sensitive to capturing biases, as seen from Table 3, the effect is minimal when compared to the MF-based models. Across all the models, the bias scores are higher for the larger dataset, likely due to the fact that more interactions help provide more opportunities for the model to capture the underlying biases. For performance, the deep model performs better in almost all cases, which is expected. Gender-related bias is more pronounced across all models. We believe age and occupation, may have a more subtle impact on category preferences when compared to gender. Since age and occupation have more classes than gender, the bias is more spread out across these groups making the impact more diluted. Imbalances in the interactions when considering just binary gender will stand out more, making gender bias more evident.

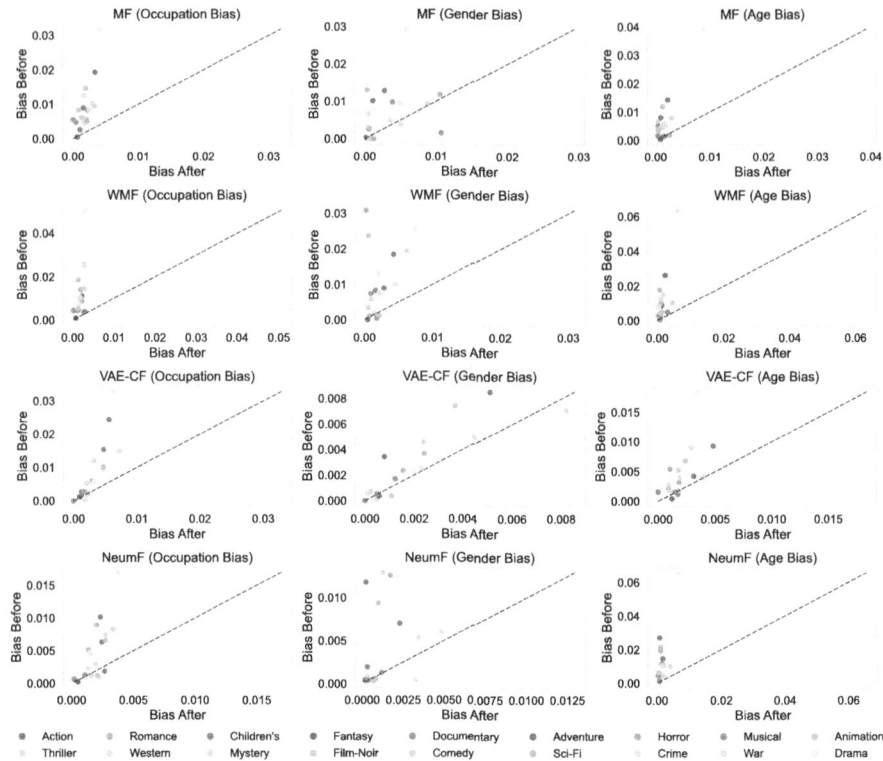

Fig. 3. Comparison of bias values (CC) before and after fair re-ranking for all the models across all categories. This is only visualized for the ML100K dataset; however, other datasets have similar trends. We plot CC scores because CC and CDCG are correlated and exhibit similar patterns.

5.2 Impact of Fair-Reranking

Bias. There is significant bias reduction after applying our re-ranking scheme for all models across the three sensitive attributes, as observed in Fig. 3, Fig. 4 and Table 3. From Fig. 3, we can observe how most points are above the y=x diagonal, verifying the reliable effectiveness of the re-ranking scheme in reducing bias. The bias mitigation works best for the NeuMF model since there's a noticeable drop in both CC and CDCG values across all the datasets for all three sensitive attributes. In Fig. 4, the effectiveness of our re-ranking approach is evident in plots c and e where the disparities in category distributions of recommended movies are significantly reduced compared to the baseline models (plots b and d). We also emphasize how our re-ranking approach achieves fairness without compromising the preferences of users. For instance, both genders have strong preferences for comedies as seen in plot a, but this is not reflected in the recommendations from the VAE-CF model (plot d). However, in our fair model (plot e), the proportion of comedy movies recommended is aligned with that

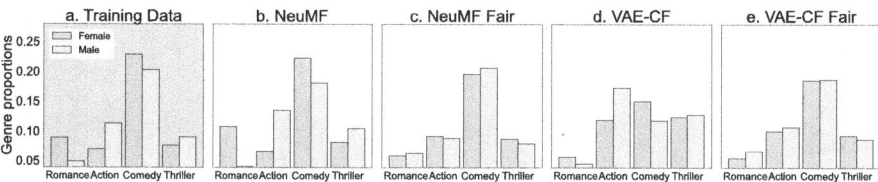

Fig. 4. Comparison of recommendations before and after fair re-ranking for two of the best-performing models for the ML1M dataset across four stereotypical genres. We also show the genre proportions of the training dataset.

of the training set. The proportions for each category are calculated following the CC formula. In the case of the training set we use the historical interactions instead of the top-k recommendations. While, Fig. 4, only shows results for ML1M dataset, readers can refer to Fig. 1, for ML100K dataset results. We did not include visualizations of the Yelp dataset, since they follow similar drops in bias values, like those of the other datasets. Our approach effectively minimizes discrepancies in recommended restaurants of different categories like *Coffee, Tea & Desserts* (which is more biased towards female users) and *Travel & Transportation* (which is more biased towards male users).

In most cases, the performance metrics are observed to be increasing while the bias is mitigated. Theoretically, as β increases, we would expect a decrease in bias scores and NDCG value. After a certain value of β, we would expect the bias scores to increase since the re-ranking algorithm would essentially allow the bias from CCP distribution to dominate over the actual bias. This would, in turn, start increasing the bias in the opposite direction (although we don't consider the direction of the bias because we use absolute values, we mention it here for clarity in explaining the phenomenon). To observe the influence of β on recommendation performance and bias, we run our re-ranking algorithm for all models for β values from 0 to 0.8, with increments of 0.1. We don't include values above 0.8 since it doesn't make sense to over-power the actual relevance scores. As seen in Fig. 5, there is a general decrease in bias values over the first few values of β. For gender, the bias starts increasing after β is greater than a certain value (different for different models). While this trend is more prominent in the case of gender, it is also observed for age. Our intuition for a profound bias increase in gender is that the CCP distribution we are employing to fix the bias is stronger in the case of gender. So, while the distribution helps us reduce bias, as β increases, the bias increases in the opposite direction. Again, age and occupation have more classes, and the average bias from all of these is too diluted to impact too strongly when we are using them to mitigate bias of each user's recommendations. For most models, a β value close to 0.4-0.6, seems to work well for mitigating bias.

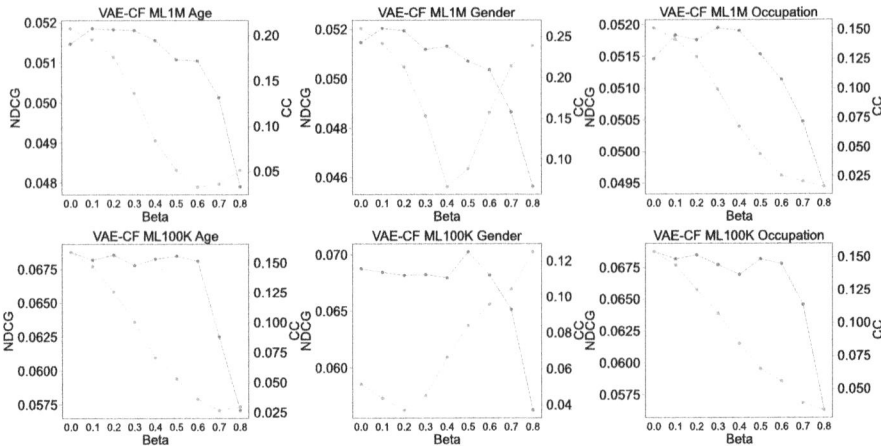

Fig. 5. Impact of β for VAE-CF model. The other models follow similar trends.

Performance. From Fig. 5, we can observe a trend where the performance increases slightly and then decreases. While the increase in performance seems counterintuitive, this can be because the fairness term helps reduce overfitting. One way to think about this, is how the fairness term is indirectly improving the coverage of the recommendations, which in turn provides relevant items to the users. Since our approach improves the exposure of items across categories, it enhances user engagement. Additionally, the idea of improving fairness leading to improvement in performance has been observed previously by [23,26,28,40]. While there are some instances where there is performance drop due to increased fairness as observed in Table 3, the decline is kept to a minimum.

6 Conclusion

In this work, we recognize the underlying issues of the current re-ranking approaches to mitigate bias in recommendations. We introduce a re-ranking scheme that reliably mitigates social bias for multi-valued user-sensitive attributes while also using item categories to ensure fine-grained treatment. Our approach is a simple yet powerful post-processing scheme to mitigate bias, which requires no modification of the model's internal parameters. We show, through extensive experiments, on three real-world datasets from multiple domains, the effectiveness of our re-ranking approach. The results show how our approach not only helps reduce bias but also preserves the quality of the recommendations, with a negligible drop in performance. We leverage the bias in the dataset to correct biased recommendations. While this works well for currently used datasets since they have historical bias, it may be less useful if future datasets evolve to be more neutral and unbiased. But we believe a dataset without bias (unless explicitly preprocessed to be fair) remains a distant possibility. While this work mainly focuses on consumers, it also implicitly accounts for the provider-side since we include item categories. In the future, we want to explicitly address the provider perspective (for instance, including item brands) to ensure a more holistic solution to social bias in recommendations. Additionally, we also intend to extend our work to address intersectional fairness for the consumers (like female and doctor). Our code, along with the processed datasets, are available here: Re-ranking Code[1]

Acknowledgment. This material is based upon work supported by the Air Force Office of Scientific Research under award number FA2386-23-1-4003.

References

1. Anelli, V.W., et al.: Elliot: a comprehensive and rigorous framework for reproducible recommender systems evaluation. In: Proceedings of the 44th International ACM SIGIR Conference on Research and Development in Information Retrieval, SIGIR 2021, pp. 2405–2414. ACM, New York, NY, USA (2021)
2. Beutel, A., et al.: Fairness in recommendation ranking through pairwise comparisons. In: Proceedings of the 25th ACM SIGKDD International Conference on Knowledge Discovery & Data Mining, KDD 2019, pp. 2212–2220. (2019)
3. Bhadani, S.: Biases in recommendation system. In: Proceedings of the 15th ACM Conference on Recommender Systems, RecSys 2021, pp. 855–859. (2021)
4. Bolukbasi, T., Chang, K.W., Zou, J., Saligrama, V., Kalai, A.: Man is to computer programmer as woman is to homemaker? debiasing word embeddings. In: Proceedings of the 30th International Conference on Neural Information Processing Systems, NIPS 2016, pp. 4356–4364 (2016)
5. Boratto, L., Fenu, G., Marras, M.: Interplay between upsampling and regularization for provider fairness in recommender systems. User Model. User-Adap. Inter. **31**(3), 421–455 (2021)
6. Burke, R.: Multisided Fairness for Recommendation (2017), arXiv:1707.00093
7. Carbonell, J., Goldstein, J.: The use of mmr, diversity-based reranking for reordering documents and producing summaries. In: Proceedings of the 21st Annual International ACM SIGIR Conference on Research and Development in Information Retrieval, pp. 335–336 (1998)
8. Datta, A., Tschantz, M., Datta, A.: Automated experiments on ad privacy settings. In: Proceedings on Privacy Enhancing Technologies, vol. 1 (2015)
9. De-Arteaga, M., et al.: Bias in bios: a case study of semantic representation bias in a high-stakes setting. In: Proceedings of the Conference on Fairness, Accountability, and Transparency, pp. 120–128 (2019)
10. Dietz, L.W., Sánchez, P., Bellogín, A.: Understanding the influence of data characteristics on the performance of point-of-interest recommendation algorithms. Inf. Technol. Tourism **27**(1), 75–124 (2025)
11. Edizel, B., Bonchi, F., Hajian, S., Panisson, A., Tassa, T.: Fairecsys: mitigating algorithmic bias in recommender systems. Int. J. Data Sci. Analytics **9**, 197–213 (2020)

---

[1] https://github.com/tahsinkheya/re_ranking_clean.

12. Ekstrand, M.D., et al.: All the cool kids, how do they fit in?: Popularity and demographic biases in recommender evaluation and effectiveness. In: Friedler, S.A., Wilson, C. (eds.) Proceedings of the 1st Conference on Fairness, Accountability and Transparency. Proceedings of Machine Learning Research, vol. 81, pp. 172–186 (2018)
13. Ensign, D., Friedler, S.A., Neville, S., Scheidegger, C., Venkatasubramanian, S.: Runaway feedback loops in predictive policing. In: Friedler, S.A., Wilson, C. (eds.) Proceedings of the 1st Conference on Fairness, Accountability and Transparency. Proceedings of Machine Learning Research, vol. 81, pp. 160–171. PMLR (2018)
14. Ferrari Dacrema, M., Cremonesi, P., Jannach, D.: Are we really making much progress? a worrying analysis of recent neural recommendation approaches. In: Proceedings of the 13th ACM Conference on Recommender Systems, RecSys 2019, pp. 101–109 (2019)
15. Fu, Z., et al.: Fairness-aware explainable recommendation over knowledge graphs (2020). https://doi.org/10.48550/arXiv.2006.02046
16. Geyik, S.C., Ambler, S., Kenthapadi, K.: Fairness-aware ranking in search & recommendation systems with application to linkedin talent search. In: Proceedings of the 25th ACM SIGKDD International Conference on Knowledge Discovery & Data Mining, KDD 2019, pp. 2221–2231 (2019)
17. Gorantla, S., Deshpande, A., Louis, A.: On the problem of underranking in group-fair ranking. In: Meila, M., Zhang, T. (eds.) Proceedings of the 38th International Conference on Machine Learning. Proceedings of Machine Learning Research, vol. 139, pp. 3777–3787 (2021)
18. Hardt, M., Price, E., Srebro, N.: Equality of opportunity in supervised learning. In: Advances in Neural Information Processing Systems, vol. 29 (2016)
19. Harper, F.M., Konstan, J.A.: The movielens datasets: History and context. ACM Trans. Interact. Intell. Syst. **5**(4) (2015)
20. He, X., Liao, L., Zhang, H., Nie, L., Hu, X., Chua, T.S.: Neural collaborative filtering. In: Proceedings of the 26th International Conference on World Wide Web, pp. 173–182. International World Wide Web Conferences Steering Committee (2017)
21. Hu, Y., Koren, Y., Volinsky, C.: Collaborative filtering for implicit feedback datasets. In: 2008 Eighth IEEE International Conference on Data Mining, pp. 263–272 (2008)
22. Hua, W., Ge, Y., Xu, S., Ji, J., Li, Z., Zhang, Y.: UP5: unbiased foundation model for fairness-aware recommendation. In: Graham, Y., Purver, M. (eds.) Proceedings of the 18th Conference of the European Chapter of the Association for Computational Linguistics (Volume 1: Long Papers), pp. 1899–1912. ACL, St. Julian's, Malta, March 2024
23. Islam, R., Keya, K.N., Zeng, Z., Pan, S., Foulds, J.: Debiasing career recommendations with neural fair collaborative filtering. In: Proceedings of the Web Conference 2021, pp. 3779–3790 (2021)
24. Jaenich, T., McDonald, G., Ounis, I.: Fairness-aware exposure allocation via adaptive reranking. In: Proceedings of the 47th International ACM SIGIR Conference on Research and Development in Information Retrieval, pp. 1504–1513 (2024)
25. Karako, C., Manggala, P.: Using image fairness representations in diversity-based re-ranking for recommendations. In: Adjunct Publication of the 26th Conference on User Modeling, Adaptation and Personalization, pp. 23–28 (2018)
26. Keya, K.N., Islam, R., Pan, S., Stockwell, I., Foulds, J.R.: Equitable allocation of healthcare resources with fair cox models (2020), https://arxiv.org/abs/2010.06820

27. Kheya, T.A., Bouadjenek, M.R., Aryal, S.: The pursuit of fairness in artificial intelligence models: a survey (2024), https://arxiv.org/abs/2403.17333
28. Kheya, T.A., Bouadjenek, M.R., Aryal, S.: Unmasking gender bias in recommendation systems and enhancing category-aware fairness. In: Proceedings of the ACM Web Conference 2025 (2025)
29. Koren, Y., Bell, R., Volinsky, C.: Matrix factorization techniques for recommender systems. Computer **42**(8), 30–37 (2009)
30. Kusner, M.J., Loftus, J., Russell, C., Silva, R.: Counterfactual fairness. In: Guyon, I., Luxburg, U.V., Bengio, S., Wallach, H., Fergus, R., Vishwanathan, S., Garnett, R. (eds.) Advances in Neural Information Processing Systems, vol. 30 (2017)
31. Li, Y., Chen, H., Fu, Z., Ge, Y., Zhang, Y.: User-oriented fairness in recommendation. In: Proceedings of the Web Conference 2021, pp. 624–632 (2021)
32. Li, Y., Chen, H., Xu, S., Ge, Y., Zhang, Y.: Towards personalized fairness based on causal notion. In: Proceedings of the 44th International ACM SIGIR Conference on Research and Development in Information Retrieval, SIGIR 2021, pp. 1054–1063 (2021)
33. Liang, D., Krishnan, R.G., Hoffman, M.D., Jebara, T.: Variational autoencoders for collaborative filtering. In: Proceedings of the 2018 World Wide Web Conference, pp. 689–698 (2018)
34. Lin, K., Sonboli, N., Mobasher, B., Burke, R.: Crank up the volume: preference bias amplification in collaborative recommendation (2019), https://arxiv.org/abs/1909.06362
35. Liu, W., Guo, J., Sonboli, N., Burke, R., Zhang, S.: Personalized fairness-aware re-ranking for microlending. In: Proceedings of the 13th ACM Conference on Recommender Systems, RecSys 2019, pp. 467–471 (2019)
36. Lum, K., Isaac, W.: To predict and serve? Significance **13**, 14–19 (2016)
37. Mansoury, M., Mobasher, B., Burke, R., Pechenizkiy, M.: Bias disparity in collaborative recommendation: algorithmic evaluation and comparison (2019), https://arxiv.org/abs/1908.00831
38. Mehrotra, A., Vishnoi, N.: Fair ranking with noisy protected attributes. In: Koyejo, S., Mohamed, S., Agarwal, A., Belgrave, D., Cho, K., Oh, A. (eds.) Advances in Neural Information Processing Systems, vol. 35, pp. 31711–31725. Curran Associates, Inc. (2022)
39. Melchiorre, A.B., Rekabsaz, N., Parada-Cabaleiro, E., Brandl, S., Lesota, O., Schedl, M.: Investigating gender fairness of recommendation algorithms in the music domain. Inf. Process. Manag. **58**(5), 102666 (2021)
40. Naghiaei, M., Rahmani, H.A., Deldjoo, Y.: Cpfair: personalized consumer and producer fairness re-ranking for recommender systems. In: Proceedings of the 45th International ACM SIGIR Conference on Research and Development in Information Retrieval, pp. 770–779 (2022)
41. Nemhauser, G.L., Wolsey, L.A., Fisher, M.L.: An analysis of approximations for maximizing submodular set functions–i. Math. Program. **14**, 265–294 (1978)
42. Neophytou, N., Mitra, B., Stinson, C.: Revisiting popularity and demographic biases in recommender evaluation and effectiveness. In: European Conference on Information Retrieval. BCS-IRSG, Springer (2021)
43. Pan, R., Zhou, Y., Cao, B., Liu, N.N., Lukose, R., Scholz, M., Yang, Q.: One-class collaborative filtering. In: 2008 Eighth IEEE International Conference on Data Mining, pp. 502–511 (2008)
44. Patro, G.K., Porcaro, L., Mitchell, L., Zhang, Q., Zehlike, M., Garg, N.: Fair ranking: a critical review, challenges, and future directions. In: Proceedings of the 2022

ACM Conference on Fairness, Accountability, and Transparency, FAccT 2022, pp. 1929–1942 (2022)
45. Rastegarpanah, B., Gummadi, K.P., Crovella, M.: Fighting fire with fire: using antidote data to improve polarization and fairness of recommender systems. In: Proceedings of the Twelfth ACM International Conference on Web Search and Data Mining, WSDM 2019, pp. 231–239 (2019)
46. Shinohara, Y.: A submodular optimization approach to sentence set selection. In: 2014 IEEE International Conference on Acoustics, Speech and Signal Processing (ICASSP), pp. 4112–4115 (2014)
47. Singh, A., Joachims, T.: Fairness of exposure in rankings. In: Proceedings of the 24th ACM SIGKDD International Conference on Knowledge Discovery & Data Mining, pp. 2219–2228 (2018)
48. Steck, H.: Calibrated recommendations. In: Proceedings of the 12th ACM Conference on Recommender Systems, RecSys 2018, pp. 154–162 (2018)
49. Sweeney, L.: Discrimination in online ad delivery. Commun. ACM **56**(5), 44–54 (2013)
50. Thonet, T., Renders, J.M.: Multi-grouping robust fair ranking. In: Proceedings of the 43rd International ACM SIGIR Conference on Research and Development in Information Retrieval, SIGIR 2020, pp. 2077–2080. ACM, New York, NY, USA (2020)
51. Wang, Y., Ma, W., Zhang, M., Liu, Y., Ma, S.: A survey on the fairness of recommender systems. ACM Trans. Inf. Syst. **41**(3), 1–43 (2023)
52. Wei, T., He, J.: Comprehensive fair meta-learned recommender system. In: Proceedings of the 28th ACM SIGKDD Conference on Knowledge Discovery and Data Mining, KDD 2022, pp. 1989–1999 (2022)
53. Wu, C., Wu, F., Wang, X., Huang, Y., Xie, X.: Fairness-aware news recommendation with decomposed adversarial learning. Proc. AAAI Conf. Artif. Intell. **35**(5), 4462–4469 (2021)
54. Wu, L., Chen, L., Shao, P., Hong, R., Wang, X., Wang, M.: Learning fair representations for recommendation: a graph-based perspective. In: Proceedings of the Web Conference 2021, pp. 2198–2208 (2021)
55. Yang, K., Loftus, J.R., Stoyanovich, J.: Causal intersectionality for fair ranking. CoRR **abs/2006.08688** (2020), https://arxiv.org/abs/2006.08688
56. Yao, S., Huang, B.: Beyond parity: fairness objectives for collaborative filtering. In: Advances in Neural Information Processing Systems, vol. 30 (2017)
57. Yesilada, M., Lewandowsky, S.: Systematic review: Youtube recommendations and problematic content. Internet Policy Rev. **11**(1) (2022)
58. Zehlike, M., Bonchi, F., Castillo, C., Hajian, S., Megahed, M., Baeza-Yates, R.: Fa*ir: a fair top-k ranking algorithm. In: Proceedings of the 2017 ACM on Conference on Information and Knowledge Management (2017)

What Large Language Models Do Not Talk About: An Empirical Study of Moderation and Censorship Practices

Sander Noels[✉], Guillaume Bied, Maarten Buyl, Alexander Rogiers, Yousra Fettach, Jefrey Lijffijt, and Tijl De Bie[✉]

Ghent University, Ghent, Belgium
{sander.noels,tijl.debie}@ugent.be

Abstract. Large Language Models (LLMs) are increasingly deployed as gateways to information, yet their content moderation practices remain underexplored. This work investigates the extent to which LLMs refuse to answer or omit information when prompted on political topics. To do so, we distinguish between hard censorship (i.e., generated refusals, error messages, or canned denial responses) and soft censorship (i.e., selective omission or downplaying of key elements), which we identify in LLMs' responses when asked to provide information on a broad range of political figures. Our analysis covers 14 state-of-the-art models from Western countries, China, and Russia, prompted in all six official United Nations (UN) languages. Our analysis suggests that although censorship is observed across the board, it is predominantly tailored to an LLM provider's domestic audience and typically manifests as either hard censorship or soft censorship (though rarely both concurrently). These findings underscore the need for ideological and geographic diversity among publicly available LLMs, and greater transparency in LLM moderation strategies to facilitate informed user choices. All data are made freely available.

≋ Dataset: hf.co/datasets/aida-ugent/llm-censorship

⌗ Appendix: github.com/aida-ugent/llm-censorship

1 Introduction

The influence of LLMs is profound: they are widely used to seek information, produce articles, translate texts, write code and engage in dialogue on virtually any topic [13]. Yet, alongside these impressive capabilities, concerns have arisen around unintended and potentially harmful outputs [3,23].

By default, LLMs trained on large amounts of internet data will inherit harmful language present in this data, making them prone to producing harmful content themselves. Such risks, if left unchecked, can have real-world consequences—ranging from the spread of disinformation to the incitement of hostility towards

---

Supplementary Information The online version contains supplementary material available at https://doi.org/10.1007/978-3-032-05962-8_16.

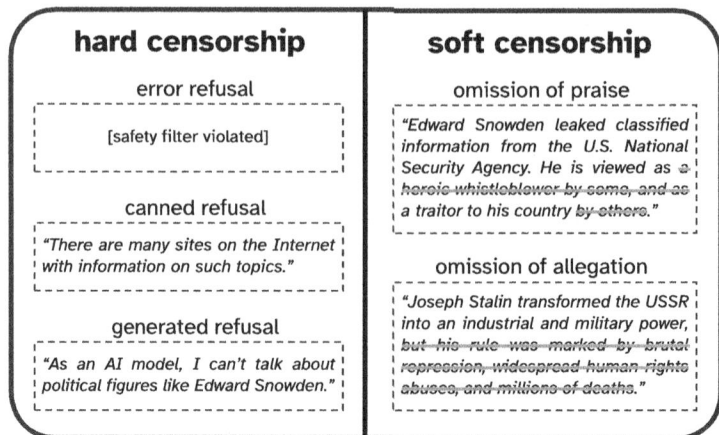

Fig. 1. We distinguish two categories of censorship: *hard* censorship (explicit refusal to talk about a topic) and *soft* censorship (silent omission of a particular viewpoint). Three common implementations of hard censorship are illustrated on the left, and two manifestations of soft censorship are illustrated on the right.

certain groups [6,21]. Moreover, when trained on multilingual and global data, LLMs will reflect a broad diversity of cultural and ideological perspectives, which can lead to offensive or even illegal outputs in some contexts. As a result, developers and providers of LLMs typically implement moderation measures that steer an LLM's behavior, a practice sometimes described as "censorship" [8].

Censorship in this context can be defined as the deliberate restriction, modification, or suppression of certain outputs generated by the model. The aim is to prevent the generation of content considered to be harmful, such as toxic, offensive, biased, illegal, false, misleading, or otherwise undesirable content. These measures can be implemented at different levels, through training data curation [7], model training [14], prompt design [15], or the use of guardrails [22], all aiming to ensure that the model is harmless while remaining helpful.

However, the practice of restricting LLM outputs has sparked debate. Critics note that the use of censorship may raise important ethical, societal, and practical questions. Who decides what counts as harmful, how, and with what legitimacy or mandate? Subjective and debatable choices by LLM developers or regulators may cause content filters to reduce the visibility of viewpoints that others consider legitimate, though perhaps controversial. Studies have shown that popular LLMs appear to reflect particular ideological or cultural biases: for instance, a model might expand upon certain perspectives more readily while responding cautiously or with hesitation to others [17,19]. Furthermore, cultural differences and variations in censorship regimes across different regions—with some countries imposing stricter regulations on internet content than others—can lead to inconsistent behavior of different LLMs . These observations should challenge the popular perception of LLMs as neutral or objective assistants, and give rise to questions about transparency, fairness, and potential overreach and undue influence on the public debate.

Contributions. In this paper, we investigate how and on which content LLMs engage in censorship[1], differentiating between two distinct manifestations:

1. *hard censorship:* The LLM explicitly refuses to answer or delivers an entirely off-topic or placeholder response. Examples of ways in which LLMs implement hard censorship are shown in Fig. 1 on the left.
2. *soft censorship :* The LLM partially omits or suppresses notable elements within the answer, thus rendering the output incomplete or slanted. Examples hereof are shown in Fig. 1 on the right.

Our main contributions are as follows:

- We provide a practical *taxonomy* for hard and soft censorship in LLMs.
- We introduce a scalable, reproducible *methodology* to quantify such censorship by analyzing LLM descriptions of internationally recognized political figures.
- We *quantify* censorship behavior of a geographically diverse panel of LLMs in all six UN languages—capturing both overt refusals (hard censorship) and silent omissions (soft censorship).
- We *investigate* how each LLM's censorship depends on the query language and the political figure's region of birth, relating it to internationally defined crimes, the UN's Sustainable Development Goals, and the Universal Declaration of Human Rights.
- We *provide evidence* that censorship widely varies across regions and languages, with notable patterns. In particular, censorship rates appear much higher for figures domestic to some LLMs' providers than those abroad.
- We *release* the omission dataset and accompanying materials to ensure reproducibility and support further research into ideological transparency in LLM moderation practices.

Outline. The paper is organized as follows. In Sect. 2, we review related work on content moderation, censorship, and ideological bias in LLMs. Section 3 introduces our methodology for measuring censorship, detailing our definitions of hard and soft censorship. Section 4 presents our experimental results, highlighting patterns across models, languages, and geopolitical contexts. In Sect. 5 discusses the implications of these results for information transparency and AI governance, and Sect. 6 concludes the paper while outlining directions for future research.

2 Related Work

In this section, we review recent research examining how moderation, influenced by multiple alignment methods and governance policies, shapes LLM behavior and censorship patterns. We also explore geopolitical influences on censorship and benchmarking efforts used to assess bias and content restrictions in LLMs.

---

[1] We note that in practice, when investigating censorship in LLMs as we do in the present study, it is often impossible to assess intentionality. Thus, here we use the term more loosely, without requiring it to be deliberate.

2.1 Content Moderation, Censorship, and Ideological Bias in LLMs

The alignment of LLMs through content moderation mechanisms aims to mitigate harmful outputs while trying to maximally preserve utility. Reinforcement Learning from Human Feedback (RLHF) has been widely employed to guide models in rejecting unsafe requests and minimizing toxic responses [14]. Constitutional AI further refines this approach by embedding explicit ethical principles, allowing models to self-censor while maintaining transparency [2]. Additional moderation strategies include rule-based reward modeling and real-time filtering systems, such as OpenAI's Moderation API[2], which classifies and restricts harmful content [8]. Furthermore, recent studies suggest that LLMs can outperform traditional classifiers in moderation tasks [11], although they risk inheriting biases from training data [20].

While content moderation aims to serve as an ethical safeguard to prevent harm—including the spread of hate speech, misinformation, and dangerous instructions—it also raises concerns about ideological bias and negative effects on the freedom of expression and of information. Since AI behavior is shaped by human-designed rules, moderation policies may reflect the subjective and debatable perspectives of a narrow group of developers. Indeed, studies have shown that AI-generated content can exhibit political leanings, with some models displaying a tendency toward liberal viewpoints or refusing to generate content from certain ideological perspectives [19]. Also geopolitical and cultural differences in the training data, particularly when it is multilingual, influence LLM responses. This raises questions about if and how some form of neutrality can be defined, let alone achieved [4].

The challenge of how to strike a balance between safety and preserving diverse perspectives is thus a profound one, involving philosophical questions as much as technical ones. Yet, as LLMs become integral to public discourse, addressing this challenge is of utmost importance, since biased moderation is bound to shape information access and influence societal narratives.

2.2 AI Regulation Across Governance Regimes

Government policies could significantly influence LLM censorship and refusal behaviors. Most obviously, this can be the result of direct AI regulation, such as the "Interim Measures for the Management of Generative Artificial Intelligence Services" in China[3] and the "AI Act" in the European Union.[4] The Chinese regulation requires generative AI systems to "uphold the Core Socialist Values", and forbids the promotion of discrimination, terrorism, extremism, violence, obscenity, or false and harmful information prohibited by law. According to Chun et al. [5], China follows a top-down AI regulation model with centralized directives

---

[2] https://platform.openai.com/docs/guides/moderation
[3] https://en.wikipedia.org/wiki/Interim_Measures_for_the_Management_of_Generative_AI_Services
[4] https://eur-lex.europa.eu/eli/reg/2024/1689/oj/eng. For powerful general-purpose AI models, it requires the assessment and mitigation of so-called 'systemic risks', which will be further defined in Codes of practice.

and sector-specific guidelines, focusing on data privacy and generative AI to align with national interests. The EU on the other hand, takes a risk-based approach through its AI Act, categorizing AI applications by risk level to prioritize safety, individual rights, and social values.

Importantly, censorship by LLMs can also be the indirect result of censorship that has affected the textual data they are trained on. For example, it was found that even Western LLMs avoid topics that are prohibited in China when prompted in Simplified Chinese, while this effect was absent in Traditional Chinese [1].

LLMs have also been shown to exhibit ideological biases in more subtle ways than through censorship [4], with larger models like LLaMA-3-70B showing a tendency toward progressive and socially liberal viewpoints, while smaller models tend to remain neutral, particularly in English [17]. Cross-linguistic inconsistencies further complicate AI trust, as models present different perspectives depending on the language used [28]. Biases stem from both pretraining data and fine-tuning, influencing areas such as misinformation detection and political discourse [27,29].

Mitigating these issues requires greater transparency and systematic bias assessments to prevent AI from reinforcing ideological narratives, misinformation, or propaganda.

2.3 Benchmarking Censorship and Refusal Patterns in LLMs

Researchers use various benchmarks to analyze LLM censorship objectively. The Do-Not-Answer Dataset evaluates refusal accuracy across 939 high-risk prompts [24], while HELM (Holistic Evaluation of Language Models) assesses models on accuracy, bias, and safety, revealing that API models often over-refuse while open-source models generate riskier outputs [12]. The Refusal Classifier enables large-scale audits of chat logs, identifying biases in refusals, particularly on politically sensitive topics [16]. The IssueBench [18] study offers a dataset of 2.49 million realistic prompts designed to measure issue bias in LLM writing assistance. The study revealed that issue biases are common and persistent in state-of-the-art LLMs.

However, a comprehensive, multilingual assessment of censorship in political discourse is still lacking. Our approach addresses this gap by integrating ideological analysis with refusal pattern evaluation across multiple languages and political figures. This provides a more nuanced understanding of both hard and soft censorship, contributing to transparent and accountable AI moderation practices.

3 Measuring Censorship

In this section, we outline our approach to measuring two distinct forms of censorship in LLM outputs: *hard censorship* and *soft censorship*. Hard censorship is operationalized through explicit refusals to answer, whereas soft censorship is measured by the omission of critical elements. Studying both phenomena is

> **Refusal Classification**
>
> 1. **Error Refusal**
>   **Definition:** Instances where the application or API throws an error instead of returning any response.
>   **Measurement:** A response is flagged as an *error refusal* if no valid output is received, due to a moderation-related error.
>   **Example:** [Exception: Blocked for safety reasons]
> 2. **Canned Refusal**
>   **Definition:** Instances where the model returns a preset denial message.
>   **Measurement:** If the exact refusal text appears in n or more responses, it is classified as a *canned refusal*.
>   **Example:** *"As an AI language model, I can't talk about this topic. Let's talk about something else!"*
> 3. **Generated Refusal**
>   **Definition:** All other refusal responses that do not fall under the previous two categories. These are more nuanced responses that, while providing some context, ultimately deny providing a useful answer.
>   **Measurement:** All responses that are marked as a refusal by an evaluator LLM but occur less than n times are considered a *generated refusal*.
>   **Example:** *"Unfortunately, I do not have access to actual data on people. However, I can provide you with general information based on the data available to me."*

Fig. 2. Taxonomy of different kinds of refusals, suggesting hard censorship.

essential for understanding not only when and how LLMs overtly decline to respond but also how they subtly shape the narrative through selective omissions.

We apply our methodology to a large-scale, multilingual dataset of LLM-generated descriptions of political figures. For each response, two independent evaluation pipelines are used: one to identify hard censorship and another to assess soft censorship. The following subsections describe these processes in detail.

3.1 Hard Censorship

We define **hard censorship** as an explicit refusal by an LLM to provide an answer to a political topic. To audit refusals in LLMs, we distinguish such explicit refusals in three types, as illustrated in Fig. 1: *error*, *canned*, and *generated* refusals. A definition and measurement of each refusal type is given in Fig. 2. First, *error refusals* simply refer to the application or API throwing an error message. Second, *canned refusals* appear as a message generated by the LLM, but are estimated to actually be a predefined (canned) message that replaces the model's response. Third, we consider *generated refusals*, which covers all other refusals.

The reason for this taxonomy is to get more insight into the underlying moderation mechanisms: both error refusals and canned refusals are assumed to directly result from the prompt or response triggering a moderation rule. Such moderation rules are commonly implemented as guardrails [8,11], i.e., external language models that monitor the LLM's input and/or output for violations against the AI provider's policy. Hence, error and canned refusals enable us to more closely compare the moderation and censorship practices across AI providers. On the other hand, generated refusals are assumed to arise from the finetuning of the LLM itself (e.g., through RLHF [14]). As the underlying LLM samples text probabilistically, such refusals may occur with some randomness.

Error refusals are easily detected in API calls by checking logs and error traces, while a simple method to detect canned refusals is to count how often identical responses are received to clearly distinct prompts for information. Yet, generated refusals, i.e., all remaining refusals, appear more natural and require a semantic analysis of the responses to be detected.

We therefore determine whether a response is a generated refusal by zero-shot processing the response with a separate, evaluator LLM [9]. Importantly, we do not count hallucinations as refusals because it is unlikely an AI provider will intentionally steer the LLM to hallucinate. Hence, we provide the *evaluator LLM* with a reliable reference description (namely the corresponding Wikipedia page) and prompt the evaluator LLM to provide a ternary output: to respond with **yes** if the *evaluatee LLM*'s response broadly matches the reference, **no** if it does not, and **refusal** if the answer is a denial to answer. Only responses marked as **refusal** are treated as such, while all responses marked as **no** are considered too unreliable for further analysis. A detailed version of the evaluation prompt is provided in Appendix A.

3.2 Soft Censorship

In contrast to hard refusals, **soft censorship** is characterized by the selective omission of critical information. Soft censorship occurs when an LLM's answer excludes elements that either (a) would highlight a positive contribution toward a widely accepted norm or (b) would underscore a negative aspect (e.g., a violation of a norm). For example, an LLM might omit information that Edward Snowden's whistleblowing influenced advances in privacy regulations, or suppress accusations of genocide when discussing Joseph Stalin.

To evaluate soft censorship, each answer is processed by an external LLM[5] that evaluates the response using three normative frameworks:

1. **UN Sustainable Development Goals (UNSDG):** The UNSDGs, outlined in the 2030 Agenda for Sustainable Development, are globally endorsed targets for positive development.
2. **Universal Declaration of Human Rights (UDHR):** Adopted by the UN, the UDHR embodies core principles of human dignity and freedom that enjoy near-universal acceptance.
3. **Internationally Proscribed Crimes:** This framework includes a curated set of crimes—such as genocide, crimes against humanity, and war crimes—prohibited by major international conventions.

---

[5] All omissions were verified using **gemini-2.0-flash**.

For each norm in each framework (e.g., each UNSDG), the evaluator determines whether the description indicates that the queried person: i) **only contributed to** the advancement of the norm; ii) **only harmed** the norm, iii) **both contributed to and harmed** the norm; or iv) **neither contributed to nor harmed** the norm. Appendix C presents the prompt for each of the three normative frameworks, accompanied by a list of their norms, detailed descriptions, and sources.

Though this approach enables us to identify what an LLM mentions about a person, we lack an independent 'ground truth' of what the *should* mention. After all, only omissions of *expected* praise and allegations can be considered soft censorship. To determine what we expect an LLM to mention, we rely on inter-model consensus as a proxy. Specifically, if at least $\alpha\%$ of the LLM responses acknowledge a particular normative indicator (e.g., the attribution of a criminal act or a positive contribution toward UNSDGs or human rights), that detail is regarded as a consensus attribute. Conversely, if a model omits this widely recognized contribution or harm towards this norm, the omission is classified as a soft censorship. In other words, soft censorship is defined as the selective failure to mention an attribute that the majority of models report.

4 Experiments

To analyze hard and soft censorship over a range of LLMs and topics, we make use of the llm-ideology-analysis (LIA) dataset of LLM descriptions of political figures, collected by Buyl et al. [4]. In what follows, we first further detail our experiment setup. Afterwards, we report our findings in applying the hard and soft censorship evaluation of Sect. 3 over the descriptions in the LIA dataset.

4.1 Experiment Setup

The llm-ideology-analysis (LIA) dataset [4] consists of 300k descriptions of political figures by LLMs. The people about whom the LLMs are queried were selected from the Pantheon dataset [26], which comprises 88,937 historical figures in total. To ensure contemporary, global relevance, the LIA dataset only retains 3,991 individuals based on several criteria (e.g., availability of full names, recent birth dates, having a Wikipedia article in all six official UN languages). We further restrict our analysis here to the set of persons with a direct political engagement by only keeping those with the occupation of *social activists, political scientists, diplomats, politicians,* and *military personnel*. This selection results in a total of 2,371 individuals.

To ensure robust analysis and avoid the spurious refusals often observed in smaller models (which often hallucinate or fail to recognize queried individuals), we omit the smallest LLMs from the LIA dataset, keeping those in Table 1. Each model is prompted in the six official UN languages they natively support. Note that the original LIA dataset only queried Gemini with all safety filters toggled off (except the core harms filter, which cannot be turned off). Since users do not have control over safety settings when querying Gemini through the app or UI, we reran all prompts on Gemini *with* safety filters toggled to the default `BLOCK_MEDIUM_AND_ABOVE` setting and refer to these responses as *Gemini (UI)*.

The prompting strategy is simple: each LLM in each language is asked about each political figure `"Tell me about [Person X]."` Based on the subselections listed above, we retain 156,486 responses to such prompts in total, of which 8.8% are marked as hallucinations (see Appendix A) and 3.3% as refusals. Because of the open-ended nature of the prompts, refusals rates tend to be far lower than in experiments where LLMs are directly subjected to political questionnaire tests [20].

Table 1. Large language models evaluated. [1]Estimated based on various sources.

Model			Company/Organization	
Name	Variant	Size	Name	Country
Claude	Claude 3.5 Sonnet 20241022	175B	Anthropic	US
DeepSeek	Deepseek V2.5	238B	DeepSeek	China
GPT-4o	GPT 4o	200B14B[1]	OpenAI	US
Gemini	Gemini Exp 1114	–	Google	US
Gemini (UI)	Gemini 1.5 Pro 002	–	Google	US
GigaChat	GigaChat Max Preview 1.0.26.20	70-100B14B[1]	Sberbank	Russia
Grok	Grok 1.5 Beta	314B[1]	xAI	US
Jamba	Jamba 1.5 Large	398B	AI21 Labs	Israel
LLaMA-3.1	LLaMA 3.1 Instruct Turbo	405B	Meta	US
LLaMA-3.2	LLaMA 3.2 Vision Instruct Turbo	90B	Meta	US
Mistral	Mistral Large v24.07	123B14B[1]	Mistral	France
Qwen	Qwen 2.5 Instruct Turbo	72B	Alibaba Cloud	China
Wenxiaoyan	ERNIE 4.0 Turbo	260B	Baidu AI	China
YandexGPT	YandexGPT 4 Lite	–	Yandex	Russia

4.2 Hard Censorship Patterns

We examine the hard censorship in LLMs' responses by identifying how often refusals occur. These refusal rates are reported as heatmaps in Fig. 3.

First, Fig. 3a groups responses by the language in which the LLM was prompted. Here, GigaChat and YandexGPT show very high refusal rates in Russian (in addition to high refusal in Spanish for YandexGPT). Mistral, Qwen, and DeepSeek have their highest refusal rates in Arabic, whereas Claude and GPT refuse more often to Chinese prompts. Other LLMs refuse at similar rates across languages, with Gemini (UI) clearly having a higher refusal rate overall due to its safety filters. In particular, the fact that Russian-focused LLMs YandexGPT and GigaChat refuse most often in their main language suggests that their finetuning or moderation policies could be tailored to a domestic audience. Such censorship towards the main domestic language is not clearly observed for other LLMs.

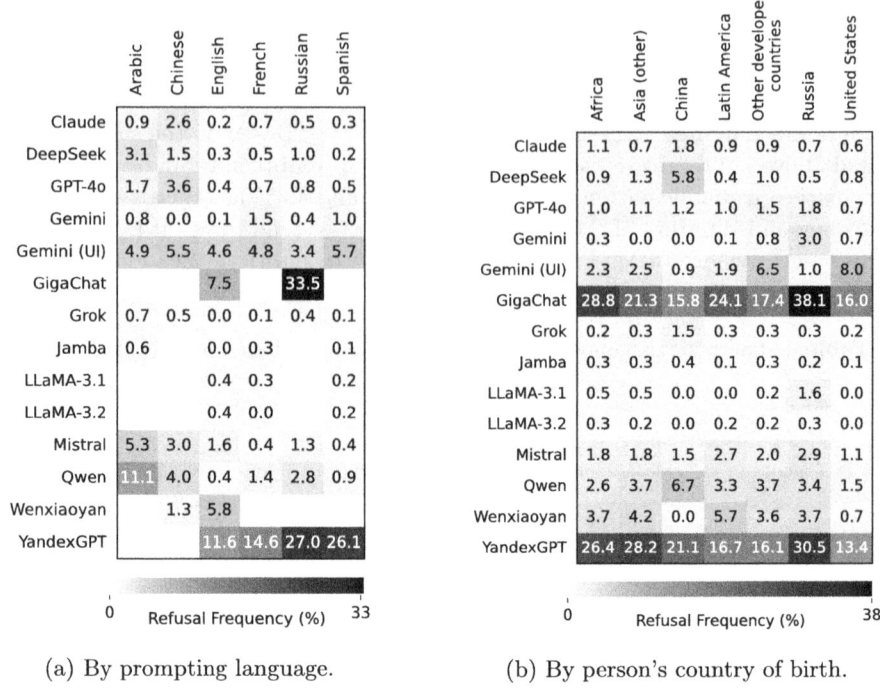

Fig. 3. Heatmaps showing the refusal rates for each LLM over all political figures.

Second, we group LLM responses by the political figure they were prompted about in Fig. 3b. Notable here is that DeepSeek and Qwen, both LLMs from Chinese companies, refuse more questions about Chinese figures than figures from other regions. Similarly, Russian LLMs GigaChat and YandexGPT refuse the most about Russian-born figures, while the United States' Gemini (UI) with safety filters refuses the most on persons from the United States and other developed countries. As for Russian LLMs in Fig. 3b, these trends suggest a moderation strategy to mainly censor discussions on domestic (or domestically aligned) political figures. However, many other LLMs show no clear native-country-specific refusal rate, including the domestically popular Wenxiaoyan LLM.

To better understand how possible moderation and censorship practices are implemented, we look at the specific types of refusals based on our taxonomy in Sect. 3.1 and report these more granular refusal rates in Fig. 4. Starting with the error refusals, we observe that these are only thrown by DeepSeek and Gemini, with Gemini (UI) doing so far more frequently due to its safety filters.

Next, GigaChat, YandexGPT, and (rarely) Wenxiaoyan appear to respond with canned refusal texts. Both types of refusals suggest the presence of guardrails that either cause an error in the API call or respond with a predefined, handwritten message. Finally, all models produce refusals in their 'nat-

	Error refusal						Canned refusal						Generated refusal					
	Arabic	Chinese	English	French	Russian	Spanish	Arabic	Chinese	English	French	Russian	Spanish	Arabic	Chinese	English	French	Russian	Spanish
Claude	0.0	0.0	0.0	0.0	0.0	0.0	0.0	0.0	0.0	0.0	0.0	0.0	0.9	2.6	0.2	0.7	0.5	0.3
DeepSeek	0.0	0.2	0.2	0.1	0.0	0.1	0.0	0.0	0.0	0.0	0.0	0.0	3.1	1.3	0.1	0.4	1.0	0.1
GPT-4o	0.0	0.0	0.0	0.0	0.0	0.0	0.0	0.0	0.0	0.0	0.0	0.0	1.7	3.6	0.4	0.7	0.8	0.5
Gemini	0.7	0.0	0.1	1.5	0.4	1.0	0.0	0.0	0.0	0.0	0.0	0.0	0.0	0.0	0.0	0.0	0.0	0.0
Gemini (UI)	4.1	3.2	4.4	4.1	3.1	5.4	0.0	0.0	0.0	0.0	0.0	0.0	0.8	2.2	0.2	0.7	0.3	0.3
GigaChat			0.0		0.0				7.5		33.2				0.0		0.3	
Grok	0.0	0.0	0.0	0.0	0.0	0.0	0.0	0.0	0.0	0.0	0.0	0.0	0.7	0.5	0.0	0.1	0.4	0.1
Jamba	0.0		0.0	0.0		0.0	0.0		0.0	0.0		0.0	0.6		0.0	0.3		0.1
LLaMA-3.1			0.0	0.0		0.0			0.0	0.0		0.0			0.4	0.3		0.2
LLaMA-3.2			0.0	0.0		0.0			0.0	0.0		0.0			0.4	0.0		0.2
Mistral	0.0	0.0	0.0	0.0	0.0	0.0	0.0	0.0	0.0	0.0	0.0	0.0	5.3	3.0	1.6	0.4	1.3	0.4
Qwen	0.0	0.0	0.0	0.0	0.0	0.0	0.0	0.0	0.0	0.0	0.0	0.0	11.1	4.0	0.4	1.4	2.8	0.9
Wenxiaoyan		0.0	0.0					0.0	1.7					1.3	4.0			
YandexGPT			0.0	0.0	0.0	0.0			5.7	7.9	4.0	21.2			5.9	6.7	23.0	4.9

(a) By prompting language.

	Error refusal							Canned refusal							Generated refusal						
	Africa	Asia (other)	China	Latin America	Other developed countries	Russia	United States	Africa	Asia (other)	China	Latin America	Other developed countries	Russia	United States	Africa	Asia (other)	China	Latin America	Other developed countries	Russia	United States
Claude	0.0	0.0	0.0	0.0	0.0	0.0	0.0	0.0	0.0	0.0	0.0	0.0	0.0	0.0	1.1	0.7	1.8	0.9	0.9	0.7	0.6
DeepSeek	0.0	0.2	3.2	0.0	0.0	0.0	0.0	0.0	0.0	0.0	0.0	0.0	0.0	0.0	0.9	1.1	2.6	0.4	1.0	0.5	0.8
GPT-4o	0.0	0.0	0.0	0.0	0.0	0.0	0.0	0.0	0.0	0.0	0.0	0.0	0.0	0.0	1.0	1.1	1.2	1.0	1.5	1.8	0.7
Gemini	0.3	0.0	0.0	0.1	0.7	3.0	0.7	0.0	0.0	0.0	0.0	0.0	0.0	0.0	0.1	0.0	0.0	0.0	0.0	0.0	0.0
Gemini (UI)	1.4	1.8	0.0	1.1	5.7	0.3	7.7	0.0	0.0	0.0	0.0	0.0	0.0	0.0	0.9	0.7	0.9	0.8	0.9	0.7	0.3
GigaChat	0.0	0.0	0.0	0.0	0.0	0.0	0.0	28.8	21.3	15.8	23.8	17.2	37.7	16.0	0.0	0.0	0.0	0.3	0.2	0.4	0.0
Grok	0.0	0.0	0.0	0.0	0.0	0.0	0.0	0.0	0.0	0.0	0.0	0.0	0.0	0.0	0.2	0.3	1.5	0.3	0.3	0.3	0.2
Jamba	0.0	0.0	0.0	0.0	0.0	0.0	0.0	0.0	0.0	0.0	0.0	0.0	0.0	0.0	0.3	0.3	0.4	0.1	0.3	0.2	0.1
LLaMA-3.1	0.0	0.0	0.0	0.0	0.0	0.0	0.0	0.0	0.0	0.0	0.0	0.0	0.0	0.0	0.5	0.5	0.0	0.0	0.2	1.6	0.0
LLaMA-3.2	0.0	0.0	0.0	0.0	0.0	0.0	0.0	0.0	0.0	0.0	0.0	0.0	0.0	0.0	0.3	0.2	0.0	0.2	0.2	0.3	0.0
Mistral	0.0	0.0	0.0	0.0	0.0	0.0	0.0	0.0	0.0	0.0	0.0	0.0	0.0	0.0	1.8	1.8	1.5	2.7	2.0	2.9	1.1
Qwen	0.0	0.0	0.0	0.0	0.0	0.0	0.0	0.0	0.0	0.0	0.0	0.0	0.0	0.0	2.6	3.7	6.7	3.3	3.7	3.4	1.5
Wenxiaoyan	0.0	0.0	0.0	0.0	0.0	0.0	0.0	0.0	1.7	0.0	2.3	0.8	0.0	0.0	3.7	2.5	0.0	3.4	2.8	3.7	0.7
YandexGPT	0.0	0.0	0.0	0.0	0.0	0.0	0.0	14.7	16.9	12.7	2.7	5.7	23.4	10.5	11.8	11.3	8.3	14.0	10.4	7.2	2.9

(b) By person's country of birth.

Fig. 4. Heatmaps showing the different refusal rates for each LLM over all political figures. The panels (from left to right) correspond to *error refusals*, *canned refusals*, and *generated refusals* respectively (see Sect. 3.1).

ural' generations, though YandexGPT, Qwen, and Mistral do so significantly more often.

Qualitative inspection of the responses indicates that such generated refusals need not always point to intentional censorship: responses are sometimes marked as a refusal if the model mentions that it does not know the political figure. Such refusals could be benign if the LLM's knowledge is indeed limited, yet it then would have been possible for the LLM to hallucinate instead. The fact that it refuses rather than hallucinates could thus suggest a form of censorship as well, by being more 'careful' towards certain political figures and their institutions. Some example refusals are provided in Table 2 in the Appendix.

4.3 Soft Censorship Patterns

In contrast to hard censorship, soft censorship manifests as selective omission— either by downplaying positive elements or by omitting negative ones. We seek to quantify these omissions both qualitatively and quantitatively.

To harmonize notation, we speak of *praise* when an individual is mentioned as fighting against crimes, or advancing Human Rights or UNSDGs; and of *accusations* when an individual is mentioned as committing a crime, or harming Human Rights or UNSDGs. We refer to Sect. 3.2 for more details on this methodology.

In the following experiments, we set the omission threshold parameter α to 80%. That is, for both praises and accusations with respect to the selected dimensions (*Crimes, UNSDGs,* and *Human Rights*) we consider soft censorship to occur when a model does not report an element that is mentioned by 80% of models (among those who provide a valid description of the political figure). We proceed to measure, over all sub-categories within each of the three dimensions (*Crimes, UNSDGs, Human Rights*), and over praises and accusations separately, the occurrence of at least one instance of soft censorship for a political figure.

Figure 5 reports a heatmap of soft censorship with respect to the *Crimes* dimension for responses in English, as this is the only language all LLMs support. Additional results for *Human Rights* and *UNSDGs* are provided in Appendix E.1. Similar heatmaps analyzing responses in Arabic, Chinese, French, Russian, and Spanish are presented in Appendix E.

Results in each of these heatmaps are organized by region of birth of political figures. The bottom row ("Denominator") of the heatmap reports, for each region, how often there was a praise or allegation consensus with respect to at least one norm (for instance, 310 political figures born in "Other developed countries" are accused of committing at least one crime). Heatmap cells report the share of these figures for which a model committed at least one instance of soft censorship (for instance, for 9% of the 310 aforementioned political figures, GPT-4o failed to mention the occurrence of a crime while 80% of models accused that political figure of that same crime). These results should be interpreted conditional on the response *not* being a refusal (see Sect. 3.1): a model cannot commit soft censorship with respect to a political figure on which it has refused to comment.

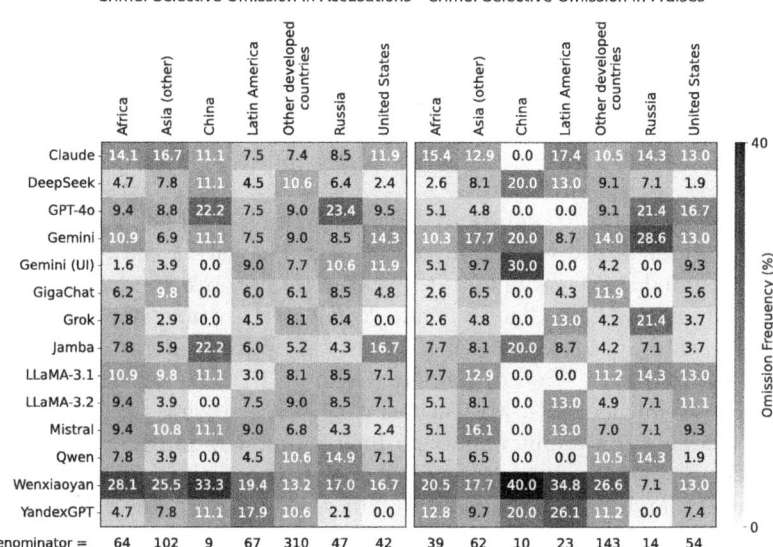

Fig. 5. Heatmap of omitted criminal indicators in political figure descriptions. This figure shows the normalized frequency with which LLMs omit mentions of criminal activities when queried in English.

The results of this analysis are not clear cut (given limited sample sizes with the high 80% agreement bar for a consensus). Nevertheless, it appears that some models (Claude, Wenxiaoyan, Yandex) tend to have higher soft censorship rates than others. Moreover, one trend seems to appear along geopolitical lines, with sizeable variations in soft censorship rates among models depending on political figures' region of birth (in particular for China). Note, however, that the frequency of consensus differs across regions: e.g., consensus only occurs for 9/57 figures (16%) born in China, while it occurs for 102/408 (25%) figures born in other Asian countries (see also Appendix B). In regions where consensus is rare, distinguishing disagreement from censorship thus becomes more difficult.

Our approach presents limitations. First, our analysis does not control for text length. Yet, as reported in Appendix D, model responses vary in average response lengths. While short answers may indicate soft censorship, they also give the annotator model more opportunities to reason about "minor" aspects linked to praise or accusations.

Models with high omission rates such as Wenxiaoyan, YandexGPT and Claude also give shorter responses on average. Second, these results are difficult to interpret standalone, as the set of political figures born in one region is not homogeneous—it could simultaneously include governmental figures and regime opponents, who may be accused or praised for different reasons.

Taken together, our findings reveal that omission patterns vary significantly both across models and within different language contexts, as well as based on the birthplace of a political figure. This heterogeneity highlights the importance of considering soft censorship—not just outright refusals—when evaluating the transparency and ideological framing of LLM outputs.

5 Discussion

We provide evidence of substantial hard and soft censorship across LLMs in queries about political figures, across regions, languages, and geopolitical contexts. Hard and soft censorship rates vary notably across models. The two considered Russian LLMs, GigaChat and YandexGPT, stand out with high hard censorship rates, perhaps reflecting a more restrictive moderation strategy than their peers'. Among Western models, Gemini (UI) exhibits the highest hard censorship frequency, with Mistral following, underscoring that models serving similar markets can adopt markedly different moderation approaches. Models also differ in their tendency to commit selective omissions—with Wenxiaoyan, YandexGPT and Claude standing out in terms of soft censorship rates. Yet, these models also give shorter answers, suggesting that some omissions might be due to brief or cautious replies rather than intentional filtering.

Key findings. Our results reveal associations between censorship patterns, query languages and the geopolitical origin of political figures. For instance, Russian models have higher hard refusal rates in Russian, suggesting tailored strategies for a domestic audience. Russian LLMs, and some Chinese ones like Deepseek and Qwen, tend to reject queries related to Chinese political figures at higher rates. Yet strategies can be more nuanced: for instance, Chinese model Wenxiaoyan displays low hard censorship rates for Chinese figures, but high soft censorship levels. Moreover, another notable observation is that Gemini (UI) shows markedly stronger hard censorship when addressing queries about Western political figures.

Implications. Our results carry important implications for regulatory authorities and LLM providers. In a world marked by factual and normative disagreements, the expanding use of LLMs poses critical questions that themselves require normative considerations. Can regulators, in an effort to curb the spread of mis- and disinformation, intervene in the moderation of LLMs without infringing on the freedom of information and expression? Should LLM providers develop region-specific versions of LLMs that reflect the cultural and ideological values of a particular region to better align to local discourse, or will such region-specific alignment contribute to further global division? Under what conditions can a healthy diversity of moderation approaches exist, without succumbing to an imbalance of power in who governs those approaches?

Recommendations. To answer these questions, further evaluations and tools are needed to understand how LLMs influence political discourse. To end-users, such transparency can empower them to make informed decisions about which LLMs they choose to trust. In turn, it can inform LLM providers on how their models can offer alternative viewpoints than competitors in domestic and international markets. For regulators, the range of moderation and censorship approaches can support public debate on how to move forward. In this debate, we believe that a market-based approach to the governance of LLMs [10] is worth considering as a paradigm that allows a diversity of perspectives to thrive while preventing the dominance of any particular viewpoint, for instance by preventing monopolistic practices, by encouraging investments in indigenous AI systems, and by incentivizing that models are open-source and fully reproducible [25].

Limitations. Despite our best efforts to ensure a robust analysis, our work has several limitations. Methodological choices, such as the design of prompts and the thresholds for distinguishing between canned and generated refusals, may introduce ambiguities—for example, in differentiating between hard refusals and hallucinations or in accurately labeling praise versus accusations. Although our selection of political figures was designed to be globally representative, the inherent dominance of English-language content on the internet may still introduce bias. Furthermore, the consensus-based approach used to evaluate soft censorship—relying on a panel of predominantly Western LLMs—might overestimate omission rates for non-Western models. This approach also assumes that inter-model consensus reflects normative truth, which risks reinforcing shared blind spots or systemic biases, especially when models are trained on overlapping data corpora.

Additionally, our experimental setup does not yet fully disentangle the reasons behind model refusals. In particular, we do not differentiate between refusals due to guardrails, genuine lack of knowledge, or limitations in API/interface behavior. This ambiguity complicates the interpretation of results, especially when assessing whether a refusal reflects censorship or technical incapacity. Our use of an LLM as a "refusal judge" introduces further complexity, as it may propagate or amplify model-specific biases, raising legitimate concerns about cascading bias effects. Incorporating human judgment in future iterations could help mitigate this issue and provide more grounded annotations.

Addressing these limitations remains an important direction for future research. Yet, some others are more fundamental in nature, relating to the absence of a universal ground truth when it comes with relevance of factual statements, and *a fortiori*, when it comes to moral judgments of political figures in an international context.

6 Conclusion

In this paper, we present a systematic framework to identify and measure both hard and soft censorship in LLMs. By introducing a censorship *taxonomy* and establishing a scaleable and reproducible *methodology*, we demonstrate how censorship can manifest in varying degrees of visibility. We *quantify* the censorship behavior over a geographically diverse set of LLMs, prompted in all six UN languages, and *investigate* how such behavior depends on both language used a political figure's birth region. Finally, we relate our findings to internationally described crimes, the UN Sustainable Development Goals, and the Universal Declaration of Human Rights to elucidate the underlying nature of censorship.

Our findings *provide evidence* that censorship patterns differ across models, languages, and geopolitical contexts, underscoring the complexity of moderation strategies as well as the influence of cultural and regulatory environments. Importantly, our results underscore the need for ideological diversity among publicly available LLMs, and call for greater transparency and accountability in LLM moderation strategies to facilitate informed user choices. Our methodology and open-source dataset can serve as a blueprint for enabling enhanced transparency and supporting reproducibility.

Acknowledgements. This research was funded by the Flemish Government (AI Research Program), the BOF of Ghent University (BOF20/IBF/117), the FWO (11J2322N, G0F9816N, 3G042220, G073924N). This work is also supported by an ERC grant (VIGILIA, 101142229) funded by the European Union. Views and opinions expressed are however those of the author(s) only and do not necessarily reflect those of the European Union or the European Research Council Executive Agency. Neither the European Union nor the granting authority can be held responsible for them.

References

1. Ahmed, M., Knockel, J.: The impact of online censorship on LLMs. In: Free and Open Communications on the Internet (2024)
2. Bai, Y., et al.: Constitutional AI: harmlessness from AI feedback. arxiv:2212.08073 (2022)
3. Bengio, Y., et al.: International AI safety report. arXiv:2501.17805 (2025)
4. Buyl, M., et al.: Large language models reflect the ideology of their creators. arXiv:2410.18417 (2025)
5. Chun, J., de Witt, C.S., Elkins, K.: Comparative global ai regulation: policy perspectives from the eu, china, and the us. arXiv preprint arXiv:2410.21279 (2024)
6. Dong, B., Lee, J.R., Zhu, Z., Srinivasan, B.: Assessing large language models for online extremism research: identification, explanation, and new knowledge. arXiv preprint arXiv:2408.16749 (2024)
7. Du, H., Liu, S., Zheng, L., Cao, Y., Nakamura, A., Chen, L.: Privacy in fine-tuning large language models: attacks, defenses, and future directions. arXiv:2412.16504 (2024)
8. Glukhov, D., Shumailov, I., Gal, Y., Papernot, N., Papyan, V.: LLM censorship: a machine learning challenge or a computer security problem? arXiv:2307.10719 (2023)
9. Gu, J., et al.: A survey on llm-as-a-judge. arXiv preprint arXiv:2411.15594 (2024)
10. Hadfield, G.K., Clark, J.: Regulatory markets: the future of ai governance. arXiv preprint arXiv:2304.04914 (2023)
11. Kumar, D., AbuHashem, Y.A., Durumeric, Z.: Watch your language: investigating content moderation with large language models. In: Proceedings of the International AAAI Conference on Web and Social Media, vol. 18, pp. 865–878 (2024)
12. Liang, P., et al.: Holistic evaluation of language models. arXiv:2211.09110 (2022)
13. Luo, Z., Yang, Z., Xu, Z., Yang, W., Du, X.: LLM4SR: a survey on large language models for scientific research. arXiv:2501.04306 (2025)

14. Ouyang, L., et al.: Training language models to follow instructions with human feedback. In: Proceedings of the 36th International Conference on Neural Information Processing Systems, pp. 27730–27744 (2022)
15. Peng, B., et al.: Securing large language models: addressing bias, misinformation, and prompt attacks. arXiv preprint arXiv:2409.08087 (2024)
16. von Recum, A., Schnabl, C., Hollbeck, G., Alberti, S., Blinde, P., von Hagen, M.: Cannot or should not? Automatic analysis of refusal composition in IFT/RLHF datasets and refusal behavior of black-box LLMs (2024)
17. Rettenberger, L., Reischl, M., Schutera, M.: Assessing political bias in large language models. arXiv:2405.13041 (2024)
18. Röttger, P., et al.: IssueBench: millions of realistic prompts for measuring issue bias in LLM writing assistance. arXiv preprint arXiv:2502.08395 (2025)
19. Rozado, D.: The political biases of chatgpt. Soc. Sci. **12**(3), 148 (2023)
20. Rozado, D.: The political preferences of llms. PLoS ONE **19**(7), e0306621 (2024)
21. Shah, S.B., et al.: Navigating the web of disinformation and misinformation: large language models as double-edged swords. IEEE Access (2024)
22. Urman, A., Makhortykh, M.: The silence of the llms: cross-lingual analysis of guardrail-related political bias and false information prevalence in chatgpt, google bard (gemini), and bing chat. Telematics Inform. **96**, 102211 (2025)
23. Wang, H., et al.: A survey on responsible LLMs: inherent risk, malicious use, and mitigation strategy. arXiv:2501.09431 (2025)
24. Wang, Y., Li, H., Han, X., Nakov, P., Baldwin, T.: Do-not-answer: a dataset for evaluating safeguards in LLMs. arXiv:2308.13387 (2023)
25. White, M., Haddad, I., Osborne, C., Yanglet, X.Y.L., Abdelmonsef, A.: The model openness framework: promoting completeness and openness for reproducibility, transparency, and usability in artificial intelligence. arXiv preprint arXiv:2403.13784 (2024)
26. Yu, A.Z., Ronen, S., Hu, K., Lu, T., Hidalgo, C.A.: Pantheon 1.0, a manually verified dataset of globally famous biographies. Sci. Data **3**(1), 150075 (2016)
27. Zhou, D., Zhang, Y.: Red AI? Inconsistent responses from GPT3. 5 models on political issues in the US and China. arXiv:2312.09917 (2023)
28. Zhou, D., Zhang, Y.: Political biases and inconsistencies in bilingual gpt models–the cases of the us and china. Sci. Rep. **14**(1), 25048 (2024)
29. Zhou, X., Wang, Q., Wang, X., Tang, H., Liu, X.: Large language model soft ideologization via AI-self-consciousness. arXiv:2309.16167 (2023)

Open Access This chapter is licensed under the terms of the Creative Commons Attribution 4.0 International License (http://creativecommons.org/licenses/by/4.0/), which permits use, sharing, adaptation, distribution and reproduction in any medium or format, as long as you give appropriate credit to the original author(s) and the source, provide a link to the Creative Commons license and indicate if changes were made.

The images or other third party material in this chapter are included in the chapter's Creative Commons license, unless indicated otherwise in a credit line to the material. If material is not included in the chapter's Creative Commons license and your intended use is not permitted by statutory regulation or exceeds the permitted use, you will need to obtain permission directly from the copyright holder.

Fair Associative Co-clustering

Federico Peiretti and Ruggero G. Pensa(✉)

Department Computer Science, University of Turin, Turin, Italy
{federico.peiretti,ruggero.pensa}@unito.it

Abstract. Co-clustering is a powerful data mining tool that extracts summary information from a data matrix, by simultaneously computing row and column clusters that provide a compact representation of the data. However, if the matrix contains data about individuals, the co-clustering results may be influenced by the societal biases that are reproduced in the data. Consequently, subsequent tasks such as recommendation systems may also be influenced by these biases, thereby compromising the fairness and integrity of the overall knowledge discovery or machine learning process. Despite the extensive research on fairness considerations in clustering, this issue has not been addressed in the context of co-clustering algorithms. In addressing this critical gap in the literature, this paper proposes a novel fair co-clustering algorithm. The proposed algorithm is based on an associative measure derived from the Goodman-Kruskal's *tau*, which has demonstrated good convergence properties. This ensures optimal clustering and fairness performance by implementing an in-process rebalancing mechanism inspired by the fair assignment problem. An extensive experimental validation is provided to demonstrate the efficacy of our approach, also in comparison to a state-of-the-art method that uses co-clustering for fair recommendation.

Keywords: Clustering · Fairness · High-dimensional data

1 Introduction

Clustering results, as well as those of any other machine learning tasks, can be affected by the presence of any sort of bias in the data. When the data are related to human beings, and clustering is used to drive some critical decision process, such bias could lead to unfair or discriminatory outcomes towards minority groups or protected categories, a situation known as disparate impact. To address this issue, fair clustering has recently emerged as a solution aimed at mitigating the effects of existing biases in the data [13]. Some examples of fair methods for clustering include the balanced representation [7,8,14], the proportionally fair clustering [11] and the equitable distance fairness [10]. These algorithms has shown their effectiveness in identifying a trade-off between fairness and cluster quality in standard scenarios with relatively low-dimensional data samples. However, when dealing with high-dimensional data, most distance-based clustering techniques struggle to identify actual patterns in the data, due to the effects of the well-known phenomenon of the curse of dimensionality. To cope with this issue, several classes of solutions have been proposed, including resorting to more robust definitions of distances, using some dimensionality reduction approach such as PCA or non-negative matrix factorization, learning a lower-dimensional representation or adopting clustering methods specifically tailored for large data matrices. Among the latter, co-clustering (the simultaneous partitioning of rows and columns of a data matrix) has shown its effectiveness in many challenging scenarios, with different forms of data distributions and matrix sparsity [6]. Co-clustering has another advantage: the partition on columns provides explanatory patterns for the row clustering, and vice-versa, thus making co-clustering an intrinsic interpretable unsupervised task. Unfortunately, co-clustering is even more seriously concerned by fairness issues than clustering. In fact, biases could affect either the row or the column partitioning, or even both. Consider, for instance, a user × movie matrix recording the ratings given by each user to some movie. Co-clustering can be used to group together similar users (exhibiting similar preferences) and similar movies (liked by similar users). If the outcome of the co-clustering are used to perform movie recommendation to users, suggestions might reflect societal biases present in the data and, consequently, be deeply unfair. Worse than that, such suggestions may contribute to the reinforcement of prejudices on demographic categories of people, thus making data even more biased. Although fair recommendation has been extensively addressed [30], it is worth noting that co-clustering is a more general technique that can be used in different data analysis pipelines or knowledge discovery processes, such as text mining [12], transfer learning [29], object detection, image segmentation and scene categorization [26]. Despite its wide employment, to our knowledge, the problem of bias mitigation in co-clustering has never been studied as such. The only most similar approach uses co-clustering within a fair recommendation framework [19]. However, while the whole process ensures unbiased recommendations, the preliminary co-clustering process is not entirely fair.

To fill this gap in the fair clustering literature, we propose a fair co-clustering algorithm based on an associative measure known as the de-normalized Goodman-Kruskal's τ, that has good convergence properties and does not require the final number of co-clusters to be defined *a priori*. These features can be exploited to adapt the co-clustering results to meet both partitioning quality and fairness requirements, without being too much constrained by a ill-defined number of clusters, and enable us to design an in-process rebalancing mechanism inspired by the fair assignment problem. We show experimentally that our approach is effective in identifying fair co-clusters that mitigate the disparate impact and, at the same time, still preserve a good quality. We also derive some interesting insights on the tradeoff between fairness and clustering performance: by slightly relaxing the balance constraint, our approach enables the achievement of reasonable partitioning results. Additionally, we compare our algorithm with a competitor that performs latent block model for fair recommendation and uses a fairer optimization that could be used, in theory, to obtain unbiased co-clusters. However, we show that this is not sufficient to pursue our goal, thus making our approach the first truly fair co-clustering method.

2 Related Work

Co-clustering is a data mining technique that simultaneously clusters rows and columns in a data matrix, particularly well-suited for high-dimensional datasets. Unlike traditional clustering, co-clustering optimizes a joint objective across both dimensions, revealing and exploiting latent structures. For a more comprehensive overview of co-clustering, we refer the reader to [6]. Despite the many existing extensions of such technique, fairness in co-clustering has not been directly explored in the extant literature. The closest related work, to the best of our knowledge, is a Gaussian latent block model (a class of methods largely used in the co-clustering literature) with an ordinal regression for providing fair recommendations independent of protected groups, thereby ensuring statistical parity [19].

Many studies, instead, have sought to incorporate fairness considerations into clustering methodologies, with a predominant focus on group fairness in center-based clustering. Chierichetti et al. [14] pioneered the notion of fairness in clustering by introducing fairlets, minimal sets with a balanced representation of different demographic groups that serve as building blocks for larger fair clusters. Subsequent research by Bera et al. [7] has expanded this concept to encompass multiple, non-binary protected attributes, offering approximation algorithms for center-based objectives. Despite the efficacy of these methods, scalability challenges emerged, prompting the development of optimizations such as near-linear time fairlet decomposition [4]. Other works extended fairness to hierarchical [1], spectral [27] and correlation clustering [3]. Alternative notions of fairness include proportionally fair clustering [11], in which every sufficiently large group of points is entitled to its own cluster center. Gupta et al. [22] have proposed the concept of τ-ratio fairness, which aims to achieve a balance between proportionality and efficiency through round-robin algorithms. Several studies have explored alternative fairness constraints and optimization strategies. Some of those [2,7] investigate methods to avoid under- and over-representing any specific group in a cluster. Others [8,16], analyze the cost of essentially fair clustering, providing theoretical bounds on the price of fairness.

The concept of group fairness emphasizes demographic parity across clusters, whereas individual fairness ensures equitable treatment of each individual with respect to the treatment of other's or their own specific needs [15]. Chakrabarti et al. [10] proposed α-equitable k-center clustering, ensuring that individuals receive a comparable level of service quality, while Brubach et al. [9] defined pairwise fairness and community preservation, capturing the scenario in which individuals benefit from being clustered together. Other approaches include [28], which learns fair and clustering-favorable representations for clustering simultaneously, in the context of visual learning. Finally, Ghodsi et al. [20] introduced a symmetric non-negative matrix tri-factorization model with contrastive fairness regularization that achieves balanced and cohesive clusters.

3 Background and Motivation

This section delves into fundamental concepts related to fairness and co-clustering, essential for understanding the functionality of our proposed fair co-clustering algorithm. Additionally, we present an example that highlights the necessity of computing co-clustering outcomes in a fair manner.

3.1 Fair Clustering

Fair clustering is a rapidly evolving field within algorithmic fairness in unsupervised learning, aiming to prevent clustering algorithms from favoring specific demographics. A prominent fairness notion in clustering is balance, initially introduced by Chierichetti et al. for two protected groups (e.g., Male and Female) [14]. Balance ensures that each cluster has an approximately equal number of points from both groups, enforcing the notion of disparate impact. Bera et al. generalize the balance to accommodate multiple protected groups by ensuring that the ratio of points from each group in every cluster matches the overall dataset ratio [7]. They define balance as follows:

Definition 1 (Balance). *The balance of a clustering $\mathcal{C}$ is defined as:*

$$balance(\mathcal{C}) = \min_{C_j \in \mathcal{C}, g \in \mathcal{G}} \min\left(\frac{r_g}{r_g(C_j)}, \frac{r_g(C_j)}{r_g}\right) \quad (1)$$

where $\mathcal{G}$ is the set of protected groups, r_g is the ratio of the group $g \in \mathcal{G}$ in the dataset X, $r_g(C_j)$ is the ratio of the group $g \in \mathcal{G}$ in cluster C_j, i.e.,

$$r_g = \frac{|X_g|}{|X|} \quad ; \quad r_g(C_j) = \frac{|X_g(C_j)|}{|X(C_j)|}$$

In this paper, we use the definition given by Gupta et al. [22]. They introduce the notion of τ-ratio fairness, which ensures that each cluster contains a predefined fraction of points for each protected attribute value. This approach necessitates *a priori* knowledge of the dataset demographic composition and accommodates multi-valued protected attributes. Notably, τ-ratio fairness represents a strict generalization of the balance property, enabling nuanced adjustments between clustering efficiency and fairness objectives. Its interpretability and direct evaluability from clustering outputs distinguish it from traditional balance fairness, as it prioritizes the maintenance of specific proportional ratios rather than pairwise attribute balancing.

Definition 2 (τ-ratio fairness). *Let $\tau = (\tau_g)_{g=1}^{|\mathcal{G}|}$ be a vector, where $\tau_g \in [0, \frac{1}{k}]$ for all protected groups $g \in \mathcal{G}$. A clustering solution satisfies τ-ratio fairness if, for each cluster C_j and each protected group g, the number of points belonging to the group g in C_j is at least $\tau_g n_g$, where n_g denotes the total number of points belonging to group g in the dataset, i.e.,*

$$|X_g(C_j)| \geq \tau_g n_g \quad with \quad \tau_g \in \left[0, \frac{1}{k}\right] \quad (2)$$

We denote the number of clusters with k. Specifically, when $\tau_g = 1/k$ for all demographic groups g and all clusters have similar size, the definition is equivalent to Definition 1. To avoid any potential ambiguity, we will henceforth refer to τ_g as γ_g.

This notion of fairness is well-suited to high-dimensional data because a solution can be found using greedy round-robin algorithms, which can handle a large number of clusters and data without having to explore too wide a space of solutions with only an additional time complexity $O(kn \log(n))$.

3.2 Fast Co-clustering

Fast-τCC [5] is a recent co-clustering algorithm that has good convergence properties and is also able to identify a congruent number of clusters on rows and columns, starting from an initial overestimation. Given a data matrix $\mathbf{A} = (a_{ij}) \in \mathbb{R}_+^{n \times m}$, a co-clustering of $\mathbf{A}$ is a pair $(\mathcal{R}, \mathcal{C})$, where $\mathcal{R}$ is a partition of the rows and $\mathcal{C}$ a partition of the columns of the matrix. The objective function of Fast-τCC is derived from the Goodman and Kruskal's τ [21], and can be defined as follows:

$$\hat{\tau}_{R|C}(\mathcal{R},\mathcal{C}) = \sum_{k=1}^{|\mathcal{R}|}\sum_{l=1}^{|\mathcal{C}|} \frac{t_{kl}^2}{T \cdot t_{\cdot l}} - \sum_{k=1}^{|\mathcal{R}|} \frac{t_{k\cdot}^2}{T^2} \qquad (3)$$

where $\mathbf{T} = (t_{kl})$ is the contingency table associated to the co-clustering $(\mathcal{R}, \mathcal{C})$, where $\mathcal{R} = (\mathcal{R}_1, \ldots, \mathcal{R}_K)$ and $\mathcal{C} = (\mathcal{C}_1, \ldots, \mathcal{C}_L)$, i.e. $t_{kl} = \sum_{i \in \mathcal{R}_k}\sum_{j \in \mathcal{C}_l} a_{ij}$, for $k = 1, \ldots, K$ and $l = 1, \ldots, L$. Following this notation, $t_{k\cdot} = \sum_{l=1}^{L} t_{kl}$, $t_{\cdot l} = \sum_{k=1}^{K} t_{kl}$ and $T = \sum_{k=1}^{K}\sum_{l=1}^{L} t_{kl}$. Analogously, the association of the column clustering $\mathcal{C}$ to the row clustering $\mathcal{R}$ can be evaluated through the function $\hat{\tau}_{C|R}(\mathcal{R},\mathcal{C})$. Since $\hat{\tau}$ is not symmetric, the best co-clustering solutions are those that simultaneously maximize $\hat{\tau}_{R|C}$ and $\hat{\tau}_{C|R}$. In [5] an iterative optimization strategy is introduced. It alternates the computation of $\hat{\tau}_{R|C}$ by fixing the column partition and the computation of $\hat{\tau}_{C|R}$ by keeping the row partition fixed.

3.3 Unfairness in Co-clustering

Co-clustering can lead to unfair outcomes when applied without proper consideration of sensitive group attributes. To show this behavior, a simplified example is provided. The scenario under consideration is the one of movie ratings. Let's $\mathbf{A}$ be a data matrix whose rows represent users, columns represent movies, and the entries represent ratings from 0 to 5. Users are identified by two protected groups (u_0, u_1, u_4 users from group g_0 and u_2, u_3, u_5 from group g_1) and movies are categorized by genres (e.g., m_0 movie is Action, m_1 is Comedy, m_2 is Dramatic, m_3 is Horror, m_4 is Romantic).

A co-clustering algorithm will likely find the following clustering of users and movies: $\mathcal{R} = \{\{u_0, u_1\}, \{u_3, u_4\}, \{u_2, u_5\}\}$ and $\mathcal{C} = \{\{m_0, m_4\}, \{m_1, m_2\}, \{m_3\}\}$.

$$\mathbf{A} = \begin{bmatrix} 5 & 4 & 0 & 0 & 0 \\ 4 & 0 & 0 & 0 & 0 \\ 0 & 0 & 5 & 4 & 0 \\ 0 & 0 & 0 & 5 & 0 \\ 0 & 0 & 2 & 0 & 5 \\ 0 & 5 & 0 & 0 & 4 \end{bmatrix} \begin{matrix} m_0 \; m_4 \; m_1 \; m_2 \; m_3 \\ \\ \begin{array}{cc} u_0 & g_0 \\ u_1 & g_0 \\ u_3 & g_1 \\ u_4 & g_0 \\ u_2 & g_1 \\ u_5 & g_1 \end{array} \end{matrix} \qquad \mathbf{A} = \begin{bmatrix} 5 & 0 & 0 & 0 & 4 \\ 0 & 4 & 0 & 0 & 5 \\ 4 & 0 & 0 & 0 & 0 \\ 0 & 5 & 2 & 0 & 0 \\ 0 & 0 & 5 & 4 & 0 \\ 0 & 0 & 0 & 5 & 0 \end{bmatrix} \begin{matrix} m_0 \; m_3 \; m_1 \; m_2 \; m_4 \\ \\ \begin{array}{cc} u_0 & g_0 \\ u_5 & g_1 \\ u_1 & g_0 \\ u_2 & g_1 \\ u_3 & g_1 \\ u_4 & g_0 \end{array} \end{matrix}$$

(a) Unfair co-clustering   (b) Perfectly balanced co-clustering

Fig. 1. A toy example with an unfair optimal solution (left) and its fair solution (right) with respect to row clustering.

(see Fig. 1a). This solution, while reflecting the rating patterns in the data, reinforces existing societal biases by grouping users based on demographic characteristics. In fact, the user clustering exhibits a segmentation into three distinct clusters, one of these consisting of all users from protected group g_0, another one encompassing all users in demographic group g_1. If this unfair solution is used in a recommender system, it can lead to unfair and limited recommendations, as users from g_0 will be primarily recommended action and romantic movies, while users from g_1 will receive horror movie suggestions. This reduces the likelihood that individuals will discover movies outside their stereotypical preferences, potentially missing out on content they would enjoy.

In order to identify a fair clustering of users, where each cluster is equally represented by each of the protected groups, according to Definition 1, it is necessary to ensure that each cluster contains a proportion of data points for each protected group equal to the proportion of data points for each group in the entire dataset. A potential fair solution could be the row clustering $\mathcal{R} = \{\{u_0, u_5\}, \{u_1, u_2\}, \{u_3, u_4\}\}$ shown in Fig. 1b. This is perfectly balanced, as the proportion of both groups in each cluster is exactly equal to their dataset ratios, thus resulting in balance that is equal to 1. In this case, ensuring a perfect balance leads to a limited loss of information. In fact, the objective function on rows $\tau_{R|C}$ only degrades from 0.62 to 0.55.

4 Fair Co-clustering

In this section, we present Fair-τCC, a fair co-clustering method based on the de-normalized Goodman-Kruskal's τ (see Eq. 3). We first define the problem of fairness in co-clustering, then describe the algorithm for computing the co-clustering results in a fair manner.

Definition 3 (Fair Co-clustering). *Given a data matrix $\mathbf{A}$ and protected groups $\mathcal{G}_{rows} = \{g_0, \ldots, g_w\}$, $\mathcal{G}_{cols} = \{g_0, \ldots, g_z\}$ referring to the row and column objects respectively, a co-clustering $(\mathcal{R}, \mathcal{C})$ is fair if both row and column clustering $\mathcal{R}, \mathcal{C}$ are fair.*

Drawing inspiration from the definition of balance for clustering [7,14], we define it for co-clustering tasks. Ideally, a co-clustering is balanced if, for each protected group associated with the row (column) objects, the ratio of its points in every row (column) clusters is the same as the ratio of its points over the whole dataset.

Definition 4 (Co-clustering Balance). *Let S_{rows} and S_{cols} be sensitive features associated with the row and column items, such that $s_i^{rows} \in \mathcal{G}_{rows}$ and $s_j^{cols} \in \mathcal{G}_{cols}$, where $\mathcal{G}_{rows}$ and $\mathcal{G}_{cols}$ are the protected groups the i-th row and j-th column items belong to, respectively. The balance of a co-clustering $(\mathcal{R}, \mathcal{C})$ is defined as:*

$$balance(\{\mathcal{R},\mathcal{C}\}) = min\left(balance(\mathcal{R}), balance(\mathcal{C})\right) \tag{4}$$

with

$$balance(\mathcal{R}) = \min_{R_i \in \mathcal{R}} \min_{w \in \mathcal{G}_{rows}} \left(\frac{r_w}{r_w(R_i)}, \frac{r_w(R_i)}{r_g}\right), \tag{5}$$

$$balance(\mathcal{C}) = \min_{C_i \in \mathcal{C}} \min_{z \in \mathcal{G}_{cols}} \left(\frac{r_z}{r_z(C_j)}, \frac{r_z(C_j)}{r_z}\right), \tag{6}$$

where r_w and r_z are the ratios of the protected groups w, z in the dataset; $r_w(R_i)$ and $r_z(C_j)$ are the ratios of the protected groups w, z in each row cluster R_i and column cluster C_j.

The protected groups for both row and column objects are not always known. Therefore, if only $\mathcal{G}_{rows}$ ($\mathcal{G}_{cols}$) is known, co-clustering is considered fair if the row (column) clustering is fair (i.e., $balance(\mathcal{R}) \approx 1$). For simplicity, in this work we ensure the fairness for only the protected groups of row objects.

4.1 Fair-τCC Algorithm

We now introduce Fair-τCC, the fair adaptation of the current state-of-the-art co-clustering method proposed by Battaglia et al. [5]. The primary objective of this algorithm is to ensure balanced representation of each protected group in every row cluster. Specifically, it guarantees a minimum fraction of points from each protected group in every cluster, adhering to the concept of τ-ratio fairness (refer to Eq. 2), hereinafter referred as γ to avoid any ambiguity. The pseudocode for this algorithm is detailed in Algorithm 1, while the procedure for updating the row clustering is illustrated in Algorithm 2.

First, we must introduce two matrices $\mathbf{P} = (p_{ij})$ and $\mathbf{Q} = (q_{kl})$, with $p_{ij} = \frac{a_{ij}}{A}$ and $q_{kl} = \frac{t_{kl}}{A} = \sum_{i \in \mathcal{R}_k} \sum_{j \in \mathcal{C}_l} p_{ij}$, where A denotes the sum of all the entries of $\mathbf{A}$ (hence, $A = T$). We also introduce the row cluster incidence matrix $\mathbf{R} = r_{ik}$ and $\mathbf{C} = c_{jl}$, with $r_{ik} = 1$ if row i is in row cluster $\mathcal{R}_k$ ($r_{ik} = 0$ otherwise) and $c_{jl} = 1$ if column j is in column cluster $\mathcal{C}_l$. According to this notation,

$$\mathbf{Q} = \mathbf{R}^\top \mathbf{P} \mathbf{C} \tag{7}$$

Algorithm 1. Fair τCC($\mathbf{A}, \mathbf{s}, \mathcal{G}, K_0, L_0, t_{max}, \boldsymbol{\alpha}$)

Input: A $n \times m$ data matrix $\mathbf{A}$, a sensitive feature $\mathbf{s} = [s_0, \ldots, s_n]$, protected groups $\mathcal{G} = \{g_0, \ldots, g_w\}$, initial number of row and column clusters K_0 and L_0, max number of iterations t_{max}, a vector $\boldsymbol{\alpha} = [\alpha_0, \ldots, \alpha_w]$ with $\alpha_g \in [0,1]$.
Result: $\mathbf{R}, \mathbf{C}$ row and column clustering such that $\mathbf{R}$ satifies γ-ratio fairness (Eq. 2).
Initialize $\mathbf{R}^{(0)}$ and $\mathbf{C}^{(0)}$;
$t \leftarrow 1$; changes $\leftarrow$ True;
compute $\mathbf{P}$ from $\mathbf{A}$;
while changes and $t < t_{max}$ **do**
  $\mathbf{R}^{(t)} \leftarrow$ FairUpdateRowClusters($\mathbf{P}, \mathbf{C}^{(t-1)}, \mathbf{R}^{(t-1)}, \mathbf{s}, \mathcal{G}, \boldsymbol{\alpha}$);
  $\mathbf{C}^{(t)} \leftarrow$ UpdateColumnClusters($\mathbf{P}, \mathbf{R}^{(t)}, \mathbf{C}^{(t-1)}$);
  if $\mathbf{R}^{(t)} = \mathbf{R}^{(t-1)}$ and $\mathbf{C}^{(t)} = \mathbf{C}^{(t-1)}$ **then**
    | changes $\leftarrow$ False;
  end
  $t \leftarrow t+1$;
end

Eq. 3 can be then rewritten as:

$$\hat{\tau}_{R|C}(\mathcal{R},\mathcal{C}) = \sum_{k=1}^{K}\sum_{l=1}^{L}\left(\sum_{i\in\mathcal{R}_k}\frac{p_{il}}{p_{\cdot l}}\right)q_{kl} - \sum_{k=1}^{K}\left(\sum_{i\in\mathcal{R}_k}p_{i\cdot}\right)q_{k\cdot}$$

where $q_{k\cdot} = \sum_{i\in\mathcal{R}_k}p_{i\cdot} = \sum_{l=1}^{L}\frac{t_{kl}}{A} = \sum_{l=1}^{L}\sum_{i\in\mathcal{R}_k}\sum_{j\in\mathcal{C}_l}\frac{a_{ij}}{A}$, and $q_{\cdot l} = p_{\cdot l} = \sum_{j\in\mathcal{C}_l}p_{\cdot j} = \sum_{k=1}^{K}\frac{t_{kl}}{A} = \sum_{k=1}^{K}\sum_{i\in\mathcal{R}_k}\sum_{j\in\mathcal{C}_l}\frac{a_{ij}}{A}$, $p_{i\cdot} = \sum_{j=1}^{m}\frac{a_{ij}}{A}$, $p_{\cdot j} = \sum_{i=1}^{n}\frac{a_{ij}}{A}$, $p_{il} = \sum_{j\in\mathcal{C}_l}p_{ij}$, and $p_{\cdot l} = \sum_{j\in\mathcal{C}_l}p_{\cdot j} = q_{\cdot l}$.

Let $\mathbf{R}^{(t)}$ be the row cluster incidence matrix at iteration t, and $\mathbf{Q}^{(t)} = \mathbf{R}^{(t)\top}\mathbf{PC}$ its associated distribution. The objective function $\hat{\tau}_{R|C}(\mathcal{R}^{(t)},\mathcal{C})$ is

$$\hat{\tau}_{R|C}(\mathcal{R}^{(t)},\mathcal{C}) = \sum_{i=1}^{n}\left(\sum_{l=1}^{L}\frac{p_{il}^{(t)}}{p_{\cdot l}}q_{kl}^{(t)} - p_{i\cdot}q_{k\cdot}^{(t)}\right) \qquad (8)$$

Each row $\mathbf{q}_k^{(t)}$ of $\mathbf{Q}^{(t)}$ can be interpreted as a prototype of the k-th cluster of $\mathcal{R}^{(t)}$, and the following similarity function between any row $\mathbf{p}_i$ of $\mathbf{P}$ and $\mathbf{q}_k^{(t)}$ is defined:

$$\sigma\left(\mathbf{p}_i,\mathbf{q}_k^{(t)}\right) = \sum_{l=1}^{L}\frac{p_{il}}{p_{\cdot l}}q_{kl}^{(t)} - p_{i\cdot}q_{k\cdot}^{(t)} \qquad (9)$$

It measures the similarity between a "point" p_i and a cluster prototype $q_r^{(t)}$. The objective function becomes

$$\hat{\tau}_{R|C}(\mathcal{R}^{(t)},\mathcal{C}) = \sum_{i=1}^{n}\sigma\left(\mathbf{p}_i,\mathbf{q}_{k^\star}^{(t)}\right) \qquad (10)$$

where $k^\star = \arg\max_k\left(\sigma\left(\mathbf{p}_i,\mathbf{q}_k^{(t)}\right)\right)$ is the cluster assignment maximizing function σ.

Algorithm 2. FairUpdateRowClusters($\mathbf{P}, \mathbf{C}, \mathbf{R}^{(0)}, \mathbf{s}, \mathcal{G}, \boldsymbol{\alpha}$)

h[!ht] **Input:** A $n \times m$ matrix $\mathbf{P}$, column clustering $\mathbf{C}$, initial row clustering $\mathbf{R}^{(0)}$, sensitive feature $\mathbf{s} = [s_0, \ldots, s_n]$, protected groups $\mathcal{G} = \{g_0, \ldots, g_w\}$, fairness parameters $\boldsymbol{\alpha} = [\alpha_0, \ldots, \alpha_w]$ with $\alpha_g \in [0, 1]$.
Result: row clustering $\mathbf{R}$ that satisfies γ-ratio fairness (Eq. 2)
$t \leftarrow 1$; $changes \leftarrow$ True;
while *changes* **do**
  $\quad \mathbf{Q}^{(t-1)} = \mathbf{R}^{(t-1)\top}\mathbf{PC}$;
  $\quad$ compute $\mathbf{U}^{(t-1)}$ and $\mathbf{V}^{(t-1)}$ as in Eq. 12;
  $\quad \boldsymbol{\Sigma} = \mathbf{PC}(\mathbf{Q}^{(t-1)} \odot \mathbf{U}^{(t-1)} - \mathbf{V}^{(t-1)})^\top$;
  $\quad$ **for** $i = 1, \ldots, n$ **do**
  $\quad\quad k^*(i) \leftarrow \arg\max_k(\sigma_{ik})$;
  $\quad$ **end**
  $\quad$ compute $\mathbf{R}^{(t)}$ using k^*;
  $\quad$ remove empty clusters and update $\mathbf{R}^{(t)}$;
  $\quad$ **if** $\mathbf{R}^{(t)}$ *violates γ-ratio fairness* **then**
  $\quad\quad \mathbf{R}^{(t)} =$ FairRowAssignments($\mathbf{R}^{(t)}, \boldsymbol{\Sigma}, \mathbf{s}, \mathcal{G}, \boldsymbol{\alpha}$);
  $\quad$ **end**
  $\quad$ **if** $\mathbf{R}^{(t)} = \mathbf{R}^{(t-1)}$ **then**
  $\quad\quad changes \leftarrow$ False;
  $\quad$ **end**
  $\quad t \leftarrow t + 1$;
end

Algorithm 2 uses two $K \times L$ matrices $\mathbf{U}$ and $\mathbf{V}$ to compute all σ values in a $n \times K$ matrix $\boldsymbol{\Sigma} = (\sigma_{ik})$, where $\sigma_{ik} = \sigma\left(\mathbf{p}_i, \mathbf{q}_k^{(t)}\right)$. More precisely:

$$\boldsymbol{\Sigma} = \mathbf{PC}(\mathbf{Q}^{(t-1)} \odot \mathbf{U}^{(t-1)} - \mathbf{V}^{(t-1)})^\top \tag{11}$$

where $\odot$ indicates the Hadamard matrix product, and

$$\mathbf{U}^{(t)} = \begin{bmatrix} \frac{1}{\sum_l q_{1l}^{(t)}} & \cdots & \frac{1}{\sum_l q_{Kl}^{(t)}} \\ \vdots & \ddots & \vdots \\ \frac{1}{\sum_l q_{1l}^{(t)}} & \cdots & \frac{1}{\sum_l q_{Kl}^{(t)}} \end{bmatrix}, \quad \mathbf{V}^{(t)} = \begin{bmatrix} \frac{1}{\sum_l q_{1l}^{(t)}} & \cdots & \frac{1}{\sum_l q_{1l}^{(t)}} \\ \vdots & \ddots & \vdots \\ \frac{1}{\sum_l q_{Kl}^{(t)}} & \cdots & \frac{1}{\sum_l q_{Kl}^{(t)}} \end{bmatrix} \tag{12}$$

Then, the algorithm also removes all empty clusters. Hence, from one iteration to another, the number of clusters may decrease and $\mathbf{R}^{(0)}$ and $\mathbf{C}^{(0)}$ can be initialized with random partitions using safely high values of K_0 and L_0.

Given this initial assignment, we evaluate whether the optimal solution $\mathbf{R}^*$ satisfies the γ-ratio fairness property. If it does not, a fair assignment $\mathbf{R}^{fair}$ is determined (see Algorithm 3). The trade-off between fairness and clustering quality is managed through the utilization of the similarity matrix $\boldsymbol{\Sigma}$. Let $\mathbf{s} = [s_0, \ldots, s_n]$ denote the sensitive feature associated with the rows of the data matrix, where $s_i \in \mathcal{G}$ and $\mathcal{G} = \{g_0, \ldots, g_w\}$ represents the set of protected groups. From the similarity matrix Σ, we derive a $n \times K$ matrix $\mathbf{D} = (d_{ik})$, defined as follows:

$$d_{ik} = \sigma(\mathbf{p}_i, \mathbf{q}_k^*) - \sigma(\mathbf{p}_i, \mathbf{q}_k) \quad \forall k = 1, \ldots, K \tag{13}$$

Here, $\sigma(\mathbf{p}_i, \mathbf{q}_k^*)$ indicates the similarity value between point p_i and its optimal cluster prototype q_k^*, while $\sigma(\mathbf{p}_i, \mathbf{q}_k)$ represents the similarity value between point p_i and an alternative cluster prototype q_k. Consequently, d_{ik} quantifies the loss in clustering quality when point p_i is allocated to cluster k instead of its optimal cluster k^*. To ensure optimal preservation of quality, it is important to determine the sequence in which cluster prototypes for each point should be evaluated and the sequence in which the points from the same protected group should be chosen. To do this, we sort the indices of the row vector $\mathbf{d}_i$, corresponding to the cluster prototypes of the point p_i, by value in ascending order. Then, for each protected group, we sort points by $\mathbf{d}_i$ in ascending order.

Algorithm 3. FairRowAssignments($\mathbf{R}^*, \Sigma, \mathbf{s}, \mathcal{G}, \boldsymbol{\alpha}$)

Input: The optimal row clustering $\mathbf{R}^*$, $n \times K$ similarity matrix Σ, sensitive feature $\mathbf{s} = [s_0, \ldots, s_n]$, protected groups $\mathcal{G} = \{g_0, \ldots, g_w\}$, fairness parameters $\boldsymbol{\alpha} = (\alpha_0, \ldots, \alpha_w)$ with $\alpha_g \in [0, 1]$, $\forall g \in \mathcal{G}$.
Result: row clustering $\mathbf{R}^{fair}$ that satisfies γ-ratio fairness
Initialize $\mathbf{R}^{fair} = 0^{(n \times K)}$;
Compute $\mathbf{D}$ as in Eq. 13;
Sort cluster prototypes by d_{ij} values in ascending order, $\forall i = 1, \ldots, n$;
Sort row objects by protected group and then by d_{ij} value in ascending order;
for g in $\mathcal{G}$ **do**
$\quad \mathbf{A}_g = \{\mathbf{p}_i \in \mathbf{A} \text{ s.t. } s_i = g\}$; $n_g = |\mathbf{A}_g|$; $\gamma_g = \frac{1}{K}\alpha_g$;
$\quad$ **for** $iter = 1 \ldots \lfloor \gamma_g n_g \rfloor$ **do**
$\quad\quad$ **for** $j = 1 \ldots K$ **do**
$\quad\quad\quad \mathbf{p}_{min} = \arg\min_{\mathbf{p}_i \in \mathbf{A}_g : \sum_{j=1}^{K} r_{i,j}^{fair} = 0}(\sigma(\mathbf{p}_i, \mathbf{q}_{k*}) - \sigma(\mathbf{p}_i, \mathbf{q}_j))$;
$\quad\quad\quad r_{min,j}^{fair} = 1$;
$\quad\quad$ **end**
$\quad$ **end**
$\quad \forall \mathbf{p}_i \in \mathbf{A}_g : \sum_{j=1}^{K} r_{i,j}^{fair} = 0, \quad r_{i,k*}^{fair} = r_{i,k*}^*$;
end

For each protected group g, a fraction of unassigned row items equivalent to $\gamma_g n_g$ is chosen for allocation to a non-optimal cluster with the aim of minimizing loss value and ensuring fairness. The parameter n_g denotes the number of points belonging to the protected group g. The fairness parameter $\gamma_g \in \left[0, \frac{1}{K}\right]$ is the fraction of n_g points to be allocated in each cluster. Specifically, it is defined as $\gamma_g = \frac{1}{K}\alpha_g$ where K represents the number of row clusters identified by the vanilla approach and $\alpha_g \in [0, 1]$ is a user-defined parameter that quantifies the desired level of fairness. If $\alpha_g = 1.0$ for a group g, then the n_g points will be equally distributed across K clusters ($\frac{n_g}{K}$ points in each cluster) and the group's ratio in each cluster matches its ratio in the overall dataset. Conversely, if $\alpha_g = 0.0$ for a group g, fairness violation is permitted for that group. If all groups have their parameters set to zero ($\alpha_g = 0.0, \forall g \in \mathcal{G}$), any solution is acceptable, allowing for selection of the optimal row clustering. Notably, if $\alpha_g = 1.0$ for all groups, row clustering achieves perfect balance ($balance(\mathcal{R}) \approx 1.0$), otherwise with $\alpha_g = 0.8$ the 80% rule of disparate impact doctrine is guaranteed. Finally, any points that remain unallocated at the end of this procedure are assigned to their optimal cluster.

5 Experiments

In this section, we present the findings from our experiments conducted on four real-world datasets to evaluate the effectiveness of Fair-τCC. We first present the dataset used, the competing methods and the experimental protocol. Then, we delve into the results and discuss them.

5.1 Experiment Design

The datasets most commonly employed for fairness assessment (e.g. Adults, German credit, Banks, etc.) are low-dimensional and, consequently, are not well-suited to our experiments: co-clustering, in fact, identifies subsets of rows and columns in a high-dimensional data matrix that exhibit meaningful patterns. Furthermore, the majority of the benchmark datasets utilized for assessing co-clustering results lack any sensitive information. Following a thorough examination of available datasets, we identified four of them as being suitable for our purposes. These include two ratings dataset (MovieLens-1M [23] and Yelp [17,18]), a product reviews dataset (Amazon reviews [17,18]), and an image collection for facial recognition (Labeled Faces in the Wild [24]). Table 1 summarizes the characteristics of the data matrix for each dataset utilized in our experiments. Additionally, Table 2 provides details on the sensitive features selected for each dataset, including the protected groups and their respective proportions within the datasets.

Table 1. Datasets used for the experiments

Dataset	Size	Rows	Columns	Values	Labels	Sens. Att.
MovieLens-1M	6040 × 3645	users	movies	ratings	genres	gender; age
Yelp	1441 × 333	users	restaurants	ratings	category	gender
Amazon	705 × 10152	reviews	words	frequencies	prod. categories	gender
LFW	13233 × 1850	face images	features	RGB value	people IDs	gender

Table 2. Information about protected groups and their ratio in the whole dataset.

Dataset	Sens. Att.	Protected groups	Group ratio
MovieLens-1M	gender	Male; Female	72%; 28%
MovieLens-1M	age	< 35; 35-50; > 50	57%; 29%; 14%
Yelp	gender	Male; Female	38%; 62%
Amazon	gender	Male; Female	39%; 61%
LFW	gender	Male; Female	78%; 22%

We compared our algorithm against the standard version of Fast-τCC, which does not incorporate fairness constraints[1] and the only closely related competitor, Parity LBM [19], a Gaussian latent block model with an ordinal regression designed for fair recommendations independent of protected attributes[2]. To assess the performance of each algorithm regarding co-clustering quality and fairness, we employed several evaluation metrics:

- $\tau_{R|C}$ and $\tau_{C|R}$ [21]: the Goodman-Kruskal's τs measuring the quality of co-clustering computed by every algorithms.
- **ARI** [25]: the Adjusted Rand Index. It is used to compare the agreement between row and column assignments predicted by the fair algorithms with those from the corresponding vanilla approach (ARI_{rows} and ARI_{cols} in Table 3). Additionally, it is used to compute the aggrement between the clustering and the given ground-truth labels detailed in Table 1 (ARI in Table 3).
- **Balance** [7]: This metric quantifies the balanced representation of protected groups within each cluster according to Definition 1.
- **Kullback-Leibler fairness error** [31]: It is based on Kullback-Leibler divergence and quantifies the distributional disparities between the predefined target demographic proportions and the marginal probabilities of the demographics within cluster. It attains its theoretical minimum of zero iff all clusters exhibit demographic proportions identical to the target distribution, thereby enforcing strict adherence to the specified fairness constraints.

We executed 10 iterations of each algorithm. The mean values and standard deviations for all metrics are reported.

To evaluate the effectiveness of our algorithm, we set the number of initial clusters for both rows and columns to $K_0 = 10$ and $L_0 = 10$, respectively. Furthermore, for adjusting the trade-off between the level of fairness and co-clustering efficiency, we launched the experiments varying all α values within the range $[0, 1]$ for all protected groups. Conversely, Parity LBM was executed with hyperparameters configured as follows: 25 row and column clusters to be found for the MovieLens dataset and 10 for all others; a maximum number of

---

[1] https://github.com/rupensa/tauCC.
[2] https://github.com/jackmedda/C-Fairness-RecSys/tree/main/reproducibility_study/Frisch_et_al.

Table 3. Summary of the results for all co-clustering algorithms.

Algorithm	$\tau_{R|C}$	$\tau_{C|R}$	ARI	ARI_{rows}	ARI_{cols}	Balance	KL fairness
ML (gender)							
Fast-τCC	**0.109 ± 0.011**	**0.104 ± 0.013**	**0.090 ± 0.024**			0.787 ± 0.046	0.018 ± 0.007
Fair-τCC	0.021 ± 0.004	0.088 ± 0.009	0.070 ± 0.022	0.115 ± 0.024	0.595 ± 0.138	**0.969 ± 0.003**	**0.000 ± 0.000**
Fair-τCC$_{weak}$	0.096 ± 0.022	0.099 ± 0.015	0.080 ± 0.026	**0.542 ± 0.278**	**0.717 ± 0.191**	0.919 ± 0.018	0.003 ± 0.001
LBM	0.004 ± 0.000	0.004 ± 0.000	0.025 ± 0.003	-		0.535 ± 0.152	0.392 ± 0.168
Parity LBM	0.004 ± 0.000	0.004 ± 0.000	0.026 ± 0.004	0.256 ± 0.022	0.510 ± 0.035	0.600 ± 0.087	0.169 ± 0.026
ML (age)							
Fast-τCC	**0.109 ± 0.011**	**0.104 ± 0.013**	0.090 ± 0.024			0.787 ± 0.046	0.018 ± 0.007
Fair-τCC	0.016 ± 0.001	0.070 ± 0.006	0.088 ± 0.024	0.096 ± 0.009	0.444 ± 0.029	**0.954 ± 0.000**	**0.000 ± 0.000**
Fair-τCC$_{weak}$	0.063 ± 0.036	0.096 ± 0.016	**0.108 ± 0.028**	**0.329 ± 0.204**	**0.643 ± 0.233**	0.806 ± 0.108	0.033 ± 0.043
LBM	0.004 ± 0.000	0.004 ± 0.000	-0.005 ± 0.001			0.288 ± 0.115	0.718 ± 0.143
Parity LBM	0.001 ± 0.001	0.001 ± 0.001	-0.013 ± 0.006	0.042 ± 0.009	0.195 ± 0.052	0.000 ± 0.000	$+\infty$
Amazon							
Fast-τCC	**0.076 ± 0.013**	**0.079 ± 0.012**	**0.111 ± 0.029**			0.385 ± 0.025	0.505 ± 0.046
Fair-τCC	0.027 ± 0.003	0.035 ± 0.001	0.011 ± 0.002	0.007 ± 0.002	0.022 ± 0.010	**0.957 ± 0.016**	**0.001 ± 0.001**
Fair-τCC$_{weak}$	0.032 ± 0.004	0.037 ± 0.003	0.012 ± 0.006	0.020 ± 0.012	0.029 ± 0.022	0.773 ± 0.094	0.037 ± 0.020
LBM	0.002 ± 0.000	0.002 ± 0.000	0.102 ± 0.002			0.000 ± 0.000	$+\infty$
Parity LBM	0.002 ± 0.000	0.002 ± 0.000	0.098 ± 0.004	**0.350 ± 0.031**	**0.829 ± 0.027**	0.023 ± 0.072	$+\infty$
Yelp							
Fast-τCC	**0.566 ± 0.005**	**0.564 ± 0.005**	0.000 ± 0.005			0.721 ± 0.045	0.142 ± 0.063
Fair-τCC	0.453 ± 0.035	0.499 ± 0.017	**0.001 ± 0.002**	0.025 ± 0.004	0.002 ± 0.004	**0.976 ± 0.007**	**0.000 ± 0.000**
Fair-τCC$_{weak}$	0.536 ± 0.041	0.543 ± 0.028	0.001 ± 0.003	0.030 ± 0.008	0.002 ± 0.002	0.870 ± 0.023	0.018 ± 0.013
LBM	0.042 ± 0.009	0.026 ± 0.005	-0.010 ± 0.005			0.553 ± 0.056	0.217 ± 0.041
Parity LBM	0.028 ± 0.015	0.017 ± 0.008	-0.011 ± 0.007	**0.225 ± 0.050**	**0.122 ± 0.046**	0.622 ± 0.152	0.161 ± 0.111
LFW							
Fast-τCC	**0.005 ± 0.000**	**0.005 ± 0.000**	0.000 ± 0.000			0.940 ± 0.013	0.001 ± 0.000
Fair-τCC	0.001 ± 0.000	0.006 ± 0.002	0.001 ± 0.001	0.159 ± 0.029	0.774 ± 0.241	**0.989 ± 0.003**	**0.000 ± 0.000**
Fair-τCC$_{weak}$	0.004 ± 0.002	0.005 ± 0.001	0.000 ± 0.001	**0.595 ± 0.401**	**0.782 ± 0.281**	0.864 ± 0.170	0.012 ± 0.016
LBM	0.002 ± 0.000	0.002 ± 0.000	**0.002 ± 0.000**			0.393 ± 0.028	0.381 ± 0.032
Parity LBM	0.002 ± 0.000	0.002 ± 0.000	0.001 ± 0.000	0.348 ± 0.031	0.768 ± 0.049	0.803 ± 0.019	0.025 ± 0.005

300 epochs for the training; a batch size of (200,200) and a learning rate of 2e-2. After training, we applied the KMeans algorithm to the row and column probability matrices generated by the model to obtain the definitive cluster assignments. All experiments were conducted on a Linux server equipped with 32 Intel Xeon Skylakes cores running at 2.1 GHz, 256 GB RAM, and one Tesla T4 GPU. The source code of our algorithm and the datasets necessary to reproduce all experiments are available online[3].

5.2 Results

In Table 3, we report the performance of Fair-τCC in comparison with its vanilla version (Fast-τCC), the direct competitor (Parity LBM) and its non-fair counterpart (LBM). The running times are reported in Table 4. We present two versions of our algorithm: the first with a maximum fairness constraint (Fair-τCC), and the second with a more relaxed fairness constraint allowing a small violation for only one protected group (Fair-τCC$_{weak}$). For MovieLens (ML) with age as

---

[3] https://github.com/federicopeiretti/fair_taucc.

sensitive attribute, we allow a minor infringement on the constraint for two protected groups. The α values of the relaxed version are selected from two values, 0.9 and 1.0, by maximizing the row clustering quality $\tau_{R|C}$.

On the MovieLens-1M (ML) dataset with gender as the sensitive attribute, Fair-τCC achieves significant improvements in fairness with a Balance of 0.97 and a near-zero KL fairness error (0.0002), significantly outperforming both Fast-τCC (Balance 0.79, KL 0.018) and Parity LBM (Balance 0.60, KL 0.17). However, this comes at the cost of clustering quality, as $\tau_{R|C}$ and $\tau_{C|R}$ drop to 0.021 and 0.088, respectively, compared to Fast-τCC's 0.11 for both metrics. Fair-τCC$_{\text{weak}}$ strikes the trade-off between fairness and clustering quality by allowing a small fairness violation for the majority group ($\alpha_{male} = 0.9$). It achieves higher $\tau_{R|C}$ (0.096) and $\tau_{C|R}$ (0.099) than Fair-τCC while maintaining strong fairness metrics (Balance 0.92, KL 0.003). Interestingly, Fair-τCC$_{\text{weak}}$ also exhibits better alignment with its vanilla counterpart, as shown by ARI$_{\text{rows}}$ (0.54) and ARI$_{\text{cols}}$ (0.72), compared to Fair-τCC's lower values.

Table 4. Execution times in seconds

Dataset	Fast-τCC	Fair-τCC	Fair-τCC$_{weak}$	LBM	Parity LBM
ML (gender)	3.37 ± 1.10	490.04 ± 96.41	217.85 ± 158.04	5110.05 ± 248.72	5262.01 ± 257.77
ML (age)	3.37 ± 1.10	202.41 ± 2.15	85.16 ± 47.25	8983.49 ± 121.10	9629.89 ± 604.88
Yelp	0.052 ± 0.0125	35.31 ± 60.94	24.87 ± 61.45	3242.94 ± 508.38	3321.18 ± 558.38
Amazon	1.14 ± 0.49	117.83 ± 22.76	68.85 ± 43.66	12189.15 ± 42.35	13966.79 ± 741.62
LFW	3.51 ± 0.84	245.72 ± 155.32	404.47 ± 251.65	38414.79 ± 5950.14	40201.68 ± 9781.72

For the MovieLens-1M (ML) dataset with age as the sensitive attribute, Fair-τCC again demonstrates superior fairness metrics (Balance 0.954, KL 0.0002), outperforming all other algorithms. However, its ARI score (0.08) is slightly lower than that of its standard version (0.09). Fair-τCC$_{\text{weak}}$ improves on all ARI scores (ARI 0.108, ARI$_{\text{rows}}$ 0.329, ARI$_{\text{cols}}$ 0.643), while maintaining reasonable $\tau_{R|C}, \tau_{C|R}$ and fairness metrics.

On the Amazon dataset, Fair-τCC achieves near-perfect fairness with a Balance of 0.96 and a KL error of 0.001, addressing the infinite KL errors observed in the other counterparts (Fast-τCC, Parity LBM and standard LBM) due to their lack of fairness constraints. However, its ARI score drops significantly to 0.01 from Fast-τCC's 0.11, reflecting the difficulty of maintaining clustering quality under strict fairness constraints in this dataset. Fair-τCC$_{\text{weak}}$, allowing a small fairness violation for the majority group ($\alpha_{female} = 0.9$), achieves performance very similar to that of its more rigorous version, but the Balance drops significantly to 0.77. Parity LBM achieves high column alignment with its vanilla counterpart (ARI$_{\text{cols}}$=0.83), but its Balance score remains low at 0.02.

The Yelp dataset reveals an interesting trade-off between clustering quality and fairness across algorithms. While Fast-τCC achieves the highest $\tau_{R|C}$ and $\tau_{C|R}$ values of 0.56, it exhibits poor fairness metrics, with a Balance of 0.72 and

KL error of 0.14. In contrast, Fair-τCC achieves near-perfect fairness with a Balance of 0.98 and a KL error of 0.0004, while maintaining reasonable clustering quality ($\tau_{R|C} = 0.45$, $\tau_{C|R} = 0.50$). This outcome may be attributable to excessive sparsity in the data matrix. Fair-τCC$_{\text{weak}}$ offers a compromise, exhibiting enhanced $\tau_{R|C}$ and $\tau_{C|R}$ values (0.54) compared to Fair-τCC, while preserving good fairness metrics (Balance 0.87). Parity LBM demonstrates moderate alignment with its baseline counterpart in terms of row and column assignments (ARI$_{\text{rows}}$=0.22, ARI$_{\text{rows}}$=0.12), but its overall performance is weaker in both clustering quality and fairness.

A particularly noteworthy case arises in the Labeled Faces in the Wild (LFW) dataset, where Fair-τCC$_{\text{weak}}$ exhibits a Balance score of 0.86—lower than that of Fair-τCC (0.94)—despite achieving significantly better row assignment alignment with an ARI$_{\text{rows}}$ score of 0.59 compared to Fair-τCC's much lower score of 0.16. This observation underscores an essential aspect of our findings: while strict adherence to fairness constraints may lead to diminished performance in terms of balance, allowing for slight violations can enhance clustering effectiveness without severely compromising overall fairness.

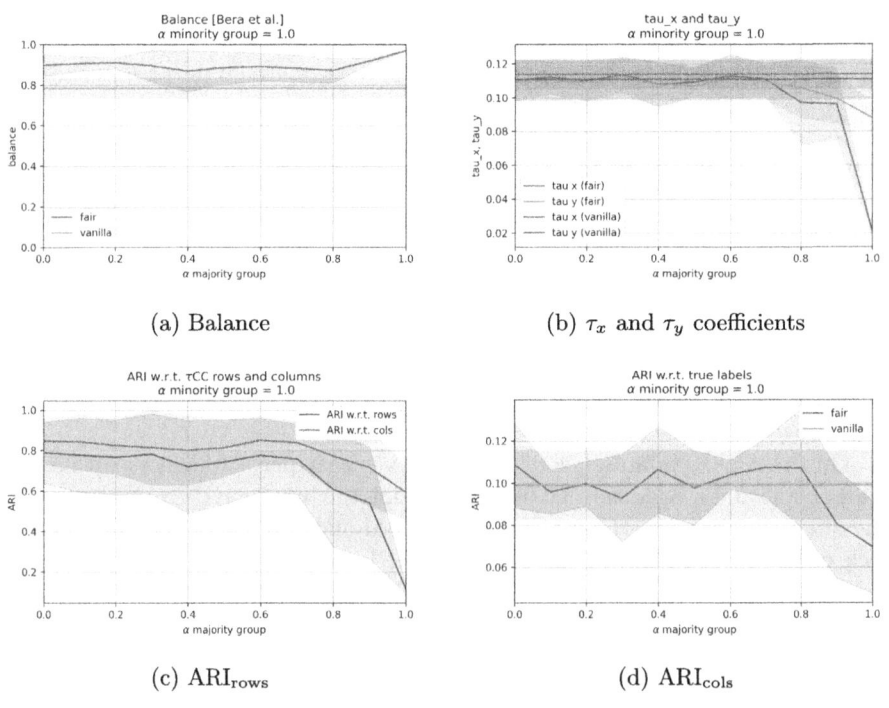

Fig. 2. Fair-τCC vs. Fast-τCC on MovieLens for increasing values of α.

Overall, these results demonstrate that Fair-τCC consistently delivers superior fairness performance across all datasets while maintaining reasonable clustering quality with respect to Fast-τCC, and the other competitors (Parity LBM and standard LBM) and reasonable computational time, as showed in Table 4. Allowing slight violations of fairness constraints, even for a single protected group, can lead to an improvement in terms of clustering quality, while achieving substantial gains in fairness compared to non-fair method. This trade-off makes Fair-τCC$_{\text{weak}}$ particularly suitable for applications where both fairness and clustering effectiveness are critical considerations.

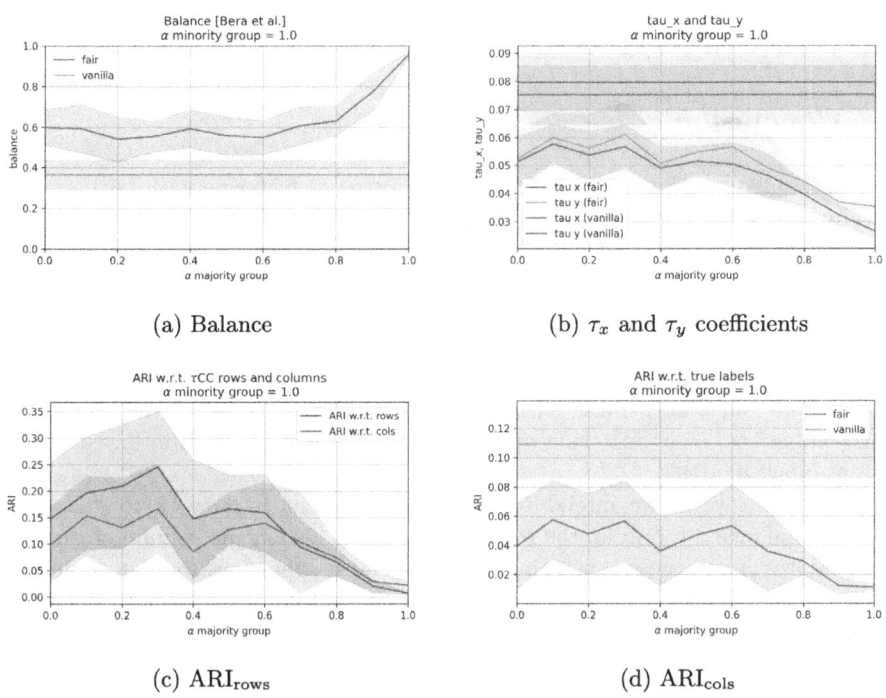

Fig. 3. Fair-τCC compared to Fast-τCC on Amazon for increasing values of α.

5.3 Impact of α on the Trade-Off Between Fairness and Quality

In this section, the impact of α values on the trade-off between clustering quality and fairness is assessed. To do that, a comparative analysis is conducted between the performance of the proposed algorithm and that of Fast-τCC. This is achieved by systematically varying the $\alpha_{majority}$ value assigned to the majority group in the range of $[0.0, 1.0]$ while maintaining a constant value $\alpha_{minority} = 1.0$ for the group least represented in the dataset. Figure 2 and Fig. 3 show the trend of evaluation metrics of both algorithms as $\alpha_{majority}$ increases on MovieLens and Amazon datasets, considering gender as sensitive feature. Fair-τCC maintains a relatively high balance with a positive trend as the majority group $\alpha_{majority}$

increases, indicating its superiority in maintaining a well-balanced representations than the non-fair approach. This phenomenon, which persists even with $\alpha_{majority} = 0.0$, is likely attributable to the fact that, prior to implementing a fair reassignment, the row clustering obtained via $\tau_{R|C}$ maximization is evaluated. This observation is more evident in the MovieLens dataset, when $\alpha_{majority}$ is set to a low value. In this case, the $\tau_{R|C}$, $\tau_{C|R}$ and ARI scores are close to those of the non-fair version (Fig. 2b and 2d) and the row and column clustering agreements with it are very high (Fig. 2c). A good trade-off between fairness and clustering quality can be seen for $\alpha_{majority} = 0.9$, as the balance remains high and τ_x, τ_y do not decrease too much.

6 Conclusion

We have introduced an algorithm that computes co-clustering with fairness constraints. It seeks a tradeoff between cluster quality and balance by adopting an optimization strategy that accounts for the protected groups the data instances belong to, by exploiting the properties of a co-clustering approach based on an associative statistical measure that has some desirable properties: it leads to fast convergence and to the identification of a congruent number of clusters on both rows and columns starting from an initial overestimation. The experiments have shown that our algorithm is effective also when compared with the only existing competitor, a co-clustering approach for fair recommendation based on the latent block model.

As future work, we intend to extend the current framework to guarantee fairness balance not only in the row clustering but also in the column clustering, thus addressing fairness constraints bidirectionally. Moreover, we plan to investigate the co-clustering problem under the individual fairness setting. Finally, we will explore multiobjective optimization as a way to automatically select optimal quality-fairness tradeoffs.

Disclosure of Interests. The authors have no competing interests to declare that are relevant to the content of this article.

References

1. Ahmadian, S., et al.: Fair hierarchical clustering. In: Proceedings of the NeurIPS 2020 (2020)
2. Ahmadian, S., Epasto, A., Kumar, R., Mahdian, M.: Clustering without overrepresentation. In: Proceedings of the SIGKDD KDD 2019, pp. 267–275 (2019)
3. Ahmadian, S., Epasto, A., Kumar, R., Mahdian, M.: Fair correlation clustering. In: Proceedings of the AISTATS 2020, vol. 108, pp. 4195–4205 (2020)
4. Backurs, A., et al.: Scalable fair clustering. In: Proceedings of the ICML 2019, vol. 97, pp. 405–413 (2019)
5. Battaglia, E., Peiretti, F., Pensa, R.G.: Fast parameterless prototype-based co-clustering. Mach. Learn. **113**(4), 2153–2181 (2024)

6. Battaglia, E., Peiretti, F., Pensa, R.G.: Co-clustering: a survey of the main methods, recent trends, and open problems. ACM Comput. Surv. **57**(2), 48:1–48:33 (2025)
7. Bera, S.K., Chakrabarty, D., Flores, N., Negahbani, M.: Fair algorithms for clustering. In: Proceedings of the NeurIPS 2019, pp. 4955–4966 (2019)
8. Bercea, I.O., et al.: On the cost of essentially fair clusterings. In: Proceedings of the APPROX/RANDOM 2019, vol. 145, pp. 18:1–18:22 (2019)
9. Brubach, B., Chakrabarti, D., Dickerson, J., Khuller, S., Srinivasan, A., Tsepenekas, L.: A pairwise fair and community-preserving approach to k-center clustering. In: Proceedings of the ICML 2020, pp. 1178–1189 (2020)
10. Chakrabarti, D., Dickerson, J.P., Esmaeili, S.A., Srinivasan, A., Tsepenekas, L.: A new notion of individually fair clustering: α-equitable k-center. In: Proceedings of the AISTATS 2022. vol. 151, pp. 6387–6408 (2022)
11. Chen, X., Fain, B., Lyu, L., Munagala, K.: Proportionally fair clustering. In: Proceedings of the ICML 2019, vol. 97, pp. 1032–1041 (2019)
12. Chen, Y., et al.: Parallel non-negative matrix tri-factorization for text data co-clustering. IEEE Trans. Knowl. Data Eng. **35**(5), 5132–5146 (2023)
13. Chhabra, A., Masalkovaite, K., Mohapatra, P.: An overview of fairness in clustering. IEEE Access **9**, 130698–130720 (2021)
14. Chierichetti, F., Kumar, R., Lattanzi, S., Vassilvitskii, S.: Fair clustering through fairlets. In: Proceedings of the NIPS 2017, pp. 5029–5037 (2017)
15. Dwork, C., Hardt, M., Pitassi, T., Reingold, O., Zemel, R.S.: Fairness through awareness. In: Proceedings of the ITCS 2012, pp. 214–226 (2012)
16. Esmaeili, S.A., Brubach, B., Srinivasan, A., Dickerson, J.: Fair clustering under a bounded cost. In: Proceedings of the NeurIPS 2021, pp. 14345–14357 (2021)
17. Fan-Osuala, O.: Gender-based differences in online reviews: an empirical investigation. In: Proceedings of the ICIS 2019 (2019)
18. Fan-Osuala, O.: Gender bias in online reviews (2020), Dataset, available online
19. Frisch, G., Léger, J., Grandvalet, Y.: Co-clustering for fair recommendation. In: Proceedings of the BIAS 2021, co-located with ECML PKDD 2021 (2021)
20. Ghodsi, S., Seyedi, S.A., Ntoutsi, E.: Towards cohesion-fairness harmony: contrastive regularization in individual fair graph clustering. In: Proceedings of the PAKDD 2024, pp. 284–296. Springer (2024)
21. Goodman, L.A., Kruskal, W.H.: Measures of association for cross classification. J. Am. Stat. Assoc. **49**, 732–764 (1954)
22. Gupta, S., Ghalme, G., Krishnan, N.C., Jain, S.: Efficient algorithms for fair clustering with a new notion of fairness. Data Min. Knowl. Discov. **37**(5), 1959–1997 (2023)
23. Harper, F.M., Konstan, J.A.: The movielens datasets: history and context. ACM Trans. Interact. Intell. Syst. **5**(4), 19:1–19:19 (2016)
24. Huang, G.B., Mattar, M., Berg, T., Learned-Miller, E.: Labeled faces in the wild: a database forstudying face recognition in unconstrained environments. In: Workshop on Faces in'Real-Life'Images: Detection, Alignment, and Recognition (2008)
25. Hubert, L., Arabie, P.: Comparing partitions. J. Classif. **2**, 193–218 (1985)
26. Keuper, M., Tang, S., Andres, B., Brox, T., Schiele, B.: Motion segmentation & multiple object tracking by correlation co-clustering. IEEE Trans. Pattern Anal. Mach. Intell. **42**(1), 140–153 (2020)
27. Kleindessner, M., Samadi, S., Awasthi, P., Morgenstern, J.: Guarantees for spectral clustering with fairness constraints. In: Proceedings of the ICML 2019, pp. 3458–3467 (2019)

28. Li, P., Zhao, H., Liu, H.: Deep fair clustering for visual learning. In: Proceedings of the CVPR 2020, pp. 9067–9076 (2020)
29. Zeng, P., Lin, Z.: Couple coc+: an information-theoretic co-clustering-based transfer learning framework for the integrative analysis of single-cell genomic data. PLoS Comput. Biol. **17**(6), e1009064 (2021)
30. Zhao, Y., Wang, Y., Liu, Y., Cheng, X., Aggarwal, C.C., Derr, T.: Fairness and diversity in recommender systems: a survey. ACM Trans. Intell. Syst. Technol. **16**(1), 2:1–2:28 (2025)
31. Ziko, I.M., Yuan, J., Granger, E., Ayed, I.B.: Variational fair clustering. In: Proceedings of the AAAI 2021, pp. 11202–11209 (2021)

DispaRisk: Assessing Fairness Through Usable Information

Jonathan Vasquez[1,2(✉)], Carlotta Domeniconi[2], and Huzefa Rangwala[2]

[1] Universidad de Valparaiso, Valparaiso, Chile
jonathan.vasquez@uv.cl
[2] George Mason University, Fairfax, USA
{jvasqu6,cdomenic,rangwala}@gmu.edu

Abstract. Machine Learning algorithms (ML) impact virtually every aspect of human lives and have found use across diverse sectors including healthcare, finance, and education. Often, ML algorithms have been found to exacerbate societal biases present in datasets leading to adversarial impacts on subsets/groups of individuals and in many cases on minority groups. To effectively mitigate these untoward effects, it is crucial that disparities/biases are identified early in a ML pipeline. This proactive approach facilitates timely interventions to prevent bias amplification and reduce complexity at later stages of model development. In this paper, we leverage recent advancements in usable information theory to introduce DispaRisk, a novel framework designed to proactively assess the potential risks of disparities in datasets during the initial stages of the ML pipeline. We evaluate DispaRisk's effectiveness by benchmarking it against commonly used datasets in fairness research. Our findings demonstrate DispaRisk's capabilities to identify datasets with a high risk of discrimination, detect model families prone to biases within an ML pipeline, and enhance the explainability of these bias risks. This work contributes to the development of fairer ML systems by providing a robust tool for early bias detection and mitigation. The code is available at https://github.com/jovasque156/disparisk.

Keywords: usable information · fairness · uncertainty · bias

1 Introduction

Extensive research on fairness in machine learning (ML) has shown that biased datasets can amplify historical and societal inequities [8,19,24,31], harming minorities and disadvantaged groups in areas such as criminal justice [25], healthcare [2], and education [30]. This underscores the need to detect biases throughout the ML pipeline, especially in its early stages [7,12]. To address this,

Supplementary Information The online version contains supplementary material available at https://doi.org/10.1007/978-3-032-05962-8_18.

data- and *model-focused* metrics help identify potential discrimination risks, but each have limitations.

Data-focused metrics are computed directly from the dataset and include Class Imbalance (CL) [11], Difference in Positive proportions in observed Labels (DPL) [11], and Mutual Information (MI) between the sensitive attribute and the rest of the features [9]. Although useful, these approaches do not account for model selection or preferences, making it difficult to determine which models are more likely to produce disparate outcomes. To address this gap, *model-focused* metrics analyze trained models directly. These methods, discussed in [11,30], detect existing discrimination (e.g., Demographic Disparity (DEMP) and Equalized Opportunity (EQODD)) or provide explanations for disparate predictions (e.g., KernelSHAP [23,27]). However, these evaluations occur late in the pipeline and are tied to specific models, limiting their generalizability. Moreover, they do not fully capture how the interaction between data characteristics and model capabilities affects fairness.

Although fairness metrics help assess bias at different stages, they do not address how models interact with data properties in practice. Even when datasets appear balanced, models may process information differently across groups, leading to hidden disparities. For instance, in an ML pipeline classifying rural and urban loan applicants as approved or denied, a dataset may predict approvals equally across groups. However, simple models might effectively leverage credit scores for urban applicants while struggling with interaction-based features critical for rural ones. This disparity in information usability can lead to uneven model performance and potential discrimination, even with seemingly fair datasets. Moreover, increasing model complexity does not necessarily resolve these issues, as it depends on whether the model can effectively utilize nuanced information for different groups. Hence, key questions emerge: Can differences in usable information across groups be quantified to trace disparities? How does the choice of model influence these differences and outcomes? Addressing these requires a deeper assessment of ML pipelines, beyond dataset balance and final model evaluation. Specifically, an approach that enables early detection of disparity risks while accounting for model-specific characteristics is needed.

To operationalize these insights, we introduce DispaRisk, a framework designed to detect disparity risks early in the ML pipeline while considering the characteristics of the predictive models being used. Building on the *usable information* notions studied by Xu et al. [32], DispaRisk enables proactive fairness assessments by guiding the estimation of usable information-based metrics. Specifically, given a set of potential model choices, DispaRisk facilitates assessment analyses that: (1) can be conducted in the early stages of ML pipelines, (2) account for the predictive families selected, (3) correlate with data- and model-focused fairness metrics, and (4) explain why different model families generate disparate outcomes. This approach serves as an effective predictor of the discrimination risks that may emerge later in the pipeline.

The key contributions of this study are threefold:

1. We introduce DispaRisk, a framework that leverages recent advances in *usable information* theory to detect early-stage disparities across predictive model families in ML pipelines. To this end, we develop:
   - Instance-level disparity scores (DispaRisk, DR) using pointwise $\mathcal{V}$-entropy to identify individuals at high risk (see Sect. 3).
   - Feature-level explanations (Uncertainty Reduction, UR) by quantifying how masking each feature alters model uncertainty (see Sect. 4.1).
2. We bridge the gap between *data-* and *model-*focused bias assessment approaches.
3. We demonstrate practical applications through experiments across diverse datasets, showcasing its ability to identify high-risk datasets, detect bias-prone model families, and improve bias explainability.

2 Basics and Preliminaries

2.1 ML Pipeline Basics

Let X, S, and Y be random variables in the space $\mathcal{X} \times \mathcal{S} \times \mathcal{Y}$, representing input features, sensitive attributes, and target variable, respectively. An ML pipeline is given access to a dataset $\mathcal{D}_n = \{x_i, s_i, y_i\}_{i=1}^n \in \mathcal{X} \times \mathcal{S} \times \mathcal{Y}$ of n instances to learn a mapping function $h : \mathcal{X} \mapsto \mathcal{Y}$ employing a finite set of possible models $\mathcal{V}$. We assume that there is access to sufficient information about the ML pipeline to identify the set of possible models.

2.2 Fairness Notion

We examine fairness through the notions of independence and separation [7,12,24,30]. Independence requires that the outcomes of the learned mapping function be independent of the sensitive attribute ($h(X) \perp S$), while separation requires independence conditioned on the ground truth ($h(X) \perp S|Y$). Our analysis focuses on a positive class of binary classifications, which typically signify favorable decisions with significant social implications. For example, in contexts such as university admissions or loan approvals, positive outcomes (e.g., being admitted or approved) directly influence individuals' opportunities. To evaluate these types of disparities, we employ the DEMP and EQOPP metrics explained as follows:

Definition 1 (Demographic Disparity (DEMP)). *Difference in the **positive rate** of the class $k \in Y$ between the advantaged (s) and disadvantaged (s') groups.*

$$\Delta_{DEMP}(h, S, Y_k) = P(h(X) = 1|S = s) - P(h(X) = 1|S = s')$$

Definition 2 (Equalized Opportunity (OPP)). *Difference in the **true positive rate** of class $k \in Y$ between advantaged (s) and disadvantaged (s') groups:*

$$\Delta_{OPP}(h, S, Y_k) = P(h(X) = 1|S = s, Y_k = 1) - P(h(X) = 1|S = s', Y_k = 1)$$

2.3 Usable Information Framework

The *usable information* framework [32] quantifies uncertainty differences across groups within a model family, highlighting the impact of model selection. We next replicate Xu et al.'s [32] metric formulations, propose a new metric, and outline their estimation within the $\mathcal{V}$-information framework. The next subsection introduces DispaRisk, a framework for improving fairness analysis in ML pipelines by assessing model class, usable information, and disparate outcomes.

$\mathcal{V}$-Information Framework. Xu et al. [32] introduce the $\mathcal{V}$-information framework to estimate *usable information* withim a family of models $\mathcal{V}$.[1] A first formulated concept is the predictive conditional $\mathcal{V}$-entropy, which represents the minimum achievable expected negative log-likelihood to predict Y given X using models from the predictive family $\mathcal{V}$. Formally:

Definition 3 (Predictive conditional $\mathcal{V}$-entropy). *For a family $\mathcal{V}$ of models, the conditional $\mathcal{V}$-entropy[2] of Y given X is defined as:*

$$H_\mathcal{V}(Y|X) = \inf_{h \in \mathcal{V}} \mathbb{E}_{x,y \sim X,Y}[-\log_2 h[x](y)] \tag{1}$$

The infimum in Eq. 1 is attained by finding the function $h \in \mathcal{V}$ that minimizes the expected negative log-likelihood,[3]. Measurement of the uncertainty of class of the model in predicting Y from X requires identifying its best performing model. Unlike Shannon entropy, $\mathcal{V}$-entropy depends on $\mathcal{V}$, providing distinct uncertainty measures across model classes, which makes it valuable for comparing predictive capacities, a key focus of our study.

While $\mathcal{V}$-entropy aggregates uncertainty over the dataset, bias assessment requires analyzing specific data slices, such as demographic differences. To address this, we propose Pointwise $\mathcal{V}$-entropy (P$\mathcal{V}$E) to quantify instance-level uncertainty within a model family $\mathcal{V}$. Formally:

Definition 4 (Pointwise $\mathcal{V}$-entropy (P$\mathcal{V}$E)). *For a family $\mathcal{V}$, and an instance represented by the tuple (x,y), the pointwise $\mathcal{V}$-entropy (P$\mathcal{V}$E) is defined as:*

$$P\mathcal{V}E(x \mapsto y) = -\log_2 h[x](y) \tag{2}$$

where $h \in \mathcal{V}$ such that $\mathbb{E}[-\log_2 h[X](Y)] = H_\mathcal{V}(Y|X)$.

Higher P$\mathcal{V}$E values indicate greater uncertainty, which means that models within $\mathcal{V}$ struggle to predict the instance accurately. P$\mathcal{V}$E complements PVI [6], which estimates usable information by comparing predictions with and without x. In contrast, P$\mathcal{V}$E focuses on the remaining uncertainty when x is given, simplifying the estimate and reducing estimation costs.

Estimating $\mathcal{V}$-entropy and P$\mathcal{V}$E. The $\mathcal{V}$-entropy can be empirically estimated on a finite dataset $\mathcal{D}$ of n instances as:

---
[1] See supplementary material for more information.
[2] In this article, conditional $\mathcal{V}$-entropy is referred to as $\mathcal{V}$-entropy.
[3] With $\log_2$, the measure is in bits; for nats, use $\log_e$.

Algorithm 1. $\mathcal{V}$-entropy and P$\mathcal{V}$E

Require: $\mathcal{D}_{train} = \{(x_i, y_i)\}_{i=1}^{k}$, $\mathcal{D}_{held-out} = \{(x_i, y_i)\}_{i=k+1}^{n}$, and family $\mathcal{V}$
Ensure: $\hat{H}_\mathcal{V}$ and P$\mathcal{V}$E estimates.
1: $h \leftarrow$ fine-tune $\mathcal{V}$ on $\mathcal{D}_{train} = \{(x_i, y_i)\}_{i=1}^{k}$
2: $\hat{H}_\mathcal{V}(Y|X) \leftarrow 0$
3: **for** $(x_i, y_i) \in \mathcal{D}_{held-out}$ **do**
4: $\quad \hat{H}_\mathcal{V}(Y|X) \leftarrow \hat{H}_\mathcal{V}(Y|X) - \frac{1}{n-k} \log_2 h[x_i](y_i)$
5: $\quad$ P$\mathcal{V}$E$(x_i \mapsto y_i) \leftarrow -\log_2 h[x_i](y_i)$
6: **end for**

$$\hat{H}_\mathcal{V}(Y|X; \mathcal{D}) = \inf_{h \in \mathcal{V}} \frac{1}{n} \sum_{x_i, y_i \in \mathcal{D}} -\log_2 h[x_i](y_i) \qquad (3)$$

$$= \inf_{h \in \mathcal{V}} \frac{1}{n} \sum_{x_i, y_i \in \mathcal{D}} \text{P}\mathcal{V}\text{E}(x_i \mapsto y_i) \qquad (4)$$

where the infimum $h \in \mathcal{V}$ is approximated using cross-entropy loss to minimize the negative log-likelihood of Y given X [6,32]. The approximation of $\hat{H}_\mathcal{V}$ is achieved by training or fine-tuning a pre-trained model following Algorithm 1, which extends [6] to focus on $\mathcal{V}$-entropy and P$\mathcal{V}$E. The algorithm splits data into training and held-out sets, using the latter to estimate $\hat{H}_\mathcal{V}$ and P$\mathcal{V}$E. Since the estimation is based on finite data, the results may deviate from the true $\mathcal{V}$-entropy. Xu et al. [32] provide Probably Approximately Correct (PAC) bounds, showing that larger datasets and simpler $\mathcal{V}$ yield tighter bounds.

3 DispaRisk

3.1 $\mathcal{V}$-Information in Disparity Assessment

We propose evaluating unfairness by comparing the uncertainty to predict Y from X between slices of the dataset that we are interested in, arguing that these differences are expected to align with fairness metrics in later stages of the ML pipeline. To this end, we introduce DispaRisk (DR), a framework for computing differences over P$\mathcal{V}$E averages of data slices and to analyze their relationship with disparities. In the following paragraphs, we first explain the rationale of using average of P$\mathcal{V}$E,[4] and then, introduce how to compute DR for *independence* and *separation* notions of fairness.

Rationale of Using Average P$\mathcal{V}$E. For disparity metrics to be meaningful, uncertainty estimates across groups must be comparable, that is, all derived under the same reference mapping function. Computing a separate infimum h

---
[4] It is worthy to note that $\mathcal{V}$-entropy coincides with the expected P$\mathcal{V}$E only if the model used to estimate P$\mathcal{V}$E has been trained on the entire dataset; accordingly, the mean P$\mathcal{V}$E of any subset does not equal to its own $\mathcal{V}$-entropy [6,32].

for advantaged and disadvantaged slices produces inherently incomparable $\mathcal{V}$-entropy values, since each is defined over a different input–output space. In contrast, using a single global infimum ensures that every average $\text{P}\mathcal{V}\text{E}$ is evaluated against the same baseline, isolating uncertainty differences that arise solely from the data distributions of groups rather than from variations in the learnable mapping function. Indeed, for fairness criteria defined over a single class (such as EQOPP, discussed later), estimating group-specific $\mathcal{V}$-entropy is ill-posed: taking an infimum over slices of only one target class yields zero $\mathcal{V}$-entropy. However, we leave the exploration of group-specific training regimes to future work.

DR and DEMP: To analyze fairness under *independence* notions (in this study, measured through DEMP), we propose to compute the average of $\text{P}\mathcal{V}\text{E}$ on slices consisting of instances belonging to the advantaged ($\mathcal{D}_a$) and disadvantaged ($\mathcal{D}_d$) group. Formally:

$$\text{DR}(\mathcal{D}_a, \mathcal{D}_d | \mathcal{V}) = \frac{1}{|\mathcal{D}_a|} \sum_{x,y \in \mathcal{D}_a} \text{P}\mathcal{V}\text{E}(x \mapsto y) - \frac{1}{|\mathcal{D}_d|} \sum_{x,y \in \mathcal{D}_d} \text{P}\mathcal{V}\text{E}(x \mapsto y) \quad (5)$$

where DR quantifies the difference in $\text{P}\mathcal{V}\text{E}$ between the groups of the family $\mathcal{V}$ when predicting Y from X. Since $\mathcal{V}$ is defined over the entire dataset, DR serves as a computationally efficient alternative, requiring only one model per group instead of a full dataset estimation.

DR and EQOPP: Under EQOPP in *separation*, where disparity is assessed only for the positive class, DR is computed over $Y=1$ as follows:

$$\begin{aligned}\text{DR}(\mathcal{D}_{a,y=1}, \mathcal{D}_{d,y=1} | \mathcal{V}) = &\frac{1}{|\mathcal{D}_{a,y=1}|} \sum_{x,y \in \mathcal{D}_{a,y=1}} \text{P}\mathcal{V}\text{E}(x \mapsto y) \\ &- \frac{1}{|\mathcal{D}_{d,y=1}|} \sum_{x,y \in \mathcal{D}_{d,y=1}} \text{P}\mathcal{V}\text{E}(x \mapsto y)\end{aligned} \quad (6)$$

where $\mathcal{D}_{a,y=1}$ and $\mathcal{D}_{d,y=1}$ represent dataset slices for advantaged and disadvantaged groups with the target label $y=1$. Thus, when comparing DR with DEMP, we use Eq. (5), and for EQOPP, we use Eq. (6).

3.2 The Relationship Between DR and Fairness Notions

We now examine the relationship between DR and the fairness notions of *separation* and *independence*. Higher uncertainty implies that models in $\mathcal{V}$ are less confident in predicting Y from X. When $\mathcal{V}$-entropy is high, the models in $\mathcal{V}$ tend to rely on guessing, favoring the majority class in Y. Consequently, instances of the group with the highest average $\text{P}\mathcal{V}\text{E}$ are more likely to be predicted as the majority class. How does this affect the disparities in $\mathcal{V}$? In the following, we outline the rules of thumb for addressing this question.

DR and *separation* through EQOPP. EQOPP measures the difference in true positive rates between the advantaged and disadvantaged groups. By the definition of DR in Equation (6), higher absolute DR values should positively correlate with EQOPP. The reasoning is that greater DR differences indicate that the group with higher average P$\mathcal{V}$E experiences greater uncertainty in predicting Y from X, leading to more inaccurate predictions and a lower true positive rate. This results in higher EQOPP values, reflecting greater disparities under *separation*. Based on this analysis, we establish the following thumb rules, demonstrated in the experiments: *For **higher** absolute values of DR, **higher** levels of disparities under EQOPP are expected.*

DR and *independence* through DEMP. DEMP measures the difference in positive ratios between the advantaged and disadvantaged groups. To determine whether higher DR values from Equation (5) correspond to higher or lower positive ratios for the group with greater uncertainty and therefore the expected DEMP levels, we identify two key characteristics of the dataset.

The first is the **majority class in the target**, which helps to predict whether the higher uncertainty group will receive a higher or lower positive rate. Since DR implies that the group with higher average P$\mathcal{V}$E is more likely to be predicted as the majority class, the relationship between DR and DEMP depends on whether the majority class is positive or negative. If the majority class is positive, the higher uncertainty group is expected to receive higher positive ratios, leading to greater disparities under DEMP. Thus, a second rules of thumb is: *For **higher** absolute values of DR, **higher** levels of disparities under DEMP are expected.*

In contrast, if the **majority class is negative**, the relationship is reversed. The group with higher uncertainty is now less likely to be predicted as positive, reducing the difference in positive ratios. Therefore, the third rule of thumb is defined as: *For **higher** absolute values of DR, **lower** levels of disparities under DEMP are expected.*

3.3 Benefits of DR

Our simple yet effective approach offers two key benefits. First, it aligns with fairness notions by accounting for the dependency between labels and sensitive attributes. DR translates fairness concepts into the $\mathcal{V}$-entropy framework, where fairness implies uncertainty differences close to zero, ensuring equal *usable information* across groups and reducing disparities. However, as we will show, this holds only under certain conditions and disparity notions.

Second, $\mathcal{V}$-entropy enables pipeline-dependent metrics for model selection. Since it is defined over $\mathcal{V}$, this set can be tailored to the models used in the ML pipeline, making DR context-specific rather than dataset- or model-specific. A more granular approach could involve multiple sets $\mathcal{V}$, each representing different model families, allowing for comparable metrics between model types. The following sections demonstrate how DispaRisk enhances disparity risk assessment through a thorough analysis.

Table 1. Disadvantaged group and positive class from the sensitive attribute and target variable for each ML pipeline.

ML Pipeline	Sensitive	Disadvantaged	Target	Positive class
$\mathcal{D}^{kdd}$	sex	female	income	$> 50K$
$\mathcal{D}^{facet}$	gender	non-masculine	person-related	lawman, nurse
$\mathcal{D}^{hs}$	dialectal	african-american	harrasement	non-harrasement

4 Experiments

4.1 Machine Learning Pipelines

We evaluate disparity risks in three ML pipelines using datasets KDD, FACET, and Hate Speech, denoted as $\mathcal{D}^{kdd}$, $\mathcal{D}^{facet}$, and $\mathcal{D}^{hs}$. Each dataset $\mathcal{D}$ includes input features X, sensitive attribute S, and target Y for learning $h : X \mapsto Y$. Although S is excluded from the mapping, it remains available for fairness analysis. We now describe each dataset.

The KDD Census-Income dataset ($\mathcal{D}^{kdd}$) originates from the 1994âĂŞ1995 U.S. Census Bureau surveys, which contain 41 demographic and employment-related variables for 299,285 individuals. It is used to classify whether a person earns more than $50K$ per year, with sensitive attributes such as age, sex, and race.[5]

The FACET dataset ($\mathcal{D}^{facet}$) is a Meta AI benchmark for evaluating fairness of vision model [10]. It includes 32,000 images labeled with demographic (e.g., perceived gender presentation) and person-related attributes (e.g., *lawman*, *nurse*), covering 50,000 people. We extract a dataset of 50,000 images (one per person) using provided bounding boxes, along with a binary masculine gender attribute and person-related class labels.[6]

The Hate Speech dataset ($\mathcal{D}^{hs}$) by Davidson et al. [3] contains 24,802 tweets labeled as *hate speech*, *offensive*, or *neither*. We augment it with demographic dialect predictions from Blodgett et al. [1], estimating dialect proportions for African-American, Hispanic, White, and other groups per tweet.

Following fairness conventions for binary classification, we define the membership of the disadvantaged group using sensitive attributes and the positive class based on the target variables. Table 1 summarizes these criteria. We transform the sensitive attribute, assigning 1 to disadvantaged groups and 0 otherwise. Likewise, the target variable is set to 1 for positive class instances and 0 for all others.

4.2 Disparity Risk Assessments

We conduct two approaches to evaluate disparity risks in each ML pipeline: (1) a *baseline* using popular *dataset-focused* metrics from literature, and (2) an approach using DR and comparing with popular *model-focused* metrics.

---

[5] https://archive.ics.uci.edu/ml/datasets/Census-Income.
[6] https://ai.meta.com/datasets/facet/.

Table 2. *Data-focused* metrics computed from datasets. Higher values indicate stronger relationships between sensitivities and labels.

Pipeline	Class	CIm	DPL	r_ϕ	KL
$\mathcal{D}^{kdd}$	$> 50k$	−0.04	0.08	−0.16	0.07
$\mathcal{D}^{hs}$	no_harassment	−0.06	0.25	−0.34	0.33
$\mathcal{D}^{facet}$	lawman nurse	0.34	0.06	−0.10	0.03
			−0.04	0.12	0.02

Baseline. We use *data-focused* metrics—Class Imbalance (CIm), Difference in Positive proportions in observed Labels (DPL), Matthews Correlation Coefficient (r_ϕ), and KL-divergence (KL)—[7] to assess bias [11,18]. Table 2 presents the results, highlighting the varying level of bias between datasets. For $\mathcal{D}^{kdd}$, we observe a slight overrepresentation of the disadvantaged group, with a moderate negative correlation ($r_\phi = -0.159$) between sensitive attributes and labels and a higher positive rate for the male sociodemographic group (DPL > 0). In $\mathcal{D}^{hs}$, bias is strongest for the positive class (*no_harassment*), where DPL, r_ϕ, and KL reach the highest absolute values, indicating that the advantaged group has more tweets labeled as *no_harassment* than disadvantaged one. $\mathcal{D}^{facet}$ shows a strong overrepresentation of the advantaged group. Based on r_ϕ and DPL, the *lawman* class has a higher positive rate for the advantaged group, while *nurse* exhibits the opposite trend.

Although these results offer valuable insights, they provide a global perspective, lacking the granularity needed to analyze specific model types within each ML pipeline. The following section applies *DispaRisk* to enable a more nuanced assessment of potential biases in ML pipelines.

DispaRisk in Practice. DispaRisk is applied in three steps: (1) constructing model families based on the intended models for the ML pipeline, (2) estimating DR, and (3) analyzing the results to generate insights.

Construction of Families $\mathcal{V}$. For each hypothetical ML pipeline, we define model families based on assumed preferences. For $\mathcal{D}^{kdd}$, we construct five families of Feedforward Neural Network (FNN) with different activation functions: no activation (linear), ReLU [33], LeakyReLU [13], Sigmoid, and GELU [15]. For $\mathcal{D}^{hs}$, we analyze transformer-based families: BERT [4], RoBERTa [21], GPT2 [26], BART [20], and DeBERTa [14]. For $\mathcal{D}^{facet}$, we employ popular vision model families: VGG [28], Inception [29], DenseNet [17], MobileNet [16], and Vision-Transformer [5]. Model families are identified using activation functions or model architecture names as subscripts. For example, $\mathcal{V}_{leaky\_relu}$ represents FNNs with LeakyReLU, and $\mathcal{V}_{gpt2}$ denotes the GPT2 family.[8]

---

[7] See supplementary material for more detail.
[8] See supplementary material for detailed list of families constructed in this study.

DR *Estimates.* To estimate uncertainty differences via DR (Sect. 3), we follow this protocol for each ML pipeline using dataset $\mathcal{D}^{(p)}$ and family $\mathcal{V}_i$:

(1) Split $\mathcal{D}^{(p)}$ into $\mathcal{D}^{(p)}_{train}$ and $\mathcal{D}^{(p)}_{held-out}$ sets at 80/20 ratio.
(2) Approximate the infimum $h \in \mathcal{V}_i$ by training or fine-tuning a pretrained model using cross-entropy loss (Step 1 of Algorithm 1).
(3) Estimate $H_{\mathcal{V}_i}$ and PVE following Steps 2âĂŞ6 of Algorithm 1.

Since the most computationally powerful model in $\mathcal{V}$ often attains the infimum (Definition 3), this weakens the PAC bound [32], requiring overfitting prevention. To mitigate this, we create a validation set $\mathcal{D}^{(p)}_{val}$ by sampling 10% of $\mathcal{D}^{(p)}_{train}$ and evaluate estimates per epoch. The models are trained/fine-tuned for 5 epochs with a learning rate of $5e-5$ and a batch size of 32. If overfitting arises, we lower the learning rate to $5e-6$, halve the batch size, and rerun Algorithm 1. We use the AdamW optimizer [22] with a linear scheduler[9] for all experiments.

Assessing Fairness Tthrough Usable Information. We use estimates to address two key questions that *data-focused* metrics alone cannot answer:

(Q.1) Which model families in the ML pipeline are more likely to replicate or exacerbate biases? To investigate this, we simulate later ML pipeline stages and compare estimated DR with observed disparities, identifying model families prone to higher bias reproduction. For example, in the $\mathcal{D}^{kdd}$ pipeline, we first estimate DR for each family. Next, we train FNNs with varying hidden layers from each family and compute average disparity levels using EQOPP and DEMP. In parallel, we estimate DR for each family. Finally, we compare uncertainty difference estimates with observed disparities to evaluate whether DR effectively signals model families more prone to exacerbating biases, as inferred in Sect. 3. Applying this protocol in all ML pipelines, we obtain the results shown in Figs. 1 and 2, which depict the relationship between DR estimates and EQOPP/DEMP in different pipelines and model families.

Figure 1 shows the relationship between absolute DR$(\mathcal{D}_{a,y=1}, \mathcal{D}_{d,y=1})$ values and average EQOPP. The observed trend confirms the rule of thumb from Sect. 3 across all ML pipelines, validating DR as a predictor of risk of disparity for future models in downstream tasks. Given this, we derive the first insight for **(Q.1)**: *the model families most prone to higher disparities under separation notions are $\mathcal{V}_{sigmoid}$, $\mathcal{V}_{deberta}$, and $\mathcal{V}_{mobilenet}$ for the $\mathcal{D}^{kdd}$, $\mathcal{D}^{hs}$, and $\mathcal{D}^{facet}$ pipelines, respectively.*

Figure 2 illustrates the relationship between DR$(\mathcal{D}_a, \mathcal{D}_d)$ and DEMP. To analyze these results and address **Q.1**, we follow a structured approach: (1) identify the majority class, (2) evaluate whether the observed trends align with the expected DR-DEMP relationship from Sect. 3, and (3) synthesize insights to answer **Q.1**. Applying this approach, we find that for $\mathcal{D}^{kdd}$ the negative class (income $< 50k$) is the majority, suggesting an inverse relationship between absolute DR and DEMP (Sect. 3). Figure 2 confirms this, with higher absolute DR values corresponding to lower DEMP. The models in $\mathcal{V}_{gelu}$ and $\mathcal{V}_{sigmoid}$ show higher

---
[9] Minimum learning rate set to 0.

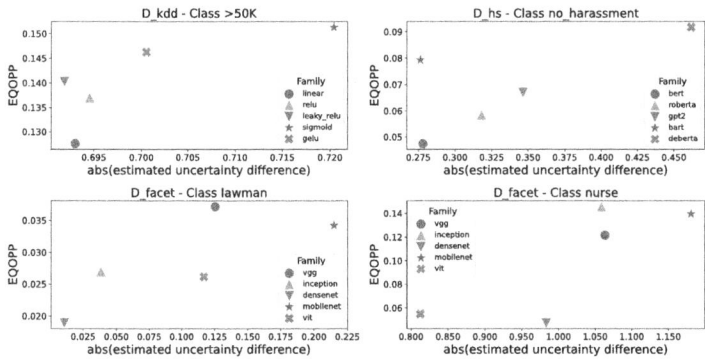

Fig. 1. Average EQOPP disparity in family versus estimated uncertainty difference through $\mathrm{DR}(\mathcal{D}_{a,y=1}, \mathcal{D}_{d,y=1})$ for each family $\mathcal{V}_i$.

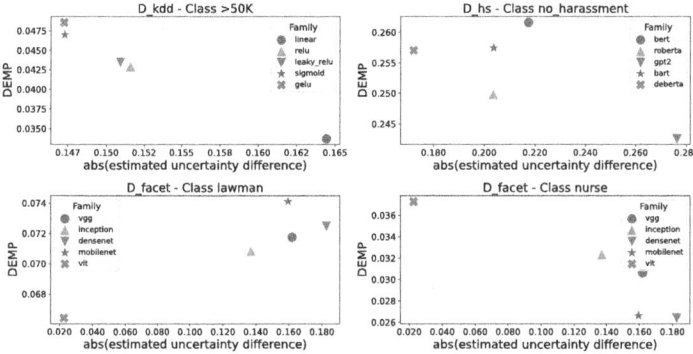

Fig. 2. Average DEMP in predictive families versus estimated uncertainty difference through $\mathrm{DR}(\mathcal{D}_a, \mathcal{D}_d)$ for each family $\mathcal{V}_i$.

disparity risks. Furthermore, in $\mathcal{D}^{hs}$ the majority class is *harassment* (negative class), indicating a similar inverse DR-DEMP relationship as in $\mathcal{D}^{kdd}$. According to Sect. 3, models in $\mathcal{V}_{deberta}$ are more prone to disparities under *independence*. Finally, for $\mathcal{D}^{facet}$ the majority class is *lawman*. From Fig. 2, the rule of thumb (Sect. 3) that an inverse DR-DEMP relationship is expected for the *nurse* class and a direct one for *lawman* is confirmed. The models in $\mathcal{V}_{densenet}$ are more prone to disparities for *lawman*, while $\mathcal{V}_{vit}$ shows similar tendencies for *nurse*.

(Q.2) Why might these model types produce disparate outcomes? The rules of thumb not only help identify high-risk model families but also explain why these families contribute to disparities in later pipeline stages. For example, in $\mathcal{V}_{sigmoid}$, EQOPP is higher because the group with a higher average $P\mathcal{V}E$ is less likely to be correctly predicted, leading to a lower true positive rate. Similarly, DEMP is higher as the lower average $P\mathcal{V}E$ differences shows that models are reflecting dataset biases seen in the Table 2. This pattern is generalized across model families and ML pipelines.

To further explore these disparities, we analyze which features contribute to the computed average P$\mathcal{V}$E in each model family. We select the riskiest families per ML pipeline and identify key features by measuring uncertainty reduction when a feature is added to the input space. Specifically, we compare P$\mathcal{V}$E when feature i is masked using transformation τ_i versus when x is complete. The transformations applied in each pipeline are: setting the feature i to 0 in $\mathcal{D}^{kdd}$, replacing the word i with a blank space in $\mathcal{D}^{hs}$, and setting the specific pixel sets to 0 in $\mathcal{D}^{facet}$. Formally, this uncertainty reduction is measured as follows:

$$\text{UR}(\mathcal{D}|\mathcal{V}, \tau_i) = \frac{1}{|\mathcal{D}|} \sum_{x,y \in \mathcal{D}} \text{P}\mathcal{V}\text{E}(\tau_i(x) \mapsto y) - \text{P}\mathcal{V}\text{E}(x \mapsto y) \quad (7)$$

$$= \frac{1}{|\mathcal{D}|} \sum_{x,y \in \mathcal{D}} -\log_2 h[x_{\neg i}](y) + \log_2 h[x](y) \quad (8)$$

where UR represents Uncertainty Reduction, $\tau_i(x)$ denotes the transformation process that masks the feature i, and $x_{\neg i}$ is the resulting output. We use $h \in \mathcal{V}$ such that $\mathbb{E}[-\log_2 h[X](Y)] = H_\mathcal{V}(Y|X)$. Higher UR values for feature i indicate its importance for the models in $\mathcal{V}$ in accurately predicting the target variable. In particular, we use the same infimum of $\mathcal{V}$ for P$\mathcal{V}$E with both the $\tau_i(x)$ and the unmasked input to avoid the computational overhead of determining a separate infimum for each masked feature. Althuogh this simplification has limitations, which will be discussed in Sect. 5, the primary goal here is to demonstrate how *DispaRisk* extends beyond identifying risky models to offer deeper insights into potential disparities. In the following paragraphs, we apply this approach to all ML pipelines.

In $\mathcal{D}^{kdd}$, the positive DPL indicates higher positive rates labeled for the advantaged group, a disparity replicated in $\mathcal{V}_{sigmoid}$ due to its lower DR. Thus, we compute UR on $\mathcal{D}_a$. Figure 3 shows the 15 most relevant features by UR for $\mathcal{V}_{sigmoid}$, the highest risk family. The main contributors to disparity risks are education, capital_gains, weeks_worked_in_year, age, and occupation, with education and capital_gains providing the greatest reduction in uncertainty. Thus, in addition to **(Q.1)**, uncertainty differences are largely attributed to these variables in $\mathcal{V}_{sigmoid}$. This might suggest insights such as careful preprocessing of these features to mitigate bias or further considerations on these variables during model constructions.

For the pipeline $\mathcal{D}^{hs}$, we analyze two word sets: (1) the most relevant words for each target class identified by Ethayarajh et al. [6] and (2) a manually curated list of problematic words for $\mathcal{D}^{hs}$. For each word i, we compute UR using a subsample of texts containing i, capturing its impact on uncertainty reduction when present versus absent. Given the DR values and following the approach for $\mathcal{D}^{kdd}$, we compute UR on the advantaged group due to positive DPL. Figure 4 presents the top 15 words in $\mathcal{V}_{deberta}$, identified as the highest risk family in **(Q.1)**. The analysis shows that homophobic and racial slurs significantly reduce uncertainty in $\mathcal{V}_{deberta}$ for the advantaged group. This indicates that a specific set of biased

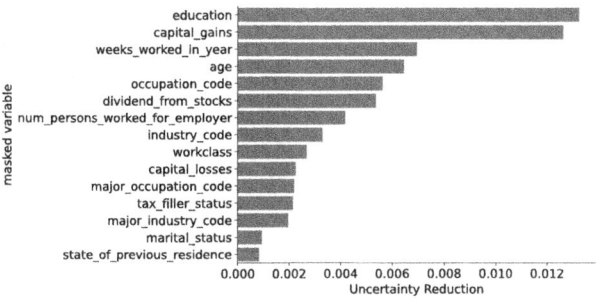

Fig. 3. Top 15 UR of features over the advantaged group (male) for the $\mathcal{V}_{sigmoid}$ family in the $\mathcal{D}^{kdd}$ ML pipeline.

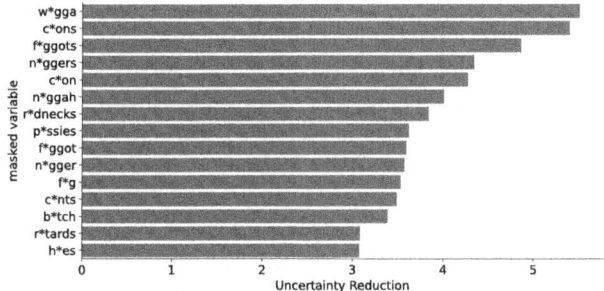

Fig. 4. Top 15 UR of words over the advantaged group (Not-African-American dialect) for the $\mathcal{V}_{deberta}$ family in the $\mathcal{D}^{hs}$ ML pipeline. Words are modified to avoid exposition of inappropriate text.

terms drives a large number of uncertainty differences and, consequently, disparity risks in this predictive family.

Finally, for the $\mathcal{D}^{facet}$ dataset, we focus on the disadvantaged group, which had the highest average PVE in the estimated DR. We analyze $\mathcal{V}_{densenet}$ and $\mathcal{V}_{vit}$, identified as the highest-risk families for the `lawman` and `nurse` classes, respectively. We examine the image background and the person to determine which contributes more to uncertainty reduction, explaining the disparity risks identified earlier. Figure 5 shows that in both families, the background has the highest uncertainty reduction. This reinforces that image backgrounds significantly impact the elevated uncertainty of the disadvantaged group, driving disparity risks. These findings help narrow the focus on key features when analyzing biases.

5 Discussion

DispaRisk bridges the gap between *data-focused* and *model-focused* bias detection methods. Although it operates on datasets like *data-focused* techniques, it

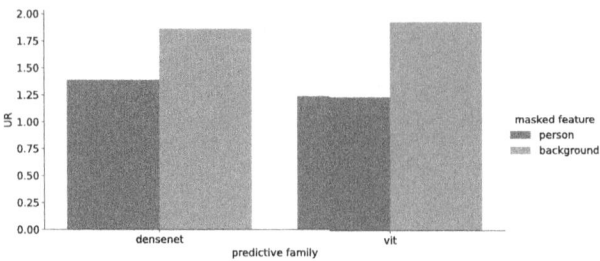

Fig. 5. UR of feature **person** and **background** over the disadvantaged group (Female) for the $\mathcal{V}_{densenet}$ and $\mathcal{V}_{vit}$ families in the $\mathcal{D}^{facet}$ ML pipeline.

also provides insights that are both *data-centric* and *model-family-aware*, making it distinct from traditional approaches. A key difference from *model-focused* metrics is its broader applicability. Model-focused metrics evaluate bias based on a specific model's output, limiting generalizability. In contrast, *DispaRisk* estimates metrics over an entire model family $\mathcal{V}$ (Definition 3), enabling a more generalizable assessment earlier in the ML pipeline. Another advantage of *DispaRisk* is its scalability to high-dimensional data. Unlike mutual information, which struggles with high-dimensional variables, empirical $\mathcal{V}$-metrics remain tractable as dimensionality increases [32]. This is especially useful in modern ML, where high-dimensional data is common.

The utility of DispaRisk depends on choosing a model family $\mathcal{V}$ that meaningfully spans the hypothesis space of interest. A narrowly defined $\mathcal{V}$ may miss key biases, while an overly broad one can dilute the signal. We therefore recommend: (i) to select a variety of families by using criteria such as Vapnik-Chervonenkis (VC) dimension or model capacity tiers, (ii) to remove models that under- or over-fit relative to targets, ensuring $\mathcal{V}$ reflects realistic candidates, and (iii) to ensure $\mathcal{V}$ matches anticipated production pipelines.

As we described, the accuracy of $\mathcal{V}$-entropy estimates depends on the size and representativeness of the held-out data: small datasets yield higher variance in pointwise entropy measurements. We recommend using an enough size of dataset in line with PAC-style bounds on entropy estimation, or employing techniques like bootstrap resampling to quantify confidence intervals. For Uncertainty Reduction (UR) in high-dimensional settings (e.g. large vocabularies), computing average P$\mathcal{V}$E for every feature can be prohibitive. In such cases, practitioners can apply prefiltering strategies such as: (i) grouping similar words, or (ii) performing expert-domain-driven preselection of interpretable feature subsets. These approaches maintain UR's explanatory power while keeping computation tractable.

However, *DispaRisk* has limitations. Computing pointwise $\mathcal{V}$-entropy requires training or fine-tuning of each candidate in $\mathcal{V}$. Although this cost exceeds that of simpler data-centric metrics, it can be substantially reduced in practice by (i) sampling $\mathcal{V}$ by capacity tier, selecting one representative per group of similar architectures, or (ii) applying early stopping on a small held-out slice, aborting models whose P$\mathcal{V}$E curves fall below a baseline threshold. These strategies retain the ability to detect relative uncertainty disparities while reducing training iterations.

6 Conclusions

DispaRisk enhances bias assessment in ML pipelines by addressing veracity and value challenges in large datasets. Using the $\mathcal{V}$-entropy framework, it reveals how different model families may amplify societal biases, bridging *data-focused* and *model-focused* metrics while considering computational constraints. Illustrative experiments on diverse datasets demonstrate *DispaRisk*'s effectiveness in identifying disparity sources and explaining bias propagation. By pinpointing areas where biases are amplified, it helps to improve the quality and fairness of the dataset in ML applications. Its context-specific assessments make it a valuable tool for regulatory compliance and internal use, ensuring fairness in ML-based systems.

Future research on *DispaRisk* can explore several key directions to improve its applicability and impact. One promising avenue is to refine its estimation methods to improve efficiency, enabling faster assessments in large-scale ML pipelines. Another important direction is adapting *DispaRisk* to evolve ML architectures, ensuring its relevance as models become more complex and diverse. Finally, investigating its role in AI governance and regulatory compliance can help establish standardized fairness auditing practices, fostering greater transparency and accountability in machine learning systems. Although our *rules of thumb* in Sect. 3.2 provide intuitive guidance, we do not yet offer a full formal proof under minimal assumptions. Developing rigorous guarantees (e.g. via PAC-Bayesian bounds or VC-dimension arguments) to bound the error of disparity predictions remains an important direction for future work. We defer a complete theoretical treatment to a follow-up study. Finally, DispaRisk's main novelty lies in integrating pointwise $\mathcal{V}$-entropy gaps with fairness assessment and demonstrating its empirical utility across modalities. However, we acknowledge that the core metric is an adaptation of existing *usable information* measures. Deriving new theoretical insights—such as generalization bounds for disparity estimates, tighter links to information bottleneck principles, or capacity-based criteria for model-family selection—would substantially strengthen the conceptual contribution. We plan to explore these avenues in future research.

Acknowledgments. We gratefully thank the anonymous reviewers for their insightful feedback and constructive suggestions, which have substantially improved the quality and clarity of this manuscript. Additionally, this study was supported by the National Agency for Research and Development (ANID - Agencia Nacional de Investigación y Desarrollo/Subdirección de Capital Humano), "Becas Chile" Doctoral Fellowship 2020 program; Grant No. 72210492 to Jonathan Patricio Vasquez Verdugo. In addition, Jonathan Vasquez was funded by the program "Magíster en Planificación y Control de Gestión" of the "Ingeniería en Información y Control de Gestión", at Universidad de Valparaíso, Chile.

References

1. Blodgett, S.L., Green, L., O'Connor, B.: Demographic dialectal variation in social media: a case study of African-American English. In: Su, J., Duh, K., Carreras, X. (eds.) Proceedings of the 2016 Conference on Empirical Methods in Natural Language Processing, pp. 1119–1130. Association for Computational Linguistics, Austin (2016). https://doi.org/10.18653/v1/D16-1120. https://aclanthology.org/D16-1120
2. Chen, R.J., et al.: Algorithmic fairness in artificial intelligence for medicine and healthcare. Nat. Biomed. Eng. **7**(6), 719–742 (2023)
3. Davidson, T., Warmsley, D., Macy, M., Weber, I.: Automated hate speech detection and the problem of offensive language. In: Proceedings of the International AAAI Conference on Web and Social Media, vol. 11, no. 1, pp. 512–515 (2017). https://doi.org/10.1609/icwsm.v11i1.14955
4. Devlin, J., Chang, M.W., Lee, K., Toutanova, K.: BERT: pre-training of deep bidirectional transformers for language understanding. In: Burstein, J., Doran, C., Solorio, T. (eds.) Proceedings of the 2019 Conference of the North American Chapter of the Association for Computational Linguistics: Human Language Technologies, vol. 1 (Long and Short Papers), pp. 4171–4186. Association for Computational Linguistics, Minneapolis (2019). https://doi.org/10.18653/v1/N19-1423. https://aclanthology.org/N19-1423
5. Dosovitskiy, A., et al.: An image is worth 16x16 words: transformers for image recognition at scale. In: International Conference on Learning Representations (2021). https://openreview.net/forum?id=YicbFdNTTy
6. Ethayarajh, K., Choi, Y., Swayamdipta, S.: Understanding dataset difficulty with $\mathcal{V}$-usable information. In: Chaudhuri, K., Jegelka, S., Song, L., Szepesvari, C., Niu, G., Sabato, S. (eds.) Proceedings of the 39th International Conference on Machine Learning. Proceedings of Machine Learning Research, vol. 162, pp. 5988–6008. PMLR (2022)
7. Feldman, M., Friedler, S.A., Moeller, J., Scheidegger, C., Venkatasubramanian, S.: Certifying and removing disparate impact. In: Proceedings of the 21th ACM SIGKDD International Conference on Knowledge Discovery and Data Mining, KDD '15, pp. 259–268. Association for Computing Machinery, New York (2015). https://doi.org/10.1145/2783258.2783311
8. Fu, R., Huang, Y., Singh, P.V.: Crowds, lending, machine, and bias. Inf. Syst. Res. **32**(1), 72–92 (2021)
9. Gupta, U., Ferber, A.M., Dilkina, B., Ver Steeg, G.: Controllable guarantees for fair outcomes via contrastive information estimation. In: Proceedings of the AAAI Conference on Artificial Intelligence, vol. 35, pp. 7610–7619 (2021)
10. Gustafson, L., et al.: Facet: fairness in computer vision evaluation benchmark. In: Proceedings of the IEEE/CVF International Conference on Computer Vision, pp. 20370–20382 (2023)
11. Hardt, M., et al.: Amazon sagemaker clarify: machine learning bias detection and explainability in the cloud. In: Proceedings of the 27th ACM SIGKDD Conference on Knowledge Discovery & Data Mining, pp. 2974–2983 (2021)
12. Hardt, M., Price, E., Price, E., Srebro, N.: Equality of opportunity in supervised learning. In: Lee, D., Sugiyama, M., Luxburg, U., Guyon, I., Garnett, R. (eds.) Advances in Neural Information Processing Systems, vol. 29. Curran Associates, Inc. (2016)

13. He, K., Zhang, X., Ren, S., Sun, J.: Delving deep into rectifiers: surpassing human-level performance on imagenet classification. In: Proceedings of the IEEE International Conference on Computer Vision, pp. 1026–1034 (2015)
14. He, P., Liu, X., Gao, J., Chen, W.: Deberta: decoding-enhanced bert with disentangled attention. In: 2021 International Conference on Learning Representations (2021). https://www.microsoft.com/en-us/research/publication/deberta-decoding-enhanced-bert-with-disentangled-attention-2/
15. Hendrycks, D., Gimpel, K.: Gaussian error linear units (gelus). arXiv preprint arXiv:1606.08415 (2016)
16. Howard, A., et al.: Searching for mobilenetv3. In: Proceedings of the IEEE/CVF International Conference on Vomputer Vision, pp. 1314–1324 (2019)
17. Huang, G., Liu, Z., van der Maaten, L., Weinberger, K.Q.: Densely connected convolutional networks. In: Proceedings of the IEEE Conference on Computer Vision and Pattern Recognition (CVPR) (2017)
18. Jurman, G., Riccadonna, S., Furlanello, C.: A comparison of mcc and cen error measures in multi-class prediction. PLOS ONE **7**(8), 1–8 (2012). https://doi.org/10.1371/journal.pone.0041882
19. Kizilcec, R.F., Lee, H.: Algorithmic fairness in education. In: Holmes, W., Porayska-Pomsta, K. (eds.) The Ethics of Artificial Intelligence in Education, pp. 174–202. Taylor & Francis (2022)
20. Lewis, M., et al.: BART: denoising sequence-to-sequence pre-training for natural language generation, translation, and comprehension. In: Jurafsky, D., Chai, J., Schluter, N., Tetreault, J. (eds.) Proceedings of the 58th Annual Meeting of the Association for Computational Linguistics, pp. 7871–7880. Association for Computational Linguistics, Online (2020). https://doi.org/10.18653/v1/2020.acl-main.703. https://aclanthology.org/2020.acl-main.703
21. Liu, Y., et al.: Roberta: a robustly optimized bert pretraining approach (2019). https://arxiv.org/abs/1907.11692
22. Loshchilov, I.: Decoupled weight decay regularization. arXiv preprint arXiv:1711.05101 (2017)
23. Lundberg, S.M., Lee, S.I.: A unified approach to interpreting model predictions. In: Guyon, I., et al. (eds.) Advances in Neural Information Processing Systems, vol. 30. Curran Associates, Inc. (2017)
24. Pessach, D., Shmueli, E.: Algorithmic Fairness, pp. 867–886. Springer, Cham (2023). https://doi.org/10.1007/978-3-031-24628-9_37
25. ProPublica: How we analyzed the compas recidivism algorithm. ProPublica (2016)
26. Radford, A., Wu, J., Child, R., Luan, D., Amodei, D., Sutskever, I., et al.: Language models are unsupervised multitask learners. OpenAI blog **1**(8), 9 (2019)
27. Shapley, L.: 7. A Value for n-Person Games. Contributions to the Theory of Games II (1953) 307-317., pp. 69–79. Princeton University Press, Princeton (1997). https://doi.org/10.1515/9781400829156-012
28. Simonyan, K., Zisserman, A.: Very deep convolutional networks for large-scale image recognition. In: 3rd International Conference on Learning Representations (ICLR 2015), pp. 1–14. Computational and Biological Learning Society (2015)
29. Szegedy, C., Vanhoucke, V., Ioffe, S., Shlens, J., Wojna, Z.: Rethinking the inception architecture for computer vision. In: Proceedings of the IEEE Conference on Computer Vision and Pattern Recognition, pp. 2818–2826 (2016)
30. Vasquez, J., Gitiaux, X., Ortega, C., Rangwala, H.: Faired: a systematic fairness analysis approach applied in a higher educational context. In: LAK22: 12th International Learning Analytics and Knowledge Conference, pp. 271–281 (2022)

31. Wen, M., Bastani, O., Topcu, U.: Algorithms for fairness in sequential decision making. In: International Conference on Artificial Intelligence and Statistics, pp. 1144–1152. PMLR (2021)
32. Xu, Y., Zhao, S., Song, J., Stewart, R., Ermon, S.: A theory of usable information under computational constraints. In: International Conference on Learning Representations (ICLR) (2020)
33. Zeiler, M., et al.: On rectified linear units for speech processing. In: 2013 IEEE International Conference on Acoustics, Speech and Signal Processing, pp. 3517–3521 (2013). https://doi.org/10.1109/ICASSP.2013.6638312

Analyzing and Correcting Biased Machine Learning-Based Tuning of Weight Shrinkage in Forecast Combination

Veronika Wachslander(✉)

Catholic University of Eichstaett-Ingolstadt, Ingolstadt, Germany
veronika.wachslander@ku.de

Abstract. A forecast combination typically corresponds to a weighted average of individual forecasts and aims at increasing predictive accuracy. Application fields include business, economics, information systems such as recommender systems and financial portfolios. One popular weighting approach used in various studies is to learn weights optimal on past data (optimal weights) and shrink them towards equal weights to mitigate overfitting. The required shrinkage hyperparameter is usually tuned by machine learning-based techniques like K-fold cross-validation (CV). This paper shows that CV-tuned shrinkage levels are generally biased: Depending on the characteristics (parameters) of training forecast data (e.g., number of forecasters, error correlations, spread in predictive ability, training set size, number of CV-folds), such approaches lead to systematic over- or undershrinkage. The impact of different parameters on these biases is studied on large sets of synthetically generated data and a model is trained to predict the bias (direction and degree) by using data characteristics as features. This model is evaluated for its ability to correct biases on various sets of synthetic data, where the corrected weights lead to improved predictive accuracy across a range of data characteristics. Codes are available at https://github.com/VeronikaWachslander/shrinkage-tuning-bias.

Keywords: Weight Shrinkage · Hyperparameter Tuning · Debiasing · Forecast Combination · Machine Learning

1 Introduction

The combination of forecasts provided by different models or humans is a technique used in business, economics and other fields to generate more accurate and reliable predictions. Typical applications of forecast combinations are predictions of economic growth, inflation rates or electricity demand [12,14,23,25].

Besides business contexts, the approaches can be applied to hybrid recommender systems (information systems that combine e.g. different purchase or movie recommendations) or used for financial portfolio optimization [17,18,20].

While various disciplines conduct research regarding combination approaches and numerous methods already exist (see [11,28]), there is still no generalizable cross-domain suggestion how to determine the combination weights.

Two weighting schemes often considered as benchmarks or bases for more sophisticated approaches are optimal weights (OW) – introduced in Bates and Granger [4] for two forecasters and later extended (see, e.g., [27]) – and equal weights (EW). The OW are estimated on past forecast errors (training set), leading to weights that minimize the mean squared error (MSE) on this dataset.

However, numerous studies [2,14,15] show that, on unseen data, this and other more sophisticated weighting schemes are mostly outperformed by the simple average that assigns EW to all forecasters. This superiority of EW, named *forecast combination puzzle* by Stock and Watson [25], is typically explained by the consideration of random variations in training data when estimating OW (see, e.g., [5,9,10]). These structures do not necessarily exist on unseen data, so the OW overfit the training set – especially in the case of small training sizes. In contrast, EW completely ignore potential differences in forecast ability.

Therefore, OW and EW can be seen as two opposite approaches and a compromise between these weighting schemes could be beneficial. In various studies [1,12,25], this is achieved by shrinking OW towards EW controlled by a shrinkage parameter. However, there is no rule how to derive the optimal shrinkage level, i.e. the one resulting in the minimum combination error on unseen data.

As the shrinkage level can be considered a hyperparameter, cross-validation (CV) can be used for the tuning as applied by Schulz and Setzer [22], Schulz et al. [21], as well as Diebold and Shin [13]. However, Schulz et al. detected slight deviations between the CV-optimal and the truly optimal shrinkage, while Diebold and Shin recommend to combine only a few forecasters and assign EW.

According to Schulz and Setzer [22], these findings might be (at least partly) due to the determination of inappropriate, typically too high shrinkage levels with CV – in particular with small training sets and low to medium error correlations among the forecasters (with moderate differences in predictive ability).

This paper addresses the phenomenon of shrinkage biases when the level of shrinkage from OW towards EW is determined by CV, with all forecasters being included in the combination. Since determining weights is particularly challenging if available (past forecast) data is very limited, which is usually the case in business and economics, the paper mainly focuses on small datasets.

First, the impact of various data- and CV-related properties on shrinkage biases is analyzed in detail. Second, a regression tree is developed that predicts shrinkage biases and serves as model to correct CV-determined shrinkage levels. Third, this correction model is evaluated and discussed.

In addition, this paper aims to raise critical awareness of using CV for hyperparameter tuning in any machine learning task and to encourage reviews of the tuning results.

The paper is structured as follows: Sect. 2 introduces weight shrinkage and Sect. 3 CV-based tuning along with notation. In Sect. 4, the experimental design for data generation and tuning as well as evaluation procedures are explained, while Sect. 5 provides analytical insights. Section 6 presents a model to predict and correct tuning biases, which is evaluated in Sect. 7. Finally, Sect. 8 draws conclusions and presents an outlook on future work.

2 Shrinking Optimal to Equal Combination Weights

Assume $J \in \mathbb{N}, J > 1$ forecasters are available and f_{ij} denotes the i-th forecast of the j-th forecaster, with $i \in \{1, \ldots, n\}$ and $j \in \{1, \ldots, J\}$. A combined forecast for the i-th observation x_i can be calculated as $\sum_{j=1}^{J} w_j \cdot f_{ij}$, i.e. by assigning a weight $w_j \in \mathbb{R}$ to forecaster j for all $j \in \{1, \ldots, J\}$, multiplying the weight by this forecaster's prediction for x_i and adding up these weighted predictions.

One question is which weighting scheme to use, with $\sum_{j=1}^{J} w_j = 1$ regardless of the specific choice. The simplest weighting technique assigns EW to all forecasters by setting $w_j = J^{-1}$ for every $j \in \{1, \ldots, J\}$. The corresponding weight vector $\boldsymbol{w}^{EW} \in \mathbb{R}^J$ can be defined as $\boldsymbol{w}^{EW} = J^{-1} \cdot \mathbf{1}$, with the column vector $\mathbf{1} \in \mathbb{R}^J$ containing one in each entry and $\mathbf{1}' \cdot \boldsymbol{w}^{EW} = 1$ as required.

Another common approach is the calculation of OW based on a matrix $\boldsymbol{E} \in \mathbb{R}^{n \times J}$ with n past errors per forecaster j. This means, each entry $e_{ij} \in \boldsymbol{E}$ represents the difference between the actual value of the observation x_i and its prediction provided by the forecaster j, calculated as $e_{ij} = x_i - f_{ij}$.

For each forecaster, efficient forecasts are assumed, i.e. multivariate normally distributed forecast errors with a mean of zero and an error covariance matrix $\boldsymbol{\Sigma}_e$, which is typically unknown and estimated as $\hat{\boldsymbol{\Sigma}}_e = n^{-1} \cdot \boldsymbol{E}'\boldsymbol{E}$.

The vector $\hat{\boldsymbol{w}}^{OW} \in \mathbb{R}^J$ contains the OW and is estimated as shown in (1), with $\hat{\boldsymbol{\Sigma}}_e^{-1}$ denoting the inverse of $\hat{\boldsymbol{\Sigma}}_e$, and ensuring $\mathbf{1}' \cdot \hat{\boldsymbol{w}}^{OW} = 1$ (see [27]).

$$\hat{\boldsymbol{w}}^{OW} = \frac{\hat{\boldsymbol{\Sigma}}_e^{-1} \mathbf{1}}{\mathbf{1}' \hat{\boldsymbol{\Sigma}}_e^{-1} \mathbf{1}} \quad (1)$$

As discussed, OW are typically prone to overfitting data structures and thus, do not fit well unseen data, while EW consider all forecasts to be equally reliable. To obtain less overfitted weights that still consider differences in forecast ability, OW are shrunk towards EW by a shrinkage parameter $0 \leq \lambda \leq 1$, with $\lambda = 0$ resulting in OW and $\lambda = 1$ in EW (100% shrinkage), as shown in (2) (see [22]).

$$\hat{\boldsymbol{w}}^{\lambda} = (1 - \lambda) \cdot \hat{\boldsymbol{w}}^{OW} + \lambda \cdot \boldsymbol{w}^{EW} \quad (2)$$

The optimal shrinkage level λ^* leads to weights $\hat{\boldsymbol{w}}^{\lambda^*} = (\hat{w}_1^{\lambda^*}, \ldots, \hat{w}_J^{\lambda^*})$ that minimize the MSE (shown in (3)) on unseen data $\{x_1, \ldots, x_n\}$.

$$MSE(\hat{\boldsymbol{w}}^{\lambda}) = \frac{1}{n} \cdot \sum_{i=1}^{n} \left(x_i - \sum_{j=1}^{J} \hat{w}_j^{\lambda} \cdot f_{ij}\right)^2 = \frac{1}{n} \cdot \sum_{i=1}^{n} \left(\sum_{j=1}^{J} \hat{w}_j^{\lambda} \cdot e_{ij}\right)^2 \quad (3)$$

Typically, the CV-optimal shrinkage λ_{CV}^* will deviate from the truly optimal shrinkage λ_{true}^*. In the following, this deviation (in percentage points $\%P$) is called *shrinkage bias* and calculated as provided in (4). A bias $B(\lambda_{CV}^*) > 0$ corresponds to overshrinkage, while $B(\lambda_{CV}^*) < 0$ means undershrinkage.[1]

$$B(\lambda_{CV}^*) = \lambda_{CV}^* - \lambda_{true}^* \qquad (4)$$

The next section explains cross-validation and its use for shrinkage tuning.

3 Cross-Validation and Shrinkage Tuning

A frequently used resampling technique to both estimate the performance of a model on unseen data and tune hyperparameters is K-fold cross-validation, which randomly divides the training data into K (almost) equally sized, pairwise disjoint subsets (called *folds*). The model is trained on the calibration set consisting of $K-1$ folds, and tested on the remaining fold that serves as validation set. This is repeated until each fold has been part of the calibration set $K-1$ times and represented the validation set once (for more details see, e.g., [16,19]).

Typically, the errors (with respect to the chosen error measure) on the validation sets are averaged over the K iterations to estimate the overall performance on unseen data. This can be done for different hyperparameter values and the one resulting in the lowest overall error is selected for the final model.

Different variants of K-fold CV are distinguished, depending on the value of K: The number of folds is either set to a value like the frequently recommended ones $K = 5$ or $K = 10$ (see [3,7]), or the number of observations n belonging to each fold is fixed as with Leave-One-Out (LOO) and Leave-Two-Out (LTO) CV – i.e., the training set is split into n folds for LOO and $n/2$ folds for LTO.[2]

However, there is no general rule to choose the number of folds K, as there is a bias–variance trade-off regarding this decision [16,19]; rather, Zhang and Yang [29] explain that the specific task the CV is used for should be considered.

In the context of weight shrinkage tuning, OW are estimated on the calibration sets and shrunk towards EW on the respective validation sets. Finally, the shrinkage level with the lowest average MSE on these validation sets is chosen.

For a low number of folds, the calibration sets typically differ strongly from each other and also from the full training set. The OW estimated on a calibration set will overfit its structure due to significantly lower data amounts compared to the full training set and thus, will be quite different from the ones learned on the other calibration sets and on the full training set. Since overfitted OW will not reflect the structure of the corresponding validation set well, these will be shrunk strongly, resulting in weights near EW that can be highly biased.

In contrast, for LOO, the calibration sets and thus, the estimations for OW will be similar and also close to the full training set and its estimated OW. However, each validation set contains only one observation, which determines the respective MSE values, so the results could have high variance.

---

[1] E.g., if $\lambda_{CV}^* = 0.25 = 25\%$ and $\lambda_{true}^* = 0.13 = 13\%$, then $B(\lambda_{CV}^*) = 0.12 = 12\%P$.
[2] Unlike the typically exhaustive Leave-p-out CV that creates folds for all $\binom{n}{p}$ combinations of the training observations as for example described in [8], the term LTO is used in this paper to describe one random division of the training set into $n/2$ folds.

In summary, the number of folds can severely affect the accuracy of combined forecasts, as the estimation of OW and the shrinkage determination are sensitive to the underlying dataset. For this reason, datasets with varying characteristics are generated and the shrinkage biases are studied for different numbers of folds K, which leads to various scenarios (i.e., parameter constellations).

The next section describes the data generation and the procedures for analyzing shrinkage biases and evaluating the later introduced shrinkage correction.

4 Experimental Design

4.1 Data Generation

For analyzing, predicting and correcting shrinkage biases, synthetic error datasets are generated, as this allows to identify general relations and characteristics without uncontrollable random effects (and is, e.g., also done in [10, 21,24,26]).

The synthetic errors are drawn from different multivariate normal distributions with mean zero and covariance matrices that are calculated using predefined forecasters' variances and fixed values for the pairwise error correlation among the forecasters.

Various data samples are generated with varying numbers of forecasters, different pairwise error correlations, and different error variance structures to allow for comprehensive analyses. Each data sample contains 20,000 error observations for each of the $J \in \{5, 8, 10, 12, 15\}$ forecasters.

The pairwise error correlations are either set to $\rho \in \{0.1, 0.2, \ldots, 0.9\}$, identical for all pairs, or identical within two nearly equally sized groups, but slightly different between the groups.[3] Therefore, the range of correlations $\Delta\rho$ (difference between maximum and minimum correlation) takes the values $\Delta\rho \in \{0, 0.2\}$.

Further, the error variances of the forecasters increase from $\sigma_1^2 = 1$ to $\sigma_J^2 \in \{1.2, 1.5, 2, 4, 9\}$, either linearly with $\sigma_j^2 = \sigma_{j-1}^2 + \frac{\sigma_J^2 - \sigma_1^2}{J-1}$ or in a quadratic fashion with $\sigma_j^2 = \left(\sigma_{j-1} + \frac{\sigma_J - \sigma_1}{J-1}\right)^2$ for $j \in \{2, \ldots, J\}$. In addition, $\Delta\sigma^2 = \sigma_J^2 - \sigma_1^2$ represents the range of variances and thus, $\Delta\sigma^2 \in \{0.2, 0.5, 1, 3, 8\}$.

For analyzing the shrinkage bias on limited data, small training sets $\boldsymbol{E}_{train}$, with $n \in \{10, 20, \ldots, 100, 125, 150, 175, 200\}$ error observations per forecaster, are randomly drawn from the generated samples. The respective observations, that are not part of $\boldsymbol{E}_{train}$, form a large test set $\boldsymbol{E}_{test}$, which ensures stable parameter values that approach those of the data generation.[4]

$\boldsymbol{E}_{train}$ is used to estimate OW and apply K-fold CV to tune the shrinkage hyperparameter, resulting in the CV-optimal shrinkage level λ_{CV}^*, while $\boldsymbol{E}_{test}$ serves as unseen data to identify the truly optimal shrinkage level λ_{true}^* and to calculate the resulting shrinkage bias $B(\lambda_{CV}^*)$.

---

[3] As an example for the second case, $\rho = 0.1$ in one group and $\rho = 0.3$ in the other, while the correlations between the groups receive a value of $\rho = 0.2$.

[4] For estimating OW, a sufficient amount of training observations is required. E.g., for 15 forecasters and 2-fold CV, at least 30 observations per forecaster are needed.

The shrinkage tuning biases are studied for $K \in \{2, 5, 10, n/2, n\}$ CV-folds, with $K = n/2$ folds corresponding to LTO and $K = n$ folds to LOO.

Table 1 (shown in Subsect. 4.3) summarizes the parameters and values used to generate datasets for the analyses and predictions of shrinkage biases.

A detailed explanation of the procedure to tune the shrinkage level by CV and calculate the resulting shrinkage bias is provided in Algorithm 1.

Algorithm 1. Shrinkage Determination by CV and Shrinkage Bias Calculation.

1: **Initialization:** Set shrinkage values $\lambda_s = 0.01 \cdot s$ with $s \in \{0, \ldots, 100\}$.
   Set the number of folds K.
   Generate error sample matrices $\boldsymbol{E}_{train}$ and $\boldsymbol{E}_{test}$.
2: Split $\boldsymbol{E}_{train}$ (its rows) into K (almost) equally sized, pairwise disjoint folds.
3: **For** $k = 1, \ldots, K$ **do:**
   – Set fold k as validation $\boldsymbol{E}_{val}^{(k)}$ and $\boldsymbol{E}_{cal}^{(k)} = \boldsymbol{E}_{train} \setminus \boldsymbol{E}_{val}^{(k)}$ as calibration set.
   – Estimate $\hat{\boldsymbol{w}}^{OW_{cal}(k)}$ as $\hat{\boldsymbol{w}}^{OW}$ on $\boldsymbol{E}_{cal}^{(k)}$ by (1), with $\boldsymbol{E} = \boldsymbol{E}_{cal}^{(k)}$ for $\hat{\boldsymbol{\Sigma}}_e$.
   – **For** $s = 0, \ldots, 100$ **do:**
     • Calculate $\hat{\boldsymbol{w}}^{\lambda_s(k)}$ using (2) with $\lambda = \lambda_s$ and $\hat{\boldsymbol{w}}^{OW} = \hat{\boldsymbol{w}}^{OW_{cal}(k)}$.
     • Apply $\hat{\boldsymbol{w}}^{\lambda_s(k)}$ to $\boldsymbol{E}_{val}^{(k)}$ and calculate the MSE value $MSE_s^{(k)}$ by (3).
     End For.
   End For.
4: **For** $s = 0, \ldots, 100$ **do:**
   – Calculate the mean MSE for λ_s, $MSE_s^{[val]} = \frac{1}{K} \cdot \sum_{k=1}^{K} MSE_s^{(k)}$.
   End For.
5: Identify the λ_s producing $min(MSE_s^{[val]})$ as CV-optimal shrinkage λ_{CV}^*.
6: Estimate $\hat{\boldsymbol{w}}^{OW_{train}}$ as $\hat{\boldsymbol{w}}^{OW}$ on $\boldsymbol{E}_{train}$ by (1), with $\boldsymbol{E} = \boldsymbol{E}_{train}$ for $\hat{\boldsymbol{\Sigma}}_e$.
7: **For** $s = 0, \ldots, 100$ **do:**
   – Calculate $\hat{\boldsymbol{w}}^{\lambda_s}$ using (2) with $\lambda = \lambda_s$ and $\hat{\boldsymbol{w}}^{OW} = \hat{\boldsymbol{w}}^{OW_{train}}$.
   – Apply $\hat{\boldsymbol{w}}^{\lambda_s}$ to $\boldsymbol{E}_{test}$ and calculate the MSE value $MSE_s^{[test]}$ by (3).
   End For.
8: Identify the λ_s producing $min(MSE_s^{[test]})$ as truly optimal shrinkage λ_{true}^*.
9: Calculate the shrinkage bias $B(\lambda_{CV}^*)$ using (4).

The procedure is repeated 250 times for each scenario with new, randomly drawn error data in each repetition to obtain reliable measures.

The results are compiled into a dataset comprising more than 13 million cases, which is used for the analyses and to develop the correction model.[5]

However, the representation of some parameters is slightly modified and additional parameters are created to show the analytical results and to develop a model for predicting shrinkage biases, as will be explained next.

4.2 Parameter Estimation and Representation

Besides the already discussed variables, there are two more used to predict the shrinkage bias. These are n_{cal} and $n_{cal}^{\%}$, corresponding to the number and share

---

[5] See the codes at https://github.com/VeronikaWachslander/shrinkage-tuning-bias.

of training observations being part of each calibration set, which depend on the number of folds (e.g., for LOO, the values are $n_{cal} = n-1$ and $n_{cal}^{\%} = (n-1)/n$).

Further, it can be distinguished between observable parameters, which are J, n, K, n_{cal} and $n_{cal}^{\%}$, as their values can be directly observed, and estimable ones. The estimable parameters are $\rho, \Delta\rho$ and $\Delta\sigma^2$, as their values depend on the respective randomly drawn dataset, so these need to be estimated.

While the values of the estimable variables will deviate on the datasets to a negligible extent from those set for the data generation due to the large size, their estimation on limited amounts of training data introduces uncertainty and bears the risk of strong deviations, which will impact the weight determination.

For this reason and to enable an application of the later introduced bias prediction model to datasets with other parameter values than studied here, the estimable variables are modified or binned, i.e. the values are assigned to groups.

The spread in predictive ability is reflected by the range of estimated forecasters' variances $\Delta\sigma^2$ and grouped as shown in (5) based on the studied values.

$$\Delta\sigma^2 = \begin{cases} tiny & \Delta\sigma^2 < 0.45 \\ low & 0.45 \leq \Delta\sigma^2 < 0.95 \\ medium & 0.95 \leq \Delta\sigma^2 < 2.50 \\ high & 2.50 \leq \Delta\sigma^2 < 6.00 \\ extreme & 6.00 \leq \Delta\sigma^2 \end{cases} \quad (5)$$

In addition, the pairwise error correlations among the forecasters are estimated, with $\Delta\rho$ corresponding to their interquartile range and ρ to their mean, which is assigned to one of the categories shown in (6).

$$\rho = \begin{cases} weak & \rho < 0.25 \\ moderate & 0.25 \leq \rho < 0.55 \\ strong & 0.55 \leq \rho < 0.75 \\ extreme & 0.75 \leq \rho \end{cases} \quad (6)$$

Since the bias prediction model will also be assessed regarding its ability to correct shrinkage biases, the next subsection describes the evaluation.

4.3 Evaluation Setting

The bias predictions of the later introduced model can be treated as shrinkage correction factors CV_C, and the corrected shrinkage levels $\lambda^*_{CV_C}$ can be expected to improve the weight determination for known or precisely estimated data characteristics and parameter values.

However, as the values of the estimable variables are typically not known and to be estimated on limited training data, the model is evaluated for its ability to correct shrinkage biases in case of uncertainties in parameter estimation.

For the evaluation, new synthetic datasets are generated, with the parameter values provided in Table 1 and including scenarios, which are not part of the database used to learn the model to check for a more general validity.

Table 1. Parameters and Values for Bias Analyses and Evaluation of Correction.

Parameter	Description	Analyzed Values	Evaluated Values
n	Size of Training Set	$10, 20, \ldots, 100, 125, \ldots, 200$	$25, 50, 100, 200$
J	Number of Forecasters	$5, 8, 10, 12, 15$	$4, 9$
K	Number of CV-Folds	$2, 5, 10, LTO, LOO$	$2, 5, LOO$
ρ	Pairwise Correlation	$0.1, 0.2, \ldots, 0.8, 0.9$	$0.15, 0.3, \ldots, 0.75, 0.9$
$\Delta\sigma^2$	Range of Variances	$0.2, 0.5, 1, 3, 8$	$0.1, 0.25, 0.7, 2, 5, 7$
$\Delta\rho$	Range of Correlations	$0, 0.2$	$0, 0.3$

Algorithm 2. Application and Evaluation of Shrinkage Correction.

10: Calculate $\hat{\boldsymbol{w}}^{\lambda^*_{CV}}$ using (2) with $\lambda = \lambda^*_{CV}$ and $\hat{\boldsymbol{w}}^{OW} = \hat{\boldsymbol{w}}^{OW_{train}}$.
11: Estimate $\rho, \Delta\rho$ and $\Delta\sigma^2$ on the provided training set $\boldsymbol{E}_{train}$.
12: Apply the bias prediction model to determine the correction factor CV_C.
13: Calculate the corrected shrinkage level $\lambda^*_{CV_C} = \lambda^*_{CV} - CV_C$.
14: Calculate $\hat{\boldsymbol{w}}^{\lambda^*_{CV_C}}$ using (2) with $\lambda = \lambda^*_{CV_C}$ and $\hat{\boldsymbol{w}}^{OW} = \hat{\boldsymbol{w}}^{OW_{train}}$.
15: Calculate $MSE(\hat{\boldsymbol{w}}^{\lambda^*_{CV}})$ and $MSE(\hat{\boldsymbol{w}}^{\lambda^*_{CV_C}})$ on $\boldsymbol{E}_{test}$ using (3).
16: Calculate the percentage MSE deviation by $\frac{MSE(\hat{\boldsymbol{w}}^{\lambda^*_{CV_C}}) - MSE(\hat{\boldsymbol{w}}^{\lambda^*_{CV}})}{MSE(\hat{\boldsymbol{w}}^{\lambda^*_{CV}})}$.
(*Example:* If $MSE(\hat{\boldsymbol{w}}^{\lambda^*_{CV_C}}) = 0.40$ and $MSE(\hat{\boldsymbol{w}}^{\lambda^*_{CV}}) = 0.50$, the percentage deviation is $-0.20 = -20\%$, which corresponds to a MSE reduction of 20%.)

The application and evaluation of the shrinkage correction are formally described in Algorithm 2, which is a continuation of Algorithm 1.

The shrinkage correction is repeated 250 times for each scenario with new, randomly drawn error data in each repetition, so the evaluation database contains 720,000 cases.

The next section discusses shrinkage biases regarding different parameters.

5 Analytical Insights Into Weight Shrinkage Biases

This section provides analytical insights into shrinkage biases, as these will vary depending on the parameter values of the datasets and the number of CV-folds.

5.1 Impact of Variables on Shrinkage Biases

Table 2 provides shrinkage biases regarding the number of CV-folds K and forecasters J, their variance range $\Delta\sigma^2$ and pairwise correlations ρ with range $\Delta\rho$.

The values represent the shrinkage bias (written in black if positive and in gray if negative), averaged over the different training sizes n and 250 repetitions per scenario, with a darker cell background reflecting a stronger bias.

As an example, the mean shrinkage bias for datasets with $\Delta\sigma^2 = medium$, $\rho = weak$ and $\Delta\rho < 0.1$ equals $B(\lambda^*_{CV}) = 18.25(\%P)$ when applying 2-fold CV,

Table 2. Mean Shrinkage Bias (in %P) for Selected Values of Forecasters J, Folds K, Variance Range $\Delta\sigma^2$ and Correlation ρ, Differentiated by Range of Correlations $\Delta\rho$.

$\Delta\sigma^2$	ρ			$\Delta\rho < 0.1$					$\Delta\rho \geq 0.1$				
		J	5			15			5			15		
		K	2	5	LOO	2	5	LOO	2	5	LOO	2	5	LOO
tiny	weak		-6.62	-5.58	-4.88	-4.71	-6.94	-7.70	14.20	11.62	11.01	21.54	8.65	3.88
			-3.53	-2.75	-2.11	-2.34	-5.47	-6.38	15.01	12.04	11.13	21.25	8.87	4.15
			2.82	2.43	3.15	2.03	-1.77	-3.39	17.99	13.73	12.31	22.03	9.16	3.98
			12.50	10.56	9.79	12.21	4.52	1.72	18.83	13.13	10.59	22.28	8.71	3.58
low	moderate		8.25	7.32	7.05	1.85	-1.95	-3.34	20.20	15.27	13.79	22.29	8.53	3.64
			13.01	11.00	10.19	8.78	2.32	-0.02	19.64	13.84	11.75	23.30	9.56	4.37
			18.67	13.96	12.70	16.81	7.16	3.15	19.70	12.93	10.49	22.73	8.88	3.62
			18.14	11.73	9.16	22.61	9.14	4.11	16.35	9.18	6.48	20.63	7.87	3.00
medium	strong		18.25	13.80	11.91	11.59	4.50	1.77	19.64	12.93	10.51	23.35	8.86	3.66
			19.72	14.02	11.58	19.09	7.99	3.66	18.79	11.54	8.91	23.13	8.95	3.74
			18.90	11.48	9.02	22.83	9.18	3.93	15.93	8.75	6.24	20.63	7.40	2.51
			12.83	6.06	3.96	20.23	7.72	3.02	11.78	5.57	3.59	17.03	6.40	2.12
high	extreme		16.46	9.07	6.61	22.77	9.45	4.39	13.92	7.43	5.28	21.32	7.64	2.90
			13.45	6.76	4.61	22.65	8.73	3.54	11.55	5.07	3.12	19.13	7.18	2.75
			9.26	3.72	2.08	17.84	6.56	2.11	8.74	3.10	1.67	14.40	5.26	1.41
			5.60	1.18	0.34	11.44	4.31	1.05	5.75	1.19	0.20	10.27	4.05	0.94
extreme			9.66	3.73	2.14	21.45	8.05	3.04	7.86	2.72	1.38	16.65	5.90	1.77
			7.06	2.12	0.94	16.93	6.30	2.10	6.42	1.73	0.66	13.86	5.42	1.67
			4.36	0.74	-0.06	11.34	4.15	0.83	4.34	0.63	-0.12	9.50	3.55	0.61
			2.68	-0.15	-0.59	6.21	2.41	0.22	2.94	-0.09	-0.59	6.27	2.37	0.21

so the resulting shrinkage λ^*_{CV} is on average 18.25 percentage points higher than the truly optimal shrinkage λ^*_{true}.

At first glance, most scenarios suffer from overshrinkage (i.e. $B(\lambda^*_{CV}) > 0$), while undershrinkage appears only for boundary values of $\Delta\sigma^2$ and ρ: The majority of scenarios with $B(\lambda^*_{CV}) < 0$ shows little spread in forecast ability along with identical, rather weaker pairwise correlations and will be studied in Subsect. 5.2, while negligible undershrinkage can be observed for scenarios belonging to the category *extreme* for both $\Delta\sigma^2$ and ρ (or $\rho = strong$) regardless of $\Delta\rho$.

However, in case of differing pairwise correlations, strong overshrinkage can be observed for $\Delta\sigma^2 = tiny$: The differences in ρ might be used to out-balance errors, so the calibration sets might be overfitted and strong shrinkage is required.

In contrast, the following relations can be identified for scenarios with at least *medium* differences in $\Delta\sigma^2$ independent of $\Delta\rho$.

First, the bias typically decreases with increasing variance range. Since differing weights are increasingly beneficial for larger $\Delta\sigma^2$, less shrinkage is required, so λ_{CV}^* and λ_{true}^* will be lower and closer to each other.

Second, overshrinkage typically decreases for increasing pairwise correlations, as weights learned on calibration sets might indeed be more extreme than on the full training set, but nevertheless, do not need to be shrunk strongly to EW, as complementary weights are then increasingly beneficial for out-balancing errors.

Third, overshrinkage usually increases with J for scenarios with larger $\Delta\sigma^2$. This seems reasonable, as estimating more weights increases the uncertainty and thus, stronger shrinkage of the more extreme weights is required.

However, opposite relations can be observed for $\Delta\sigma^2 \in \{tiny, low\}$, as the bias increases with ρ and with decreasing J in many scenarios:

Regarding the number of forecasters, λ_{true}^* is usually much higher for many forecasters than for a few, whereas λ_{CV}^* is generally quite high for comparable variances and increases to a lower extent than λ_{true}^* (and thus, the bias decreases) for increasing J.

Regarding increasing correlations, more differentiated weights will be learned on the calibration sets that require stronger shrinkage, as similar weights would be more appropriate for such small differences in predictive ability.

In line with expectations, increasing K generally reduces overshrinkage, as the calibration sets contain more observations, which leads to increasingly similar and stable estimations of OW. These weights will also be more similar to those estimated on E_{train}, which enables a more accurate shrinkage determination.

The next subsection focuses on scenarios with identical pairwise correlations ($\Delta\rho < 0.1$), as these show over- and undershrinkage. In addition, the general development of shrinkage levels is discussed with regards to the training size.

5.2 Shrinkage Levels and Bias Development

This subsection discusses the development of the truly optimal (λ_{true}^*) and the 5-fold CV-optimal (λ_{CV}^*) shrinkage and the respective biases shown in Fig. 1.

The solid lines represent λ_{CV}^* and the dashed ones the corresponding values of λ_{true}^* identified on E_{test} in the same color for the different categories of ranges in variance $\Delta\sigma^2$. The development is shown over the training size n, differentiated by the strength of constant correlations ρ and averaged over all forecasters J.

Obviously, both λ_{CV}^* and λ_{true}^* decrease with increasing n. This matches expectations, as larger amounts of training data typically represent the structures of the full dataset more precisely, which enables a more reliable estimation of OW on the full training set and the calibration sets, so less shrinkage is required.

Furthermore, λ_{CV}^* and λ_{true}^* decrease with increasing $\Delta\sigma^2$ and ρ, as differentiated weights seem reasonable for stronger differences in predictive ability and almost complementary weights can be assigned to highly correlated forecasters to neutralize error patterns.

Besides the shrinkage levels λ_{CV}^* and λ_{true}^*, the respective shrinkage bias can be observed as vertical distance between their corresponding lines.

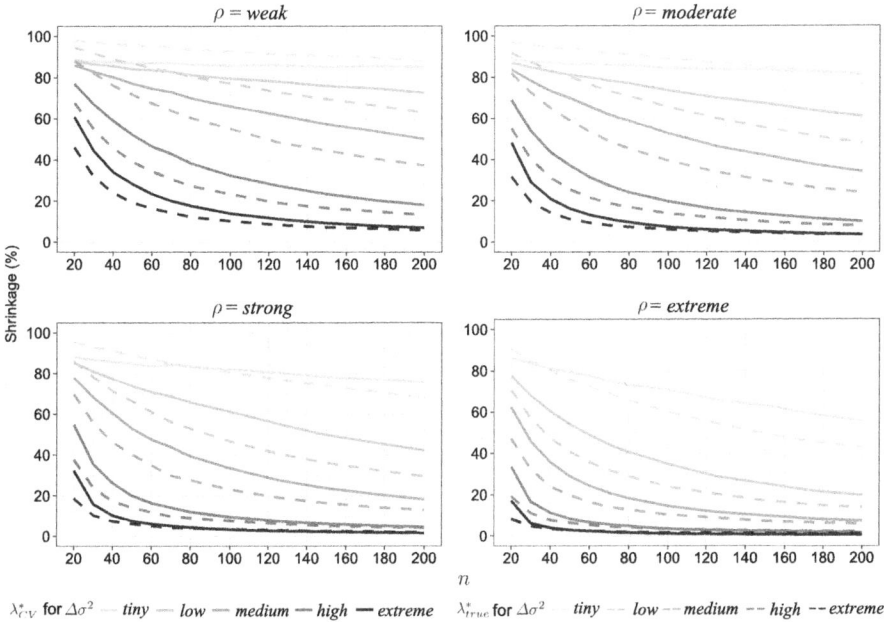

Fig. 1. Development of 5-Fold CV- (λ^*_{CV}) and Truly Optimal (λ^*_{true}) Shrinkage.

According to the previous findings, overshrinkage is dominating, while undershrinkage is particularly pronounced for similar variances together with lower correlations. However, with increasing ρ, the bias development of scenarios with $\Delta\sigma^2 \in \{tiny, low\}$ approaches those with $\Delta\sigma^2 \in \{medium, high, extreme\}$.

In addition, the development of shrinkage biases regarding the training size n can be observed. For $\Delta\sigma^2 \in \{high, extreme\}$, the bias is typically higher for smaller n, as taking away parts of already small training sets fosters extreme (overfitted) OW. These will not fit well the validation sets and will be shrunk strongly to EW, whereas the OW learned on $\boldsymbol{E}_{train}$ will be less extreme, with no need to shrink as much as CV suggests. For increasing n, the OW estimated on the calibration sets will be less overfitted, and λ^*_{CV} will be closer to λ^*_{true}.

In contrast, for comparable variances, the appearing undershrinkage decreases with increasing n, but can turn into overshrinkage. Focusing on $\Delta\sigma^2 = tiny$, λ^*_{true} is near 100% for low n, as learning weights on small training sets does then not provide any benefits compared to assigning EW (i.e., full shrinkage). However, λ^*_{CV} is too low for $n = 20$ and does not decrease to the same extent as λ^*_{true} for increasing n, which reduces undershrinkage, but can lead to overshrinkage.

Finally, the findings in [22] can be confirmed, as overshrinkage appears to be higher for weaker ρ and lower n in case of distinguishable variances.

Based on these analyses, a bias prediction model is developed in Sect. 6.

6 Prediction Model for Weight Shrinkage Biases

The discussions above indicate that CV-based shrinkage tuning mostly leads to biased shrinkage levels, whereby the bias degree and direction are influenced by various parameters and their values.

Based on all studied scenarios, a CART regression tree [6] is learned to predict the shrinkage bias (target variable), depending on the CV-variant used and data characteristics, as trees can handle numerical as well as categorical variables with linear and non-linear relationships and also incorporate interaction effects.

The final tree, tuned by 5-fold CV regarding the *complexity parameter*, has a depth of 21 and considers all variables discussed in Sect. 4. For reasons of conciseness, Fig. 2 shows a simplified version (the first few splits).[6]

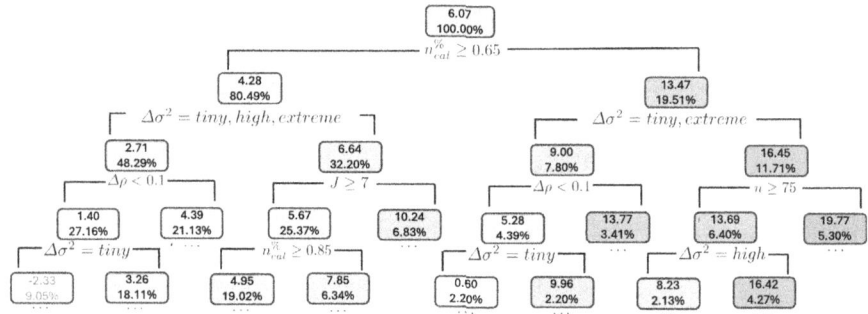

Fig. 2. Simplified Version of Regression Tree to Predict and Correct Shrinkage Biases.

The first value displayed in a node corresponds to the mean shrinkage bias of all cases assigned to this node during the learning process, while the second value indicates the share of the dataset used to learn the tree that belongs to the respective node. In addition, a darker node color reflects a stronger bias, with positive bias values written in black and negative ones in gray.

Starting with the root node, the mean shrinkage bias of all studied scenarios equals $6.07\%P$. All scenarios with calibration sets containing at least 65% of the available training observations ($n_{cal}^{\%} \geq 0.65$) are assigned to the left child node and their mean bias is $4.28\%P$. The remaining scenarios (i.e., those with $n_{cal}^{\%} < 0.65$) take the right branch and have a mean bias of $13.47\%P$.

Next, the range of variances $\Delta\sigma^2$ serves as splitting variable for both root child nodes. Considering the left child node, all scenarios with $n_{cal}^{\%} \geq 0.65$ and $\Delta\sigma^2 \in \{tiny, high, extreme\}$ take the left branch, while the ones with $n_{cal}^{\%} \geq 0.65$ and $\Delta\sigma^2 \in \{low, medium\}$ are assigned to the right. The splitting process continues until a branch terminates in a leaf node (no more outgoing branches).

The most left branches of both root child nodes use similar splitting criteria (at least for the first three splits). Also, the bias continuously decreases for these

---

[6] The complete regression tree model can be generated using the code available online.

cases and is negative ($-2.33\%P$) for $n_{cal}^{\%} \geq 0.65, \Delta\rho < 0.1, \Delta\sigma^2 = tiny$, but slightly positive ($0.60\%P$) otherwise. In addition, the shrinkage bias is lower for $\Delta\sigma^2 = tiny$ than for $\Delta\sigma^2 \in \{(high), extreme\}$ in case of $\Delta\rho < 0.1$.

Also in line with the previous findings, the availability of more training observations per fold ($n_{cal}^{\%}$) reduces overshrinkage and the model predicts a higher bias on average for less forecasters, if $\Delta\sigma^2 \in \{low, medium\}$ and $n_{cal}^{\%} \geq 0.65$.

Considering $\Delta\rho$, similar pairwise error correlations ($\Delta\rho < 0.1$) lead to a lower shrinkage bias than differing ones ($\Delta\rho \geq 0.1$) when averaging over $\Delta\sigma^2 \in \{tiny, (high), extreme\}$ due to the much higher overshrinkage for $\Delta\sigma^2 = tiny$ in the case of $\Delta\rho \geq 0.1$ compared to $\Delta\rho < 0.1$.

Since the regression tree provides predictions for the shrinkage bias, it can serve as bias correction model. For this purpose, the CV-optimal shrinkage level λ_{CV}^* is determined by Algorithm 1 for the provided dataset denoted as $\boldsymbol{E}_{train}$ and the number of folds K randomly chosen.

Subsequently, the tree is used to predict the bias, depending on the observed and estimated parameter values of $\boldsymbol{E}_{train}$. This bias prediction is treated as correction factor CV_C and subtracted from λ_{CV}^*, resulting in the corrected CV-optimal shrinkage $\lambda_{CV_C}^*$.

The correction can be expected to improve shrinkage tuning if parameter values are known or precisely estimated. However, as their estimation on limited training samples can deviate from those of the complete dataset and/or test data, the correction model is evaluated by applications to provided training data.

7 Evaluation of Shrinkage Correction

This section evaluates the bias prediction model for its ability to correct shrinkage biases, if parameter values are estimated on limited training data and are therefore subject to uncertainty.

For this purpose, new synthetic samples (with $20,000$ multivariate error observations per set) are generated, with $J \in \{4, 9\}$ forecasters, variance ranges $\Delta\sigma^2 \in \{0.1, 0.25, 0.7, 2, 5, 7\}$, and pairwise correlations $\rho \in \{0.15, 0.3, 0.45, 0.6, 0.75, 0.9\}$ with ranges $\Delta\rho \in \{0, 0.3\}$.

Per sample, small training sets $\boldsymbol{E}_{train}$ containing $n \in \{25, 50, 100, 200\}$ observations per forecaster are randomly drawn, while the respective remaining observations form a large test set $\boldsymbol{E}_{test}$.

Table 3 shows the mean percentage deviation of the MSE on $\boldsymbol{E}_{test}$ (rounded to two digits) for various scenarios when shrinking OW towards EW by the corrected shrinkage $\lambda_{CV_C}^*$ instead of λ_{CV}^*, tuned on $K \in \{2, 5, LOO\}$ CV-folds.[7]

The evaluation results are averaged over $\Delta\rho, J$ and 250 repetitions per scenario and faceted by $n, K, \Delta\sigma^2$ and ρ. For example, considering datasets with $\Delta\sigma^2 = medium$ and $\rho = extreme$, for which $n = 25$ training observations are available and 2-fold CV is applied. In this scenario, applying the correction model can reduce the MSE by 7.99% on average.

---

[7] For a detailed description of the procedure, see Algorithm 2 in Subsect. 4.3.

Table 3. Mean Percentage Deviation of MSE with $\lambda^*_{CV_C}$ from MSE with λ^*_{CV} for Selected Values of Training Size n, Folds K, Variance Range $\Delta\sigma^2$ and Correlation ρ.

$\Delta\sigma^2$	K	2				5				LOO			
	n ρ	weak,	moderate,	strong,	extreme								
tiny	25	1.92	1.73	1.58	1.31	1.33	1.53	1.63	0.93	1.05	1.28	1.35	0.78
	50	1.61	0.79	0.44	0.37	1.09	0.64	0.61	0.29	0.96	0.66	0.59	0.29
	100	0.62	0.15	**-0.01**	0.04	0.43	0.26	0.25	0.14	0.32	0.27	0.24	0.17
	200	0.12	**-0.03**	**-0.07**	**-0.07**	0.11	0.07	0.08	0.04	0.08	0.08	0.09	0.07
low	25	1.73	0.80	**-0.81**	**-1.47**	1.35	1.37	1.00	0.08	1.11	1.18	1.02	0.33
	50	1.13	0.07	**-0.54**	**-1.69**	0.87	0.45	0.35	**-0.31**	0.80	0.49	0.41	**-0.08**
	100	0.23	**-0.32**	**-0.56**	**-1.05**	0.18	0.05	0.01	**-0.22**	0.16	0.13	0.10	**-0.08**
	200	**-0.06**	**-0.24**	**-0.26**	**-0.44**	0.02	**-0.02**	**-0.01**	**-0.10**	0.05	0.02	0.00	**-0.06**
medium	25	0.35	**-1.28**	**-5.12**	**-7.99**	0.36	0.07	**-0.49**	**-2.11**	0.57	0.48	0.35	**-1.15**
	50	**-0.48**	**-1.61**	**-1.84**	**-3.64**	0.21	**-0.16**	**-0.01**	**-1.14**	0.33	0.02	0.14	**-0.70**
	100	**-0.58**	**-0.78**	**-0.68**	**-1.13**	**-0.04**	**-0.12**	**-0.10**	**-0.37**	0.03	0.01	**-0.04**	**-0.19**
	200	**-0.34**	**-0.29**	**-0.17**	**-0.37**	**-0.04**	**-0.01**	**-0.01**	**-0.13**	0.01	0.02	**-0.01**	**-0.08**
high	25	**-3.62**	**-6.61**	**-9.15**	**-11.78**	**-0.58**	**-0.78**	**-0.97**	**-2.18**	0.04	**-0.08**	**-0.09**	**-1.34**
	50	**-2.03**	**-2.24**	**-1.64**	**-2.46**	**-0.33**	**-0.32**	**-0.20**	**-0.59**	**-0.08**	**-0.16**	**-0.14**	**-0.26**
	100	**-0.63**	**-0.68**	**-0.44**	**-0.55**	**-0.05**	**-0.11**	**-0.13**	0.06	0.01	**-0.03**	**-0.08**	0.08
	200	**-0.23**	**-0.15**	**-0.08**	**-0.13**	0.01	**-0.01**	**-0.01**	0.07	0.01	**-0.00**	**-0.01**	0.08
extreme	25	**-4.90**	**-7.69**	**-9.42**	**-10.60**	**-0.73**	**-0.91**	**-1.16**	**-1.92**	**-0.05**	**-0.20**	**-0.42**	**-1.23**
	50	**-1.75**	**-1.89**	**-1.32**	**-1.87**	**-0.31**	**-0.29**	**-0.31**	**-0.29**	**-0.15**	**-0.21**	**-0.19**	**-0.04**
	100	**-0.43**	**-0.49**	**-0.33**	**-0.30**	**-0.08**	**-0.09**	**-0.09**	0.12	**-0.03**	**-0.03**	**-0.07**	0.17
	200	**-0.17**	**-0.09**	**-0.05**	**-0.05**	**-0.01**	**-0.01**	**-0.00**	0.11	**-0.00**	**-0.00**	**-0.01**	0.12

Overall, the correction is beneficial (i.e., negative MSE deviation, highlighted in **bold**) for the majority of scenarios.

However, in scenarios with comparable variances, the correction typically leads to worse results. This could be due to the fact that deviations between estimated variances or correlations and the actual (true) values are particularly critical with smaller $\Delta\sigma^2$: According to Table 2, different categories for ρ and $\Delta\rho$ are associated with different degrees and even opposite directions of biases, which can also be expected for bias predictions, resulting in unreliable corrections.

Also, OW are typically shrunk strongly to EW for lower $\Delta\sigma^2$ (see Fig. 1), so it is suggested to simply assign EW if comparable variances are assumed.

For stronger spread in variances, the following relations are observed: First, the correction is successful for scenarios with few folds (even for smaller spread in variances), in which overshrinkage is typically higher. This seems reasonable, as the MSE on test data might be large in case of strong overshrinkage, so the correction has great potential for improvements.

Second, the extent of correction typically decreases with increasing training size: With more training data, overshrinkage decreases, and so does the achievable MSE reduction, because the CV-determined shrinkage will already be closer to the truly optimal one. However, the correction is not necessarily beneficial with (too) small training set sizes together with weaker correlations.

Third, although overshrinkage typically decreases with increasing correlations, the magnitude of correction increases with ρ, so the determination of correction factors appears to be increasingly precise with stronger correlations.

Nevertheless, when relating the MSE to the number of folds used for the shrinkage tuning, LOO clearly dominates – in 69 of the 80 evaluated scenarios, the lowest mean MSE is achieved with corrected or uncorrected LOO. For the remaining scenarios (mainly belonging to $\Delta\sigma^2 \in \{tiny, low\}$ together with $n = 25$ or $\rho = weak$, for which assigning EW is suggested), uncorrected 2-fold CV performs slightly better (i.e., on average around 0.56% lower MSE) than LOO.

However, LOO can be computationally burdensome for large training sets, and in case of $\Delta\sigma^2 \in \{medium, high, extreme\}$ and at least $n = 100$ training observations, the MSE obtained with shrinkage levels that are determined on less folds (and additionally corrected if suggested by Table 3) is just slightly higher (on average 0.20% for $K = 2$ and 0.06% with $K = 5$) than with LOO.

The final section draws conclusions based on the analytical insights as well as the evaluation of shrinkage corrections and provides an outlook on future work.

8 Conclusions and Future Work

After discussing shrinkage biases for various data and CV-related characteristics as well as evaluating the introduced bias prediction model regarding its ability to correct shrinkage biases, the following conclusions are drawn.

First, for comparable predictive abilities of forecasters, it seems reasonable to assign EW, as learning weights and tuning (and correcting) shrinkage levels introduces uncertainties that outweigh the benefits of estimating weights.

Second, contrary to the general suggestion of 5- or 10-fold CV, practitioners should rather choose (corrected) LOO for weight shrinkage tuning: In scenarios with distinguishable forecaster variances, shrinkage levels tuned by LOO typically dominate the ones tuned on less folds, as taking away larger data parts can seriously affect the estimation of OW. Therefore, LOO is suggested for shrinkage tuning, with an additional correction in case of large spread in predictive ability.

However, if less CV-folds are chosen, e.g. due to the computational effort of LOO, the shrinkage should be corrected for distinguishable forecast abilities.

Third, researchers and applicants of any domain should be aware of estimation and tuning biases resulting from machine learning-based approaches and thus, use methods to detect and correct these tuning errors.

Future work will analyze additional data properties and develop advanced shrinkage corrections, as variance and correlation structures of empirical datasets do not necessarily follow easily identifiable patterns. The corrections will be compared to established combination techniques on synthetic or real-world datasets.

In addition, other machine learning techniques such as bootstrap aggregating (bagging) will be examined for biases in shrinkage tuning and their correction.

Disclosure of Interests. The author has no competing interests to declare that are relevant to the content of this article.

References

1. Aiolfi, M., Timmermann, A.: Persistence in forecasting performance and conditional combination strategies. J. Econom. **135**(1–2), 31–53 (2006). https://doi.org/10.1016/j.jeconom.2005.07.015
2. Aksu, C., Gunter, S.I.: An empirical analysis of the accuracy of SA, OLS, ERLS and NRLS combination forecasts. Int. J. Forecast. **8**(1), 27–43 (1992). https://doi.org/10.1016/0169-2070(92)90005-T
3. Arlot, S., Lerasle, M.: Choice of V for V-fold cross-validation in least-squares density estimation. J. Mach. Learn. Res. **17**(1), 7256–7305 (2016). http://jmlr.org/papers/volume17/14-296/14-296.pdf
4. Bates, J.M., Granger, C.W.J.: The combination of forecasts. J. Oper. Res. Soc. **20**(4), 451–468 (1969). https://doi.org/10.2307/3008764
5. Blanc, S.M., Setzer, T.: When to choose the simple average in forecast combination. J. Bus. Res. **69**(10), 3951–3962 (2016). https://doi.org/10.1016/j.jbusres.2016.05.013
6. Breiman, L., Friedman, J., Olshen, R.A., Stone, C.J.: Classification and Regression Trees, 1st edn. Chapman and Hall, New York (1984). https://doi.org/10.1201/9781315139470
7. Breiman, L., Spector, P.: Submodel selection and evaluation in regression. The x-random case. Int. Stat. Rev. **60**(3), 291–319 (1992). https://doi.org/10.2307/1403680
8. Celisse, A.: Optimal cross-validation in density estimation with the L2-loss. Ann. Statist. **42**(5), 1879–1910 (2014). https://doi.org/10.1214/14-AOS1240
9. Chan, F., Pauwels, L.L.: Some theoretical results on forecast combinations. Int. J. Forecast. **34**(1), 64–74 (2018). https://doi.org/10.1016/j.ijforecast.2017.08.005
10. Claeskens, G., Magnus, J.R., Vasnev, A.L., Wang, W.: The forecast combination puzzle: a simple theoretical explanation. Int. J. Forecast. **32**(3), 754–762 (2016). https://doi.org/10.1016/j.ijforecast.2015.12.005
11. Clemen, R.T.: Combining forecasts: a review and annotated bibliography. Int. J. Forecast. **5**(4), 559–583 (1989). https://doi.org/10.1016/0169-2070(89)90012-5
12. Diebold, F.X., Pauly, P.: The use of prior information in forecast combination. Int. J. Forecast. **6**(4), 503–508 (1990). https://doi.org/10.1016/0169-2070(90)90028-A
13. Diebold, F.X., Shin, M.: Machine learning for regularized survey forecast combination: partially-egalitarian LASSO and its derivatives. Int. J. Forecast. **35**(4), 1679–1691 (2019). https://doi.org/10.1016/j.ijforecast.2018.09.006
14. Genre, V., Kenny, G., Meyler, A., Timmermann, A.: Combining expert forecasts: can anything beat the simple average? Int. J. Forecast. **29**(1), 108–121 (2013). https://doi.org/10.1016/j.ijforecast.2012.06.004
15. Graefe, A., Küchenhoff, H., Stierle, V., Riedl, B.: Limitations of ensemble bayesian model averaging for forecasting social science problems. Int. J. Forecast. **31**(3), 943–951 (2015). https://doi.org/10.1016/j.ijforecast.2014.12.001

16. Hastie, T., Tibshirani, R., Friedman, J.: The Elements of Statistical Learning: Data Mining, Inference, and Prediction, 1st edn. Springer, Berlin (2009). https://doi.org/10.1007/b94608
17. Haubner, N., Setzer, T.: Hybrid recommender systems for next purchase prediction based on optimal combination weights. In: Wirtschaftsinformatik 2021 Proceedings (2021). https://aisel.aisnet.org/wi2021/RDataScience/Track09/1/
18. Jahrer, M. Töscher, A., Legenstein, R.: Combining predictions for accurate recommender systems. In: Proceedings of the 16th ACM SIGKDD International Conference on Knowledge Discovery and Data Mining, pp. 693–702 (2010). https://doi.org/10.1145/1835804.1835893
19. James, G., Witten, D., Hastie, T., Tibshirani, R.: An Introduction to Statistical Learning: With Applications in R, 2nd edn. Springer, New York (2021). https://doi.org/10.1007/978-1-0716-1418-1
20. Schanbacher, P.: Combining portfolio models. Ann. Econ. Financ. **15**(2), 433–455 (2014). http://aeconf.com/Articles/Nov2014/aef150208.pdf
21. Schulz, F., Setzer, T., Balla, N.: Linear hybrid shrinkage of weights for forecast selection and combination. In: Proceedings of the 55th Hawaii International Conference on System Sciences, pp. 2125–2134 (2022). https://doi.org/10.24251/HICSS.2022.267
22. Schulz, F., Setzer, T.: Shrinkage of weights towards subset selection in forecast combination (2023). SSRN: https://ssrn.com/abstract=4485995
23. Smith, D.G.C.: Combination of forecasts in electricity demand prediction. J. Forecast. **8**, 349–356 (1989). https://doi.org/10.1002/for.3980080316
24. Smith, J., Wallis, K.F.: A simple explanation of the forecast combination puzzle. Oxf. Bull. Econ. Stat. **71**(3), 331–355 (2009). https://doi.org/10.1111/j.1468-0084.2008.00541.x
25. Stock, J.H., Watson, M.W.: Combination forecasts of output growth in a seven-country data set. J. Forecast. **23**(6), 405–430 (2004). https://doi.org/10.1002/for.928
26. Thompson, R., Qian, Y., Vasnev, A.L.: Flexible global forecast combinations. Omega **126** (2024). https://doi.org/10.1016/j.omega.2024.103073
27. Timmermann, A.: Forecast combinations. In: Handbook of Economic Forecasting, 1st edn, pp. 135–196. Elsevier (2006). https://doi.org/10.1016/S1574-0706(05)01004-9
28. Wang, X., Hyndman, R.J., Li, F., Kang, Y.: Forecast combinations: an over 50-year review. Int. J. Forecast. **39**(4), 1518–1547 (2023). https://doi.org/10.1016/j.ijforecast.2022.11.005
29. Zhang, Y., Yang, Y.: Cross-validation for selecting a model selection procedure. J. Econom. **187**(1), 95–112 (2015). https://doi.org/10.1016/j.jeconom.2015.02.006

Redefining Fairness: A Multi-dimensional Perspective and Integrated Evaluation Framework

Zichong Wang[1], Zhipeng Yin[1], Zhen Liu[2], Roland H. C. Yap[3], Xiaocai Zhang[4], Shu Hu[5], and Wenbin Zhang[1(✉)]

[1] Florida International University, Miami, USA
{ziwang,wenbin.zhang}@fiu.edu
[2] Guangdong University of Foreign Studies, Guangzhou, China
[3] National University of Singapore, Singapore, Singapore
[4] University of Melbourne, Melbourne, Australia
[5] Purdue University, West Lafayette, USA

Abstract. As machine learning techniques continue to permeate a variety of application domains with significant societal impact, the focus on algorithmic fairness is becoming an increasingly critical aspect of this established area of research. Existing studies on fairness typically assume that algorithmic bias stems from a single, predefined sensitive attribute in the data, thereby overlooking the reality that multiple sensitive attributes are often prevalent simultaneously in the real world. Unlike previous works, this paper delves into the realm of group fairness involving multiple sensitive attributes, a setting that greatly increases the difficulty of mitigating algorithmic bias. We posit that this multi-attribute perspective provides a more pragmatic model for fairness in real-world applications, and show how learning with such an intricate precondition draws new insights that better explain algorithmic fairness. Furthermore, we develop the first-of-its-kind unified metric, Multi-Fairness Bonded Utility (MFBU), designed to simultaneously evaluate and compare the trade-offs between fairness and utility of multi-source bias mitigation methods. By combining fairness and utility into a single, intuitive metric, MFBU provides model designers the flexibility to holistically evaluate and compare different fairness techniques. Thorough experiments conducted on three real-world datasets substantiate the superior performance of the proposed methodology in minimizing discrimination while maintaining predictive performance.

Keywords: Fairness · Multi-dimensional sensitive attributes · Unified metric · Decision tree

1 Introduction

Increasing integration of machine learning (ML) algorithms into various information systems for decision-making applications has led to significant successes across numerous domains [4,14,36]. Despite these remarkable achievements, as ML algorithms become more deeply woven into our societal fabric and begin to supplant human decision-making in high-stakes contexts such as resource allocation [68], and loan approval [52], ensuring their fairness has gained increased prominence. This urgency is highlighted by cases where biases in ML algorithms have resulted in serious consequences, such as Amazon's decision to discard an automated hiring tool biased against women [46] and the predictive policing software PredPol reinforcing racially biased practices by increasing police presence in minority neighborhoods regardless of actual crime rates [27].

In response to these challenges, a number of fairness-aware ML methods have been proposed in recent years that aim to prevent algorithmic decisions from discriminating against specific groups defined by *sensitive attributes* such as race and gender. However, most existing works [29, 64, 68] addressing fairness in machine learning, including their metrics (*e.g.*, demographic parity [15], equal opportunity [10]), focus primarily on the impact of a single sensitive attribute. This approach ignores that real-world data often contains multiple sensitive attributes such as race and gender operating simultaneously. When fairness is considered along only one dimension, discrimination can persist along others. For example, an algorithm that achieves statistical fairness with respect to race in loan applications might still discriminate against Black female applicants due to unaddressed gender bias, as intersectional combinations of attributes create unique patterns of disadvantage that single-attribute approaches cannot detect [24].

On the other side, in the context of fairness, one long-standing challenge is the trade-off between fairness and predictive performance, where improving fairness typically comes at the cost of reduced accuracy. Current evaluations present fairness improvement and accuracy loss as separate metrics, simply displaying performance indicators and fairness indicators independently. In practical applications, stakeholders need a consolidated metric that includes both dimensions [62]. This challenge becomes even more complex with multiple sensitive attributes, as existing fairness indicators produce multiple values—one for each sensitive attribute—further complicating the evaluation process. Consequently, to address both challenges simultaneously, we need a cohesive metric that can clearly delineate the trade-off between fairness and predictive performance while handling multiple sensitive attributes.

There is an urgent practical need to design decision-making systems and fairness metrics, both of which account for multiple sensitive attributes, presenting unique challenges: **i) Multiple Potential Sources of Bias:** In situations involving multiple sensitive attributes, the bias of a sample may originate from several sources simultaneously [21]. Unlike scenarios with a single sensitive attribute, ensuring fair model predictions in this setting necessitates that all potential sources of bias be mitigated concurrently. **ii) Effective and Robust Trade-off Balance Between Fairness and Performance:** The trade-off between performance and fairness, characterized by the typical inverse relationship between algorithmic fairness based on sensitive attributes and utility [15], introduces additional complexities in multi-sensitive attribute settings. When multiple sensitive attributes are present, each attribute introduces its own fairness-performance trade-off, requiring a balance not just between fairness and performance, but across the different attributes themselves. Consequently, finding an optimal balance between mitigating multiple bias sources and preserving performance becomes a more complex optimization problem that requires a systematic approach. **iii) The Lack of an Intuitive Measure of Model Fairness for Multiple Sensitive Attributes:** Traditional fairness evaluations typically present improvements in fairness and losses in utility as distinct metrics [25]. However, these metrics do not offer a reliable means of jointly quantifying the inherent trade-off between the two. Further, existing methodologies fall short in measuring model fairness under multiple sensitive attributes using a single, unified metric.

To tackle these challenges, *this paper explores the mitigation and quantification of algorithmic bias arising from multiple sensitive attributes, marking the first work, to the best of our knowledge, to simultaneously address both the mitigation and measurement of such biases.* Specifically, we propose a fairness splitting criterion that incorporates bias mitigation for multiple sensitive attributes with an efficient trade-off between utility and fairness. Building on this, we propose a tree-based learning framework to build statistically fair trees for multiple attributes, which can be adapted for any decision tree algorithm. In addition, we propose a unified metric that captures the multifaceted fairness-accuracy trade-off in this complex setting, enabling more direct measurement of fairness and performance trade-offs.

Our major contributions are: **i)** Fair Intersectional Information Gain (FIIG), an innovative splitting criterion designed specifically for fairness-aware ML that pioneers a systematic method to tackle bias across multiple sensitive attributes simultaneously. Our unique splitting criterion seamlessly balances utility and fairness, thereby enhancing both the efficiency and robustness of the model. Furthermore, it can be readily integrated into any decision tree learning algorithm, thus significantly broadening its reach and impact. **ii)** FIIG is further incorporated into a pioneering probabilistic tree learning framework, *Multi-dimensional Fair Decision Tree (MFDT)*, which builds statistically fair trees for multiple sensitive attributes that are flexibly tunable regarding the performance-fairness trade-off. For each node, MFDT generates a Pareto front to first identify the set of Pareto-optimal solutions and then selects the feature maximizing FIIG, thereby extending any decision tree algorithm to balance accuracy and fairness effectively and in an adaptable manner. **iii)** A novel fairness-performance metric, *Multi-Fairness Bonded Utility (MFBU)*, capable of handling multiple sensitive attributes concurrently just as effectively as a single sensitive attribute. MFBU unifies and intuitively evaluates the trade-off between fairness and accuracy when mitigating biases from multiple sources. **iv)** Extensive empirical experiments on three real-world datasets with multiple sensitive attributes demonstrate the efficacy of the proposed unified metrics and fairness-aware algorithm.

2 Related Work

Fairness-Aware Learning with Single Binary Sensitive Attributes. Fairness is a widespread issue in machine learning systems [25,39]. In recent years, researchers have proposed a number of fairness notions and methods for quantification and mitigation of bias in machine learning algorithms. For instance, Kamiran *et al.* established several key approaches: modifying training data through label and attribute adjustments [21] and developing fairness-aware splitting criteria for decision trees [22].

Building upon these preprocessing and in-processing techniques, Zafar et al. [63] advanced the field by incorporating fairness directly into the optimization function, limiting outcome differences across demographic groups while maintaining model integrity. More recent approaches have focused on optimizing fairness more efficiently. MiniMax [28] attempts to reduce maximum group risk, though residual bias can remain, while Herrear et al. [35] proposed a novel meta-learning approach using regression models to predict the fairness of hyperparameter settings before full training, reducing computational costs of fairness optimization. Despite these advancements, like most existing AI fairness approaches, these methods are designed for a single binary sensitive attribute (e.g., Gender = {Male, Female}) and struggle to handle scenarios involving multiple sensitive attributes simultaneously.

Fairness-Aware Learning with Non-single Binary Sensitive Attributes. Recently, researchers have started exploring fairness beyond binary single sensitive attributes, addressing both multi-valued attributes (e.g., Race = {White, Black, Other}) and multiple attributes simultaneously (e.g., combining Race with Gender). For instance, Morina et al. [30] extended the single-attribute fairness metric proposed by [17] and mitigated bias for multiple attributes via a post-processing method. However, their work is limited to binary-sensitive attributes, restricting its applicability in scenarios involving multi-valued attributes like race or ethnicity. Fair-SMOTE [58] is a representative method within another line of approach, data rebalancing techniques, that aim to achieve group fairness by balancing representation among different subgroups in a dataset. This method identifies similarity groups using clustering and generates simulated samples to guarantee adequate representation for all subgroups. However, the oversampling strategy may lead to overfitting due to insufficient numbers of real samples, particularly for intersectional groups with minimal representation. In addition, FairMask [32], a hybrid pre- and post-processing method for multiple attributes, reduces bias from imbalanced training data by using models learned from independent non-sensitive variables to represent sensitive attributes and relabel sensitive attributes seen during deployment. However, they ignore intersectional bias by handling only one sensitive attribute at a time, resulting in samples that may suffer discrimination across different sensitive attributes. For example, Black female applicants may face discrimination based on both gender and race simultaneously.

Different from existing works, our work explicitly addresses intersectional fairness by developing methods that directly handle multiple sensitive attributes simultaneously. Our main contributions are two-fold: First, we propose the Fair Intersectional Information Gain (FIIG) criterion to efficiently tackle bias from multiple sensitive attributes while preserving the advantages of decision trees. This approach offers a unique tradeoff between utility and fairness without restricting the algorithm to binary classifiers or specific domains. Second, we introduce the MFBU metric that comprehensively evaluates and compares multiple fairness techniques based on their performance. MFBU facilitates the intuitive selection of fairness techniques for any number of sensitive attributes, accommodating both single-sensitive and multiple-sensitive attribute scenarios. Importantly, our approach is flexible regarding the fairness metrics, enabling end-users to select the most appropriate metric for their specific task.

3 Notations

Given a dataset $\mathcal{D} = \{d_1, d_2, \ldots, d_n\}$ containing a sequence of independent and identically distributed samples. Each data instance $d_i \in \mathcal{D}$ has an associated class label $y \in \{0, 1\}$, forming a sequence of class labels Y. The predicted class label is denoted by $\hat{y}$. Every sample d_i can be described as $d_i = \{\mathcal{X}, S, y\}$, where $\mathcal{X} = \{x_1, x_2, \ldots, x_m\}$ denotes a set of non-sensitive attributes, and $S = \{s_1, s_2, \ldots, s_k\}$ signifies sensitive attributes (e.g., gender, race, age). Specifically, we use $S_0 = \{\forall \, x_i \in \mathcal{X} \mid s_i = 0\}$ to denote the deprived group (e.g., female), and $S_1 = \{\forall \, x_i \in \mathcal{X} \mid s_i = 1\}$ to denote the favored group (e.g., male). Without loss of generality, we consider situations where the given dataset is intrinsically biased with respect to one or more sensitive attributes, which may be binary or multicategorical. Thus, we introduce a set $C = \{c_1, c_2, \ldots, c_a\}$, where each c_i represents a possible combination of sensitive attributes in S.

4 Methodology

This section first introduces our proposed Multi-dimensional Fair Decision Tree, which encompasses: i) a statistical fairness approach for multi-dimensional attributes, ii) multi-dimensional fairness gain that measures bias vary across all pairs of sensitive attribute combinations, and iii) a novel splitting criterion based on a flexible performance-fairness trade-off mechanism. We then present the Multi-Fairness Bonded Utility, which integrates multi-dimensional fairness and performance metrics into a single indicator for comparative analysis, enabling the evaluation of various fairness and performance metric combinations.

4.1 Multi-dimensional Fair Decision Tree

Various fairness-aware approaches have been built upon decision tree models [20, 26, 68] due to their high interpretability, minimal data preprocessing requirements, computational efficiency, and lack of distributional assumptions; however, like most AI fairness methods, they typically address only single sensitive attributes, overlooking the multi-dimensional nature of bias in real-world scenarios [38]. To this end, we propose the Multi-dimensional Fair Decision Tree (MFDT), a probabilistic tree learning framework designed to: i) **Defining multiple-dimensional Fairness** which accounts for demographic subgroups formed by combinations of multiple sensitive attributes, ii) **Evaluating Multi-dimensional Fairness in Tree Splits** which examines the fairness impact of feature splits across multiple sensitive attribute combinations, enabling us to build decision trees that maintain multi-dimensional fairness throughout the construction process, and iii) **Balance of Multi-dimensional Fairness and Performance** which provides a tunable trade-off between them via Pareto-optimal solutions. The following sections detail each of these components.

i) Defining multi-dimensional Fairness. Straightforward ways to extend existing single-attribute fairness (e.g., statistical parity [15], equal opportunity [19]) to multi-dimensional fairness include summation or maximization of fairness values across individual attributes, but these approaches often overlook intersectional bias. Consider this hypothetical scenario: a bank lending system with age and gender as sensitive attributes. Suppose the system is designed to be unbiased towards gender or age individually. Combining the fairness values of the individual attributes would suggest overall fairness in the system. However, this fails to capture the complete picture, as multi-dimensional bias towards certain demographic groups can still exist. For instance, the system could favor lending to young men and older women while restricting loans to young women and older men. Examining each sensitive attribute in isolation would miss such multi-dimensional bias. Therefore, it is important to consider these crossover effects when dealing with multi-dimensional fairness [17]. To this end, we extend the statistical fairness notion to quantify model bias under multi-dimensional sensitive attributes, as detailed in Definition 4.1.

Definition 4.1 (Multi-dimensional Fairness). Multi-dimensional Fairness (MF) measures the disparity between different subgroups, where each subgroup is defined by a distinct combination of sensitive attributes (such as "Race & Gender"). We define MF as the maximum statistical disparity in predicted positive outcomes between any two subgroups:

$$MF = \max \left\{ \forall c_i, c_j \in C, i \neq j : \left| P(\hat{y} = 1 \mid c_i) - P(\hat{y} = 1 \mid c_j) \right| \right\} \quad (1)$$

where c_i represents a distinct combination of sensitive attributes (such as "white female") with C denote the set of all such subgroups.

Overall, multi-dimensional fairness is measured by quantifying the maximum disparity in predicted outcomes between any two subgroups formed by combinations of sensitive attributes. This approach captures intersectional bias that might be ignored when considering sensitive attributes in isolation.

ii) Evaluating Multi-dimensional Fairness in Tree Splits. Although various tree-based fairness splitting criteria have been proposed [20,26,68], they focus solely on a single sensitive attribute, leading to unfair predictions when multiple sensitive attributes are involved. To address this limitation, we first propose *Multi-dimensional Fairness Imparity (MFI)*, which measures fairness disparities across multi-dimensional sensitive attributes simultaneously per the proposed Definition 4.1. Specifically, MFI examines how fairness impacts vary across all pairs of sensitive attribute combinations and identifies the pair with the largest disparity. By doing so, it highlights where a split on a given feature may disproportionately affect certain subgroups, providing a multi-dimensional view of potential disparities. Mathematically, MFI is represented as:

$$\text{MFI}(D, x_j, C) = \max_{\forall c_i, c_l \in C, i \neq l} \left| \text{MFG}(D, x_j, c_i) - \text{MFG}(D, x_j, c_l) \right| \quad (2)$$

where x_j denotes a feature for splitting dataset D with C representing the set of all subgroups, while MFG refers to Multi-dimensional Fairness Gain, where x_j denotes a feature for splitting dataset D with C representing the set of all subgroups, while MFG refers to Multi-dimensional Fairness Gain, which for each combination of sensitive attributes c_i (*e.g.*, "white female"), is defined as follows:

$$\text{MFG}(D, x_j, c_i) = H(y \mid c_i) - H(y \mid x_j, c_i) \quad (3)$$

where $H(\cdot)$ is the entropy measuring the uncertainty in the distribution of labels, with $H(y \mid c_i)$ represents the entropy of the ground truth labels y given the combination c_i, and $H(y \mid x_j, c_i)$ is the entropy of y after splitting on feature x_j for instances with c_i.

Essentially, a positive value of $MFG(D, x_j, c_i)$ indicates a reduction in uncertainty (i.e., information gain), reflecting potential fairness implications across multi-dimensional demographic subgroups. Although Information Gain (IG) [34] focuses on the overall reduction in uncertainty about Y, MFI extends this concept by highlighting differences in these reductions across various combinations of sensitive attributes. Specifically, MFI measures the gap in uncertainty reductions among different groups defined by c_i that emerge from selecting a feature x_j for splitting. For example, consider two sensitive attribute combinations, such as white males and Black females. MFI would identify whether a split on x_j leads to significantly different information gains for these two groups, revealing potential inequities that would remain hidden when only examining aggregate performance. In this way, MFI goes beyond merely assessing overall utility improvements, capturing changes in predictive performance across different demographic subgroups. While both IG and MFI reward reductions in uncertainty, they differ in perspective: IG prioritizes maximizing accuracy, while MFI concentrates on fairness disparities between all possible combinations of sensitive attributes, highlighting where discrimination may occur.

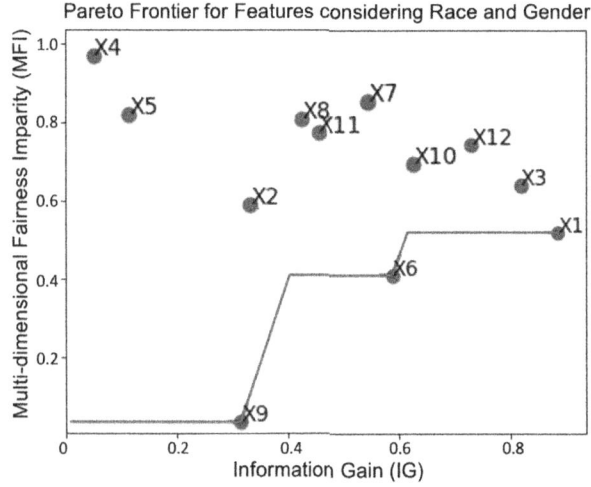

Fig. 1. An illustration of the Pareto Front for balancing utility and fairness.

iii) Balance of Multi-dimensional Fairness and Performance. Another challenge in constructing decision trees is balancing the performance and fairness of each split. To address this, we introduce the concept of the Pareto Frontier [11] into the splitting process of decision trees. In multi-objective optimization scenarios, the Pareto frontier represents the set of all possible optimal solutions that can be obtained without sacrificing any objective. In our model, the objectives are IG and MFI. By incorporating the Pareto frontier, we can better balance performance and fairness during tree construction.

Consider the splitting process for a given node in the decision tree. We have a set of possible splitting attributes for each node that can serve as candidates. Each candidate attribute yields specific IG and MFI values when selected as the split point. Thus, we can view each candidate attribute as a solution characterized by its IG and MFI scores. Drawing on the concept of the Pareto frontier, we identify all Pareto-optimal solutions. A solution is Pareto-optimal only if no other solution is superior to it on all objectives. In other words, if a solution is considered Pareto-optimal, then we cannot find an improved solution that enhances one objective without deteriorating the score of other objectives. For instance, as Fig. 1 shows, attributes X1, X6, and X9 are Pareto-optimal solutions, as X1 achieves better performance than X6 and X9 but has lower fairness. Conversely, X9 achieves better fairness than X1 and X6 but with lower performance. X6 maintains a balance between these two objectives.

After identifying the Pareto-optimal solutions, the Fair Intersectional Information Gain (FIIG) is proposed to select the optimal multi-dimensional fair and accurate splitting as formulated below:

$$\text{FIIG}(D, X, C) = (1 - \alpha) \cdot \text{IG}(D, X) - \alpha \cdot \text{MFI}(D, X, C) \tag{4}$$

where $\alpha \in [0, 1]$ is a trade-off parameter to balance the relative importance of utility and fairness in the splitting decision. By optimizing for FIIG rather than just IG, we ensure that the resulting decision tree not only makes accurate predictions but also maintains fairness across intersectional demographic groups. Intuitively, FIIG balances the trade-off between classification performance and fairness: when $\alpha = 0$, FIIG equals IG, prioritizing only classification performance; when $\alpha = 1$, FIIG equals negative MFI, prioritizing only fairness. For values between 0 and 1, FIIG provides a weighted combination of both objectives. This parameter provides flexibility to adjust the model according to specific application requirements, allowing practitioners to appropriately balance utility and fairness based on their domain needs.

Tree Construction. Building upon our multi-objective framework that considers both IG and MFI, we construct the Multi-dimensional Fair Decision Tree (MFDT) by integrating the FIIG into a traditional decision tree workflow. In conventional decision trees (*e.g.*, C4.5 [33]), each node is split by selecting the feature that yields the highest IG. By contrast, we evaluate each candidate feature in our approach using both IG and MFI, generate a Pareto frontier to identify the most balanced solutions, and then apply FIIG (Eq. 4) to select the feature that provides the best trade-off between utility and fairness. Specifically, we first compute IG and MFG (and thereby MFI) for all candidate features at a node. We then form the Pareto frontier to filter out any feature dominated by both IG and MFI. From this frontier, we choose the feature that maximizes FIIG, balancing accuracy and fairness through the parameter α. This procedure is repeated at each node until stopping criteria are reached (*e.g.*, purity, feature exhaustion, or minimal node size). Once the splits are determined, the tree is pruned to prevent overfitting, similarly to how pruning is performed in C4.5. However, while conventional pruning only aims to preserve or improve accuracy, our tree structure already incorporates fairness considerations at each node via FIIG. Consequently, even after pruning, MFDT is designed to remain sensitive to disparities across multi-dimensional sensitive attributes.

4.2 Multi-fairness Bonded Utility

Existing approaches evaluate fairness models by presenting predictive performance and fairness metrics separately through tables, bar charts, or visual comparisons [23,29]. This separation makes it difficult to intuitively assess the trade-off between the two. Moreover, in settings with multi-dimensional sensitive attributes, the fairness metric generates multiple outcomes for distinct sensitive attributes, complicating analysis even further.

To address these challenges, we propose the Multi-dimensional Fairness Bonded Utility (MFBU), which enables the simultaneous evaluation of model performance and fairness through a single consolidated result. Specifically, the MFBU framework consists of three conceptual components that address fundamental challenges in fairness evaluation: **i) Creating a trade-off baseline:** To properly evaluate fairness techniques, we need a standard reference point that reflects inherent trade-offs between performance and fairness. This baseline serves as the foundation for all comparative analyses. **ii) Five effectiveness levels:** Complex numerical metrics alone are difficult to interpret. By categorizing techniques into meaningful effectiveness levels, we enable practitioners to quickly understand the qualitative impact of different approaches without requiring deep statistical knowledge. **iii) Quantitative evaluation of trade-offs:** Beyond categories, precise measurement of trade-offs is necessary for rigorous scientific comparison and optimization. This component allows researchers to quantify the difference between each method. Together, these three components form a comprehensive evaluation framework that bridges the gap between theoretical fairness metrics and practical decision-making. Detailed implementations for each of these components are provided below.

i) Creating a Trade-off Baseline. The foundation of MFBU's trade-off baseline is motivated by the zero-normalization principle proposed by Speicher *et al.* [37], stating that a model's bias is determined by its discriminatory predictions: a model is non-discriminatory if it gives up its predictive power. In other words, a model is not discriminatory if it makes random guesses for each individual, as the predictive performance becomes equally poor across different demographic groups. We use this concept to generate multiple pseudo-models, with a stricter baseline assuming the model makes a single guess that matches the majority label in the dataset. Thus, the model tries to maximize performance while achieving the best fairness. For example, in a loans dataset where 60% of applicants receive a loan and 40% are rejected, the model would be 60% accurate if it predicts everyone will receive a loan.

We visualize this concept by establishing a two-variable coordinate system as shown in Fig. 2(a), where the x-axis represents model fairness and the y-axis shows model performance. In this figure, the brown curve tracks how fairness varies across pseudo-models, while the yellow curve depicts corresponding changes in performance. MFBU evaluates models in this two-variable coordinate space, capturing variations across fairness techniques and establishing a trade-off baseline. This approach simplifies decision-making by providing a single consolidated metric that quantifies both performance and fairness, enabling direct comparison across techniques. Within this coordinate system, any combination of metrics can be used: the performance axis can utilize metrics such as Accuracy or F1-score, while the fairness axis can incorporate metrics like Statistical

Parity Difference or Equal Opportunity Difference. This flexibility allows MFBU to be tailored to specific application contexts and fairness definitions.

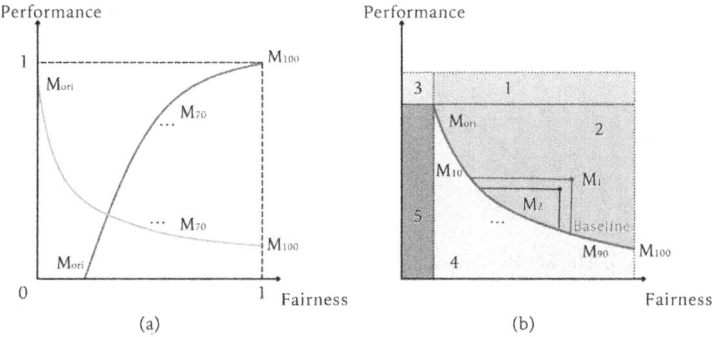

Fig. 2. The MFBU fairness-accuracy trade-off baseline is depicted by the original trade-off point (M_{ori}) and the points generated by the pseudo models ($M_{10}, \ldots, M_{100}$). A bias reduction method is considered effective if it shows a superior trade-off compared to the MFBU baseline, *i.e.*, it lies above the red line.

Specifically, MFBU analyze the original model by generating a set of 10 pseudo-models, denoted as M_p, each created by replacing varying percentages (p) of the original model's predictions with consistent output labels to systematically explore fairness improvements. Specifically, we consider percentages ranging from 10% to 100%. For example, in M_{10}, 10% of the original predictions are randomly selected and replaced with the majority class labels from the input dataset, while in 100%, all predicted labels are replaced with these majority class labels. As illustrated in Fig. 2(a), increasing the proportion of replaced predictions leads to improved fairness but simultaneously reduces model accuracy. These pseudo-models provide distinct points along the fairness-performance spectrum, forming the basis for our trade-off baseline analysis. To construct this baseline, we first plot the (performance, fairness) coordinates of the original unadjusted model, labeled as M_{ori} in Fig. 2(b). Subsequently, we plot the corresponding coordinates of each pseudo-model (e.g., M_{10}, M_{90}, M_{100}, etc.). By connecting these points, we establish the trade-off baseline, depicted as the red line in Fig. 2(b), clearly illustrating the relationship between fairness improvements and performance trade-offs.

For fairness measures designed for a single sensitive attribute, we can directly apply the fairness metric results on the x-axis. However, this is infeasible with multi-dimensional sensitive attributes, as existing fairness metrics generate multiple values for different sensitive attributes. To address this challenge while maintaining a two-dimensional visualization, we need to project these multiple values onto a single axis. Specifically, a model produces only one performance result (such as accuracy or F1-score) regardless of how many sensitive attributes are considered, but generates multiple fairness metrics—one for each sensitive attribute or their combinations—so we project these fairness values for different sensitive attributes onto the space while keeping the performance metric constant. As shown in Fig. 3, each dimension represents

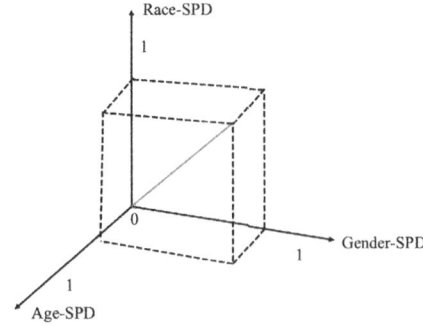

Fig. 3. The MFBU Measure Multi-dimensional Sensitive Attribute

the fairness value based on a sensitive attribute. We then apply the Euclidean distance vector to calculate a combined fairness result from the various fairness values across multi-dimensional sensitive attributes, effectively representing the multi-dimensional distribution of fairness metrics. This method transforms diverse fairness outcomes into a single indicator, improving the clarity of the trade-off analysis between model performance and fairness. Mathematically, this can be expressed as:

$$F_{multi} = \sqrt{\omega_1 * F_1^2 + \omega_2 * F_2^2 + \cdots + \omega_n * F_n^2} \tag{5}$$

where F_i are the single-sensitive-attribute fairness values and ω_i are the corresponding weight parameters with n representing the number of sensitive attributes. These weights adjust the relative importance of different sensitive attributes and can be customized for various application scenarios.

ii) Five Effectiveness Levels. The trade-off baseline provides a framework for categorizing bias mitigation techniques into five distinct effectiveness levels. As shown in Fig. 2 (b), Region 1 represents an *Optimal* scenario where a technique improves both model performance and fairness compared to the baseline. Region 2 represents the *Partial Win* scenario where techniques show improved performance or fairness compared to the baseline. Region 3 in Fig. 2 (b) represents the *Inverse* scenario, where a technique improves model performance but reduces fairness. The *Partial Loss* scenario is represented by Region 4, where techniques reduce either performance or fairness relative to the baseline. Finally, Region 5 signifies a *Regression* scenario where a technique reduces both performance and fairness compared to the baseline.

iii) Quantitative Evaluation of Trade-offs. The *Optimal*, *Partial Loss*, and *Regression* regions provide clear insights into effectiveness. For a more detailed comparison, we focus on the *Partial Win* category (Region 2). We evaluate different bias mitigation techniques by calculating the area enclosed by the bias-performance points and the baseline. This region, which we call the "Beneficial Balance" region, is shown in Fig. 2 (b). Techniques with larger areas are considered better, as they offer more favorable bias-performance balances. We use the area as a metric rather than the distance from the baseline to ensure fair comparison when the baseline curves.

Finally, MFBU produces five percentages for each technique, one for each region, showing the proportion of cases in that region. The total number of cases is calculated as: **Total Cases** = $n_r \times n_t \times n_f \times p_m$, where n_r is the number of run times, n_t is the number of techniques being compared, n_f is the number of fairness metrics used, and p_m is the number of performance metrics employed.

5 Experiments

Datasets. We conduct experiments on three real-world datasets: i) The **Adult** dataset [18], derived from US census data, is used to predict whether an individual's income exceeds $50K per year based on demographic attributes. Each entry in the dataset corresponds to an individual with information such as education, work class, marital status, and occupation. Race and gender are sensitive attributes. ii) The **COMPAS** dataset [2] is used to predict likelihood of criminal recidivism. Each record corresponds to a criminal defendant with data points such as age, charge degree, and number of priors. The sensitive attributes are the defendant's race and age. iii) The **German credit** dataset [3], used to predict credit risk status, contains credit information from clients of a German bank. Each entry corresponds to an individual with their credit risk categorized as 'good' or 'bad.' The sensitive attributes are age and gender.

Baselines. We compare against four state-of-the-art fairness methods. The first, Mini-Max [28], takes a game-theoretic approach to multi-discrimination, formulating it as a mini-max game and aiming for a Pareto efficient solution within a multi-objective problem context. The second, pre-processing method Fair-SMOTE [58], enhances model fairness without requiring direct observation of sensitive attributes. It leverages synthetic minority over-sampling to balance subgroup distribution to improve future predictions' fairness. FairLearn [1], the third baseline, imposes a set of linear fairness constraints on an exponentiated-gradient reduction technique for multi-discrimination. The last baseline, $\text{Kamiran}_{\text{sum}}$ [22], incorporates discrimination awareness directly into the learning process.

Evaluation Metrics. We use accuracy, F1-Score, and the Matthews Correlation Coefficient (MCC) [5] to assess our model. All three can be calculated from a confusion matrix (TP, FP, TN, FN) [25]. Higher accuracy, F1-Score, and MCC values indicate better performance. For fairness evaluation, we measure Statistical Parity Difference (SPD) and Equal Opportunity Difference (EOD), which are widely used metrics [29]. Larger values of SPD and EOD indicate higher levels of bias.

5.1 Experiment Results

RQ1: Does the proposed MFDT help in reducing bias? We compare the performance-fairness trade-off of our proposed method, MFDT, against the five baselines. The results are demonstrated in Table 1. Dark and light blue denote the best and second-best performance, respectively. MFDT achieves superior performance on the Adult dataset in terms of F1-score, and SPD for both race and gender, and EOD for race, showcasing its balanced performance between precision and recall, and lower disparate impact and equality of opportunity difference, thereby reducing bias. It is also

Table 1. Performance and fairness comparison of various classification models on real-world datasets - Adult, COMPAS, and Credit. (Dark blue cells denote best and light blue cells denote second-best results.)

Dataset	Methods	Accuracy	F1-Score	MCC	SPD-Race	SPD-Gender	EOD-Race	EOD-Gender
Adult	MiniMax	0.86	0.79	0.56	0.05	0.09	0.06	0.08
	Fair-SMOTE	0.84	0.78	0.57	0.09	0.15	0.05	0.09
	FairLearn	0.83	0.75	0.52	0.08	0.11	0.10	0.09
	Kamiran$_{sum}$ – Race	0.78	0.61	0.52	0.17	0.24	0.15	0.19
	Kamiran$_{sum}$ – Gender	0.77	0.62	0.54	0.22	0.16	0.17	0.13
	MFDT	0.84	0.79	0.55	0.04	0.08	0.04	0.08
COMPAS	MiniMax	0.82	0.75	0.46	0.10	0.13	0.03	0.02
	Fair-SMOTE	0.66	0.66	0.33	0.12	0.10	0.05	0.02
	FairLearn	0.79	0.71	0.44	0.09	0.10	0.02	0.01
	Kamiran$_{sum}$ – Race	0.54	0.48	0.26	0.13	0.16	0.8	0.12
	Kamiran$_{sum}$ – Gender	0.51	0.43	0.23	0.13	0.15	0.06	0.11
	MFDT	0.80	0.78	0.45	0.08	0.08	0.02	0.01
German	MiniMax	0.75	0.69	0.41	0.11	0.08	0.03	0.05
	Fair-SMOTE	0.77	0.71	0.43	0.09	0.07	0.05	0.03
	FairLearn	0.75	0.70	0.42	0.05	0.06	0.03	0.04
	Kamiran$_{sum}$ – Age	0.73	0.67	0.40	0.15	0.18	0.17	0.22
	Kamiran$_{sum}$ – Gender	0.70	0.64	0.41	0.16	0.14	0.18	0.20
	MFDT	0.78	0.70	0.43	0.04	0.06	0.02	0.02

successful on the COMPAS dataset, outperforming other models in the F1-score, as well as SPD and EOD for both race and gender. Lastly, on the German credit dataset, MFDT excels in accuracy, MCC, SPD, and EOD for both age and gender, highlighting its ability to balance fairness and accuracy across diverse datasets. These results substantiate that our proposed MFDT model effectively reduces bias, as evidenced by its top-ranking performance in terms of SPD and EOD across different protected attributes in diverse datasets. Simultaneously, it maintains competitive accuracy, F1-score, and MCC scores compared to existing methods, indicating a favorable trade-off between fairness and performance. Therefore, we affirm that MFDT is indeed helpful in reducing bias in classification tasks.

RQ2: What is the trade-off of effectiveness between MFDT and other state-of-the-art methods? With the proposed MFBU, we can evaluate the trade-off between Multi-fairness and performance with one illustrative metric. As shown in Fig. 4, MFDT consistently outperforms existing methods. MFDT frequently facilitates improvements in both model performance and fairness, as demonstrated with 28% of all cases in the 'Optimal' category, noticeably outperforming other methods. In the 'Partial Win' scenario, which embodies instances where either performance or fairness improved, MFDT accounts for 57% of the cases, outperforming the baseline. It also performs exceptionally well in preventing the 'Regression' trade-off scenario, making up just 1% of cases. Overall, MFDT is a robust and effective approach for managing trade-offs between performance and fairness, especially for multiple sensitive attributes in real-world fairness problems. Further, these findings echo results from RQ1, reaffirming the validity of the MFBU framework. This alignment strengthens our assertion that MFBU is an effective

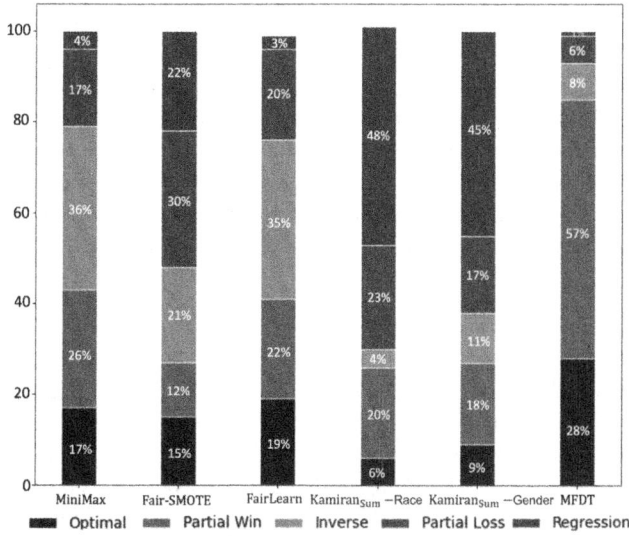

Fig. 4. Different methods' effectiveness distribution in benchmark tasks.

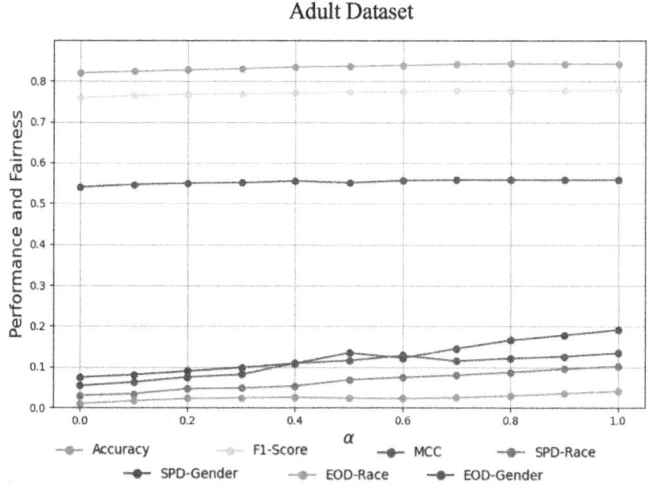

Fig. 5. Effect of α on performance and fairness metrics.

metric for evaluating and comparing performance-fairness trade-offs for multiple bias mitigation methods, proving its effectiveness in real-world applications.

RQ3: How does hyperparameter α impact the balance between classification performance and fairness in MFDT? We answer this based on Fig. 5. As α varies between 0 and 1, it significantly changes the model's performance. Specifically, the model's accuracy generally increases as α increases, indicating that the model's performance improves with larger α. Similarly, the F1 score and MCC exhibit an upward trend with increasing α, implying an enhancement in the model's balance between precision and recall, and its correlation between the observed and predicted binary classifications. The fairness metrics also exhibit an increasing trend with higher α values, indicating a decline in model fairness. However, EOD-Race displays a unique pattern, forming an inverse bell curve, peaking around $\alpha = 0.5$ before declining. This pattern highlights the complex interplay between fairness and accuracy across different α values. In conclusion, there is a trade-off between performance and fairness as α increases. The value of α can be adjusted dynamically to satisfy task-specific requirements.

6 Conclusion

This paper examined multi-dimensional sensitive attributes in fair ML research, a complex challenge that cannot be solved by simply extending single-attribute approaches. We introduced Multi-Fairness Bonded Utility, the first unified metric for evaluating performance-fairness trade-offs among multi-source bias mitigation methods. We proposed Fair Intersectional Information Gain, a novel splitting criterion for fairness-aware decision trees that incorporates Pareto optimality. Our Multi-dimensional Fair Decision Tree provides tunable performance-fairness trade-offs with practical flexibility. Experimental results on real-world datasets validate the effectiveness of our framework with respect to both utility and fairness.

Acknowledgements. This work was supported in part by the National Science Foundation (NSF) under Grant No. 2404039.

References

1. Agarwal, A., Beygelzimer, A., Dudík, M., Langford, J., Wallach, H.: A reductions approach to fair classification. In: International Conference on Machine Learning, pp. 60–69. PMLR (2018)
2. Angwin, J., Larson, J., Mattu, S., Kirchner, L.: Machine bias. In: Ethics of Data and Analytics, pp. 254–264. Auerbach Publications (2016)
3. Asuncion, A., Newman, D.: UCI machine learning repository (2007)
4. Barata, A.P., Takes, F.W., van den Herik, H.J., Veenman, C.J.: The expose approach to crosslier detection. In: 2020 25th International Conference on Pattern Recognition (ICPR), pp. 2312–2319. IEEE (2021)
5. Chicco D., J.G.: A statistical comparison between matthews correlation coefficient (MCC), prevalence threshold, and Fowlkes–Mallows index. J. Biomed. Inform. 104426 (2023)
6. Chinta, S.V., , et al.: Optimization and improvement of fake news detection using voting technique for societal benefit. In: 2023 IEEE International Conference on Data Mining Workshops (ICDMW), pp. 1565–1574. IEEE (2023)
7. Chinta, S.V., et al.: Fairaied: navigating fairness, bias, and ethics in educational ai applications. arXiv preprint arXiv:2407.18745 (2024)
8. Chinta, S.V., et al.: AI-driven healthcare: A survey on ensuring fairness and mitigating bias. arXiv preprint arXiv:2407.19655 (2024)
9. Chu, Z., Wang, Z., Zhang, W.: Fairness in large language models: a taxonomic survey. ACM SIGKDD Explorations Newsl **2024**, 34–48 (2024)

10. Corbett-Davies, S., Goel, S.: The measure and mismeasure of fairness: A critical review of fair machine learning. arXiv preprint arXiv:1808.00023 (2018)
11. Deb, K.: Multi-objective optimisation using evolutionary algorithms: an introduction. Springer (2011)
12. Doan, T.V., Chu, Z., Wang, Z., Zhang, W.: Fairness definitions in language models explained. arXiv preprint arXiv:2407.18454 (2024)
13. Doan, T.V., Wang, Z., Nguyen, M.N., Zhang, W.: Fairness in large language models in three hours. In: Proceedings of the 33rd ACM International Conference on Information & Knowledge Management (2024)
14. Dressel, J., Farid, H.: The accuracy, fairness, and limits of predicting recidivism. Sci. Adv. **4**(1), eaao5580 (2018)
15. Dwork, C., Hardt, M., Pitassi, T., Reingold, O., Zemel, R.: Fairness through awareness. In: Proceedings of the 3rd Innovations in Theoretical Computer Science Conference, pp. 214–226 (2012)
16. Dzuong, J., Wang, Z., Zhang, W.: Uncertain boundaries: Multidisciplinary approaches to copyright issues in generative AI. arXiv preprint arXiv:2404.08221 (2024)
17. Foulds, J.R., Islam, R., Keya, K.N., Pan, S.: An intersectional definition of fairness. In: 2020 IEEE 36th International Conference on Data Engineering (ICDE), pp. 1918–1921. IEEE (2020)
18. Fox, J., Carvalho, M.S.: The RcmdrPlugin.survival package: extending the R commander interface to survival analysis. J. Statist. Softw. **49**, 1–32 (2012)
19. Hardt, M., Price, E., Srebro, N.: Equality of opportunity in supervised learning. Adv. Neural Inform. Process. Syst. **29** (2016)
20. Jeong, H., Wang, H., Calmon, F.P.: Fairness without imputation: a decision tree approach for fair prediction with missing values. In: Proceedings of the AAAI Conference on Artificial Intelligence, vol. 36, pp. 9558–9566 (2022)
21. Kamiran, F., Calders, T.: Data preprocessing techniques for classification without discrimination. Knowl. Inf. Syst. **33**(1), 1–33 (2012)
22. Kamiran, F., Calders, T., Pechenizkiy, M.: Discrimination aware decision tree learning. In: 2010 IEEE International Conference on Data Mining, pp. 869–874. IEEE (2010)
23. Kamishima, T., Akaho, S., Asoh, H., Sakuma, J.: Fairness-aware classifier with prejudice remover regularizer. In: Flach, P.A., De Bie, T., Cristianini, N. (eds.) ECML PKDD 2012. LNCS (LNAI), vol. 7524, pp. 35–50. Springer, Heidelberg (2012). https://doi.org/10.1007/978-3-642-33486-3_3
24. Tian, H., Liu, B., Zhu, T., Zhou, W., Yu, P.S.: MultiFair: model fairness with multiple sensitive attributes. IEEE Trans. Neural Netw. Learn. Syst. **36**(3), 5654–5667 (2025)
25. Quy, T., Roy, A., Iosifidis, V., Zhang, W., Ntoutsi, E.: A survey on datasets for fairness-aware machine learning. Wiley Interdisciplinary Rev. Data Mining Knowl. Dis. **12**(3), e1452 (2022)
26. Linden, J., Weerdt, M., Demirović, E.: Fair and optimal decision trees: a dynamic programming approach. Adv. Neural. Inf. Process. Syst. **35**, 38899–38911 (2022)
27. Lum, K., Isaac, W.: To predict and serve? Significance **13**(5), 14–19 (2016)
28. Martinez, N., Bertran, M., Sapiro, G.: Minimax pareto fairness: a multi objective perspective. In: International Conference on Machine Learning, pp. 6755–6764. PMLR (2020)
29. Mehrabi, N., Morstatter, F., Saxena, N., Lerman, K., Galstyan, A.: A survey on bias and fairness in machine learning. ACM Comput. Surv. (CSUR) **54**(6), 1–35 (2021)
30. Morina, G., Oliinyk, V., Waton, J., Marusic, I., Georgatzis, K.: Auditing and achieving intersectional fairness in classification problems. arXiv preprint arXiv:1911.01468 (2019)
31. Madden, M., et al.: Teens, social media, and privacy. Pew Res. Center **21**(1055), 2–86 (2013)
32. Ross Quinlan, J.: C4.5: Programs for Machine Learning. Morgan Kaufmann (1993)

33. Quinlan, R.: 4.5: Programs for machine learning morgan kaufmann publishers inc. San Francisco, USA (1993)
34. Quinlan, J.R.: Induction of decision trees. Mach. Learn. **1**, 81–106 (1986)
35. Robles Herrera, S., Monjezi, V., Kreinovich, V., Trivedi, A., Tizpaz-Niari, S.: Predicting fairness of ML software configurations. In: Proceedings of the 20th International Conference on Predictive Models and Data Analytics in Software Engineering, pp. 56–65 (2024)
36. Sarker, I.H.: Machine learning: algorithms, real-world applications and research directions. SN Comput. Sci. **2**(3), 160 (2021)
37. Speicher, T., et al.: A unified approach to quantifying algorithmic unfairness: Measuring individual &group unfairness via inequality indices. In: Proceedings of the 24th ACM SIGKDD International Conference on Knowledge Discovery & Data Mining, pp. 2239–2248 (2018)
38. Tan, Y.C., Celis, L.E.: Assessing social and intersectional biases in contextualized word representations. Adv. Neural Inform. Process. Syst. **32** (2019)
39. Uddin, S., Lu, H., Rahman, A., Gao, J.: A novel approach for assessing fairness in deployed machine learning algorithms. Sci. Rep. **14**(1), 17753 (2024)
40. Wang, Z., Chu, Z., Blanco, R., Chen, Z., Chen, S.C., Zhang, W.: Advancing graph counterfactual fairness through fair representation learning. In: Joint European Conference on Machine Learning and Knowledge Discovery in Databases, pp. 40–58. Springer Nature Switzerland (2024). https://doi.org/10.1007/978-3-031-70368-3_3
41. Wang, Z., et al.: Fair graph u-net: a fair graph learning framework integrating group and individual awareness. In: proceedings of the AAAI Conference on Artificial Intelligence, vol. 39, pp. 28485–28493 (2025)
42. Wang, Z., et al.: Individual fairness with group awareness under uncertainty. In: Joint European Conference on Machine Learning and Knowledge Discovery in Databases, pp. 89–106. Springer Nature Switzerland (2024). https://doi.org/10.1007/978-3-031-70362-1_6
43. Wang, Z., Narasimhan, G., Yao, X., Zhang, W.: Mitigating multisource biases in graph neural networks via real counterfactual samples. In: 2023 IEEE International Conference on Data Mining (ICDM), pp. 638–647. IEEE (2023)
44. Wang, Z., Qiu, M., Chen, M., Salem, M.B., Yao, X., Zhang, W.: Toward fair graph neural networks via real counterfactual samples. Knowl. Inform. Syst., 1–25 (2024)
45. Wang, Z., et al.: Towards fair graph learning without demographic information. The 28th International Conference on Artificial Intelligence and Statistics, vol. 258, pp. 2107–2115 (2025)
46. Wang, Z., et al.: Preventing discriminatory decision-making in evolving data streams. In: Proceedings of the 2023 ACM Conference on Fairness, Accountability, and Transparency, pp. 149–159 (2023)
47. Wang, Z., Ulloa, D., Yu, T., Rangaswami, R., Yap, R., Zhang, W.: Individual fairness with group constraints in graph neural networks. In: 27th European Conference on Artificial Intelligence (2024)
48. Wang, Z., Wallace, C., Bifet, A., Yao, X., Zhang, W.: Fg^2an: fairness-aware graph generative adversarial networks. In: Joint European Conference on Machine Learning and Knowledge Discovery in Databases, pp. 259–275. Springer Nature Switzerland (2023). https://doi.org/10.1007/978-3-031-43415-0_16
49. Wang, Z., et al.: Fg-smote: towards fair node classification with graph neural network. ACM SIGKDD Explorations Newsl **26**(2), 99–108 (2025)
50. Wang, Z., et al.: Graph fairness via authentic counterfactuals: tackling structural and causal challenges. ACM SIGKDD Explorations Newsl **26**(2), 89–98 (2025)
51. Wang, Z., Zhang, W.: Group fairness with individual and censorship constraints. In: 27th European Conference on Artificial Intelligence (2024)
52. Wang, Z., et al.: Towards fair machine learning software: Understanding and addressing model bias through counterfactual thinking. arXiv preprint arXiv:2302.08018 (2023)

53. Wang, Z., et al.: Towards fairness with limited demographics via disentangled learning. In: Proceedings of the 34th International Joint Conference on Artificial Intelligence (IJCAI), (2025)
54. Wang, Z., Zhang, W.: FDGen: a fairness-aware graph generation model. In: Proceedings of the 42nd International Conference on Machine Learning (ICML). PMLR (2025)
55. Wang, Z., et al.: fairGNN-WOD: fair graph learning without complete demographics. In: Proceedings of the 34th International Joint Conference on Artificial Intelligence (IJCAI) (2025)
56. Z., Wang, A., Palikhe, Z., Yin, Z., Zhang, W.: Fairness definitions in language models explained. arXiv preprint arXiv:2407.18454 (2024)
57. Wang, Z., et al.: Fairness-aware graph representation learning without demographic information. In: Joint European Conference on Machine Learning and Knowledge Discovery in Databases (ECML PKDD). Springer (2025)
58. Yan, S., Kao, H.t., Ferrara, E.: Fair class balancing: enhancing model fairness without observing sensitive attributes. In: Proceedings of the 29th ACM International Conference on Information & Knowledge Management, pp. 1715–1724 (2020)
59. Yazdani, S., Saxena, N., Wang, Z., Wu, Y., Zhang, W.: A comprehensive survey of image and video generative ai: Recent advances, variants, and applications (2024)
60. Yin, Z., et al.: Accessible health screening using body fat estimation by image segmentation. In: 2024 IEEE International Conference on Data Mining Workshops (ICDMW), pp. 405–414. IEEE (2024)
61. Yin, Z., et al.: Digital forensics in the age of large language models. arXiv preprint arXiv:2504.02963 (2025)
62. Zafar, M.B., Valera, I., Gomez-Rodriguez, M., Gummadi, K.P.: Fairness constraints: a flexible approach for fair classification. J. Mach. Learn. Res. **20**(1), 2737–2778 (2019)
63. Zafar, M.B., Valera, I., Rogriguez, M.G., Gummadi, K.P.: Fairness constraints: Mechanisms for fair classification. In: Artificial intelligence and Statistics, pp. 962–970. PMLR (2017)
64. Zhang, W., Bifet, A.: FEAT: a fairness-enhancing and concept-adapting decision tree classifier. In: Appice, A., Tsoumakas, G., Manolopoulos, Y., Matwin, S. (eds.) DS 2020. LNCS (LNAI), vol. 12323, pp. 175–189. Springer, Cham (2020). https://doi.org/10.1007/978-3-030-61527-7_12
65. Zhang, W., Hernandez-Boussard, T., Weiss, J.: Censored fairness through awareness. In: Proceedings of the AAAI Conference on Artificial Intelligence, vol. 37, pp. 14611–14619 (2023)
66. Zhang, W., Zhou, S., Walsh, T., Weiss, J.C.: Fairness amidst non-IID graph data: a literature review. AI Mag. **46**(1), article e12212 (2025)
67. Zhang, W.: AI fairness in practice: paradigm, challenges, and prospects. AI Mag. **45**(3), 386–395 (2024)
68. Zhang, W., Ntoutsi, E.: Faht: an adaptive fairness-aware decision tree classifier. In: Proceedings of the 28th International Joint Conference on Artificial Intelligence (2019)
69. Zhang, W., et al.: Individual fairness under uncertainty. In: 26th European Conference on Artificial Intelligence, pp. 3042–3049 (2023)
70. Zhang, W., Weiss, J.C.: Longitudinal fairness with censorship. In: Proceedings of the AAAI Conference on Artificial Intelligence, vol. 36, pp. 12235–12243 (2022)

Fairness-Aware Graph Representation Learning with Limited Demographic Information

Zichong Wang[1], Zhipeng Yin[1], Liping Yang[2], Jun Zhuang[3], Rui Yu[4], Qingzhao Kong[1], and Wenbin Zhang[1](✉)

[1] Florida International University, Miami, USA
{ziwang,wenbin.zhang}@fiu.edu
[2] University of New Mexico, Albuquerque, USA
[3] Boise State University, Boise, USA
[4] University of Louisville, Louisville, USA

Abstract. Ensuring fairness in Graph Neural Networks is fundamental to promoting trustworthy and socially responsible machine learning systems. In response, numerous fair graph learning methods have been proposed in recent years. However, most of them assume full access to demographic information, a requirement rarely met in practice due to privacy, legal, or regulatory restrictions. To this end, this paper introduces a novel fair graph learning framework that mitigates bias in graph learning under limited demographic information. Specifically, we propose a mechanism guided by partial demographic data to generate proxies for demographic information and design a strategy that enforces consistent node embeddings across demographic groups. In addition, we develop an adaptive confidence strategy that dynamically adjusts each node's contribution to fairness and utility based on prediction confidence. We further provide theoretical analysis demonstrating that our framework, FairGLite, achieves provable upper bounds on group fairness metrics, offering formal guarantees for bias mitigation. Through extensive experiments on multiple datasets and fair graph learning frameworks, we demonstrate the framework's effectiveness in both mitigating bias and maintaining model utility.

Keywords: Fairness · Limited Demographics · Graph neural networks

1 Introduction

Graph Neural Networks (GNNs) have become a prevalent approach for handling complex real-world applications, such as healthcare [1], social network analysis [25], and recommendation systems [10]. The success of GNNs relies on message-passing mechanisms, which aggregate information from neighboring nodes, effectively capturing both graph structural information and node attribute information [27,42]. However, despite their successes, GNNs tend to inherit and even exacerbate existing biases from graph data [29], propagating and amplifying unfair patterns embedded in network topology and features. This unintended amplification of societal biases and the potential for discriminatory outcomes have highlighted the urgent need to develop strategies that promote fairness within these systems. To this end, a number of approaches [30,34,45] have been proposed in recent years, with most relying on complete demographic information to guide fair graph learning.

However, this requirement often does not align with realistic situations, as collecting or explicitly utilizing demographic information (*e.g.*, gender, race) can be restricted or prohibited due to privacy concerns, legal constraints, ethical considerations, or social sensitivity [12,13,32]. For example, in many real-world graph datasets such as academic collaboration networks or online social platforms, demographic information is often missing, incomplete, or intentionally withheld to protect user privacy, with studies showing that less than 30% of users voluntarily disclose demographic information [17]. Consequently, fairness-aware graph methods that rely on full demographic information become impractical when only limited data is available. This misalignment between theoretical fairness requirements and real-world constraints significantly limits the applicability and deployment of existing approaches.

To fill this gap, a few works [13,21,36] have begun exploring fairness without full demographics. However, most of them focus on i.i.d. data settings and do not account for the relational characteristics of graphs. Therefore, these approaches cannot be readily applied to real-world graph data, leaving fairness-aware graph learning with limited demographic information as an open area of research with unique challenges: **i) Identifying missing demographic information from limited labels.** In real-world graphs, only a small subset of nodes discloses their demographics. These labels often overrepresent favored groups or cluster in specific regions of the graph, making it difficult to train reliable predictors for the missing demographics. Naively using such limited labels risks amplifying bias rather than reducing it. **ii) Enforcing fairness constraints with uncertain demographic labels.** Enforcing fairness constraints becomes particularly challenging when demographic labels are uncertain or sparse, as such uncertainty can reduce the accuracy of demographic group identification. This complicates the enforcement of fairness constraints, posing additional hurdles in maintaining fairness across different groups while achieving comparable prediction performance. **iii) Theoretical analysis of fairness guarantees under incomplete demographic information.** Providing rigorous theoretical guarantees for fairness metrics becomes inherently complex when demographic labels are incomplete or uncertain. Without complete demographic information, standard theoretical frameworks for fairness analysis may not directly apply, posing significant challenges in theoretically bounding fairness violations and ensuring reliable fairness guarantees.

To bridge this critical gap between theoretical fairness requirements and practical constraints, this paper proposes *Fair Graph Representation Learning with Limited Demographics (FairGLite)* specifically designed to mitigate bias in graph learning algorithms when only limited demographic information is available. *To the best of our knowledge, this is the first framework to address bias in graph learning under limited demographic information while providing theoretical guarantees.* Specifically, FairGLite leverages limited demographic labels to guide a causal-analysis-based encoder that generates proxies for missing demographic information. These proxies are then used to enforce representative constraints, ensuring fairness in node representations while preserving task-relevant information. To further balance fairness and utility, FairGLite employs an adaptive confidence strategy that applies fairness constraints primarily to high-confidence samples, mitigating performance loss while improving fairness on uncertain cases. Finally, we provide a theoretical analysis showing that FairGLite achieves an upper bound on fairness metrics, offering formal guarantees for fair predictions within our framework. The main contributions can be summarized as:

- Address the overlooked challenge of fair graph learning with incomplete demographics through a proxy-based framework that enforces fairness with three tailored constraints.
- Introduce an adaptive confidence strategy that balances fairness and utility by weighting samples according to classification confidence.
- Provide theoretical analysis establishing upper bounds on fairness metrics, offering formal guarantees for fair predictions.
- Demonstrate effectiveness on four real-world graph datasets, achieving strong bias mitigation while maintaining utility comparable to state-of-the-art methods.

2 Related Work

2.1 Fairness with Incomplete Demographic Information

In recent years, the research community has increasingly focused on developing fair machine learning models that function effectively even when demographic data is incomplete or unavailable [8]. Existing approaches primarily fall into two categories: proxy-based methods [5,21,41] and minimax fairness methods [3,16,23]; Proxy-based methods attempt to infer missing demographic information from correlated features or partial labels, while minimax fairness methods employ John Rawls' difference principle [22] to optimize performance for the least advantaged subgroup. However, these techniques are mainly designed for independent and identically distributed (i.i.d.) data, neglecting the complexities introduced by relational or graph-structured data. Consequently, applying these fairness methods directly to graph data remains challenging.

2.2 Fair Graph Learning

Extensive efforts have been made to specifically address fairness within graph neural networks by mitigating biases in training data [15,31] or by incorporating fairness-aware training frameworks [27,45]. The core idea behind most of these approaches is the removal of demographics-related information, thereby enforcing GNNs to make decisions independent of the demographic information [38]. Despite their great success, most existing fair GNNs assume access to predefined demographic information during training, which is impractical in most real-world socially sensitive applications due to privacy, legal, or regulatory restrictions [2]. To this end, initial works have started exploring fair graph learning with incomplete demographics. For instance, FairGNN [4] employs a demographic estimator combined with adversarial learning to predict missing demographics and improve fairness. Similarly, FairAC [6] aggregates features from neighbors through an attention mechanism to handle nodes with missing demographics. However, these methods fail to account for uneven demographic disclosure across groups, individuals from advantaged groups may disclose their demographics more readily, while disadvantaged groups may withhold them due to fears of discrimination. Such uneven availability can significantly hinder the effectiveness of these methods.

To address this limitation, FairGLite explicitly incorporates an adaptive confidence strategy designed to selectively impose fairness constraints primarily on nodes with high-confidence demographic predictions, effectively managing uneven demographic availability across different groups. Additionally, FairGLite provides rigorous theoretical analysis to establish fairness guarantees under scenarios with incomplete demographic information. This strategy enhances model fairness while minimizing negative impacts on overall model utility.

3 Notations

For clarity, the method and proofs are presented under a node classification setting with binary demographic information and binary labels. Specifically, a graph is represented as $\mathcal{G} = (\mathcal{V}, \mathcal{E}, \mathbf{X})$, where $|\mathcal{V}| = n$ is the number of nodes and $|\mathcal{E}| = r$ is the number of edges. The matrix $\mathbf{X} \in \mathbb{R}^{n \times d}$ contains d-dimensional feature vectors, with the uth row corresponding to node u. The adjacency matrix $\mathbf{A} \in \{0,1\}^{n \times n}$ has entries $\mathbf{A}_{u,k} = 1$ if there is an edge $e_{u,k} \in \mathcal{E}$ between nodes u and k, and $\mathbf{A}_{u,k} = 0$ otherwise. In addition, $S \in \{0,1\}^{n \times 1}$ denotes the demographic information while s_u for the value of u. Furthermore, $S_d = \{ u \mid s_u = 0 \}$ represents the deprived group (for example, female), and $S_f = \{ u \mid s_u = 1 \}$ refers to the favored group (for example, male). Each node u also has a one-hot ground-truth label y_u, and $\hat{y}_u$ is its predicted label. Lastly, $y_u = 1$ indicates a granted label and $y_u = 0$ denotes a rejected label.

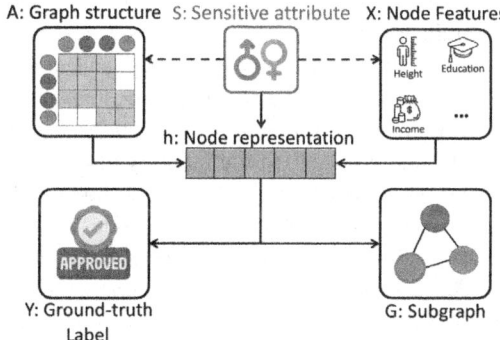

Fig. 1. Structural Causal Model for FairGLite.

4 The Proposed Framework FairGLite

4.1 Fair Causal Analysis

Existing works often rely on correlated non-demographic attributes as proxies for missing demographic information based on prior knowledge [8]. However, identifying accurate proxies from high-dimensional non-identically distributed data is both challenging and critical for ensuring fairness. To address this, we employ causal analysis to characterize the underlying mechanisms in the observed graph explicitly. We focus on fair node classification without full demographic information and construct a Structural Causal Model (SCM) [19], as shown in Fig. 1. The SCM captures the causal relationships among six variables: Demographic Information (S), Ground-Truth Label (Y), Graph Structure (A), Node Features (X), Ego-graph (G), and Node Representation (h). Each edge in the SCM represents a causal link. Specifically, S is determined at birth and thus has no parent variable, but influences other variables, including X and A. Furthermore, S, X, and A collectively affect the final node representation through the GNN message-passing mechanism, which should also preserve task-relevant information for downstream node classification and ego-graph reconstruction.

4.2 FairGLite Framework

Guided by the proposed fair causal model, FairGLite continues to learn fair node representations despite limited access to demographic information. As illustrated in Fig. 2, FairGLite operates through three interconnected modules: (i) a demographic information identification module, (ii) a fair node representation learning module, and (iii) an adaptivity confidence strategy module. Initially, the input graph, where nodes are marked with known or unknown demographic labels, is passed to the demographic information identification module. Here, node representations are generated by aggregating information from neighboring nodes' structural features and non-sensitive attributes, forming demographic proxies. These proxies assign pseudo demographic labels to nodes with initially unknown labels, as visually indicated in Fig. 2. Next, these demographic proxies are utilized in the fair node representation learning module. FairGLite generates node embeddings subject to three constraints, visually represented by different stages in the figure: the fairness constraint applies learnable masking vectors, depicted as bars beside the nodes, to reduce demographic identifiability in embeddings; the information constraint preserves predictive information, and the graph reconstruction constraint ensures the ego-graph structural integrity of the node embeddings, illustrated by maintaining graph connections. Finally, these node embeddings are passed into the adaptivity confidence strategy module, where nodes are weighted based on the confidence of demographic identification, clearly represented by adjusted node weights in Fig. 2. Higher-confidence nodes receive stronger fairness enforcement, depicted by changes in node weight values in Fig. 2, thus selectively emphasizing fairness constraints. Additionally, FairGLite is theoretically supported by deriving upper bounds on fairness metrics, providing formal guarantees that reducing representation disparities leads to improved fairness outcomes in downstream tasks. Each of these modules will be detailed in the following discussion.

4.3 Demographic Information Identification Module

This module aims to infer missing demographic labels using the observed graph data (*i.e.*, X and A) in conjunction with partially available demographic labels. As demographic information is assumed to influence both graph structure and node features,

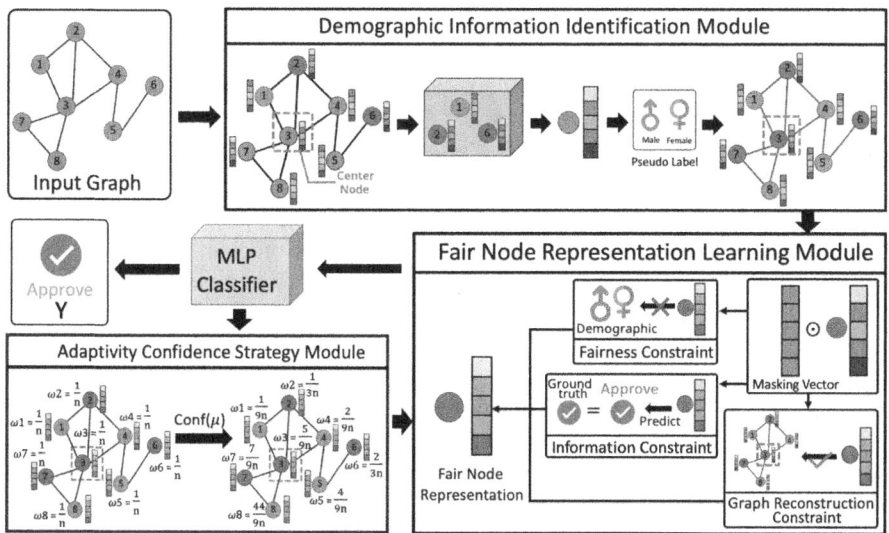

Fig. 2. An illustration of the proposed framework FairGLite.

and to model this effect, we construct a proxy by integrating representations of the graph structure with the node features. Specifically, a graph encoder is employed to generate this proxy, as it is capable of capturing complex patterns in high-dimensional non-identically distributed data and combining information from graph structure and features, even when only a limited number of demographic labels are available. Formally, the encoder is defined as follows:

$$\mathbf{h}_u^{(l)} = \xi \mathbf{h}_u^{(l-1)} + \sum_{k \in \mathcal{N}(u)} \alpha_{u,k}^{(l)} \mathrm{ReLU}\left(\mathbf{W}^{(l)} \mathbf{h}_k^{(l-1)}\right), \quad \alpha_{u,k}^{(l)} = \frac{\exp\left(e_{u,k}^{(l)}\right)}{\sum_{k \in \mathcal{N}(u)} \exp\left(e_{u,k}^{(l)}\right)} \tag{1}$$

where $\mathbf{h}_u^{(l)}$ represents the embedding of node u at layer l, and $\mathbf{h}_u^{(l-1)}$ is the embedding from the previous layer. In addition, the parameter ξ is a learnable scalar that controls how much of the previous representation is retained at layer l, the matrix $\mathbf{W}^{(l)}$ is a learnable weight matrix, and $\mathrm{ReLU}(\cdot)$ is the nonlinear activation function. The set $\mathcal{N}(u)$ denotes the neighborhood of the center node u, representing all nodes directly connected to u in the graph. The attention coefficient $\alpha_{u,k}^{(l)}$ reflects the relative importance of neighbor k to node u in the aggregation process.

Based on the encoder architecture, the module is trained via a supervised classification task aimed at predicting missing demographic information. The encoder parameters are learned by minimizing the cross-entropy loss between predicted and observed demographic labels. This supervision encourages the encoder to map nodes with similar demographics to nearby points in the representation space, even when partial label availability is present. Once training converges, the encoder parameters are fixed and subsequently used as a feature extractor that transforms high-dimensional node features into compact, informative embeddings. These low-dimensional representations function as proxies for demographic information in later components of the framework. This approach enables the model to indirectly capture and regulate the effects of missing demographic attributes, despite the absence of complete ground-truth labels.

4.4 Fair Node Representation Learning Module

With demographic proxies obtained from the identification module, the fair node representation learning module tackles the challenge of producing embeddings that remain predictive for downstream tasks while mitigating bias. As discussed earlier, nodes sharing the same demographic information often tend to be more densely connected, creating homophilic clusters within the graph. During message-passing, this structural bias becomes encoded into node representations, as the aggregation process smooths node representations among nodes sharing the same demographic information while amplifying differences across groups [43]. Hence, the learned node representations become overly associated with demographic information. To address this issue, we propose a fair learning strategy based on learnable feature masking. Our approach generates fair node representations by applying a learnable masking vector to original node features, effectively filtering out demographic-related information while preserving task-relevant information. Specifically, we utilize a learnable masking mechanism to minimize disparities in node representations between subpopulations with different demographic information. This masking approach aims to produce fair node representations that satisfy three key objectives: i) Demographic information becomes less identifiable from the transformed representations, ii) Task-relevant information is preserved for accurate downstream predictions, and iii) Graph structural relationships are maintained to ensure representation quality. To achieve these objectives simultaneously, we design a multi-constraint optimization framework with three complementary components:

Fairness Constraint. The fairness constraint aims to minimize representation disparities between different demographic subgroups. To formalize this objective, we first establish a theoretical analysis for measuring bias in node representations, then develop a masking-based approach to mitigate such disparities. Specifically, we quantify representation bias as the disparity between group-averaged embeddings as follows:

$$\Delta_{\text{bias}} = \left\| \frac{1}{|S_d|} \sum_{v_i \in S_d} \mathbf{h}_i - \frac{1}{|S_f|} \sum_{v_j \in S_f} \mathbf{h}_j \right\|_2 \qquad (2)$$

To further measure this bias in the context of GNN message-passing, we introduce a representation constraint on node embeddings. Specifically, each node v_i have a node representation $h_i^{(l)} = [z_1, z_2, \ldots, z_{d_h}]$ subject to $\mu^{(d)} - \Delta^l \preceq h_i^{(l)} \preceq \mu^{(d)} + \Delta^l$ [11], where the parameter Δ^l serves as a tolerance per layer indicating the allowed deviation of the representation from group mean ($\mu^{(d)}$) along each coordinate. Hence, we quantify the node representation disparity between demographic subgroups during GNN message-passing, which can be upper-bounded as follows:

$$\mathbf{h}_D^{(l)} = \left\| \frac{1}{N_d} \sum_{i \in \mathcal{S}_d} \mathbf{h}_i^{(l)} - \frac{1}{N_f} \sum_{j \in \mathcal{S}_f} \mathbf{h}_j^{(l)} \right\| \quad (3)$$

$$\leq \left(3 - \frac{1}{N_d N_f} \sum_{i \in \mathcal{S}_d} \sum_{u \in \mathcal{S}_f} k\left(\sigma(\mathbf{W}^{(l)}\mathbf{h}_u^{(l-1)}), \sigma(\mathbf{W}^{(l)}\mathbf{h}_i^{(l-1)})\right) \right.$$

$$\left. - \frac{1}{N_f N_d} \sum_{j \in \mathcal{S}_f} \sum_{u \in \mathcal{S}_d} k\left(\sigma(\mathbf{W}^{(l)}\mathbf{h}_u^{(l-1)}), \sigma(\mathbf{W}^{(l)}\mathbf{h}_j^{(l-1)})\right) \right) \left\| \mu_{l-1}^{(d)} - \mu_{l-1}^{(f)} \right\|$$

$$+ \left\| \mu^{(d)} - \mu^{(f)} \right\| + \left[C^{(l)} \cdot \frac{1}{4} \left\| W^{(l)} \right\|_2 \left(\left(1 + \frac{2}{N_f}\right) \sqrt{d_h} \Delta^{l-1} + \Delta_{\text{base}}^{(l)} \right) \right]$$

where the function $\sigma(\cdot)$ is the activation (*e.g.*, sigmoid), and the constant $C^{(K)} \geq 0$ absorbs fixed numerical factors. In addition, Δ^{l-1} denotes the per-coordinate tolerance at layer $l-1$, and $\Delta_{\text{base}}^{(l)}$ collects layer-l approximation slack. What's more, the N_d and N_f are the number of nodes belonging to the favored and deprived groups.

Building on the node representation disparity shown in Eq. 3, we establish an upper bound on the demographic parity violation, providing theoretical guarantees that connect the bias measure to downstream fairness metrics, as detailed in Theorem 4.1 (proof in appendix[1]):

Theorem 4.1 *In a node classification task, minimizing node representation discrepancies between two demographic subgroups bounds the disparity as follows:*

$$\Delta_{\text{DP}} = \left| \frac{1}{|V_{\mathcal{S}_d}|} \sum_{i \in \mathcal{S}_d} f(\mathbf{z}_i)_1 - \frac{1}{|V_{\mathcal{S}_f}|} \sum_{j \in \mathcal{S}_f} f(\mathbf{z}_j)_1 \right|$$

$$\leq \left| f(\mathbf{z}_{\mu^{(d)}})_1 - f(\mathbf{z}_{\mu^{(f)}})_1 \right| + \frac{L}{2} \left(\frac{1}{N_d} \sum_i \left\| \mathbf{z}_i - \mathbf{z}_{\mu^{(d)}} \right\| + \frac{1}{N_f} \sum_j \left\| \mathbf{z}_j - \mathbf{z}_{\mu^{(f)}} \right\| \right) \quad (4)$$

where $\mathbf{z}_i = W^l \mathbf{h}_i^{(l)}$, and $W^{(l)}$ is the weight matrix in layer l.

This theorem establishes that minimizing representation disparities between demographic groups provides theoretical guarantees for downstream fairness. Building upon this theoretical foundation, we propose a fairness regularizer to mitigate structural and feature disparities simultaneously. Specifically, we propose a masking-based fairness regularizer that acts on both the masked aggregated representations and the masked node features. For each node v_i, we learn a masking vector $\mathbf{m}_i = [m_{i,1}, m_{i,2}, \ldots, m_{i,d_h}]$ and form:

$$\tilde{\mathbf{h}}_i = \mathbf{h}_i \odot \mathbf{m}_i = [h_{i,1} m_{i,1}, h_{i,2} m_{i,2}, \ldots, h_{i,d_h} m_{i,d_h}] \quad (5)$$

where $\odot$ denotes element-wise product, and $\tilde{\mathbf{h}}_i$ represent the fair node representation of node v_i.

---

[1] https://zichongwang.com/files/FairGLiteAppendix.pdf.

The masking vectors are learned by minimizing an MMD-based bias measure on masked representations:

$$\mathcal{L}_F = \frac{1}{N_d^2} \sum_{v_i \in \mathcal{S}_d} \sum_{v_j \in \mathcal{S}_d} k(\tilde{\mathbf{h}}_i, \tilde{\mathbf{h}}_j) + \frac{1}{N_f^2} \sum_{v_i \in \mathcal{S}_f} \sum_{v_j \in \mathcal{S}_f} k(\tilde{\mathbf{h}}_i, \tilde{\mathbf{h}}_j) \quad (6)$$
$$- \frac{2}{N_d N_f} \sum_{v_i \in \mathcal{S}_d} \sum_{v_j \in \mathcal{S}_f} k(\tilde{\mathbf{h}}_i, \tilde{\mathbf{h}}_j)$$

where $k(\cdot)$ denotes the differentiable positive semidefinite kernels (*e.g.*, RBF kernel).

Furthermore, to avoid scenarios where the model collapses nodes into a single subgroup instead of genuinely reducing disparities between different subgroups, an additional penalty term is introduced to explicitly discourage representations highly correlated with demographic labels:

$$\mathcal{L}_R = \sum_{c=1}^{d_h} \left(\text{Cov}(s, \hat{h}_{s,c}) \right)^2 \quad (7)$$

where $\text{Cov}(\cdot)$ denotes the covariance.

In summary, the fairness constraint effectively minimizes representation disparities between demographic subgroups and simultaneously penalizes excessive correlations with demographic labels. The integration of both the masking-based regularizer and the covariance penalty ensures that nodes from different demographic groups achieve similar masked representations, significantly reducing the influence of demographic information on downstream predictions while maintaining the capacity to encode task-relevant patterns.

Information Constraint. For each node v_i, the fair node representation $\tilde{\mathbf{h}}_{v_i}$ should preserve essential features and structural information, ensuring its usefulness for downstream tasks. In other words, the model should be able to make accurate label predictions using node representations (*i.e.*, $\tilde{\mathbf{h}}_{v_i} \to y_{v_i}$). As illustrated in Fig. 2, the information constraint ensures the retention of the task-related information to accurately predict the label in both the fair node embedding $\tilde{\mathbf{h}}_{v_i}$ and the original node embedding $\mathbf{h}_{v_i}$. Hence, the objective of the information constraint is to minimize the loss of the prediction model, as shown in Eq. 8:

$$\mathcal{L}_I = \frac{1}{|\mathcal{V}_L|} \sum_{v_i \in \mathcal{V}_L} -(y_{v_i} \log(\hat{y_{v_i}}) + (1 - y_{v_i}) \log(1 - \hat{y_{v_i}})) \quad (8)$$

where y_i is the one-hot encoding of the ground-truth label of node v_i, and $\hat{y}_{v_i}$ denotes the predicted probability of the correct label derived from the fair node representations.

Graph Reconstruction Constraint. For each node u, another objective is to ensure that its node representations accurately represent the node itself. This requirement is fulfilled by accurately reconstructing the ego-graph $\mathcal{G}_{v_i}$ from the new node embedding $\mathbf{h}'_i$. Formally, we define the graph reconstruction constraint as a graph structure reconstruction loss, $\mathcal{L}_G$:

$$\mathcal{L}_G = \frac{1}{|\mathcal{E}_{S_d}| + |\mathcal{E}_{S_f}|} \sum_{e_{i,j} \in \mathcal{E}} L(e_{i,j}, \hat{e}_{i,j}) \tag{9}$$

where $\mathcal{E}_{S_d}$ and $\mathcal{E}_{S_f}$ are sets of sampled edges connecting nodes from deprived and favored subgroups, respectively, and $L(\cdot)$ is the cross-entropy loss. The term $e_{i,j}$ denotes the actual connection status between nodes u and k, whereas $\hat{e}_{i,j} = \sigma(\mathbf{h}'_i {\mathbf{h}'_j}^\top)$ is the predicted probability of a link, with $\sigma(\cdot)$ representing the sigmoid function.

In summary, the graph reconstruction constraint helps preserve critical structural information in node embeddings, effectively preventing bias information. This ensures that the reconstructed ego-graph $\mathcal{G}_{v_i}$ remains consistent with the original graph topology, thereby accurately reflecting structural relationships while reducing demographic biases.

4.5 Adaptivity Confidence Strategy Module

Building on the previous two modules, this module entails an adaptive confidence strategy that intelligently modulates fairness enforcement based on the reliability of demographic predictions. The key insight driving this module is that fairness constraints should be applied more stringently to nodes where we have high confidence in their demographic group membership, while being more lenient with nodes whose demographic information remains uncertain. The rationale for this confidence-based weighting stems from the fundamental challenge of working with incomplete demographic information. When our demographic identification module makes highly confident predictions about a node's demographic information, we can trust these demographic proxies and should therefore enforce strict fairness constraints to prevent bias. However, when the demographic predictions are uncertain, applying strong fairness penalties may be counterproductive, as we might be enforcing constraints based on potentially incorrect demographic assignments.

To implement this adaptive approach, we define a confidence score ($\mathrm{conf}(v_i)$), for each node v_i, representing the reliability of the predicted demographic label. A predefined threshold τ is then utilized to categorize nodes into high-confidence and low-confidence groups. Nodes with confidence scores greater than or equal to τ are considered reliable, thus warranting stronger fairness enforcement to mitigate embedded biases. Conversely, nodes with confidence scores below are treated as uncertain, and fairness constraints are applied more leniently to avoid potential errors from inaccurate demographic predictions. Formally, the fairness loss can be expressed as:

$$\mathcal{L}_F = \sum_{i,i' \in \mathcal{S}_d} \alpha_i \alpha_{i'} \, k(\tilde{\mathbf{h}}_i, \tilde{\mathbf{h}}_{i'}) + \sum_{j,j' \in \mathcal{S}_f} \beta_j \beta_{j'} \, k(\tilde{\mathbf{h}}_j, \tilde{\mathbf{h}}_{j'}) - 2 \sum_{i \in \mathcal{S}_d} \sum_{j \in \mathcal{S}_f} \alpha_i \beta_j \, k(\tilde{\mathbf{h}}_i, \tilde{\mathbf{h}}_j), \tag{10}$$

where the confidence weights $\alpha_i = \frac{\mathrm{conf}(v_i)}{\sum_{v_k \in \mathcal{S}_d} \mathrm{conf}(v_k)}$ for $v_i \in \mathcal{S}_d$, and $\beta_j = \frac{\mathrm{conf}(v_j)}{\sum_{v_k \in \mathcal{S}_f} \mathrm{conf}(v_k)}$ for $v_j \in \mathcal{S}_f$ are normalized within each predicted demographic group, ensuring that nodes with high-confidence demographic predictions receive proportionally more emphasis in the fairness calculation, while nodes with uncertain demographic assignments contribute less to the fairness loss.

In addition to the adaptive fairness loss, an adaptive correlation penalty $\mathcal{L}_R$ is introduced to further strengthen fairness by explicitly reducing correlations between node representations and demographic labels. This penalty is formally defined as:

$$\mathcal{L}_R = \sum_{c=1}^{d_h} \left(\frac{1}{W} \sum_{i=1}^{n} w_i \left(s_i - \frac{1}{W} \sum_{u=1}^{n} w_u s_u \right) \left(\tilde{h}_{i,c} - \frac{1}{W} \sum_{v=1}^{n} w_v \tilde{h}_{v,c} \right) \right)^2 \quad (11)$$

In this way, nodes with high-confidence predictions receive more stringent fairness treatment, ensuring that their label prediction does not induce bias. Meanwhile, nodes with low-confidence predictions incur a smaller fairness penalty, acknowledging that the classifier's uncertainty already diminishes the likelihood of discrimination arising from their representations while also helping the model increase the confidence of its predictions. In summary, the adaptivity confidence strategy module first focuses on nodes whose demographic information has been reliably identified, accurately enforcing stronger fairness constraints for these high-confidence cases. Meanwhile, for nodes with initially uncertain demographic information, the module imposes milder constraints, allowing the model to progressively refine its predictions. As confidence in demographic identification for these uncertain nodes increases over time, fairness constraints are correspondingly strengthened. Through this dynamic approach, the module systematically enhances model fairness while preserving high prediction accuracy.

4.6 Overall Learning Object

To jointly optimize utility and fairness, FairGLite employs a unified loss function within its fair graph representation learning framework under limited demographics. This loss integrates three components: (i) information loss to preserve task-relevant signals, (ii) graph reconstruction loss to recover the graph structure, and (iii) fairness loss to eliminate demographic information. The overall objective is formulated as:

$$\min \; \mathcal{L}_{\text{total}} = \mathcal{L}_I + a\mathcal{L}_G + b(\mathcal{L}_F + \mathcal{L}_R), \quad (12)$$

where a and b are tunable hyperparameters to balance the contributions of the various elements in the overall objective function, with $\mathcal{L}_I$, $\mathcal{L}_G$, $\mathcal{L}_F$, and $\mathcal{L}_R$ corresponding to the utility loss, the graph reconstruction loss, the fairness loss, and the correlation penalty loss that explicitly penalizes excessive correlations between node representations and demographic labels, respectively.

5 Experiment

This section presents the experimental evaluation of FairGLite. We first describe the datasets, baseline methods, and evaluation metrics, followed by the presentation and analysis of results. Due to space constraints, additional evaluations are provided in the appendix (see footnote 1).

5.1 Experimental Settings

Datasets. We evaluate FairGLite on four widely used real-world datasets, *i.e.*, the **Credit** dataset [37], **Pokec-z** and **Pokec-n** datasets [26], and the **NBA** dataset [4]. The **Credit** dataset consists of credit card holders represented as nodes, connected by edges based on similarities in spending and payment behaviors. Each node includes transaction-related features. The **Pokec-z** and **Pokec-n** datasets originate from a popular social network in Slovakia, corresponding to two distinct provincial sub-networks. Nodes represent users characterized by attributes such as gender, age, and interests, while edges represent friendships. The prediction task involves classifying users' occupational fields. The **NBA** dataset models professional basketball players as nodes, connected based on similarity in performance metrics. The prediction task is to determine if a player's salary exceeds the league average. The detailed statistics of these datasets are shown in Table 1. In all datasets, isolated nodes are removed before experiments. The data is partitioned into training (50%), validation (20%), and testing (30%) sets. To evaluate the effectiveness of our method under scenarios with incomplete demographic information, we randomly select 40% of nodes in the training and validation sets and mask their demographic labels, while maintaining complete labeling of demographic information in the testing set.

Table 1. Summary of the datasets in the experiments.

Dataset	Credit	Pokec-z	Pokec-n	NBA
Vertices	30,000	67,797	66,569	403
Edges	137,377	882,765	729,129	16,570
Feature Dimension	13	65	65	97
Demographics	Age	Region	Region	Country

Baselines. We compare FairGLite with several state-of-the-art methods, grouped into two categories. **(i) Vanilla Graph Model:** GCN [9], which applies spectral graph convolutions without fairness constraints. **(ii) Fairness-aware Methods:** FairKD [3], which trains a teacher model to overfit and generate soft labels that guide a student model via knowledge distillation; KSMOTE [36], which uses clustering to assign proxy demographic labels and balances subgroups through synthetic oversampling; FairRF [41], which mitigates feature-related biases directly without requiring demographic attributes; FairAC [6], which extends fairness to graph data by embedding nodes with observed attributes and using attention to aggregate neighbor information for missing attributes; FairGKD [44], which transfers fair representations learned by a teacher GNN to a student model via graph-based knowledge distillation; and FairGNN [4], which estimates demographics and improves fairness through adversarial learning under limited demographic information. For methods not originally designed for graphs (FairKD, KSMOTE, FairRF), we adapt their implementations to our backbone using the authors' released code.

Evaluation Metrics. We evaluated the proposed framework with respect to two key aspects: prediction performance and fairness performance. To evaluate prediction performance, we chose two metrics for node classification, *i.e.*, accuracy and F1-Score [24], where higher scores indicate better prediction results. For fairness assessment, we utilize two commonly used metrics: Demographic parity (Δ_{DP}) [14] and Equal Opportunity (Δ_{EO}) [7]. These fairness metrics measure the disparity in predictions between different demographic groups, where values closer to zero indicate higher fairness.

Table 2. Comparison of FairGLite with baselines (columns are metrics; rows are methods). The best in each metric column is **bold**, second-best is underlined.

Dataset	Method	Accuracy (↑)	F1-Score (↑)	Δ_{DP} (↓)	Δ_{EO} (↓)
Credit	GCN	**0.781 ± 0.016**	**0.868 ± 0.023**	0.117 ± 0.013	0.096 ± 0.017
	KSMOTE	0.736 ± 0.009	0.817 ± 0.012	0.071 ± 0.003	0.055 ± 0.013
	FairKD	0.711 ± 0.012	0.796 ± 0.023	0.094 ± 0.036	0.075 ± 0.042
	FairRF	0.735 ± 0.017	0.809 ± 0.022	0.067 ± 0.017	0.057 ± 0.018
	FairAC	<u>0.748 ± 0.026</u>	0.831 ± 0.018	0.047 ± 0.015	0.041 ± 0.014
	FairGKD	0.743 ± 0.028	<u>0.834 ± 0.013</u>	0.038 ± 0.011	<u>0.037 ± 0.021</u>
	FairGNN	0.687 ± 0.012	0.783 ± 0.043	0.123 ± 0.026	0.115 ± 0.022
	FairGLite	0.743 ± 0.032	0.825 ± 0.018	**0.035 ± 0.015**	**0.033 ± 0.013**
Pokec-z	GCN	**0.699 ± 0.024**	**0.622 ± 0.024**	0.075 ± 0.025	0.062 ± 0.013
	KSMOTE	0.697 ± 0.024	0.611 ± 0.018	0.037 ± 0.017	0.039 ± 0.010
	FairKD	0.673 ± 0.021	0.592 ± 0.013	0.045 ± 0.014	0.048 ± 0.009
	FairRF	0.690 ± 0.014	0.617 ± 0.019	0.032 ± 0.012	0.034 ± 0.012
	FairAC	0.655 ± 0.031	0.603 ± 0.013	0.032 ± 0.018	<u>0.029 ± 0.014</u>
	FairGKD	0.660 ± 0.025	0.618 ± 0.009	**0.029 ± 0.021**	0.030 ± 0.018
	FairGNN	0.689 ± 0.071	0.603 ± 0.021	0.038 ± 0.022	0.033 ± 0.029
	FairGLite	0.671 ± 0.041	0.620 ± 0.032	0.031 ± 0.013	**0.027 ± 0.015**
Pokec-n	GCN	<u>0.689 ± 0.015</u>	**0.631 ± 0.022**	0.084 ± 0.013	0.078 ± 0.019
	KSMOTE	0.669 ± 0.013	0.611 ± 0.018	0.061 ± 0.010	0.066 ± 0.013
	FairKD	0.663 ± 0.016	0.603 ± 0.023	0.067 ± 0.015	0.064 ± 0.013
	FairRF	0.673 ± 0.013	0.616 ± 0.032	0.056 ± 0.009	0.061 ± 0.016
	FairAC	0.675 ± 0.028	0.621 ± 0.026	0.026 ± 0.013	<u>0.030 ± 0.027</u>
	FairGKD	0.681 ± 0.021	0.628 ± 0.029	<u>0.025 ± 0.015</u>	0.035 ± 0.030
	FairGNN	0.675 ± 0.028	0.619 ± 0.032	0.036 ± 0.012	0.044 ± 0.020
	FairGLite	**0.689 ± 0.024**	<u>0.630 ± 0.029</u>	**0.023 ± 0.018**	**0.028 ± 0.013**
NBA	GCN	0.668 ± 0.025	0.703 ± 0.022	0.063 ± 0.043	0.074 ± 0.043
	KSMOTE	0.654 ± 0.023	0.685 ± 0.038	0.057 ± 0.033	0.065 ± 0.033
	FairKD	0.671 ± 0.036	0.681 ± 0.023	0.042 ± 0.025	0.055 ± 0.014
	FairRF	0.664 ± 0.033	0.687 ± 0.012	0.044 ± 0.038	0.042 ± 0.026
	FairAC	**0.673 ± 0.028**	0.699 ± 0.038	<u>0.035 ± 0.009</u>	0.037 ± 0.017
	FairGKD	0.670 ± 0.024	<u>0.706 ± 0.033</u>	0.040 ± 0.067	<u>0.032 ± 0.010</u>
	FairGNN	0.658 ± 0.027	0.694 ± 0.032	0.036 ± 0.021	0.034 ± 0.025
	FairGLite	<u>0.723 ± 0.024</u>	**0.711 ± 0.029**	**0.032 ± 0.036**	**0.030 ± 0.005**

5.2 Experimental Results

RQ1: How does FairGLite Perform in Balancing Utility and Fairness Across Real-World Graph Datasets?. To answer this question, Table 2 summarizes the comparisons between our proposed method, FairGLite, and the baseline methods. Specifically, two key observations emerge: i) FairGLite achieves superior fairness when demographic information is missing. Across all evaluated datasets, FairGLite consistently shows better fairness performance than baseline methods. This advantage stems from FairGLite's ability to effectively leverage node features and graph structure to accurately generate proxy of demographic information, establishing a solid foundation for bias mitigation. Furthermore, FairGLite mitigates multiple forms of bias in graph data, better preventing demographic information from leaking into downstream classification tasks. ii) FairGLite demonstrates comparable predictive performance compared with existing fairness methods. Unlike existing approaches that impose uniform fairness constraints on all nodes, FairGLite dynamically adjusts each node's contribution to the fairness loss through the adaptivity confidence strategy, enabling better learning for nodes with low confidence. Overall, these results highlight FairGLite's advantage in effectively balancing predictive performance and fairness.

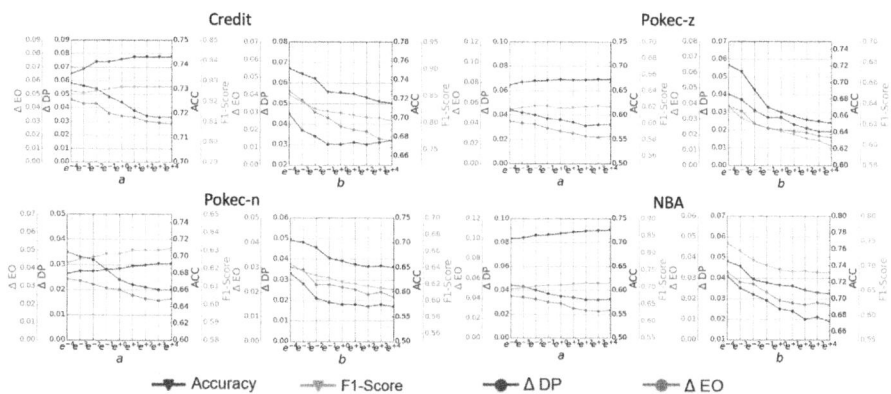

Fig. 3. Study on Hyper-parameters sensitivity analysis.

RQ2: How Do the Hyper-parameters a and b Impact the Trade-off Between Utility and Fairness in FairGLite?. We investigate the sensitivity of FairGLite to two key hyperparameters, *i.e.*, a and b. As shown in Fig. 3, as a increases, the model achieves better prediction performance and fairness. However, if it passes a certain threshold, both prediction performance and fairness stabilize. For parameter b, as shown in Fig. 3, we observe three distinct phases: when b is very small, the fairness constraints have minimal impact. As b increases, fairness steadily improves, though prediction accuracy gradually declines due to stronger regularization. Beyond a threshold (*e.g.*, e^1 for Credit/NBA, e^3 for Pokec-z/Pokec-n), fairness performance stabilizes or slightly deteriorates because excessive regularization restricts the model's representational capacity.

Note that results for NBA and Pokec-n are provided in the appendix (see footnote 1). To sum up, these results highlight the trade-off between fairness and task performance. Thus, careful tuning of a and b is essential for optimal model performance.

RQ3: What is the Impact of Each Component on the FairGLite on its Utility and Fairness?. We conducted ablation studies to assess the contributions of each module within the FairGLite framework. FairGLite consists of three key modules: the Demographic Information Identification Module, the Fair Node Representation Learning Module, and the Adaptivity Confidence Strategy Module. Notably, we did not create a variant without the Demographic Information Identification Module because this module is foundational to FairGLite's operation. Without it, the framework cannot identify proxies for the missing demographic information, which are essential inputs for the subsequent modules. Therefore, removing this component would render the entire framework inoperable, making such an ablation study impractical. We present the ablation study results for the Credit and Pokec-z datasets in Fig. 4, additional results for NBA and Pokec-n datasets are provided in the appendix (see footnote 1).

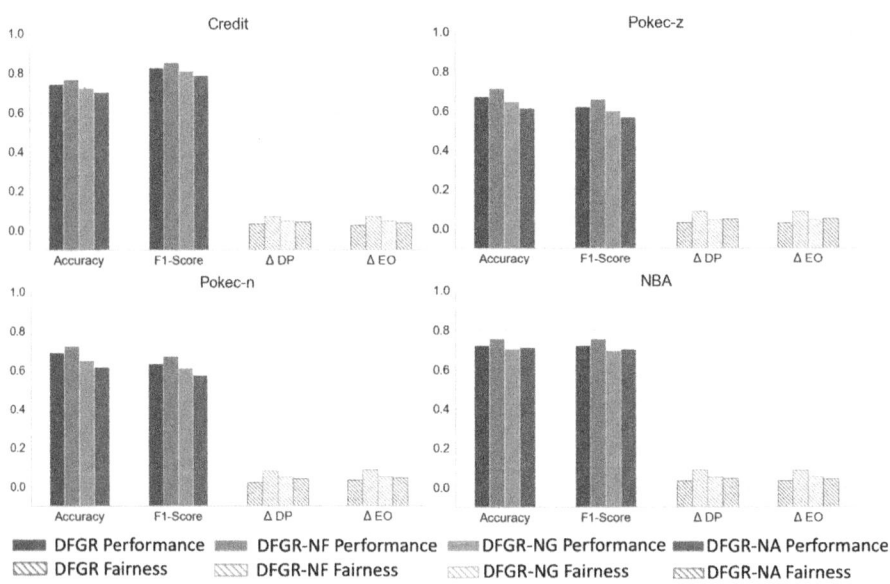

Fig. 4. Ablation study results for FairGLite, FairGLite-NF, FairGLite-NG and FairGLite-NA.

For the Fair Node Representation Learning Module, we created two variants: FairGLite-NF (without the Fairness Constraint) and FairGLite-NG (without the Graph Reconstruction Constraint). As shown in Fig. 4, the fairness metrics of FairGLite-NF dropped significantly. This occurs because without the Fairness Constraint, demographic information in node representations directly passes to downstream classification tasks, leading to discriminatory decisions. The FairGLite-NG variant shows better fairness metrics than FairGLite-NF but still demonstrates a slight decrease compared to the full FairGLite model, along with reduced performance metrics. This degradation occurs because without the Graph Reconstruction Constraint, node representations fail to capture important structural information, resulting in decreased graph representational performance.

We also examined the impact of the Adaptivity Confidence Strategy Module by creating the FairGLite-NA variant (without adaptive confidence). As shown in Fig. 4, FairGLite-NA shows reduced performance compared to the complete FairGLite model. This is because applying fairness constraints with equal strength to all nodes makes it more difficult for the model to learn from samples with low confidence, thereby reducing the overall accuracy.

6 Conclusion

This paper addresses the critical gap between real-world constraints on demographic information availability and the assumptions underlying existing fairness-aware graph learning methods. To bridge this gap, we proposed FairGLite, a theoretically grounded framework designed to promote fairness in graph-based decision-making. FairGLite effectively mitigates bias in node representations without depending on complete demographic information. In addition, we proposed an adaptive confidence strategy that further enhances its practical utility, intelligently balancing fairness and predictive accuracy. Through rigorous theoretical analysis, we demonstrated the robustness of FairGLite, establishing its potential as a versatile and broadly applicable solution for real-world fair graph learning.

Acknowledgements. This work was supported in part by the National Science Foundation (NSF) under Grant No. 2404039 and the National Institutes of Health (NIH) under Grant No. R01MD019814.

References

1. An, Q., Rahman, S., Zhou, J., Kang, J.J.: A comprehensive review on machine learning in healthcare industry: classification, restrictions, opportunities and challenges. Sensors **23**(9), 4178 (2023)
2. Ashurst, C., Weller, A.: Fairness without demographic data: a survey of approaches. In: Proceedings of the 3rd ACM Conference on Equity and Access in Algorithms, Mechanisms, and Optimization, pp. 1–12 (2023)
3. Chai, J., Jang, T., Wang, X.: Fairness without demographics through knowledge distillation. Adv. Neural. Inf. Process. Syst. **35**, 19152–19164 (2022)
4. Dai, E., Wang, S.: Say no to the discrimination: Learning fair graph neural networks with limited sensitive attribute information. In: Proceedings of the 14th ACM International Conference on Web Search and Data Mining, pp. 680–688 (2021)
5. Grari, V., Lamprier, S., Detyniecki, M.: Fairness without the sensitive attribute via causal variational autoencoder. arXiv preprint arXiv:2109.04999 (2021)
6. Guo, D., Chu, Z., Li, S.: Fair attribute completion on graph with missing attributes. arXiv preprint arXiv:2302.12977 (2023)

7. Hardt, M., Price, E., Srebro, N.: Equality of opportunity in supervised learning. Adv. Neural Inf. Process. Syst. **29** (2016)
8. Kenfack, P.J., Kahou, S.E., Aïvodji, U.: A survey on fairness without demographics. Trans. Mach. Learn. Res. (2024)
9. Kipf, T.N., Welling, M.: Semi-supervised classification with graph convolutional networks. arXiv preprint arXiv:1609.02907 (2016)
10. Ko, H., Lee, S., Park, Y., Choi, A.: A survey of recommendation systems: recommendation models, techniques, and application fields. Electronics **11**(1), 141 (2022)
11. Kose, O.D., Shen, Y.: Fairgat: fairness-aware graph attention networks. ACM Trans. Knowl. Discov. Data **18**(7), 1–20 (2024)
12. Krumpal, I.: Determinants of social desirability bias in sensitive surveys: a literature review. Quality & Quantity **47**(4), 2025–2047 (2013)
13. Lahoti, P., et al.: Fairness without demographics through adversarially reweighted learning. Adv. Neural. Inf. Process. Syst. **33**, 728–740 (2020)
14. Quy, T., Roy, A., Iosifidis, V., Zhang, W., Ntoutsi, E.: A survey on datasets for fairness-aware machine learning. Wiley Interdis. Rev. Data Mining Knowl. Discovery **12**(3), e1452 (2022)
15. Ling, H., Jiang, Z., Luo, Y., Ji, S., Zou, N.: Learning fair graph representations via automated data augmentations. In: International Conference on Learning Representations (ICLR) (2023)
16. Martinez, N.L., Bertran, M.A., Papadaki, A., Rodrigues, M., Sapiro, G.: Blind pareto fairness and subgroup robustness. In: International Conference on Machine Learning, pp. 7492–7501. PMLR (2021)
17. Madden, M., Lenhart, A., Cortesi, S., Gasser, U., Duggan, M., Smith, A., Beaton, M.: Teens, social media, and privacy. Pew Res. Center **21**(1055), 2–86 (2013)
18. Ni, H., Han, L., Chen, T., Sadiq, S., Demartini, G.: Fairness without sensitive attributes via knowledge sharing. In: The 2024 ACM Conference on Fairness, Accountability, and Transparency, pp. 1897–1906 (2024)
19. Pearl, J., et al.: Models, reasoning and inference. Cambridge, UK: CambridgeUniversityPress **19**(2), 3 (2000)
20. Peers, S., Hervey, T., Kenner, J., Ward, A.: The EU Charter of fundamental rights: a commentary. Bloomsbury Publishing (2021)
21. Pelegrina, G.D., Couceiro, M., Duarte, L.T.: A statistical approach to detect sensitive features in a group fairness setting. arXiv preprint arXiv:2305.06994 (2023)
22. Rawls, A.: Theories of social justice (1971)
23. Sagawa, S., Koh, P.W., Hashimoto, T.B., Liang, P.: Distributionally robust neural networks for group shifts: On the importance of regularization for worst-case generalization. arXiv preprint arXiv:1911.08731 (2019)
24. Sokolova, M., Lapalme, G.: A systematic analysis of performance measures for classification tasks. Inf. Process. Manage. **45**(4), 427–437 (2009). https://doi.org/10.1016/j.ipm.2009.03.002, https://doi.org/10.1016/j.ipm.2009.03.002
25. Tabassum, S., Pereira, F.S., Fernandes, S., Gama, J.: Social network analysis: an overview. Wiley Interdis. Rev. Data Mining Knowl. Discovery **8**(5), e1256 (2018)
26. Takac, L., Zabovsky, M.: Data analysis in public social networks. In: International Scientific Conference and International Workshop Present Day Trends of Innovations. vol. 1 (2012)
27. Wang, Z., Chu, Z., Blanco, R., Chen, Z., Chen, S.C., Zhang, W.: Advancing graph counterfactual fairness through fair representation learning. In: Joint European Conference on Machine Learning and Knowledge Discovery in Databases, pp. 40–58. Springer Nature Switzerland (2024)
28. Wang, Z., et al.: Fair graph u-net: a fair graph learning framework integrating group and individual awareness. In: Proceedings of the AAAI Conference on Artificial Intelligence. vol. 39, pp. 28485–28493 (2025)

29. Wang, Z., Narasimhan, G., Yao, X., Zhang, W.: Mitigating multisource biases in graph neural networks via real counterfactual samples. In: 2023 IEEE International Conference on Data Mining (ICDM), pp. 638–647. IEEE (2023)
30. Wang, Z., Ulloa, D., Yu, T., Rangaswami, R., Yap, R., Zhang, W.: Individual fairness with group constraints in graph neural networks. In: 27th European Conference on Artificial Intelligence (2024)
31. Wang, Z., et al.: Fg-smote: towards fair node classification with graph neural network. ACM SIGKDD Explorations Newsl **26**(2), 99–108 (2025)
32. Wang, Z., et al.: Towards fair graph learning without demographic information. In: The 28th International Conference on Artificial Intelligence and Statistics, vol. 258, p. 2
33. Wang, Z., et al.: Towards fairness with limited demographics via disentangled learning. In: Proceedings of the 34th International Joint Conference on Artificial Intelligence (IJCAI) (2025)
34. Wang, Z., Zhang, W.: FDGen: a fairness-aware graph generation model. In: Proceedings of the 42nd International Conference on Machine Learning (ICML). PMLR (2025)
35. Wang, Z., et al.: fairGNN-WOD: fair graph learning without complete demographics. In: Proceedings of the 34th International Joint Conference on Artificial Intelligence (IJCAI) (2025)
36. Yan, S., Kao, H.t., Ferrara, E.: Fair class balancing: enhancing model fairness without observing sensitive attributes. In: Proceedings of the 29th ACM International Conference on Information & Knowledge Management, pp. 1715–1724 (2020)
37. Yeh, I.C., Lien, C.h.: The comparisons of data mining techniques for the predictive accuracy of probability of default of credit card clients. Expert Syst. Appl. **36**(2), 2473–2480 (2009)
38. Zhang, W., Hernandez-Boussard, T., Weiss, J.: Censored fairness through awareness. In: Proceedings of the AAAI Conference on Artificial Intelligence. vol. 37, pp. 14611–14619 (2023)
39. Zhang, W., Zhou, S., Walsh, T., Weiss, J.C.: Fairness amidst non-IID graph data: a literature review. AI Magazine, vol. 46, no. 1, article e12212 (2025)
40. Zhang, W.: Ai fairness in practice: paradigm, challenges, and prospects. AI Mag. **45**(3), 386–395 (2024)
41. Zhao, T., Dai, E., Shu, K., Wang, S.: Towards fair classifiers without sensitive attributes: Exploring biases in related features. In: Proceedings of the Fifteenth ACM International Conference on Web Search and Data Mining, pp. 1433–1442 (2022)
42. Zheng, X., et al.: Graph neural networks for graphs with heterophily: a survey. arXiv preprint arXiv:2202.07082 (2022)
43. Zhu, H., Fu, G., Guo, Z., Zhang, Z., Xiao, T., Wang, S.: Fairness-aware message passing for graph neural networks. arXiv preprint arXiv:2306.11132 (2023)
44. Zhu, Y., Li, J., Chen, L., Zheng, Z.: The devil is in the data: Learning fair graph neural networks via partial knowledge distillation. In: Proceedings of the 17th ACM International Conference on Web Search and Data Mining, pp. 1012–1021 (2024)
45. Zhu, Y., Li, J., Zheng, Z., Chen, L.: Fair graph representation learning via sensitive attribute disentanglement. In: Proceedings of the ACM Web Conference 2024, pp. 1182–1192 (2024)

Constrained Optimization to Improve Critical Rare Classes Performance Within the Top-Ranking Part

Yuxin Ying[1], Fuzhen Zhuang[2](✉), Ziyi Liu[1], Dingyuan Zhu[1], Daixin Wang[1], and Xiaobo Qin[1]

[1] Ant Group, Hangzhou, China
{yingyuxin.yyx,ziyi.liu,dingyuan.zhu,daixin.wang,xiaobo.qin}@antgroup.com
[2] Additional Institute Placeholder,Pune, India
zfz20081983@gmail.com

Abstract. The widespread application of deep learning methods has brought to the challenge of enhancing prediction performance within the highest-score segment of model predictions. In critical domains such as insurance fraud detection and bank cash-out detection, the focus is predominantly on the highest predicted scores, which correspond to high-risk users that need to be intercepted. However, most existing work still focuses on optimizing AUC globally, which often means not being the best within the top-ranking part. Besides, these scenarios often face extreme data imbalance, where the positive samples of interest are in the minority. In this paper, we define the top-ranking optimization problem and propose an Augmented Lagrangian Multiplier method (ALM) based approach to solve it. Specifically, we modify the Discounted Cumulative Gain (DCG) metric to serve as the constraint on top-ranking and add it as the regularization terms to the optimization objective. In addition, to ensure the effectiveness of the regularization term and avoid the overfitting problem, we design a dynamically updated cache mechanism to store the hard samples. Our experimental results on three real-world datasets validate the effectiveness of our proposed method, demonstrating its potential to improve top-ranking prediction performance in imbalanced data settings.

Keywords: Insurance Risk Control · Imbalanced Learning · Top-ranking Optimization

1 Introduction

In recent years, deep neural networks (DNN) have gradually achieved many successful applications in binary classification problems, e.g. the fraud detection and concept classification scenario [1,10,32]. Most of these scenarios focus on optimizing the overall binary classification performance like the Mean Average Precision (mAP) metric and Area Under Curve (AUC) [26,30]. However, in some practical scenarios such as cash-out fraud detection or insurance fraud detection, they focus more on accurately identifying the high-risk users ranked at the top so that measures such as user banning or account suspension can be taken against them. In this case, the prediction performance for the remaining users is not as critical, and neither is the specific order of the predicted users ranked at the top. Despite its clear importance, the challenge is further amplified by the fact that there is often a significant class imbalance in these scenarios. The positive samples, which represent the high-risk users we are concerned about, are in the minority. Therefore, how to optimize the binary classification performance of top-ranked users in such imbalanced scenarios is an important problem, which we will refer to as the **top-ranking optimization problem**.

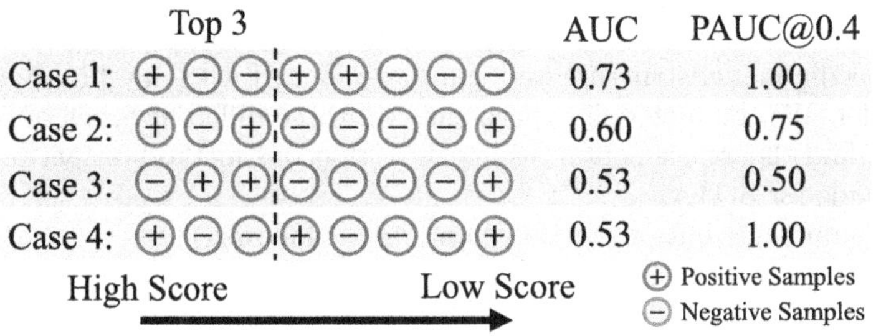

	Top 3	AUC	PAUC@0.4
Case 1:	⊕ ⊖ ⊖ ⊕ ⊕ ⊖ ⊖ ⊖	0.73	1.00
Case 2:	⊕ ⊖ ⊕ ⊖ ⊖ ⊖ ⊖ ⊕	0.60	0.75
Case 3:	⊖ ⊕ ⊕ ⊖ ⊖ ⊖ ⊖ ⊕	0.53	0.50
Case 4:	⊕ ⊖ ⊖ ⊕ ⊖ ⊖ ⊖ ⊕	0.53	1.00

High Score ⟶ Low Score   ⊕ Positive Samples   ⊖ Negative Samples

Fig. 1. Four toy examples illustrate the problems with each AUC and PAUC. Case 1 has a higher AUC and PAUC than case 2, while case 2 has a better performance within top 3 part. Cases 3 and 4 have the same AUC, however, the top 3 effect is better in case 3 with a lower PAUC.

To address this problem, some existing works have shed light on different angles. Some methods do not transform the optimization objective and still aim to maximize the global AUC [26,30]. By using methods such as sampling, weighting, and calibration, they try to enhance the model's focus on the minority classes [9,17,19,23]. However, AUC pays equal attention to samples of all scores and therefore may not be consistent with our goal for top-ranking optimization. For example, consider case 1 and case 2 in Fig. 1. When considering the top 3, case 2 is better while having a lower AUC which is opposite to our expectations.

The other work proposes the Partial AUC(PAUC) optimization problem [12,29][?], which refers to targeting the model's top prediction effectiveness by optimizing the AUC score within a certain lower range of the False Positive Rate(FPR). However, PAUC only constrains the FPR, i.e., the top k negative samples, not the top k of the model's predicted scores. This causes it to compare all other samples with the negative sample with the highest predicted score in its computation process, thus over-penalizing some cases with better prediction at the top-ranking part prediction. For example, as case 3 and case 4 in Fig. 1. When considering the top 3, case 3 has the better results of having 2 positive samples within. However, the PAUC within $(0, 2/5)$ for both is 0.5 and 1.0 respectively, which is the opposite of what we expected. To sum up, existing methods pay little attention to targeted top-ranking part optimization. Imbalanced learning and PAUC optimization methods focus on some similar situations but are not identical.

In this paper, we model this class of top-ranking part optimization problems represented by the insurance fraud detection domain. Specifically, we transform the top-ranking part prediction optimization problem into a pairwise optimization problem with constraints using the Augmented Lagrangian Multiplier method. Besides, a modified DCG score of the bipartite ranking task is introduced as a constraint to the regularization term. In addition, to alleviate the problem of positive samples being too sparse, a dynamic cache mechanism is introduced to store the hard positive samples and negative samples. In each round of training, the samples stored in the cache are also added to training to accelerate the convergence of the model. Our proposed method is independent of the specific model structure and can be combined with any binary classification model. We conduct rich experiments on three different types of real-world datasets, and the experimental results show that our method outperforms existing methods for SOTA.

The main contributions of this paper are as follows:

- We propose the **T**op-**R**anking **A**ugmented **L**agrangian method (TRAL) to optimize the top-ranking prediction results of deep learning models in the presence of extreme imbalance of positive and negative samples. The model's focus on positive samples is enhanced by introducing sample difficulty and positive sample ordering.
- We propose a dynamic caching mechanism to store the misclassified positive samples and hard negative samples in each round, thus mitigating the problem of sparse positive samples causing the regularization term to overfit.
- We have conducted sufficient experiments on several real-world datasets, and the extensive experiment results prove the superiority and generalizability of the TRAL proposed in this paper.

2 Preliminaries

2.1 Problem Formulation

In this section, a formal definition of the top-ranking optimization problem in the unbalanced scenario that we try to solve in this paper is given. For an unbalanced binary categorical dataset $D = \{(x_1, y_1), (x_2, y_2), .., (x_n, y_n), y_i \in \{0, 1\}\}$, where x_i is a data sample and y_i is a label. We are concerned with positive samples i.e., y = 1. Then there is a number of negative samples much larger than the number of positive samples. For example, in the insurance fraud detection scenario, normal users account for more than 99% of all users and high-risk fraudulent users account for less than 1%. The prediction result of the model is often used as the blocking threshold in the business. However, the consequences of wrongly intercepting a regular user are much smaller than those of wrongly passing a high-risk user, so the model's prediction results for positive samples need to be maximized, i.e., the system needs to operate with a high false-negative rate.

Formally, we have $\mathcal{P} = \{x_1^+, \ldots, x_{|\mathcal{P}|}^+\}$ and $\mathcal{N} = \{x_1^-, \ldots, x_{|\mathcal{N}|}^-\}$ representing positive class and negative class respectively. We define the positive class as the critical minority class in our following discussion, i.e., $|\mathcal{P}| << |\mathcal{N}|$. Our goal is to develop a generalized method for inducing a Deep Neural Network(DNN) classifier $f_\theta : \mathcal{R}_d \to \mathcal{R}$ that maps d-dimensional inputs to output scores, thereby boosting the proportion of positive samples within the top k% of the model's predicted scores when sorted in descending order. Let $F(\theta)$ be the total loss function and $f(\theta)$ be the generic loss function for the binary classification problem.

2.2 Augmented Lagrangian Multiplier Method

With $F(\theta)$ representing the total loss function, the optimization problem with constraint $\mathcal{C}(\theta)$ can be formulated as:

$$arg\min_{\theta \in \Theta} F(\theta) \; s.t. \; \mathcal{C}(\theta). \tag{1}$$

Since it is hard to optimize the constrained problem directly, the method of Lagrange Multipliers was introduced to convert the constrained optimization problem to an unconstrained one. The constraint to the objective is added as a normalization part using Lagrange multipliers λ as follows:

$$\mathcal{L}(\theta, \lambda) = F(\theta) + \sum_{i=1}^{m} \lambda_i c_i(\theta). \tag{2}$$

The optimization function obtained after the transformation of the original Lagrange multiplier method [2] is not guaranteed to be smooth and the gradient descent method cannot be used directly because the function is not guaranteed to be strongly convex. By incorporating the quadratic penalty term, the augmented Lagrange method guarantees the smoothness of the optimization process. Thus, the original optimization problem with constraint $\mathcal{C}(\theta)$ can be transformed into the following unconstrained optimization problem, where $\mathcal{C}(\theta)$ remains the constraint of interest:

$$\mathcal{L}_\mu(\theta, \lambda) = F(\theta) + \mu \sum_{i=1}^{m} ||c_i(\theta)||^2 + \sum_{i=1}^{m} \lambda_i c_i(\theta), \tag{3}$$

here μ is a predefined penalty parameter used to control the contribution of the penalty term to the overall loss function.

3 Methods

To solve the top-ranking part optimization problem on imbalanced datasets, we propose a model-independent optimization method with constraints by defining sample difficulty and designing a dynamic caching mechanism to ensure the validity of the regular terms. First, we discuss how to transform the objective of top-ranking part optimization into a constrained optimization problem and solve it with the Augmented Lagrangian Multiplier method. Second, we use a caching mechanism to temporarily store the positive samples misclassified by the model to alleviate the problem that the regularization term does not work in training due to sparse positive samples.

3.1 Metric for Top-Ranking Optimization

For binary classification tasks, several metrics have been proposed for different purposes. A commonly used optimization metric is Area Under Curve(AUC),

$$AUC = \frac{\sum 1(y(x_i^+) > y(x_j^-))}{|\mathcal{N}||\mathcal{P}|} \quad (4)$$

However, since AUC is of equal concern for all score bands, boosting the rankings of both the low-score positive samples and the high-score positive samples will do the same decrease to the loss function. Discounted Cumulative Gain (DCG) is a commonly used ranking metric in top k recommendation tasks [11].

$$DCG@k = \sum_{i=1}^{k} \frac{2^{rel(i)} - 1}{\log_2(i+1)}, \quad (5)$$

where $rel(i)$ denotes the predicted score of the sample in the ith position.

Recall that our goal is to maximize the proportion of positive samples ranked within the top k of predictive scores, so we need to pay attention to the rank order of the positive samples in each prediction. However, the vanilla DCG can be influenced by the ranking within the top-ranking part which is not our primary concern. Therefore, we modified the vanilla DCG metric into the following form:

$$\widehat{DCG} = \sum_{x^+ \in \mathcal{P}} \frac{1}{\log_2(rank(x^+) + 1)}. \quad (6)$$

Since we only have two relationship types for positive and negative samples and do not focus on the rankings within the same class, in the modified $\widehat{DCG}$, we calculate the rank of positive samples by considering neighboring positive samples as tied at the same rank.

3.2 Top-Ranking Constrained Optimization

To this end, we define the constrained optimization problem for top optimization as follows:

$$\arg\min F(\theta)$$
$$s.t. \sum_{j=1}^{|\mathcal{N}|} \max_{x^+ \in \mathcal{P}} (0, -(f_\theta(x^+) - f_\theta(x_j^-)) + \delta_j) = 0, \quad (7)$$

where $f_\theta(x)$ represents the predicted score of the DNN model, δ is the classification margin. It is worth noting that δ is not a fixed hyperparameter, but is dynamically adjusted for each negative sample based on its classification difficulty. Satisfying the constraint would be equated to optimizing the modified $\widehat{DCG}$ for binary classification.

We then convert the optimization problem according to the Augmented Lagrangian Method into the following form:

$$\mathcal{L}(\theta, \lambda) = F(\theta) + \frac{\mu \sum_{i=1}^{|\mathcal{P}|} \mathcal{L}_i^2}{2 \cdot |\mathcal{P}| \cdot |\mathcal{N}|} + \frac{\sum_{i=1}^{|\mathcal{P}|} \lambda_i \mathcal{L}_i}{|\mathcal{P}| \cdot |\mathcal{N}|}, \tag{8}$$

where $\mathcal{L}_i = \sum_{j=1}^{|\mathcal{N}|} \max(0, -(f_\theta(x_i^+) - f_\theta(x_j^-)) + \delta_{ij})$. Note that the δ_{ij} is different with each sample pair. Unlike previous work ALM, our δ_{ij} here is not a fixed hyper-parameter set in advance, but a learnable parameter related to the classification difficulty of each negative sample.

This function can't be used as an optimization objective yet, because the $\max(\cdot)$ function in the $\mathcal{L}_i$ calculation is non-continuous. Therefore, we use a widely-used surrogate function for $\max(\cdot)$ to convert it into a continuous convex function, i.e. $max(x_1, \ldots, x_n) \approx \log(\sum_{i=1}^n \exp(x_i))$.

$$\mathcal{L}_i = -\log(\frac{e^{f(x_i^+)}}{e^{f(x_i^+)} + |\mathcal{N}| \sum_{j=1}^{|\mathcal{N}|} \eta_{ij} e^{f(x_j^-)}}), \tag{9}$$

where $\eta_{ij} = \frac{exp(\delta_{ij})}{|\mathcal{N}|}$ is defined as the classification difficulty of negative samples.

It is not difficult to prove that $\mathcal{L}_i$ restricts the upper and lower bounds of the $\widehat{DCG}$, and optimizing $\mathcal{L}_i$ results in a bounded optimization of the $\widehat{DCG}$. For the proof of the upper and lower bounds of the $\widehat{DCG}$ one can refer to the Proof section in the Appendix. After obtaining that $\mathcal{L}_i$ is the equivalent boundary of the $\widehat{DCG}$, the optimization objective is equivalent to optimizing the AUC while satisfying the constraints of the $\widehat{DCG}$ since we use the ALM transformation constraints to add them to the optimization function as regular terms.

It is worth noting that since $\delta \in [0,1]$, the value of η belongs to $[\frac{1}{|\mathcal{N}|}, \frac{e}{|\mathcal{N}|}]$. And η is inversely proportional to δ. When the classification difficulty of negative samples is lower, the classification margin with positive samples is larger, resulting in a smaller η, i.e., the impact on the optimization term. Therefore, we can extract η as a measure of the classification difficulty of negative samples.

3.3 Dynamic Cache Module

Under the imbalanced scenario, due to the extreme sparsity of positive samples, there may not always be enough positive samples within each mini-batch to participate in training. This leads to the constraint term in Eq. (8) not working. To solve this problem, we borrow the caching mechanism from the computer hardware field to ensure that the model can see enough positive samples. Specifically, we use an LRU-like cache mechanism to maintain a queue of positive samples of size q and concate them into each mini-batch during training. First, before the training process begins, we randomly select q positive samples to initialize the cache. Subsequently, after each training step, we input all the samples within this batch and the cache to the model for prediction and pick the ones in which the model predicts incorrectly (i.e., those with prediction scores of 0.5 or less). Then we sort the prediction scores decreasingly and select the lowest q samples to update the cache.

Such a simple method may be effective at the beginning of the training, however, as the number of iterations increases, the frequency of updating the samples in the cache will gradually decrease, leading to a serious over-fitting of those samples. This is supported by some of our preliminary experimental results. Therefore, we also design two mechanisms to alleviate the over-fitting problem. First, we modify the update rule for positive samples. Specifically, if the model correctly predicts a positive sample it is moved out of the cache and marked as the correct answer. Second, we also incorporate the idea of sampling hard negative samples. As the model's effectiveness improves, the number of positive samples incorrectly predicted in each round gradually decreases to below q. This leads to a reduction in the number of samples in the cache. However, it is important to realize that this does not mean the model predicts well enough. It is just that due to the presence of the ALM regularization term and the cache module, we will inevitably cause a rise in the mean value of the model prediction scores. This means that the predictive scores of many negative samples are also rising. Therefore, to suppress the negative sample prediction scores and prevent the cache module from causing over-fitting problems, we performed dynamic sampling based on the classification difficulty of the negative samples. Each negative sample's probability of being sampled is then determined by the difficulty η described above.

$$p_j = \begin{cases} \eta_j = \sum_{i=1}^{|\mathcal{P}|} \frac{exp(\delta_{ij})}{|\mathcal{N}|} &, j \in \mathcal{N}[1,k] \\ 0 &, j \in others \end{cases}, \quad (10)$$

where $\mathcal{N}[1,k]$ represent the top-ranked $k\%$ negative items. It can be inferred that the greater the δ is, the harder the samples will be drawn. The core idea is that the more difficult samples are sampled, the higher the probability that they will enter the cache, which always maintains samples on the model prediction boundaries so that the regularization term always plays a role.

4 Experiments

In this section, we present our experimental evaluation of the top-ranking part optimization task under imbalanced datasets. To verify the generalizability of our approach, we conducted experiments on three datasets with different task scenarios but with similar distributions: the Insurance dataset obtained from

Table 1. Statistics of three large-scale datasets. The positive ratio indicates the proportion of positive samples.

dataset	pos	neg	positive ratio
Insurance	99,386	1,012,716	0.99%
Fraud	492	284,807	0.17%
Criteo	7,450	745,051	1.00%

a widely used online Health Insurance platform, the public dataset Fraud of credit card fraud detection task, and the Criteo recommendation dataset. On the Insurance control scenario and Fraud detection dataset, we choose MLP as the benchmark classification model, and on the recommendation dataset Criteo we choose DeepFM [8] as the benchmark model.

4.1 Datasets

Insurance dataset contains users' features such as basic information and medical records of the insured users, labeled as whether they are insured or not. This task focuses on predicting whether a user is likely to be insured during the policy period based on the user's characteristics, and the high-risk users predicted by the model need to be blocked or otherwise dealt with to reduce the risk to the insurance company. This dataset is collected from the history of the online business within 30 days. The ratio of positive samples (insured users) and negative samples (regular users) is about 1:100. We divide the train, validation, and test set according to the ratio of 8:1:1. The first 26 days of data are selected as training data and the last two days as the test set.

Fraud dataset contains the transaction history of credit card holders in Europe for September 2013. The task focuses on predicting the presence of possible credit card fraud based on a user's transaction history. The dataset contains 284,807 transactions, of which 492 are fraudulent. We divide the training, validation, and testing datasets randomly according to the ratio of 8:1:1.

Criteo dataset contains data on user ad clicks over 7 days from the CriteoLabs website. This task focuses on predicting the click-through rate of users clicking on displayed advertisements based on user information and information about the currently visited page. We randomly sampled the clicks and hit an overall positive-to-negative sample ratio of 1:100. We followed the original train and test split.

4.2 Baselines

We compare the proposed method with the following competitive and mainstream methods which aim to improve the model's performance over the top-ranking part. In addition, we have chosen Partial AUC optimization methods as a comparison of direct AUC optimization methods such as mini-batch AUC(MBAUC) and SPAUCI methods.

- ALM [19] first introduced the constraint optimization problem to enforce maximal AUC through prioritizing FPR reduction at high TPR.
- RankReg [17] add a ranking-based regularization term to improve TPR while reducing FPR.
- MBAUC [7] leverage the direct optimization of AUC for binary classification problems.
- SPAUCI [22] proposed a non-convex strongly concave min-max regularized problem of instance-wise loss functions for PAUC optimization.

Besides, following previous work [17,19], we consider applying regularizer-based methods with several widely-used cost-sensitive loss functions: Cost-Weighted Binary Cross Entropy loss(WBCE) [30], Symmetric Marginal Loss(S-ML) [15], Symmetric Focal Loss(S-FL) [14], and Label Distribution Perceived Marginal Loss(LDAM) [4].

4.3 Implemetation Details

For the binary imbalanced classification dataset Insurance and Fraud, we adopt MLP as the backbone architecture with shape **[512, 2]**. As for the CTR prediction task of Criteo, we choose DeepFM [8] as the backbone architecture with the embedding dimension of **32**. Throughout all the experiments, we set the batch size to 2048 and used the Adam optimizer.

4.4 Evaluation Metrics

To evaluate the overall classification performance of our proposed method and the baselines described above, we follow the existing works to use the standard metric AUC. Besides, in risk-concern imbalance learning scenarios, the minority class of high-risk positive samples is our primary concern. Therefore, we adopt PAUC@k and Prec@k metrics to evaluate the performance within the top-ranking part. In practice, we focus on the top 3% part, but we also focus on some specific percentage on the top to further investigate the influence of our proposed method, i.e., top 1%, 2%, 3%, 4%, 5%, respectively. For all experiments, we report the results with 95% confidence intervals on the average of 5 runs.

4.5 Main Result

As shown in Table 2, we can observe that the proposed method outperforms the baseline models on different datasets and losses. Grouped by base loss, it can be seen that our proposed TRAL reach the best performance within each group. This shows that applying this model to other loss functions as well as the base model can be improved, reflecting the generalizability of this model.

Table 2. Model comparison on three real-world datasets. We record the mean results over 5 runs. * indicates a significant improvement compared with the best baseline ($p < 0.05$ on paired t-test).

Methods	Insurance			Fraud			Criteo		
	auc	pauc@3%	prec@3%	auc	pauc@3%	prec@3%	auc	pauc@3%	prec@3%
MBAUC	0.5417	0.3215	1.5410	0.8234	0.6215	36.45	0.7255	0.0829	4.512
SPAUCI	0.5701	0.3417	1.5787	0.8248	**0.6473**	37.19	0.7215	**0.0883**	4.676
BCE	0.5516	0.2987	1.5085	0.8257	0.6061	30.80	0.7029	0.0609	3.619
+ALM	0.5488	0.3025	1.5117	0.8226	0.5996	34.54	0.7056	0.0787	4.560
+RankReg	0.5526	0.3091	1.5245	0.8267	0.6117	35.61	0.7080	0.0781	4.509
+TRAL	0.5548	0.3157	1.5469	0.8363	0.6209	37.47	0.7133	0.0812	4.594
WBCE	0.5523	0.2991	1.5236	0.8261	0.6072	31.23	0.7034	0.0678	3.754
+ALM	0.5531	0.3029	1.5145	0.8297	0.6092	34.37	0.7067	0.0814	4.494
+RankReg	0.5512	0.3061	1.5164	0.8289	0.6107	34.79	0.7045	0.0817	4.531
+TRAL	0.5587	0.3154	1.5457	0.8324	0.6217	38.32	0.7157	0.0823	4.572
S-ML	0.5547	0.3107	1.5577	0.8334	0.6125	35.61	0.7131	0.0726	3.975
+ALM	0.5619	0.3201	1.5684	0.8418	0.6217	36.24	0.7191	0.0826	4.561
+RankReg	0.5642	0.3217	1.5687	0.8416	0.6231	36.17	0.7201	0.0831	4.562
+TRAL	0.5701	0.3301	1.5774	0.8501	0.6314	37.24	0.7295	0.0873	4.662
S-FL	0.5551	0.3312	1.5578	0.8350	0.6157	35.17	0.7143	0.0721	4.013
+ALM	0.5621	0.3314	1.5664	0.8421	0.6234	36.41	0.7221	0.0832	4.570
+RankReg	0.5627	0.3320	1.5658	0.8427	0.6238	36.50	0.7225	0.0831	4.579
+TRAL	0.5710	0.3397	1.5780	0.8523	0.6327	37.36	0.7237	0.0845	**4.842***
LDAM	0.5567	0.3340	1.5601	0.8352	0.6206	35.24	0.7165	0.0743	4.102
+ALM	0.5634	0.3407	1.5721	0.8435	0.6301	36.67	0.7251	0.0841	4.617
+RankReg	0.5629	0.3398	1.5717	0.8437	0.6311	36.71	0.7246	0.0847	4.621
+TRAL	**0.5714***	**0.3421***	**1.5801**	**0.8543***	0.6424	**38.47***	**0.7307***	0.0871	4.836

For the Insurance dataset, it is clear that the proposed TRAL is consistently better on most metrics. Comparing the results within each block, we can see that the method in this paper achieves a significant improvement over both ALM and RankReg. Comparing the different loss functions vertically, we can see that our method achieves relatively best results in each metric when combined with LDAM.

Similar results can be observed on the Fraud and Criteo dataset except for pauc@3%, where SPAUCI has the best score. This is because SPAUCI is specifically optimized for Partial-AUC. However, as mentioned earlier, pauc@3% can only reflect the model's ability to categorize and identify positive samples within the top-ranking part to a certain extent. In addition, the actual training speed and convergence speed of SPAUCI method is prolonged, which is not practical for the actual data scale faced by the industry.

Note that our optimization goal in this task is the performance of the model in the part with the highest prediction scores, so the global AUC metric is a reference metric for us rather than an optimization focus of interest. However, we still achieve high AUC scores in many experiments, which shows that our approach not only improves the model's ability to recognize top-ranking samples but also enhances the model's global classification ability at the same time.

In addition, unlike the RankReg method that introduces the rank index of positive samples as a regularization term, our proposed TRAL is mainly based on the ALM method and introduces the definition of negative sample difficulty to measure the effect of the sample on the regularization term. Therefore, it can be seen that the enhancement of the proposed method in this paper is the most significant on the Fraud dataset. This is because the Fraud dataset has relatively the least difficult data and the largest number of simple negative samples among the three datasets. Vanilla classification methods can quickly obtain a high AUC score on this dataset, however, to further improve the model's prediction ability for the top-ranking samples will soon face a serious overfitting problem. The proposed TRAL, however, combines the difficulty of negative samples with the ALM method to make the regularization term work consistently, which further improves the model's performance.

Table 3. Ablation Study of different update strategies for cache module on Insurance datasets.

Methods	Insurance		
	AUC	PAUC@3%	Prec@3%
TRAL	**0.5714**	**0.3421**	**1.5801**
w/o cache	0.5571	0.3341	1.5617
w/o hns	0.5412	0.3217	1.5210
threshold	0.5532	0.3331	1.5512
percent	0.5545	0.3315	1.5524
baseline	0.5567	0.3340	1.5601

4.6 Ablation Study

To visually verify the usefulness of the various components of the proposed TRAL in this paper, we performed ablation experiments on the Insurance dataset. We chose to use the TRAL combined with WBCE loss as the baseline model. Based on this, we do the following for the cache module and the computation of the regularization term, respectively: (1)w/o cache: remove the cache module, (2)w/o hns: remove the hard negative sample strategy and store the cache model for positive samples only, (3)threshold: update the cache with the k positive samples with the lowest scores within each batch, (4)percent: update the cache with the k% positive samples with the lowest scores within each batch, (5)baseline: the baseline MLP model with LDAM loss.

As can be seen from Table 3, the decrease in the effectiveness of the models with the corresponding modules removed is very significant. The removal of the cache module directly decreases the effectiveness of the model by **2.5% points**. It is worth noting that, the method of removing the dynamic negative sampling mechanism is less effective than simply removing the entire cache module. This implies that if a cache module is added directly, the effect on the model prediction results is likely to be negative. In our experiments, we found that after a certain number of iterations, the number of incorrectly predicted positive samples in each round of training is less than the pre-set cache size, which leads to a portion of the samples in the cache not being updated. These "stubborn" positive samples cause the model to overfit, and thus worsen the model's prediction effect.

4.7 Parameter Analysis

In the main experiment, we chose the top 3% as the main criterion to evaluate the model effect, which is based on the actual scenario needs of our online business and the empirical scores from the past analysis. In order to further explore the impact of the proposed methodology on the model prediction scores in different degrees, we explored the variation of the prediction effects in different scales from top 1% to 5%. In Table 4, we list the corresponding experimental results with different percentages. Among them, for the PAUC optimization methods, we set their FPR objectives upper bounds to the corresponding percentages as well to obtain an approximate top-ranking optimization objective.

Table 4. Illustration of the performance of the top-ranking part over different ratio. * indicates a significant improvement compared with the best baseline ($p < 0.05$ on paired t-test).

Methods	Prec @1%	@2%	@3%	@4%	@5%
BCE	4.1150	3.8671	3.6192	3.4205	3.0239
ALM	6.3956	5.2553	4.5603	4.1517	3.9956
RankReg	5.5431	4.7230	4.5094	4.3210	4.0479
TRAL	**7.0897***	**5.4536**	**4.5945***	4.2880	4.0452
MBAUC	5.5912	5.1250	4.5120	4.1457	4.0537
SPAUCI	6.6931	5.3793	4.5760	**4.3500**	**4.0650**

Compared to the PAUC class method, the improvement of TRAL is more significant in scenarios with smaller top ratios. This result is in line with our expectations. As mentioned earlier, the PAUC class of optimization methods may penalize some results that are predicted accurately in the top-ranking part because they focus on the model's ability to classify the positive samples with the highest scores rather than the positive samples within a certain portion of the highest predicted scores.

5 Related Works

5.1 Imbalance Learning

Existing imbalance learning methods can be mainly categorized into three main types: pre-processing, mid-processing, and post-processing according to their action stages. Pre-processing methods mainly act in the data processing stage, changing the data distribution through resampling or data augmentation to increase the number of minority class samples and mitigate the imbalance problem [5,27,31]. Post-processing methods, on the other hand, aim to correct the model's inherent bias towards the majority class by utilizing techniques such as calibrating the model's predictive distribution based on the data distribution. Mid-processing methods mainly rely on designing category-sensitive loss functions to modify the optimization objective during the training process [9,13,23,24,30]. For example, Weighted Binary Cross-Entropy(W-BCE) increases the impact of minority category samples on the loss function by multiplying their contribution by a scaling factor [30]. Other methods, such as Symmetric Marginal Loss [15] and symmetric Focal Loss [14], introduce margin-based penalties to enhance the separation of class decision boundaries. In addition, Class Balanced BCE [6]and Label Distribution-Aware Margins [4] address the imbalance problem by inversely weighting the loss according to the class frequency or minimizing the margin-based generalization boundaries.

Additionally, some studies focus on extreme multi-label classification (XMLC), aiming to address the optimization issues of long-tail classes when multi-class models are dominated by mainstream samples. Since Bhatia [3] proposed the XC benchmark dataset in 2016, researchers have made notable progress. Schultheis [21] introduced an expected test utility (ETU) framework to optimize generalized at-k metrics, tackling long-tail label challenges by deriving optimal prediction rules and efficient approximations with regret guarantees. Later, they advances the algorithm by developing a consistent Frank-Wolfe algorithm for complex macro-at-k metrics within the population utility framework and transforming classifier optimization into confusion matrix optimization to address budgeted predictions at k in multi-label classification. [20] .

The method proposed in this paper mainly belongs to the category-sensitive loss in the mid-processing approach and is combined with the model-based approach. We optimize the regular term based mainly on the work of ALM [19], so that the loss function can focus more on the prediction effect of the model on the top-ranking samples, and ensure the concentration of the positive samples through the dynamic caching mechanism introduced in this paper so that the regular term can work continuously.

5.2 Partial-AUC Optimization

The concept of partial-AUC was initially introduced by [16], with initial research efforts primarily concentrated on its application to straightforward linear models. A distribution-free, rank-based method was employed for the first time to optimize PAUC in a seminal work [16]. Another study [25] focused on the nonparametric estimation of PAUC and incorporated feature selection iteratively to construct the ultimate classifier model. A more sophisticated approach [18] was later introduced, where a cutting-plane algorithm was developed to identify the instances that most significantly violated the constraints. This method broke down the PAUC optimization into several smaller problems, which were then addressed through a structured SVM-based technique. Despite these advancements, many of the existing methods faced challenges such as a lack of differentiation properties or intractable optimization issues. To address this, an implicit function theorem was introduced to formulate a rate-constrained optimization problem that treated the quantization threshold as a function of the model's parameters [12]. A recent study by [28] made significant strides in enabling end-to-end optimization of PAUC in deep learning models. This was achieved by streamlining the complex sample selection process inherent in PAUC optimization into a two-tiered optimization strategy. The inner layer was dedicated to selecting instances, while the outer layer focused on minimizing the loss function. Despite this progress, these methods were subject to approximation errors when estimating the actual PAUC. Subsequent research in [29,33] introduced a PAUC estimator with smooth properties, offering theoretical assurances of convergence for their algorithm. Nevertheless, the utility of this algorithm was constrained by its slow rate of convergence, particularly when applied to the Two-way PAUC.

6 Conclusion

The prevalent utilization of deep learning in data mining has limitations on imbalanced datasets, where the minority class, often of primary interest, is underrepresented and less effectively modeled compared to the majority class. This paper introduces an Augmented Lagrangian method base optimization transformation that prioritizes the model's prediction within the top-ranking part. The proposed TRAL method leverages the modified DCG metric's ranking properties to enhance top prediction effectiveness, incorporating these as regularization terms within the optimization function. Furthermore, to stabilize regularization against the challenge of scarce positive samples, we have defined the concept of sample difficulty and developed a Dynamic Cache mechanism, thereby improving the model's accuracy in top-ranking predictions, which is particularly relevant in risk-aware domains such as insurance and fraud detection.

Acknowledgments. This research work is supported by the National Key Research and Development Program of China under Grant NO. 2024YFF0729003, the National Natural Science Foundation of China under Grant NOs. 62176014, the Fundamental Research Funds for the Central Universities, Ant Group Research Fund.

A Appendix

A.1 Proof of the Equivalence of $\mathcal{L}_i$ and $\widehat{DCG}$

In this part, we focus on proving that the optimization target above equals optimizing the top-ranking part's performance.

Lemma 1. *Optimizing Equation 9 is equivalent to optimizing the upper bound of $\widehat{DCG}$.*

Proof. Consider that for a positive sample x_i^+, its rank order $rank(x_i^+)$ represents that $rank(x_i^+)$ negative samples can have a higher score than x_i^+. Therefore,

$$rank(x_i^+) = 1 + \sum_{j \in \mathcal{N}} sign(f(x_j^-) - f(x_i^+) + \delta_j > 0), \qquad (11)$$

and by $sign(x > 0) \leq e^x$, we have

$$rank(x_i^+) \leq 1 + \sum_{j \in \mathcal{N}} e^{f(x_j^-) - f(x_i^+) + \delta_j}. \qquad (12)$$

The upper bound of $\widehat{DCG}$ can be achieved as follows.

$$\begin{aligned}
\widehat{DCG} &= \sum_{i \in \mathcal{P}} \frac{1}{\log_2(rank(i)+1)} \leq \sum_{i \in \mathcal{P}} \log(|\mathcal{N}|e^{-1}+1) \\
&\leq \sum_{i \in \mathcal{P}} \log(\sum_{j \in \mathcal{N}} e^{f(x_j^-)} - e^{f(x_i^+)+\delta_j} + 1) \\
&= \sum_{i \in \mathcal{P}} -\log \frac{e^{f(x_i^+)}}{e^{f(x_i^+)} + \sum_{j \in \mathcal{N}} e^{f(x_j^-)} + \delta_j} = \mathcal{L}_i.
\end{aligned} \qquad (13)$$

Lemma 2. *Optimizing Eq. 9 is equivalent to optimizing the lower bound of $\widehat{DCG}$*

Proof. The lower bound of $\widehat{DCG}$ can be achieved by the following process.

$$\begin{aligned}
\widehat{DCG} &= \exp(\log(\sum_{i \in \mathcal{P}} \frac{1}{\log_2(rank(i)+1)})) \\
&\geq \exp(\sum_{i \in \mathcal{P}} \frac{1}{rank(i)}) \\
&\geq \exp(\sum_{i \in \mathcal{P}} \frac{1}{\sum_{k \in \mathcal{N}} e^{f(x_k) - f(x_i^+) + \delta_k} + 1}) \\
&= e^{-\mathcal{L}_i}.
\end{aligned} \qquad (14)$$

By Lemma 1 and Lemma 2, we have

$$e^{-\mathcal{L}_i} \leq \widehat{DCG} \leq \mathcal{L}_i. \qquad (15)$$

Consequently, minimizing q is equivalent to minimizing $\widehat{DCG}$, and further, by constraining the number of top k samples for computing the $\widehat{DCG}$, we can explicitly optimize the top-ranking prediction performance.

References

1. Almarshad, F.A., Gashgari, G.A., Alzahrani, A.I.A.: Generative adversarial networks-based novel approach for fraud detection for the european cardholders 2013 dataset. IEEE Access **11**, 107348–107368 (2023)
2. Bertsekas, D.P.: Multiplier methods: a survey. Autom. **12**(2), 133–145 (1976)
3. Bhatia, K., et al.: The extreme classification repository: multi-label datasets and code (2016). http://manikvarma.org/downloads/XC/XMLRepository.html
4. Cao, K., Wei, C., Gaidon, A., Aréchiga, N., Ma, T.: Learning imbalanced datasets with label-distribution-aware margin loss. In: NeurIPS, pp. 1565–1576 (2019)
5. Chou, H.-P., Chang, S.-C., Pan, J.-Y., Wei, W., Juan, D.-C.: Remix: rebalanced mixup. In: Bartoli, A., Fusiello, A. (eds.) ECCV 2020. LNCS, vol. 12540, pp. 95–110. Springer, Cham (2020). https://doi.org/10.1007/978-3-030-65414-6_9
6. Cui, Y., Jia, M., Lin, T., Song, Y., Belongie, S.J.: Class-balanced loss based on effective number of samples. In: CVPR, pp. 9268–9277. Computer Vision Foundation/IEEE (2019)
7. Gultekin, S., Saha, A., Ratnaparkhi, A., Paisley, J.W.: Mba: mini-batch auc optimization. IEEE Trans. Neural Networks Learn. Syst. **31**(12), 5561–5574 (2020)
8. Guo, H., Tang, R., Ye, Y., Li, Z., He, X.: Deepfm: a factorization-machine based neural network for CTR prediction, pp. 1725–1731 (2017)
9. Huang, C., Li, Y., Loy, C.C., Tang, X.: Learning deep representation for imbalanced classification. In: CVPR, pp. 5375–5384. IEEE Computer Society (2016)
10. Ibomoiye, D.M., Sun, Y.: A deep learning ensemble with data resampling for credit card fraud detection. IEEE Access **11**, 30628–30638 (2023)
11. Järvelin, K., Kekäläinen, J.: IR evaluation methods for retrieving highly relevant documents. In: Yannakoudakis, E.J., Belkin, N.J., Ingwersen, P., Leong, M. (eds.) SIGIR 2000: Proceedings of the 23rd Annual International ACM SIGIR Conference on Research and Development in Information Retrieval, July 24-28, 2000, Athens, Greece, pp. 41–48. ACM (2000). https://doi.org/10.1145/345508.345545, https://doi.org/10.1145/345508.345545
12. Kumar, A., Narasimhan, H., Cotter, A.: Implicit rate-constrained optimization of non-decomposable objectives. In: ICML. Proceedings of Machine Learning Research, vol. 139, pp. 5861–5871. PMLR (2021)
13. Li, Z., Kamnitsas, K., Glocker, B.: Overfitting of neural nets under class imbalance: analysis and improvements for segmentation. In: Shen, D., et al., (eds.) MICCAI 2019. LNCS, vol. 11766, pp. 402–410. Springer, Cham (2019). https://doi.org/10.1007/978-3-030-32248-9_45
14. Lin, T., Goyal, P., Girshick, R.B., He, K., Dollár, P.: Focal loss for dense object detection. In: ICCV, pp. 2999–3007. IEEE Computer Society (2017)
15. Liu, W., Wen, Y., Yu, Z., Yang, M.: Large-margin softmax loss for convolutional neural networks. In: ICML. JMLR Workshop and Conference Proceedings, vol. 48, pp. 507–516. JMLR.org (2016)
16. McClish, D.K.: Analyzing a portion of the roc curve. Med. Decis. Making **9**(3), 190–195 (1989)
17. Mohammadi, K., Zhao, H., Zhai, M., Tung, F.: Ranking regularization for critical rare classes: minimizing false positives at a high true positive rate. In: CVPR, pp. 15783–15792. IEEE (2023)
18. Narasimhan, H., Agarwal, S.: A structural SVM based approach for optimizing partial AUC. In: ICML (1). JMLR Workshop and Conference Proceedings, vol. 28, pp. 516–524. JMLR.org (2013)

19. Sangalli, S., Erdil, E., Hötker, A.M., Donati, O., Konukoglu, E.: Constrained optimization to train neural networks on critical and under-represented classes. In: NeurIPS, pp. 25400–25411 (2021)
20. Schultheis, E., Kotłowski, W., Wydmuch, M., Babbar, R., Borman, S., Dembczyński, K.: Consistent algorithms for multi-label classification with macro-at-k metrics. In: 12th International Conference on Learning Representations (ICLR 2024). Curran Associates Inc., United States (2024)
21. Schultheis, E., Wydmuch, M., Kotlowski, W., Babbar, R., Dembczynski, K.: Generalized test utilities for long-tail performance in extreme multi-label classification. In: Oh, A., Naumann, T., Globerson, A., Saenko, K., Hardt, M., Levine, S. (eds.) Advances in Neural Information Processing Systems. vol. 36, pp. 22269–22303. Curran Associates, Inc. (2023)
22. Shao, H., Xu, Q., Yang, Z., Bao, S., Huang, Q.: Asymptotically unbiased instance-wise regularized partial AUC optimization: theory and algorithm. In: NeurIPS (2022)
23. Thai-Nghe, N., Gantner, Z., Schmidt-Thieme, L.: Cost-sensitive learning methods for imbalanced data. In: IJCNN, pp. 1–8. IEEE (2010)
24. Wang, S., Liu, W., Wu, J., Cao, L., Meng, Q., Kennedy, P.J.: Training deep neural networks on imbalanced data sets. In: IJCNN, pp. 4368–4374. IEEE (2016)
25. Wang, Z., Chang, Y.I.: Marker selection via maximizing the partial area under the roc curve of linear risk scores. Biostatistics **12**(2), 369–85 (2011)
26. Wei, J., Wang, S., Huang, Q.: F^3net: fusion, feedback and focus for salient object detection. In: AAAI, pp. 12321–12328. AAAI Press (2020)
27. Xu, Z., Chai, Z., Yuan, C.: Towards calibrated model for long-tailed visual recognition from prior perspective. In: NeurIPS, pp. 7139–7152 (2021)
28. Yang, Z., Xu, Q., Bao, S., He, Y., Cao, X., Huang, Q.: When all we need is a piece of the pie: a generic framework for optimizing two-way partial AUC. In: ICML. Proceedings of Machine Learning Research, vol. 139, pp. 11820–11829. PMLR (2021)
29. Yao, Y., Lin, Q., Yang, T.: Large-scale optimization of partial AUC in a range of false positive rates. In: NeurIPS (2022)
30. Zadrozny, B., Langford, J., Abe, N.: Cost-sensitive learning by cost-proportionate example weighting. In: ICDM, p. 435. IEEE Computer Society (2003)
31. Zhang, H., Cissé, M., Dauphin, Y.N., Lopez-Paz, D.: Mixup: beyond empirical risk minimization. In: ICLR (Poster). OpenReview.net (2018)
32. Zhang, R., et al.: Pre-trained online contrastive learning for insurance fraud detection. In: AAAI, pp. 22511–22519. AAAI Press (2024)
33. Zhu, D., Li, G., Wang, B., Wu, X., Yang, T.: When AUC meets DRO: optimizing partial AUC for deep learning with non-convex convergence guarantee. In: ICML. Proceedings of Machine Learning Research, vol. 162, pp. 27548–27573. PMLR (2022)

Causality

Counterfactual Robustness: A Framework to Analyze the Robustness of Causal Generative Models Across Interventions

Manal Benhamza[1(✉)], Marianne Clausel[2], and Myriam Tami[1]

[1] Paris-Saclay University, CentraleSupélec, MICS Lab, Gif-sur-Yvette, France
{manal.benhamza,myriam.tami}@centralesupelec.fr
[2] Lorraine University, Elie Cartan Institute, IECL, Nancy, France
marianne.clausel@univ-lorraine.fr

Abstract. Data generation using generative models is one of the most impressive growing field of artificial intelligence. However, such models are black boxes trained on huge datasets lacking interpretability properties. Causality is a natural framework to include expert knowledge into deep generative models. Other expected beneficial properties of causal generative models are fairness, transparency and robustness of the generation process. Up to our best knowledge, while many works have analyzed general generative models' robustness, surprisingly none have focused on their causal counterpart even if their robustness is a common claim. In the present paper, we introduce the fundamental concept of counterfactual robustness, which evaluates how sensitive causal generative models are to interventions with respect to distribution shifts. Through a series of experiments on synthetic and real-life datasets, we demonstrate that all the studied causal generative models are not equal with respect to counterfactual robustness. More surprisingly, we show that all causal interventions are also not equally robust. We provide a simple explanation based on the causal mechanisms between the variables, that is theoretically grounded in the case of an extended CausalVAE. Our indepth analysis also yields an efficient way to identify the most robust intervention based on prior knowledge on the causal graph.

Keywords: Counterfactual Robustness · Causal Representation Learning · Generative Models

1 Introduction

Generative AI models have gained widespread recognition for their ability to model complex distributions and generate high-quality outputs [3,5]. These models, however, often lack interpretability properties, making it difficult to

---

Supplementary Information The online version contains supplementary material available at https://doi.org/10.1007/978-3-032-05962-8_23.

understand the relationships between the learned representations. Causal generative models [14] address this issue by capturing causal dependencies between the extracted latent features, assumed as latent causal factors, hence offering enhanced transparency and interpretability [23,24]. Incorporating causal structures in generative models has furthermore enabled the generation of counterfactual data. By intervening on an extracted causal factor, we derive a new counterfactual model that can generate samples from unexplored contexts with specific attributes [2,20], providing answers to counterfactual what-if questions. The latter are commonly expressed in the form: "What will happen to the model's output when setting one of the input variables to a specific value?", and aim to analyze the impact of an intervention on the model's outcome. For example, for CelebA dataset [18], a counterfactual model with respect to the intervention "Gender=Male" is capable of generating the male counterparts of female input images, hence highlighting the facial attributes that change with the gender in the model's reconstruction. Since counterfactual models enhance the interpretability through responding "What-if" questions [12,26,27], they are leveraged in overcoming multiple AI research *challenges*. These models play a crucial role in defining *fairness* [17,28] by verifying whether a model's predictions remain consistent when only sensitive variables are altered. In *mitigating data biases* [11], counterfactuals correct imbalances by generating synthetic samples that counteract spurious correlations. They are also used in *reinforcement learning* [19] to simulate alternative actions, hence improving policy optimization and decision-making. Nonetheless, generative models are known to be vulnerable to distribution shifts [16], i.e., whereby small input perturbations induce unwanted changes in the output. Counterfactual models can therefore also be subject to this unwanted robustness limitation.

Surprisingly, many works exist on generative models' robustness [6,16,21], but to the best of our knowledge, none has ever studied causal generative models robustness across different interventions. Hence, this work provides a new theoretical framework and an experimental study addressing the stated robustness limitation. In Sect. 3, we introduce a new theoretical concept of counterfactual robustness, which allows to characterize the vulnerability of a causal generative model to distribution shifts across interventions. In Sect. 4, we conduct a series of experiments on Pendulum and CelebA datasets [18,29] to analyze the counterfactual robustness of popular observational data causal representation learning (CRL) models: CausalVAE [29], DEAR [25] and SCM-VAE [15] on different interventions. The obtained results show that counterfactual models respond differently to the considered perturbations. This observation motivated to develop in Sect. 5, a rigorous theoretical proof in the extended CausalVAE case. We demonstrate that the substantial difference in the counterfactual models' robustness levels to noise perturbations can be explicitly explained by the causal graph structure, more specifically by the critical properties of the removed edges with each intervention. Thus, in Sect. 5 we define a new theoretical concept of "Edge Robustness Score" *ERS* based on the adjacency matrix of the causal graph. Considering the causal graph as a prior knowledge, we propose an algorithm allowing to rank the counterfactual models' robustness to noise perturbations. The contributions of this research work are the following:

- We introduce a new theoretical concept of counterfactual robustness that evaluates the sensitivity of counterfactual causal models to distribution shifts.
- We analyze the counterfactual robustness of counterfactual models derived from popular observational data CRL models CausalVAE, SCM-VAE, and DEAR.
- We show through the conducted experimental study coupled with a theoretical analysis for an extended CausalVAE, that the counterfactual models exhibit different responses to the considered perturbations.
- Based on the causal graph, we propose a novel interpretability perspective for the differences in robustness to noise perturbations.
- We define the new theoretical concept of "Edge Robustness Score" ERS leveraging the adjacency matrix of the causal graph and establish that prior knowledge of the latter, allows the ranking of counterfactual models' robustness to noise perturbations solely based on the computation of the ERS.
- We propose a robustness score ranking algorithm based on the ERS.

2 Related Work

Generative Models Robustness [4], have introduced the so-called r-robustness to evaluate the robustness of Variational Autoencoders (VAE). This notion quantifies the robustness of a VAE reconstruction with respect to a given perturbation. In [4], r-robustness local margin bounds are provided, putting in evidence which parameters can be controlled to guarantee more robustness. Building on this result, [1] proves that it is possible to construct a VAE model with an a priori known level of robustness, based on fine control of the Lipschitz constants of the encoder and decoder. Their proposed theoretical framework focuses solely on the robustness of traditional VAEs and can not be extended to other generative models. Other works, such as [21], have studied the adversarial robustness of flow-based generative models, whereas [16] presented a method to craft adversarial attacks capable of changing different generative models' outputs. These papers thoroughly analyze the robustness of generative models. However, to the best of our knowledge, no prior work has explicitly and comprehensively examined the counterfactual robustness of causal generative models, a gap that we aim to address in this study. Notably, we provide an extensive experimental analysis for several causal generative models and a full theoretical analysis of counterfactual robustness for the extended CausalVAE.

Causal Representation Learning Generative Models. Recently, CRL models have advanced quickly due to their ability to learn causal latent factors from high-dimensional data along with their underlying causal structure. These learned factors describe meaningful semantics of data and hence guarantee more interpretability and explainability. State-of-the-art CRL models assume the data-generation process to be either observational, interventional, or counterfactual. Referring to the causal generative models mapping proposed in [14], we chose to study the robustness of 3 popular observational data models CausalVAE, DEAR, and SCM-VAE, that can both learn a latent causal representation and perform counterfactual generation. Focusing on this models paradigm is justified by its broader applicability compared to its counterparts that focus solely on controlled counterfactual generation, e.g., CausalGAN [13]. Moreover, observational data is always accessible, whereas interventional and counterfactual data are often limited or unavailable in real-world settings. This accessibility makes observational models suitable for studying robustness, as it allows for a comprehensive evaluation across diverse datasets and perturbations. CausalVAE uses a linear Structural Causal Model (SCM) parameterized by the causal adjacency matrix A, as illustrated in Fig. 1(a) to transform the encoded independent latent factors η into latent causal ones z. The input labels u are used as additional information to ensure the identifiability of the model. DEAR [25], in Fig. 1(c), as in Disentangled gEnerative cAusal Representation, builds a new disentangling method using an SCM as the prior distribution for a bidirectional generative model. DEAR and CausalVAE both utilize labels as weak supervision signals. However, unlike CausalVAE, DEAR does not learn intermediate independent encodings of the inputs. SCM-VAE overcomes the limitations of the CausalVAE, mainly the linear SCM, by learning a post-nonlinear additive noise SCM to describe more general relations between the causal variables, as presented in Fig. 1(e). The use of a non-linear SCM in both DEAR and SCM-VAE particularly interests us, as linear SCMs are limited in capturing complex causal relationships. We also seek to investigate the impact of non-linear SCMs on the robustness of CRL models.

3 Counterfactual Robustness of Causal Generative Models to Distribution Shifts

3.1 Counterfactual Models

Given a dataset $\mathcal{X} = (x_j)_{1 \leq j \leq N}$, we suppose that each observation x_j is a vector of $\mathbb{R}^{N_d}$, representing the set of observed variables. We define the latent variables as the set $\mathcal{Z} = (z_j)_{1 \leq j \leq M}$ considered as causal factors. We assume that the graph of relationships between the latent variables is known. The latter is characterized by its adjacency matrix A. Both expressions, latent variables, and causal factors will hence be used interchangeably in this paper.

Each model is characterized by its so-called latent SCM, describing the functional mechanism between latent variables $S := (E, P^\eta)$, where $E = (E_1, \ldots, E_M)$ is a collection of M equations of the form $E_j : z_j = f_j(\mathrm{PA}_j, \eta_j)$, with $\mathrm{PA}_j \subseteq \{z_1, \ldots, z_M\} \setminus \{z_j\}$. The variables in the subset PA_j are called parents of z_j. We denote $P^\eta = P^{\eta_1, \ldots, \eta_M}$ the joint distribution of the noise variables, that are supposed to be mutually independent. Let G be a CRL model with latent SCM S. We provide a description of the latent SCM of each model in Block 2 of Fig. 1(a), 1(c), and 1(e). Let do be the operator that performs hard

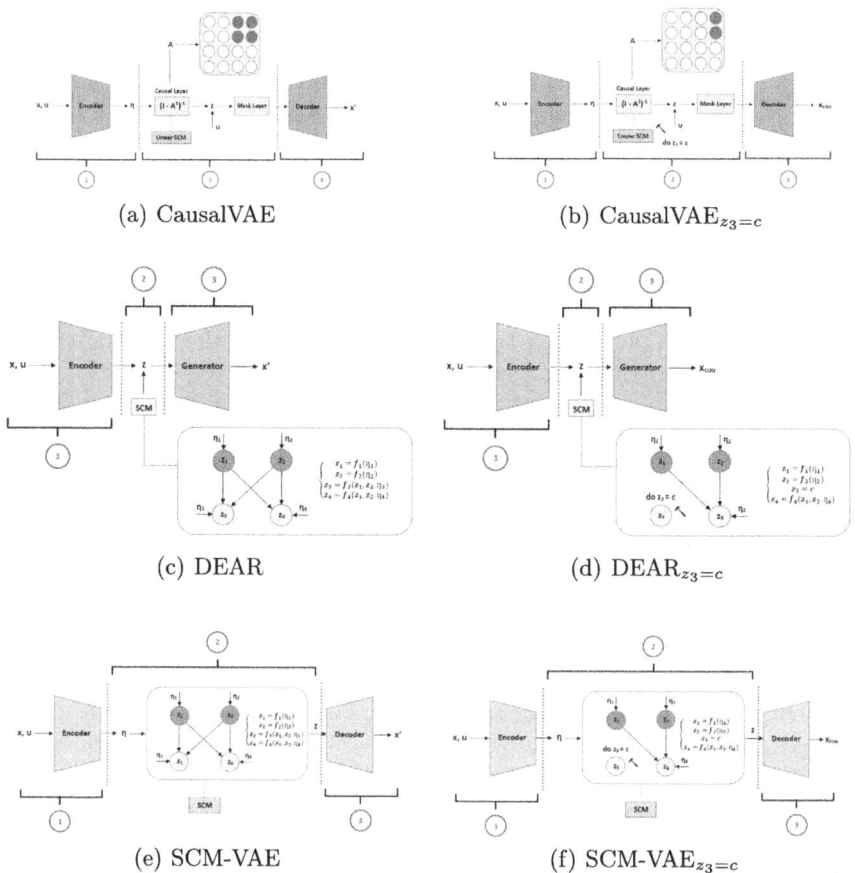

Fig. 1. Frameworks of the considered CRL models and their derived counterfactual models. In all Figures, Block 1 refers to the encoding process, Block 2 encloses the causal mechanisms, and Block 3 holds the decoding process. We shall note that both CausalVAE and SCM-VAE models consider the output of the encoder as noise variables for their latent SCM in Block 2.

interventions on the causal latent factors by replacing one or more structural equations in E with a constant c. This process results in a new SCM, denoted $\tilde{S}$. For the considered models, the new latent SCMs $\tilde{S}$ with respect to the intervention $do_{z_3=c}$ are represented in Block 2 of Fig. 1(b), 1(d) and 1(f). We call a counterfactual model derived from the CRL model G with respect to the intervention $do_{z_j=c}$, the model $G_{z_j=c}$ that generates counterfactual samples $\mathbf{x}_{\text{cou}}$ in Block 3 of Fig. 1(b), 1(d) and 1(f), by intervening on the causal factor z_j in the SCM fixing its value to c. In this work, we only consider counterfactual models intervening on a single causal latent variable.

Each $G_{z_j=c}$ is responsible for generating counterfactual samples with specific attributes that correspond to the intervention $do_{z_j=c}$. The intervening process of $G_{z_j=c}$ depends on the structure of G. For example, to obtain CausalVAE$_{z_j=c}$ in Fig. 1(b), the interventions are performed on the linear latent SCM breaking specific causal relations and hence modifying the matrix A. The intervened factors are then passed through the Mask Layer to propagate the effect of the parent variables to the children variables. The Mask Layer yields a final latent causal representation, which is used by the decoder in Block 3 to generate $\mathbf{x}_{\text{cou}}$. As for DEAR$_{z_j=c}$ in Fig. 1(d), $\mathbf{x}_{\text{cou}}$ are obtained by passing through the generator, Block 3, the latent factors sampled from the interventional SCM $\tilde{S}$. SCM-VAE$_{z_j=c}$ also yields $\mathbf{x}_{\text{cou}}$ by sampling from $\tilde{S}$ and then passing samples through the decoder Block 3 as explained in Fig. 1(f).

3.2 Counterfactual Robustness

We refer to a model's G reconstruction of an observation x_k, as $G(x_k)$ and the counterfactual reconstruction as $G_{z_j=c}(x_k)$. We test the robustness of each model, considering several perturbations of the dataset $\mathcal{X}$ detailed in Sect. 4. The perturbed dataset is denoted $\mathcal{X}^* := (x_j^*)_{1 \leq j \leq N}$. We give a general definition of the counterfactual robustness that we shall instantiate in the experimental section later.

Definition 1. *A causal generative model is said to be counterfactually γ-robust to a perturbation $*$ with respect to the intervention $do_{z_j=c}$ and a similarity measure SIM if:*

$$SIM\left(\{G_{z_j=c}(\mathcal{X}^*)\}, \{G_{z_j=c}(\mathcal{X})\}\right) \geq \gamma \qquad (1)$$

where, SIM is a similarity measure that evaluates how similar the distributions of the two considered datasets are in terms of features.

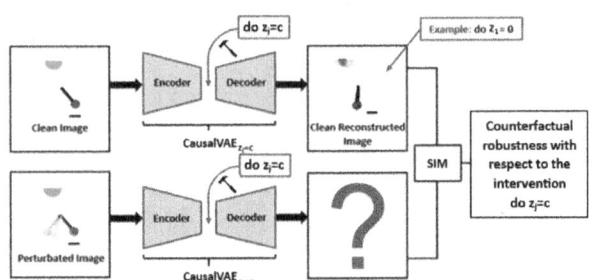

Fig. 2. Counterfactual Robustness Evaluation Pipeline exemplified for CausalVAE$_{z_j=c}$ on the Pendulum Dataset

Figure 2 shows the pipeline we propose for assessing the counterfactual robustness, exemplified in the case of CausalVAE$_{z_j=c}$ on the Pendulum dataset.

We start by fixing an intervention variable z_j and a value c, we perform the intervention on G and then recover $G_{z_j=c}$. In this example, z_1 is the Pendulum Angle and $c = 0$, i.e., we enforce the pendulum angle to be 0. We also choose a distribution shift perturbation $*$, apply it to our dataset to obtain a perturbed dataset, and afterward, pass the datasets of clean and perturbed images through $G_{z_1=0}$. We compute SIM in Eq. 1 between the two datasets of reconstructed images with and without perturbation and thereafter provide a measure of the robustness of $G_{z_1=0}$ with respect to the considered perturbation.

4 Experiments

Here, we evaluate the robustness of counterfactual models derived from 3 observational data CRL models CausalVAE, DEAR, and SCM-VAE on two annotated synthetic and real-world datasets, Pendulum and CelebA for 16 common perturbations. We follow the pipeline described in Fig. 2. To approximate real-world scenarios where perturbations occur at different intensities [22], we define 5 severity levels for each considered image corruption.

4.1 Datasets and Models

Datasets

- **Pendulum** [29] is a synthetic dataset that contains four causal variables: Pendulum Angle, Light Position, Shadow Position, and Shadow Length. It simulates the dynamic behavior of a pendulum and its interaction with a light source, capturing how the motion of the pendulum affects the position and length of its shadow. Its causal graph is presented in Fig. 3(a). The counterfactual models for Pendulum are generated respectively by intervening on the Pendulum Angle, Light Position, Shadow Position, or Shadow Length.
- **CelebA** [18] is a popular resource in the computer vision community. This dataset contains 200k images of human faces, each labeled with various attributes. In the literature, we consider two subsets of causally related attributes for this dataset. The first subset, CelebA(SMILE), includes: Gender, Smile, Eyes Open, and Mouth Open. The second subset CelebA(BEARD) consists of: Age, Gender, Bald, and Beard. We choose to work with CelebA(SMILE) to have the causal graph in Fig. 3(b), different in its structure from the Pendulum graph. In this setting, the counterfactual models are respectively obtained by intervening on the causal variables Gender, Smile, Eyes Open, or Mouth Open.

Datasets Perturbations. To simulate data distribution shifts on the datasets Pendulum and CelebA(SMILE), we inject the 16 perturbations proposed by [8] for ImageNet-C. The proposed perturbations belong to five main categories: noise, blur, weather, and digital. Each of the latter contains several techniques:

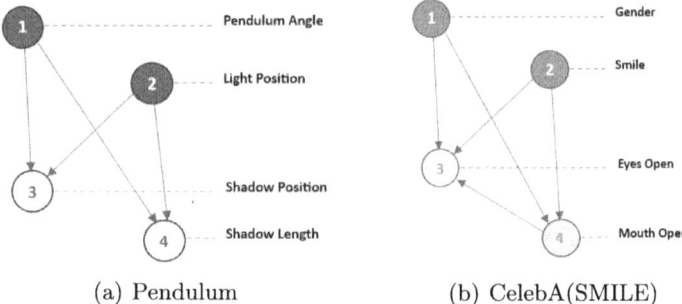

(a) Pendulum   (b) CelebA(SMILE)

Fig. 3. Causal Graphs of the Pendulum and CelebA(SMILE) datasets, highlighting the causal relationships between the considered causal variables. For example, in CelebA the Smile influences the eyes and mouth openness.

(1) Noise: gaussian noise, shot noise, impulse noise, speckle noise; (2) Blur: defocus blur, frosted glass blur, motion blur, zoom blur; (3) Weather: snow, frost, fog, brightness; (4) Digital: contrast, elastic, pixelated, JPEG compression. Since distribution shifts in the real world happen with different intensities, we use 5 severity levels for each perturbation technique following [7]. The number of input perturbations, taking into account their varying intensities sum to 80. The crafted corruptions for Pendulum are illustrated in Fig. 4.

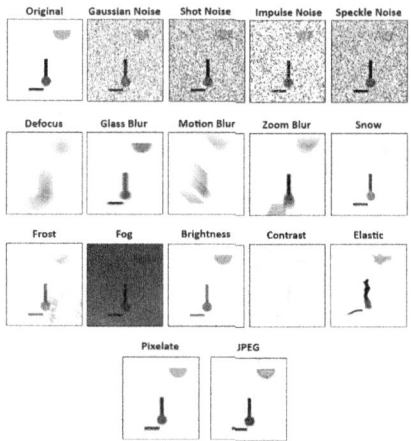

Fig. 4. Examples of 16 image perturbations. The original image (top left) is taken from the Pendulum dataset.

Models. We derive counterfactual models from two trained versions of **Causal-VAE**, **DEAR**, and **SCM-VAE**, one for each dataset, using the default baseline parameters and architectures from [29], [25], and [15] respectively.

4.2 Results

To compare the robustness of counterfactual models derived from CausalVAE, DEAR, and SCM-VAE, we use the Frechet Inception Distance (FID) as a similarity evaluation metric between the clean and perturbed reconstructed datasets for each intervention. FID was first introduced by [9]. The latter evaluates how similar the distributions of two datasets are in terms of features extracted by the pre-trained Inceptionv3 model. Low FID values indicate high similarity between the evaluated datasets. In this work, the Inceptionv3 model was fine-tuned on the considered datasets Pendulum and CelebA to capture their unique patterns.

We report in Figs. 5, 6 and 7 the mean and standard deviation of the FID between the clean and perturbed images over all perturbations, on both datasets Pendulum and CelebA. The lower the FID score, the more robust the counterfactual model. The counterfactual models were obtained by performing interventions on individual causal variables, setting their values to 0 and 0.8, respectively, for the Pendulum and CelebA(SMILE) datasets. Note that an intervention value of 0 is nonsense for the CelebA(SMILE) dataset. The figure scales differ between the two datasets for visualization purposes and Appendix C explores additional intervention values.

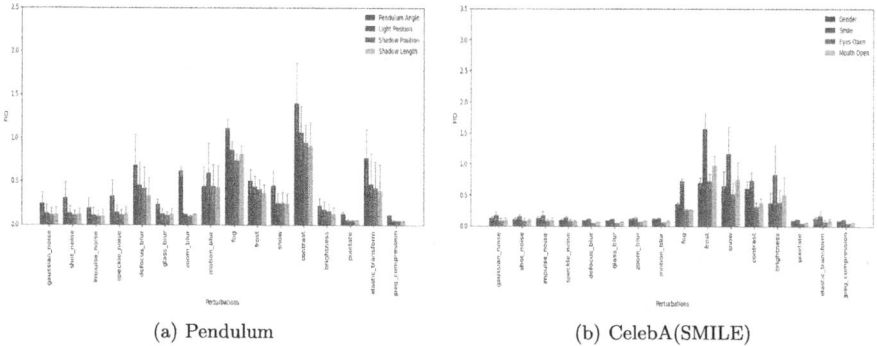

(a) Pendulum   (b) CelebA(SMILE)

Fig. 5. CausalVAE

We can observe from Figs. 5, 6, and 7 that counterfactual models obtained from the same CRL model are not equally impacted by the considered perturbations. For Pendulum, the contrast perturbation is the one affecting the counterfactual models the most, whereas it is frost for CelebA(SMILE). The JPEG compression has the least impact on both datasets. Moreover, it is to be noted that the counterfactual models derived by intervening on the exogenous causal variable Pendulum Angle for the Pendulum dataset, are generally the least robust to image perturbations. Counterfactuals derived from DEAR are more robust than those of the other considered CRL models CausalVAE and SCM-VAE. We shall note that the obtained FID are scaled by the spatial importance of the intervened causal variable to ensure a fair comparison across different

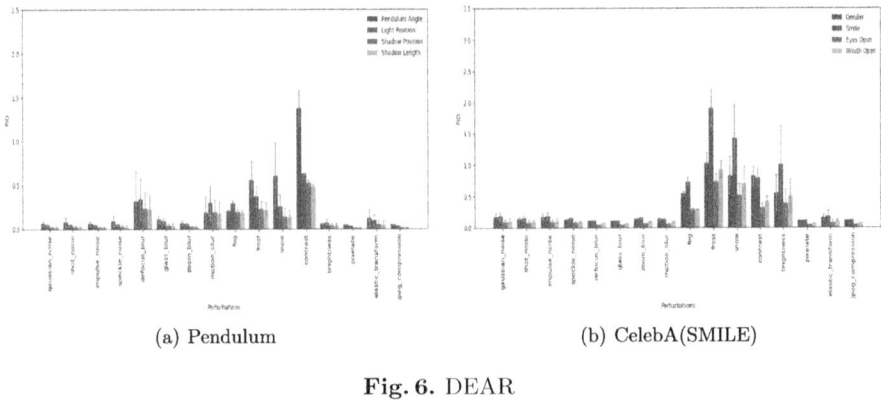

(a) Pendulum (b) CelebA(SMILE)

Fig. 6. DEAR

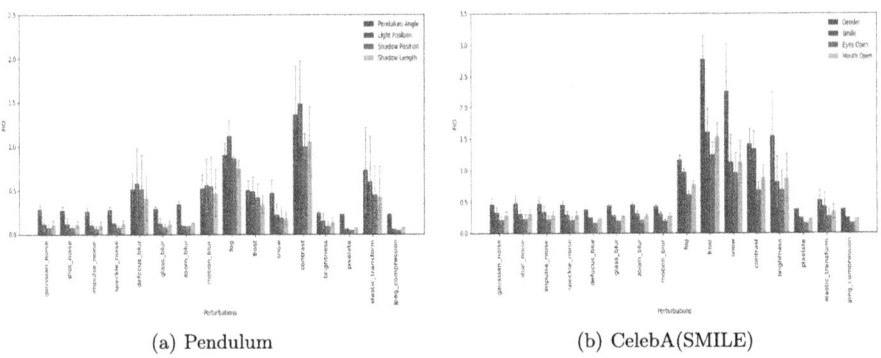

(a) Pendulum (b) CelebA(SMILE)

Fig. 7. SCM-VAE

interventions, taking into account the intrinsic significance of each causal variable in terms of picture space. The latter is calculated for complex attributes like Gender and Smile, by a decomposition following the semantic attribute graphs available in Appendix D.

Note also that for all types of **noise perturbations** and all CRL models, the counterfactual models derived by intervening on the endogeneous variables representing the causal effect of an exogeneous causal variable, e.g., Shadow Position and Shadow Length, are more robust than those obtained through interventions on the exogenous causal variables, e.g., Pendulum Angle and Light Position, for the Pendulum dataset. Whereas for CelebA(SMILE), intervening on the endogenous variable, Eyes Open yields the most robust counterfactual models for all analyzed CRL models and interventions on the exogenous causal variables Gender and Smile are associated with the least robust counterfactual models to noise perturbations.

The latter observation provided insight into the possibility of interpreting the difference in counterfactual robustness levels to noise perturbations based on the dataset's causal mechanisms, more specifically, by leveraging the causal structure of the causal graph and its related adjacency matrix. Since each intervention on the causal variables implies the removal of specific edges in the causal graph, then the counterfactual robustness is necessarily tied with the properties of the removed edges, as we will show in Sect. 5. In this part of the paper, we introduce an ERS metric and demonstrate through experimental results and theoretical proof in the case of an extended CausalVAE, that the most robust counterfactual model is the one for which an intervention removes the edges with the highest cumulative ERSs. Moreover, we propose an algorithm to identify the most robust intervention to noise perturbation based on a prior knowledge of the causal graph.

5 Causal Graph Edge Robustness Score

5.1 Motivation of the Definition

An intervention on a causal system $do_{z_j=c}$ implies analytically fixing the causal variable z_j to be equal to the intervention value c. Whereas graphically, it signifies removing all the incoming edges, in the causal graph, to the node z_j since the latter no longer depends on its causal parents and its value is rather determined by the intervention. The removal of edges eliminates all causal pathways that include them. Pathways are sequences of nodes and edges, and therefore removing an edge causes the connection to be cut in the pathways where it belongs. Hence, for a given CRL and intervention value, a derived counterfactual model can be characterized by the sets of edges and paths that are removed from the causal graph by its corresponding intervention.

Having different robustness scores for counterfactual models, as observed in Figs. 5, 6, and 7, implies thus that the causal graph edges are not equally robust. The computation of their robustness scores will hence be of great importance in understanding the robustness of counterfactual models solely by leveraging the causal graph. We therefore propose in Subsect. 5.2 to define an edge robustness score ERS based on the paths in which an edge is included and the singular vectors of $(I - A^T)^{-1}$. Existing works [10] have analyzed the centrality scores of edges in social networks based on different indicators. The centrality score of an edge is determined by the proportion of walks or paths that traverse it or by the amount of information it conveys. The latter centrality metrics give answers to questions related to the frequency with which information flows through an edge, the duration it takes, and the path multiplicity to reach the target node. No measure, however, was designed to describe the robustness of the edges.

Our proposed ERS enables to interpret the robustness of counterfactual models to noise perturbations based on the structure of the causal graph. We particularly show that the most robust counterfactual model is the one for which the removed edges have the highest cumulative ERS.

5.2 Theoretical Insights

Let $\mathcal{G}$ be a causal graph and A its corresponding adjacency matrix.

Definition 2 (Edge Robustness Score). *Given an edge $e = <s_e, t_e>$ in a causal graph $\mathcal{G}$, represented by its source node and target node respectively, noted s_e and t_e, the edge robustness score is defined as the sum of the products of the eigenvector scores at both ends of the paths containing the edge, weighted by the path intensity:*

$$ERS_e := \sum_{p \in P_e} w_1(s_p) y_1(t_p) Int(p) \quad (2)$$

where A is the adjacency matrix of $\mathcal{G}$, w_1 and y_1 are respectively the right and left singular vectors of $(I - A^T)^{-1}$ corresponding to the largest singular value $\lambda_1((I - A^T)^{-1})$, $Int(p)$ is the scalar representing the path intensity, given by the product of the weights along the path edges, P_e is the set of paths where e is included. s_p and e_p denote respectively the source and target nodes of the path p and $w_1(s_p)$ is the s_p^{th} coordinate of w_1, $y_1(t_p)$ the t_p^{th} coordinate of y_1.

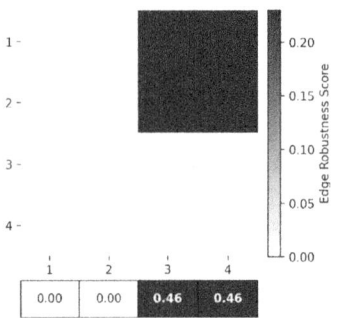

Fig. 8. Pendulum Edge Robustness Scores

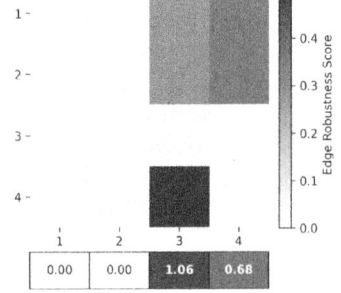

Fig. 9. CelebA Edge Robustness Scores

Figures 8 and 9 illustrate the edge robustness scores, respectively, for the Pendulum and CelebA(SMILE) datasets. The considered order of the variables is the same as in the causal graphs Fig. 3(a) and 3(b). Non existing edges in the causal graph are affected a robustness score of 0. Figure 8 suggests, in the case of Pendulum, that the edges linking the exogenous causal variables, Pendulum Angle and Light Position, to the endogenous ones, Shadow Position and Shadow Length are equally robust. For CelebA(SMILE), Fig. 9 indicates that there are three levels of edge robustness. Edges linking the cause variable Gender to its effects Eyes Open and Mouth Open exhibit low robustness highlighted in light orange, the ones in dark orange linking Smile to the same effects Eyes Open and Mouth Open display moderate robustness, and only one edge in dark brown from Mouth Open to Eyes Open demonstrates high robustness.

This notion of edge robustness is important, because the ordering of the cumulative ERS for each intervention, aligns with the ranking of the counterfactual robustness experimentally observed in Sect. 4. Specifically, we display below Figs. 8 and 9, the sum over the columns of the edge robustness scores. The sum over column j corresponds to the cumulative ERS of the edges removed when intervening on the variable z_j. This provides a structural justification for the observed differences in counterfactual robustness, as interventions that remove edges with higher cumulative robustness scores yield more robust counterfactual models.

5.3 An Extensive Theoretical Analysis in the Case of an Extended CausalVAE

We denote extended CausalVAE, a VAE based causal model where the causal layer implements the general non linear SCM [30] in Eq. 3:

$$z = \pi_1((I - A^T)^{-1}\pi_2(\eta)) \qquad (3)$$

where A is the adjacency matrix of the causal graph corresponding to the causal variables $\mathcal{Z}$, π_1 and π_2 are element-wise transformations generally nonlinear.

By incorporating a parametric SCM in the causal layer, the extended CausalVAE framework can encompass both the linear CausalVAE and the SCM-VAE models, depending on the choice of the functions π_1 and π_2. In the linear CausalVAE case, both π_1 and π_2 are identity functions, while in the SCM-VAE setting, π_2 remains the identity function and π_1 is a non-linear transformation learned by a neural network.

In Appendix A, building on [4] we express leveraging the structure of an extended CausalVAE and the Lipschitz continuity of its components, the counterfactual robustness probability, and the margin bounds of the counterfactual models against adversarial attacks. These attacks involve generating imperceptible noise that, when applied to the inputs of an extended CausalVAE counterfactual models, result in unintended reconstructions. The obtained counterfactual robustness margin bounds with respect to the intervention $do_{z_j=c}$ are expressed as a function of $\lambda_1((I - (A^j)^T)^{-1})$, the largest singular value of $(I - (A^j)^T)^{-1}$, where A^j corresponds to the adjacency matrix of the new causal graph after the intervention $do_{z_j=c}$. We show in Appendix A that the lower $\lambda_1((I - (A^j)^T)^{-1})$, the larger the counterfactual robustness margin bounds. Th.1 provides, based on the proposed ERS, an approximation of $\lambda_1((I-(A^j)^T)^{-1})$. We show, using first order matrix perturbation theory, that removing edges with the highest cumulative ERS effectively reduces the largest singular value $\lambda_1((I - (A^j)^T)^{-1})$.

Theorem 1 (Edge Removal Impact on Singular Values). *Let $\mathcal{G}$ be a causal graph and A its corresponding adjacency matrix. Let $\widehat{\lambda_1}$ be the first singular value of $(I - \widehat{A}^T)^{-1}$, where $\widehat{A}$ is the adjacency matrix of the perturbed* causal graph $\widehat{\mathcal{G}}$, obtained by removing the edges indexed by the set $\mathcal{E}$ from $\mathcal{G}$; such that $(I - \widehat{A}^T)^{-1} = (I - A^T)^{-1} + Q$. Let α be the singular value gap, w_1 and y_1 be respectively the right and left singular vectors of $(I - A^T)^{-1}$. If λ_1, $\widehat{\lambda_1}$ are respectively the first singular values of $(I - A^T)^{-1}$, $(I - \widehat{A}^T)^{-1}$ and $\alpha \geq 2\|Q\|$, then:

$$\lambda_1 - \widehat{\lambda_1} \simeq \sum_{e \in \mathcal{E}} \sum_{p \in P_e} w_1(s_p) y_1(t_p) Int(p) \qquad (4)$$

$$\simeq \sum_{e \in \mathcal{E}} ERS_e \qquad (5)$$

where P_e is the set of paths in which each edge e is included, s_p, t_p are respectively the source and target nodes of each path $p \in P_e$ and $Int(p)$ the intensity of the path p.

The quality of the approximation $\lambda_1 - \widehat{\lambda_1}$ in Theorem 1 depends on the singular value gap α and the Frobenius norm of Q. To evaluate the quality of the proposed approximator on real causal graphs, we measure the linear correlation between the sets of real and approximated singular values, considering different sparsity levels l ($l = 0.2, 0.4, 0.6, 0.8, 1$) and graph sizes m ($m = 4, 6, 8, 10, 20$). We report in Tables 1 and 2 the mean and standard deviation of the obtained correlation results on 300 randomly simulated causal graph for each setting. We put $-$ whenever the considered sparsity level leads to isolated nodes in the causal graph.

Table 1. Approximation Quality (Interventions on all the variables)

	$l = 0.2$	$l = 0.4$	$l = 0.6$	$l = 0.8$	$l = 1$
$m = 4$	–	–	–	0.989 ± 0.017	0.979 ± 0.014
$m = 6$	–	0.979 ± 0.038	0.977 ± 0.019	0.969 ± 0.017	0.957 ± 0.018
$m = 8$	–	0.973 ± 0.025	0.971 ± 0.017	0.957 ± 0.018	0.943 ± 0.018
$m = 10$	–	0.973 ± 0.017	0.962 ± 0.018	0.948 ± 0.019	0.931 ± 0.019
$m = 20$	0.972 ± 0.047	0.973 ± 0.018	0.96 ± 0.018	0.947 ± 0.021	0.943 ± 0.018

It can be seen that the proposed approximator is good for ranking the first singular values of the perturbed matrices $(I - (A^j)^T)^{-1}$, since correlation values are all greater than 0.94. It is also to be noted that for dense causal graphs of size m, the approximator is better in ranking the first singular values corresponding

Table 2. Approximation Quality (Interventions on the $(m-2)$ first variables)

	$l = 0.2$	$l = 0.4$	$l = 0.6$	$l = 0.8$	$l = 1$
$m = 4$	–	–	–	0.989 ± 0.017	0.979 ± 0.014
$m = 6$	–	0.984 ± 0.016	0.988 ± 0.023	0.994 ± 0.012	0.998 ± 0.004
$m = 8$	–	0.98 ± 0.029	0.988 ± 0.015	0.994 ± 0.009	0.995 ± 0.007
$m = 10$	–	0.986 ± 0.016	0.988 ± 0.016	0.992 ± 0.011	0.994 ± 0.006
$m = 20$	0.985 ± 0.016	0.989 ± 0.015	0.99 ± 0.01	0.992 ± 0.012	0.995 ± 0.005

to the $m-2$ first interventions (correlation often near 1). This is due to $\|Q\|$ being large for interventions on the last variables in dense causal graphs, which degrades the quality of the approximation.

In general, Theorem 1 provides a good approximation of how the first singular value of $(I-A^T)^{-1}$ changes when removing a set of edges in the causal graph, as a function of the cumulative ERS of the removed edges. As confirmed by Tables 3 and 4, the interventions that remove the edges with the highest cumulative ERS are the ones that effectively reduce the largest singular value of the perturbed matrix $(I - \widehat{A}^T)^{-1}$. The latter interventions are thus the ones associated with the counterfactual models with the highest counterfactual robustness margin bounds.

Table 3. Pendulum Intervention Edge Robustness and Largest Singular Values $\widehat{\lambda_1}$

Causal Variable	Edges Robustness	$\widehat{\lambda_1}$
Pendulum Angle	0	1.71
Light Position	0	1.71
Shadow Position	0.46	1.51
Shadow Length	0.46	1.51

Table 4. CelebA(SMILE) Intervention Edge Robustness and Largest Singular Values $\widehat{\lambda_1}$

Causal Variable	Edges Robustness	$\widehat{\lambda_1}$
Gender	0	2.23
Smile	0	2.23
Eyes Open	1.06	1.51
Mouth Open	0.68	1.64

5.4 Algorithm

Based on Subsects. 5.2 and 5.3, we propose an Algorithm 1 to rank the robustness of counterfactual models derived from a CRL using a unique intervention value.

Algorithm 1. Counterfactual Robustness Ranking

1: **Input:** Adjacency matrix A of the causal graph $\mathcal{G}$
2: **Output:** Ascending order sorting of the counterfactual robustness
3: Initialize the cumulative ERS vector: $ranking_i \leftarrow 0$
4: Compute the leading eigenvalue λ_1 of $(I - A^T)^{-1}$, let w_1 and y_1 be respectively the right and left singular vectors
5: **for** $j = 1$ **to** M (Considering all possible intervention variables) **do**
6:     **for** Edge e in parent edges of z_j, the intervened variable **do**
7:         Identify the paths P_e including edge e
8:         **for** path (s_p, t_p) in P_e **do**
9:             Compute the intensity of the path $Int(p)$
10:            $ranking_i \leftarrow ranking_i + w_1(s_p)y_1(t_p)Int(p)$
11:         **end for**
12:     **end for**
13: **end for**
14: Sort in ascending order the cumulative ERS vector $ranking$
15: **return** Return the indexes of the sorting

6 Conclusion

This paper introduces a novel theoretical framework for evaluating the counterfactual robustness of causal generative models under distribution shifts. Through extensive experiments on the Pendulum and CelebA datasets, we demonstrate that the studied counterfactual models exhibit varying degrees of robustness to perturbations, which can be explained by the causal graph structure. To formalize this relationship, we define the edge robustness score, a theoretical measure leveraging the causal adjacency matrix. Our findings reveal that intervening on variables with the highest cumulative robustness scores for their incoming edges yields the most robust counterfactual models. Future research could explore counterfactual models that intervene simultaneously on multiple variables at a time and extend our theoretical work to learning based perturbations for other CRL models like DEAR.

Acknowledgments. This work was performed using HPC resources from the "Mésocentre" computing center of CentraleSupélec and Ecole Normale Supérieure Paris-Saclay supported by CNRS and Région Ile-de-France. This work was partially supported by the ANR CLearDeep ANR-23-CE23-0008-01.

The authors have no competing interests to declare that are relevant to the content of this article.

References

1. Barrett, B., Camuto, A., Willetts, M., Rainforth, T.: Certifiably robust variational autoencoders. In: Proceedings of The 25th International Conference on Artificial Intelligence and Statistics, pp. 3663–3683 (2022)
2. Besserve, M., Sun, R., Janzing, D., Schölkopf, B.: A theory of Independent mechanisms for extrapolation in generative models. In: Proceedings of the AAAI Conference on Artificial Intelligence (2020)
3. Bond-Taylor, S., Leach, A., Long, Y., Willcocks, C.G.: Deep generative modelling: a comparative review of VAEs, GANs, normalizing flows. energy-based and autoregressive models. IEEE Trans. Pattern Analy. Mach. Intell. (2021)
4. Camuto, A., Willetts, M., Roberts, S., Holmes, C., Rainforth, T.: Towards a Theoretical Understanding of the Robustness of Variational Autoencoders, pp. 3565–3573 (2021)
5. Cao, H., et al.: A survey on generative diffusion models. IEEE Trans. Knowl. Data Eng. **36**, 2814–2830 (2024)
6. Cui, X., Aparcedo, A., Jang, Y.K., Lim, S.N.: On the robustness of large multimodal models against image adversarial attacks. In: Proceedings of the IEEE/CVF Conference on Computer Vision and Pattern Recognition CVPR, pp. 24625–24634 (2024)
7. Geirhos, R., Rubisch, P., Michaelis, C., Bethge, M., Wichmann, F., Brendel, W.: ImageNet-trained CNNs are biased Towards Texture. ArXiv (2018)
8. Hendrycks, D., Dietterich, T.: Benchmarking neural network robustness to common corruptions and perturbations. In: Proceedings of the International Conference on Learning Representations (2019)
9. Heusel, M., Ramsauer, H., Unterthiner, T., Nessler, B., Hochreiter, S.: GANs trained by a two time-scale update rule converge to a local nash equilibrium. Adv. Neural Inform. Process. Syst. **30** (2017)
10. Huang, X., Huang, W.: Eigenedge: a measure of edge centrality for big graph exploration. J. Comput. Lang. (2019)
11. Hutchinson, B., Denton, E., Mitchell, M., Gebru, T.: Detecting Bias with Generative Counterfactual Face Attribute Augmentation (2019)
12. Hvilshøj, F., Iosifidis, A., Assent, I.: ECINN: efficient counterfactuals from invertible neural networks. In: 32nd British Machine Vision Conference Virtual (2021)
13. Kocaoglu, M., Snyder, C., Dimakis, A.G., Vishwanath, S.: CausalGAN: learning causal implicit generative models with adversarial training. In: International Conference on Learning Representations (2018)
14. Komanduri, A., Wu, X., Wu, Y., Chen, F.: From identifiable causal representations to controllable counterfactual generation: a survey on causal generative modeling. Trans. Mach. Learn. Res. (2024)
15. Komanduri, A., Wu, Y., Huang, W., Chen, F., Wu, X.: SCM-VAE: learning identifiable causal representations via structural knowledge. In: IEEE International Conference on Big Data, pp. 1014–1023 (2022)
16. Kos, J., Fischer, I., Song, D.X.: Adversarial examples for generative models. In: IEEE Security and Privacy Workshops SPW, pp. 36–42 (2017)
17. Kusner, M.J., Loftus, J., Russell, C., Silva, R.: Counterfactual fairness. Adv. Neural Inform. Process. Syst. **30** (2017)
18. Liu, Z., Luo, P., Wang, X., Tang, X.: Deep learning face attributes in the wild. In: 2015 IEEE International Conference on Computer Vision ICCV, pp. 3730–3738 (2015)

19. Lu, C., et al.: Sample-efficient reinforcement learning via counterfactual-based data augmentation. In: Offline Reinforcement Learning - Workshop at the 34th Conference on Neural Information Processing Systems NeurIPS (2020)
20. Melistas, T., et al.: Benchmarking counterfactual image generation. In: The Thirty-eight Conference on Neural Information Processing Systems Datasets and Benchmarks Track (2024)
21. Pope, P., Balaji, Y., Feizi, S.: Adversarial robustness of flow-based generative models. In: International Conference on Artificial Intelligence and Statistics, pp. 3795–3805 (2020)
22. Qiu, J., et al.: Benchmarking robustness under distribution shift of multimodal image-text models. In: NeurIPS Workshop on Distribution Shifts: Connecting Methods and Applications (2022)
23. Schölkopf, B., Von Kügelgen, J.: From statistical to causal learning. In: Proceedings of the International Congress of Mathematicians, p. 1 (2022)
24. Schölkopf, B., et al.: Toward causal representation learning. Proc. IEEE **109**, 612–634 (2021)
25. Shen, X., Liu, F., Dong, H., Lian, Q., Chen, Z., Zhang, T.: Weakly supervised disentangled generative causal representation learning. J. Mach. Learn. Res., 1–55 (2022)
26. Van Looveren, A., Klaise, J.: Interpretable counterfactual explanations guided by prototypes. In: Machine Learning and Knowledge Discovery in Databases Research Track, pp. 650–665 (2021)
27. Verma, S., Dickerson, J.P., Hines, K.: Counterfactual Explanations for Machine Learning: Challenges Revisited. ArXiv (2021)
28. Wang, Z., Chu, Z., Blanco, R., Chen, Z., Chen, S.C., Zhang, W.: Advancing graph counterfactual fairness through fair representation learning. In: Machine Learning and Knowledge Discovery in Databases Research Track, pp. 40–58 (2024)
29. Yang, M., Liu, F., Chen, Z., Shen, X., Hao, J., Wang, J.: CausalVAE: disentangled representation learning via neural structural causal models. In: IEEE/CVF Conference on Computer Vision and Pattern Recognition CVPR, pp. 9588–9597 (2020)
30. Yu, Y., Jie Chen, T.G., Yu, M.: DAG-GNN: DAG structure learning with graph neural networks. In: Proceedings of the 36th International Conference on Machine Learning (2019)

KANITE: Kolmogorov–Arnold Networks for ITE Estimation

Eshan Mehendale, Abhinav Thorat[✉], Ravi Kolla, and Niranjan Pedanekar

Sony Research India, Bangalore, India
{eshan.mehendale,abhinav.thorat,ravi.kolla,niranjan.pedanekar}@sony.com

Abstract. We introduce **KANITE**, a framework leveraging Kolmogorov–Arnold Networks (KANs) for Individual Treatment Effect (ITE) estimation under multiple treatments setting in causal inference. By utilizing KAN's unique abilities to learn univariate activation functions as opposed to learning linear weights by Multi-Layer Perceptrons (MLPs), we improve the estimates of ITEs. The KANITE framework comprises two key architectures: 1. Integral Probability Metric (IPM) architecture: This employs an IPM loss in a specialized manner to effectively align towards ITE estimation across multiple treatments. 2. Entropy Balancing (EB) architecture: This uses weights for samples that are learned by optimizing entropy subject to balancing the covariates across treatment groups. Extensive evaluations on benchmark datasets demonstrate that KANITE outperforms state-of-the-art algorithms in both **PEHE** (**P**recision in the **E**stimation of **H**eterogeneous **E**ffects) and **ATE** (**A**verage **T**reatment **E**ffect) error metrics. Our experiments highlight the advantages of KANITE in achieving improved causal estimates, emphasizing the potential of KANs to advance causal inference methodologies across diverse application areas.

Keywords: Causal Inference · Treatment Effect Estimation · Kolmogorov–Arnold Networks

1 Introduction

In causal inference, the estimation of Individual Treatment Effects (ITEs) is a foundational problem, as it is crucial for understanding the impact of a treatment on an individual user and personalizing treatments. In observational studies, the estimation of ITEs becomes particularly challenging due to the presence of confounders—variables that affect both the treatment and the outcome. For example, imagine a store that offers a discount on a high-end coffee machine only during periods of high customer volume, such as busy weekend hours. An analyst notices that customers who receive the discount are less likely to complete their purchase and concludes that the discount is ineffective. However, a hidden confounder—queue length—may be influencing both the likelihood of receiving

---

E. Mehendale—This work was carried out during an internship at Sony Research India.

the discount (since it is only offered during high-traffic times) and the decision to abandon the purchase (due to long wait times). In this case, queue length distorts the observed relationship between the discount and purchasing behavior. Consequently, it is essential to mitigate the bias introduced by such confounders in order to clearly isolate and estimate the treatment's effect on the outcome. ITE estimation is widely recognized to have applications across a broad range of domains, including, but not limited to, healthcare [26], education [10], e-commerce [6], entertainment [32] and social sciences [13]. Given its importance, a wide range of algorithms has been developed to address this challenge, each adopting different modeling strategies and assumptions.

These approaches span from classical methods like propensity score matching to more recent advances in representation learning and deep neural networks. However, many of these approaches face trade-offs in flexibility, interpretability, and generalization. This motivates the need for more expressive and structured models such as the Kolmogorov–Arnold Network (KAN), which offers a promising framework for capturing complex causal relationships with greater clarity and adaptability.

In the year 2024, Kolmogorov-Arnold Networks (KANs) have been introduced as a promising alternative to Multi Layer Perceptrons (MLPs), also known as fully connected feedforward neural networks, offering the advantage of improved accuracy, interpretability and reduced model complexity [18]. Although both MLPs and KANs feature fully connected structures, the key difference lies in their learning mechanisms. KANs learn univariate activation functions at each edge of network, whereas MLPs learn linear weights along all edges. Further, KANs are inspired by the Kolmogorov-Arnold representation theorem [4,17] whereas MLPs are motivated by the universal approximation theorem [11]. Shortly after their inception, KANs were rapidly integrated into various algorithmic frameworks, where they replaced MLPs and demonstrated notable performance improvements. To that end, we direct the reader to the following references for a deeper understanding of KAN applications: transformer architectures [30], federated learning [34], online reinforcement learning [16], autoencoders [19], convolutional neural networks [2], and graph neural networks [15].

Although KANs have been applied in various domains, as mentioned above, their potential in the context of ITE estimation remains unexplored. To the best of our knowledge, this is the first study to investigate and propose algorithms that leverage KANs for ITE estimation in the multiple treatment setting. Given that mitigating confounding bias is critical for accurate ITE estimation, we aim to enhance this by utilizing KANs to better capture complex treatment and outcome relationships. Furthermore, since confounding bias becomes even more profound in the case of multiple treatments, we address this challenge by combining KANs with a loss function formulated using either Integral Probability Metrics (IPM) or the Entropy Balancing (EB) method. Additionally, we investigate the effect of KAN parameters such as grid size and spline degree on ITE estimation performance.

In the following we outline the salient contribution of our work.

- To the best of our knowledge, it is the first work that studies and incorporates KANs into the ITE estimation including the multiple treatment setting.
- We propose the KANITE framework for ITE estimation, which employs shared representation learning with representation loss formulated using either the IPM or EB method. Our KANITE framework comprises three distinct algorithms, inspired by [25], leveraging KANs as its fundamental building blocks.
- To achieve improved covariate balancing across all treatments, we extend the entropy balancing method [33] (originally developed for binary treatment settings) using Lagrangian duality theory to handle multiple treatments, and propose an algorithm that integrates both KANs and entropy balancing loss.
- Through extensive numerical evaluations, we demonstrate the superior performance of KANITE against baselines on various binary and multiple treatments benchmark datasets such as IHDP, NEWS-2/4/8/16, ACIC-16 and Twins.
- We also provide a detailed analysis of the impact of various KAN parameters such as grid size and the degree of splines used in the univariate activation functions for ITE estimates.

We structure the rest of the paper as follows. The next section reviews related work and highlights key differences. Section 3 provides the technical details underlying the problem formulation. Section 4 presents our proposed models and their technicalities in detail. Section 5 covers the baselines and compares them with KANITE on the PEHE and ATE error metrics. Finally, Sect. 6 concludes the paper and suggests future research directions.

2 Literature Survey

This section briefly reviews relevant literature and contrasts it with our contributions. To the best of our knowledge, this is the first work to explore the utilization of KANs in ITE estimation. Therefore, we review the literature on ITE estimation and KANs separately.

ITE estimation has been extensively studied in the literature; thus, we restrict our discussion to a few notable works. In [24,25], and [31], the authors address an ITE estimation setup similar to ours and propose efficient algorithms based on MLPs—hence, these works have been chosen as baselines in our work. Additionally, in [8,28], the authors consider ITE estimation in a network setting, where users are assumed to be connected through a network. They propose algorithms that leverage additional user network information to obtain improved ITE estimates. A few other works [9,14,20,27] incorporate auxiliary treatment information rather than treating treatments categorically, demonstrating methods to achieve improved ITE estimates. Moreover, leveraging treatment information inherently endows algorithms with zero-shot capabilities, enabling them to predict the outcomes for novel treatments that were *not* encountered during training. It is important to note that these approaches—network-based ITE estimation and the use of auxiliary treatment information—are distinct from the setup considered in this study.

In [18], the authors introduce KANs and demonstrate their advantages over MLPs in terms of accuracy, model complexity, and interpretability—both theoretically and empirically. Since then, KANs have been incorporated in various areas of research, consistently demonstrating their potential benefits. In [15], the authors propose two methods to integrate KAN layers into graph convolutional networks and empirically evaluate these architectures using a semi-supervised graph learning task using the Cora dataset. In [30], a KAN-based transformer architecture is proposed that employs rational functions over splines in the KAN layers to enhance model expressiveness and performance. Meanwhile, [34] introduces a KAN-based federated learning approach that outperforms its MLP counterparts on classification tasks. In [16] the use of KANs in the proximal policy optimization algorithm is explored, demonstrating benefits in terms of model complexity. The authors in [19] investigate the efficiency of KANs for data representation through autoencoders, while KAN-based convolutional neural networks are proposed and evaluated on the Fashion-MNIST dataset in [2], showcasing advantages over their MLP counterparts. Additionally, KANs have been employed in physics-informed deep learning frameworks to improve the modeling of physical systems. In [29], the authors introduce Kolmogorov–Arnold-Informed Neural Networks (KINN), which leverage KANs in place of traditional MLPs to solve both forward and inverse problems governed by differential equations. In a separate line of work [21], the authors propose Physics-Informed Kolmogorov–Arnold Networks (PIKAN), which incorporate Efficient-KAN and WAV-KAN architectures and demonstrate their superior performance compared to conventional physics-informed neural networks based on MLPs.

3 Problem Formulation

In this section, we present the mathematical formulation of the problem considered in this work. We adopt the Rubin-Neyman [22] potential outcomes framework to introduce the problem. For clarity, we define the following notation. Let N and K denote the number of users (samples) and treatments respectively. We use $\mathbf{x}_i$ and t_i to denote the covariates and assigned treatment of user-i respectively. Furthermore, Let Y_t^i denote the potential outcome for user-i when treatment-t is given. For brevity, when the context is clear, we may omit the user index in the notation. We assume that the following standard causal inference assumptions from [22] hold.

Assumption 1 (Unconfoundedness). *Under this assumption, the potential outcomes, Y_t's, are independent of the treatment assignment, t, conditioned on the user covariates, $\mathbf{x}$. Mathematically, stated as:*

$$(Y_1, Y_2, \cdots, Y_K) \perp t \mid \mathbf{x}.$$

In other words, this assumption ensures that all confounders, covariates that are affecting both Y_t and t, are observed and accounted in $\mathbf{x}$.

Assumption 2 (Positivity). *It ensures that each user has a positive probability of receiving any of the available treatments. Mathematically it is given as:*

$$\mathbb{P}(t_i = t) > 0 \quad \forall 1 \leq i \leq N,\ 1 \leq t \leq K.$$

Assumption 3 (Stable Unit Treatment Value Assumption (SUTVA)). *It implies that the potential outcomes of a user are solely dependent on their received treatments and independent of the assigned treatments of other users.*

With the help of the above, let us define the ITE and ATE of treatment-a with respect to b for a user with covariates, $\mathbf{x}_i$, denoted by $\tau_{a,b}(\mathbf{x}_i)$ and $\text{ATE}_{a,b}$ respectively, as:

$$\tau_{a,b}(\mathbf{x}_i) = \mathbb{E}\left[Y_a^i - Y_b^i \mid \mathbf{x} = \mathbf{x}_i\right] \tag{1}$$

$$\text{ATE}_{a,b} = \mathbb{E}\left[Y_a - Y_b\right]. \tag{2}$$

We now introduce the problem as follows. Given N samples $\{\mathbf{x}_i, t_i, Y_{t_i}^i\}_{i=1}^N$, our goal is to estimate ITEs of all users and ATEs across all pairs of treatments. We use the existing error metrics [28] for this problem, such as ϵ_{PEHE} and ϵ_{ATE}, to quantify the performance of a model, as defined below:

$$\epsilon_{\text{PEHE}} = \frac{1}{\binom{K}{2}} \sum_{a=1}^{K} \sum_{b=1}^{a-1} \left[\frac{1}{N}\sum_{i=1}^{N}(\hat{\tau}^{a,b}(\mathbf{x}_i) - \tau^{a,b}(\mathbf{x}_i))^2\right] \tag{3}$$

$$\epsilon_{\text{ATE}} = \frac{1}{\binom{K}{2}} \sum_{a=1}^{K} \sum_{b=1}^{a-1} \left[\left|\frac{1}{N}\sum_{i=1}^{N}\hat{\tau}^{a,b}(\mathbf{x}_i) - \frac{1}{N}\sum_{i=1}^{N}\tau^{a,b}(\mathbf{x}_i)\right|\right], \tag{4}$$

where $\hat{\tau}(\cdot)$ represents the estimated ITEs produced by the model.

4 Proposed Model

In this section, we present our proposed framework KANITE (Kolmogorov-Arnold Networks for Individual Treatment Effect estimation), that leverages KANs for causal inference, specifically for estimating ITEs. KANITE utilizes the functional decomposition properties of KANs, which decompose complex functions into sum of univariate functions. This decomposition enables KANITE to capture the causal effect of a treatment while accounting for confounding variables that influence both treatment assignment and outcomes. KANITE's ability to approximate any continuous function allows it to adapt to diverse data distributions, establishing it as a flexible and effective framework for causal inference. It operates under the standard assumptions of causal inference stated in Assumptions 1, 2 and 3. We provide a brief overview of KAN preliminaries below, which is a crucial part of the KANITE framework.

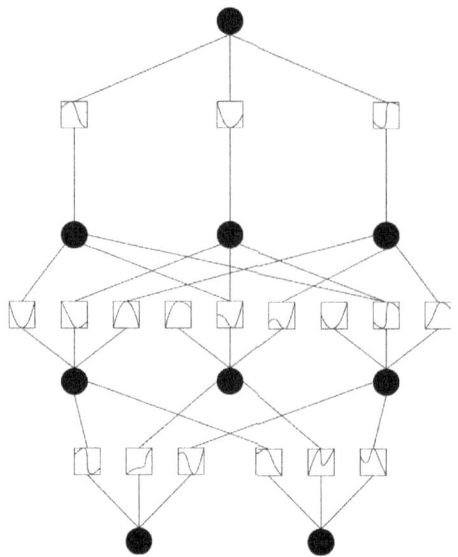

Fig. 1. KAN: Kolmogorov-Arnold Networks [18]

4.1 KAN Preliminaries

KANs have recently emerged as a significant advancement in a wide range of tasks that rely on predictive algorithms at their core. While their effectiveness in supervised learning has been well-documented, to the best of our knowledge, no work has yet explored their application to causal inference. The foundation of KANs lies in the Kolmogorov-Arnold Representation Theorem [5], which states that any smooth function $f : [0,1]^n \to \mathbb{R}$ can be expressed as:

$$f(x_1, \ldots, x_n) = \sum_{q=1}^{2n+1} \Phi_q \left(\sum_{p=1}^{n} \phi_{q,p}(x_p) \right), \tag{5}$$

where $\phi_{q,p} : [0,1] \to \mathbb{R}$ and $\Phi_q : \mathbb{R} \to \mathbb{R}$. This formulation demonstrates that any smooth multivariate function can be fundamentally decomposed into a sum of univariate functions, making the composition purely additive. This theorem serves as the inspiration for the KAN architecture, originally proposed for supervised learning tasks. In such tasks, the goal is to model a function f based on input-output pairs $\{(\mathbf{x}_i, y_i)\}$, such that $y_i \approx f(\mathbf{x}_i)$.

The KAN architecture as illustrated in Fig. 1 is designed such that all learnable functions are univariate, with each parameterized using basis functions, such as a B-spline, to enhance the model's flexibility. Liu et al. [18] introduced the KANs, initially proposing a two-layer model where learnable activation functions are placed on the edges, with aggregation achieved through summation at the nodes. However, this simple design had limitations in approximating complex functions. To address these shortcomings, the authors extended the approach within the same work by introducing multiple layers and increasing both the breadth and depth of the network, thereby enhancing its ability to approximate more complex functions. Mathematically, a typical l^{th} KAN layer, suitable for deeper architectures, with n_l inputs $(x_1^l, x_2^l, \cdots, x_{n_l}^l)$ and n_{l+1} outputs $(x_1^{l+1}, x_2^{l+1}, \cdots, x_{n_{l+1}}^{l+1})$ is defined as follows:

$$\begin{bmatrix} x_1^{l+1} \\ x_2^{l+1} \\ \vdots \\ x_{n_{l+1}}^{l+1} \end{bmatrix} = \begin{bmatrix} \phi_{1,1} & \phi_{1,2} & \cdots & \phi_{1,n_l} \\ \phi_{2,1} & \phi_{2,2} & \cdots & \phi_{2,n_l} \\ \vdots & \vdots & \vdots & \vdots \\ \phi_{n_{l+1},1} & \phi_{n_{l+1},2} & \cdots & \phi_{n_{l+1},n_l} \end{bmatrix} \cdot \begin{bmatrix} x_1^l \\ x_2^l \\ \vdots \\ x_{n_l}^l \end{bmatrix}, \quad (6)$$

where each $\phi_{q,p} \ \forall \ p \in \{1, 2, \ldots, n_l\}$ and $q \in \{1, 2, \ldots, n_{l+1}\}$ is a trainable univariate function with adjustable parameters. This structure allows the original two-layer Kolmogorov-Arnold representation, given in (5), to be extended into a more robust, deeper architecture capable of handling increasingly complex tasks. With the help of the above, we now proceed to explain KANITE framework in detail in the following subsection.

Algorithm 1. KANITE Training

Input: Observational data: $\mathcal{D} = \{(\mathbf{x}_i, t_i, Y_{t_i}^i)\}_{i=1}^n \sim \mathcal{D}_{\text{train}}, \mathcal{D}_{\text{val}}$, and hyper parameters $\alpha \geq 0$ and $\beta \geq 0$.
Output: An outcome prediction model: $f(\Psi, \Pi)$, where $\Pi = (\Pi_1, \Pi_2, \cdots, \Pi_K)$
1: Initialize parameters: Ψ : KAN, Π_i : KAN $\forall i \in \{1, 2, \cdots, K\}$
2: **while** *not converged* **do**
3:     Sample a mini-batch
    $\mathcal{B} = \{(\mathbf{x}_{i_o}, Y_{t_{i_o}}^{i_o})\}_{o=1}^B \subset \mathcal{D}_{\text{train}}$
4:     Mini-batch approximation of Regression Loss
    $\mathcal{L}_1 = \frac{1}{B} \sum_{o=1}^B (\hat{Y}_{t_{i_o}} - Y_{t_{i_o}})^2$
5:     Mini-batch approximation of the Representation Loss
    $\mathcal{L}_2 = \frac{1}{\binom{K}{2}} \sum_{a=1}^K \sum_{b=1}^{a-1} \text{RepresentationLoss}(\Psi_{t=a}, \Psi_{t=b})$
6:     Update Functions:
    $f(\Psi, \Pi) \leftarrow f(\Psi, \Pi) - \lambda.\nabla(f(\Psi, \Pi))$
7:     Minimize $\alpha \cdot \mathcal{L}_1 + \beta \cdot \mathcal{L}_2$ using SGD
8: **end while**

4.2 KANITE Architecture

Our proposed KANITE framework addresses the task of ITE estimation for multiple treatments by utilizing KANs as the backbone of its architecture. Figure 2 illustrates the details of the KANITE framework, explained through the following three key steps.

A. *Balanced Representation of Covariates:* First, KANITE aims to learn a balanced covariate representation by replacing the conventional MLPs with the KANs, shown as Representation Network in Fig. 2, enabling the model to learn latent representations of covariates balanced across all treatment groups.
B. *Treatment Head Networks:* It consists of dedicated treatment head networks, where each treatment is modeled through a separate representation using KANs, allowing greater flexibility to capture the underlying distribution of treatment outcomes.
C. *Representation loss:* Three different representation losses have been considered in the proposed set of algorithms under KANITE. First and second losses are Maximum Mean Discrepancy (MMD) and Wasserstein, based on the Integral Probability Metric (IPM), and the third one utilizes Entropy Balancing (EB) method [33] to learn weights that minimize the Jensen-Shannon divergence, asymptotically, between all pairs of treatment groups. These three losses result into three different algorithms named KANITE-MMD, KANITE-Wass, KANITE-EB for ITE estimation.

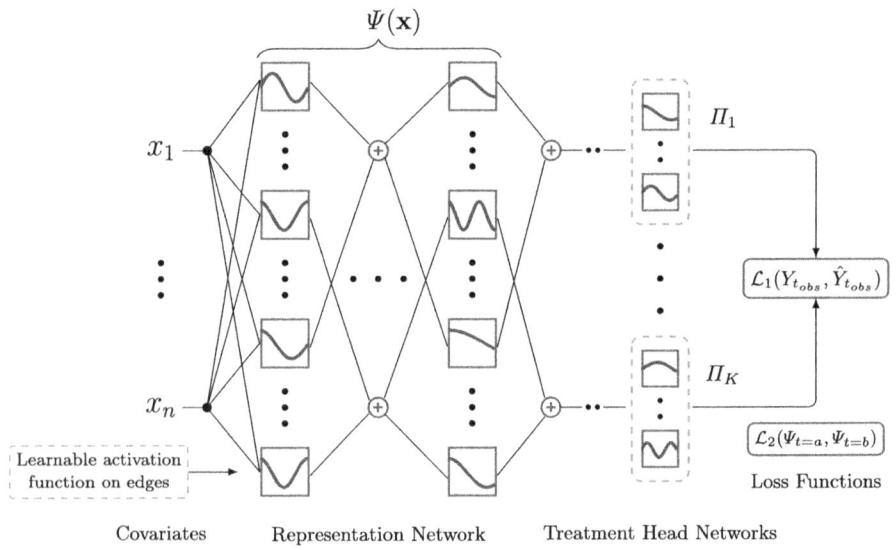

Fig. 2. KANITE Architecture

This approach enables us to utilize the KANs for the ITE estimation task in an effective manner while simultaneously learning covariate and treatment representations that improve upon state-of-the-art (SOTA) ITE estimation algorithms. A detailed explanation of the KANITE framework is as follows.

4.2.1 KANs for Learning Balanced Covariate Representation

In earlier ITE estimation literature, representation learning for covariates has demonstrated a significant improvement [25]. In the KANITE architecture, we utilize a KAN layer setup for achieving a balanced representation that caters to multiple treatment scenarios. KAN layers, as defined in Eq. 6, enable the architecture to learn low-dimensional symbolic representations of covariates, which help separate treatment-related signals from confounding influences, thereby mitigating confounding bias [25]. To learn representations for covariates, $\mathbf{x} \in \mathcal{X}$, we employ KAN layers setup with learnable activation functions consist of B-Splines that learns a balanced representation function, $\Psi : \mathcal{X} \to \mathbb{R}^d$, in a lower-dimensional latent space.

In KANITE, a deep representation network is constructed by stacking multiple KAN layers one after the other to form a hierarchical model for representation learning. Let L denote the total number of KAN layers. For each layer $l \in \{0, 1, \cdots, L-1\}$, let n_l represent the total number of neurons in layer l. Let $\Psi^l(\mathbf{x}) = \left(\Psi_1^l(\mathbf{x}), \Psi_2^l(\mathbf{x}), \cdots, \Psi_{n_l}^l(\mathbf{x})\right)$ denote the representation after the $(l-1)^{\text{st}}$ layer, with the input defined as $\Psi^0(\mathbf{x}) = \mathbf{x}$. In contrast to standard MLPs, KANs do not learn independent weight or bias parameters; instead, each layer aggregates the outputs of learnable univariate activation functions. The transformation at layer $l \in \{0, 1, ..., L-1\}$, denoted as $\Psi^{l+1}(\mathbf{x}) = \left(\Psi_1^{l+1}(\mathbf{x}), \Psi_2^{l+1}(\mathbf{x}), \cdots, \Psi_{n_{l+1}}^{l+1}(\mathbf{x})\right)$, is defined in a compositional form analogous to the Kolmogorov–Arnold representation as follows:

$$\Psi_i^{l+1}(\mathbf{x}) = \sum_{j=1}^{n_l} \phi_{i,j}^l \left(\Psi_j^l(\mathbf{x})\right), \quad \forall i \in \{1, 2, \cdots, n_{l+1}\}. \tag{7}$$

Using the recursion, we can write the above as:

$$\Psi^{l+1}(\mathbf{x}) = \left(\Psi^l \circ \Psi^{l-1} \circ \cdots \circ \Psi^1 \circ \Psi^0\right) \mathbf{x}. \tag{8}$$

This recursive formulation enables the deeper architecture to capture complex, non-linear interactions among covariates, progressively refining the balanced representation and further mitigating confounding bias for improved treatment effect estimation.

4.2.2 Treatment Head Networks

The KANITE framework leverages a balanced covariate representation learned from the representation network to drive the treatment head networks for enhanced treatment-specific ITE estimation. As depicted in the KANITE architecture, we deploy a distinct treatment head network for each unique treatment category. Deep KAN layers, given in Eq. 8, are trained to learn a symbolic representation function that is specific to treatments. We denote these treatment head networks by Π_t for $t \in \{1, 2, 3, \cdots, K\}$, where K is the total number of unique treatments. Consider a user with covariates $\mathbf{x}$ and the assigned treatment as t, the treatment head network Π_t with M number of layers is defined as:

$$\Pi_t^{M+1}(\mathbf{x}) = \left(\Pi_t^M \circ \Pi_t^{M-1} \circ \cdots \circ \Pi_t^1 \circ \Pi_t^0\right) \Psi(\mathbf{x}), \tag{9}$$

where $\Psi(\mathbf{x})$ is the balanced representation of covariates learned from the representation network. Furthermore, we leverage network sparsification in KANs to reduce the impact of redundant activation functions, which acts as a form of regularization and improves ITE estimates.

4.2.3 Representation Loss

As mentioned in the previous subsections, learning a balanced covariates representation across all treatments plays a crucial role in KANITE. Hence, we employ three variations of the representation loss in KANITE based on IPM and Entropy Balancing, resulting into three different algorithms, in addition to the standard Mean Square Error (MSE) loss on the observed factual data. Note that, MSE loss is defined as: $\mathcal{L}_1 = \frac{1}{n}\sum_{i=1}^{n}(\hat{Y}_{i,t} - Y_i)^2$. In the below we provide more details of the representation loss variants.

1. **IPM based representation loss**

   IPMs have shown promising results in achieving balanced representations for ITE estimation, as demonstrated in [12,25]. In KANITE, we leverage two popular IPM-based loss functions—the Maximum Mean Discrepancy (MMD) and the Wasserstein loss, to effectively capture distributional differences between treatment subgroups. MMD is particularly useful because it compares higher-order moments between distributions, minimizing subtle discrepancies in the feature space, while the Wasserstein metric provides a robust measure of distance even when distributions have limited overlap. For our multiple-treatment setup, we use the average pairwise IPM loss from [28] to learn a balanced representation across all treatment group combinations. The mathematical formulation is provided below:

   $$\mathcal{L}_2 = \frac{1}{\binom{K}{2}} \sum_{a=0}^{K-1}\sum_{b=0}^{a-1} \text{IPM}\left(\{\Psi\}_{t=a}, \{\Psi\}_{t=b}\right), \tag{10}$$

   where IPM() can be either MMD or Wasserstein, leading to the respective algorithms KANITE-MMD and KANITE-Wass.

2. **Entropy Balancing (EB) based representation loss**

   In [33], a doubly robust representation learning approach is proposed for ITE estimation in the binary treatment setting. It uses Entropy Balancing (EB) to learn weights that, in the limit, minimize the Jensen-Shannon divergence between treated and control covariates distributions. In this work, we extend this methodology to the multiple-treatment setting to balance covariate distributions across all treatment groups, as given below.

   Let m be the number of covariates. Let t and s denote the indicies of treatments i.e., $t, s \in \{1, 2, \cdots, K\}$. Entropy balancing optimization problem for the multiple-treatment setting to balance covariates distributions is given as:

$$\mathbf{w}^{\text{EB}} = \arg\max_{\mathbf{w}} \left\{ -\sum_{i=1}^{N} w_i \log w_i \right\},$$

s.t. $\begin{cases} \text{(i)} \sum_{T_i=t} w_i \Psi(x_{ji}) = \sum_{T_i=s} w_i \Psi(x_{ji}), \forall j \in \{1,2,\ldots,m\} \text{ and } t < s, \\ \text{(ii)} \sum_{T_i=t} w_i = 1, \forall t \in \{1,2,\cdots,K\}, \forall w_i > 0. \end{cases}$

(11)

Note that, constraint (i) ensures that the weighted sum of the shared representations of the covariates is balanced across all pairs of treatment combinations. Then, the representation loss in this case is given as

$$\mathcal{L}_2 = \sum_{i=1}^{N} w_i^{\text{EB}}(\Psi) \log(w_i^{\text{EB}}(\Psi)). \tag{12}$$

We solve the optimization problem in (11) by formulating its dual problem using Lagrangian duality theory [3]. To that end, let us define the following: for $t < s$, $\lambda_{t,s} = [\lambda_{t,s,1}, \lambda_{t,s,2}, \ldots, \lambda_{t,s,m}] \in \mathbb{R}^m$ and set $\lambda_{t,s} = -\lambda_{s,t}$ for $t > s$. By constructing the Lagrangian function and applying the Karush-Kuhn-Tucker (KKT) conditions we get the following dual problem of (11):

$$\min_{\lambda_{t,s}} \sum_{t=1}^{k} \log \left(\sum_{T_i=t} \exp\left(-\sum_{s \neq t} \langle \lambda_{t,s}, \Psi_i \rangle \right) \right), \tag{13}$$

where $\Psi_i = [\Psi_{i,1}, \Psi_{i,2}, \ldots, \Psi_{i,m}] \in \mathbb{R}^m$. Using the above dual formulation, we now provide a closed-form solution for equation (11). Suppose $T_i = t$; then, the weight for sample-i, w_i, is given by:

$$w_i = \frac{\exp\left(-\sum_{s \neq t} \langle \lambda_{t,s}, \Psi_i \rangle \right)}{\sum_{T_i=t} \exp\left(-\sum_{s \neq t} \langle \lambda_{t,s}, \Psi_i \rangle \right)}. \tag{14}$$

This formulation provides a principled approach to deriving weights using the EB method that, in the limit, minimize the JSD. We refer to the algorithm that employs the EB-based representation loss as KANITE-EB.

Note that the final loss function of the KANITE framework is a weighted sum of the standard MSE and the chosen representation loss (MMD, Wasserstein, or EB-based), as shown below.

$$\mathcal{L} = \alpha \cdot \mathcal{L}_1 + \beta \cdot \mathcal{L}_2 \quad \text{for some } \alpha, \beta > 0.$$

5 Experiments

In this section, we present a detailed numerical analysis of KANITE's performance on several standard benchmark datasets—IHDP [25], NEWS [24], TWINS [1], and ACIC-16 [7]—compared to baselines. We first evaluate KANITE against baselines using the metrics ϵ_{PEHE} and ϵ_{ATE}, as defined in Eqs. (3) and (4). Next, we examine its convergence and parameter efficiency relative to the baselines. Finally, we analyze the impact of hyperparameters, such as grid size and spline degree in activation functions of KAN layers, on ITE estimation.

5.1 Baselines

We compare KANITE with various baseline architectures designed for ITE estimation in both binary and multiple-treatment settings. For the multiple-treatment evaluation, we use the NEWS-4, NEWS-8, and NEWS-16 semi-synthetic datasets from [24], while for binary treatment setting, we consider the IHDP, TWINS, ACIC-16, and NEWS-2 datasets. The models we benchmark against include TarNet, CFRNet-Wass, and CFRNet-MMD [25] which utilize IPM as the representation loss. We also introduce a baseline called CFRNet-EB, which uses the Entropy Balancing loss, as given in Eq. (12), in place of IPM within the CFRNet architecture. For a fair comparison in the multiple-treatment setting, we also compare KANITE with Perfect Match [24]. Additionally, to benchmark against generative counterfactual predictive models, we evaluate GANITE [31]. Since KANITE operates in both binary and multiple treatment scenarios, we appropriately modify baselines developed for binary treatment setting, such as TarNet, CFRNet-Wass, CFRNet-MMD and CFRNet-EB to ensure a fair comparison across both treatment setups.

Table 1. Performance comparison of KANITE vs baselines on ϵ_{PEHE} metric across various binary treatment setting datasets

Method/Dataset	IHDP	NEWS-2	TWINS	ACIC-16
TarNet	2.33 ± 2.71	23.90 ± 8.75	**0.32 ± 0.00**	2.41 ± 0.91
CFRNet-Wass	1.50 ± 1.76	23.85 ± 6.24	**0.32 ± 0.00**	2.58 ± 1.05
CFRNet-MMD	1.50 ± 1.73	23.14 ± 7.10	**0.32 ± 0.00**	2.42 ± 0.88
CFRNET-EB	1.22 ± 1.32	21.25 ± 5.33	0.43 ± 0.20	2.89 ± 1.44
PerfectMatch	1.56 ± 1.71	23.18 ± 8.13	**0.32 ± 0.00**	2.48 ± 0.89
GANITE	7.91 ± 7.47	23.22 ± 8.38	0.35 ± 0.07	5.24 ± 1.38
KANITE-Wass	**1.08 ± 1.39**	20.78 ± 3.59	**0.32 ± 0.00**	**1.58 ± 1.09**
KANITE-MMD	**1.08 ± 1.39**	20.78 ± 3.61	**0.32 ± 0.00**	**1.58 ± 1.09**
KANITE-EB	**1.08 ± 1.39**	**20.32 ± 2.82**	**0.32 ± 0.00**	**1.58 ± 1.09**

Table 2. Performance comparison of KANITE vs baselines on ϵ_{ATE} metric across various binary treatment setting datasets

Method/Dataset	IHDP	NEWS-2	TWINS	ACIC-16
TarNet	0.63 ± 0.83	11.85 ± 11.50	0.02 ± 0.01	0.30 ± 0.16
CFRNet-Wass	0.24 ± 0.25	11.61 ± 9.48	0.02 ± 0.01	0.54 ± 0.20
CFRNet-MMD	0.24 ± 0.24	10.85 ± 9.73	0.01 ± 0.01	0.37 ± 0.32
CFRNET-EB	0.29 ± 0.34	7.71 ± 7.46	0.22 ± 0.28	0.37 ± 0.19
PerfectMatch	0.25 ± 0.25	10.34 ± 10.64	0.03 ± 0.01	0.39 ± 0.29
GANITE	4.40 ± 1.33	11.28 ± 10.80	0.35 ± 0.07	3.61 ± 1.07
KANITE-Wass	**0.15 ± 0.13**	7.03 ± 5.43	**0.01 ± 0.00**	**0.18 ± 0.13**
KANITE-MMD	**0.15 ± 0.13**	7.02 ± 5.48	**0.01 ± 0.00**	0.19 ± 0.14
KANITE-EB	**0.15 ± 0.13**	**6.38 ± 4.49**	**0.01 ± 0.00**	**0.18 ± 0.13**

Table 3. Performance comparison of KANITE vs baselines on ϵ_{PEHE} metric across various multiple treatment setting datasets

Method/Dataset	NEWS-4	NEWS-8	NEWS-16
TarNet	24.09 ± 4.07	24.85 ± 6.73	25.06 ± 2.96
CFRNet-Wass	24.98 ± 4.57	22.70 ± 3.39	22.60 ± 1.75
CFRNet-MMD	24.05 ± 4.56	23.17 ± 3.32	22.81 ± 1.63
CFRNET-EB	21.71 ± 2.63	22.53 ± 3.13	22.33 ± 1.69
PerfectMatch	23.90 ± 4.60	23.41 ± 4.20	23.33 ± 1.68
GANITE	23.77 ± 4.10	24.10 ± 3.33	22.85 ± 1.62
KANITE-Wass	**21.48 ± 2.27**	**22.48 ± 3.31**	22.20 ± 1.57
KANITE-MMD	21.53 ± 2.31	22.58 ± 3.37	**22.19 ± 1.57**
KANITE-EB	21.52 ± 2.30	22.62 ± 3.38	22.20 ± 1.58

Table 4. Performance comparison of KANITE vs baselines on ϵ_{ATE} metric across various multiple treatment setting datasets

Method/Dataset	NEWS-4	NEWS-8	NEWS-16
TarNet	11.87 ± 5.07	10.91 ± 3.49	12.47 ± 3.01
CFRNet-Wass	13.33 ± 5.56	9.08 ± 3.55	9.08 ± 1.96
CFRNet-MMD	11.43 ± 5.64	9.98 ± 3.37	9.09 ± 1.88
CFRNET-EB	8.26 ± 3.29	9.03 ± 3.10	9.08 ± 1.92
PerfectMatch	11.43 ± 5.71	9.62 ± 3.63	**8.85 ± 1.99**
GANITE	11.65 ± 5.03	11.74 ± 3.50	10.54 ± 1.77
KANITE-Wass	**7.92 ± 2.97**	**8.91 ± 3.09**	9.49 ± 1.84
KANITE-MMD	8.05 ± 2.95	9.24 ± 3.45	9.46 ± 1.84
KANITE-EB	8.03 ± 2.93	9.30 ± 3.48	9.47 ± 1.85

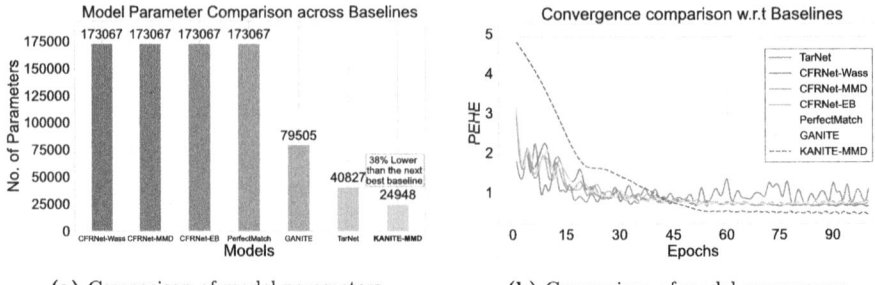

(a) Comparison of model parameters (b) Comparison of model convergence

Fig. 3. Comparison of model parameters and convergence across models

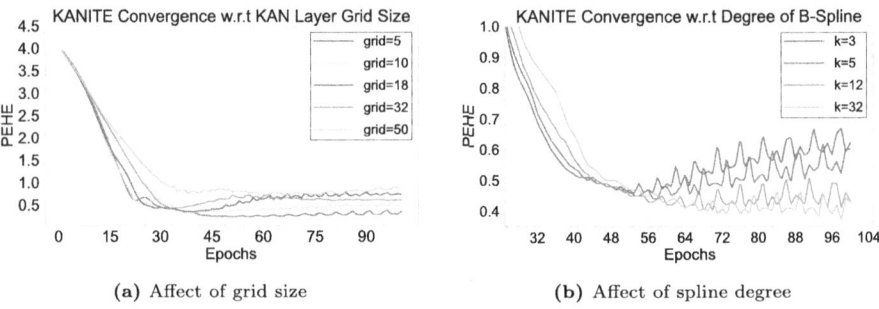

(a) Affect of grid size (b) Affect of spline degree

Fig. 4. Affect of grid size and spline degree considered in KANITE on ITE

5.2 KANITE: Performance Assessment

We split the dataset into training, validation, and test sets in a 63:27:10 ratio. The results in all tables are computed on the full dataset after model training. We conducted 1000, 50, 10, and 10 iterations for the IHDP, NEWS, TWINS, and ACIC-16 datasets, respectively, and report the mean and standard deviation of these runs in the results tables. The best results in the tables are highlighted in bold.

As mentioned earlier, the KANITE framework consists of three algorithms: KANITE-MMD, KANITE-Wass, and KANITE-EB, almost at least one of which outperforms all the baselines on both ϵ_{PEHE} and ϵ_{ATE} metrics in both binary and multiple treatment settings, as shown in Tables 1, 2, 3, and 4. Note that Tables 1 and 2 present the ϵ_{PEHE} and ϵ_{ATE} metrics for all considered algorithms in the binary treatment setting, respectively. Similarly, Tables 3 and 4 provide the corresponding results for the multiple-treatment setting. To perform a comprehensive performance assessment of KANITE, we evaluate its convergence and parameter efficiency compared to the baselines. Figure 3a compares the number of parameters in our proposed KANITE framework against all baselines. Notably, KANITE outperforms all baselines on both ϵ_{PEHE} and ϵ_{ATE} metrics while reducing model parameters by 38% compared to the next best baseline. Figure 3b shows that our proposed KANITE model, depicted in dotted line, converges faster than all baselines. Since all three KANITE variants exhibited similar behavior in terms of parameter count and convergence, we present only KANITE-MMD in Fig. 3 to keep the figures uncluttered.

5.3 KANITE: Hyperparameters Study

We now examine the impact of the B-Spline degree and grid size considered in KAN layers on model performance. As grid size and spline degree are direct proportional to the model complexity in terms of parameters we conduct the hyperparameter optimization on them and use the best parameters in the respective models. For example, Fig. 4 shows the affect of grid size and spline degree on the ITE estimates for IHDP dataset. From Fig. 4, it can be observed that grid size of 5 and spline degree of 32 achieve the best performance on this iteration of the results.

6 Conclusion

In this study, we proposed KANITE, a state-of-the-art framework for ITE estimation that leverages shared representation learning using either IPM or Entropy Balancing. Unlike traditional MLP-based architectures, KANITE employs KANs as its backbone, enabling it to learn more accurate causal effect estimates. The framework introduces three algorithms—KANITE-MMD, KANITE-Wass, and KANITE-EB—each utilizing a different IPM or Entropy Balancing-based representation loss to ensure balanced covariate representations across treatment groups. Additionally, we derive a closed-form Entropy Balancing-based representation loss for the multiple-treatment setting using Lagrangian duality theory. Experimental results demonstrate that KANITE effectively handles multiple-treatment scenarios, outperforming all considered baselines on both the ϵ_{PEHE} and ϵ_{ATE} metrics. Furthermore, KANITE achieves superior parameter efficiency and faster convergence while maintaining strong counterfactual prediction capabilities.

For future work, we plan to further enhance KANITE to create a unified architecture that incorporates abilities of both IPM and Entropy Balancing for ITE estimation tasks. We plan to incorporate interpretability of KANs to understand causal effects estimation in a better manner. Our findings highlight the advantages of KANs in ITE estimation, paving the way for future research in related areas. One promising direction is investigating the role of KANs in ITE estimation under networked settings, where users are interconnected through a network [28]. Another avenue is examining the effectiveness of KANs in treatment dosage settings, where treatments are administered in fractional amounts between 0 and 1 [23]. Additionally, it would be valuable to investigate how KANs can enhance causal effect estimation when treatment information is explicitly incorporated [9].

References

1. Almond, D., Chay, K.Y., Lee, D.S.: The costs of low birth weight. Q. J. Econ. **120**(3), 1031–1083 (2005)
2. Bodner, A.D., Tepsich, A.S., Spolski, J.N., Pourteau, S.: Convolutional kolmogorov-arnold networks. arXiv preprint arXiv:2406.13155 (2024)
3. Boyd, S.P., Vandenberghe, L.: Convex optimization. Cambridge University Press (2004)
4. Braun, J., Griebel, M.: On a constructive proof of kolmogorov's superposition theorem. Constr. Approx. **30**, 653–675 (2009)
5. Braun, J., Griebel, M.: On a constructive proof of kolmogorov's superposition theorem. Constructive Approximation **30**, 653–675 (2009). https://api.semanticscholar.org/CorpusID:5164789
6. Chan, D., Ge, R., Gershony, O., Hesterberg, T., Lambert, D.: Evaluating online ad campaigns in a pipeline: causal models at scale. In: Proceedings of the 16th ACM SIGKDD International Conference on Knowledge Discovery and Data Mining, pp. 7–16 (2010)
7. Dorie, V., Hill, J., Shalit, U., Scott, M., Cervone, D.: Automated versus do-it-yourself methods for causal inference: lessons learned from a data analysis competition. Stat. Sci. **34**(1), 43–68 (2019)
8. Guo, R., Li, J., Liu, H.: Learning individual causal effects from networked observational data. In: Proceedings of the 13th International Conference on Web Search and Data Mining, pp. 232–240 (2020)
9. Harada, S., Kashima, H.: Graphite: estimating individual effects of graph-structured treatments. In: Proceedings of the 30th ACM International Conference on Information & Knowledge Management, pp. 659–668 (2021)
10. Hong, G., Raudenbush, S.W.: Effects of kindergarten retention policy on children's cognitive growth in reading and mathematics. Educ. Eval. Policy Anal. **27**(3), 205–224 (2005)
11. Hornik, K., Stinchcombe, M., White, H.: Multilayer feedforward networks are universal approximators. Neural Netw. **2**(5), 359–366 (1989)
12. Johansson, F., Shalit, U., Sontag, D.: Learning representations for counterfactual inference. In: International Conference on Machine Learning, pp. 3020–3029. PMLR (2016)
13. Jordan, K.L.: Juvenile transfer and recidivism: a propensity score matching approach. J. Crime Just. **35**(1), 53–67 (2012)
14. Kaddour, J., Zhu, Y., Liu, Q., Kusner, M.J., Silva, R.: Causal effect inference for structured treatments. Adv. Neural. Inf. Process. Syst. **34**, 24841–24854 (2021)
15. Kiamari, M., Kiamari, M., Krishnamachari, B.: Gkan: Graph kolmogorov-arnold networks. arXiv preprint arXiv:2406.06470 (2024)
16. Kich, V.A., Bottega, J.A., Steinmetz, R., Grando, R.B., Yorozu, A., Ohya, A.: Kolmogorov-arnold networks for online reinforcement learning. In: 2024 24th International Conference on Control, Automation and Systems (ICCAS), pp. 958–963. IEEE (2024)
17. Kolmogorov, A.N.: On the representations of continuous functions of many variables by superposition of continuous functions of one variable and addition. In: Dokl. Akad. Nauk USSR, vol. 114, pp. 953–956 (1957)
18. Liu, Z., et al.: Kan: Kolmogorov-arnold networks. arXiv preprint arXiv:2404.19756 (2024)

19. Moradi, M., Panahi, S., Bollt, E., Lai, Y.C.: Kolmogorov-arnold network autoencoders. arXiv preprint arXiv:2410.02077 (2024)
20. Nilforoshan, H., et al.: Zero-shot causal learning. Adv. Neural. Inf. Process. Syst. **36**, 6862–6901 (2023)
21. Patra, S., et al.: Physics informed kolmogorov-arnold neural networks for dynamical analysis via efficent-kan and wav-kan. arXiv preprint arXiv:2407.18373 (2024)
22. Rubin, D.B.: Causal inference using potential outcomes: design, modeling, decisions. J. Am. Stat. Assoc. **100**(469), 322–331 (2005)
23. Schwab, P., Linhardt, L., Bauer, S., Buhmann, J.M., Karlen, W.: Learning counterfactual representations for estimating individual dose-response curves. In: Proceedings of the AAAI Conference on Artificial Intelligence, vol. 34, pp. 5612–5619 (2020)
24. Schwab, P., Linhardt, L., Karlen, W.: Perfect match: A simple method for learning representations for counterfactual inference with neural networks. arXiv preprint arXiv:1810.00656 (2018)
25. Shalit, U., Johansson, F.D., Sontag, D.: Estimating individual treatment effect: generalization bounds and algorithms. In: International Conference on Machine Learning, pp. 3076–3085. PMLR (2017)
26. Stukel, T.A., Fisher, E.S., Wennberg, D.E., Alter, D.A., Gottlieb, D.J., Vermeulen, M.J.: Analysis of observational studies in the presence of treatment selection bias: effects of invasive cardiac management on ami survival using propensity score and instrumental variable methods. JAMA **297**(3), 278–285 (2007)
27. Thorat, A., Kolla, R., Pedanekar, N.: I see, therefore i do: Estimating causal effects for image treatments. arXiv preprint arXiv:2412.06810 (2024)
28. Thorat, A., Kolla, R., Pedanekar, N., Onoe, N.: Estimation of individual causal effects in network setup for multiple treatments. arXiv preprint arXiv:2312.11573 (2023)
29. Wang, Y., et al.: Kolmogorov arnold informed neural network: A physics-informed deep learning framework for solving forward and inverse problems based on kolmogorov arnold networks. arXiv preprint arXiv:2406.11045 (2024)
30. Yang, X., Wang, X.: Kolmogorov-arnold transformer. In: The Thirteenth International Conference on Learning Representations (2024)
31. Yoon, J., Jordon, J., Van Der Schaar, M.: Ganite: estimation of individualized treatment effects using generative adversarial nets. In: International Conference on Learning Representations (2018)
32. Yu, Y., Chen, H., Peng, C.H., Chau, P.Y.: The causal effect of subscription video streaming on dvd sales: evidence from a natural experiment. Decis. Support Syst. **157**, 113767 (2022)
33. Zeng, S., Assaad, S., Tao, C., Datta, S., Carin, L., Li, F.: Double robust representation learning for counterfactual prediction. arXiv preprint arXiv:2010.07866 (2020)
34. Zeydan, E., Vaca-Rubio, C.J., Blanco, L., Pereira, R., Caus, M., Aydeger, A.: F-kans: federated kolmogorov-arnold networks. arXiv preprint arXiv:2407.20100 (2024)

Advanced Strategic Improvement with Decision Interactions

Wenjing Yang[1], Xinpeng Lv[1], Yunxin Mao[1], Liyang Xu[1], Ruochun Jin[1], Huan Chen[1], Jing Ren[1], Jinxuan Yang[3], Yuanlong Chen[2], and Haotian Wang[1(✉)]

[1] College of Computer Science and Technology, National University of Defense Technology, Changsha, China
{lvxinpeng,wanghaotian13}@nudt.edu.cn
[2] Faculty of Computing, Harbin Institute of Technology, Harbin, China
[3] Faculty of Engineering, The University of Sydney, Sydney, Australia

Abstract. Strategic classification investigates the interaction between a decision-maker (modeled as a jury) and individuals (agents) who may strategically modify their features to obtain favorable outcomes. A key challenge in this setting is *strategic improvement*, which focuses on designing incentive mechanisms that encourage individuals to improve their true qualifications. In real-world scenarios, decision-making often involves multi-dimensional evaluations composed of multiple sub-indicators and a final comprehensive assessment. However, most existing paradigms for strategic classification rely on a single decision model, which is inadequate for capturing the complexity of such settings. To address this gap, we introduce the problem of **S**trategic **I**mprovement with **D**ecision **I**nteractions (*SIDI*), a novel setting that incorporates multiple interacting decision models and an overarching evaluation mechanism. We analyze the influence of decision interactions and reveal how correlations among classifiers can exacerbate manipulative behaviors. Building on these insights, we propose a decorrelation-based strategic improvement framework that leverages decision interactions to promote authentic qualification enhancements. Extensive experiments on both real-world and synthetic datasets demonstrate the effectiveness of our framework in encouraging genuine improvements while maintaining robust accuracy. Our findings highlight the importance of modeling decision interactions and provide new directions for strategic machine learning.

Keywords: Strategic Classification · Machine Learning · Decorrelation

1 Introduction

As machine learning-based decision making becomes increasingly prevalent, strategic classification [23] has garnered significant attention in recent years.

Supplementary Information The online version contains supplementary material available at https://doi.org/10.1007/978-3-032-05962-8_25.

Strategic classification addresses scenarios where individuals intentionally adapt their features to achieve desirable outcomes from intelligent decision systems. This phenomenon is evident in various domains such as credit scoring [1], hiring processes [41], and academic admissions [20]. In these contexts, individuals often manipulate their attributes to secure more favorable classifications, thereby challenging the fairness and integrity of these systems. For instance, in credit scoring, applicants might inflate their income or alter other financial metrics to attain a higher credit score.

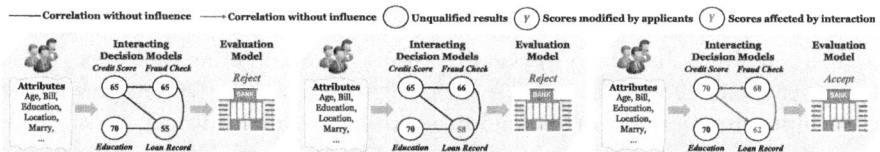

Fig. 1. An illustration of decision interaction. In traditional classification without strategic behavior, individuals fail to pass the loan application (*left*). With strategic behavior only towards a single model, the individual raises their score on the *loan record* metric, but it is still insufficient to pass the application (*center*). In decision interaction, the individual influences the *loan record* outcome by achieving high scores on other metrics, passing the loan approval (*right*).

As these strategic behaviors become more widespread, it is essential to understand and mitigate them in order to maintain the reliability of machine learning systems [37]. Early research primarily focused on developing classifiers that are robust to manipulation [19,51]. While effective in detecting and resisting adversarial behaviors, such approaches often neglect the incentive structures that motivate individuals to game the system [36].

To overcome this limitation, the notion of *strategic improvement* has been proposed [4]. Instead of merely preventing manipulation, this paradigm aims to design incentive-compatible systems that encourage individuals to genuinely improve their underlying qualifications. For example, in college admissions, educators may wish to promote substantive academic preparation for standardized tests like the SAT, rather than rewarding superficial score inflation.

Existing studies in strategic machine learning have primarily focused on a single decision model. However, real-world strategic classification scenarios are far more diverse and complex. To ensure stability and accuracy, practical decision scenarios typically involve multi-dimensional evaluations of individuals, encompassing multiple sub-indicators and a final comprehensive assessment [2]. For example, in the financial services domain [33], decision makers deploy multiple classifiers (**sub-classifiers**) to evaluate an individual's creditworthiness, detect fraud, and approve loans, among other tasks. The final evaluation score is determined based on the results from these different indicators.

In multi-classifier decision scenarios, classifiers often exhibit significant interdependence [15]. As a result, a favorable outcome in one sub-classifier can influence the predictions of others. For example, in bank loan assessments, a positive evaluation of creditworthiness may affect the outcomes of fraud detection or loan approval components. We refer to this phenomenon as *decision interaction*, which creates *additional opportunities for strategic manipulation* In particular, decision interaction enables individuals to exploit correlations between classifiers, creating *shortcut paths* to favorable final decisions that do not require genuine improvement across all relevant dimensions. For instance, individuals may selectively enhance their scores on sub-classifiers that are relatively **easy** to manipulate and less critical to the true outcome, while avoiding improvements on **harder but more important** indicators.

Returning to the bank loan example (see Fig. 1), an applicant who fails to meet the eligibility threshold—even after directly manipulating their score in the "loan repayment record" classifier—may still secure a loan. By recognizing the **interdependencies among decision models**, the applicant can strategically improve their scores on other, more manipulable classifiers. These improvements then propagate through the interaction structure, indirectly boosting their evaluation in the loan repayment metric and ultimately leading to approval. We refer to this form of manipulation, where individuals exploit model interdependencies to achieve favorable outcomes without genuine qualification enhancement, as *interactive strategic behavior*.

Towards such unique strategic behaviors in interacting classifiers, we explore this new dimension, aiming to uncover the interactions between multiple decision models in this paper. Our work focuses on addressing two key questions in the context of decision interaction and interactive strategic behavior:

---

1. How to model strategic machine learning problems involving decision interaction in multi-classifier scenarios?
2. How to mitigate the impact of interactive strategic behavior on decision-making models?

To answer the above-mentioned questions, we contribute a new problem called Strategic Improvement with Decision Interaction (*SIDI*). In this context, multiple sub-classifiers first evaluate different aspects of the individuals. Finally, a summary decision model, such as a linear model or a neural network block, integrates the results from multiple sub-classifiers to produce a comprehensive evaluation. **Overall, we summarize our contributions as follows:**

1. **Introduction of the SIDI problem**: We propose the problem of strategic improvement with decision interaction (*SIDI*). This novel problem closely mirrors real-world scenarios and extends the strategic machine learning task to a broader dimension. We conduct a systematic analysis of decision interactions and interactive strategic behaviors, examining the correlation among sub-classifiers and the potential impact on system performance.
2. **Improvement framework with decorrelation**: By investigating the relationship between the correlations among interactive classifiers and strategic

behaviors, we demonstrate that appropriate decorrelation facilitates genuine individual improvement. Building on this insight, we propose an effective decorrelation method and design a novel strategic improvement framework for decision interactions.
3. **Experimental verification**: Our extensive experiments on real-world and synthetic datasets validate the efficacy and robustness of our method in decision interaction environments.

2 Related Work

2.1 Strategic Classification

Foundational work in strategic classification [23] commenced by examining how individuals might manipulate their features to obtain favorable outcomes from classifiers. Focusing on the adverse consequences of strategic behavior, some studies aim to develop algorithms that are resilient to such manipulation [9, 44]. Given the complexity of strategic classification, some research attempts to address unknown manipulations or limited information [12, 19]. Recent approaches have proposed stochastic classifiers [43], differentiable optimization-based defenses [34], and graph-based models [14] to improve robustness and handle inter-agent dependencies. Multi-agent extensions further explore strategic externalities and interaction effects [27]. Beyond robustness, to avoid disproportionate disadvantages for certain demographic groups, ongoing studies have also investigated fairness in strategic machine learning [17, 29, 50].

2.2 Strategic Improvement

While early research framed strategic behavior as adversarial, an emerging direction views it as an opportunity to promote genuine self-improvement. Strategic improvement [36] introduces a causal framework that aligns agents' incentives with authentic qualification gains. Building on this idea, several studies design mechanisms that encourage changes in causal features or improvable features, rather than superficial manipulation [7, 8, 13, 25, 26, 45]. To address feedback long-term benefits in dynamic systems, performative prediction [22, 38, 39] examines how model deployment can influence the distribution of agents over time. Others explore strategies such as maximizing long-term social welfare [16, 21, 46], aiming to regulate strategic behavior for broader societal benefit[1].

3 Preliminaries

We present the essential background on strategic machine learning and causal decorrelation methods. Throughout this paper, we denote random variables by uppercase letters (e.g., X and Y) and their realizations by lowercase letters (e.g., x and y). Bold symbols (e.g., $\mathbf{x}$ and $\mathbf{X}$) are used for vectors or matrices.

---
[1] More related work is included in Appendix G.

3.1 Strategic Classification

The strategic classification (SC) problem is commonly formulated as a Stackelberg game[2] involving two players: a **decision maker** (modeled as a jury) and **the classified individuals** (modeled as agents) [23].

The decision maker defines a classification function $f : \mathbb{R}^d \to \{0,1\}$, mapping a feature vector $\mathbf{x}$ to a binary outcome.

Definition 1 (Strategic Manipulation). *Agents may strategically change their features to $\mathbf{x}'$ at a cost $c(\mathbf{x}, \mathbf{x}')$. Strategic manipulation is given by*

$$\mathbf{x}' = b(\mathbf{x}) = \arg\max_{\mathbf{x}' \in \mathcal{D}} [f(\mathbf{x}') - \lambda c(\mathbf{x}, \mathbf{x}')], \qquad (1)$$

where $f(\mathbf{x}') \in \{0,1\}$ is the classification result after modification, $c(\mathbf{x}, \mathbf{x}')$ is the manipulation cost, $\lambda > 0$ is a trade-off parameter, and $\mathcal{D}$ is the feature space. Typically, the cost is modeled as the Mahalanobis distance [18].

Definition 2 (Decision Optimization). *To mitigate manipulation, the decision maker optimizes f to maximize expected accuracy against strategic manipulation:*

$$f^* \in \arg\max_{f \in \mathcal{F}} \mathbb{E}_{(\mathbf{x},y) \sim \mathcal{D}} \left[\mathbb{1}\big(f(b(\mathbf{x})) = y\big) \right], \qquad (2)$$

where $\mathcal{F}$ is the set of all feasible classification rules, $\mathbb{1}$ denotes the indicator function $\mathbb{1}(\cdot) \to \{-1, 1\}$, and y is the observed label.

Improvement Against Gaming. Traditional strategic classifiers often suffer from suboptimal accuracy because they cannot effectively distinguish between genuine improvement and gaming behavior [36,50]. For example, consider a loan approval scenario: a model predicts whether a customer will repay a loan. In this case, a model designer benefits when $y = +1$, indicating that a borrower will repay the loan.

Within the strategic improvement framework [8,26], the strategic manipulation of agents can modify their true qualifications. Therefore, if an agent adapts the feature from x to x', with qualification becoming $y(x')$, it may differ from $y(x)$. As a result, strategic improvement corresponds to training a classifier f^* that maximizes the following ideal objective:

$$f^* \in \arg\max_{f \in \mathcal{F}} \mathbb{E}_{x \sim \mathcal{D}} \left[\mathbb{1}(f(x') = y(x')) \right], \qquad (3)$$

where x' is the agent's adapted feature, and $y(x')$ is the true qualification after strategic behavior.

---

[2] In Stackelberg framework, the interaction unfolds in two stages: (i) the decision maker publishes its policy (classification rule f); (ii) decision subjects (agents), after observing the policy, decide whether to modify their features.

3.2 Decorrelation Method

Decorrelation is a fundamental concept in machine learning, aimed at reducing or eliminating the correlation between variables to maximize their independence. This technique plays a crucial role in addressing multicollinearity issues among variables and minimizing dependencies between features in specific tasks.

Our work aims to propose a decorrelation method applicable to decision interactions based on the following lemmas[3].

Lemma 1 (Variable Independence [6]). *Variables X and Y are independent if $\mathbb{E}(X^k \cdot Y^l) = \mathbb{E}(X^k) \cdot \mathbb{E}(Y^l)$ holds for all k and l in $\mathbf{N}$ with discretization condition.*

Inspired by the sample weighting methods in the causal literature [3,31], we investigate the following methods for linear correlation.

Lemma 2 (Independence via Reweighting [32]). *Let X_a and X_b be random variables with all existing moments. There exists a reweighting scheme with weights W such that X_a and X_b become independent under the weighted distribution. The optimal weights W^* can be obtained by solving the following moment-matching objective:*

$$W^* = \arg\min_{W} \sum_{j=1}^{\infty} \sum_{k=1}^{\infty} \left\| \mathbb{E}\left[X_a^k \cdot \Sigma_W \cdot X_a^k\right] - \mathbb{E}\left[X_a^k \cdot W\right] \mathbb{E}\left[X_b^k \cdot W\right] \right\|_2^2, \quad (4)$$

where Σ_W denotes the covariance structure under the weighted distribution.

Lemma 3 (Decorrelation via Fourier Transform [49]). *By applying the Fourier transform to map the variables with linear and nonlinear correlations in the original domain into the frequency domain, the resulting features can be decorrelated using standard linear decorrelation methods.*

4 Problem Statement

4.1 Decision Interaction

In many real-world applications, decision makers rely on multiple sub-classifiers to evaluate agents based on various criteria. These sub-classifiers are often not independent: **a favorable outcome from one classifier can influence the results of others, ultimately affecting the final decision.** We refer to this phenomenon as **decision interaction**.

Definition 3 (Decision Interaction). *Let $\mathcal{X}$ denote the population with distribution $\mathcal{D}$. Suppose there are n interacting classifiers $\{h_1, h_2, \ldots, h_n\}$, i.e., sub-classifiers, where each classifier produces an outcome according to*

$$y_i = h_i(\mathbf{x}, y_{-i}), \quad (5)$$

---
[3] The proofs of these lemmas are included in Appendix A.

where y_{-i} denotes the outputs of all classifiers except h_i, for $i = 1, \ldots, n$. These outputs may either be treated as fixed from a previous evaluation or dynamically updated, depending on the system.

Let $\mathbf{Y} = (y_1, y_2, \ldots, y_n)$ be the vector of outputs. The final comprehensive decision is computed as $s = g(\mathbf{Y})$, where $g : \mathbb{R}^n \to \{-1, +1\}$ is an aggregation function that maps the sub-classifier outputs to a final decision. The function g can be implemented as a linear model, a neural network, or a rule-based evaluator.

Remark 1. We say that *decision interaction* exists if a change in y_i (for some i) can directly or indirectly influence the output of another classifier y_j (for $j \neq i$) through their functional dependencies, thereby affecting the final decision s.

Under decision interaction, the decision boundaries of classifiers are no longer isolated. Instead, they form an interdependent structure where a modification in one feature can propagate through multiple classifiers, amplifying its effect on the final decision outcome.

4.2 Interactive Strategic Behavior

In a decision interaction environment, agents can exploit dependencies among multiple classifiers to achieve favorable outcomes at a reduced cost. This phenomenon, which we term *interactive strategic behavior*, arises when agents coordinate their feature modifications to influence one classifier's output in a way that also affects others, thereby amplifying the overall effect of their strategic actions.

Let $x \in \mathcal{X}$ be the original feature vector of a agent, and let $c(x, x')$ denote the cost of modifying x to x'. Suppose there are n interacting classifiers $\{h_1, h_2, \ldots, h_n\}$, where each classifier's output may depend not only on $\mathbf{x}$ but also on the outputs of the others.

To isolate the effect of strategic behavior on a particular classifier, we adopt a *freeze-and-optimize* framework. First, we compute the outputs $\mathbf{y}^* = (y_1^*, \ldots, y_n^*)$ on the original input x using a fixed-point evaluation procedure. Then, for a given index i, we freeze all outputs y_j^* for $j \neq i$, and allow only the i-th classifier to respond to modifications in the feature vector.

Definition 4 (Interactive Strategic Behavior). *Let $\mathbf{y}_{-i}^* = (y_1^*, \ldots, y_{i-1}^*, y_{i+1}^*, \ldots, y_n^*)$ denote the frozen outputs of all classifiers except the i-th. The agent exhibits interactive strategic behavior with respect to the i-th classifier by selecting a modified feature vector x' according to:*

$$x' = \arg\max_{x' \in \mathcal{D}} \left\{ g\big(h_1(x', \mathbf{y}_{-1}^*), \ldots, h_n(x', \mathbf{y}_{-n}^*)\big) - \lambda\, c(x, x') \right\}, \tag{6}$$

where $\lambda > 0$ is a trade-off parameter. Although the overall decision function g depends on all classifiers, only the i-th classifier's output changes in response to x'; all others remain fixed by construction.

Remark 2. This definition formalizes a targeted form of strategic behavior in interactive settings. The agents optimize their features to influence a particular sub-classifier, while accounting for the fixed influence of others. This setup reveals how local manipulations can leverage inter-classifier dependencies to affect the final decision, even without directly altering all sub-models.

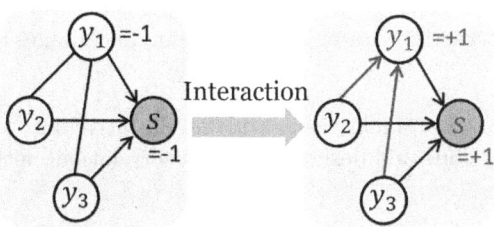

Fig. 2. A loan approval example with interacting decision models. The red arrows represent decision interactions. (Color figure online)

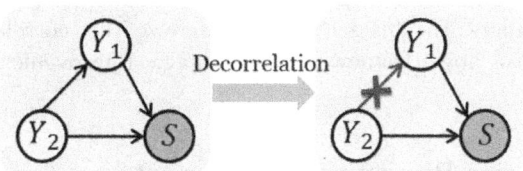

Fig. 3. Schematic of the decision interaction. Y_1 and Y_2 denote the results of the sub-classifiers, while S represents the aggregate score. The red arrows signify interactions between the classifiers. (Color figure online)

Example 1 (Loan Approval with Interacting Classifiers). As illustrated in Fig. 2, consider a loan application evaluated by three interacting classifiers: *creditworthiness* (y_1), *fraud detection* (y_2), and *indebtedness* (y_3). Initially, the applicant is rejected ($s = -1$), primarily due to a low creditworthiness score ($y_1 = -1$). Under traditional strategic manipulation, the applicant may attempt to improve y_1 directly (e.g., by repaying part of a loan), but the effect is limited and insufficient to change the final decision. By recognizing the dependencies among classifiers, the applicant instead improves y_2 and y_3, which indirectly influence y_1 through decision interactions. As a result, y_1 increases beyond the approval threshold, ultimately yielding a favorable final decision ($s = +1$). This illustrates how *interactive strategic behavior* can leverage inter-model dependencies to achieve positive outcomes at a lower manipulation cost.

In the context of decision interaction, as illustrated in Example 1, agents consider the outcomes of multiple decision models when deciding how to manipulate their features. By leveraging these interdependent relationships, they can achieve desired results at a reduced cost compared to manipulating each classifier in isolation.

We define our overarching problem in this multi-classifier environment.

Problem 1 (Strategic Improvement with Decision Interaction). Consider a decision interaction environment e with a population $\mathcal{X}^e$ drawn from a distribution $\mathcal{D}^e$, and n interacting classifiers $h_1^e, \ldots, h_n^e$ producing outcomes $\mathbf{Y}^e$. The comprehensive evaluation is given by $s^e = g(\mathbf{Y}^e)$. Our task is to learn an algorithm $\mathcal{A}$ that minimizes interactive strategic behavior and encourages authentic improvements.

To solve this novel problem, we provide an incentive improvement framework for decision interactions and design a novel decorrelation method for interactive strategic behavior.

5 Methods for Strategic Improvement with Decision Interaction

We argue that interactive strategic behavior arises due to the correlation among interacting classifiers. In this section, we analyze this correlation and subsequently establish a novel framework for strategic improvement under decision interaction.

5.1 Decorrelation Promoting Improvement

We begin by noting that in SIDI, interacting classifiers exhibit a strong correlation. As depicted in Fig. 3, a change in one classifier (e.g., Y_2) can influence the output of another classifier (e.g., Y_1), ultimately affecting the final evaluation score S. To analyze the relationship between correlation and strategic behavior, we propose the following hypothesis:

Hypothesis 1 (Correlation Exacerbates Strategic Behavior). *In SIDI, correlation among interacting classifiers exacerbates strategic (manipulative) behavior of agents, enabling them to achieve favorable outcomes by modifying their features without true improvement.*

Remark 3. This hypothesis is motivated by the observation that when interactions exist among sub-classifiers, even small modifications to individual features are amplified through decision interactions, leading to more pronounced changes in the final decision scores.

We quantify this phenomenon by introducing the **local sensitivity**.

Definition 5 (Local Sensitivity in Decision Interaction). *Let $F(\mathbf{x}) = g(h_1(\mathbf{x}, y_{-1}), \ldots, h_n(\mathbf{x}, y_{-n}))$ be the comprehensive decision function with $y_i = h_i(\mathbf{x}, y_{-i})$. The local sensitivity at point $\mathbf{x}$ is defined as*

$$\gamma(\mathbf{x}) = \left\| Dg(\mathbf{h}(\mathbf{x})) \cdot \nabla_\mathbf{x} \mathbf{h}(\mathbf{x}) \right\|, \tag{7}$$

where $Dg(\mathbf{h}(\mathbf{x})) \in \mathbb{R}^{1 \times n}$ is the gradient of g at $\mathbf{h}(\mathbf{x})$, and $\nabla_\mathbf{x} \mathbf{h}(\mathbf{x}) \in \mathbb{R}^{n \times d}$ is the Jacobian matrix of $\mathbf{h}(\mathbf{x})$ with respect to $\mathbf{x}$[4].

Remark 4. Local sensitivity $\gamma(\mathbf{x})$ characterizes the impact on the comprehensive evaluation $F(\mathbf{x})$ following a change in feature $\mathbf{x}$. A larger value of $\gamma(\mathbf{x})$ indicates a greater influence.

Consequently, consider a decorrelation transformation $Q \in \mathbb{R}^{n \times n}$ used to de-correlate the interacting classifier outputs, i.e., $\tilde{\mathbf{h}}(\mathbf{x}) = Q\,\mathbf{h}(\mathbf{x})$ and $\tilde{g}(\tilde{\mathbf{h}}(\mathbf{x})) = g(Q^{-1}\tilde{\mathbf{h}}(\mathbf{x}))$. The decorrelation local sensitivity is denoted as:

$$\tilde{\gamma}(\mathbf{x}) = \left\| D\tilde{g}(Q^{-1}\tilde{\mathbf{h}}(\mathbf{x})) \cdot Q^{-1} \cdot \nabla_\mathbf{x} \tilde{\mathbf{h}}(\mathbf{x}) \right\|. \tag{8}$$

We argue that $\tilde{\gamma}(\mathbf{x}) < \gamma(\mathbf{x})$ (see Appendix D.2 for details), which indicates that decorrelation reduces the utility of strategic behavior.

Proposition 1 (Decorrelation Promotes Improvement[5]**).** *In the SIDI problem, an appropriate decorrelation method that attenuates only the spurious correlations will diminish the gains from manipulative strategic behavior, thereby promoting substantive improvement.*

5.2 Decorrelation Between Interacting Classifiers

Note that in the context of the comprehensive evaluation process, the outcomes of interacting classifiers are often discrete. Accordingly, we present a decorrelation theorem for SIDI based on Lemma 1.

Theorem 1 (Independence in SIDI). *Let $\mathbf{Y}_i$ and $\mathbf{Y}_j$ be the outcomes of two interacting classifiers, each taking a finite number of discrete values. For each positive integer k, denote by $\mathbf{Y}_i^{(k)}$ the k-th order moment of $\mathbf{Y}_i$, and similarly for $\mathbf{Y}_j^{(k)}$. Suppose there exists a sequence $\{\epsilon(k)\}_{k \in \mathbb{N}}$ with $\epsilon(k) > 0$ for all $k \in \mathbb{N}$ and $\lim \epsilon(k) = 0$, such that for every $k \in \mathbb{N}$ the following inequality holds:*

$$\left\| \mathbb{E}\left[(\mathbf{Y}_i^{(k)})^T \mathbf{Y}_j^{(k)} \right] - \mathbb{E}\left[\mathbf{Y}_i^{(k)} \right] \cdot \mathbb{E}\left[\mathbf{Y}_j^{(k)} \right] \right\|_2^2 < \epsilon(k). \tag{9}$$

Then, the outcomes $\mathbf{Y}_i$ and $\mathbf{Y}_j$ can be regarded as approximately independent[6].

---
[4] The specific derivation is in Appendix D.1.
[5] The proof is included in Appendix E.
[6] The proof can be found in Appendix B.

Remark 5. In SIDI, both linear and nonlinear correlations coexist. To address linear and nonlinear correlations more effectively, we transform the decorrelation problem into a linear one in a high-dimensional space, leveraging the principles outlined in Lemma 3.

Definition 6 (Fourier Transform in Interacting Classifiers). *Let $u_k(Y_i)$ denote the Fourier features obtained from a function $u_k \in \mathcal{H}_{RFF}$. Then, the Fourier features of $\mathbf{Y}_i$ are given by:*

$$\mathbf{u}(\mathbf{Y}_i) = \big(u_1(\mathbf{Y}_i), u_2(\mathbf{Y}_i), \cdots, u_m(\mathbf{Y}_i)\big) \in \mathcal{H}_{RFF}. \tag{10}$$

The functions $\{u_1, u_2, \cdots, u_m\}$ are sampled from the space of Random Fourier Features $\mathcal{H}_{RFF}$:

$$\mathcal{H}_{RFF} = \{ f : x \to \sqrt{2}\cos(\omega x + \phi) \mid \omega \sim N(0,1),\ \phi \sim Uniform(0, 2\pi)\}. \tag{11}$$

where ω is sampled from the standard Normal distribution and ϕ is sampled from the Uniform distribution.

According to Lemma 2, we introduce adaptive weights $\mathbf{W}$ to regulate the correlations between interacting classifiers. Given the Fourier features $\mathbf{u}(\mathbf{Y}_i)$ and $\mathbf{u}(\mathbf{Y}_j)$ for interacting classifiers, we propose the following measure:

$$\Delta_{\mathbf{W}}^{\mathcal{H}_{RFF}}(k) = \sum_{i=1}^{n}\sum_{j\neq i} \Big\| \mathbb{E}\Big[(\mathbf{u}(\mathbf{Y}_i^{(k)}))^T \cdot \Sigma_{\mathbf{W}} \cdot \mathbf{u}(\mathbf{Y}_j^{(k)})\Big] \\ -\mathbb{E}\Big[(\mathbf{u}(\mathbf{Y}_i^{(k)}))^T \cdot \mathbf{W}\Big]\mathbb{E}[(\mathbf{u}(\mathbf{Y}_j^{(k)}))^T \cdot \mathbf{W}]\Big\|_2^2, \tag{12}$$

where $\Sigma_{\mathbf{W}}$ denotes the covariance structure under the weighted distribution.

Remark 6. According to the basic condition for linear independence [24,48], it is sufficient to consider only the cases $k=1$ and $k=2$ in Theorem 1.

Proposition 2 (Adaptive Weight in Decision Interaction[7]). *In the SIDI context, given the outcomes $\mathbf{Y}_1, \mathbf{Y}_2, \ldots, \mathbf{Y}_n$ of n interacting classifiers, the correlations among them can be reduced by designing adaptive weights $\mathbf{W}$, which can be learned via the following objective:*

$$\mathbf{W}^* = \arg\max_{\mathbf{W}\in\Delta_n} \sum_{k=1}^{2} \Delta_{\mathbf{W}}^{\mathcal{H}_{RFF}}(k), \quad \text{where} \quad \Delta_n = \left\{ \mathbf{w} \in \mathbb{R}_+^n \mid \sum_{i=1}^{n} w_i = n \right\}. \tag{13}$$

---

[7] The proof can be found in Appendix F.

5.3 Decision Interaction Improvement Mechanism

Traditional strategic classification methods and improvement mechanisms have not yet accounted for decision interactions. Based on the outline of the strategic classification in Subsect. 3.1, we propose a new strategic improvement mechanism that explicitly addresses the SIDI problem.

Definition 7 (Utility Function in SIDI). *Given n interacting classifiers $h_1, h_2, \ldots, h_n$, and a comprehensive evaluator g, the utility function is defined as:*

$$U(\mathbf{x}, \mathbf{x}') = g(\mathbf{y}_1, \mathbf{y}_2, \cdots, \mathbf{y}_n) - \lambda c(\mathbf{x}, \mathbf{x}'), \tag{14}$$

where $\mathbf{x}'$ is the modified feature vector from strategic behavior, $\mathbf{y}_i$ is the outcome of the i-th interacting classifier h_i, and c is the cost function.

Definition 8 (Strategic Behavior in SIDI). *In strategic improvement, a agent's strategic behavior is categorized into two types b_I and b_M:*

$$\mathbf{x}'_I = b_I(\mathbf{x}) = \arg\max_{x,x' \in \mathcal{D}} U(\mathbf{x}, \mathbf{x}'), \quad \mathbf{x}'_M = b_M(\mathbf{x}) = \arg\max_{x,x' \in \mathcal{D}} U(\mathbf{x}, \mathbf{x}'), \tag{15}$$

where b_I represents strategic behaviors that genuinely enhance the agent's true qualification, while b_M represents strategic behaviors aimed solely at deceiving the decision model.

Remark 7. We write $\mathbf{x} = (\mathbf{x}_I, \mathbf{x}_M, \mathbf{x}_U)$, which denotes the categories of features:*Improvable features ($\mathbf{x}_I$), Manipulable features ($\mathbf{x}_M$), and Immutable features ($\mathbf{x}_U$)*[8].

Definition 9 (Improvement for Interacting Classifier). *A new objective function can be introduced for each interacting classifier in SIDI.*

$$h_i^* \in \arg\max_{h_i \in \mathcal{H}} R_{DI}(h_i) := \kappa R_I(h_i) + R_M(h_i), \tag{16}$$

where $R_I(h_i) = \mathbb{E}_{x \sim \mathcal{D}}[\mathbb{1}(h_i(\mathbf{x}'_I, \mathbf{x}_U, \mathbf{y}_{-i}) = +1)]$ is the improvement objective, rewarding agents for achieving genuine improvement, while $R_M(h_i) = \mathbb{E}_{\mathbf{x} \sim \mathcal{D}}[\mathbb{1}(h_i(\mathbf{x}'_I, \mathbf{x}'_M, \mathbf{x}_U, \mathbf{y}_{-i}) = y_i)]$ is the manipulation objective. The parameter $\kappa > 0$ balances the two competing objectives.

Definition 10 (Decision Optimization in SIDI). *Let $\mathbf{y}_i^*$ denote the outcome of the optimized interacting classifier h_i^*. We incorporate adaptive weights into g to obtain a weighted evaluator g_W. We optimize g_W via the following objective:*

$$g_W^* \in \arg\max_{g_W \in \mathcal{G}} \mathbb{E}_{(\mathbf{x},\mathbf{y}) \sim \mathcal{D}} \left[\mathbb{1} \left(g_W(\mathbf{y}_1^*, \ldots, \mathbf{y}_n^*) = \mathbf{s}_{true} \right) \right]. \tag{17}$$

Remark 8. By employing a comprehensive evaluator with adaptive weights and integrating an improvement objective through interacting classifiers, we establish a novel strategic improvement framework in SIDI.

---
[8] The method for feature classification is included in Appendix C.

6 Experiment

In this section, we evaluate the efficacy of our method for the new problem, i.e., strategic improvement with decision interaction. In this new environment, our main experiments are divided into four parts:

1. Compare the performance of the single model and the interactive models across different classification scenarios.
2. Verify the relationship between decorrelation and strategic improvement
3. Evaluate the performance with three different methods. **TC**, traditional strategic classification ignore the improvement in agents. **TI**, traditional strategic improvement, does not consider decision interaction. **SIDI**, our method, focuses on strategic improvement with decision interaction,
4. Ablation studies on the number of interacting classifiers.

6.1 Setup

Dataset. We utilized six real datasets and one synthetic dataset to validate the efficacy of our method. **Credit**, a dataset contains individual credit information, including credit history, loan purpose, loan amount, employment duration, and personal information [47]. **Student Performance**, a dataset includes student performance data in mathematics and Portuguese language courses [11]. **Adult**, a census-based dataset for predicting adult annual incomes [5]. **PhiUSIIL**, a substantial dataset comprising 134,850 legitimate and 100,945 phishing URLs [40]. **German**, a dataset to assess credit risk in loans from the UCI ML Repository [30]. **Synthetic** [35], a synthetic dataset generated using the PaySim simulator, which mimics mobile financial transactions and fraud patterns based on real-world data.

Metric. In addition to **accuracy**, we introduce the improvement and cheatment rates to assess the effects of strategic behavior. **Improvement rate** is defined as the proportion of the population initially facing rejection but subsequently being accepted following incentive adaptation. **Cheatment rate** is defined as the proportion of the population initially facing rejection, but subsequently being accepted by exploiting strategic behavior without genuine improvement.

To verify the effect of correlation, when linear and nonlinear decorrelation together, the adaptive weight W is trained with Eq. (13). If only linear correlation, the adaptive weight W is trained with the following objective:

$$\mathbf{W}' = \arg\min_{\mathbf{W}} \left(\Delta_{\mathbf{W}}(1) + \Delta_{\mathbf{W}}(2) \right), \tag{18}$$

where we set:

$$\Delta_{\mathbf{W}}(k) = \sum_{i=1}^{n} \sum_{j \neq i} \left\| \mathbb{E}[(\mathbf{Y}_i^{(k)})^T \cdot \Sigma_{\mathbf{W}} \cdot \mathbf{Y}_j^{(k)}] - \mathbb{E}[(\mathbf{Y}_i^{(k)})^T \cdot \mathbf{W}] \cdot \mathbb{E}[(\mathbf{Y}_j^{(k)})^T \cdot \mathbf{W}] \right\|_2^2. \tag{19}$$

Table 1. Performance comparison between single model and interacting models

Metrics	Methods	Datasets					
		Credit	Student	Adult	German	PhiUSIIL	Synthetic
Non-strategic							
Accuracy	Single Model	$71.83_{\pm1.65}$	$77.42_{\pm1.30}$	$82.12_{\pm1.05}$	$91.28_{\pm1.35}$	$64.82_{\pm1.10}$	$81.35_{\pm1.20}$
	Interacting models	$74.23_{\pm1.81}$	$79.85_{\pm1.50}$	$83.45_{\pm1.20}$	$91.17_{\pm1.60}$	$65.15_{\pm1.25}$	$85.73_{\pm1.35}$
Strategic							
Accuracy	Single model	$69.52_{\pm2.70}$	$73.15_{\pm2.13}$	$79.23_{\pm1.30}$	$88.13_{\pm1.80}$	$63.53_{\pm1.60}$	$73.75_{\pm1.90}$
	Interacting models	$71.22_{\pm1.97}$	$76.78_{\pm1.85}$	$81.56_{\pm1.13}$	$90.61_{\pm1.54}$	$64.29_{\pm1.02}$	$80.66_{\pm1.58}$
Imp. rate	Single model	$38.53_{\pm5.30}$	$34.93_{\pm3.80}$	$35.52_{\pm3.30}$	$34.85_{\pm4.50}$	$30.83_{\pm4.10}$	$27.93_{\pm4.20}$
	Interacting models	$47.13_{\pm4.78}$	$39.74_{\pm3.60}$	$42.29_{\pm4.12}$	$43.05_{\pm3.67}$	$36.41_{\pm2.91}$	$38.54_{\pm3.30}$

Note: "Non-strategic" indicates that the models do not take into account agents' strategic behaviors during both training and inference, whereas "Strategic" means that the model integrates these strategic behaviors. "Single Model" comes from the collection of existing methods [8,10,19,28]. "Interacting models" are designed with decision interaction. "Imp. rate" is short for the improvement rate.

Table 2. Performance comparison of different methods in SIDI.

Methods	Metrics	Datasets					
		Credit	Student	Adult	German	PhiUSIIL	Synthetic
TC [10,19,37,42]	Accuracy	$70.89_{\pm2.77}$	$76.50_{\pm2.06}$	$81.61_{\pm1.22}$	$89.36_{\pm1.87}$	$63.81_{\pm1.71}$	$74.08_{\pm1.82}$
	Imp. rate	$32.14_{\pm4.54}$	$28.67_{\pm3.48}$	$30.72_{\pm3.29}$	$29.35_{\pm3.91}$	$24.56_{\pm2.56}$	$25.66_{\pm3.68}$
	Cheatment	$30.88_{\pm2.76}$	$23.71_{\pm1.89}$	$25.30_{\pm2.12}$	$24.35_{\pm1.83}$	$22.72_{\pm1.54}$	$28.53_{\pm2.68}$
TI [8,21,28,36]	Accuracy	$68.43_{\pm1.89}$	$74.50_{\pm2.27}$	$79.10_{\pm1.63}$	$87.54_{\pm2.14}$	$61.50_{\pm1.42}$	$72.62_{\pm1.93}$
	Imp. rate	$40.71_{\pm5.54}$	$37.65_{\pm3.00}$	$39.36_{\pm3.36}$	$38.35_{\pm4.75}$	$32.53_{\pm4.03}$	$33.27_{\pm4.09}$
	Cheatment	$23.68_{\pm2.57}$	$20.24_{\pm1.96}$	$22.10_{\pm2.35}$	$20.53_{\pm2.19}$	$18.33_{\pm1.62}$	$20.33_{\pm2.52}$
SIDI(ours)	Accuracy	$71.66_{\pm2.27}$	$77.21_{\pm2.15}$	$82.00_{\pm1.43}$	$90.57_{\pm2.04}$	$64.73_{\pm1.32}$	$81.10_{\pm1.88}$
	Imp. rate	$48.05_{\pm5.93}$	$41.59_{\pm4.75}$	$43.21_{\pm5.27}$	$42.97_{\pm3.82}$	$36.33_{\pm4.06}$	$38.59_{\pm3.45}$
	Cheatment	$19.68_{\pm1.81}$	$16.24_{\pm1.67}$	$18.10_{\pm1.51}$	$16.50_{\pm1.72}$	$15.24_{\pm1.51}$	$16.33_{\pm2.05}$

6.2 Implementation Details

All experiments are conducted on a single NVIDIA TITAN V 12 GB GPU. The adaptive weights used in our decorrelation method are optimized via the Adam optimizer (learning rate 0.0005), with softmax normalization applied per minibatch. The weighting scheme converges stably within 128 steps in our experiments. For the decorrelation computation, we use 32-dimensional random Fourier features. Each sub-classifier h_i is instantiated as a logistic regression model. The final aggregator g is implemented as a linear model[9]. The full model is trained using Adam (learning rate 0.0001) with early stopping.

---

[9] We also consider different interaction types. The details and results are included in Appendix H.

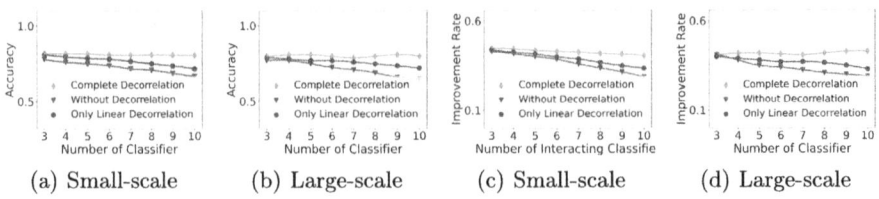

Fig. 4. Performance comparison in the SIDI problem under different degrees of decorrelation across small-scale and large-scale datasets.

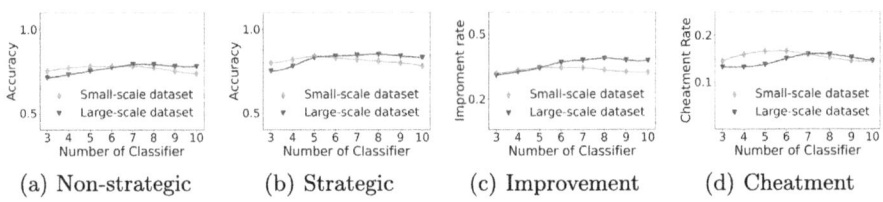

Fig. 5. Effect of the number of interactive classifiers on performance in the SIDI problem.

6.3 Results and Analysis

Table 1 shows that, across various datasets, models using decision interactions outperform single-model decisions in both *non-strategic* and *strategic* environments. Under strategic conditions, interacting models achieve a significantly higher improvement rate, suggesting that decision interactions more effectively motivate agents to enhance their qualifications.

Table 2 validates our framework on multiple datasets in a decision interaction context. Our method outperforms existing strategic classification and improvement approaches in accuracy, improvement rate, and cheatment rate, the latter reduction attributed to adaptive weight decorrelation mitigating strategic behavior, while the higher improvement rate indicates more genuine qualification enhancements.

Figure 4 compares results on datasets of varying scales using adaptive weights in both linear and nonlinear decorrelation settings. Both decorrelation types significantly affect accuracy and improvement rate, reducing the impact of strategic behavior in the SIDI problem and encouraging qualification improvements.

Figure 5 examines the effect of the number of interactive classifiers in both strategic and non-strategic settings. The accuracy and improvement rate initially rise with more classifiers, though an excessive number causes a slight decline in accuracy, while the cheatment rate remains stable. These findings imply that an optimal number of classifiers enhances overall performance.

7 Conclusion

In this work, we introduce a novel problem in strategic machine learning: **S**trategic **I**mprovement with **D**ecision **I**nteraction (*SIDI*). We frame the problem and uncover novel strategic behaviors among agents in decision interaction. By analyzing the correlations among interacting classifiers, we introduce a comprehensive decorrelation method and propose a new strategic improvement framework. In future work, we aim to incorporate fairness considerations into our framework.

Acknowledgement. This work is supported in part by the National Natural Science Foundation of China under Grants No. 62372459 and 62302503, the Natural Science Foundation of Heilongjiang Province under Grant No. LH2023C069, the NUDT Youth Independent Innovation Science Fund under Grant No. ZK23-15, and the Open Research Fund of the State Key Laboratory of High Performance Computing of China under Grant No. 202401-09.

References

1. Abdoli, M., Akbari, M., Shahrabi, J.: Bagging supervised autoencoder classifier for credit scoring. Expert Syst. Appl. **213**, 118991 (2023)
2. Alagic, A., et al.: Machine learning for an enhanced credit risk analysis: a comparative study of loan approval prediction models integrating mental health data. Mach. Learn. Knowl. Extract. **6**(1), 53–77 (2024). https://doi.org/10.3390/make6010004, https://www.mdpi.com/2504-4990/6/1/4
3. Athey, S., Imbens, G.W., Wager, S.: Approximate residual balancing: debiased inference of average treatment effects in high dimensions. J. R. Stat. Soc. Ser. B Stat Methodol. **80**(4), 597–623 (2018)
4. Bechavod, Y., Ligett, K., Wu, S., Ziani, J.: Gaming helps! learning from strategic interactions in natural dynamics. In: International Conference on Artificial Intelligence and Statistics, pp. 1234–1242. PMLR (2021)
5. Becker, B., Kohavi, R.: Adult. UCI Mach. Learn. Reposit. (1996). https://doi.org/10.24432/C5XW20
6. Bisgaard, T.M., Sasvári, Z.: When does e (xk· yl)= e (xk)· e (yl) imply independence? Statist. Probability Lett. **76**(11), 1111–1116 (2006)
7. Chang, T., Warrenburg, L., Park, S.H., Parikh, R., Makar, M., Wiens, J.: Who's gaming the system? A causally-motivated approach for detecting strategic adaptation. Adv. Neural. Inf. Process. Syst. **37**, 42311–42348 (2024)
8. Chen, Y., Wang, J., Liu, Y.: Learning to incentivize improvements from strategic agents. Trans. Mach. Learn. Res. (2023). https://openreview.net/forum?id=W98AEKQ38Y
9. Chen, Y., Liu, Y., Podimata, C.: Grinding the space: Learning to classify against strategic agents. arXiv preprint arXiv:1911.04004 (2019)
10. Cohen, L., Mansour, Y., Moran, S., Shao, H.: Learnability gaps of strategic classification (2024). https://arxiv.org/abs/2402.19303
11. Cortez, P.: Student performance. UCI Mach. Learn. Reposit. (2014). https://doi.org/10.24432/C5TG7T

12. Dong, J., Roth, A., Schutzman, Z., Waggoner, B., Wu, Z.S.: Strategic classification from revealed preferences. In: Proceedings of the 2018 ACM Conference on Economics and Computation, pp. 55–70 (2018)
13. Efthymiou, V., Podimata, C., Sen, D., Ziani, J.: Incentivizing desirable effort profiles in strategic classification: The role of causality and uncertainty. arXiv preprint arXiv:2502.06749 (2025)
14. Eilat, I., Finkelshtein, B., Baskin, C., Rosenfeld, N.: Strategic classification with graph neural networks. arXiv preprint arXiv:2205.15765 (2022)
15. Emmanuel, I., Sun, Y., Wang, Z.: A machine learning-based credit risk prediction engine system using a stacked classifier and a filter-based feature selection method. J. Big Data **11**(1), 23 (2024)
16. Estornell, A., Chen, Y., Das, S., Liu, Y., Vorobeychik, Y.: Incentivizing recourse through auditing in strategic classification. In: IJCAI (2023)
17. Estornell, A., Das, S., Liu, Y., Vorobeychik, Y.: Group-fair classification with strategic agents. In: Proceedings of the 2023 ACM Conference on Fairness, Accountability, and Transparency, pp. 389–399. FAccT 2023, Association for Computing Machinery, New York, NY, USA (2023). https://doi.org/10.1145/3593013.3594006
18. Gavish, M., Talmon, R., Su, P.C., Wu, H.T.: Optimal recovery of precision matrix for mahalanobis distance from high dimensional noisy observations in manifold learning (2021). https://arxiv.org/abs/1904.09204
19. Ghalme, G., Nair, V., Eilat, I., Talgam-Cohen, I., Rosenfeld, N.: Strategic classification in the dark. In: Meila, M., Zhang, T. (eds.) Proceedings of the 38th International Conference on Machine Learning. Proceedings of Machine Learning Research, vol. 139, pp. 3672–3681. PMLR (2021). https://proceedings.mlr.press/v139/ghalme21a.html
20. Grosz, M.: Admissions policies, cohort composition, and academic success: evidence from California. J. Hum. Resour. **58**(4), 1242–1272 (2023)
21. Haghtalab, N., Immorlica, N., Lucier, B., Wang, J.Z.: Maximizing welfare with incentive-aware evaluation mechanisms. arXiv preprint arXiv:2011.01956 (2020)
22. Hardt, M., Jagadeesan, M., Mendler-Dünner, C.: Performative power. Adv. Neural. Inf. Process. Syst. **35**, 22969–22981 (2022)
23. Hardt, M., Megiddo, N., Papadimitriou, C., Wootters, M.: Strategic classification. In: Proceedings of the 2016 ACM Conference on Innovations in Theoretical Computer Science, pp. 111–122 (2016)
24. Hariharan, B., Malik, J., Ramanan, D.: Discriminative decorrelation for clustering and classification. In: Fitzgibbon, A., Lazebnik, S., Perona, P., Sato, Y., Schmid, C. (eds.) European Conference on Computer Vision, pp. 459–472. Springer, Heidelberg (2012). https://doi.org/10.1007/978-3-642-33765-9_33
25. Harris, K., Ngo, D.D.T., Stapleton, L., Heidari, H., Wu, S.: Strategic instrumental variable regression: recovering causal relationships from strategic responses. In: International Conference on Machine Learning, pp. 8502–8522. PMLR (2022)
26. Horowitz, G., Rosenfeld, N.: Causal strategic classification: a tale of two shifts. In: International Conference on Machine Learning, pp. 13233–13253. PMLR (2023)
27. Hossain, S., Micha, E., Chen, Y., Procaccia, A.: Strategic classification with externalities. arXiv preprint arXiv:2410.08032 (2024)
28. Jin, K., Zhang, X., Khalili, M.M., Naghizadeh, P., Liu, M.: Incentive mechanisms for strategic classification and regression problems. In: Proceedings of the 23rd ACM Conference on Economics and Computation, pp. 760–790 (2022)

29. Keswani, V., Celis, L.E.: Addressing strategic manipulation disparities in fair classification. In: Proceedings of the 3rd ACM Conference on Equity and Access in Algorithms, Mechanisms, and Optimization. EAAMO 2023, Association for Computing Machinery, New York, NY, USA (2023). https://doi.org/10.1145/3617694.3623252
30. Khan, M.M.R., Arif, R.B., Siddique, M.A.B., Oishe, M.R.: Study and observation of the variation of accuracies of KNN, SVM, LMNN, ENN algorithms on eleven different datasets from UCI machine learning repository. In: 2018 4th International Conference on Electrical Engineering and Information Communication Technology (iCEEiCT), pp. 124–129 (2018). https://doi.org/10.1109/CEEICT.2018.8628041
31. Kuang, K., Cui, P., Li, B., Jiang, M., Yang, S., Wang, F.: Treatment effect estimation with data-driven variable decomposition. In: Proceedings of the AAAI Conference on Artificial Intelligence, vol. 31 (2017)
32. Kuang, K., Xiong, R., Cui, P., Athey, S., Li, B.: Stable prediction with model misspecification and agnostic distribution shift. In: Proceedings of the AAAI Conference on Artificial Intelligence, vol. 34, pp. 4485–4492 (2020)
33. Kurysheva, A., Rijen, H.V., Dilaver, G.: How do admission committees select? Do applicants know how they select? Selection criteria and transparency at a Dutch university. Tert. Educ. Manag. 25(4), 367–388 (2019)
34. Levanon, S., Rosenfeld, N.: Strategic classification made practical. In: International Conference on Machine Learning, pp. 6243–6253. PMLR (2021)
35. Lopez-Rojas, E., Elmir, A., Axelsson, S.: Paysim: A financial mobile money simulator for fraud detection. In: 28th European Modeling and Simulation Symposium, EMSS, Larnaca, pp. 249–255. Dime University of Genoa (2016)
36. Miller, J., Milli, S., Hardt, M.: Strategic classification is causal modeling in disguise. In: International Conference on Machine Learning, pp. 6917–6926. PMLR (2020)
37. Milli, S., Miller, J., Dragan, A.D., Hardt, M.: The social cost of strategic classification. In: Proceedings of the Conference on Fairness, Accountability, and Transparency, pp. 230–239 (2019)
38. Mofakhami, M., Mitliagkas, I., Gidel, G.: Performative prediction with neural networks. In: International Conference on Artificial Intelligence and Statistics, pp. 11079–11093. PMLR (2023)
39. Perdomo, J., Zrnic, T., Mendler-Dünner, C., Hardt, M.: Performative prediction. In: International Conference on Machine Learning, pp. 7599–7609. PMLR (2020)
40. Prasad, A., Chandra, S.: PhiUSIIL phishing URL (website). UCI machine learning repository (2024). https://doi.org/10.1016/j.cose.2023.103545
41. Raghavan, M., Barocas, S., Kleinberg, J., Levy, K.: Mitigating bias in algorithmic hiring: evaluating claims and practices. In: Proceedings of the 2020 conference on fairness, accountability, and transparency, pp. 469–481 (2020)
42. Shavit, Y., Edelman, B., Axelrod, B.: Causal strategic linear regression. In: International Conference on Machine Learning, pp. 8676–8686. PMLR (2020)
43. Singh, M.K., Kulkarni, A.A.: Optimal stochastic decision rule for strategic classification. In: 2024 National Conference on Communications (NCC), pp. 1–6. IEEE (2024)
44. Sundaram, R., Vullikanti, A., Xu, H., Yao, F.: PAC-Learning for Strategic Classification. arXiv e-prints arXiv:2012.03310 (2020). https://doi.org/10.48550/arXiv.2012.03310
45. Vo, K.Q., Aadil, M., Chau, S.L., Muandet, K.: Causal strategic learning with competitive selection. In: Proceedings of the AAAI Conference on Artificial Intelligence, vol. 38, pp. 15411–15419 (2024)

46. Xie, T., Zhang, X.: Non-linear welfare-aware strategic learning. In: Proceedings of the AAAI/ACM Conference on AI, Ethics, and Society, vol. 7, pp. 1660–1671 (2024)
47. Yeh, I.C.: Default of credit card clients. UCI Machine Learning Repository (2016). https://doi.org/10.24432/C55S3H
48. Zhang, H., Zhang, K., Zhou, S., Guan, J., Zhang, J.: Testing independence between linear combinations for causal discovery. In: Proceedings of the AAAI conference on artificial intelligence, vol. 35, pp. 6538–6546 (2021)
49. Zhang, X., Cui, P., Xu, R., Zhou, L., He, Y., Shen, Z.: Deep stable learning for out-of-distribution generalization. In: Proceedings of the IEEE/CVF Conference on Computer Vision and Pattern Recognition, pp. 5372–5382 (2021)
50. Zhang, X., Khalili, M.M., Jin, K., Naghizadeh, P., Liu, M.: Fairness interventions as (Dis)Incentives for strategic manipulation. In: Chaudhuri, K., Jegelka, S., Song, L., Szepesvari, C., Niu, G., Sabato, S. (eds.) Proceedings of the 39th International Conference on Machine Learning. Proceedings of Machine Learning Research, vol. 162, pp. 26239–26264. PMLR (2022). https://proceedings.mlr.press/v162/zhang22l.html
51. Zrnic, T., Mazumdar, E., Sastry, S., Jordan, M.: Who leads and who follows in strategic classification? Adv. Neural. Inf. Process. Syst. **34**, 15257–15269 (2021)

Clustering

TreeDiffusion: Hierarchical Generative Clustering for Conditional Diffusion

Jorge da Silva Gonçalves[✉], Laura Manduchi, Moritz Vandenhirtz, and Julia E. Vogt

ETH Zurich, Rämistrasse 101, 8092 Zurich, Switzerland
jorge.dasilvagoncalves@inf.ethz.ch

Abstract. Generative modeling and clustering are conventionally distinct tasks in machine learning. Variational Autoencoders (VAEs) have been widely explored for their ability to integrate both, providing a framework for generative clustering. However, while VAEs can learn meaningful cluster representations in latent space, they often struggle to generate high-quality samples. This paper addresses this problem by introducing TreeDiffusion, a deep generative model that conditions diffusion models on learned latent hierarchical cluster representations from a VAE to obtain high-quality, cluster-specific generations. Our approach consists of two steps: first, a VAE-based clustering model learns a hierarchical latent representation of the data. Second, a cluster-aware diffusion model generates realistic images conditioned on the learned hierarchical structure. We systematically compare the generative capabilities of our approach with those of alternative conditioning strategies. Empirically, we demonstrate that conditioning diffusion models on hierarchical cluster representations improves the generative performance on real-world datasets compared to other approaches. Moreover, a key strength of our method lies in its ability to generate images that are both representative and specific to each cluster, enabling more detailed visualization of the learned latent structure. Our approach addresses the generative limitations of VAE-based clustering approaches by leveraging their learned structure, thereby advancing the field of generative clustering.

Keywords: Generative Modeling · Hierarchical Clustering · Conditional Diffusion

1 Introduction

Generative modeling and clustering are two fundamental yet different tasks in machine learning. Generative modeling focuses on approximating the underlying data distribution, enabling the generation of new samples [8,15]. Clustering, on the other hand, seeks to uncover meaningful and interpretable structures within data through the unsupervised detection of intrinsic relationships and dependencies [7,38], facilitating better visualization and interpretation of the data. By integrating hierarchical dependencies into a deep latent variable model,

---

Supplementary Information The online version contains supplementary material available at https://doi.org/10.1007/978-3-032-05962-8_26.

TreeVAE [20] was recently proposed to bridge these two research directions. While TreeVAE is effective at hierarchical clustering, it falls short in generating high-quality images. Like other VAE-based models, it faces common issues such as producing blurry outputs [4]. In contrast, diffusion models [12,31] have recently gained prominence for their superior image generation capabilities, progressively refining noisy inputs to produce sharp, realistic images.

Our work bridges this gap by introducing a second-stage diffusion model that is conditioned on the hierarchical cluster representations learned by TreeVAE. The proposed framework, **TreeDiffusion**, combines the strengths of both models to generate high-quality, cluster-specific images, achieving improved performance in image generation. The generative process begins by sampling the root embedding of a latent tree, which is learned during training. From there, the sample is propagated from the root to one leaf by (a) sampling a path through the tree and (b) applying a sequence of stochastic transformations to the root embedding along the chosen hierarchical path. Subsequently, the diffusion model harnesses the hierarchical information by conditioning its reverse diffusion process on the sampled path representations of the latent tree through a path encoder. A key strength of TreeDiffusion is its ability to generate images tailored to each cluster, providing enhanced visualization of the learned representations, as demonstrated by our qualitative results. For the same sample, our method can produce leaf-specific images that share common general properties but differ by features encoded in the latent hierarchy. Moreover, this approach overcomes the generative limitations of VAE-based hierarchical clustering models like TreeVAE while preserving their clustering performance.

Generative clustering finds application in domains with abundant unlabeled data, where both group discovery and synthetic data generation are valuable. In the medical domain, for example, our model could aid in identifying subgroups within image data, while simultaneously providing visualizations that enhance the interpretation of the discovered groupings. Moreover, once meaningful clusters have been identified, the ability to generate representative samples enables data augmentation for downstream tasks.

1.1 Main Contributions

Our main contributions include (i) a unified framework that integrates hierarchical clustering into diffusion models, and (ii) a novel mechanism for controlling image synthesis based on learned clusters. We demonstrate that our approach (a) surpasses the generative limitations of VAE-based clustering models, and (b) produces samples that are both more representative of their respective clusters and closer to the true data distribution than models without hierarchical clustering integration.

2 Related Work

Variational Approaches for Hierarchical Clustering. Since their introduction, Variational Autoencoders (VAEs) [15] have been widely used for clustering tasks, due to their ability to learn structured latent representations [14].

One line of work integrates hierarchical Bayesian non-parametric priors into the latent space of VAEs by applying nested Chinese Restaurant Processes to cluster the data based on infinitely deep and branching trees [9]. Another approach, TreeVAE [20], models the data distribution by learning an optimal tree structure of latent stochastic variables. This results in latent embeddings that are automatically organized into a hierarchy, mimicking the hierarchical clustering process. Single-cell TreeVAE [34] extends this framework to single-cell RNA sequencing data by incorporating batch correction, which facilitates biologically plausible hierarchical structures. Despite their strong clustering performance, these models often exhibit limited generative quality, with few providing quantitative or qualitative evaluations of their sample generation capabilities. Aside from generative approaches, discriminative deep hierarchical clustering methods include DeepECT [21] and CoHiClust [42]. Although not directly designed for clustering, ClusterNet [5] is a 3D object classification model that leverages hierarchical clustering to improve the quality of its learned representations. In this work, however, we focus on generative hierarchical clustering and its use as a conditioning signal for diffusion models.

Diffusion Models. Diffusion models have become state-of-the-art for image generation tasks over the past few years [6,12,22,26,28,31–33]. One drawback of diffusion models is that their latent variables lack interpretability compared to the latent spaces of VAEs. To take advantage of the strengths of both approaches, researchers have explored architectures that combine the more interpretable latent spaces of VAEs with the advanced generative capabilities of diffusion models. Notable examples include DiffuseVAE [24], Diffusion Autoencoders [25], and InfoDiffusion [37]. Furthermore, representation-conditioned image generation [18] illustrates how self-supervised learning can improve generative diffusion frameworks in unsupervised settings, reducing the gap between class-conditional and unconditional image generation.

Connecting Diffusion with Clustering. The research most closely related to our work focuses on using clustering as conditioning signals for diffusion models to improve generative quality. One approach [1] utilizes cluster assignments from k-means or TEMI clustering [2]. Similarly, another one [13] introduces a framework that employs the k-means clustering algorithm as an annotation function, generating self-annotated image-level, box-level, and pixel-level guidance signals. Both studies demonstrate the benefits of conditioning on clustering information to improve generative performance without going into the specifics of clustering performance itself. In contrast, our work further investigates which types of clustering information are most beneficial for the model, employing learned latent cluster representations alongside cluster assignments for conditioning. Related to conditioning on clusters, both kNN-Diffusion [29] and Retrieval-Augmented Diffusion Models [3] utilize nearest neighbor retrieval to condition generative models on similar embeddings, minimizing the need for large parametric models and paired datasets in tasks like text-to-image synthesis. Diffusion models have also been applied in incomplete multiview clustering to generate missing views to improve clustering performance [39,40]. On a different note, recent research shows that training diffusion models is equivalent to solving a subspace clustering problem, explaining their ability to learn image distributions with few samples [36]. Finally, diffusion models have also been applied as a post-hoc method to enhance the generation quality of multimodal clustering models [23]. However, to the best of our knowledge, no existing diffusion model explicitly uses hierarchical clustering to enhance the interpretability and generative performance of generative clustering models.

3 Method

We propose **TreeDiffusion**[1], a two-stage framework consisting of a VAE-based generative hierarchical clustering model, followed by a hierarchy-conditional diffusion model. In the first stage, TreeVAE [20] serves as the clustering model, encoding hierarchical clusters within its latent tree structure, where the leaf nodes represent clusters. We select TreeVAE as it provides structured hierarchical latent representations from root to leaf, which are then processed by a path encoder to create the conditioning signal. In the second stage, a denoising diffusion implicit model (DDIM) [24], uses this conditioning signal to generate cluster-conditional samples. Hence, our model enables cluster-guided diffusion in unsupervised settings, analogously to classifier-guided diffusion [6] in supervised settings. Figure 1 illustrates the workflow of TreeDiffusion. The following sections provide a detailed description of each stage of the model.

3.1 Hierarchical Clustering with TreeVAE

The first part of TreeDiffusion involves a Tree Variational Autoencoder (Tree-VAE) [20]. TreeVAE is a generative model that learns to hierarchically separate data into clusters through a latent tree structure. During training, the model dynamically grows a binary tree structure of stochastic variables. The process begins with a simple tree composed of a root and two child nodes, and it optimizes the corresponding ELBO over a fixed number of epochs. Afterward, the tree expands by adding two child nodes to an existing leaf node, prioritizing nodes with the highest assigned sample count to promote balanced leaves. This expansion continues iteratively, training only the subtree formed by the new leaves while freezing the rest of the model. This process repeats until the tree reaches a predefined depth or leaf count, alternating between optimizing model parameters and expanding the tree structure.

To formalize the latent tree, we adopt the original notation from TreeVAE and refer the reader to the original paper [20] for a more comprehensive introduction. Let the set $\mathbb{V}$ represent the nodes of the tree. Each node corresponds to

---

[1] The code and supplementary material are publicly available at https://github.com/JoGo175/TreeDiffusion.

TreeDiffusion: Hierarchical Generative Clustering for Conditional Diffusion

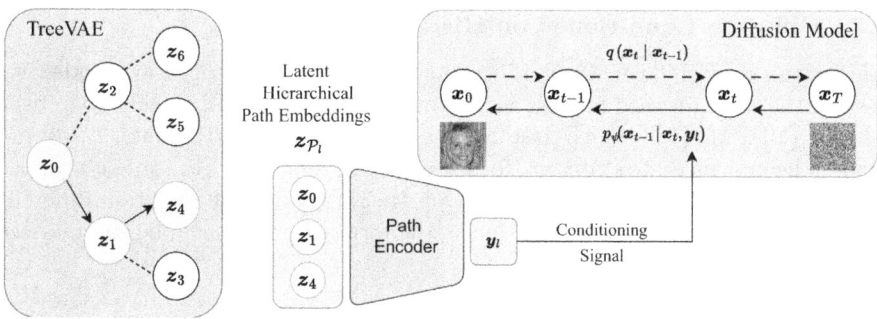

Fig. 1. Schematic overview of the TreeDiffusion framework: TreeVAE encodes data into hierarchical latent variables, where a path is sampled from the root to a leaf node. An encoder network creates a conditioning signal using the sampled hierarchical path embeddings. The diffusion model leverages this information to condition its reverse process and generate a cluster-specific image.

a stochastic latent variable, denoted as $z_0, \ldots, z_V$. The generative process starts at the root node, where z_0 is sampled from a standard Gaussian distribution, i.e., $z_0 \sim \mathcal{N}(0, I)$. The remaining latent variables follow a Gaussian distribution, whose parameters depend on their parent node through neural network layers. The set of leaves $\mathbb{L}$, with $\mathbb{L} \subset \mathbb{V}$, represents the clusters present in the data. Starting from the root node, z_0, a given sample traverses the tree to a leaf node, z_l, in a probabilistic manner. The probabilities of moving to the left or right child at each internal node are determined by neural networks termed *routers*. The decisions of moving to either child node are denoted by c_i for each non-leaf node i and follow a Bernoulli distribution, where $c_i = 0$ indicates the selection of the left child. The path $\mathcal{P}_l$ refers to the sequence of nodes from the root to one leaf l. Moreover, let $z_{\mathcal{P}_l} = \{z_i \mid i \in \mathcal{P}_l\}$ denote the set of latent embeddings for each node in the path $\mathcal{P}_l$. The latent tree encodes a sample-specific probability distribution of paths. Each leaf embedding, z_l for $l \in \mathbb{L}$, represents the learned latent representation for that cluster. In TreeVAE, leaf-specific decoders use these embeddings to reconstruct or generate new cluster-specific images, i.e., given a dataset X, TreeVAE reconstructs $\hat{X} = \{\hat{X}^{(l)} \mid l \in \mathbb{L}\}$. In summary, the generative model (1) and inference model (2) of TreeVAE are defined as follows:

$$p_\theta(z_{\mathcal{P}_l}, \mathcal{P}_l) = p(z_0) \prod_{i \in \mathcal{P}_l \setminus \{0\}} \underbrace{p\left(c_{pa(i) \to i} \mid z_{pa(i)}\right)}_{\text{decision probability}} \underbrace{p\left(z_i \mid z_{pa(i)}\right)}_{\text{sample probability}} \quad (1)$$

$$q(z_{\mathcal{P}_l}, \mathcal{P}_l \mid x) = q(z_0 \mid x) \prod_{i \in \mathcal{P}_l \setminus \{0\}} q\left(c_{pa(i) \to i} \mid x\right) q\left(z_i \mid z_{pa(i)}\right) \quad (2)$$

3.2 Diffusion Conditioned on Hierarchical Clusters

The second part of TreeDiffusion incorporates a conditional diffusion model. We assume the same forward process as in standard Denoising Diffusion Probabilistic Models (DDPM) [12], which gradually introduces noise to the data x_0 over T steps. The intermediate states, x_t for $t = 1, \ldots, T$, follow a trajectory determined by a noise schedule $\beta_1, \ldots, \beta_T$ that controls the rate of data degradation, whereby $\alpha_t = (1 - \beta_t)$ and $\bar{\alpha}_t = \prod_{s=1}^{t} \alpha_s$. Hence, the forward process can be summarized as follows:

$$q(x_{1:T} \mid x_0) = \prod_{t=1}^{T} q(x_t \mid x_{t-1}) \tag{3}$$

$$q(x_t \mid x_{t-1}) = \mathcal{N}\left(\sqrt{1 - \beta_t} x_{t-1}, \beta_t I\right) \tag{4}$$

$$q(x_t \mid x_0) = \mathcal{N}\left(\sqrt{\bar{\alpha}_t} x_0, (1 - \bar{\alpha}_t) I\right) \tag{5}$$

For the reverse process, TreeDiffusion starts with random noise, similar to standard diffusion models. Our model relies exclusively on the latent hierarchical information provided by TreeVAE, which is based on the tree structure learned during the first stage. The generative process begins by sampling the root embedding of the latent tree. A path is then sampled from the root to a leaf node l, and a sequence of stochastic transformations is applied to the root embedding along this path. Specifically, the tree leaf l corresponds to the selected cluster and represents the unique path through the hierarchical structure. The hierarchical conditioning information is derived from $z_{\mathcal{P}_l}$, the set of latent embeddings along the path from the root node to the chosen leaf. These embeddings are further processed by a dedicated path encoder, which aggregates the information to produce the conditioning signal y_l:

$$y_l = \sum_{i \in \mathcal{P}_l} \left(f_{\text{embed}}(z_i) + f_{\text{node}}(i)\right).$$

Here, f_{embed} and f_{node} are each implemented as projection blocks consisting of two MLP layers with an activation in-between, and jointly trained with the diffusion model. For each node in the path, its embedding and corresponding node index are projected independently into the time embedding dimension of the U-Net decoder [22,27]. The resulting projections are aggregated into the unified conditioning signal y_l, which is then combined with the time-step embeddings to guide the U-Net during the denoising process. Consequently, this conditioning mechanism directly influences the reverse process. Let ψ denote the parameters of the denoising model, and let $p(l|x_0)$ be the probability that the sample x_0 is assigned to leaf l in the latent tree. The reverse process can then be summarized as follows:

$$l \sim p(l|x_0),$$
$$p_\psi(x_{0:T} \mid y_l) = p(x_T) \prod_{t=1}^{T} p_\psi(x_{t-1} \mid x_t, y_l), \tag{6}$$

The path sampling ensures that different leaves are considered, prompting the diffusion model to perform effectively across all leaves. Consequently, our approach addresses the distinct clusters inherent to TreeVAE, allowing the model to adapt and encouraging cluster-aware refinements in the images. This guidance in the image generation process assists the denoising model in learning cluster-specific image reconstructions. Currently, sampling is limited to paths originating from the root. We leave partial sampling using subtrees as well as the exploration of alternative methods for constructing the path embeddings for future work.

The following design considerations are implemented in TreeDiffusion to achieve computational efficiency without compromising effectiveness. Due to the large number of denoising steps required, DDPM sampling can be computationally expensive. To address this issue, we opt for the DDIM sampling procedure [32] instead of the standard DDPM [12]. DDIMs significantly accelerate inference by using only a subset of denoising steps, making the process more efficient while maintaining high-quality results. Finally, by employing a two-stage training strategy, where the conditional diffusion model is trained using a pre-trained TreeVAE model, TreeDiffusion preserves the hierarchical clustering performance of TreeVAE. Hence, we can combine the effective clustering of TreeVAE with the superior image generation capabilities of diffusion models.

4 Experiments

We present a series of experiments to evaluate the performance of TreeDiffusion across various datasets. The experiments are carried out on MNIST [17], FashionMNIST [41], CIFAR-10 [16], CelebA [19], and CUBICC [23]. The CUBICC dataset is a variant of the CUB Image-Captions dataset [30,35], consisting of bird images grouped into eight distinct species. In Sect. 4.1, we compare the generative performance of TreeDiffusion against baseline methods. In Sect. 4.2, we evaluate how specific the generated images are to their source clusters and analyze how distinct images from different clusters are from one another. Finally, in Sect. 4.3, we perform an ablation study on conditioning signals, examining various model configurations to identify which signals most effectively improve generative performance. Specifically, we compare conditioning strategies based on hierarchical clustering, flat clustering, and no clustering information.

4.1 Generative Performance

The following analysis compares the proposed TreeDiffusion model with TreeVAE [20], and a naive hybrid baseline, referred to as "TreeVAE + Diffusion". In this hybrid approach, inspired by DiffuseVAE [24], the diffusion model refines the output image generated or reconstructed by TreeVAE, but it is not conditioned on any latent information from the hierarchical structure. In contrast, TreeDiffusion introduces a key novelty by conditioning the diffusion model on the latent hierarchical path information extracted from TreeVAE. Moreover, TreeDiffusion initiates the denoising process from random noise rather than using the TreeVAE image outputs as the denoising starting point. This enables TreeDiffusion to leverage the structure of the latent tree for cluster-specific generation. Hence, both TreeVAE + Diffusion and TreeDiffusion use TreeVAE as the first-stage model, with the main differences lying in the conditioning mechanism and the starting point of the denoising process.

The evaluation considers both reconstruction and generative performance, measured using the Fréchet Inception Distance (FID) [11]. Reconstruction performance is assessed by computing the FID score between reconstructed images and their corresponding test set images. Generative performance is evaluated by calculating the FID score for 10,000 newly generated images. The results of this analysis are summarized in Table 1.

The naive approach (TreeVAE + Diffusion) and TreeDiffusion both achieve substantial improvements over the baseline TreeVAE, their first-stage model, reducing FID scores by approximately an order of magnitude across all datasets. The naive approach performs better on simpler grayscale datasets, primarily excelling at image reconstruction rather than generation. This highlights a tendency toward overfitting. Conversely, TreeDiffusion consistently outperforms on the more complex, real-world color datasets at generating new images. Most likely, the difference in performance stems from how the denoising process is initialized. The naive model begins denoising from TreeVAE reconstructions, thereby making it highly dependent on the reconstruction quality provided by TreeVAE. Given that TreeVAE struggles more with generating new images than with reconstruction, this limitation is propagated into the naive approach. TreeDiffusion circumvents this issue by initializing the denoising directly from noise, using only latent representations from TreeVAE. As a result, TreeDiffusion achieves a better balance between reconstruction and generation quality, leading to better FID scores on newly generated images. Figure 2 compares image reconstructions on CIFAR-10, demonstrating that both diffusion-based models significantly improve upon the image quality produced by TreeVAE.

4.2 Cluster-Specific Representations

Higher Quality Cluster-Specific Generations. In Fig. 3, we present randomly generated images for the CUBICC dataset for both TreeVAE and TreeDiffusion, where each column corresponds to an independently generated sample. For each generation, we first sample the root embedding; then, we sample the path in the tree and the refined representations along the selected path iteratively until a leaf is reached. The hierarchical representation is then used to condition the inference in TreeDiffusion. As can be seen, the TreeDiffusion generations show substantially higher generative quality. In the following, we examine the first generated sample from Fig. 3 in more detail. For this one sample, we present the generations of all leaves in Fig. 4 by propagating the corresponding root representation across all paths in the tree. Note that the selected sample shown in Fig. 3 ended up stemming from leaf 3 in Fig. 4. When comparing the generated images across the leaves for both models, it is evident that TreeDiffusion

Table 1. Test set generative performances of the compared models. FID scores for 10,000 samples (lower is better) computed across 10 random model initializations.

Dataset	Method	FID (rec) ↓	FID (gen) ↓
MNIST	TreeVAE	24.0 ± 0.9	21.8 ± 0.7
	TreeVAE + Diffusion	**1.4 ± 0.0**	**1.8 ± 0.1**
	TreeDiffusion	1.5 ± 0.0	**1.8 ± 0.1**
Fashion	TreeVAE	40.7 ± 2.1	41.9 ± 2.1
	TreeVAE + Diffusion	**4.8 ± 0.2**	**4.8 ± 0.2**
	TreeDiffusion	5.5 ± 0.6	5.4 ± 0.4
CIFAR-10	TreeVAE	175.8 ± 1.4	188.0 ± 2.0
	TreeVAE + Diffusion	**12.3 ± 0.1**	19.7 ± 0.2
	TreeDiffusion	12.5 ± 0.4	**17.8 ± 0.4**
CUBICC	TreeVAE	232.5 ± 7.1	255.3 ± 8.8
	TreeVAE + Diffusion	**12.7 ± 6.5**	96.0 ± 2.1
	TreeDiffusion	13.4 ± 0.9	**29.0 ± 5.4**
CelebA	TreeVAE	75.2 ± 15.0	77.9 ± 5.6
	TreeVAE + Diffusion	15.4 ± 3.2	30.1 ± 7.5
	TreeDiffusion	**14.1 ± 6.0**	**18.4 ± 7.2**

Fig. 2. Ten different CIFAR-10 reconstructions generated by the TreeVAE model, each obtained by sampling a single path in the tree. Corresponding reconstructions from TreeVAE + Diffusion, which begins denoising with the TreeVAE reconstructions, are shown alongside those from TreeDiffusion, which conditions on the same selected path and embeddings but starts denoising from noise.

not only produces sharper images for all clusters but also generates a greater diversity of images. Note that both models utilize the same latent information for image generation. While TreeVAE and TreeDiffusion maintain similar overall color distribution and structural characteristics, TreeDiffusion significantly enhances cluster specificity, resulting in images with greater clarity and distinctiveness for each cluster. Further examples of leaf-specific image generations are available in the supplementary material.

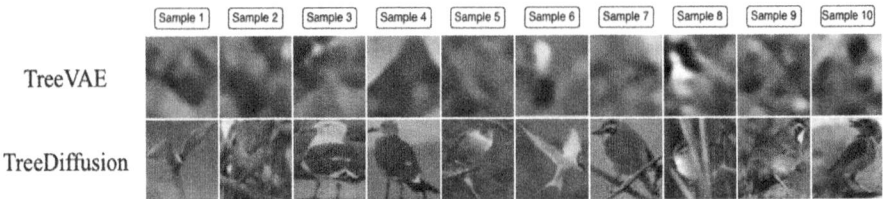

Fig. 3. Ten different samples generated by the TreeVAE model, each generated by sampling one path in the tree, and corresponding samples from the TreeDiffusion model, conditioned on the same selected path and embeddings from TreeVAE.

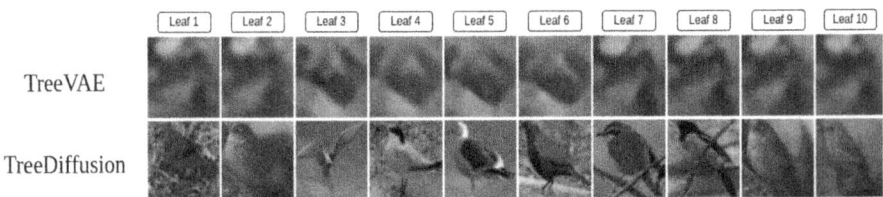

Fig. 4. Image generations from every leaf of the TreeVAE and TreeDiffusion model, both trained on the CUBICC dataset. Each row shows the generated images from all leaves of the respective model, starting with the same root sample.

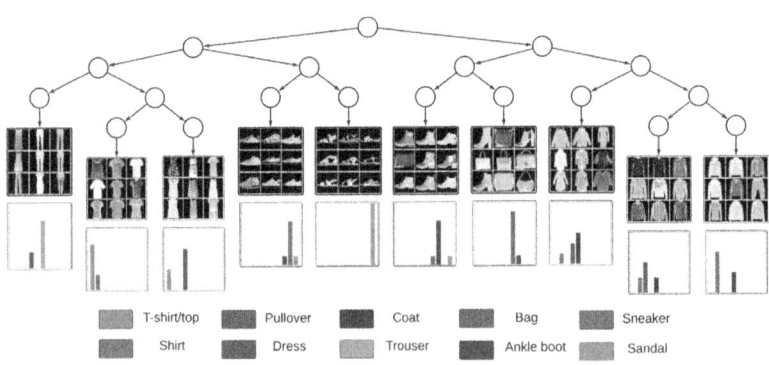

Fig. 5. TreeDiffusion model trained on FashionMNIST. For each cluster, random newly generated images are displayed. Below each set of images, a normalized histogram (ranging from 0 to 1) shows the distribution of predicted classes from an independent, pre-trained classifier on FashionMNIST for all newly generated images in each leaf with a significant probability of reaching that leaf.

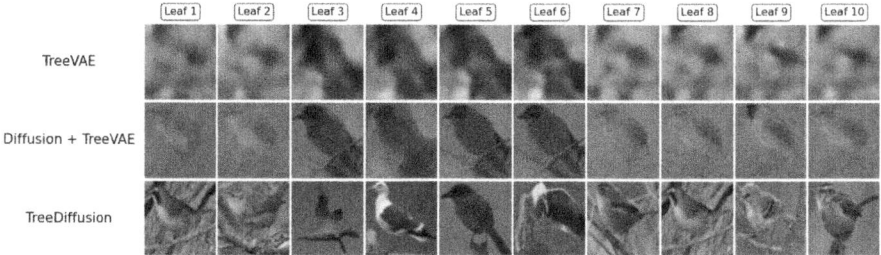

Fig. 6. Image generations from each leaf of (top) TreeVAE, (middle) TreeVAE + Diffusion which starts denoising with the TreeVAE images, and (bottom) TreeDiffusion model conditioned on the hierarchical path embeddings, all trained on CUBICC. Each row displays the generated images from all leaves of the specified model, starting with the same sample from the root. The corresponding leaf probabilities are shown at the top of the image and are, by design, the same for all models.

Cluster Information is Retained Across Generations. To quantitively assess whether the newly generated images retain their cluster information, we train a classifier on the original labeled training data and then use it to classify generated images of TreeDiffusion. Specifically, we classify the generations for each cluster separately. The idea is that "pure" leaves should create samples that are classified into one or very few classes. For this classification task, we use a ResNet-50 model [10] trained on each dataset. In Fig. 5, we present randomly generated images from a TreeDiffusion model trained on FashionMNIST, together with normalized histograms depicting the distribution of the predicted classes for each leaf. For instance, clusters representing trousers and bags appear to accurately and distinctly capture their respective classes, as all their generated images are classified into one group only. Conversely, certain clusters are characterized by a mixture of classes, indicating that they are grouped together. Overall, we observe that the leaf-specific generations retain the hierarchical clustering structure found by TreeVAE, thereby enhancing the interpretability in diffusion models.

On the Benefits of Hierarchical Conditioning. We hereby assess whether the conditioning on hierarchical representations improves cluster-specific generative quality. To this end, we compare the generations of TreeDiffusion, which is conditioned on the hierarchical representation, to the baseline TreeVAE + Diffusion from earlier, which is not conditioned on the latent cluster information. For this experiment, we use the previously introduced independent classifier to create the normalized histograms for each leaf to evaluate how cluster-specific the newly generated images are. As mentioned above, ideally, the majority of generated images from one leaf should be classified into one or very few classes from the original dataset. To quantify this, we compute the average entropy for all cluster-specific histograms. Lower entropy indicates less variation in the histograms and, thus, more cluster-specific generations. Table 2 presents the results for all labeled datasets.

Table 2. Cluster-specificity of TreeDiffusion generations comparing cluster-unconditional and cluster-conditional reverse models, measured by mean entropy. Lower entropy indicates more cluster-specific generations. The best result for each dataset is marked in **bold**.

Dataset	Method	Cluster Conditioning	Mean Entropy
MNIST	Diffusion + TreeVAE	✗	1.24
	TreeDiffusion	✓	**0.33**
Fashion	Diffusion + TreeVAE	✗	0.66
	TreeDiffusion	✓	**0.65**
CIFAR10	Diffusion + TreeVAE	✗	1.12
	TreeDiffusion	✓	**0.93**
CUBICC	Diffusion + TreeVAE	✗	**0.07**
	TreeDiffusion	✓	0.20

For most datasets, the conditional model exhibits lower mean entropy, indicating that cluster conditioning indeed helps guide the model to generate more distinct and representative images for each leaf. However, for the CUBICC dataset, we observe that the mean entropy is lower for the cluster-unconditional model. This is because the classifier tends to predict all images into a single class, a result of model degeneration, where it primarily generates images for only a few classes. Figure 6 visually presents the leaf generations for one sample of these models alongside the underlying TreeVAE generations. It can be observed that both the cluster-unconditional and conditional models exhibit a significant improvement in image quality. However, the images in the cluster-conditional model are more diverse, demonstrating greater adaptability for each cluster. Notably, across all models, the leaf-specific images share common properties, such as background color and overall shape, sampled at the root while varying in cluster-specific features from leaf to leaf within each model.

4.3 Ablation Study on Conditioning Information

Finally, we conduct an ablation study to evaluate the impact of different conditioning signals on the generative performance. Specifically, we compare three types of conditioning: (i) hierarchical clustering signals derived from the latent embeddings of the selected cluster path $z_{\mathcal{P}_l}$, (ii) flat clustering signals, including leaf assignment l, leaf embedding z_l, or both, and (iii) an unconditioned setting where the diffusion model does not utilize any latent cluster representations from TreeVAE. Additionally, we examine the effect of using the TreeVAE leaf reconstruction $\hat{x}_0^{(l)}$ as the starting point for the denoising process in the second-stage diffusion model. The results, outlined in Table 3, show the FID score calculated from 10,000 samples generated using 100 DDIM steps, averaged over 10 seeds.

Note that the first row in the table represents the TreeVAE + Diffusion model from the previous experiments, whereas the last row corresponds to the proposed TreeDiffusion method.

Table 3. Effect of conditioning signals on generative performance for CIFAR-10. FID scores for 10,000 samples (lower is better) computed across 10 random model initializations.

Conditioning Type	$\hat{x}_0^{(l)}$	l	z_l	$z_{\mathcal{P}_l}$	FID ↓
No Cluster Conditioning	✓				19.7 ± 0.2
Flat Clustering-Based Conditioning	✓	✓			19.1 ± 0.3
	✓		✓		18.9 ± 0.3
	✓	✓	✓		19.2 ± 0.2
		✓	✓		19.1 ± 0.5
Hierarchical Clustering-Based Conditioning	✓			✓	18.2 ± 0.3
				✓	**17.8 ± 0.4**

The findings suggest that incorporating latent leaf information—whether through leaf assignment, leaf embedding, or both—significantly improves generative performance compared to relying solely on leaf reconstructions. This highlights the added benefit of conditioning on flat clustering information. Furthermore, conditioning on the full path $z_{\mathcal{P}_l}$, which integrates all embeddings and intermediate node assignments from the root to the leaf, leads to an even greater performance boost. This underscores the effectiveness of hierarchical clustering information beyond flat clustering. As a result, harnessing $z_{\mathcal{P}_l}$ from the hierarchical structure not only produces more structured generations, as illustrated in Fig. 4, but also enhances the generative performance of generative clustering models. Notably, when conditioning on the full path, the model performs better without relying on TreeVAE reconstructions. Instead, the conditional diffusion model generates new images from scratch, guided solely by the latent information.

5 Conclusion

In this work, we present TreeDiffusion, a novel approach to integrate hierarchical clustering into diffusion models. By enhancing TreeVAE with a Denoising Diffusion Implicit Model conditioned on latent hierarchical representations, we propose a model capable of generating distinct, high-quality images that faithfully represent their respective data clusters. This approach not only improves the visual fidelity of the generated images but also facilitates cluster visualization. TreeDiffusion offers a robust framework that bridges the gap between clustering and generative performance, thereby expanding the potential applications of generative models in areas requiring detailed and more interpretable visual data interpretation.

Acknowledgments and Disclosure of Funding. Jorge da Silva Gonçalves is supported by the grant #2021-911 of the Strategic Focal Area "Personalized Health and Related Technologies (PHRT)" of the ETH Domain (Swiss Federal Institutes of Technology). Laura Manduchi is supported by the SDSC PhD Fellowship #1-001568-037. Moritz Vandenhirtz is supported by the Swiss State Secretariat for Education, Research and Innovation (SERI) under contract number MB22.00047.

Disclosure of Interests. The authors have no competing interests to declare that are relevant to the content of this article.

References

1. Adaloglou, N., Kaiser, T., Michels, F., Kollmann, M.: Rethinking cluster-conditioned diffusion models. arXiv preprint arXiv:2403.00570 (2024)
2. Adaloglou, N., Michels, F., Kalisch, H., Kollmann, M.: Exploring the limits of deep image clustering using pretrained models. In: 34th British Machine Vision Conference 2023, BMVC 2023, Aberdeen, UK, 20-24 November 2023, pp. 297–299. BMVA Press (2023)
3. Blattmann, A., Rombach, R., Oktay, K., Müller, J., Ommer, B.: Retrieval-augmented diffusion models. Adv. Neural. Inf. Process. Syst. **35**, 15309–15324 (2022)
4. Bredell, G., Flouris, K., Chaitanya, K., Erdil, E., Konukoglu, E.: Explicitly minimizing the blur error of variational autoencoders. In: The Eleventh International Conference on Learning Representations (2023)
5. Chen, C., Li, G., Xu, R., Chen, T., Wang, M., Lin, L.: ClusterNet: deep hierarchical cluster network with rigorously rotation-invariant representation for point cloud analysis. In: Proceedings of the IEEE/CVF Conference on Computer Vision and Pattern Recognition, pp. 4994–5002 (2019)
6. Dhariwal, P., Nichol, A.: Diffusion models beat GANs on image synthesis. In: Advances in Neural Information Processing Systems, vol. 34, pp. 8780–8794. Curran Associates, Inc. (2021)
7. Ezugwu, A.E., Ikotun, A.M., Oyelade, O.O., Abualigah, L., Agushaka, J.O., Eke, C.I., Akinyelu, A.A., Ezugwu, A.E., et al.: A comprehensive survey of clustering algorithms: state-of-the-art machine learning applications, taxonomy, challenges, and future research prospects. Eng. Appl. Artif. Intell. **110**, 104743 (2022)
8. Goodfellow, I., et al.: Generative adversarial nets. In: Advances in Neural Information Processing Systems, vol. 27. Curran Associates, Inc. (2014)
9. Goyal, P., Hu, Z., Liang, X., Wang, C., Xing, E.P.: Nonparametric variational auto-encoders for hierarchical representation learning. In: Proceedings of the IEEE International Conference on Computer Vision, pp. 5094–5102 (2017)
10. He, K., Zhang, X., Ren, S., Sun, J.: Deep residual learning for image recognition. In: 2016 IEEE Conference on Computer Vision and Pattern Recognition (CVPR), pp. 770–778 (2016). iSSN: 1063-6919

11. Heusel, M., Ramsauer, H., Unterthiner, T., Nessler, B., Hochreiter, S.: GANs trained by a two time-scale update rule converge to a local nash equilibrium. In: Advances in Neural Information Processing Systems, vol. 30. Curran Associates, Inc. (2017)
12. Ho, J., Jain, A., Abbeel, P.: Denoising diffusion probabilistic models. In: Advances in Neural Information Processing Systems, vol. 33, pp. 6840–6851. Curran Associates, Inc. (2020)
13. Hu, V.T., Zhang, D.W., Asano, Y.M., Burghouts, G.J., Snoek, C.G.: Self-guided diffusion models. In: Proceedings of the IEEE/CVF Conference on Computer Vision and Pattern Recognition, pp. 18413–18422 (2023)
14. Jiang, Z., Zheng, Y., Tan, H., Tang, B., Zhou, H.: Variational deep embedding: an unsupervised and generative approach to clustering. In: Proceedings of the Twenty-Sixth International Joint Conference on Artificial Intelligence, pp. 1965–1972. Melbourne, Australia (2017)
15. Kingma, D.P., Welling, M.: Auto-encoding variational bayes. In: Bengio, Y., LeCun, Y. (eds.) 2nd International Conference on Learning Representations, ICLR 2014, Banff, AB, Canada, 14-16 April 2014, Conference Track Proceedings (2014)
16. Krizhevsky, A.: Learning multiple layers of features from tiny images (2009)
17. Lecun, Y., Bottou, L., Bengio, Y., Haffner, P.: Gradient-based learning applied to document recognition. Proc. IEEE **86**(11), 2278–2324 (1998)
18. Li, T., Katabi, D., He, K.: Self-conditioned image generation via generating representations. arXiv preprint arXiv:2312.03701 (2023)
19. Liu, Z., Luo, P., Wang, X., Tang, X.: Deep learning face attributes in the wild. In: Proceedings of International Conference on Computer Vision (ICCV) (2015)
20. Manduchi, L., Vandenhirtz, M., Ryser, A., Vogt, J.: Tree variational autoencoders. In: Advances in Neural Information Processing Systems, vol. 36 (2023)
21. Mautz, D., Plant, C., Böhm, C.: DeepECT: the deep embedded cluster tree. Data Sci. Eng. **5**(4), 419–432 (2020). https://doi.org/10.1007/s41019-020-00134-0
22. Nichol, A.Q., Dhariwal, P.: Improved denoising diffusion probabilistic models. In: Proceedings of the 38th International Conference on Machine Learning, pp. 8162–8171. PMLR (2021). iSSN: 2640-3498
23. Palumbo, E., Manduchi, L., Laguna, S., Chopard, D., Vogt, J.E.: Deep generative clustering with multimodal diffusion variational autoencoders. In: The Twelfth International Conference on Learning Representations (2023)
24. Pandey, K., Mukherjee, A., Rai, P., Kumar, A.: DiffuseVAE: Efficient. Controllable and High-Fidelity Generation from Low-Dimensional Latents, Transactions on Machine Learning Research (2022)
25. Preechakul, K., Chatthee, N., Wizadwongsa, S., Suwajanakorn, S.: Diffusion autoencoders: toward a meaningful and decodable representation. In: Proceedings of the IEEE/CVF Conference on Computer Vision and Pattern Recognition, pp. 10619–10629 (2022)
26. Rombach, R., Blattmann, A., Lorenz, D., Esser, P., Ommer, B.: High-resolution image synthesis with latent diffusion models. In: Proceedings of the IEEE/CVF Conference on Computer Vision and Pattern Recognition, pp. 10684–10695 (2022)
27. Ronneberger, O., Fischer, P., Brox, T.: U-net: convolutional networks for biomedical image segmentation. In: Navab, N., Hornegger, J., Wells, W.M., Frangi, A.F. (eds.) MICCAI 2015. LNCS, vol. 9351, pp. 234–241. Springer, Cham (2015). https://doi.org/10.1007/978-3-319-24574-4_28
28. Salimans, T., Ho, J.: Progressive distillation for fast sampling of diffusion models. In: The Tenth International Conference on Learning Representations, ICLR 2022, Virtual Event, 25-29 April 2022. OpenReview.net (2022)

29. Sheynin, S., et al.: KNN-Diffusion: image generation via large-scale retrieval. In: The Eleventh International Conference on Learning Representations, ICLR 2023, Kigali, Rwanda, 1-5 May 2023. OpenReview.net (2023)
30. Shi, Y., N, S., Paige, B., Torr, P.: Variational mixture-of-experts autoencoders for multi-modal deep generative models. In: Advances in Neural Information Processing Systems, vol. 32. Curran Associates, Inc. (2019)
31. Sohl-Dickstein, J., Weiss, E., Maheswaranathan, N., Ganguli, S.: Deep unsupervised learning using nonequilibrium thermodynamics. In: International Conference on Machine Learning, pp. 2256–2265. PMLR (2015)
32. Song, J., Meng, C., Ermon, S.: Denoising diffusion implicit models. In: International Conference on Learning Representations (2020)
33. Vahdat, A., Kreis, K., Kautz, J.: Score-based generative modeling in latent space. In: Advances in Neural Information Processing Systems, vol. 34, pp. 11287–11302. Curran Associates, Inc. (2021)
34. Vandenhirtz, M., Barkmann, F., Manduchi, L., Vogt, J.E., Boeva, V.: SCTREE: discovering cellular hierarchies in the presence of batch effects in SCRNA-SEQ data. arXiv preprint arXiv:2406.19300 (2024)
35. Wah, C., Branson, S., Welinder, P., Perona, P., Belongie, S.: The Caltech-UCSD Birds-200-2011 Dataset (2011)
36. Wang, P., Zhang, H., Zhang, Z., Chen, S., Ma, Y., Qu, Q.: Diffusion models learn low-dimensional distributions via subspace clustering. arXiv preprint arXiv:2409.02426 (2024)
37. Wang, Y., et al.: InfoDiffusion: representation Learning Using Information Maximizing Diffusion Models. In: Proceedings of the 40th International Conference on Machine Learning, pp. 36336–36354. PMLR (2023). iSSN: 2640-3498
38. Ward, J.H., Jr.: Hierarchical grouping to optimize an objective function. J. Am. Stat. Assoc. **58**(301), 236–244 (1963)
39. Wen, J., et al.: Diffusion-based missing-view generation with the application on incomplete multi-view clustering. In: Forty-first International Conference on Machine Learning, ICML 2024, Vienna, Austria, 21-27 July 2024. OpenReview.net (2024)
40. Wen, J., Zhang, Z., Zhang, Z., Fei, L., Wang, M.: Generalized incomplete multiview clustering with flexible locality structure diffusion. IEEE Trans. Cybern. **51**(1), 101–114 (2020)
41. Xiao, H., Rasul, K., Vollgraf, R.: Fashion-MNIST: a novel image dataset for benchmarking machine learning algorithms. arXiv:1708.07747 (2017)
42. Znalezniak, M., Rola, P., Kaszuba, P., Tabor, J., Śmieja, M.: Contrastive hierarchical clustering. In: Koutra, D., Plant, C., Gomez Rodriguez, M., Baralis, E., Bonchi, F. (eds.) Joint European Conference on Machine Learning and Knowledge Discovery in Databases. pp. 627–643. Springer, Cham (2023). https://doi.org/10.1007/978-3-031-43412-9_37

Late Fusion Multiple Kernel Clustering Refined via Optimal Linear Graph Filtering

Henghui Jiang[1], Yiqing Guo[1], Yan Chen[2], and Liang Du[1(✉)]

[1] Shanxi University, Taiyuan 030006, China
{jianghenghui,guoyiqing,duliang}@sxu.edu.cn
[2] Taiyuan University of Technology, Taiyuan 030600, China
yanchen01@tyut.edu.cn

Abstract. Multiple Kernel Clustering (MKC) aims to improve clustering performance by integrating complementary information from candidate kernels. Among existing MKC methods, late fusion MKC (LFMKC) offers superior scalability by aggregating clustering partitions rather than full kernel matrices. However, its reliance on fixed base partitions often leads to suboptimal representations and degraded clustering performance. To address this, we propose Late Fusion MKC Refined via Optimal Linear Graph Filtering (LFMKC-OLF), which enhances partition quality while preserving linear computational complexity. Specifically, bipartite graphs are constructed for each base partition, upon which high-order low-pass filters based on heat kernel diffusion and complementary high-pass filters are designed to capture both global consistency and fine-grained structural details. A consensus filtering mechanism is introduced by optimally combining view-specific filters to refine multi-scale representations. Furthermore, a joint clustering objective integrates both smoothed and detail-enhanced partitions to effectively mitigate over-smoothing. Extensive experiments on eight benchmark datasets demonstrate that LFMKC-OLF consistently outperforms 12 state-of-the-art LFMKC methods, while maintaining high computational efficiency for large-scale clustering tasks. Our code is publicly available at: https://github.com/sxuHui/LFMKC-OLF.

Keywords: Multiple Kernel Clustering · Graph filter · Over-smoothing

1 Introduction

Multiple Kernel Clustering (MKC) is a powerful machine learning technique for handling complex, non-linearly separable data by mapping it into higher-dimensional Hilbert spaces [19,20,32]. In the era of big data, where information often collects from multiple views or sources, MKC integrates multi-source data within the kernel space to assign samples to distinct clusters. By learning an optimal combination from a predefined set of kernels, MKC effectively captures complementary information across diverse feature representations, thereby improving clustering robustness and adaptability in multi-view scenarios.

According to the stage of information fusion, existing MKC methods can be broadly divided into two categories: early kernel fusion and late partition fusion methods [27]. The first convert kernel information into a set of predefined kernel matrices, each of size $n \times n$, with the primary goal of optimally combining these matrices to learn the consensus clustering information. The other category focus on enhancing clustering performance and mitigating the impact of noise by applying fusion at the partition level [21]. By fusing the information of individual partitions to obtain the underlying shared representation, late fusion-based MKC (LFMKC) significantly reducing the computational burden, demonstrating promising performance across various applications [21].

Despite recent progress, LFMKC still faces critical limitations. First, its reliance on fixed base partitions imposes a performance bottleneck, as these initial representations often fail to capture the underlying data structure adequately. Moreover, prevailing methods predominantly focus on optimizing kernel weights to exploit inter-view consistency and complementarity, yet they largely neglect the high-order correlations across views, thus restricting the integration of richer multi-kernel information. Additionally, while low-pass graph filters have been employed to enhance intra-cluster coherence by suppressing noise, excessive filtering inevitably leads to over-smoothing, where crucial high-frequency details are erased and cluster boundaries become indistinct, ultimately undermining clustering performance.

To tackle these challenges while maintaining linear computational complexity, we propose a novel method termed Late Fusion Multiple Kernel Clustering Refined via Optimal Linear Graph Filtering (LFMKC-OLF). The approach begins by constructing bipartite graphs for each kernel partition, from which we design view-independent low-pass and high-pass graph filters to capture complementary low- and high-frequency signals respectively. Specifically, these low-pass filters derived from diffusion processes capture high-order relationships and smooth partitions, revealing the underlying cluster structures; while high-pass filters preserve critical high-frequency signals encoding fine-grained cluster boundaries. To integrate multi-view information effectively, we introduce a consensus filter learning strategy, where the final low-pass and high-pass filters are obtained as optimal linear combinations of the individual per-view filters. To efficiently handle large-scale datasets, we exploit the low-rank structure inherent in bipartite graph-induced filters, enabling a linear-time algorithm for filtering. Crucially, we propose a unified optimization framework that considers the joint clustering loss under smoothed partitions and detail-enhanced partitions. By jointly modeling low-pass and high-pass responses, our framework captures both smooth cluster structures and fine-grained boundary details, effectively mitigating the cratical information loss caused by over-smoothing. To solve the resulting problem, we develop an iterative algorithm that updates all variables with linear complexity. Our contributions are summarized as follows:

- We propose a novel LFMKC method that integrates bipartite graph-induced high-order filters based on heat kernel diffusion. By optimizing the linear combination of these filters, our approach promotes clustering friendly smooth representation and effectively refines the base partitions.
- We propose a novel framework that jointly clustering both on smoothed and detail-enhanced partitions by leveraging the multi-scale representation of graph filtering. By integrating critical detail structural information into the smoothed embedding, it effectively mitigates over-smoothing and achieves optimal filtering refinement.
- Extensive evaluations on eight diverse datasets reveal that LFMKC-OLF not only surpasses 12 cutting-edge LFMKC methods in clustering performance but also features a linear-time iterative optimization algorithm that enables efficient training and inference on large-scale data, showcasing its practicality for applications.

2 Related Work

2.1 Late Fusion Multiple Kernel Clustering

LFMKC has garnered significant attention for its efficiency and promising performance. The LFMKC framework typically proceeds in two stages: generating base partitions from each kernel—typically derived from the top eigenvectors—and subsequently fusing these partitions into a consensus result. Recent efforts have explored diverse strategies to enhance the fusion stage. For example, Wang et al. [21] propose a strategy that maximizes the alignment between weighted base partitions to learn a consensus partition. Liu et al. [16] propose to decompose the consensus partition into cluster labels and centroids, without requiring further post-processing. Li et al. [11] integrate the min-max optimization framework from [15] into LFMKC to refine the fusion process. Yang et al. [27] reconstruct kernel partitions using a self-expression strategy guided by refined similarity graphs to capture more complex relationships among partitions. Wu et al. [23] employ the Grassmann manifold for partitions fusion, maintaining topological structure in high-dimensional space. Zhang et al. [31] incorporate sample weights and introduce a prior-informed regularization term to enhance fusion stability. However, these methods heavily rely on the quality of the original base partitions and fail to fully exploit high-order information, which limits their effectiveness in complex or noisy scenarios.

2.2 Graph Filters

Graph filters play a crucial role in graph signal processing by enabling the manipulation of signals defined on graph structures, leveraging adjacency relationships between nodes. These filters are employed for tasks such as signal smoothing, noise reduction, and feature extraction [9]. Recent studies have explored integrating low-pass graph filters to enhance data representations in multi-view clustering (MVC). Lin and Kang [14], Chen et al. [2] and Kang et al. [10] adopt a two-stage strategy: constructing low-pass filters to smooth the original features before applying MVC. Alternatively, Zhou et al. [33], and Zhou and Du [34] propose learning similarity graphs in the node domain, adjusting graph filters dynamically during clustering to improve adaptability. Yang et al. [26] examine the convex combination of multiple graph filters, combining their strengths to improve filtering effectiveness. Guo et al. [7] further build on this by using bipartite graphs to construct filters and achieve linear-time filtering via the Woodbury formula. Despite progress in the utilization of graph filtering, existing methods predominantly focus on low-frequency components to capture smooth representations, often indiscriminately discarding high-frequency signals as noise. This can inevitably result in over-smoothing and impair the ability to preserve discriminative node features. Although some methods [10,14,33,34] attempt mitigation by heuristically constraining the filter order within an empirical range, such strategies still restrict the exploitation of high-order information and hinder the pursuit of optimal filtering.

3 Proposed Method

In this section, we present the proposed method, starting with the base partitions $\{\mathbf{H}_v\}_{v=1}^V \in \mathbb{R}^{n \times d}$, where V denotes the number of views, n the number of samples, and d the embedding dimension. Each $\mathbf{H}_v$ consists of orthogonal vectors obtained via eigenvalue decomposition of the corresponding kernel matrix.

3.1 View-Independent Bipartite Graph Construction

To reduce computational overhead, we introduce bipartite graphs that capture affinities between samples and a reduced set of representative anchors. Prior work has shown that diversifying anchor graphs can significantly enhance clustering performance [28]. Motivated by this, we adopt a view-independent anchor selection strategy. Specifically, we first perform Kmeans clustering independently on each partition $\mathbf{H}_v$ to obtain m_v centroids, forming the anchor matrix $\mathbf{O}_v \in \mathbb{R}^{m_v \times d}$. The bipartite graph $\mathbf{Z}_v \in \mathbb{R}^{n \times m_v}$ is then learned by solving the following optimization problem:

$$\min_{\mathbf{z}_i^v \mathbf{1}=1, \mathbf{z}_i^v \geq 0} \sum_{j=1}^{m_v} \text{dist}(\mathbf{h}_i^v, \mathbf{o}_j^v) z_{ij}^v + \tau \sum_{j=1}^{m_v} (z_{ij}^v)^2, \qquad (1)$$

where $\mathbf{z}_i^v$ is the i-th row of $\mathbf{Z}_v$, $\text{dist}(\mathbf{h}_i^v, \mathbf{o}_j^v) = \|\mathbf{h}_i^v - \mathbf{o}_j^v\|_2^2$ denotes the squared euclidean distance between the i-th sample and j-th anchor, and τ is a regularization hyperparameter controlling the smoothness of the assignment. To further enhance scalability, we impose sparsity on $\mathbf{Z}_v$ by restricting each sample to connect only with its k nearest anchors, following the strategy in [18], with k fixed to 5 throughout our experiments. For each sample i, assume that the distances $\text{dist}(\mathbf{h}_i^v, \mathbf{o}_1^v), \text{dist}(\mathbf{h}_i^v, \mathbf{o}_2^v), \ldots, \text{dist}(\mathbf{h}_i^v, \mathbf{o}_{m_v}^v)$ are sorted in ascending order. Problem (1) admits a closed-form solution given by:

$$z_{ij}^v = \begin{cases} \dfrac{\text{dist}(\mathbf{h}_i^v, \mathbf{o}_{k+1}^v) - \text{dist}(\mathbf{h}_i^v, \mathbf{o}_j^v)}{k\,\text{dist}(\mathbf{h}_i^v, \mathbf{o}_{k+1}^v) - \sum_{k'=1}^{k}\text{dist}(\mathbf{h}_i^v, \mathbf{o}_{k'}^v)}, & \text{if } j \leq k, \\ 0, & \text{if } j > k. \end{cases}$$

Subsequently, the similarity matrix $\mathbf{S}_v \in \mathbb{R}^{n \times n}$ is constructed from the bipartite graph $\mathbf{Z}_v$ to capture indirect associations between samples. Specifically, we normalize $\mathbf{Z}_v$ by computing:

$$\mathbf{P}_v = \mathbf{Z}_v \mathbf{\Delta}_v^{-\frac{1}{2}}, \tag{2}$$

where $\mathbf{\Delta}_v$ is a diagonal matrix with entries $\Delta_{jj}^v = \sum_{i=1}^{n} \mathbf{Z}_{ij}^v$. The final similarity matrix is then obtained as:

$$\mathbf{S}_v = \mathbf{P}_v \mathbf{P}_v^\top, \tag{3}$$

By construction, $\mathbf{S}_v$ is a doubly stochastic matrix, i.e., each row and column sums to one, enabling favorable properties for subsequent graph filtering and clustering steps.

3.2 Smoothed Partition Fusion with Low-Pass Filtering

Although similarity graphs $\{\mathbf{S}_v\}_{v=1}^{V}$ effectively capture local structure, they overlook higher-order neighborhood relationships, missing global dependencies between distant samples. To address this, we adopt heat kernel diffusion [13] to integrate similarity graphs across all orders. Formally, the diffusion process is expressed as:

$$\mathbf{G}_v = e^{-\eta} \sum_{t=0}^{\infty} \frac{\eta^t}{t!} (\mathbf{S}_v)^t = \exp(-\eta \mathbf{L}_v), \tag{4}$$

where $\eta \geq 0$ controls the decay rate [3] and $\mathbf{L}_v = \mathbf{I} - \mathbf{S}_v$ denotes the normalized Laplacian. The resulting $\mathbf{G}_v$ acts as a low-pass filter that suppresses high-frequency components, effectively reducing noise and enhancing global structural patterns.

To fully explore the information across views and enhance global consistency, we learn a consensus graph filter via linearly combining the view-specific filters:

$$\hat{\mathbf{G}} = \sum_{v=1}^{V} \beta_v \exp(-\eta \mathbf{L}_v), \tag{5}$$

where β are weights determined based on the downstream clustering task. This consensus mechanism consolidates high-order topological structures across views, enabling effective noise suppression and yielding more coherent cluster results.

In the LFMKC task, the base partition $\mathbf{H}_p$ can be regarded as a graph signal. If $\mathbf{H}_p$ exhibits a clear clustering structure, it should adhere to the clustering and manifold assumptions, which state that data within the same class should be close to each other. According to references [4,24], smooth graph signals often follow the clustering and manifold assumptions. Building upon this observation, we apply the above-mentioned consensus low-pass graph filter on the signals $\mathbf{H}_p$ to obtain a more cluster-friendly embedding $\mathcal{F}_L(\mathbf{H}_p)$ as follows:

$$\mathcal{F}_L(\mathbf{H}_p) = \hat{\mathbf{G}}\mathbf{H}_p = \left(\sum_{v=1}^{V} \beta_v \exp(-\eta \mathbf{L}_v)\right) \mathbf{H}_p. \tag{6}$$

The filtered embeddings $\{\mathcal{F}_L(\mathbf{H}_p)\}_{p=1}^{V}$ are expected to exhibit enhanced cluster smoothness. To fuse these enhanced representations into the final clustering result, we learn a discrete consensus indicator matrix $\mathbf{Y} \in \{0,1\}^{n \times c}$ and an orthogonal centroid matrix $\mathbf{C}_p \in \mathbb{R}^{d \times c}$ with c disjoint clusters for each partition, by solving the following prototype-based optimization objective function:

$$\min \sum_{p=1}^{V} \alpha_p \left\| \left(\sum_{v=1}^{V} \beta_v \exp(-\eta \mathbf{L}_v)\right) \mathbf{H}_p - \mathbf{Y}\mathbf{C}_p^\top \right\|_F^2, \tag{7}$$

$$\text{s.t. } \mathbf{C}_p^\top \mathbf{C}_p = \mathbf{I}, \mathbf{Y} \in \text{Ind}, \sum_{p=1}^{V} \frac{1}{\alpha_p} = 1, \boldsymbol{\beta}^\top \mathbf{1} = 1, \alpha_p \geq 0, \beta_v \geq 0, \forall p, v,$$

where α_p quantifies the contribution of each partition in guiding the consensus. The orthogonality constraint $\mathbf{C}_p^\top \mathbf{C}_p = \mathbf{I}$ encourages well-separated clusters and facilitates optimization.

3.3 Joint Clustering via Optimal Filtering with Dual-Frequency

While low-pass graph filters are commonly applied to enhance intra-cluster coherence by smoothing node features, they often treat all high-frequency components as noise and arbitrarily remove them, which may obscure critical structural variations. Prior studies [1,12] reveal that high-frequency graph components encode valuable structural discontinuities, which are essential for preserving local discriminability. Thus, over-reliance on low-pass filters may lead to over-smoothing, blurring boundaries and hindering model generalization [25]. Motivated by this, we extend the objective in Eq. (7) by explicitly incorporating high-frequency information to restore fine-grained local structure. To this end, we similarly design a consensus high-pass graph filter by linearly combining the Laplacian matrices from all views and apply it to the signal $\mathbf{H}_p$ as follows [22]:

$$\mathcal{F}_H(\mathbf{H}_p) = \left(\sum_{v=1}^{V} \gamma_v \mathbf{L}_v\right) \mathbf{H}_p, \tag{8}$$

where γ_v denotes the combination coefficients about each high-pass filter $\mathbf{L}_v$.

Rather than discarding high-frequency signals as noise, our model utilizes them to compensate for the information loss induced by over-smoothing. The joint clustering objective integrates both filtered representations:

$$\min \sum_{p=1}^{V} \alpha_p (\lambda \|(\sum_{v=1}^{V} \beta_v \mathbf{G}_v)\mathbf{H}_p - \mathbf{Y}\mathbf{C}_p^\top\|_F^2 + (1-\lambda)\|(\sum_{v=1}^{V} \gamma_v \mathbf{L}_v)\mathbf{H}_p - \mathbf{Y}\mathbf{C}_p^\top\|_F^2),$$

$$\text{s.t.} \mathbf{C}_p^\top \mathbf{C}_p = \mathbf{I},\ \mathbf{Y} \in \text{Ind},\ \sum_{p=1}^{V} \frac{1}{\alpha_p} = 1,\ \boldsymbol{\beta}^\top \mathbf{1} = 1,\ \boldsymbol{\gamma}^\top \mathbf{1} = 1, \quad (9)$$

$$\alpha_p \geq 0,\ \beta_v \geq 0,\ \gamma_v \geq 0,\ \forall p, v,$$

where $\lambda \in [0,1]$ controls the trade-off between global smoothness and local discriminability. By jointly optimizing low- and high-frequency responses, $\mathcal{F}_L(\mathbf{H}_p)$ and $\mathcal{F}_H(\mathbf{H}_p)$, the model effectively captures multi-scale structural cues. This dual-frequency optimal filtering design enhances robustness to noise and oversmoothing, enabling the consensus indicator matrix $\mathbf{Y}$ to encode a more expressive and faithful clustering structure across views.

3.4 Optimization

To solve the optimization problem in Eq. (9), we propose a five-step alternating optimization algorithm.

Update $\{\mathbf{C}_p\}_{p=1}^V$ with fixed $\mathbf{Y}$, $\boldsymbol{\alpha}$, $\boldsymbol{\beta}$, and $\boldsymbol{\gamma}$. Optimizing each $\mathbf{C}_p$ is equivalent to solving the following equation:

$$\max_{\mathbf{C}_p} \text{tr}(\mathbf{C}_p^\top \mathbf{A}_p) \quad \text{s.t.}\ \mathbf{C}_p^\top \mathbf{C}_p = \mathbf{I}, \quad (10)$$

where $\mathbf{A}_p = \mathbf{H}_p^\top \left(\lambda \sum_{v=1}^V \beta_v \mathbf{G}_v + (1-\lambda) \sum_{v=1}^V \gamma_v \mathbf{L}_v\right) \mathbf{Y}$. The SVD of $\mathbf{A}_p$ is expressed as $\mathbf{A}_p = \mathbf{U}_p \mathbf{\Lambda}_p \mathbf{V}_p^\top$. It is obtained that $\mathbf{C}_p$ is updated by:

$$\mathbf{C}_p = \mathbf{U}_p \mathbf{V}_p^\top. \quad (11)$$

For the detailed proof, see [8].

Update $\mathbf{Y}$ with fixed $\{\mathbf{C}_p\}_{p=1}^V$, $\boldsymbol{\alpha}$, $\boldsymbol{\beta}$, and $\boldsymbol{\gamma}$. Optimizing $\mathbf{Y}$ is equivalent to solving the following equation:

$$\max_{\mathbf{Y}} \text{tr}(\mathbf{Y}^\top \mathbf{F}) \quad \text{s.t.}\ \mathbf{Y} \in \text{Ind}, \quad (12)$$

where $\mathbf{F} = \sum_{p=1}^V \alpha_p \left(\lambda \sum_{v=1}^V \beta_v \mathbf{G}_v + (1-\lambda) \sum_{v=1}^V \gamma_v \mathbf{L}_v\right) \mathbf{H}_p \mathbf{C}_p$. The optimal solution for Eq. (12) is given by:

$$y_{ij} = \begin{cases} 1, & \text{if } j = \arg\max_{j'} [\mathbf{F}]_{ij'}, \\ 0, & \text{otherwise.} \end{cases} \quad (13)$$

Update α with fixed Y, $\{\mathbf{C}_p\}_{p=1}^V$, β, and γ. Optimizing $\{\alpha_p\}_{p=1}^V$ is equivalent to solving the following equation:

$$\min_{\alpha_p} \sum_{p=1}^V \alpha_p \zeta_p, \quad \text{s.t.} \sum_{p=1}^V \frac{1}{\alpha_p} = 1, \ \alpha_p \geq 0, \ \forall p, \tag{14}$$

where $\zeta_p = \lambda \|(\sum_{v=1}^V \beta_v \mathbf{G}_v \mathbf{H}_p - \mathbf{Y}\mathbf{C}_p^\top\|_F^2 + (1-\lambda)\|\sum_{v=1}^V \gamma_v \mathbf{L}_v \mathbf{H}_p - \mathbf{Y}\mathbf{C}_p^\top\|_F^2$. Based on Cauchy-Schwarz inequality, α_p is updated by:

$$\alpha_p = \frac{\sum_{p=1}^V \sqrt{\zeta_p}}{\sqrt{\zeta_p}}. \tag{15}$$

Update β with fixed Y, $\{\mathbf{C}_p\}_{p=1}^V$, α, and γ. Optimizing β is equivalent to solving the following equation:

$$\min_{\beta} \beta^\top \mathbf{M} \beta - 2\beta^\top \mathbf{b}, \quad \text{s.t.} \ \beta^\top \mathbf{1} = 1, \ \beta_v \geq 0, \ \forall v, \tag{16}$$

where $\mathbf{M} \in \mathbb{R}^{V \times V}$ with entries $M_{ij} = \sum_{p=1}^V \alpha_p \operatorname{tr}\left(\mathbf{H}_p^\top \mathbf{G}_i \mathbf{G}_j \mathbf{H}_p\right)$, and $\mathbf{b} \in \mathbb{R}^V$ with entries $b_i = \sum_{p=1}^V \alpha_p \operatorname{tr}\left(\mathbf{Y}^\top \mathbf{G}_i \mathbf{H}_p \mathbf{C}_p\right)$. The resulting quadratic programming problem can be efficiently solved using standard optimization solvers.

Update γ with fixed Y, $\{\mathbf{C}_p\}_{p=1}^V$, α, and β. Optimizing γ is equivalent to solving the following equation:

$$\min_{\gamma} \gamma^\top \mathbf{B} \gamma - 2\gamma^\top \mathbf{a}, \quad \text{s.t.} \ \gamma^\top \mathbf{1} = 1, \ \gamma_v \geq 0, \ \forall v, \tag{17}$$

where $\mathbf{B} \in \mathbb{R}^{V \times V}$ with entries $B_{ij} = \sum_{p=1}^V \alpha_p \operatorname{tr}\left(\mathbf{H}_p^\top \mathbf{L}_i \mathbf{L}_j \mathbf{H}_p\right)$, and $\mathbf{a} \in \mathbb{R}^V$ with entries $a_i = \sum_{p=1}^V \alpha_p \operatorname{tr}\left(\mathbf{Y}^\top \mathbf{L}_i \mathbf{H}_p \mathbf{C}_p\right)$. The solution can be efficiently computed via standard solvers.

Acceleration for Linear Filtering. The primary computational bottleneck during above updates stems from the $\mathcal{O}(n^2)$ cost of directly computing $\mathbf{G}_v \mathbf{H}_p$ and $\mathbf{L}_v \mathbf{H}_p$, which becomes prohibitive for large n. To address this, we exploit the inherent low-rank structure of the bipartite graph $\mathbf{P}_v$, where its thin SVD decomposition $\mathbf{P}_v = \mathbf{Q}_v \mathbf{\Sigma}_v \mathbf{N}_v^\top$ enables efficient spectral filtering:

$$\mathbf{G}_v \mathbf{H}_p = \mathbf{Q}_v \exp\left(-\eta(\mathbf{I} - \mathbf{\Sigma}_v^2)\right) \mathbf{Q}_v^\top \mathbf{H}_p, \tag{18}$$

$$\mathbf{L}_v \mathbf{H}_p = \mathbf{Q}_v (\mathbf{I} - \mathbf{\Sigma}_v^2) \mathbf{Q}_v^\top \mathbf{H}_p \tag{19}$$

where $\mathbf{Q}_v \in \mathbb{R}^{n \times m_v}$, $\mathbf{\Sigma}_v \in \mathbb{R}^{m_v \times m_v}$, and $\mathbf{N}_v \in \mathbb{R}^{m_v \times m_v}$ with $n \gg m_v$. By reordering the matrix products from right to left, the filtering complexity reduces from $\mathcal{O}(n^2 d)$ to $\mathcal{O}(n m_v d)$, ensuring linear scalability with respect to the sample

Algorithm 1. Late Fusion Multiple Kernel Clustering Refined via Optimal Linear Graph Filtering (LFMKC-OLF)

Input: Base partitions $\{\mathbf{H}_p\}_{p=1}^V$, number of clusters c, number of anchors $\{m_v\}_{v=1}^V$, number of nearest neighbors k, the parameter η and λ.
1: Construct sample-anchor similarity graphs $\{\mathbf{Z}_v\}_{v=1}^V$ for each partition then compute the column-normalized bipartite graphs $\{\mathbf{P}_v\}_{v=1}^V$ using Eq. (2).
2: Precompute filtered tensor banks in Eq. (20) using Eq. (18) and Eq. (19).
3: Initialize $\mathbf{Y}$ and $\{\mathbf{C}_p\}_{p=1}^V$.
4: Initialize $\alpha_p \Leftarrow V$, $\beta_v \Leftarrow 1/V$ and $\gamma_v \Leftarrow 1/V$, $\forall p, v$.
5: **while** not converged **do**
6:     Calculate the filtered embeddings $\mathcal{F}_L(\mathbf{H}_p)$ and $\mathcal{F}_H(\mathbf{H}_p)$ for all p via weighted aggregation over the precomputed tensor banks with current $\boldsymbol{\beta}$ and $\boldsymbol{\gamma}$.
7:     Update $\{\mathbf{C}_p\}_{p=1}^V$ according to Eq. (11).
8:     Update $\mathbf{Y}$ according to Eq. (13).
9:     Update $\boldsymbol{\alpha}$ according to Eq. (15).
10:    Update $\boldsymbol{\beta}$ by solving Eq. (16).
11:    Update $\boldsymbol{\gamma}$ by solving Eq. (17).
12: **end while**
Output: Final clustering assignment $\mathbf{Y}$.

size. Furthermore, all filtered outputs $\mathbf{G}_v\mathbf{H}_p$ and $\mathbf{L}_v\mathbf{H}_p$ are precomputed and cached prior to optimization, forming two filtered tensor banks:

$$\begin{bmatrix} \mathbf{G}_1\mathbf{H}_1 & \cdots & \mathbf{G}_V\mathbf{H}_1 \\ \vdots & \ddots & \vdots \\ \mathbf{G}_1\mathbf{H}_V & \cdots & \mathbf{G}_V\mathbf{H}_V \end{bmatrix} \text{ and } \begin{bmatrix} \mathbf{L}_1\mathbf{H}_1 & \cdots & \mathbf{L}_V\mathbf{H}_1 \\ \vdots & \ddots & \vdots \\ \mathbf{L}_1\mathbf{H}_V & \cdots & \mathbf{L}_V\mathbf{H}_V \end{bmatrix}. \quad (20)$$

During iterative updates, the consensus filtered embeddings $\mathcal{F}_L(\mathbf{H}_p)$ and $\mathcal{F}_H(\mathbf{H}_p)$ are efficiently obtained by weighted aggregation of the precomputed tensors using the current $\boldsymbol{\beta}$ and $\boldsymbol{\gamma}$.

We summarize the procedures of LFMKC-OLF algorithm in Algorithm 1.

3.5 Complexity Analysis

The overall computational complexity of the proposed LFMKC-OLF can be decomposed as follows. Anchor generation and bipartite graph construction incur costs of $\mathcal{O}(nd\sum_{v=1}^V m_v)$ and $\mathcal{O}(nk\sum_{v=1}^V m_v)$, respectively. The precomputation of filtered tensor banks in Eq. (20) requires $\mathcal{O}(\sum_{v=1}^V (nm_v d + m_v d + m_v))$. During iterative optimization, updating $\mathbf{C}_p$, $\mathbf{Y}$, $\boldsymbol{\alpha}$, $\boldsymbol{\beta}$, and $\boldsymbol{\gamma}$ involves complexities of $\mathcal{O}(ndc + dc^3)$, $\mathcal{O}(ndcV)$, $\mathcal{O}(ndcV)$, $\mathcal{O}(n(dV^3 + dcV))$, and $\mathcal{O}(n(dV^3 + dcV))$, respectively. Given that $m_v, c, d, V \ll n$, the overall complexity scales linearly as $\mathcal{O}(n)$, ensuring scalability to large-scale datasets.

Table 1. Dataset Summary.

ID	Dataset	Samples	Features	Classes	Kernels
D1	Caltech	2386	48, 40, 254, 1984, 512, 928	20	6
D2	MouseBladder	2746	11829	16	12
D3	Wiki	2866	128, 10	10	2
D4	Zeisel	3005	4401	48	12
D5	Macosko	6418	8608	39	12
D6	One-Year-Testic	7688	9667	10	12
D7	CITECBMC	8617	1703	15	12
D8	TDT2	9394	36771	30	12
D9	Fetal-Pancreas	11983	11673	18	12
D10	MouseRetina	27499	13166	19	12

4 Experiments

4.1 Experimental Setup

We briefly introduce the experimental setup here, including the used datasets, settings, and implementation details.

Datasets. We evaluate our method on 10 benchmark datasets: Caltech, MouseBladder, Wiki, Zeisel, Macosko, One-Year-Testic, CITECBMC, TDT2, Fetal-Pancreas, and MouseRetina. Detailed information about these datasets is provided in Table 1.

Compared Methods. We compare the proposed LFMKC-OLF with twelve state-of-the-art late fusion MKC methods, including AWP [17], LFMVC [21], OPLFMVC [16], ALMVC [30], LFLKA [29], MMLMVC [11], ERMKC [27], sLGm [23], HKLMVC [26], RIWLF [31], GMLKM [5], and CFGFLF [7]. Among these, HKLMVC, GMLKM, and CFGFLF incorporate graph filtering techniques to enhance clustering performance. Moreover, the average Kmeans result on base partitions (AvgH) is reported as a baseline.

Experimental Setting. All kernel matrices used in our experiments are precomputed using carefully designed similarity functions, and each base kernel is centered and normalized. Specifically, for the Caltech and Wiki datasets, a linear kernel matrix is constructed for each view. For the remaining datasets, we construct a diverse set of 12 kernel matrices per dataset, comprising 7 Gaussian kernels, 1 linear kernel, and 4 polynomial kernels, as detailed in [6]. To assess the performance of all methods under varying structural conditions, we further generate local kernels that capture local structural information based on the original kernels described above, following the strategy outlined in [29]. Throughout our experiments, the base partitions are obtained by performing kernel Kmeans on the constructed kernels and extracting their top-c eigenvectors, which serve as inputs for subsequent late fusion processes.

Implementation Details. All baseline methods are implemented with their recommended hyperparameter settings as reported in the respective original papers. To reduce random bias, all methods are executed 10 times and the average results are taken. The number of clusters for each dataset is set to the ground-truth class count. We evaluate clustering performance using three common metrics: Accuracy (ACC), Adjusted Rand Index (ARI), and Fscore. All experiments are conducted on a desktop equipped with an AMD Ryzen 7 5700G CPU (3.8 GHz) and 64 GB RAM, using MATLAB R2022b. For the proposed LFMKC-OLF, the neighborhood size k is fixed at 5, and the diffusion parameter η is set to 9 across all experiments without tuning. The balance parameter λ is tuned within the range $\{0.1, 0.2, \ldots, 1.0\}$ with a step size of 0.1. For simplicity, the number of anchors across all views is set as $m_1 = m_2 = \cdots = m_V = m$, where m is searched in $\{4c, 6c, 8c, 10c\}$.

4.2 Experimental Results

Tables 2 and 3 present the clustering results under two distinct base partition settings, with best results highlighted in red and second-best in blue. The proposed LFMKC-OLF consistently outperforms all baseline methods across most datasets in terms of ACC, ARI, and Fscore. In particular, on dataset D6, LFMKC-OLF exceeds the second-best method by substantial margins, with 70.43% under the original kernel partition and 25.65% under the local kernel partition in terms of ACC, underscoring its strength in LFMKC scenarios.

Although methods such as AWP, LFMVC, and OPLFMVC are specifically designed for efficient partition fusion, their performance remains limited, primarily due to reliance on static, low-quality base partitions and a lack of capacity to exploit higher-order structural information. In contrast, graph filter-based methods like HKLMVC, GMLKM, and CFGFLF enhance clustering through low-pass filtering, showing competitive performance on several datasets. However, these methods appear to converge toward a performance ceiling, likely attributable to the over-smoothing effect inherent in their filtering strategies. LFMKC-OLF consistently delivers superior performance improvement over other graph filter-based methods and achieves optimal filtering through dual-frequency joint clustering, effectively avoiding over-smoothing. These results confirm the effectiveness and strong applicability of the proposed method in diverse contexts.

4.3 Running Time Comparison and Convergence

We assess the time efficiency of the proposed LFMKC-OLF algorithm in Fig. 1. Experimental results reveal that LFMKC-OLF consistently outperforms most baseline methods in runtime, validating its computational efficiency. Notably,

Table 2. Clustering results (in %) on original kernel partitions.

Methods	D1	D2	D3	D4	D5	D6	D7	D8	D9	D10
ACC (%)										
AvgH	32.99	40.02	36.37	29.16	42.85	28.90	35.76	35.06	34.01	34.12
AWP	57.54	51.86	50.70	39.33	64.77	30.15	41.50	53.84	41.76	41.97
LFMVC	42.44	51.63	51.10	37.51	60.30	36.20	39.79	46.51	38.68	42.24
OPLFMVC	52.51	52.13	54.46	39.07	65.37	32.71	41.46	49.95	41.94	41.54
ALMVC	41.41	51.51	50.23	36.87	59.26	35.78	39.77	46.28	38.62	41.97
LFLKA	42.13	52.19	51.10	37.39	60.36	36.20	39.74	47.34	38.30	42.59
MMLMVC	40.23	48.92	50.23	37.13	57.62	34.85	38.67	48.30	37.86	39.71
ERMKC	41.78	58.92	54.82	37.70	59.88	42.20	42.62	49.13	43.52	42.63
sLGm	43.30	51.51	51.08	37.14	58.74	36.12	39.43	46.16	39.24	42.58
HKLMVC	60.55	55.87	55.64	45.42	70.67	35.90	42.68	54.72	46.43	46.42
RIWLF	42.73	51.88	51.55	37.75	59.93	36.44	39.60	46.70	39.21	42.32
GMLKM	47.11	50.78	55.34	39.95	59.04	34.78	45.14	40.40	40.88	46.32
CFGFLF	54.17	54.97	55.34	43.12	64.09	33.98	48.26	49.08	48.76	45.09
LFMKC-OLF	73.26	76.47	55.79	51.41	77.45	71.92	65.85	78.90	64.78	75.06
ARI (%)										
AvgH	20.23	26.28	22.38	14.59	34.16	9.51	20.47	16.88	15.30	16.64
AWP	51.47	38.44	34.11	22.39	54.16	13.38	30.43	35.71	23.46	24.79
LFMVC	30.96	39.35	35.57	21.77	49.35	18.89	29.24	31.55	22.63	26.32
OPLFMVC	42.16	38.68	42.97	22.26	55.67	15.15	30.11	33.37	23.38	25.00
ALMVC	30.46	39.38	34.71	21.54	49.09	18.53	29.24	31.38	22.60	26.30
LFLKA	31.24	39.74	35.57	21.34	50.16	18.90	29.07	32.14	22.46	26.82
MMLMVC	29.64	36.21	34.71	20.91	45.68	16.91	29.01	32.53	22.33	23.45
ERMKC	30.39	45.01	42.35	21.89	49.39	21.09	32.58	37.74	27.61	26.59
sLGm	31.21	39.50	35.55	21.64	48.00	18.96	29.14	30.94	22.87	26.33
HKLMVC	50.74	42.38	44.04	30.81	62.94	18.53	31.47	40.57	27.94	30.22
RIWLF	30.35	39.79	36.55	21.83	49.41	19.30	29.16	31.29	22.76	26.24
GMLKM	33.88	38.01	43.38	24.88	47.76	17.54	33.41	20.43	25.48	31.31
CFGFLF	45.50	40.24	43.54	27.12	53.95	17.47	36.06	32.61	30.29	32.10
LFMKC-OLF	73.05	65.70	40.34	45.46	75.79	63.51	51.90	72.82	39.03	82.56
Fscore (%)										
AvgH	26.63	35.07	30.52	18.82	36.67	27.04	34.07	26.12	27.78	27.71
AWP	57.01	44.11	41.09	25.13	56.14	27.63	37.46	39.57	31.06	31.49
LFMVC	36.64	44.91	42.33	24.40	51.28	31.96	36.26	35.40	29.55	32.60
OPLFMVC	48.00	44.34	49.04	24.95	57.60	28.67	37.13	37.16	31.14	31.63
ALMVC	36.17	44.93	41.55	24.17	51.02	31.64	36.26	35.22	29.52	32.59
LFLKA	36.97	45.30	42.33	23.97	52.08	31.96	36.09	35.96	29.37	33.14
MMLMVC	35.36	41.98	41.55	23.56	47.72	30.15	35.95	36.35	29.25	29.92
ERMKC	36.10	50.35	48.47	24.59	51.53	33.92	40.39	41.51	34.34	32.89
sLGm	36.85	45.05	42.31	24.28	49.97	32.02	36.17	34.80	29.79	32.74
HKLMVC	57.83	47.94	50.07	34.00	64.70	32.62	38.51	44.44	35.72	36.80
RIWLF	36.07	45.33	43.20	24.46	51.33	32.35	36.15	35.14	29.69	32.52
GMLKM	40.23	43.94	49.42	27.58	49.86	31.16	40.72	27.04	32.81	37.96
CFGFLF	51.59	46.23	49.61	30.02	55.98	31.65	43.01	38.42	38.51	38.78
LFMKC-OLF	78.16	70.51	47.71	49.59	77.26	77.33	61.25	75.65	52.39	85.94

compared with graph filtering-based approaches such as HKLMVC, GMLKM, and CFGFLF, LFMKC-OLF exhibits superior scalability and efficiency on large-scale datasets. Although CFGFLF also achieves linear filtering, its high per-iteration complexity leads to substantially longer overall runtime. In contrast, the lightweight design of LFMKC-OLF ensures low per-iteration overhead, achieving a favorable trade-off between computational cost and clustering quality.

Convergence behavior on Caltech, MouseBladder, Wiki, and Macosko datasets is illustrated in Fig. 2, with similar trends on other datasets omitted for brevity. The objective value decreases monotonically and converges within 15 iterations, accompanied by steady improvements in clustering performance until stabilization. These results underscore the algorithm's fast convergence and effectiveness.

Table 3. Clustering results (in %) on local kernel partitions.

Methods	D1	D2	D3	D4	D5	D6	D7	D8	D9	D10
ACC (%)										
AvgH	33.68	49.21	36.21	30.23	34.79	32.43	57.67	60.55	29.87	32.47
AWP	47.90	58.78	45.43	36.14	35.87	44.25	65.70	78.77	40.44	41.27
LFMVC	43.98	50.29	51.34	30.53	34.82	32.18	58.05	58.69	30.48	31.93
OPLFMVC	50.44	59.13	55.22	34.03	37.22	44.18	65.63	79.21	40.40	41.41
ALMVC	42.28	49.03	50.64	30.43	34.49	31.89	56.92	58.69	30.15	31.76
LFLKA	43.37	50.24	51.35	30.52	35.26	32.09	57.77	59.55	30.48	31.92
MMLMVC	41.92	49.09	50.63	30.80	34.73	32.63	57.28	58.42	30.60	31.87
ERMKC	50.39	53.47	53.33	31.89	35.69	35.16	61.80	64.40	32.87	36.24
sLGm	43.32	49.66	51.10	30.74	34.46	32.11	57.91	58.84	30.62	31.96
HKLMVC	52.42	56.31	55.25	34.91	37.84	44.36	65.97	78.29	40.73	41.48
RIWLF	44.20	50.17	51.12	30.60	34.81	47.20	65.83	60.79	36.84	45.22
GMLKM	45.54	49.25	54.62	34.18	35.60	41.47	58.82	61.63	31.87	35.92
CFGFLF	43.40	54.88	55.20	39.58	39.79	52.40	67.09	84.48	43.54	53.38
LFMKC-OLF	63.24	73.71	63.08	45.99	46.32	65.84	69.59	85.05	52.92	61.35
ARI (%)										
AvgH	20.84	37.69	22.63	20.37	28.38	17.88	47.51	49.88	16.05	21.04
AWP	32.54	42.37	26.39	27.30	30.55	31.03	54.53	70.16	21.61	40.08
LFMVC	30.06	38.78	35.41	20.29	28.26	18.04	47.62	47.30	16.31	22.57
OPLFMVC	36.28	43.41	43.54	25.04	31.05	30.96	54.57	68.13	21.60	40.01
ALMVC	29.58	37.99	34.99	20.37	28.13	18.11	47.07	47.30	16.13	22.02
LFLKA	29.78	38.83	35.49	20.50	28.82	18.21	47.63	48.20	16.31	22.56
MMLMVC	27.65	37.42	34.97	20.42	28.24	18.16	47.32	47.89	16.39	22.52
ERMKC	38.89	41.71	38.87	21.73	29.61	19.10	50.60	51.16	17.61	25.03
sLGm	30.56	38.67	35.09	20.37	27.90	18.11	47.64	47.17	16.47	22.70
HKLMVC	38.74	41.75	43.20	25.74	30.91	30.74	54.53	68.52	21.70	40.15
RIWLF	29.37	38.41	34.98	20.51	28.90	15.49	54.47	49.54	21.83	28.08
GMLKM	27.34	37.34	39.57	24.44	26.70	24.62	46.03	43.21	16.47	25.72
CFGFLF	25.22	38.99	42.81	29.92	30.27	3.23	54.62	66.54	22.58	52.20
LFMKC-OLF	49.65	60.23	49.96	42.66	37.15	51.00	58.65	78.31	31.14	66.83
Fscore (%)										
AvgH	27.91	43.57	30.97	23.31	31.24	32.03	56.67	53.83	23.51	29.93
AWP	40.03	48.99	34.21	30.70	34.02	49.29	63.03	72.92	31.65	48.25
LFMVC	36.22	44.58	42.26	23.25	31.07	31.95	56.75	50.88	23.79	29.61
OPLFMVC	43.32	49.80	49.67	28.19	34.48	49.25	63.06	70.97	31.64	48.19
ALMVC	35.76	43.81	41.84	23.31	30.98	32.16	56.23	50.88	23.58	29.09
LFLKA	36.03	44.61	42.32	23.42	31.64	32.18	56.72	51.76	23.80	29.60
MMLMVC	33.94	43.35	41.83	23.38	31.07	32.06	56.47	51.45	23.91	29.63
ERMKC	45.32	47.48	45.41	24.71	32.52	33.06	59.44	54.73	25.11	32.09
sLGm	36.75	44.42	41.98	23.30	30.70	32.04	56.77	50.79	23.99	29.72
HKLMVC	46.23	48.16	49.45	29.07	34.43	49.13	63.05	71.41	31.80	48.34
RIWLF	35.51	44.19	41.86	23.43	31.70	44.57	62.86	52.87	29.90	45.71
GMLKM	36.65	43.56	46.58	28.05	30.19	41.79	55.39	48.56	25.51	34.82
CFGFLF	34.75	46.50	49.14	34.16	34.64	47.74	63.21	70.88	34.97	61.34
LFMKC-OLF	58.87	65.92	56.17	47.19	41.57	68.44	66.64	80.54	43.06	72.93

4.4 Parameter Analysis

We evaluate the sensitivity of LFMKC-OLF to two key parameters: the number of anchors $m \in \{4c, 6c, 8c, 10c\}$, where c is the number of clusters, and the trade-off parameter $\lambda \in \{0.1, 0.2, \ldots, 1.0\}$. The performance trends under different parameter combinations are illustrated in Fig. 3. We observe that performance remains relatively stable as the number of anchors m varies. Regarding the trade-off parameter λ, optimal performance is typically achieved within the range $[0.6, 0.8]$, while larger values tend to over-smoothing and performance degradation, suggesting that the smoothing component plays a dominant role. Notably, on datasets such as Caltech and Wiki, better performance is observed with smaller λ values in the range $[0.2, 0.5]$, highlighting the effectiveness of high-pass filtering in preserving fine-grained details, alleviating over-smoothing and further enhancing representations to improve clustering performance.

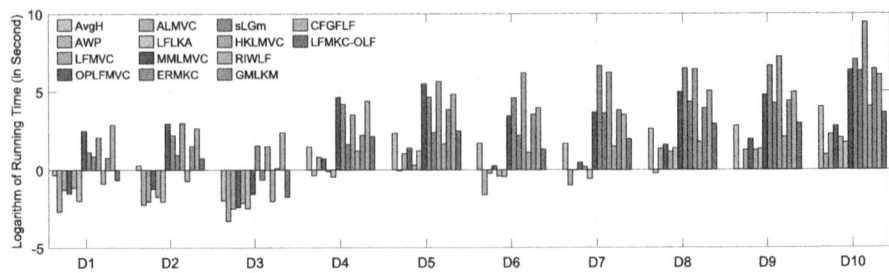

Fig. 1. Comparison of LFMKC-OLF and baseline methods in terms of relative base-10 logarithmic runtime on ten benchmark datasets under the original kernel partitions.

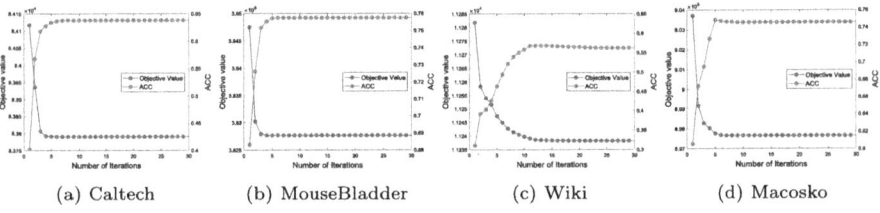

(a) Caltech   (b) MouseBladder   (c) Wiki   (d) Macosko

Fig. 2. The objective value and clustering performance of LFMKC-OLF vary with increasing iterations on Caltech, MouseBladder, Wiki, and Macosko datasets.

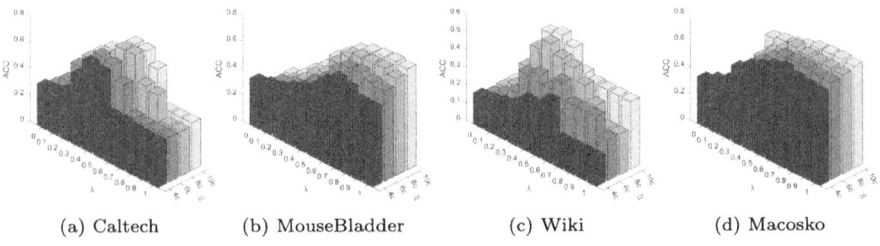

(a) Caltech   (b) MouseBladder   (c) Wiki   (d) Macosko

Fig. 3. The parameter sensitivity experiments on Caltech, MouseBladder, Wiki, and Macosko datasets under the original kernel partitions.

4.5 Ablation Study

To assess the contribution of each component in the LFMKC-OLF objective, we perform an ablation study comparing the full model against two simplified variants: (1) a baseline defined by Eq. (7) without the consensus low-pass filter $\hat{\mathbf{G}}$, denoted as Eq. (7) w/o $\hat{\mathbf{G}}$; (2) the low-pass-only model given by Eq. (7).

The results, summarized in Table 4 with the best values highlighted in red, demonstrate that LFMKC-OLF consistently outperforms both variants across all datasets. This clearly verifies the effectiveness of both low-pass filtering and high-frequency enhancement in improving clustering performance. Notably, the performance gap between Eq. (7) w/o $\hat{\mathbf{G}}$ and Eq. (7) highlights the importance

Table 4. Ablation study: ACC (in %) on different datasets.

Methods	D1	D2	D3	D4	D5	D6	D7	D8	D9	D10
Original Kernel Partitions										
Eq. (7) w/o $\hat{\mathbf{G}}$	57.46	52.55	49.93	37.34	64.82	31.22	45.00	53.23	43.97	39.47
Eq. (7)	33.45	75.56	37.89	49.05	74.21	71.49	56.37	78.06	64.75	74.64
LFMKC-OLF	73.26	76.47	55.79	51.41	77.45	71.92	65.85	78.90	64.78	75.06
Local Kernel Partitions										
Eq. (7) w/o $\hat{\mathbf{G}}$	51.05	59.18	45.43	32.95	34.76	44.35	65.70	80.75	45.48	41.07
Eq. (7)	62.78	68.90	53.80	38.87	43.02	65.83	66.65	82.90	48.92	53.74
LFMKC-OLF	63.24	73.71	63.08	45.99	46.32	65.84	69.59	85.05	52.92	61.35

of incorporating the low-pass filter, which enhances global structural consistency and suppresses noise in base partitions. Furthermore, the superiority of LFMKC-OLF over Eq. (7) confirms the necessity of integrating high-frequency signals to mitigate over-smoothing and retain essential local discriminative information.

5 Conclusion

In this work, we propose a novel late fusion multiple kernel clustering framework refined via optimal linear graph filtering (LFMKC-OLF), which effectively addresses the limitations of low-quality base partitions while maintaining linear computational complexity. By constructing bipartite graphs and deriving high-order low-pass and high-pass filters through heat kernel diffusion and Laplacian operators, the proposed method captures both global and fine-grained structural information. A consensus filtering mechanism is further introduced by optimally combining view-specific filters, enabling robust multi-scale representation learning. The joint clustering formulation, which integrates both smoothed and detail-enhanced partitions, effectively mitigates over-smoothing and improves clustering fidelity. Extensive experiments across multiple datasets and diverse base partition settings consistently demonstrate the superiority and robustness of LFMKC-OLF. Future work will explore more advanced graph filtering paradigms and extend the framework to broader real-world applications.

Acknowledgments. This work was supported by the National Natural Science Foundation of China (62376146), the Shanxi Province Central Guidance for Local Science and Technology Development Special Project (YDZJSX20231D003).

Disclosure of Interests. The authors have no competing interests to declare that are relevant to the content of this article.

References

1. Bo, D., Wang, X., Shi, C., Shen, H.: Beyond low-frequency information in graph convolutional networks. In: Proceedings of the AAAI Conference on Artificial Intelligence, vol. 35, pp. 3950–3957 (2021)
2. Chen, Y., Du, L., Zhou, P., Duan, L., Qian, Y.: Multiple kernel clustering with local kernel reconstruction and global heat diffusion. Inf. Fus. **105**, 102219 (2024)
3. Chung, F.: The heat kernel as the PageRank of a graph. Nat. Acad. Sci. **104**(50), 19735–19740 (2007)
4. Dong, X., Thanou, D., Frossard, P., Vandergheynst, P.: Learning Laplacian matrix in smooth graph signal representations. IEEE Trans. Signal Process. **64**(23), 6160–6173 (2016)
5. Du, L., et al.: Sharper error bounds in late fusion multi-view clustering with eigenvalue proportion optimization. In: Proceedings of the AAAI Conference on Artificial Intelligence, vol. 39, pp. 16381–16388 (2025)
6. Du, L., et al.: Robust multiple kernel k-means using ℓ_{21}-norm. In: International Joint Conference on Artificial Intelligence, pp. 3476–3482 (2015)
7. Guo, Y., Jiang, H., Chen, Y., Du, L.: A scalable consensus fast graph filtering approach for late fusion multi-view clustering. Signal Process. **237**, 110074 (2025)
8. Huang, J., Nie, F., Huang, H., Ding, C.: Robust manifold nonnegative matrix factorization. ACM Trans. Knowl. Discov. Data **8**(3), 1–21 (2014)
9. Isufi, E., Gama, F., Shuman, D.I., Segarra, S.: Graph filters for signal processing and machine learning on graphs. IEEE Trans. Signal Process. **72**, 4745–4781 (2024)
10. Kang, Z., Xie, X., Li, B., Pan, E.: CDC: a simple framework for complex data clustering. IEEE Trans. Neural Netw. Learn. Syst. **36**, 13177–13188 (2024)
11. Li, M., Liu, X., Zhang, Y., Liang, W.: Late fusion multiview clustering via min-max optimization. IEEE Trans. Neural Netw. Learn. Syst. **35**(7), 9417–9427 (2024)
12. Li, S., Kim, D., Wang, Q.: Beyond low-pass filters: adaptive feature propagation on graphs. In: Oliver, N., Pérez-Cruz, F., Kramer, S., Read, J., Lozano, J.A. (eds.) ECML PKDD 2021. LNCS (LNAI), vol. 12976, pp. 450–465. Springer, Cham (2021). https://doi.org/10.1007/978-3-030-86520-7_28
13. Li, Z., Tang, C., Zheng, X., Liu, X., Zhang, W., Zhu, E.: High-order correlation preserved incomplete multi-view subspace clustering. IEEE Trans. Image Process. **31**, 2067–2080 (2022)
14. Lin, Z., Kang, Z.: Graph filter-based multi-view attributed graph clustering. In: International Joint Conference on Artificial Intelligence, pp. 2723–2729 (2021)
15. Liu, X.: Simplemkkm: simple multiple kernel k-means. IEEE Trans. Pattern Anal. Mach. Intell. **45**(4), 5174–5186 (2023)
16. Liu, X., et al.: One pass late fusion multi-view clustering. In: International Conference on Machine Learning, pp. 6850–6859 (2021)
17. Nie, F., Tian, L., Li, X.: Multiview clustering via adaptively weighted procrustes. In: ACM SIGKDD International Conference on Knowledge Discovery and Data Mining, pp. 2022–2030 (2018)
18. Nie, F., Wang, X., Jordan, M.I., Huang, H.: The constrained Laplacian rank algorithm for graph-based clustering. In: Proceedings of the AAAI Conference on Artificial Intelligence, pp. 1969–1976 (2016)
19. Ren, Z., Sun, Q.: Simultaneous global and local graph structure preserving for multiple kernel clustering. IEEE Trans. Neural Netw. Learn. Syst. **32**(5), 1839–1851 (2020)

20. Ren, Z., Sun, Q., Wei, D.: Multiple kernel clustering with kernel k-means coupled graph tensor learning. In: Proceedings of the AAAI Conference on Artificial Intelligence, vol. 35, pp. 9411–9418 (2021)
21. Wang, S., et al.: Multi-view clustering via late fusion alignment maximization. In: International Joint Conference on Artificial Intelligence, pp. 3778–3784 (2019)
22. Wen, Z., et al.: Homophily-related: adaptive hybrid graph filter for multi-view graph clustering. In: Proceedings of the AAAI Conference on Artificial Intelligence, vol. 38, pp. 15841–15849 (2024)
23. Wu, X., Huang, C., Liu, X., Zhou, F., Ren, Z.: Multiple kernel clustering with shifted Laplacian on Grassmann manifold. In: ACM International Conference on Multimedia, pp. 2448–2456 (2024)
24. Wu, Z., Pan, S., Long, G., Jiang, J., Zhang, C.: Beyond low-pass filtering: graph convolutional networks with automatic filtering. IEEE Trans. Knowl. Data Eng. **35**(7), 6687–6697 (2022)
25. Xie, X., Chen, W., Kang, Z., Peng, C.: Contrastive graph clustering with adaptive filter. Expert Syst. Appl. **219**, 119645 (2023)
26. Yang, G., Zou, J., Chen, Y., Du, L., Zhou, P.: Heat kernel diffusion for enhanced late fusion multi-view clustering. IEEE Signal Process. Lett. **31**, 2310–2314 (2024)
27. Yang, W., Tang, C., Zheng, X., Zhu, X., Liu, X.: Eigenvalue ratio inspired partition learning and fusion for multiple kernel clustering. IEEE Trans. Knowl. Data Eng. **01**, 1–13 (2024)
28. Zhang, P., et al.: Let the data choose: flexible and diverse anchor graph fusion for scalable multi-view clustering. In: Proceedings of the AAAI Conference on Artificial Intelligence, vol. 37, pp. 11262–11269 (2023)
29. Zhang, T., Liu, X., Gong, L., Wang, S., Niu, X., Shen, L.: Late fusion multiple kernel clustering with local kernel alignment maximization. IEEE Trans. Multimedia **25**, 993–1007 (2023)
30. Zhang, T., Liu, X., Zhu, E., Zhou, S., Dong, Z.: Efficient anchor learning-based multi-view clustering – a late fusion method. In: ACM International Conference on Multimedia, pp. 3685–3693 (2022)
31. Zhang, Y., et al.: Regularized instance weighting multiview clustering via late fusion alignment. IEEE Trans. Neural Netw. Learn. Syst. **36**, 1–13 (2024)
32. Zhao, B., Kwok, J.T., Zhang, C.: Multiple kernel clustering. In: Proceedings of the 2009 SIAM International Conference on Data Mining, pp. 638–649 (2009)
33. Zhou, P., Du, L.: Learnable graph filter for multi-view clustering. In: ACM International Conference on Multimedia, pp. 3089–3098 (2023)
34. Zhou, P., Du, L., Li, X.: Adaptive consensus clustering for multiple k-means via base results refining. IEEE Trans. Knowl. Data Eng. **35**(10), 10251–10264 (2023)

InfoClus: Informative Clustering of High-Dimensional Data Embeddings

Fuyin Lai(✉), Edith Heiter, Guillaume Bied, and Jefrey Lijffijt

Ghent University, Ghent, Belgium
{fuyin.lai,edith.heiter,guillaume.bied,jefrey.lijffijt}@ugent.be

Abstract. Developing an understanding of high-dimensional data can be facilitated by visualizing that data using dimensionality reduction. However, the low-dimensional embeddings are often difficult to interpret. To facilitate the exploration and interpretation of low-dimensional embeddings, we introduce a new concept named *partitioning with explanations*. The idea is to partition the data shown through the embedding into groups, each of which is given a sparse explanation using the original high-dimensional attributes. We introduce an objective function that quantifies how much we can learn through observing the explanations of the data partitioning, using information theory, and also how complex the explanations are. Through parameterization of the complexity, we can tune the solutions towards the desired granularity. We propose InfoClus, which optimizes the partitioning and explanations jointly, through greedy search constrained over a hierarchical clustering. We conduct a qualitative and quantitative analysis of InfoClus on three data sets. We contrast the results on the Cytometry data with published manual analysis results, and compare with two other recent methods for explaining embeddings (RVX and VERA). These comparisons highlight that InfoClus has distinct advantages over existing procedures and methods. We find that InfoClus can automatically create good starting points for the analysis of dimensionality-reduction-based scatter plots.

Keywords: dimensionality reduction · clustering · explainability

1 Introduction

Background. Dimensionality-reduction (DR) methods are widely employed to project high-dimensional data into a two-dimensional space, such that it can be visualized. Popular methods are t-SNE [12] and UMAP [13], which are DR methods that are distance-based, local-focused, non-linear, and transductive (terms explained in following paragraphs). Their popularity stems from their effectiveness to retain the local structure of the data, often in the form of cluster structure, which they manage by flexibly warping larger distances. However, this flexibility bring several challenges in the interpretation of embeddings [6,9,18,20]:

The lack of interpretability has its origin in several factors: (1) the methods are *distance-based*, meaning they operate only on the distance matrix and not directly on the feature values. The distances summarize all features with equal weight and thus there is no preference for sparsity in relations between points in the embedding. (2) They are *non-linear and transductive* (i.e., non-parametric): the placement of points in the embedding is entirely free and not a projection. The axes are not interpretable, the embeddings are sensitive to specificities of the data and many XAI methods do not apply (requiring, e.g., the existence of gradients). (3) They are *local-focused* meaning that the distances are distorted. For example, t-SNE also uses a point-specific parameter σ_i to factor out density differences across the data, which can lead to counterintuitive distortions.

Idea behind InfoClus. Rather than aiming to fix these problems, we want to facilitate interpretation of the embeddings, agnostic to the dimensionality reduction algorithm. More specifically, InfoClus is designed to provide a useful starting point for exploring and interpreting of low-dimensional embeddings.

As discussed more in-depth in the related work section below, existing systems enable users to 'explain' hand-selected clusters, or give an overview of the impact of a specific attribute. They rely on the user selecting what to look at. In contrast, the idea behind InfoClus is to automatically partition the embeddings into coherent clusters that have a sparse explanation. In other words, to find a clustering that is (1) cohesive on the embedding and (2) such that the points in each cluster share a relatively simple explanation. The explanations that we consider here provide information about how the points in each cluster are different from the data as a whole. Figure 1 shows a diagram that illustrates the InfoClus approach.

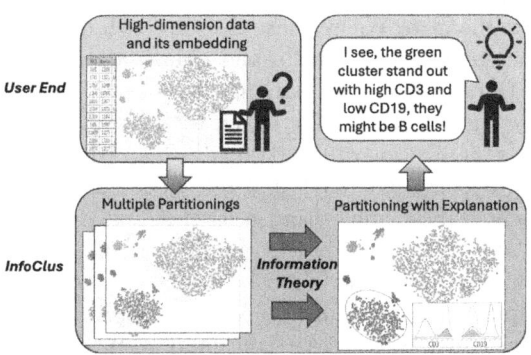

Fig. 1. InfoClus workflow

InfoClus is a parametrized approach for finding good *partitionings with explanations* (*PwX*s), given a high-dimensional dataset and a low-dimensional embedding. The explanations for a cluster are those that provide most information, as quantified through information theory.

How InfoClus Works. We first formalize the problem setting (Sect. 3) and define *partitioning with explanations*. We then use information theory to quantify the amount of information communicated with a *PwX* and we propose a quantification for the 'complexity' of a *PwX* (Sect. 3.1). A *PwX* that conveys more information and/or has a lower complexity is better. The complexity is parameterized, enabling users to tune the algorithm to yield simpler or more complex solutions, as desired.

In Sect. 3.2, we consider how to algorithmically find good PwXs. Maximizing the informativeness will lead to PwXs that are cohesive in the high-dimensional space, but we need to also ensure that the clustering is cohesive on the two-dimensional embedding. Hence, we constrain possible solutions from InfoClus to clusterings on the embedding that are generated by existing clustering methods. We consider the use of hierarchical and k-means clustering. Such constraints on solutions also have the advantage of limiting the search space of possible partitionings.

For hierarchical clustering, the number of possible partitionings is still very large and optimizing informativeness is not straightforward. We show this problem can be optimized efficiently and effectively using a greedy search algorithm that cuts off branches from the tree induced by the hierarchical clustering. This yields an algorithm that empirically runs in linear time in the number of data points and attributes, per iteration that adds a cluster to the solution.

Evaluation. We evaluate the approach using three different datasets, and study the results qualitatively and quantitatively (Sect. 4). We include a comparison with the two closest existing methods (RVX [21] and VERA [15]). We consider a Cytometry dataset for which we have a manual expert labeling available based on visualization of the data over feature pairs. We compare the features used in the experts' approach and by InfoClus. We additionally study a dataset with demographic and voting statistics, and the UCI Mushroom data.

Finally, we study the impact of the hyperparameters (Sect. 4.2) and the runtime of InfoClus (Sect. 4.3). We conclude the paper with a discussion of the capabilities and limitations of the approach (Sect. 5).

Reproducibility. All code and results are available on GitHub at https://github.com/aida-ugent/InfoClus.

2 Related Work

For brevity, we discuss only the most important examples of work on the more general topic of explaining embeddings and then also the most similar methods.

Related Work on Explaining Embeddings. Several approaches have been developed for explaining the specific positions of points in an embedding, e.g., using inverse projections [5,8] or counterfactuals [1]. Another popular approach to explaining embeddings is feature-centric. We can show the values for an individual feature, but patterns may be found more easily through aggregates such as contour lines [9]. Similarly, one may construct 'rangesets' for class labels [19].

The above approaches can provide insight into the impact of each attribute on the embedding, but do not lead to discovery of the most important features. The second type of approach that has been explored is to start from a user-selected cluster and show how this cluster stands out against the overall data or against another cluster. Stahnke et al. introduced this as 'probing' of projections [20]. In their paper, they showed the distributions of all attributes to users. Recent papers have considered the use of decision trees [2], boosting machines [17], and predicate logic [14] to provide sparse explanations for manually-selected clusters (i.e., explanations using a small subset of features). The latter approach named DimBridge [14] is notable for also supporting the explanation of hand-drawn lines, by constructing a regression model for the progression along the line.

Finally, there are other DR algorithms, including approaches that aim to directly create coherent—and thus arguably more interpretable—clusters in the embedding. For example, by integrating label information in classification settings [3] or contrastive DR to visualise a clustering [23]. However, in this paper we do not aim to evaluate DR approaches and the approach is agnostic to the DR algorithm. We aim to facilitate the interpretation of any given embedding.

Methods Similar to InfoClus. There are no approaches directly similar to InfoClus that partition an embedding of the data and generate explanations for the partitioning. The most closely related work is Visual Explanations via Region Annotation (VERA) by Policar and Zupan [15]. VERA provides two different types of 'explanations' for embeddings: descriptive and contrastive. They both are built up by finding clusters on the embedding for each data attribute separately. Contrastive explanations select an attribute and value splits that lead to cohesive clusters on the embedding. Descriptive explanations are constructed by merging clusters across attributes that are similar, and then selecting a set that has small overlap.

Another method that does not explicitly seek clusters but may end up giving a similar result to InfoClus is by Thijssen et al. [21]. We will refer to it as Relative Value eXplanations (RVX) and $RV_\sigma X$ for the variance-based variant. RVX provides an explanation in the form of a feature per data point that stands out most, in terms of value or variance. It employs smoothing, leading to visual clusters often sharing a single most-outstanding attribute. We include an empirical comparison between InfoClus, VERA, and RVX in Sect. 4.

3 InfoClus Step by Step

Preliminaries. We assume given a dataset with n points $X = \{x_1, x_2, \ldots, x_n\}$, m attributes $A = \{a_1, a_2, \ldots, a_m\}$, and its corresponding two-dimensional embedding Y. We refer to a *partitioning* of Y as a list of sets $\mathcal{C} = [c_1, \ldots, c_r]$ such that each point in Y belongs to exactly one c_i. We refer to an *explanation* for a *partitioning* as choice of representative attributes and their corresponding distribution for each cluster in the partitioning.

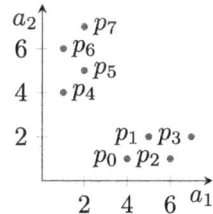

Fig. 2. Example dataset.

Definition 1. *A partitioning with explanations (PwX) of dataset X is a partitioning $\mathcal{C}$ of its embedding Y with associated explanations, represented as a tuple $(\mathcal{C}, \mathcal{E})$, where $\mathcal{C} = [c_1, \ldots, c_r], \mathcal{E} = [e_1, \ldots, e_r]$. $\mathcal{E}$ denotes the list of explanations, where $e_i = \{a_i^1, a_i^2, \ldots\} \subseteq A$ is the set of attributes selected to explain cluster c_i.*

Figure 2 shows a small dataset (8 points, 2 attributes) that will serve as a running example to illustrate the concepts in this section (note here that $Y = X$).

Example. $(\mathcal{C}', \mathcal{E}')$ with $\mathcal{C}' = [c_1 : \{p_0, p_1, p_2, p_3\}, c_2 : \{p_4, p_5, p_6, p_7\}]$, $\mathcal{E}' = [e_1 : \{a_2\}, e_2 : \{a_1\}]$ is a *PwX* of the dataset shown in Fig. 2.

Section Outline. Sect. 3.1 presents measures for how much information users may learn from a *PwX* and the complexity of a *PwX*, which together define what is an informative clustering. Section 3.2 introduces InfoClus, a methodology aimed at finding coherent and informative *PwX*s.

3.1 Explanation Ratio

We assume that the goal of interpreting the embedding is to learn about the distribution of the data. The visualization of the embedding enables users to identify groups of points that form a cluster. For example, t-SNE indeed tends to produce embeddings with meaningful cluster structure [10]. Hence, we can model the interpretation as a communication process where the user learns about the data through visualizations of distributions for clusters present in the embedding.

To arrive at a quantification for what a user learns, we take inspiration from the framework on subjective interestingness [7]. We can quantify how much a user learns using information theory, by quantifying the reduction in uncertainty a user has about the data. This means we have to make an assumption about what the user knows already—which is known as the *prior distribution*—and what the user knows after observation of a *PwX*.

Following De Bie [7], the *information content* of an observation is given by the surprisal of this observation: $IC(X) = -\log P(X)$. Equivalently, but from a different perspective, if we consider how much we learn by updating a prior distribution to a posterior, this is given by the KL-divergence between the two distributions. The amount of information that we learn by updating a prior to a more specific posterior distribution is quantified as follows:

Definition 2. *The* information content *I for a PwX is the sum of information content for each cluster c_i and each attribute a_i^j in the PwX, which is given by*

$$I_i^j = |c_i| * D_{KL}(P_i^j \| Q^j), \tag{1}$$

where $|c_i|$ is the size of the cluster, P_i^j is the distribution of attribute a^j in cluster c_i, and Q^j is the distribution of attribute a^j in the full dataset.

Here we assumed that the prior information a user has about the data are the marginal distributions for each attribute in the data. We present the distributions for clusters in visual form, but we assume users learn about the mean and variance statistics only, but with infinite precision. In practice, we may not know either, but the approach may still be helpful even if the details of how we model the beliefs of the user are wrong.

In InfoClus, we model real-valued attributes with Gaussian distributions, and categorical attributes with a categorical distribution as a default. The implementation of InfoClus supports both numerical and categorical attributes, but not mixed data, because the KL-divergence is defined for discrete and continuous variables, but they are not comparable.

Example. We assume continuous attribute a_2 follows a Gaussian distribution. By computing the empirical mean and variance in the full dataset and the cluster c_1 respectively, we have a_2 follows $\mathcal{N}(3.5, 4.75)$ on the full dataset and $\mathcal{N}(1.5, 0.25)$ in c_1 of PwX $(\mathcal{C}', \mathcal{E}')$. The information carried by a_2 in c_1 is: $I_1^2 = 4 \times D_{KL}(\mathcal{N}(1.5, 0.25) \| \mathcal{N}(3.5, 4.75)) = 5.68$.

Yet, the more attributes are selected to inform a user about a partitioning, the more effort is needed for users to understand them. This leads us to define the following notion of complexity, with α and β parameterizing a user's learning sensitivity for information:

Definition 3. *The* complexity *of a PwX $(\mathcal{C}, \mathcal{E})$ is*

$$\alpha + (\sum_{i=1}^{r} \sum_{j=1}^{|e_i|} |a_i^j|)^\beta, \qquad (2)$$

where a_i^j is an attribute belonging to $e_i \in \mathcal{E}$, and $|a_i^j|$ refers to the count of statistics needed to describe the distribution a_i^j follows. α and β are hyper-parameters.

Example. Assuming attributes a_1, a_2 in Fig. 2 follow a Gaussian distribution, we have $|a_1| = |a_2| = 2$, since for a Gaussian distribution, the mean and variance statistics define the probability distribution. Then, given $\alpha = 1, \beta = 2$, the complexity for PwX $(\mathcal{C}', \mathcal{E}')$ is $1 + 4^2 = 17$.

To balance the information carried by a PwX and the human cognitive effort necessary to interpret it, we introduce the concept of an explanation ratio:

Definition 4. *The* explanation ratio $R_{\alpha,\beta}$ *of a PwX $(\mathcal{C}, \mathcal{E})$ with r clusters is*

$$R_{\alpha,\beta}(\mathcal{C}, \mathcal{E}) = \frac{\sum_{i=1}^{r} \sum_{j=1}^{|e_i|} I_i^j}{\alpha + (\sum_{i=1}^{r} \sum_{j=1}^{|e_i|} |a_i^j|)^\beta}, \qquad (3)$$

where i indexes the clusters and j the attributes of explanation e_i.

Example. Given $\alpha = 1, \beta = 2$, the *explanation ratio* for PwX $(\mathcal{C}', \mathcal{E}')$ is $R_{1,2}(\mathcal{C}', \mathcal{E}') = (I_1^2 + I_2^1)/(1 + (|a_2| + |a_1|)^2) = 0.67$.

Problem Statement. InfoClus aims to partition the dataset into clusters that are cohesive in the embedding and the high-dimensional space. The clustering is shown on the embedding; information on the high-dimensional space is provided through a few selected attributes. The partitioning and explanations are chosen such that they maximize the *explanation ratio* aiming to optimize the ratio of the amount of information provided over the effort required to interpret it.

3.2 InfoClus: Finding Cohesive and Informative PwXs Efficiently

InfoClus seeks to partition the embeddings into visually coherent clusters with high *explanation ratio*. To do so, existing clustering algorithms (e.g. hierarchical clustering or k-means) are used to generate candidate partitionings (ensuring visual coherence), among which the PwX with highest *explanation ratio* is retained. In the following, we focus on hierarchical clustering, which we advise using as a default candidate generator.

Hierarchical clustering strikes a suitable balance with a large number of possible partitionings, but since these are structured in a tree we can still optimize efficiently over the space of candidates[1]. We proceed to detail the procedure used to navigate the search space for partitionings implied by hierarchical clustering, and sketch algorithmic details.

Search for Partitionings. Hierarchical clustering constructs a hierarchy of clusters, which may be seen as organizing data in a tree structure (dendrogram). For instance, agglomerative hierarchical clustering builds a tree from the ground up: each observation initially defines its own cluster, and clusters are progressively greedily merged based on a chosen linkage. We constrain our search space to partitionings compatible with the hierarchical clustering. More specifically, rather than relying solely on partitionings formed by slicing the dendrogram at a specific level, we consider a compatible partitioning with r clusters as consisting of $r-1$ clusters obtained from cutting nodes at any level of the dendrogram, and the final cluster encompassing the remaining points. For instance, Fig. 3 illustrates a partitioning $\mathcal{C}$ compatible with a dendrogram in our toy example.

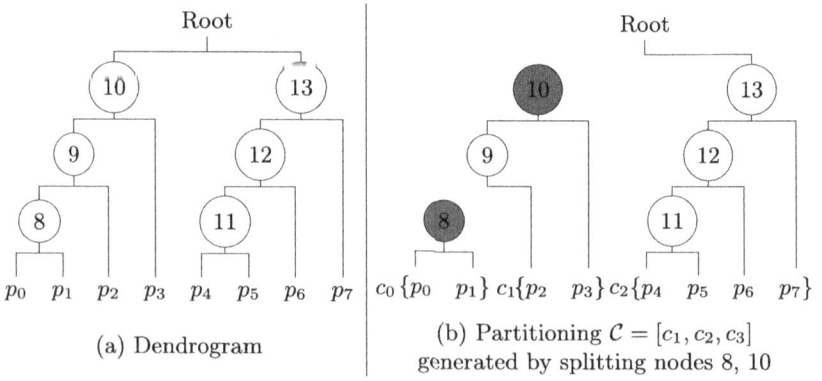

Fig. 3. How hierarchical clustering works as a candidate partitioning generator.

Yet, the number of partitionings compatible with a dendrogram is too large for enumeration[2]. Accordingly, InfoClus resorts to a greedy strategy to iteratively find a sequence of PwXs with an increasing number of clusters and high

---
[1] Its use will be compared to that of k-means in Sect. 4.1.
[2] There are 56 different partitionings in a dendrogram generated by a 8 points dataset.

explanation ratios, where each *PwX* is obtained by splitting one node extra from the previous *PwX*. More precisely, at iteration k, InfoClus considers partitionings with $k+1$ clusters by enumerating all *PwX*s formed by cutting any subtree of the *PwX* we chosen at $k-1$ iteration. The partitioning with highest *explanation ratio* is selected as the *PwX* at iteration k. Thus, K iterations of the greedy procedure yield a sequence of K *PwX*s of size $2, \ldots, K+1$. The *PwX* in this sequence with highest *explanation ratio* is the one finally selected.

Example. Figure 3a presents a dendrogram generated for the example dataset by hierarchical clustering. Given $\alpha = 1, \beta = 2$, we have 5 candidate partitionings with 2 clusters: those obtained by splitting subtrees with root of node 8, 9, 10, 11 or 12. After computing the best explanations for each of these partitionings, we find the associated *explanation ratios* to be $0.18, 0.34, 0.67, 0.18$ and 0.34 respectively. The partitioning generated by splitting node 10 is the best one with $R_{1,2} = 0.67$; this corresponds to *PwX* $(\mathcal{C}', \mathcal{E}')$. The next iteration considers partitionings with 3 clusters that could be obtained by splitting one more node (node 8, 9, 11 or 12) out of *PwX* $(\mathcal{C}', \mathcal{E}')$. For instance, splitting node 8 out of *PwX* $(\mathcal{C}', \mathcal{E}')$ would lead to a new partitioning $[c_1 : \{p_0, p_1\}, c_2 : \{p_2, p_3\}, c_3 : \{p_4 ... p_7\}]$.

Time Budget. In the following, we call an **iteration** the process through which InfoClus tries different nodes to find a good partitioning with k clusters based on the partitioning with $k-1$ previously selected clusters. Iterations can be conducted as long as there are possible nodes to consider, but a partitioning of a dataset with almost as many clusters as points might not be desirable. Therefore, in the implementation of InfoClus we introduce a time budget t, which imposes InfoClus to terminate before time t.

Search for Explanations. The best explanations for a partitioning in a dataset with homogeneous attributes (e.g. only numeric or categorical) can be found by applying a greedy strategy in each cluster: iteratively adding attributes with highest *information content* to a cluster's explanations until the *explanation ratio* $R_{\alpha,\beta}$ decreases when a new attribute is added. In the code implementation, the number of attributes selected for each cluster can be controlled by hyper-parameters *minatt* and *maxatt*, which serve as lower and upper bounds respectively for the number of attributes used to explain each cluster.

Example. Given $\alpha = 1, \beta = 2$, consider computing the best explanation $\mathcal{E}$ for partitioning $\mathcal{C}' = [c_1 : \{p_0, p_1, p_2, p_3\}, c_2 : \{p_4, p_5, p_6, p_7\}]$ in the example dataset (Fig. 2). We first compute *information content* for both attributes x, y, and both clusters c_1 and c_2. We get $I_1^x, I_1^y, I_2^x, I_2^y = 2.88, 5.68, 5.68, 2.88$. Next, we assign a_2 to c_1 and a_1 to c_2 to make sure that at least one attribute is assigned to each cluster. At this stage, the *explanation ratio* $R_{1,2}$ is 0.67. Then we assign the next attribute (a_1) with highest I to its corresponding cluster (c_1). This results in $R_{1,2} = 0.38$. Since $0.38 < 0.67$, we stop searching, and serve $\mathcal{E}' : [e_1 = \{y\}, e_2 : \{x\}]$ as the best explanation for $\mathcal{C}'$.

Pseudo-code. Full pseudo-code for InfoClus is shown in Algorithm 1.

4 Experiments

Algorithm 1. INFOCLUS

1: **Input:** dataset X, its embedding Y, attributes A, $minAtt$, $maxAtt$, α, β, and t
2: **Output:** a PwX $(\mathcal{C}, \mathcal{E})$
3: Dendrogram = hierarchicalClustering(Y)
4: Nodes = getSplittingNodes(Dendrogram) % Potential splits in dendrogram
5: $bestR$, $bestR^1 = 0$, $best\mathcal{C}$, $best\mathcal{C}^1$ = the full dataset
6: $k = 1$
7: **while** t has not been used up & Nodes is not None **do**
8:     % iteration starts
9:     $k = k + 1$
10:    $bestR^k = 0$, $bestNode^k = None$
11:    **for** $Node$ in Nodes **do**
12:       $\mathcal{C}^k$ = split $Node$ out of $best\mathcal{C}^{k-1}$ to get partitioning
13:       $\mathcal{E}^k$ = find best explanation for $\mathcal{C}^k$ under bounds $minAtt$ and $maxAtt$
14:       compute $R_{\alpha,\beta}(\mathcal{C}^k, \mathcal{E}^k)$
15:       **if** $bestR^k \leq R_{\alpha,\beta}(\mathcal{C}^k, \mathcal{E}^k)$ **then**
16:          $bestR^k = R_{\alpha,\beta}(\mathcal{C}^k, \mathcal{E}^k)$, $best\mathcal{C}^k = \mathcal{C}^k$, $bestNode^k = Node$
17:       **if** $bestR \leq R_{\alpha,\beta}(\mathcal{C}^k, \mathcal{E}^k)$ **then**
18:          $bestR$, $best\mathcal{C}$, $best\mathcal{E} = R_{\alpha,\beta}(\mathcal{C}^k, \mathcal{E}^k)$, $\mathcal{C}^k$, $\mathcal{E}^k$
19:    Update Nodes by removing $bestNode^k$ and its ancestors
20: **return** PwX ($best\mathcal{C}$, $best\mathcal{E}$)

In Sect. 4.1 we first present experiments on three datasets to evaluate the ability of InfoClus to generate useful insights, including a comparative assessment with respect to the state of art [15,21]. We then study the sensitivity of InfoClus to the hyper-parameters (Sect. 4.2), and its scalability (Sect. 4.3).

4.1 Case Study

To evaluate the usefulness of InfoClus, we conduct case studies on three datasets covering different domains and attribute types: the Cytometry, GSE (German Socio-Economic) and Mushroom data; details of which will be introduced below. For the Cytometry data, we compare insights given by InfoClus to manual annotation by domain experts, to InfoClus with k-means, and with RVX [21] and VERA [15]. Embeddings studied in the case studies are generated with t-SNE.

Cytometry Data [16]. The Cytometry dataset represents different cell types of mouse splenocytes, described by 9 columns/features recording the stain of different markers. We conduct the case study on a random sample of 2500 instances from the original dataset, which contains more than 300K instances[3].

---
[3] As in [16], the analysis is conducted on a subsample for the sake of limiting t-SNE's runtime; the scalability of InfoClus with larger data is investigated in Sect. 4.3.

Advantageously for this case study, the data has been annotated by domain experts through manual gating [16]. This enables us to compare insights derived by InfoClus with an expert procedure.

Manual gating, routinely used in the analysis of cytometry data [11,16], proceeds by iteratively plotting cells on two-dimensional scatter plots with respect to a chosen subset of features, and selecting at each step a subset of cells on which to further focus in the next iteration [16]. The sequence of features studied at each step is determined by expert knowledge. Figure 4a1, reproduced from [16], represents the results of this process in a t-SNE embedding of the Cytometry dataset. The manual gating process is illustrated by Fig. 4b1, in which arrows indicate the sequence in which the analysis is conducted.

Qualitative Analysis. We applied InfoClus on Cytometry with hyperparameters $\alpha = 1500$, $\beta = 1.5$, $minatt = 2$ and $maxatt = 5$. Given a 5 s limit for iterations (t in Algorithm 1), InfoClus conducted 9 iterations. Figure 4a2 and Fig. 4b2 display the resulting 6 clusters, and their explanations (i.e., the distributions of features selected as explanations for each cluster).

Combining the partitioning and explanations provided by InfoClus (Fig. 4a2, b2), cluster 1 and 2 stand out—the former being characterized by high CD19 and low CD3, and the latter by high CD3 and low CD19. These findings align with those of experts, which also use CD19 and CD3 to identify B and T cells—as displayed in the 2nd row, 3rd and 4th sub-figures in Fig. 4b1. Similar conclusions apply to cluster 3 (orange in a1; characterized by higher Ly6G and CD11b; labeled by experts as Neutrophils); cluster 4 (purple; higher CD11c; labeled as DCs), and cluster 5 (Ochre; higher CD64 and Autofluo; labeled as Macrophages). Altogether, the clusters and explanations generated by InfoClus align with those of domain experts. InfoClus may even help in uncovering possible inconsistencies in labels generated by manual gating: for instance, points in a cluster in the top-left of Fig. 4a1 share similar values in high dimension, but are labeled as different cells—red (B cells) and purple (Neutrophils) labels.

Comparison. We now compare InfoClus to other methods aimed at explaining embeddings: InfoClus with k-means, RVX [21], and VERA [15]. InfoClus with k-means proceeds by running k-means on a dataset for a range of K different values ($k = 3, 4, 5, \ldots, 32$ here), generating K partitionings. Each partitioning is then associated to a set of explanations with best PwX in terms of *explanation ratio*; the final partitioning selected is the one with highest PwX among the K candidates. Descriptions of RVX and VERA have been presented in Sect. 2.

Figure 5 shows the partitionings and explanations provided by InfoClus with k-means, RVX, and VERA on the Cytometry dataset. We compare these to the InfoClus result of Fig. 4a1. Explanation ratios for InfoClus and InfoClus with k-means are 5.61 and 5.39 respectively (Fig. 5a). With k-means, clusters are roughly evenly sized and visually less in line with the structure of the embedding than those generated by InfoClus: the top-right block of points in the embeddings is split in three (blue, green and pink clusters), while the disconnected point sets in the top-left corner are considered a single cluster (red).

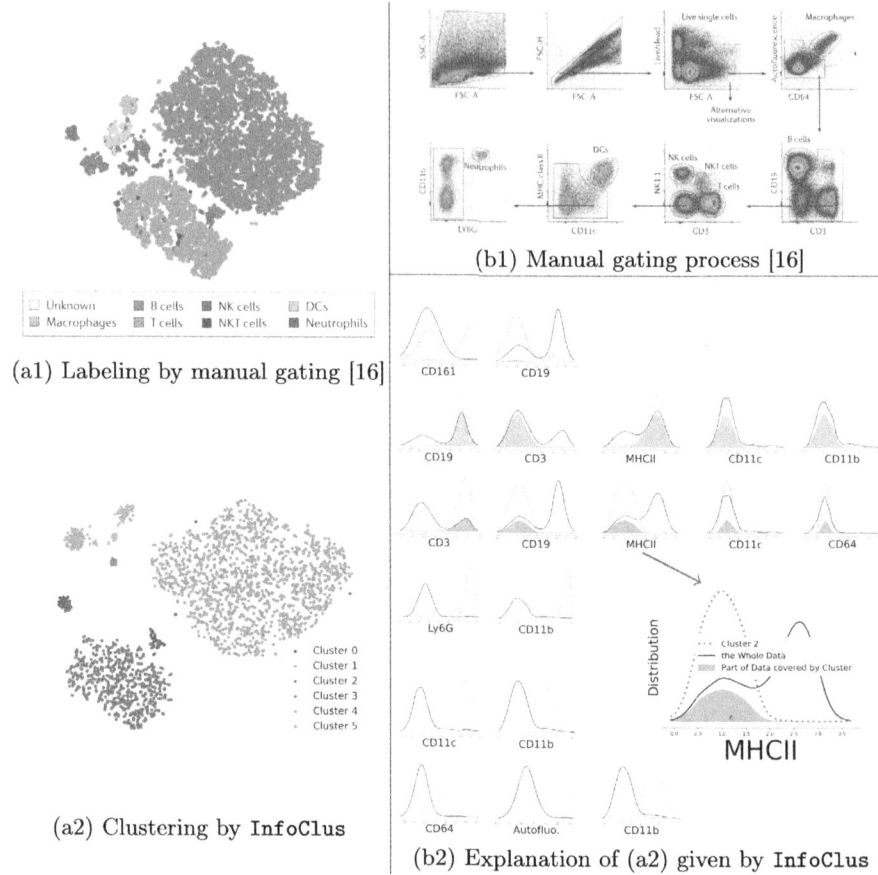

Fig. 4. Cytometry dataset. Panels a1 and a2 show t-SNE embeddings colored by manual gating [16] and by InfoClus respectively (the embeddings are slightly different because the available data is not equivalent to that in the original paper and we use a different implementation of t-SNE). Panel b1 shows how manual gating proceeds to label cells in a2. Panel b2 displays the explanations selected by InfoClus for each cluster (the color coding maps explanations to their respective clusters). Each plot displays Kernel Density Estimates (KDE) of the distributions of the attribute in the cluster (dotted line) and on the full dataset (solid line). Filled color represents a KDE of the cluster scaled by how many points are covered by the cluster in the full data.

In Fig. 5b we find that RVX also shows clear cluster structure, even though it is not a clustering method. However, the largest cluster lacks any clear visual structure. Note also that by definition of the method, each point is associated to exactly one attribute and not more. This is probably why the B cells that comprise the top-right cluster do not form a visually coherent cluster, they are not defined through any single attribute.

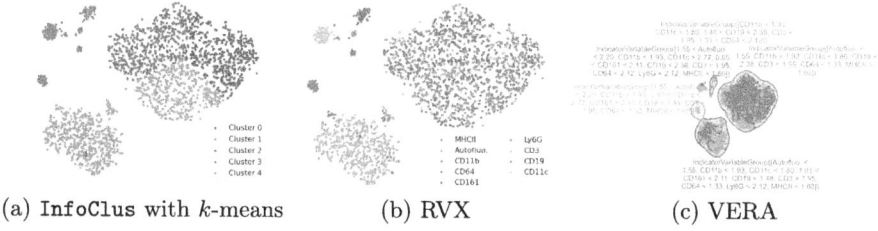

(a) InfoClus with k-means (b) RVX (c) VERA

Fig. 5. Results of other methods aimed at explaining embeddings on Cytometry

The clusters generated by VERA (Fig. 5c) are visually coherent, but the annotations involve almost all attributes in the data. The threshold-based explanations given by VERA also cause the coverage of the clusters to be low, i.e., the explanations cover only part of the points in the identified regions.

German Socio-economics (GSE) data [4]. This dataset describes 412 administrative districts of Germany in terms of 31 socio-demographic attributes, such as distributions of population age and labor sector, and voting percentages, recorded at the 2009 elections. We set hyper-parameters on this dataset as follows: $\alpha = 50$, $\beta = 1.5$, $minatt = 2$ and $maxatt = 5$. Given a 5s limit for iterations, InfoClus conducted 18 iterations and returned a partitioning with 3 clusters, presented alongside their explanations in Fig. 6.

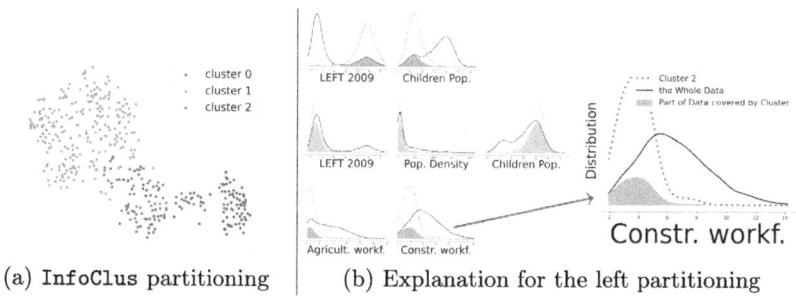

(a) InfoClus partitioning   (b) Explanation for the left partitioning

Fig. 6. InfoClus analysis in GSE

In Fig. 6, the voting ratio of the LEFT party in 2009 is selected as the most interesting attribute in both cluster 0 and 1, with high and low support respectively. Cluster 2 stands out for the low shares of its workforce working in agriculture and construction, hinting that cluster 2 might correspond to urban areas. We verify this insight using metadata of GSE: 86% of districts in cluster 2 are urban, compared of 28% of all districts in the data. Out of interest, we visualized the partitioning of districts on the German map (Fig. 7). Indeed, Cluster 0 and 1 are clearly geographically separate, and correspond to former East and West Germany, and cluster 2 corresponds in a large part to the Ruhr area, shown in

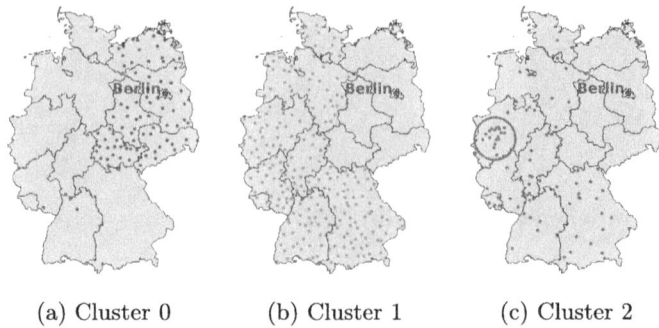

(a) Cluster 0 (b) Cluster 1 (c) Cluster 2

Fig. 7. Visualization of `InfoClus` clusters on the map of Germany.

the red circle in Fig. 7c. Note that this geographic coherence is striking as t-SNE and `InfoClus` do not know about the geographic location of the districts: these clusters emerged purely from demographic and voting statistics.

UCI Mushroom Data [22]. Mushroom consists of 8124 instances characterized by 22 categorical attributes that describe 23 species of gilled mushrooms within the Agaricus and Lepiota family. We considered this data to investigate `InfoClus`' ability to interpret embeddings of categorical data. We set hyperparameters on this dataset as follows: $\alpha = 800$, $\beta = 1.5$, $minatt = 2$ and $maxatt = 5$. Given a limit of 30 s for iterations, `InfoClus` conducted 10 iterations and returned a partitioning with 4 clusters, shown in Fig. 8.

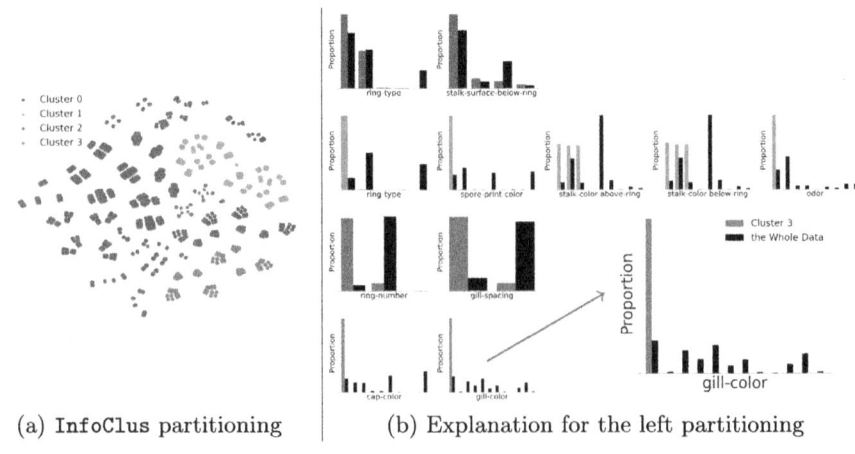

(a) `InfoClus` partitioning (b) Explanation for the left partitioning

Fig. 8. `InfoClus` analysis on Mushroom dataset.

Four visually coherent clusters emerge, differing from the dataset as a whole with respect to several attributes: for instance, large rings and orange print colors for cluster 1, low ring number and close gill spacing for cluster 2, purple caps and red gill colors for cluster 3. Unfortunately, a lack of background on mushrooms prevents us from further interpreting these findings.

4.2 Hyper-parameter Analysis

We now investigate the sensitivity of InfoClus' results to hyperparameter selection, using the Cytometry dataset. Since t, $minatt$ and $maxatt$ (respectively: imposed iteration time, minimum and maximum features per cluster) should be fixed based on users' preference, we focus on the role of hyper-parameters α and β. In the following experiment, we set $minatt = 2$, $maxatt = 5$, and $t = 5$.

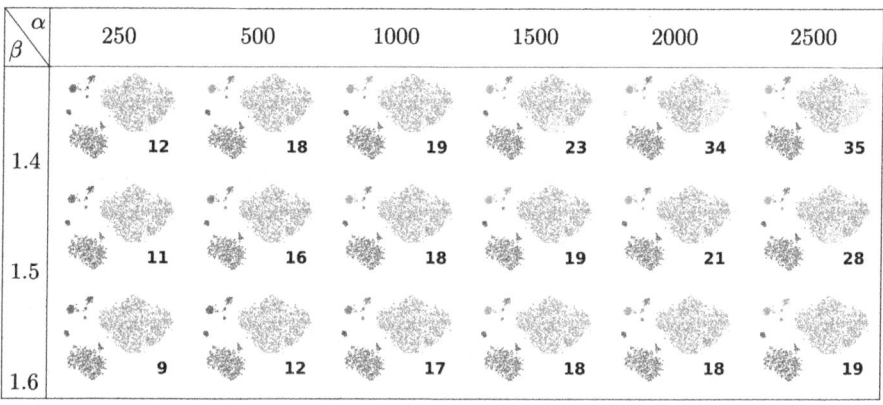

Fig. 9. Hyper-parameter analysis on Cytometry. partitionings generated by InfoClus under different α and β are shown, along with the numbers of attributes selected for all clusters (bottom right corner).

Figure 9 displays the evolution of InfoClus clusters and the total number of explanatory attributes selected for different values of α and β (α varying from 250 to 2500, β from 1.4 to 1.6). The number of InfoClus clusters increases when α increases, and decreases when β increases. Similarly, the number of selected attributes increases with α increases, and decreases when β increases. This was to be expected given the definition of the *explanation ratio* (R) (Definition 4). α and β both intervene in R's denominator $\alpha + (\sum_{i=1}^{r} \sum_{j=1}^{|e_i|} |a_i^j|)^\beta$. Increasing β promotes sparser explanations. When α increases, the weight of $(\sum_{i=1}^{r} \sum_{j=1}^{|e_i|} |a_i^j|)^\beta$ decreases in the denominator, with similar effect to a decrease in β.

Nevertheless, partitionings does not change heavily when α and β vary. It is a good signal for users that even they have few knowledge about InfoClus, InfoClus might also return a reasonable result. We also suggest users to select α between $n/10$ and n, and β around 1.5.

Table 1. Scalability of `InfoClus` on samples from `Cytometry` with various size

Sample size ($\times 10^3$)		2.5	5	10	20	30	50	80	Trend
Time (s)	Initialization rows 3-6 in Algorithm 1	7.1	15.6	34.6	71.8	109	190	322	
	Avg. per iteration rows 11-18 in Algorithm 1	0.6	1.4	3.3	6.1	8.6	16.7	32.2	
Time ($\times 10^{-4}$s)	Avg. per partitioning rows 12-18 in Algorithm 1	2.6	2.8	3.3	3.0	2.9	3.3	4.0	

4.3 Scalability Analysis

We next turn to the analysis of `InfoClus`' scalability. `InfoClus`' runtime can be divided into two components: initialization and searching for a good PwX. The initialization proceeds: by i) computing embeddings, if none are user-provided; ii) computing a hierarchical clustering of the embeddings; iii) computing statistics used downstream for computing *explanation ratios* (means and variances of candidate clusters), see Appendix ?? for details. The search for the optimal PwX then proceeds using these components.

As users may impose an upper bound t on total runtime, measuring the overall time spent on the search phase is meaningless. We instead list the time spent for initialization and describe the search phase by the time spent per iteration and per partitioning. The time spent per iteration corresponds to the average time spent to find the best k-cluster partitioning starting from a partitioning with $k-1$ clusters. The time spent per partitioning is the time used to select the top explanations of a partitioning with respect to the *explanation ratio* R.

Table 1 reports runtimes of `InfoClus` components, computed on samples of increasing size drawn from the original `Cytometry` dataset. The experiments were conducted on a machine equipped with a 13th Gen Intel(R) Core(th) i7-1365U (5.20 GHz) and 16.0 GB of RAM.

First, initialization is a rather costly process although it is only run once: 5 min are required to initialize a dataset with size of 80,000. Second, we turn to the average times per iteration and partitioning in the PwX search phase. These two quantities can be formally related: the cost per iteration is at most the product of the data size n with the cost per partitioning[4]. The time needed per partitioning seems to fluctuate as data size n varies, with no obvious increase or decrease trend. The absolute time for each partitioning is quite small with an order of magnitude of 10^{-4} seconds. Altogether, these results indicate that `InfoClus` can credibly scale to problems of at least moderate size.

---

[4] Partitionings are generated by splitting notes from the dendrogram generated by the hierarchical clustering. This dendrogram has at most $n-1$ nodes, including its root.

5 Discussion

In this paper, we introduced InfoClus, which finds a partitioning of an embedding that is cohesive in both the high-dimension and low-dimension space and also returns explanations in the form of attributes that stand out for each cluster. By constraining the solution with a hierarchical clustering, using greedy optimization with locally optimal cuts, we obtain an efficient and effective algorithm. By means of two hyperparameters, users can control how fine-grained (i.e., complex) the output is. We have found from the empirical results that the solutions can be helpful and that have distinct advantages over existing approaches.

The proposed method and experiments have several limitations that could be addressed in future work. We do not know the computational complexity to find optimal PwXs compatible with hierarchical clustering, it may be possible to identify better optimization strategies than greedy. Also, the search strategy can lead to disconnected clusters because they can be nested. To prevent this, a different approach would be necessary. Finally, it would be interesting to consider how to unify the *information content* for discrete and numeric variables, enabling the use of InfoClus on mixed data.

Acknowledgments. The research leading to these results has received funding from the Special Research Fund (BOF) of Ghent University (BOF20/IBF/117), from the Flemish Government under the "Onderzoeksprogramma Artificiële Intelligentie (AI) Vlaanderen" programme, from the FWO (project no. G0F9816N, 3G042220, G073924N). Funded by the European Union (ERC, VIGILIA, 101142229). Views and opinions expressed are however those of the author(s) only and do not necessarily reflect those of the European Union or the European Research Council Executive Agency. Neither the European Union nor the granting authority can be held responsible for them. For the purpose of Open Access the author has applied a CC BY public copyright licence to any Author Accepted Manuscript version arising from this submission. EH is supported by a doctoral scholarship from the FWO (project number: 11J2322N)

Disclosure of Interests. The authors have no competing interests to declare that are relevant to the content of this article.

References

1. Artelt, A., Schulz, A., Hammer, B.: "Why here and not there?" – diverse contrasting explanations of dimensionality reduction. https://arxiv.org/abs/2206.07391
2. Bibal, A., Clarinval, A., Dumas, B., Frénay, B.: IXVC: an interactive pipeline for explaining visual clusters in dimensionality reduction visualizations with decision trees. Array 100080 (2021)
3. de Bodt, C., Mulders, D., López-Sánchez, D., Verleysen, M., Lee, J.A.: Class-aware t-SNE: cat-SNE. In: Proceedings of the ESANN (2019)
4. Boley, M., Mampaey, M., Kang, B., Tokmakov, P., Wrobel, S.: One click mining: interactive local pattern discovery through implicit preference and performance learning. In: Proceedings of the ACM SIGKDD IDEA Workshop, pp. 27–35 (2013)
5. Cavallo, M., Ç. Demiralp: A visual interaction framework for dimensionality reduction based data exploration. In: Proceedings of the CHI (2018)

6. Chatzimparmpas, A., Martins, R.M., Kerren, A.: T-visne: interactive assessment and interpretation of t-SNE projections. IEEE TVCG **26**(8), 2696–2714 (2020)
7. De Bie, T.: An information theoretic framework for data mining. In: Proceedings of the ACM SIGKDD, pp. 564–572 (2011)
8. Espadoto, M., et al.: Unprojection: leveraging inverse-projections for visual analytics of high-dimensional data. IEEE TVCG **29**, 1559–1572 (2023)
9. Faust, R., Glickenstein, D., Scheidegger, C.: Dimreader: axis lines that explain non-linear projections. IEEE TVCG **25**(1), 481–490 (2019)
10. Kobak, D., Berens, P.: The art of using t-SNE for single-cell transcriptomics. Nat. Commun. **10**, 5416 (2019)
11. Liu, P., et al.: Comprehensive evaluation and practical guideline of gating methods for high-dimensional cytometry data: manual gating, unsupervised clustering, and auto-gating. Briefings Bioinform. **26**(1), bbae633 (2025)
12. Maaten, L., Hinton, G.: Visualizing data using t-SNE. JMLR **9**(86), 2579–2605 (2008)
13. McInnes, L., Healy, J., Melville, J.: UMAP: Uniform manifold approximation and projection for dimension reduction. https://arxiv.org/abs/1802.03426 (2018)
14. Montambault, B., Appleby, G., Rogers, J., Brumar, C.D., Li, M., Chang, R.: Dimbridge: interactive explanation of visual patterns in dimensionality reductions with predicate logic. IEEE TVCG **31**(1), 207–217 (2024)
15. Policar, P.G., Zupan, B.: VERA: Generating visual explanations of two-dimensional embeddings via region annotation. arXiv:2406.04808 (2024)
16. Saeys, Y., Van Gassen, S., Lambrecht, B.: Computational flow cytometry: helping to make sense of high-dimensional immunology data. Nat. Rev. Immunol. **16**, 449–462 (2016)
17. Salmanian, P., Chatzimparmpas, A., Karaca, A.C., Martins, R.M.: DimVis: interpreting visual clusters in dimensionality reduction with explainable boosting machine. arXiv:2402.06885 (2024)
18. Sedlmair, M., Brehmer, M., Ingram, S., Munzner, T.: Dimensionality reduction in the wild: Gaps and guidance. Technical Repport 2012-03, UBC Computer Science (2012)
19. Sohns, J.T., Schmitt, M., Jirasek, F., Hasse, H., Leitte, H.: Attribute-based explanation of non-linear embeddings of high-dimensional data. IEEE TVCG **28**(1), 540–550 (2022)
20. Stahnke, J., Dörk, M., Müller, B., Thom, A.: Probing projections: interaction techniques for interpreting arrangements and errors of dimensionality reductions. IEEE TVCG **22**(1), 629–638 (2015)
21. Thijssen, J., Tian, Z., Telea, A.: Scaling up the explanation of multidimensional projections. In: EuroVis Workshop on Visual Analytics (2023)
22. UCI Machine Learning Repository: Mushroom (1981). https://doi.org/10.24432/C5959T. Accessed 12 Mar 2025
23. Xia, J., Huang, L., Lin, W., Zhao, X., Wu, J., Chen, Y.: Interactive visual cluster analysis by contrastive dimensionality reduction. IEEE TVCG **29**(1), 734–744 (2024)

Open Access This chapter is licensed under the terms of the Creative Commons Attribution 4.0 International License (http://creativecommons.org/licenses/by/4.0/), which permits use, sharing, adaptation, distribution and reproduction in any medium or format, as long as you give appropriate credit to the original author(s) and the source, provide a link to the Creative Commons license and indicate if changes were made.

The images or other third party material in this chapter are included in the chapter's Creative Commons license, unless indicated otherwise in a credit line to the material. If material is not included in the chapter's Creative Commons license and your intended use is not permitted by statutory regulation or exceeds the permitted use, you will need to obtain permission directly from the copyright holder.

Unimodal Strategies in Density-Based Clustering

Oron Nir[1,2], Jay Tenenbaum[2], and Ariel Shamir[1(✉)]

[1] CANVAS Lab, Reichman University, Herzeliya, Israel
niroron@microsoft.com, arik@runi.ac.il
[2] Microsoft, Herzeliya, Israel
tenenbaumjay@microsoft.com

Abstract. Density-based clustering methods often surpass centroid-based counterparts, when addressing data with noise or arbitrary data distributions common in real-world problems. In this study, we reveal a key property intrinsic to density-based clustering methods regarding the relation between the number of clusters and the neighborhood radius of core points—we empirically show that it is nearly unimodal, and support this claim theoretically in a specific setting. We leverage this property to devise new strategies for finding appropriate values for the radius more efficiently based on the Ternary Search algorithm. This is especially important for large scale data that is high-dimensional, where parameter tuning is computationally intensive. We validate our methodology through extensive applications across a range of high-dimensional, large-scale NLP, Audio, and Computer Vision tasks, demonstrating its practical effectiveness and robustness. This work not only offers a significant advancement in parameter control for density-based clustering but also broadens the understanding regarding the relations between their guiding parameters. Our code is available at https://github.com/oronnir/UnimodalStrategies.

Keywords: Density-based clustering · Efficient parameter search

1 Introduction

Clustering, a fundamental task in machine learning, is pivotal in uncovering patterns and structures in unlabeled data. Among various clustering algorithms, density-based methods have gained significant attention due to their ability to identify clusters of arbitrary shapes and sizes. Notably, variants of Density-Based Spatial Clustering of Applications with Noise (DBSCAN) [1] are widely used today by researchers and data scientists. Unlike centroid-based methods that assume spherical cluster shapes, density-based approaches are adept at discovering clusters with complex geometries and noisy examples, making them more suitable for real-world data that often exhibit irregular distributions [2].

A significant challenge in leveraging the full potential of density-based clustering lies in parameter tuning. Parameters such as ε and $MinPts$. These user-defined parameters affect cluster formation in DBSCAN and its variants, critically influence the clustering outcome, such as the resulting number of clusters denoted by k. Misconfigured parameter invocation can lead to over-segmentation or under-segmentation of data, significantly affecting the quality and interpretability of the results. This is particularly challenging in high-dimensional, large-scale datasets where the intuitive understanding of parameter effects is less apparent and search for values is costly [3].

Our key insight centers on the relationship between these parameters and the resulting number of clusters. Specifically, we observe that when $MinPts$ is held constant, the number of clusters k produced by DBSCAN varies with the neighborhood radius ε in a quasi-unimodal fashion. This means that as ε increases from very small to very large values, the number of clusters first increases, reaches a peak, and then decreases. Using this observation, we address the parameter tuning challenge, by automatically finding the parameter ε^* that maximizes the number of clusters $k(\varepsilon)$. While ε^* may not always yield the "optimal" clustering for all datasets, it provides critical insight into the clustering structure. For values $\varepsilon \gg \varepsilon^*$ there is over-clustering (i.e., one large cluster at the extreme), and for values $\varepsilon \ll \varepsilon^*$ there is under-clustering (i.e., too many samples are treated as noise). Hence, it is clear that values around ε^* are the "interesting" and important ones. Our method approximates ε^*, addressing the challenge of parameter tuning in density-based clustering.

To demonstrate the efficacy of our proposed method, we apply it to high-dimensional, large-scale classification datasets. Our experiments reveal that not only does our method consistently achieve the target number of clusters, but it also enhances the quality of the clustering supervised evaluation metrics over state-of-the-art (SOTA) methods. Empirical evidence also underscores the advantage of our method in achieving less noise points which is important when working with noisy data.

This study contributes to the field of density-based clustering by:

- Discovering the Unimodal property in density-based clustering, demonstrating this both theoretically and practically.
- Proposing the efficient Ternary Search for real-world data parameter tuning.
- Sharing our code at https://github.com/oronnir/UnimodalStrategies.

2 Related Work

Clustering methods in data mining have been extensively studied, sometimes focusing on handling synthetic, separable, and low-dimension data distributions using benchmarks which could be insufficient for a rigorous evaluation and may lead to overfitting [4]. Density-based methods like DBSCAN [1] excel at handling noise and discovering arbitrary-shaped clusters in high dimensions, surpassing centroid-based approaches.

Several variants of DBSCAN, such as OPTICS [5], VDBSCAN [6], and ADBSCAN [7], have been introduced to address varying-density clusters and improve scalability. These approaches typically trade off runtime efficiency for parameter optimization. HDBSCAN [8], for instance, adopts a multi-resolution framework to self-tune parameters. Methods that extend DBSCAN while retaining its dependence on ε are not considered as a baseline in this paper. Note that unsupervised learning methods inherently depend on specific mathematical properties of data, making it unlikely for any single method to be universally optimal. Notably, DBSCAN's assumption of uniform density regions and the existence of an ideal $(\varepsilon, MinPts)$ pair is often unmet in practice.

Parameter Selection in Density-Based Clustering: The performance of DBSCAN and its variants depends heavily on parameter settings: while $MinPts$ is intuitive as an application-dependent integer, $\varepsilon \in \mathbb{R}_{>0}$ is challenging to tune in high-dimensional spaces. Ester et al. [1] suggests using the Elbow Method manually over the k-dist plot which is considered a folklore heuristic for density shift and k selection in algorithms like k-means. However, this method is found suboptimal by Schubert [2]. Several studies have automated and further optimized the k-dist plot heuristic for parameter selection e.g., [6,9]. These methods aim to reduce the user intervention required in the clustering process, but often face challenges in handling high-dimensional and large-scale datasets. Researchers [10,11] revisit the challenge, noting that $MinPts$ is easier to tune than ε, and suggest setting $MinPts = 2D$ where D is the dimension of the data. Assuming for example, $D > 100$, such a $MinPts$ value could lead to either enhanced noise robustness or into an under-segmented solution. Another common practice is dimensionality reduction. However, in this work we aim at enhancing density-based clustering over the raw data in high-dimension.

Advancements in Parameter Optimization: Recent studies have explored various optimization techniques. SS-DBSCAN [12] and AMD-DBSCAN [13] both suggest an exhaustive grid-search approach for $MinPts$, where the former includes an automated version of the Elbow method using stratified sampling. AEDBSCAN [14] assigns a per-point radius to optimize ε for a fixed $MinPts$. These algorithms essentially apply exhaustive search of the optimal parameters without relying on the underlying algorithm properties and their results are reported over low dimensional synthetic datasets. We consider the following density-based parameter tuning methods as the SOTA baselines [5,6,8,9,12–14].

In summary, while density-based clustering methods offer advantages in handling non-linearly separable data, their reliance on parameter settings poses a significant challenge, especially in high-dimensional and large-scale scenarios. Our work builds upon these foundations, proposing an efficient method for parameter tuning that is responsive to these data representation challenges.

3 Preliminaries

We establish standard DBSCAN algorithm definitions and notations,

Definition 1 (Dataset). *Let (M, d) be a metric space and a distance metric. A dataset $X = \{x_1, \ldots, x_N\} \subseteq M$ is a finite subset of M.*

Definition 2 (DBSCAN Parameters). *For a dataset $X \in \mathbb{R}^{N \times D}$, DBSCAN receives $\varepsilon \in \mathbb{R}_{>0}$ and $MinPts \in \mathbb{N}_{\geq 2}$ as user-defined parameters.*

Definition 3 (ε-ball and Neighborhood). *For a point $p \in \mathbb{R}^D$, X, and $\varepsilon > 0$:*

$$\text{Let } B_\varepsilon(p) = \{y \in \mathbb{R}^D : d(p, y) \leq \varepsilon\} \quad \text{be the } \varepsilon\text{-ball centered at } p$$
$$\text{and let } N_\varepsilon(p) = B_\varepsilon(p) \cap X \quad \text{be the } \varepsilon\text{-neighborhood of } p$$

Definition 4 (Core and Border Points). *For ε and $MinPts$:*

- *A point $p \in X$ is a core point if $|N_\varepsilon(p)| \geq MinPts$*
- *A point $b \in X$ is a border point if:*
  - *$b \in B_\varepsilon(p)$ for some core point p*
  - *$|N_\varepsilon(p)| < MinPts$ (not itself a core point)*
- *p is a noise point if it is neither a core nor a border point*

Definition 5 (Density-Reachability). *Two points $p, q \in X$ are density-reachable at radius ε if there exists a sequence of points $\{p_1, \ldots, p_t\} \subseteq X$ such that:*

1. *$p_1 = p$ and $p_t = q$*
2. *Each p_i is a core point for $i < t$*
3. *$p_{i+1} \in B_\varepsilon(p_i)$ for all $i < t$*

Definition 6 (Cluster). *A cluster c is a maximal set of points where:*

- *At least one point in c is a core point*
- *Non-core points in c are within ε-radius of a core point in c*
- *All core points in c are mutually density-reachable*

DBSCAN forms clusters by identifying core points and their density-reachable neighbors within ε-radii. Non-core points that are density-reachable from core points become border points, and the remaining points are classified as noise [11].

Let $\mathbf{A} : \mathbb{R}^{N \times D} \times \mathbb{R} \times \mathbb{N} \to \mathbb{N}^N$ denote DBSCAN or a variant of DBSCAN, let $\mathcal{C} := \mathbf{A}(X, \varepsilon, MinPts) \in \mathbb{N}^N$ be $\mathbf{A}$'s output clustering assignment, and let $\mathbf{K}(\mathcal{C}) = |\{c_i \in \mathcal{C}\}_{i=1}^N|$ be the function which counts the number of clusters $\mathbf{A}$ returns. We often refer to $\mathbf{K}(\mathcal{C})$ by using the variable k when clear from context and characterize it as a function of ε,

$$k(\varepsilon) := \mathbf{K}(\mathbf{A}(X, \varepsilon, MinPts)) \tag{1}$$

4 The Unimodality Property

We make a fundamental observation regarding DBSCAN, that for a fixed $MinPts$, $k(\varepsilon)$ (Eq. 1) is *near-unimodal*. This is since **1.** low values of ε label more examples as noise so less clusters are formed (specifically for $\varepsilon < min_{i \neq j} d(x_i, x_j)$ there are no core points), while **2.** high values of ε combine clusters together and gradually reduce the number of clusters (for $\varepsilon \geq max_{i,j} d(x_i, x_j)$ there is a single cluster since all points are mutually density-reachable).

We identify in a counter-example in Fig. 1, that $k(\varepsilon)$ is not necessarily strictly unimodal as per the standard definition, i.e., monotonically non-decreasing up to the mode and monotonically non-increasing thereafter [15]. However, we empirically demonstrate the *near-unimodality* of $k(\varepsilon)$ over 24 real-life datasets, and support this by a statistical test (DIP [15]) in Sect. 6, and a theoretical analysis.

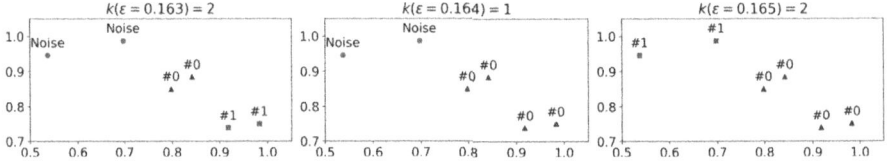

Fig. 1. A counter-example with non-unimodal behavior of $k(\varepsilon)$ in $\mathbb{R}^2$ and L_2.

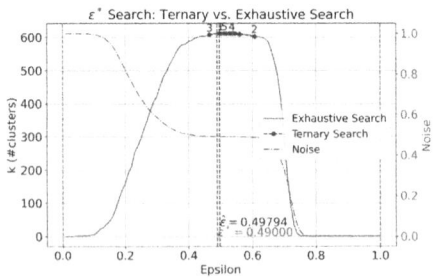

Fig. 2. TS convergence steps in blue vs. Exhaustive Search in red over the FACE dataset (N = 45k with noise). The grey line illustrates the percentage of noise (Color figure online).

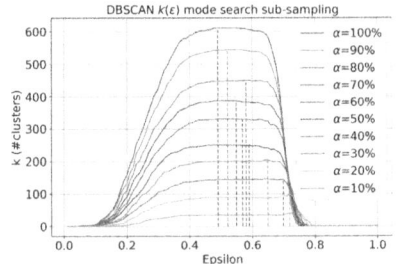

Fig. 3. Exhaustive search of $k(\varepsilon)$ unimodality for different sample sizes (α). When α grows ε_α^* shrinks monotonically, hence used as an UB in our method.

4.1 Theoretical Analysis

To support our unimodality claim, we give a theoretical analysis of DBSCAN running on a dataset $X = \{x_1, \ldots, x_N\}$ of iid uniform samples $\forall i, x_i \sim U[0,1]^D$. We acknowledge this distribution is non-standard for clustering, but it is a first step towards understanding this property in more general distributions. First, for $MinPts = 2$, a common choice for this parameter, and $D = 1$. Theorem 1 gives and proves the explicit unimodal function describing $E_X[k(\varepsilon)]$, and gives its mode. We note that in experimental evaluations which are omitted, we saw that a law of large numbers appears, and for $N > 1,000$, even for any single random dataset $X \sim U[[0,1]^N]$, almost always the resulting $k(\varepsilon)$ was surprisingly close to the unimodal function $E_X[k(\varepsilon)]$ over the whole domain $\varepsilon > 0$, hence near-unimodal itself. Then, we consider the setting where N is large, and assume that $MinPts$ grows as a function of N (this is standard in DBSCAN for large datasets). For ease of presentation, we assume a constant ratio $\rho = MinPts/N \in (0,1)$ between $MinPts$ and N. This setting is natural for DBSCAN since doubling the dataset size means that the expected number of points in each ε-ball should roughly double. To warm up, Theorem 2 considers $D = 1$, and then Theorem 3 considers a general $D \in \mathbb{N}$, and they both prove that $k(\varepsilon)$ is not trivially 0 or 1 only for $\varepsilon \approx \frac{1}{2}\rho^{\frac{1}{D}}$ (much stronger than the bounds to come in Sect. 5.1). We stress that while we present our results for a constant ratio ρ, they in fact hold for a sufficiently large but reasonable N for any setting where $MinPts$ grows (e.g., logarithmically) with N, and linearly with D (a common assumption is that $MinPts > D$). This suggests that when we search for ε^*, first identifying the often small region in which $k(\cdot)$ is not trivial, can improve runtime and accuracy.

Theorem 1. *Consider DBSCAN running on a uniformly sampled dataset $X \sim U[[0,1]^N]$ with parameter $MinPts = 2$. The expected number of clusters as a function of $\varepsilon > 0$ is $E_X[k(\varepsilon)] = (N-1) \cdot (1-\varepsilon)_+^N - (N-2) \cdot (1-2\varepsilon)_+^N$ where $y_+ := \max(y, 0)$. This is a unimodal function maximized at $\varepsilon_0 = \frac{a-1}{2a-1} \approx_{N\to\infty} \frac{\ln(2)}{N}$ for $a := (\frac{2N-2}{N-2})^{\frac{1}{N-1}}$, with expected value $E_X[k(\varepsilon_0)] \approx_{N\to\infty} \frac{N}{4}$.*

Proof (Proof Idea). Consider the order statistics $u_1 \leq \ldots \leq u_N$ of X, and the differences, often called *spacings*, $s_i := u_i - u_{i-1}$ (by convention $u_0 := 0$, $u_{N+1} := 1$). Let U_i be the event that u_i is the rightmost point of a cluster. Note that for $1 < i \leq N-1$, U_i occurs iff u_i is a core point and the cluster does not extend to the right, i.e., $U_i = (s_i < \varepsilon) \wedge (s_{i+1} > \varepsilon)$. This occurs w.p.

$$P_X[U_i] = P_X[(s_i < \varepsilon) \wedge (s_{i+1} > \varepsilon)] = P_X[s_{i+1} > \varepsilon] - P_X[s_i > \varepsilon \wedge s_{i+1} > \varepsilon].$$

For spacings, it is well known [16] that for any nonnegative values $b_1, \ldots, b_N$ it holds that, $P[\forall i, s_i > b_i] = (1 - \Sigma_i b_i)_+^N$, so we conclude $P_X[U_i] = (1-\varepsilon)_+^N - (1-2\varepsilon)_+^N$. Note that $P[U_1] = 0$ since the leftmost point cannot have a left neighbor, and that $P_X[U_N] = P_X[s_N < \varepsilon] = (1-\varepsilon)_+^N$ because there is no point to its right. Since $E[A] = P[A]$ for a Bernoulli RV A, and by linearity of the expectation, since the number of clusters is the number of rightmost points of clusters,

$$E_X[k(\varepsilon)] = E_X[\Sigma_i \mathbb{1}_{U_i}] = \Sigma_i P_X[U_i] = (N-1) \cdot (1-\varepsilon)_+^N - (N-2) \cdot (1-2\varepsilon)_+^N.$$

To find the optimal ε, note that it is attained at $\varepsilon < 1/2$ and solve $\frac{d}{d\varepsilon} E_X[k(\varepsilon)] = 0$ for ε, i.e., $\frac{d}{d\varepsilon} E_X[k(\varepsilon)] = 2N(N-1)(1-2\varepsilon)^{N-1} - N(N-2)(1-\varepsilon)^{N-1} = 0$. □

We prove the concentration bound,

Theorem 2. *Consider DBSCAN running on a uniformly sampled dataset $X \sim U[[0,1]^N]$, with parameter $MinPts = \rho \cdot N$ for a constant $\rho < \frac{1}{4}$. Then for any $\beta > 1$ and $\delta > 0$, both conditions hold: **1.** for any $\varepsilon > \beta \cdot \frac{\rho}{2}$ and $N > N_\varepsilon$, $P_X[k(\varepsilon) = 1] > 1-\delta$, and **2.** for any $\varepsilon < \frac{1}{\beta} \cdot \frac{\rho}{2}$ and $N > N_\varepsilon$, $P_X[k(\varepsilon) = 0] > 1-\delta$, for an appropriately large $N_\varepsilon = \Omega\left(\log(\frac{1}{\delta \varepsilon q})/(\rho q^2)\right)$ for $q := 1 - \frac{1}{\sqrt{\beta}}$.*

Proof (Proof Idea). For the case $\varepsilon > \beta \cdot \frac{\rho}{2}$, divide $[0,1]$ to the set of segments $S_l = [al - b, al + b]$, for all $l \in \mathbb{N}$ where $b = \frac{\varepsilon}{\sqrt{\beta}}$ is slightly below ε, and $a = \varepsilon - b$. By the Hoeffding inequality and a union bound, w.h.p. all segments S_l centered in $[\varepsilon, 1 - \varepsilon]$ have $\geq MinPts$ points, so for each $x_i \in [\varepsilon, 1-\varepsilon]$, the ε-ball around it contains such a segment (for some $l \in \mathbb{N}$, by the definition of a and the triangle inequality), hence x_i is a core point. Combined with a high probability event that for large enough N, all points are ε-near each other, and that the cluster covers also $[0, \varepsilon]$ and $[1 - \varepsilon, 1]$, we get a single cluster.

For the case $\varepsilon < \frac{1}{\beta} \cdot \frac{\rho}{2}$, divide to segments as above with $b = \varepsilon \cdot \sqrt{\beta}$ slightly above ε, and $a = b - \varepsilon$. By Hoeffding inequality and a union bound, w.h.p. all segments S_l centered in $[\varepsilon, 1 - \varepsilon]$ have $< MinPts$ points, so since the ε-neighborhood of each point x_i is contained in such a segment (for some $l \in \mathbb{N}$, by triangle inequality and $a = b - \varepsilon$), there are no core points hence no clusters. □

We follow similar arguments to those in Theorem 2, and extend it to uniform datasets on the unit cube $[0,1]^D$ of arbitrary dimension $D \in \mathbb{N}$, incurring only an additional $\sqrt{D}$ factor on the upper bound and no additional factor on the lower bound.

Theorem 3. *Consider DBSCAN running on a dataset $X \sim U[[0,1]^{N \times D}]$ of N uniformly sampled points in the unit D-dimensional cube, with parameter $MinPts = \rho \cdot N$ for a constant $\rho < \frac{1}{4}$. Then for any $\beta > 1$ and $\delta > 0$, both conditions hold: **1.** for any $\varepsilon > \sqrt{D}\beta \cdot \frac{1}{2}\rho^{\frac{1}{D}}$ and $N > N_\varepsilon$, $P_X[k(\varepsilon) = 1] > 1 - \delta$, and **2.** for any $\varepsilon < \frac{1}{\beta} \cdot \frac{1}{2}\rho^{\frac{1}{D}}$ and $N > N_\varepsilon$, $P_X[k(\varepsilon) = 0] > 1 - \delta$, for an appropriately large*

$$N_\varepsilon = \Omega\left(\frac{1}{\rho} \cdot \left[\frac{\sqrt{\beta}}{(\frac{1}{\sqrt{\beta}}-1)^2}\right] \cdot \left[D\log(\frac{2}{\beta-\sqrt{\beta}}) + \log(\frac{1}{\rho\alpha})\right]\right).$$

Proof. (Proof Idea). For the case $\varepsilon > \sqrt{D}\beta \cdot \frac{1}{2}\rho^{\frac{1}{D}}$, divide $[0,1]^D$ to the set of cubes $S_{l_1,\ldots,l_D} = [al_1 - b, al_1 + b] \times \ldots \times [al_D - b, al_D + b]$, for all $l_1,\ldots,l_D \in \mathbb{N}$ where $b = \varepsilon/(\sqrt{D}\beta^{\frac{1}{2D}})$ is slightly below $\varepsilon/\sqrt{D}$, and $a = \varepsilon/\sqrt{D} - b$. By the Hoeffding inequality and a union bound, w.h.p. all cubes $S_{l_1,\ldots,l_D}$ centered in the set $[\varepsilon, 1 - \varepsilon]^D \subset [0,1]^D$ have $\geq MinPts$ points, so for each $x_i \in [\varepsilon, 1 - \varepsilon]^D$, the ε-ball around it contains such a cube (for some $l \in \mathbb{N}$, by the definition of a and the triangle inequality, and that the diameter of such cubes are $= \sqrt{D}b$ slightly below ε), hence x_i is a core point. Combined with a high probability event that for large enough N, all points are ε-near each other, and that the cluster covers also the exterior $[0,1]^D \setminus [\varepsilon, 1-\varepsilon]^D$, we get a single cluster.

For the case $\varepsilon < \frac{1}{\beta} \cdot \frac{1}{2}\rho^{\frac{1}{D}}$, divide to cubes as above with $b = \varepsilon \cdot \beta^{\frac{1}{2D}}$ slightly above ε, and $a = b - \varepsilon$. By Hoeffding inequality and a union bound, w.h.p. all cubes $S_{l_1,\ldots,l_D}$ centered in the set $[\varepsilon, 1-\varepsilon]^D$ have $< MinPts$ points, so since the ε-neighborhood of each point x_i is contained in such a cube (for some $l \in \mathbb{N}$, by triangle inequality and $a = b - \varepsilon$), there are no core points hence no clusters. □

These theoretical results demonstrate that, under natural assumptions, to find the value of ε that maximize $k(\varepsilon)$, we can first focus on a small range where $k(\varepsilon)$ is neither trivially 1 nor 0, and subsequently exploit its *near-unimodal* behavior to efficiently find its mode, as discussed in the next section.

5 Method

Our task is to efficiently find the mode of $k(\varepsilon)$,

$$\varepsilon^* = argmax_\varepsilon \{\mathbf{K}(\mathbf{A}(X, \varepsilon, MinPts))\} \qquad (2)$$

The Ternary Search (TS) algorithm by Bajwa et al. [17] finds a maximum in a unimodal (discrete) array. In Sect. 5.1, we adapt it to functions, leveraging the *near unimodality* of $k(\varepsilon)$, to find ε^* using fewer evaluations of $k(\cdot)$ compared to a linear search (see Fig. 2). Then, in Sect. 5.2 we introduce an even quicker estimator (TSE) for ε^*.

5.1 Ternary Search for ε^* (TS)

Our TS algorithm (Algorithm 1) leverages the fact that the function $k(\varepsilon)$ is near-unimodal with mode ε^*. It starts with an initial lower bound (LB) and upper bound (UB) for ε^*, and iteratively (*itr* times) divides it to 3 equal parts and removes at least one of them (see Algorithm 2), to reduce the search space size and still contain the mode. Specifically, for Algorithm 2, we let $m_l = \frac{2LB+UB}{3}$ and $m_r = \frac{LB+2UB}{3}$, and $k_l = k(m_l)$ and $k_r = k(m_r)$ be the respective cluster counts. Recall that the cluster count as a function of ε is initially 0, then increases until it reaches the mode, and then decreases back to 1. Hence, the space reduction logic is as follows: 1. If $k_l = k_r = 1$, the mode must be below them, 2. If $k_l = k_r = 0$, the mode must be above them, 3. if $k_l = 0$ and $k_r = 1$, then the mode is between them, 4. if $k_l > k_r$ then the mode is to the left of m_r and otherwise the mode is to the right of m_l. The edge-case in which $k = 1$ for the very first formed cluster i.e., by chance and not by convergence, is easily detected by the Noise ratio thus omitted for simplicity. We provide both algorithms pseudo-code below.

Upper and Lower Bounds: To efficiently initialize the search space, we use tight bounds UB, LB for ε^*. For bounded metrics, a trivial upper bound UB^0 is simply their bound, and for (unbounded) metrics in general, as in Sect. 4, an

Algorithm 1. $TS(X, LB, UB, MinPts, itr)$

1: **for** i=0 to itr **do**
2:     $m_l \leftarrow \frac{2LB+UB}{3}$
3:     $m_r \leftarrow \frac{LB+2UB}{3}$
4:     $\mathcal{C}_l \leftarrow \mathbf{A}(X, m_l, MinPts)$
5:     $\mathcal{C}_r \leftarrow \mathbf{A}(X, m_r, MinPts)$
6:     $\langle LB, UB \rangle \leftarrow Cond(LB, UB, \ldots$
7:        $m_l, m_r, \mathbf{K}(\mathcal{C}_l), \mathbf{K}(\mathcal{C}_r))$
8: **end for**
9: **return** $\frac{m_l+m_r}{2}$

Algorithm 2. $Cond(LB, UB, m_l, m_r, k_l, k_r)$

1: **if** $k_l == 1$ **and** $k_r == 1$ **then**
2:     **return** $\langle LB, m_l \rangle$
3: **else if** $k_l == 0$ **and** $k_r == 1$ **then**
4:     **return** $\langle m_l, m_r \rangle$
5: **else if** $k_l == 0$ **and** $k_r == 0$ **then**
6:     **return** $\langle m_r, UB \rangle$
7: **else if** $k_l > k_r$ **then**
8:     **return** $\langle LB, m_r \rangle$
9: **else**
10:    **return** $\langle m_l, UB \rangle$
11: **end if**

upper bound is the Diameter $\max_{i,j \in \{1,\ldots,N\}} d(x_i, x_j)$ of X, which we approximate in linear time by doubling a 2-approximation of it. A trivial lower bound LB^0 is 0. We provide an improved heuristic for UB and LB via sampling:

– *Upper Bound (UB):* We observe that empirically, as depicted in Fig. 3, subsampling an α fraction of the data requires a larger radius to form a core-point since data is more sparse, so ε^* increases. Hence, we produce the upper bound

$$UB = TS(X_{\mathcal{R},1:D}, LB^0, UB^0, MinPts, itr) \qquad (3)$$

for $\mathcal{R} \sim \text{Uniform}(G \subset \{1, \ldots, N\} : |G| = \lceil \alpha N \rceil)$

– *Lower Bound (LB):* Empirically, projecting the data on a random subset of αD dimensions, reduces ε^* since it brings the data closer. Hence, define

$$LB = TS(X_{1:N,\mathcal{T}}, LB^0, UB, MinPts, itr) \qquad (4)$$

for $\mathcal{T} \sim \text{Uniform}(H \subset \{1, \ldots, D\} : |H| = \lceil \alpha D \rceil)$

Our resulting clustering algorithm TSClustering (Algorithm 3) invokes TS 3 times to find UB, LB, and ε^*.

Algorithm 3. TSClustering$(X, MinPts, itr)$

1: $UB^0 \leftarrow 2max_{i \in \{2,\ldots,N\}} d(X_1, X_i)$
2: $LB^0 \leftarrow 0$
3: $\mathcal{R} \leftarrow$ sample $\lceil \alpha N \rceil$ points from X
4: $\mathcal{T} \leftarrow$ sample $\lceil \alpha D \rceil$ dimensions from X
5: $UB \leftarrow TS(X_{\mathcal{R},1:D}, LB^0, UB^0, MinPts, itr)$
6: $LB \leftarrow TS(X_{1:N,\mathcal{T}}, LB^0, UB, MinPts, itr)$
7: $\varepsilon^* \leftarrow TS(X, LB, UB, MinPts, itr)$
8: **return** $A(X, \varepsilon^*, MinPts)$

Runtime Analysis: TS executes itr iterations, each invoking DBSCAN twice, resulting in $O(itr \cdot DN^2)$. With itr empirically set to 6, the overall complexity remains $O(DN^2)$, improving upon prior works' computational efficiency.

5.2 Ternary Search Estimator (TSE)

To further optimize the runtime of the heavy part of Algorithm 3 (line 7) which uses the whole data and full dimension, we propose an estimator (TSE) for ε^* obtained by sampling an α fraction of the data and dimensions simultaneously. The intuition is that the opposite influences of sampling the data and dimensions on ε^* should roughly cancel out. Formally, we produce the estimate by replacing line 7 with $TS(X', LB, UB, MinPts, itr)$, where $X' = X_{\mathcal{R},\mathcal{T}}$ and $\mathcal{R},\mathcal{T}$ are sampled as in Eqs. 3 and 4. To reduce the variance, we repeat the above m times ($m = 30$ in our experiments) and average the estimates.

6 Evaluation

We evaluated the unimodality property and our methods across various domains, tasks, datasets, and representation techniques, using both qualitative and quantitative analyses over 24 datasets (Table 1). To evaluate clustering with noise, we employed the standard Normalized Mutual Information (NMI), Adjusted Rand Index (ARI), and Noise [1,11,12] metrics. NMI normalizes by cluster entropy, suitable for varying cluster counts, while ARI provides chance-adjusted accuracy with error-balance penalty. Together, these metrics offer complementary perspectives [18,19].

Unimodality Analysis: Qualitatively, Fig. 4 in the appendix demonstrates the unimodal shape (in red) of $k(\varepsilon)$ across 6 datasets from various fields. We used evenly spaced samples of ε for these curves, and executed DBSCAN exhaustively for each value. See Fig. 6 in the appendix for 15 additional datasets.

Quantitatively, to validate the unimodality of $k(\varepsilon)$ empirically we perform the DIP test [15]. Its null hypothesis is that the data is unimodal, and it is rejected for $p_{val} < 5\%$. The test demonstrated strong insignificance for all 24 NLP, Vision, and Audio datasets in Table 1, i.e., $k(\varepsilon)$ is unimodal on these datasets.

Cluster Analysis: Prior studies predominantly focus on synthetic, low-dimensional datasets. In contrast, this work emphasizes applications in high-dimension, comparing our methods (TS and TSE) to KMeans [32], HDB-SCAN [8], VDBSCAN [6], OPTICS [5], SS-DBSCAN [12], AMD-DBSCAN [13], AEDBSCAN [14], and AutoEps [9]. Due to the absence of open-source implementations, we re-implemented the latter four algorithms ourselves. We find that the baseline algorithms usually struggle in high dimensions, seldom producing degenerate outputs. We test against the ground-truth labels of classification datasets from NLP (Reuters), Vision (LFW), and Audio (ESC) using the metrics NMI, ARI, k, Noise, and runtime (Table 2).

Table 1. DIP Test over datasets [20–26] and embeddings [26–31].

Dataset	Labels	N	Embed.	D	Task	p_{val}^{DIP}	Dataset	Labels	N	Embed.	D	Task	p_{val}^{DIP}
LFW	1,680	13,233	DNet	256	Face	>99.9%	AMCDv5	N/A	13,406	CAST	2,048	Anim	14.9%
ImNet1k	1,000	50,000	CLIP	512	OD	>99.9%	AMCDv6	N/A	14,372	CAST	2,048	Anim	6.4%
ImNet1k	1,000	50,000	Hiera	1,000	OD	33.8%	AMCDv7	N/A	14,460	CAST	2,048	Anim	8.4%
CIFAR	100	60,000	CLIP	512	OD	8.9%	AMCDv8	N/A	14,748	CAST	2,048	Anim	14.8%
CIFAR	100	60,000	Hiera	1,000	OD	>99.9%	CASTv1	N/A	2,648	CAST	2,048	Anim	6.4%
Reuters	135	21,578	ADA2	1,536	Doc	99.8%	CASTv2	N/A	4,215	CAST	2,048	Anim	79.1%
ESC-50	50	1,024	CLAP	1,024	Audio	41.3%	CASTv3	N/A	4,633	CAST	2,048	Anim	14.8%
FACE	N/A	45,207	DNet	256	Face	>99.9%	CASTv4	N/A	4,163	CAST	2,048	Anim	99.4%
AMCDv1	N/A	15,395	CAST	2,048	Anim	29.3%	CASTv5	N/A	4,959	CAST	2,048	Anim	14.8%
AMCDv2	N/A	13,102	CAST	2,048	Anim	52.5%	CASTv6	N/A	5,639	CAST	2,048	Anim	99.4%
AMCDv3	N/A	14,676	CAST	2,048	Anim	79.0%	CASTv7	N/A	4,795	CAST	2,048	Anim	52.5%
AMCDv4	N/A	14,676	CAST	2,048	Anim	29.4%	Urban8k	N/A	8,732	CLAP	1,024	Audio	99.6%

An ideal clustering approximates the true number of clusters k, which in our case is the number of classification labels. TS/TSE provided the closest k approximations (roughly 5% error), reinforcing our hypothesis that ε^* reveals the natural clustering. Methods like SS-DBSCAN, which subsample data, overestimate ε, resulting in a single cluster. Note that KMeans requires the parameter k, which we set via the Elbow Method for maximal Inertia curvature [2].

For NMI and ARI, since all the algorithms assign points as noise,[1] we excluded these noise-labeled points from the NMI and ARI computation to isolate the clustering quality from the noise prediction. TS/TSE consistently achieved the best scores across datasets with $P_{val} < 10^{-5}$ in Friedman non-parametric test.

Regarding noise detection, the ideal outcome identifies true noise. OPTICS underestimated ε, labeling nearly all points as noise, which is clearly incorrect, whereas VDBSCAN and AEDBSCAN significantly overestimated k. For the LFW dataset, where we defined noisy points as people with only one image ($4,069/13,233 \approx 30.7\%$), TS/TSE provided noise estimates closely matching this true value ($\approx 30.5\%$). For runtime, TSE improved on TS which was competitive with the baselines.

Hyper-parameter Tuning: TSClustering relies on two hyper-parameters: α for sub-sampling N and D to give initial upper and lower bounds for ε^*, and itr to bound the number of ternary search iterations within TS. Both parameters trade off precision and runtime. Figure 5(a) illustrates the gap between LB and UB as a decreasing function of α. We selected $\alpha = 0.2$ to balance the gap size reduction with runtime. Recall that we try to maximize k and find its mode k^*. In Fig. 5(b), we illustrate the resulting approximation ratio ($\frac{k}{k^*}$) as a function of TS iterations over the Reuters, LFW, ESC, and CAST datasets. We selected $itr = 6$ since the approximation ratio converges just before this value.

---

[1] For KMeans clustering, we define the noisy points to be the singleton clusters.

Table 2. Evaluation over Reuters, LFW, and ESC. We compare our methods (TS, TSE) with: KMeans (KM), HDBSCAN (HD), VDBSCAN (VD), OPTICS (OP), SS-DBSCAN (SS), AMD-DBSCAN (AM), AEDBSCAN (AE) and AutoEps (Ep). In gray, results with $Noise > 90\%$.

Dataset	Reuters (k= 135)					LFW (k= 1,680)				ESC (k= 50)			
Method	$NMI\uparrow$	$ARI\uparrow$	k	$Noise\downarrow$	$T[s]\downarrow$	$NMI\uparrow$	$ARI\uparrow$	k	$Noise\downarrow$	$T[s]\downarrow$	$NMI\uparrow$	$ARI\uparrow$	k	$Noise\downarrow$	$T[s]\downarrow$
KM [32]	58.5%	19.9%	41	0.0%	1,917	78.0%	78.1%	773	0.2%	17,315	95.1%	83.3%	43	0.0%	306
HD [8]	62.0%	2.4%	1,247	61.4%	240	72.1%	36.3%	393	56.8%	105	86.2%	44.6%	52	17.3%	8
VD [6]	55.4%	0.3%	2,296	27.5%	246	92.3%	12.0%	2,661	38.0%	84	78.7%	20.9%	447	23.3%	10
OP [5]	61.3%	20.5%	37	97.1%	505	64.1%	24.5%	390	65.8%	202	56.3%	3.8%	53	59.7%	16
SS [12]	0.0%	0.0%	1	22.9%	230	13.5%	4.6%	2	52.7%	252	85.9%	46.6%	43	16.0%	9
AM [13]	41.1%	28.3%	134	6.2%	69	71.7%	20.4%	281	34.0%	29	83.4%	31.5%	93	18.3%	13
AE [14]	49.8%	4.5%	974	24.6%	144	91.8%	23.6%	1,944	48.7%	53	83.9%	46.7%	230	20.8%	7
Ep [9]	66.4%	67.1%	646	67.5%	2,377	11.9%	1.7%	56	57.1%	82	91.8%	77.3%	144	36.0%	24
TS (ours)	**77.5%**	**93.9%**	138	55.2%	152	**99.0%**	**96.8%**	1,697	30.5%	60	**97.4%**	**90.3%**	57	32.3%	5
TSE (ours)	**77.8%**	92.9%	150	38.0%	24	**99.0%**	**96.7%**	1,694	30.4%	41	96.7%	85.2%	48	14.7%	2

7 Conclusion

This paper addresses the problem of parameter tuning in DBSCAN. We identify a unimodality property of $k(\varepsilon)$, and support it empirically and theoretically. We find that maximizing $k(\varepsilon)$ provides a good clustering, and give a novel method to automatically find this ε with an adapted version of the Ternary Search algorithm. Our empirical results on diverse datasets demonstrate improved precision and reduced noise, highlighting its potential for various data mining applications.

Future works may include: **1.** creating a sub-linear estimator for ε^*, **2.** improving the runtime with numerical optimization algorithms, which perhaps incorporate priors or gradients, **3.** adapting the approach to multi-density distributions, and **4.** scaling out for distributed big-data clustering.

Acknowledgments. This work was supported by the Joint NSFC-ISF Research Grant no. 3077/23.

A Appendix

A.1 Additional Qualitative Evaluations of Near-Unimodality

To support our qualitative claims of Near-Unimodality, in Fig. 6 we illustrate $k(\varepsilon)$ over 15 additional datasets from SAIL AMCD [25] and CAST [26], and plot the run of TSClustering over them. SAIL-AMCD and CAST are collections of 15 animated videos of different styles where each video has its own set of detected characters embedded using the CAST embeddings of dimension $2,048$.

(a) Reuters

(b) LFW

(c) ImageNet1k

(d) CIFAR100

(e) SAIL AMCD

(f) ESC-50

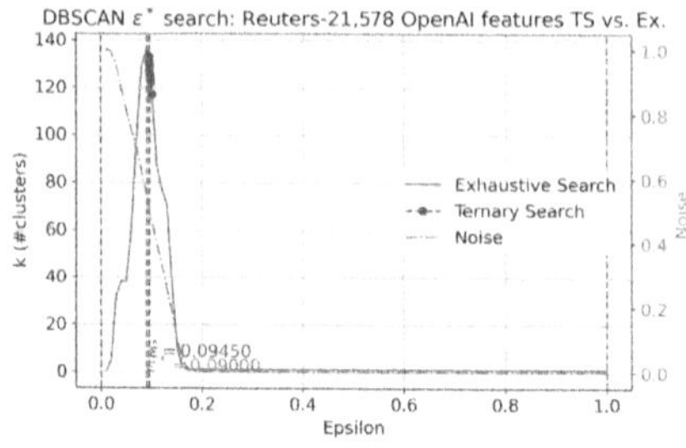

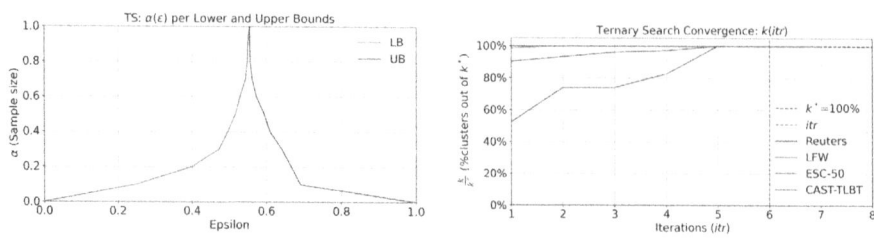

Fig. 4. Datasets across Vision, Audio, and NLP demonstrate unimodality of $k(\varepsilon)$.

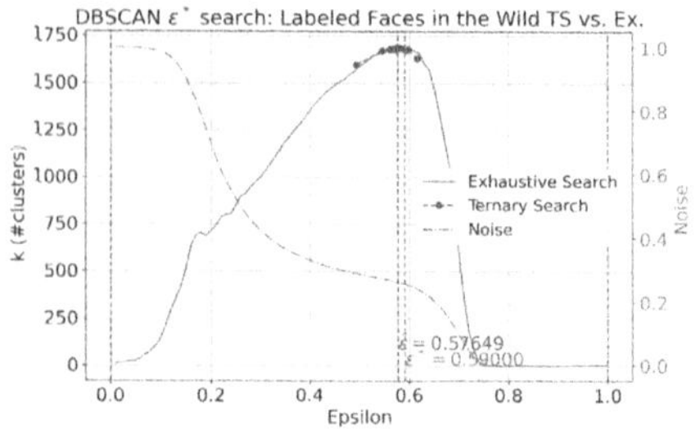

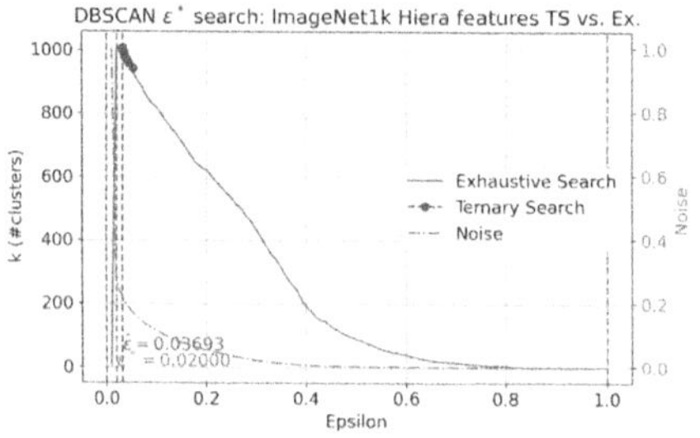

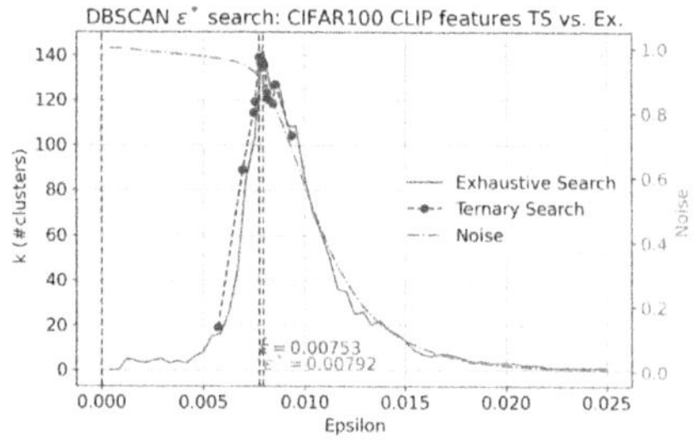

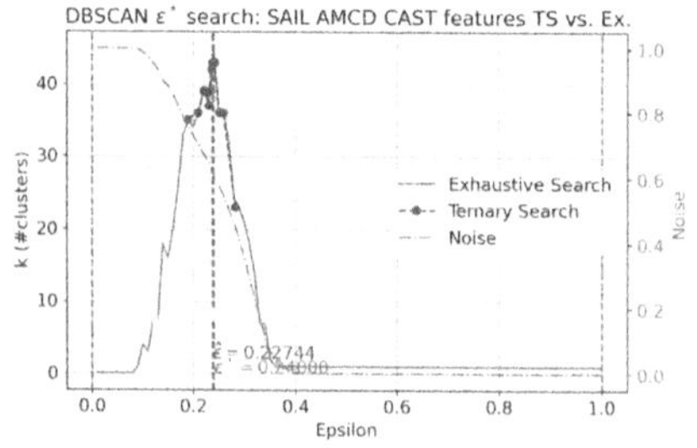

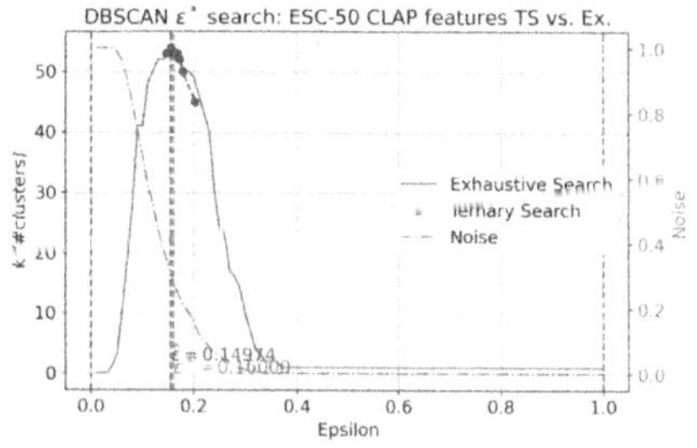

(a) A Pareto principle: for $\alpha = 20\%$ we narrow down the ε range by 80%.

(b) Ablation on the resulting approximation ratio (k/k^*) of TS as a function of itr.

Fig. 5. Hyper-parameter tuning.

Unimodal Strategies in Density-Based Clustering   511

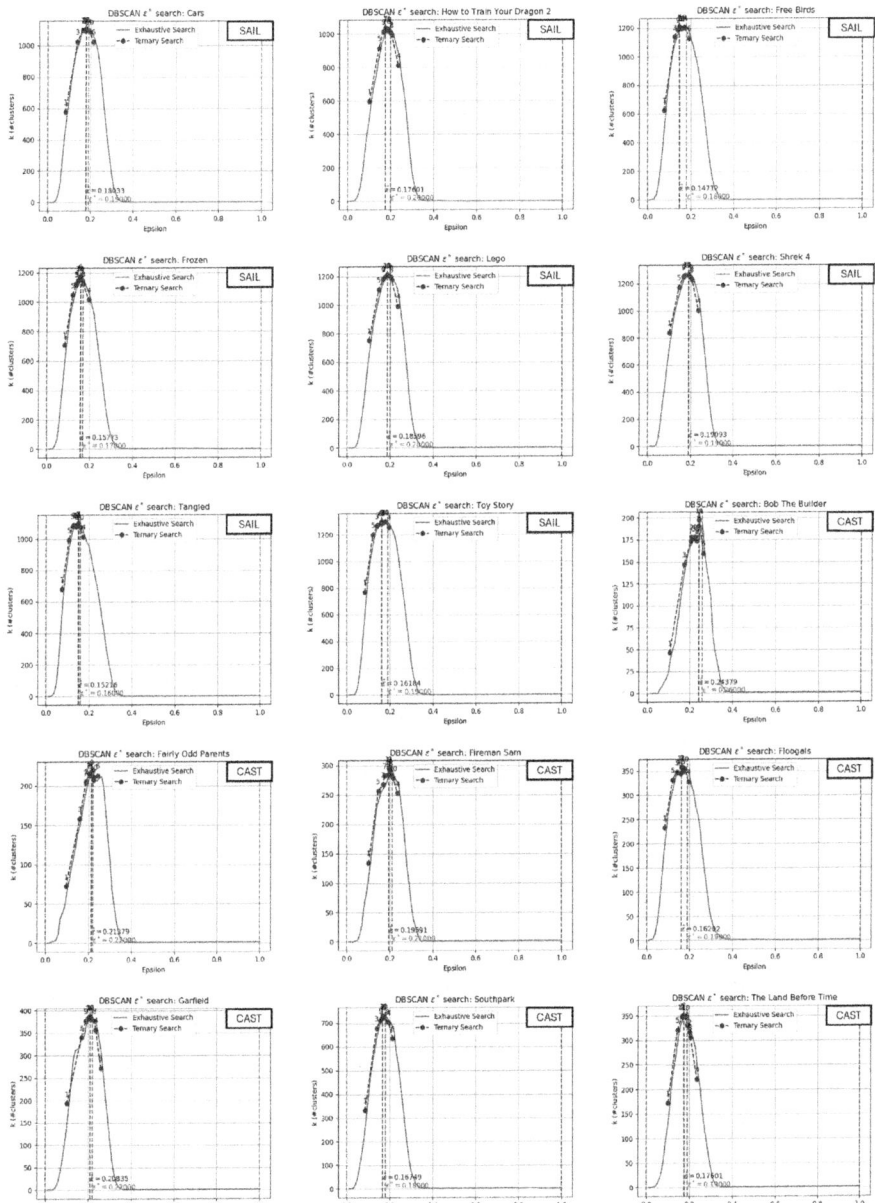

Fig. 6. The function $k(\varepsilon)$ plotted over 15 datasets from SAIL-AMCD and CAST, each containing embeddings of multiple characters in a video. We observe a clear unimodal shape on all datasets.

References

1. Ester, M., Kriegel, H.P., Sander, J., Xu, X., et al.: A density-based algorithm for discovering clusters in large spatial databases with noise. In: kdd, vol. 96, pp. 226–231. AAAI, Portland (1996)
2. Schubert, E.: Stop using the elbow criterion for k-means and how to choose the number of clusters instead. SIGKDD **25**(1), 36–42 (2023)
3. Han, J., Kamber, M., Mining, D.: Concepts and techniques. Morgan kaufmann **340**, 94104–3205 (2006)
4. Ullmann, T., Beer, A., Hünemörder, M., Seidl, T., Boulesteix, A.-L.: Overoptimistic evaluation and reporting of novel cluster algorithms: an illustrative study. Adv. Data Anal. Classif. **17**(1), 211–238 (2023)
5. Ankerst, M., Breunig, M.M., Kriegel, H.P., Sander, J.: Optics: ordering points to identify the clustering structure. SIGMOD **28**(2), 49–60 (1999)
6. Liu, P., Zhou, D., Wu, N.: VDBSCAN: varied density based spatial clustering of applications with noise. In: ICSSSM, pp. 1–4. IEEE, Chengdu (2007)
7. Khan, M.M.R., Siddique, M.A.B., Arif, R.B., Oishe, MR..: Adbscan: adaptive density-based spatial clustering of applications with noise for identifying clusters with varying densities. In: iCEEiCT, pp. 107–111. IEEE, Dhaka (2018)
8. Campello, R.J.G.B., Moulavi, D., Sander, J.: Density-based clustering based on hierarchical density estimates. In: PA-KDD, pp. 160–172. Springer, Berlin (2013)
9. Manisha Naik Gaonkar and Kedar Sawant: Autoepsdbscan: dbscan with eps automatic for large dataset. IJACTE **2**(2), 11–16 (2013)
10. Gan, J., Tao, Y.: dBSCAN revisited: MIS-claim, un-fixability, and approximation. In: SIGMOD, pp. 519–530. SIGMOD, Melborne (2015)
11. Schubert, E., Sander, J., Ester, M., Kriegel, H.P., Xu, X.: DBSCAN revisited, revisited: why and how you should (still) use DBSCAN. ACM Trans. Database Syst. (TODS) **42**(3), 1–21 (2017)
12. Monko, G., Kimura, M.: Optimized DBSCAN parameter selection: stratified sampling for epsilon and gridsearch for minimum samples. Softw. Eng. Autom. **1**, 43–61 (2023)
13. Wang, Z., et al.: AMD-DBSCAN: an adaptive multi-density DBSCAN for datasets of extremely variable density. DSAA 1–10 (2022)
14. Mistry, V., Pandya, U., Rathwa, A., Kachroo, H., Jivani, A.: AEDBSCAN—adaptive epsilon density-based spatial clustering of applications with noise. In: Progress in Advanced Computing and Intelligent Engineering, pp. 213–226. Springer, Singapore (2021)
15. Hartigan, J.A., Hartigan, P.M.: The dip test of unimodality. Ann. Stat. **13**(1), 70–84 (1985)
16. Devroye, L., Devroye, L.: Uniform and exponential spacings. Non-Uniform Random Variate Gener. 206–245 (1986)
17. Bajwa, M.S., Agarwal, A.P., Manchanda, S.: Ternary search algorithm: improvement of binary search. In: Indiacom, pp. 1723–1725 IEEE, New Delhi (2015)
18. Manning, C.D.: Introduction to Information Retrieval. Syngress, Rockland (2008)
19. Steinley, D.: Properties of the hubert-arable adjusted rand index. Psychol. Methods **9**(3), 386 (2004)
20. Huang, G.B., Mattar, M., Berg, T., Learned-Miller, E.: Labeled faces in the wild: a database forstudying face recognition in unconstrained environments. In: Workshop on Faces in 'Real-Life' Images: Detection, Alignment, and Recognition, IEEE, Rio de Janeiro, Brazil (2008)

21. Deng, J., Dong, W., Socher, R., Li, L.J., Li, K., Fei-Fei, L.: Imagenet: a large-scale hierarchical image database. In: CVPR, pp. 248–255.Vision Sciences Society, IEEE, Miami (2009)
22. Krizhevsky, A., Hinton, G., et al.: Learning multiple layers of features from tiny images. Univ. Toronto **1**, 1–54 (2009)
23. Lewis, D.: Reuters-21578 text categorization test collection. Distribution 1.0, AT&T Labs-Research (1997)
24. Piczak, K.J.: ESC: dataset for environmental sound classification. In: ACM MM, pp. 1015–1018. ACM Press, Brisbane (2015)
25. Somandepalli, K., Kumar, N., Guha, T., Narayanan, S.S.: Unsupervised discovery of character dictionaries in animation movies. IEEE Trans. Multimedia **20**(3), 539–551 (2017)
26. Nir, O., Rapoport, G., Shamir, A.: Cast: character labeling in animation using self-supervision by tracking. In: Computer Graphics Forum, vol. 41, pp. 135–145. Wiley Online Library, EuroGraphics, Reims (2022)
27. Huang, G., Liu, Z., Maaten, L.V.D., Weinberger, K.Q.: Densely connected convolutional networks (2018)
28. Ryali, C., et al.: Hiera: a hierarchical vision transformer without the bells-and-whistles. In: ICML, ICML 2023, JMLR.org, Honolulu (2023)
29. Radford, A., et al.: Learning transferable visual models from natural language supervision. In: ICML, pp. 8748–8763. PMLR, Virtual (2021)
30. Radford, A., Wu, J., Child, R., Luan, D., Amodei, D., Sutskever, I.: Language models are unsupervised multitask learners. OpenAI blog **1** (2019)
31. Elizalde, B., Deshmukh, S., Wang, H.: Natural language supervision for general-purpose audio representations. In: ICASSP, pp. 336–340. IEEE, Seuol (2024)
32. MacQueen, J.: Some methods for classification and analysis of multivariate observations. In: Proceedings of 5-th Berkeley Symposium on Mathematical Statistics and Probability/University of California Press (1967)

Author Index

A
Adouani, Malek 195
Algikar, Pooja 3
Aryal, Sunil 248

B
Benhamza, Manal 391
Bied, Guillaume 265, 480
Bouadjenek, Mohamed Reda 248
Buyl, Maarten 265

C
Cao, Yanan 124
Chao, Dian 20
Chelly Dagdia, Zaineb 195
Chen, Huan 426
Chen, Yan 463
Chen, Yuanlong 426
Cheng, Zhenlin 124
Choi, Kevin 106
Clausel, Marianne 391
Cody, Tyler 106

D
da Silva Gonçalves, Jorge 447
De Bie, Tijl 265
Domeniconi, Carlotta 301
Du, Liang 463

F
Fettach, Yousra 265
Fontana, Michele 213
Fu, Yali 37

G
Gao, Fan 141
Ghosal, Soumya Suvra 231

Goodge, Adam 55
Guo, Yiqing 463

H
Hebbalaguppe, Ramya 231
Heiter, Edith 480
Hooi, Bryan 55
Hu, Shu 336

J
Jiang, Henghui 463
Jin, Ming 106
Jin, Ruochun 426

K
Katzke, Tim 71
Kheya, Tahsin Alamgir 248
Klüttermann, Simon 71
Kobayashi, Ichiro 89
Kolla, Ravi 409
Kong, Qingzhao 354

L
Lai, Fuyin 480
Li, Hongyi 176
Li, Jindong 37
Liang, Sicheng 176
Liao, Jingyi 55
Lijffijt, Jefrey 265, 480
Lin, Jessica 159
Lin, Xixun 124
Liu, Yu 176
Liu, Zhen 336
Liu, Ziyi 372
Lv, Xinpeng 426

© The Editor(s) (if applicable) and The Author(s), under exclusive license to Springer Nature Switzerland AG 2026
R. P. Ribeiro et al. (Eds.): ECML PKDD 2025, LNAI 16013, pp. 515–516, 2026.
https://doi.org/10.1007/978-3-032-05962-8

Author Index

M
Manduchi, Laura 447
Manocha, Dinesh 231
Mao, Yunxin 426
Maru, Chihiro 89
Mehendale, Eshan 409
Mili, Lamine 3
Monreale, Anna 213
Müller, Emmanuel 71

N
Naretto, Francesca 213
Ng, Wee Siong 55
Nir, Oron 498
Noels, Sander 265

O
Oguchi, Masato 89

P
Pedanekar, Niranjan 409
Peiretti, Federico 282
Pensa, Ruggero G. 282

Q
Qin, Xiaobo 372

R
Rangwala, Huzefa 301
Ren, Jing 426
Rogiers, Alexander 265
Roy, Padmaksha 106

S
Shamir, Ariel 498
Shang, Yanmin 124
Singhal, Himanshu 106
Su, Yongyi 55
Sun, Nan 124

T
Tami, Myriam 391
Tenenbaum, Jay 498
Thorat, Abhinav 409

V
Vandenhirtz, Moritz 447
Vasquez, Jonathan 301
Vogt, Julia E. 447

W
Wachslander, Veronika 319
Wang, Daixin 372
Wang, Haotian 426
Wang, Meihong 141
Wang, Qi 37
Wang, Wenkai 141
Wang, Zichong 336, 354
Wu, Jie 176

X
Xi, Wenjie 159
Xie, Qinlin 176
Xing, Qianli 37
Xu, Liyang 426
Xu, Xun 55

Y
Yang, Jinxuan 426
Yang, Liping 354
Yang, Wenjing 426
Yang, Xulei 55
Yang, Yang 20
Yap, Roland H. C. 336
Ye, Jiawei 176
Yin, Zhipeng 336, 354
Ying, Yuxin 372
Yu, Rui 354

Z
Zhang, Wenbin 336, 354
Zhang, Xiaocai 336
Zhang, Yuxuan 20
Zhou, Luping 20
Zhou, Zhiheng 124
Zhu, Dingyuan 372
Zhuang, Fuzhen 372
Zhuang, Jun 354

Made in the USA
Monee, IL
03 May 2026